Lecture Notes in Computer Scie T0238143

Commenced Publication in 1973
Founding and Former Series Editors:
Gerhard Goos, Juris Hartmanis, and Jan van Leeuwen

Jérôme Durand-Lose
Maurice Margenstern (Eds.)

Machines, Computations, and Universality

5th International Conference, MCU 2007
Orléans, France, September 10-13, 2007
Proceedings

 Springer

Volume Editors

Jérôme Durand-Lose
Laboratoire d'Informatique Fondamentale d'Orléans
Université d'Orléans
B.P. 6759, F-45067 ORLÉANS Cedex 2,
E-mail: Jerome.Durand-Lose@univ-orleans.fr

Maurice Margenstern
Université Paul Verlaine - Metz
UFR MIM, LITA, EA 3097
Ile du Saulcy, 57045 Metz Cédex, France
E-mail: margens@univ-metz.fr

Library of Congress Control Number: Applied for

CR Subject Classification (1998): B.6.1, F.1.1, K.1

LNCS Sublibrary: SL 1 – Theoretical Computer Science and General Issues

ISSN   0302-9743
ISBN-10   3-540-74592-0 Springer Berlin Heidelberg New York
ISBN-13   978-3-540-74592-1 Springer Berlin Heidelberg New York

Springer is a part of Springer Science+Business Media

springer.com

© Springer-Verlag Berlin Heidelberg 2007
Printed in Germany

Typesetting: Camera-ready by author, data conversion by Scientific Publishing Services, Chennai, India
Printed on acid-free paper   SPIN: 12115495   06/3180   5 4 3 2 1 0

Preface

In this volume, the reader will first find the invited talks given during the conference. Then, in a second part, he/she will find the contributions that were accepted for the conference after selection. In both cases, papers are given in the alphabetical order of the authors.

MCU 2007 was the fifth edition of the conference in theoretical computer science, *Machines, Computations and Universality*. The first and second editions, MCU 1995 and MCU 1998, at that time called *Machines et calculs universels*, were organized by Maurice Margenstern, in Paris and in Metz (France), respectively. The third edition, MCU 2001, was the first one to be organized outside France, and it was held in Chişinău (Moldova). Its co-organizers were Maurice Margenstern and Yurii Rogozhin. The proceedings of MCU 2001 were the first to appear in Lecture Notes in Computer Science, see LNCS 2055. The fourth edition, MCU 2004, was held in Saint-Petersburg. Its co-organizers were Maurice Margenstern, Anatoly Beltiukov and Nikolai Kossovski. The proceedings of the invited papers and the papers presented at the conference after selection were published in an issue of Lecture Notes in Computer Science, LNCS 3354, after the conference, as revised selected papers.

From its very beginning, the MCU conference has been an international scientific event, and also from the very beginning, it has always aimed to be of a high scientific standard. This edition confirmed the initial goal of the MCU conference with its triennial periodicity. Every three years, we are able to measure the advances made in the field. And on each occasion we have witnessed some very interesting results.

MCU 2007 was held in Orléans (France) in September 2007. The topics covered proved the vitality of the domains featured in the previous edition, namely cellular automata, molecular computing and super-Turing computations. This time, new results were presented in cellular automata, namely for solutions of the synchronization problem, as well as a new approach for the theoretical study of cellular automata in connection with their neighborhoods. Universality results in molecular computing continued to be a topic of interest, with the modelizations becoming more and more refined and getting closer to biological phenomena. Also included was a very interesting modelization of the Kolmogorov-Uspensky Machine by bio-chemical reactions organized in a reaction-diffusion computer.

Super-Turing computations played an important role this year. We saw continuations of models presented in Saint-Petersburg where recursivity and universality results on reals were investigated. We also saw new aspects of super-Turing computations with infinite time machines and inductive Turing machines. With respect to the infinite time Turing machine, a very good survey was presented giving important results obtained in this domain in recent years.

A number of papers focussed on the various problems surrounding the theory of formal languages connected with universality or decidability procedures.

We also witnessed a renewal of the traditional core of the MCU conference with a new universal reversible Turing machine and new small universal Turing machines, the first new result of this kind since MCU 2001: although it is now much more difficult, the race for the smallest universal Turing machine goes on. These proceedings also include new results from an older field of research, that of tag-systems, intensively used in small universal Turing machines but not studied for themselves since Pager's results in 1970.

We hope that the reader will be impressed by the well-written papers and the important results presented in this volume.

We would like to take this opportunity to thank the referees of the submitted papers for their very efficient work. Submission, refereeing and preparation of the proceedings was carried out with the help of EasyChair (http://www.easychair.org). We would like to express our appreciation of this conference system.

The members of the program committee gave us decisive help on this occasion. Thanks to them, namely Erzsébet Csuhaj-Varjú, Ansheng Li, Jean-Yves Marion, Gheorghe Păun, Yurii Rogozhin, Grzegorz Rozenberg, Jiři Wiedermann, Damien Woods, we can offer the reader this issue of LNCS.

MCU 2007 was supported by a number of sponsors, who are listed on the next page. We would like to extend our gratitude to all of them.

July 2007   Jérôme Durand-Lose
                                                             Maurice Margenstern

Sponsors

 Laboratoire d'Informatique Fondamentale d'Orléans

 Université d'Orléans

 LITA, Université de Metz

 Conseil Régional Région Centre

 Conseil Général du Loiret

 Mairie d'Orléans

GDR 673 du CNRS Informatique Mathématique

Table of Contents

Encapsulating Reaction-Diffusion Computers

Andrew Adamatzky

Faculty of Computing, Engineering and Mathematical Sciences,
University of the West of England, Bristol BS16 1QY, United Kingdom
andrew.adamatzky@uwe.ac.uk

Abstract. Reaction-diffusion computers employ propagation of chemical and excitation waves to transmit information; they use collisions between traveling wave-fronts to perform computation. We increase applicability domain of the reaction-diffusion computers by encapsulating them in a membrane, in a form of vegetative state, plasmodium, of true slime mold. In such form reaction-diffusion computers can also realize Kolmogorov-Uspensky machine.

1   From Reaction-Diffusion Computers to Plasmodium

In reaction-diffusion computers [2,4] data are presented by initial concentration profile or configuration of disturbance (e.g. sites of stimulation of excitable media), information is transfered by spreading wave patterns, computation is implemented in collisions of wave-fronts, and final concentration profile represents results of the computation. Reaction-diffusion computers are theoretically and experimentally proved to be capable for quite sophisticated computational tasks, including image processing, computational geometry, logics and arithmetics, and robot control, see extensive overview of theoretical and experimental results in [4].

There is a particular feature of reaction-diffusion chemical computers. In their classical, and so far commonly accepted form, the media are 'fully conductive' for chemical or excitation waves. Every point of a two- or three-dimensional medium can be involved in propagation of chemical waves and reactions between diffusing chemical species. Once reaction is initiated in a point, it spreads all over the computing space by target and spiral waves. Such, analogues to one-to-all broadcasting in massive-parallel systems, phenomena of wave-propagation are employed to solve problems ranging from Voronoi diagram construction to robot navigation [2,4]. We could not however quantize information (e.g. assign logical values to certain waves) or implement one-to-one transmission in fully reactive media.

Till quite recently the only way to direct and quantize information in a chemical medium was to geometrically constrain the medium. Thus, only reactive or excitable channels are made, along which wave travel. The waves collide with other waves at the junctions between the channels, and implement certain logical gates in result of the collision, see overview in Chapter 1 of e.g. [4].

J. Durand-Lose and M. Margenstern (Eds.): MCU 2007, LNCS 4664, pp. 1–11, 2007.
© Springer-Verlag Berlin Heidelberg 2007

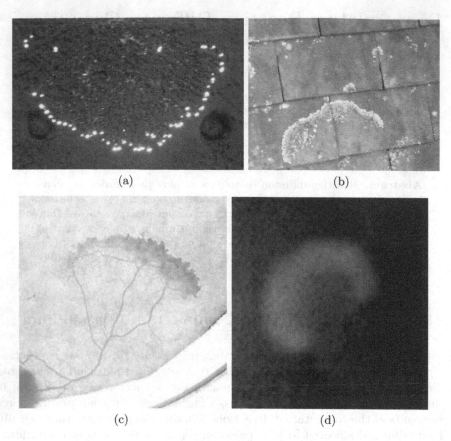

Fig. 1. Examples of localized propagations in real-world systems: (a) localized waves of combustion, (b) fragment of wave front of lichen colony, (b) propagating plasmodium, (c) wave-fragment in sub-excitable Belousov-Zhabotinsky system

Using sub-excitable media is yet another way of quantizing information. In sub-excitable media a local disturbance leads to generation of mobile localization, wave-fragment which travels for a reasonably long distance without changing its shape [36]. Presence of a wave-fragment in a given domain of space signifies logical truth, absence of the fragment logical falsity. A full power of collision-based computing can be applied then [3]. Such mobile localization are typical natural phenomena occurring in situations when system lacks resources to realize in full its development potential (Fig.1), e.g. experience deficiency of combustive material (Fig.1a), illumination (Fig.1b), nutrients in substate (Fig.1c), and excitability (Fig.1d).

Also there is a range of problems, where chemical processor could not cope without external support. Shortest path is one of such problems. One can use excitable medium to outline a set of all collision-free paths in a space with obstacles [4], but to select and visualize the shortest path amongst all possible one needs to use external cellular-automaton processor, or conceptually supply excitable chemical medium with some kind of field of local pointers [4]. Experimental setups, e.g. [39] which claim to directly compute a shortest path in chemical media are indeed employing external computing resources to store time-lapsed snapshots of propagating wave-fronts and to calculate intersection of wave-fronts. Such usage of external resources dramatically reduce fundamental values of the computing with propagating patterns. This is caused mainly by uniformity of spreading wave-fronts, their inability to sharply select directions toward locations of data points, and also because excitable systems usually do not form stationary structures or standing waves.

Ideally, we would prefer to combine advantages of 'free space'[1] computing in fully reactive media with precision and simplicity of logical representation of geometrically constrained media. This can be done by encapsulating reaction-diffusion system in an elastic membrane.

There is a real-world system which strongly resembles encapsulated reaction-diffusion system. *P. Polycephalum* is a single cell with many nucleus which behave like amoeba, or even young neuroblast and this is why it play so perfectly role of computing substrate for our algorithm of growing spanning tree. In its main vegetative phase, called plasmodium, slime mold actively searches for nutrients. When next source of food is located plasmodium forms a vein of protoplasm between previous and current sources of food. Growing and feeding plasmodium exhibits characteristic rythmic contractions with articulated sources. The contraction waves are associated with waves of potential change, and the waves observed in plasmodium [48] are similar that found in excitable chemical systems, like Belousov-Zhabotinsky medium. The following wave phenomena were discovered experimentally [48]: undisturbed propagation of contraction wave inside the cell body, collision and annihilation of contraction waves, splitting of the waves by inhomogeneity, and formation of spiral waves of contraction. These are closely matching dynamics of pattern propagation in in excitable reaction-diffusion chemical systems.

The plasmodium has already proved to be a unique fruitful object to design various schemes of non-classical computation [10,11,45], including shortest path [31,31,33] and even design of controllers for robots [46].

In the paper we highlight novel aspects of our studies in computing with propagating localizations. Firstly, we demonstrate the spanning tree construction – the problem unsolvable in 'classical' reaction-diffusion computer without help of external hardware devices – can be solved in plasmodium of *Physarum polycephalum*. Secondly, we outline a refreshing approach to universality of biological substrates by constructing Physarum machine, which is an experimental implementation of Kolmogorov-Uspensky machine.

2   Spanning Trees

In 1991 we proposed an algorithm of computing spanning tree of a finite planar set based on formation of a neurite tree in a development of a single neuron [1]. Our

---

[1] Thanks to Jonathan Mills for the term.

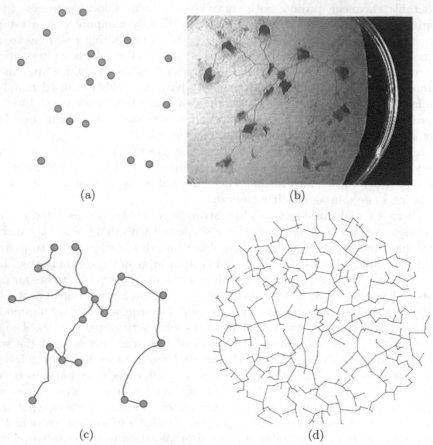

Fig. 2. Approximating spanning tree by plasmodium: (a) data set of planar points, (b) tree represented by protoplasmic strands/veins of the plasmodium, (c) extracted spanning tree, (d) spanning tree of 500 points computed by simulated plasmodium

idea was to place a neuroblast somewhere on the plane amongst drops of chemical attractants, positions of which represent points of a given planar set. Then neurite tree starts to grow and spans the given planar set of chemo-attractants with acyclic graph of axonal and dendritic branches. Due to lateral circumstances experimental implementation of the algorithm was not possible at the time of its theoretical investigation [1]. Recent experimental developments in foraging behaviour of *P. Polycephalum* [31,31,33,46,10,11,45] convinced us that our algorithm for growing spanning tree can be implemented by living plasmodium.

The scoping experiments were designed as follows. We either covered container's bottom with a piece of wet filter paper and placed a piece of living plasmodium on it, or just planted plasmodium on a bottom of bare container and fixed wet paper on the container's cover to keep humidity high. Oat flakes placed at the positions of given planar points to be spanned by a tree. The containers were stored in the dark except during periods of observation.

Once placed in the container and recovered the plasmodium starts to explore the surrounding space. Numerous pseudopodia emerge, frequently branch and proceed. The plasmodium growth from its initial position by protoplasmic pseudopodia detecting, by chemotaxis, relative locations of closest sources of nutrients. When another source of nutrients, element of the given planar set, is reached the relevant part of the plasmodium reshapes and shrinks to a protoplasmic strand, or a tube. This tube connects initial and newly acquired sites. This protoplasmic strand represents an edge of the computed spanning tree. Planar points distributed in a Petri dish are usually spanned by a protoplasmic vein tree in 1-3 days, depending on diameter of the planar set, substrate and other conditions.

Let us have a closer look at the set of 16 points (Fig. 2a) to be spanned. We represented the set by a positions of oat flakes (source of nutrients), placed flakes on the moistened filter paper, placed a piece of plasmodium at one of the flakes. In two days plasmodium spanned set of flakes. Edges of the tree are visible as dark protoplasmic strands, connecting dark irregular shapes of oat flakes (Fig. 2b). Manually enhances picture of the spanning tree is shown in Fig. 2c. Tree computed by plasmodium in our experiments satisfactory match trees computed by clasical techniques, e.g. by Jaromczyk-Supowit method [24,40], see [8]. Even when represented in simulation, the algorithm works pretty well on large data sets (Fig. 2d).

3   Phyrasum Machines

We demonstrate that plasmodium of *Physarum polycephalum* is an ideal biological sibstrate for implementation of Kolmogorov-Uspensky machines [7].

Kolmogorov-Uspensky machine (KUM) [28,29] is defined on a colored/labeled undirected graph with bounded degrees of nodes and bounded number of colors/labels. KUM operates, modify their storage, as follows. Select an active node in the storage graph. Specify local active zone, the node's neighborhood. Modify the active zone: add new node with the pair of edges, connecting the new node with the active node; delete a node with the pair of incident edges; add/delete edge between the nodes. A program for KUM specifies how to replace neighborhood of active node with new neighborhood, depending on labels of edges connected to the active node and labels of the nodes in proximity of the active node [14]. All previous and modern models of real-world computation are heirs of KUM: Knuth's linking automata [27], Tarjan's Reference Machines [41], Schönhage's storage modification machines [34,35]. When restrictions on bounded in- and out-degrees of the machine's storage graph are lifted, the machine becomes Random Access Machine.

Functions computable on Turing machines (TM) are computed in on KUM, and any sequential device are simulated by KUM [23]. KUM can simulate TM in real time, but not *vice verse* [22]. KUM's topology is much more flexible than that of TM, and KUM is stronger then any 'tree-machine' [38].

In 1988 Gurevich [23] suggested that an edge of KUM is not only informational but also physical entity and reflects physical proximity of the nodes (thus e.g. even in three-dimensional space number of neighbors of each node is polynomially bounded). What would be the best natural implementation of KUM? A potential candidate should be capable for growing, unfolding, graph-like storage structure, dynamically manipulating nodes and edges, and should have a wide range of functioning parameters. Vegetative stage, plasmodium, of a true slime mold *Physarum polycephalum* satisfies all these requirements.

The scoping experiments were designed as follows. We either covered container's bottom with a piece of wet filter paper and placed a piece of living plasmodium[2] on it, or just planted plasmodium on a bottom of a bare container and fixed wet paper on the container's cover to keep humidity high. Oat flakes were distributed in the container to supply nutrients and represent part, or data-nodes, of Physarum machine. The containers were stored in the dark except during periods of observation. To color oat flakes, where required, we used SuperCook Food Colorings[3]: blue (colors E133, E122), yellow (E102, E110, E124), red (E110, E122), and green (E102, E142). Flakes were saturated with the colorings, then dried.

Nodes: Physarum machine has two types of nodes: stationary nodes, presented by sources of nutrients (oat flakes), and dynamic nodes, sites where two or more protoplasmic veins originate (Fig. 3). At the beginning of computation, stationary nodes are distributed in the computational space, and plasmodium is placed at one point of the space. Starting in the initial conditions the plasmodium exhibits foraging behavior, and occupies stationary nodes (Fig. 3).

Edges: An edge of Physarum machine is a strand, or vein, of protoplasm connecting stationary and/or dynamic nodes. KUM machine is an undirected graph, i.e. if nodes x and y are connected then they are connected by two edges (xy) and (yx). In Physarum machine this is implemented by a single edge but with periodically reversing flow of protoplasm [25,30].

Data, results and halting: Program and data are represented by a spatial configuration of stationary nodes. Result of the computation over stationary data-node is presented by configuration of dynamics nodes and edges. The initial state of a Physarum machines, includes part of input string (the part which represents position of plasmodium relatively to stationary nodes), empty output string, current instruction in the program, and storage structure consists of one isolated node. That is the whole graph structure developed by plasmodium is the result of its computation, "if S is a terminal state, then the connected component of the initial vertex is considered to be the "solution"" [29]. Physarum machine halts when all data-nodes are utilized.

Active zone: In KUM storage graph must have some active node. This is an inbuilt feature of Physarum machine. When plasmodium resides on a substrate

---

[2] Thanks to Prof. Soichiro Tsuda for providing me with *P. polycephalum* culture.
[3] www.supercook.co.uk

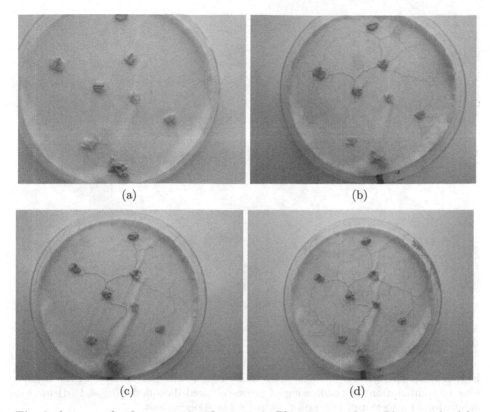

(a)   (b)

(c)   (d)

Fig. 3. An example of computational process in Physarum machine. Photographs (a)–(d) are taken with time lapse circa 24 hours.

with poor or no nutrients, then just one or few nodes generate actively spreading protoplasmic waves. In these cases the protoplasm spreads as mobile localizations similarly to wave-fragments in sub-excitable Belousov-Zhabotinsky medium [36]. An example of single active node, which is just started to develop its active zone, is shown in (Fig. 4). At every step of computation in KUM there is an active node and some active zone, usually nodes neighboring to active node. The active zone has limited complexity, in a sense that all elements of the zone are connected by some chain of edges to the initial node. In general, size of active zone may vary depending on computational task. In Physarum machine an active node is a trigger of contraction/excitation waves, which spread all over the plasmodium tree and cause pseudopodia to propagate, shape to change and even protoplasmic veins to annihilate. Active zone is comprised of stationary or dynamic nodes connected to active node with veins of protoplasm.

Bounded connectivity: In contrast to Schönhage machine KUM has bounded in- and out-degree of the storage graph. Graphs developed by Physarum are predominantly planar graphs. Moreover, if we put a piece of vein of protoplasm on top of another vein of protoplasm, the veins fuse [37]. Usually, not more

Fig. 4. Basic operations: (a) single active node is generating active zone at the beginning of computation, (b) addressing of green-coloured data-node, (c) and (d) implementation of ADD NODE, ADD EDGE, REMOVE EDGE operations

then three protoplasmic strands join each other in one given point of space. It is reported that average degree of minimum spanning tree is around 1.99, and of relative neighborhood graph around 2.6 [17]. Graphs produced by standard procedures for generating combinatorial random planar graphs show a limited growth of average degree with number of nodes or edges, the degree stays around 4 when number of edges increase from 100 to 4000 [9]. We could assume that average degree of storage graph in Physarum machines is a bit higher then degree of spanning trees but less then degree of random planar graphs.

Addressing and labeling: Every node of KUM must be uniquely addressable and nodes and edges labeled [29]. There is no direct implementation of such addressing in Physarum machine. With stationary nodes this can be implemented either by coloring the nodes, or by tuning humidity of the oat flakes. Coloring the stationary nodes could be another solution. An example of experimental implementation of addressing is shown in Fig. 4b.

Basic operations: A possible set of instructions for Physarum machine could be as follows. Common instruction would include INPUT, OUTPUT, GO, HALT, and internal instructions: NEW, SET, IF [19]. At present state of experimental implementation we assume that INPUT is done via distribution of sources of nutrients, while OUTPUT is recorded optically. Instruction SET causes pointers redirection, and can be realized by placing fresh source of nutrients in the experimental container, preferably on top of one of the old sources of nutrients. When new node is created all pointers from the old node point to the new node. Let us look at the experimental implementation of core instructions.

ADD NODE: To add a stationary node b to node a's neighborhood, plasmodium must propagate from a to b, and form a protoplasmic vein representing edge (ab). To form a dynamic node, propagating pseudopodia must branch into two or more pseudopodia, and the site of branching will represent newly formed node.

REMOVE NODE: To remove stationary node from Physarum machine, plasmodium leaves the node. Annihilating protoplasmic strands forming a dynamic node at their intersection, remove the dynamic node.

ADD EDGE: To add an edge to a neighborhood, active node generates propagating processes which establish a protoplasm vein with one or more neighboring nodes.

REMOVE EDGE: When protoplasmic vein annihilates, e.g. depending on global state or when source of nutrients exhausted, edge represented by the vein is removed from Physarum machine (Fig. 4cd). The following sequence of operations is demonstrated in Fig. 4cd: node 3 is added to the structure by removing edge (12) and forming two new edges (13) and (23).

References

1. Adamatzky, A.: Neural algorithm for constructing minimal spanning tree. Neural Network World 6, 335–339 (1991)
2. Adamatzky, A.: Computing in non-linear media and automata collectives. IoP, Bristol (2001)
3. Adamatzky, A. (ed.): Collision-Based Computing. Springer, Heidelberg (2003)
4. Adamatzky, A., De Lacy Costello, B., Asai, T.: Reaction-Diffusion Computers. Elsevier, Amsterdam (2005)
5. Adamatzky, A., Teuscher, C.: From Utopian to Genuine Unconventional Computers. Luniver Press (2006)
6. Adamatzky, A.: Physarum machines: encapsulating reaction-diffusion to compute spanning tree (submitted)
7. Adamatzky, A.: Physarum machine: implementation of Kolmogorov-Uspensky machine in biological substrate. Parallel Processing Letters (in press, 2007)
8. Adamatzky, A.: Growing spanning trees in plasmodium machines, Kybernetes (in press, 2007)
9. Alber, J., Dornm, F., Niedermeier, R.: Experiments on Optimally Solving NP-complete Problems on Planar Graphs. Manuscript (2001),
http://www.ii.uib.no/~frederic/ADN01.ps
10. Aono, M., Gunji, Y.-P.: Resolution of infinite-loop in hyperincursive and nonlocal cellular automata: Introduction to slime mold computing. In: Computing Anticiaptory Systems. AIP Conference Proceedings, vol. 718, pp. 177–187 (2001)
11. Aono, M., Gunji, Y.-P.: Material implementation of hyper-incursive field on slime mold computer. In: Computing Anticiaptory Systems. AIP Conference Proceedings, vol. 718, pp. 188–203 (2004)

12. Bardzin's, J.M.: On universality problems in theory of growing automata. Doklady Akademii Nauk SSSR 157, 542–545 (1964)
13. Barzdin', J.M., Kalnins, J.: A universal automaton with variable structure. Automatic Control and Computing Sciences 8, 6–12 (1974)
14. Blass, A., Gurevich, Y.: Algorithms: a quest for absolute definitions. Bull. Europ. Assoc.TCS 81, 195–225 (2003)
15. van Emde Boas, P.: Space measures for storage modification machines. Information Process. Lett. 30, 103–110 (1989)
16. Calude, C.S., Dinneen, M.J., Păun, G., Rozenberg, G., Stepney, S.: UC 2006. LNCS, vol. 4135. Springer, Heidelberg (2006)
17. Cartigny, J., Ingelrest, F., Simplot-Ryl, D., Stojmenovic, I.: Localized LMST and RNG based minimum-energy broadcast protocols in ad hoc networks. Ad Hoc Networks 3, 1–16 (2005)
18. Cloteaux, B., Rajan, D.: Some separation results between classes of pointer algorithms. In: DCFS '06: Proceedings of the Eighth Workshop on Descriptional Complexity of Formal Systems, pp. 232–240 (2006)
19. Dexter, S., Doyle, P., Gurevich, Y.: Gurevich abstract state machines and Schönhage storage modification machines. J. Universal Computer Science 3, 279–303 (1997)
20. Dijkstra, E.A.: A note on two problems in connection with graphs. Numer. Math. 1, 269–271 (1959)
21. Gacs, P., Leving, L.A.: Casual nets or what is a deterministic computation, STAN-CS-80-768 (1980)
22. Grigoriev, D.: Kolmogorov algorithms are stronger than Turing machines. Notes of Scientific Seminars of LOMI (in Russian) 60, 29–37 (1976) (English translation in J. Soviet Math. 14(5) 1445–1450 (1980))
23. Gurevich, Y.: On Kolmogorov machines and related issues. Bull. EATCS 35, 71–82 (1988)
24. Jaromczyk, J.W., Kowaluk, M.: A note on relative neighborhood graphs. In: Proc. 3rd Ann. Symp. Computational Geometry, pp. 233–241 (1987)
25. Kamiya, N.: The protoplasmic flow in the myxomycete plasmodium as revealed by a volumetric analysis. Protoplasma 39, 3 (1950)
26. Kirkpatrick, D.G., Radke, J.D.: A framework for computational morphology. In: Toussaint, G.T. (ed.) Computational Geometry, pp. 217–248. North-Holland, Amsterdam (1985)
27. Knuth, D.E.: The Art of Computer Programming. Fundamental Algorithms, vol. 1. Addison-Wesley, Reading, Mass (1968)
28. Kolmogorov, A.N.: On the concept of algorithm. Uspekhi Mat. Nauk 8(4), 175–176 (1953)
29. Kolmogorov, A.N., Uspensky, V.A.: On the definition of an algorithm. Uspekhi Mat. Nauk (in Russian), 13, 3–28 (1958) (English translation: ASM Translations 21(2), 217–245 (1963))
30. Nakagakia, T., Yamada, H., Ueda, T.: Interaction between cell shape and contraction pattern in the *Physarum plasmodium*. Biophysical Chemistry 84, 195–204 (2000)
31. Nakagaki, T.: Smart behavior of true slime mold in a labyrinth. Research in Microbiology 152, 767–770 (2001)
32. Nakagaki, T., Yamada, H., Toth, A.: Maze-solving by an amoeboid organism. Nature 407, 470 (2000)
33. Nakagaki, T., Yamada, H., Toth, A.: Path finding by tube morphogenesis in an amoeboid organism. Biophysical Chemistry 92, 47–52 (2001)

34. Schönhage, A.: Real-time simulation of multi-dimensional Turing machines by storage modification machines. Project MAC Technical Memorandum, vol. 37. MIT, Cambridge (1973)
35. Schönhage, A.: Storage modification machines. SIAM J. Comp. 9, 490–508 (1980)
36. Sedina-Nadal, I., Mihaliuk, E., Wang, J., Perez-Munuzuri, V., Showalter, K.: Wave propagation in subexcitable media with periodically modulated excitability. Phys. Rev. Lett. 86, 1646–1649 (2001)
37. Shirakawa, T.: Private communication (February 2007)
38. Shvachko, K.V.: Different modifications of pointer machines and their computational power. In: Tarlecki, A. (ed.) Mathematical Foundations of Computer Science 1991. LNCS, vol. 520, pp. 426–435. Springer, Heidelberg (1991)
39. Steinbock, O., Tóth, A., Showalter, K.: Navigating complex labyrinths: optimal paths from chemical waves. Science 267, 868–871 (1995)
40. Supowit, K.J.: The relative neighbourhood graph, with application to minimum spanning tree. J. ACM 30, 428–448 (1988)
41. Tarjan, R.E.: Reference machines require non-linear time to maintain disjoint sets, STAN-CS-77-603 (March 1977)
42. Tero, A., Kobayashi, R., Nakagaki, T.: A coupled-oscillator model with a conservation law for the rhythmic amoeboid movements of plasmodial slime molds. Physica D 205, 125–135 (2005)
43. Teuscher, C., Adamatzky, A. (eds.): Unconventional Computing 2005: From Cellular Automata to Wetware. Luniver Press (2005)
44. Tirosh, R., Oplatka, A., Chet, I.: Motility in a "cell sap" of the slime mold *Physarum Polycephalum*. FEBS Letters 34, 40–42 (1973)
45. Tsuda, S., Aono, M., Gunji, Y.-P.: Robust and emergent Physarum-computing. BioSystems 73, 45–55 (2004)
46. Tsuda, S., Zauner, K.P., Gunji, Y.P.: Robot Control: From Silicon Circuitry to Cells. In: Ijspeert, A.J., Masuzawa, T., Kusumoto, S. (eds.) BioADIT 2006. LNCS, vol. 3853, pp. 20–32. Springer, Heidelberg (2006)
47. Uspensky, V.A.: Kolmogorov and mathematical logic. The Journal of Symbolic Logic 57, 385–412 (1992)
48. Yamada, H., Nakagaki, T., Baker, R.E., Maini, P.K.: Dispersion relation in oscillatory reaction-diffusion systems with self-consistent flow in true slime mold. J. Math. Biol. (2007)

On the Computational Capabilities of Several Models

Olivier Bournez and Emmanuel Hainry

LORIA/INRIA, 615 Rue du Jardin Botanique
54602 Villers-Lès-Nancy, France
{Olivier.Bournez,Emmanuel.Hainry}@loria.fr

Abstract. We review some results about the computational power of several computational models. Considered models have in common to be related to continuous dynamical systems.

1 Dynamical Systems and Polynomial Cauchy Problems

A polynomial Cauchy problem is a Cauchy problem of type

$$\begin{cases} \mathbf{x}' = p(\mathbf{x}, t) \\ \mathbf{x}(0) = \mathbf{x}_0 \end{cases}$$

where $p(\mathbf{x}, t)$ is a vector of polynomials, and $\mathbf{x}_0$ is some initial condition.

The class of functions that are solution of a polynomial Cauchy problem turns out to be a very robust class [14]. It contains almost all natural mathematical functions. It is closed under addition, subtraction, multiplication, division, composition, differentiation, and compositional inverse [14].

Actually, every continuous time dynamical system $\mathbf{x}' = f(\mathbf{x}, t)$ where each component of f is defined as a composition of functions in the class and polynomials can be shown equivalent to a (possibly higher dimensional) polynomial Cauchy problem [14]. This implies that almost all continuous time dynamical systems considered in books like [17], or [22] can be turned in the form of (possibly higher dimensional) polynomial Cauchy problems.

For example, consider the dynamic of a pendulum $x'' + p^2 \sin(x) = 0$. Because of the sin function, this is not directly a polynomial ordinary differential equation. However, define $y = x'$, $z = \sin(x)$, $u = \cos(x)$. A simple computation of derivatives show that we must have

$$\begin{cases} x' = y \\ y' = -p^2 z \\ z' = yu \\ u' = -yz \end{cases},$$

which is a polynomial ordinary differential equation.

This class of dynamical systems becomes even more interesting if one realizes that it captures all what can be computed by some models of continuous time machines, such as the General Purpose Analog Computer (GPAC) of Shannon [26].

J. Durand-Lose and M. Margenstern (Eds.): MCU 2007, LNCS 4664, pp. 12–23, 2007.

2   The GPAC

The GPACs was introduced in 1941 by Shannon [26] as a mathematical model of an analog device: the Differential Analyzer [11]. The Differential Analyzer was used from the 1930s to the early 60s to solve numerical problems. For example, differential equations were used to solve ballistics problems. These devices were first built with mechanical components and later evolved to electronic versions.

A GPAC may be seen as a circuit built of interconnected black boxes, whose behavior is given by Figure 1, where inputs are functions of an independent variable called the *time* (in an electronic Differential Analyzer, inputs usually correspond to electronic voltages). These black boxes add or multiply two inputs, generate a constant, or solve a particular kind of Initial Value Problem defined with an ordinary differential equation.

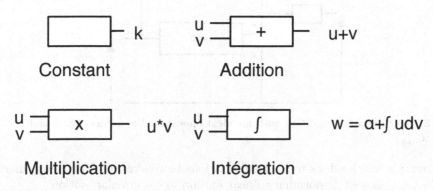

Fig. 1. The basic units of a GPAC (the output w of an integration operator satisfies $w'(t) = u(t)v'(t)$, $w(t_0) = \alpha$ for some initial condition α)

The model was further refined in [25,20,15,16]. For the more robust class of GPACs defined in [16], the following property holds:

Theorem 1 (GPAC Generated Functions [16]). *A scalar function $f : \mathbb{R} \to \mathbb{R}$ is generated by a GPAC iff it is a component of the (necessarily unique) solution of a polynomial Cauchy problem. A function $f : \mathbb{R} \to \mathbb{R}^k$ is generated by a GPAC iff all of its components are.*

From previous closure properties, GPAC can be considered as a faithful model of (today's) analog electronics [9]. Figure 3 shows how to realize an integration with an ideal operational amplifier, a resistor and a condenser.

3   Planar Mechanisms

The power of planar mechanisms made of rigid bars linked by their end by rivets attracted much attention in England and in France in the late 19th century, with a new birth of interest in Russia at the end of the forties: see for example [6], [27]. The

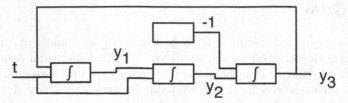

Fig. 2. Generating cos and sin by a GPAC. In form of a system of equations, we have $y_1' = y_3$, $y_2' = y_1$, $y_3' = -y_1$. It follows that $y_1 = \cos$, $y_2 = \sin$, $y_3 = -\sin$, if $y_1(0) = 1$, $y_2(0) = y_3(0) = 0$.

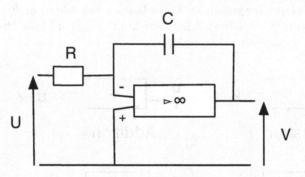

Fig. 3. Realizing an integration with an ideal operational amplifier: one has $V(t) = -1/RC \int_0^t U(t)dt$

pantograph, which allows to realize dilatations is well-known. The Peaucellier's mechanism allows transforming a linear motion into a circular motion.

More generally, this is natural to ask what is the power of such devices. This is given by the following very nice result (see for e.g. [6], [27]) attributed to Kempe [19]: this corresponds to semi-algebraic sets.

Theorem 2 (Completeness of planar mechanism)

- *For any non-empty semi-algebraic set S, there exists a mechanism with n points that move on linear segments, but that are free to move on these segments, and that forces the relation $(x_1, \ldots, x_n) \in S$, where x_i are the distances on the linear segments.*
- *Conversely, the domain of evolution of any finite planar mechanism is semi-algebraic.*

4   Distributed Computations

4.1   Populations Protocols

We present the recent *population protocol model* of [2], proposed as a model for passively mobile sensor networks.

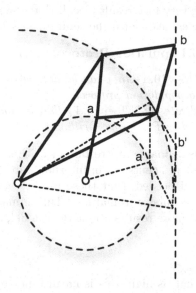

Fig. 4. Peaucellier's mechanism. The circular motion of a is transformed into a linear motion of b.

In this model, a protocol consists in giving a finite set of internal states $Q = \{1, 2, \ldots, k\}$, and transition rules given by $\delta : Q \times Q \to Q \times Q$. For $\delta(p, q) = (p', q')$, write $\delta_1(p, q) = p'$, $\delta_2(p, q) = q'$.

A configuration of a system at a given time is given by the internal states of each of the n individuals.

We suppose that the individuals are completely indiscernible. It follows that the state of a system can be described by the number n_i of individuals in state i, for $1 \leq i \leq k$, better than by the state of each individual.

At each discrete round, a unique individual i is put in relation with some other individual j: at the end of this meeting, the individual i is in state $\delta_1(q_i, q_j)$, and individual j is in state $\delta_2(q_i, q_j)$.

We suppose that we cannot control the interactions, and that there is a notion of fairness: if in a configuration C one can go to configuration C' in one step (denoted by $C \to C'$) then in any derivation $C_0 C_1 \cdots$, with $C_i \to C_{i+1}$ for all i, if C appears infinitely often, then C' also.

One wants to consider population protocols as predicate recognizers $\psi : \mathbb{N}^m \to \{0, 1\}$.

To do so, fix a subset $Q^+ \subset Q$, and say that an tuple $(n_1, \ldots, n_m) \in \mathbb{N}^m$, for $m \leq k$, is accepted (respectively rejected) by the protocol, if starting from any configuration with n_i individuals in state i, eventually all the individuals will be in some internal state that belongs to Q^+ (resp. its complement), and this stays true at any time afterward.

One says that the protocol recognizes $\psi : \mathbb{N}^m \to \{0, 1\}$ if for all tuple $(n_1, \ldots, n_m)$, it is accepted when $\psi(n_1, \ldots, n_m) = 1$ and it is rejected when $\psi(n_1, \ldots, n_m) = 0$.

We have the following very nice result (recall that the sets that are definable in Presburger arithmetic coincide with the semi-linear sets over the integers).

Theorem 3 (Power of Population Protocols [4])

- *Any predicate $\psi : \mathbb{N}^m \to \{0, 1\}$ that can be defined in Presburger arithmetic can be computed by a population protocol.*
- *Conversely, any predicate $\psi : \mathbb{N}^m \to \{0, 1\}$ that is computed by a population protocol can be defined in Presburger arithmetic.*

For example, since this is definable in Presburger arithmetic, there is a protocol to decide if more than 5% of agents are in internal state 1.

This theorems shows, if needed, that these models are really different from classical models, such as cellular automata, or Turing machines.

Refer to [1], [5], [3] for more results about this model, and some variants.

4.2 Another Model

If the number of individuals is high, this is natural not to talk about numbers, but about proportions or statistics.

For example, consider the following protocol: we have a population of n agents. Each agent is either in the state +, or in state −. Hence, a configuration corresponds to a point of $S = \{+, -\}^n$.

We suppose that time is discrete. At each discrete time (round), all (or a fixed fraction of) the agents interact in pairs, according to the following rules:

$$++ \to 1/2+, 1/2-$$
$$+- \to +$$
$$-+ \to +$$
$$-- \to 1/2+, 1/2-$$

One must interpret the second rule in the following way: if an individual of type + interacts with an individual of type −, then it becomes of type +. One must interpret the first rule in the following way: if an individual is of type + interacts with an individual of type +, he becomes of type + with probability $1/2$, and of type − with probability $1/2$.

We suppose that the pairings are chosen at random uniformly.

Experimentally, the proportion of + in the population converges towards $\sqrt{2}/2$, when the number of individuals increases. This could be expected, since, if p denotes the proportion of +, with probability p an individual meets a +, and $1 - p$ a −. Now, the first and fourth rule destroy in mean $1/2+$ each, whereas the second and third rules create one + each. By doing the sum, one can write that in expectation, the number of + that are created at each round is

$$1/2p^2 + 2p(1 - p) + 1/2(1 - p)^2 = 1/2 + p - p^2.$$

Now, at equilibrium, there must be conservation, and so it must be equal to p. Hence $p^2 = 1/2$, i.e. $p = \sqrt{2}/2$.

The previous system converges towards $\sqrt{2}/2$, and hence can be considered as computing this value. Which numbers are computable by such protocols? Of course, by assuming using pairwise pairing, rational probabilities, and a finite number of internal states for each agent.

5   Computing with Distributed Games

More generally, in previous two models, rules of interactions can be considered as games between participants. When the number of individuals n becomes high, models of dynamics of population, and of dynamics in game theory become natural and relevant. We review some of them.

5.1   Game Theory Models

To introduce some dynamism in game theory, there are two main approaches. The first consists in repeating games. The second in using models from evolutionary game theory.

Let's first present the simplest concepts from Game Theory [24]. We focus on non-cooperative games, with complete information, in extensive form.

The simplest game is a two player games, called I and II, with a finite set of options, called *pure strategies*, $Strat(I)$ and $Strat(II)$. Denote by $a_{i,j}$ (respectively: $b_{i,j}$) the score (or if it is a random variable its expected value) for player I (resp. II) when I uses strategy $i \in Strat(I)$ and II strategy $j \in Strat(II)$. The scores are given by $n \times m$ matrices A and B, where n and m are the cardinality of $Strat(I)$ and $Strat(II)$.

Example 1 (Prisonner dilemma). The case where A and B are the following matrices

$$A = \begin{pmatrix} 3 & 0 \\ 5 & 1 \end{pmatrix}, B = \begin{pmatrix} 3 & 5 \\ 0 & 1 \end{pmatrix}$$

is called the *game of prisoners*, or *prisoner dilemma*. We denote by C (for cooperation) the first pure strategy, and by D (for defection) the second pure strategy of each player.

A *mixed strategy* of player I, which consists in using $i \in Strat(I)$ with probability x_i, will be denoted by vector $\mathbf{x} = (x_1, \ldots, x_n)^T$. One must have $\sum_{i=1}^{n} x_i = 1$, i.e. $\mathbf{x} \in S_n$, where S_n is the unit simplex of $\mathbb{R}^n$, generated by the vectors $\mathbf{e}_i$ of the unit standard basis of $\mathbb{R}^n$. In a similar way, a mixed strategy for II corresponds to $\mathbf{y} = (y_1, \ldots, y_m)^T$ with $\mathbf{y} \in S_m$. If player II uses mixed strategy $\mathbf{x}$, and player II mixed strategy $\mathbf{y}$, then the first has mean score $\mathbf{x}^T A \mathbf{y}$ and the second $\mathbf{x}^T B \mathbf{y}$. A strategy $\mathbf{x} \in S_n$ is said to be a best response to strategy $\mathbf{y} \in S_m$, denoted by $\mathbf{x} \in BR(\mathbf{y})$ if

$$\mathbf{z}^T A \mathbf{y} \leq \mathbf{x}^T A \mathbf{y} \qquad (1)$$

for all strategy $\mathbf{z} \in S_n$. A pair $(\mathbf{x}, \mathbf{y})$ is a *mixed Nash equilibrium* if $\mathbf{x} \in BR(\mathbf{y})$ and $\mathbf{y} \in BR(\mathbf{x})$. Nash theorem [23] claims, by a fixed point argument, that such an equilibrium always exists. However, it is not necessarily unique.

5.2   Repeated Games

Repeating k times a game is equivalent to extend the space of choices into $Strat(I)^k$ and $Strat(II)^k$: player I (respectively II) chooses its action $\mathbf{x}(t) \in Strat(I)$, (resp. $\mathbf{y}(t) \in Strat(II)$) at time t for $t = 1, 2, \cdots, k$. Hence, this is equivalent to a two-players game with respectively n^k and m^k choices for players.

In practice, player I (respectively II) has to solve the following problem at each time (round) t: given the history of the game up to now, that is to say $X_{t-1} = \mathbf{x}(1), \cdots, \mathbf{x}(t-1)$ and $Y_{t-1} = \mathbf{y}(1), \cdots, \mathbf{y}(t-1)$ what should I play at time t? That is to say how to choose $\mathbf{x}(t) \in Strat(I)$? (resp. $\mathbf{y}(t) \in Strat(II)$?).

This is natural to suppose that the answer of each of the players is given by some behavior rules: $\mathbf{x}(t) = f(X_{t-1}, Y_{t-1})$, $\mathbf{y}(t) = g(X_{t-1}, Y_{t-1})$ for some functions f and g. For example, the question of the best behavior rule to use for the prisoner lemma gave birth to an important literature, in particular, after the book [7].

5.3   Games on a Graph

An example of behavior for the prisoner lemma is $PAVLOV$.

Example 2 (PAVLOV). The $PAVLOV$ behavior consists, in the iterated prisoner lemma, in fixing a threshold, say 3, and at time t, replaying the previous pure action if the last score is above this threshold, and changing the action otherwise.

Concretely, if we denote $+$ for C, and $-$ for D, one checks easily that this corresponds to rules

$$\begin{cases} ++ \rightarrow ++ \\ +- \rightarrow -- \\ -+ \rightarrow -- \\ -- \rightarrow ++, \end{cases} \tag{2}$$

where the left hand side of each rule denotes $\mathbf{x}(t-1)\mathbf{y}(t-1)$, and the right hand side the corresponding result for $\mathbf{x}(t)\mathbf{y}(t)$.

From a set of such rules, this is easy to obtain a distributed dynamic. For example, let's follow [12]: Suppose that we have a connected graph $G = (V, E)$, with N vertices. The vertices correspond to players. An instantaneous configuration of the system is given by an element of $\{+, -\}^N$, that is to say by the state $+$ of $-$ of each vertex. Hence, there are 2^N configurations.

At each round t, one chooses randomly and uniformly one edge (i, j) of the graph. At this moment, players i and j play the prisoner dilemma with the $PAVLOV$ behavior, that is to say the rules of the equation 2 are applied.

What is the final state reached by the system?

The underlying model is a huge Markov chain with 2^N states. The state $E^* = \{+\}^N$ is absorbing. If the graph G does not have any isolated vertex, this is the unique absorbing state, and there exists a sequence of transformations that transforms any state E into this state E^*. As a consequence, from well-known classical results for Markov chains, whatever the initial configuration is, with probability 1, the system will be in state E^* [10]. The system is *self-stabilizing*. Several results about the convergence time towards this stable state can be found in [12], and [13], for rings, and complete graphs.

What is interesting in this example is that it shows how to go from a game, and behaviors to a distributed dynamic on a graph. Clearly this is easy to associate a similar dynamic to any[1] Markovian behavior on a symmetric game.

5.4 Myopic Dynamic

In the general case, to every 2-players repeated game, one can associate the *myopic* behavior. It consists in the fact that each player makes systematically the hypothesis that the opposite player will replay at time t the same thing as he played at time $t - 1$. As a consequence, this behavior consists in choosing systematically at time t the (or a) best response to the action of the opposite player at time $t - 1$:

$$f(X_{t-1}, Y_{t-1}) \in BR(\mathbf{y}(t - 1)).$$

Take, like [8], the example of the Cournot duopoly game. The Cournot duopoly game is a well-known economical model of the competition of two producers of a same good. In this model, the production of a unit article of this good costs c. One makes the hypothesis that the total demand is of the form $q = q_1 + q_2 = M - p$, where p is the sold price, and q_1 and q_2 the number of produced articles by each of the firms.

The problem of firm I (respectively II) is to fix q_1 (resp. q_2) in order to maximize its profit $(p - c)q_1$ (resp. $(p - c)q_2$). One shows easily (see [8]), that the best response to q_2 is to choose $q_1 = 1/2(M - c - q_2)$, and that the best response to q_1 is to choose $q_2 = 1/2(M - c - q_1)$, so that the unique Nash equilibrium corresponds to the intersection of the two lines defined by these equations.

The myopic dynamic for the two players then gives on this game

$$\begin{cases} q_1(t) = 1/2(M - c - q_2(t - 1)) \\ q_2(t) = 1/2(M - c - q_1(t - 1)). \end{cases}$$

This is easy to show that whatever the initial point is, such a dynamic converges towards the Nash equilibrium. The collective dynamic converges towards the rational equilibrium. Unfortunately, as shown in [8], this is not always the case.

5.5 Fictious Player Dynamic

The myopic behavior can be considered as very too basic. A more reasonable behavior seems to be the following: to predict what will play the opposite player at time t, let's use the statistic of what he did at time $1, 2, \cdots, t - 1$: if he

---

[1] But not necessarily Pavlovian. Actually, the behavior $PAVLOV$, as described here, is not ambiguous only on 2 by 2 matrices.

played action i n_i times, let's estimate that he will play action i with probability $x_i = n_i/(t-1)$ at time t. This is what is called the *fictious player dynamic*.

To simplify things, let's follow [8], and suppose that $n = m = 2$, and that the matrices are given by

$$A = \begin{pmatrix} 0 & 3 \\ 2 & 1 \end{pmatrix}, \quad B = \begin{pmatrix} 2 & 0 \\ 1 & 3 \end{pmatrix}.$$

If at time $1, 2, \cdots, t-1$, player 2 used n_i times action number i, player I will estimate that player II will play at time t action i with probability $y_i(t) = n_i/(t-1)$. Player II will evaluate probability $x_i(t)$ that player I play action i in a symmetric way.

To study the dynamic, as this is shown in [8], one just needs to go from discrete time to continuous time: a simple analysis (see [8]) shows that as long as $(x_2(t), y_2(t))$ stays in zone A of the left part of Figure 5, player I will use its second pure strategy, and player II its first pure strategy as a best response to what he or she expects from the opposite player.

The dynamic $(x_2(t), y_2(t))$ will stay in this zone up to time $t + \tau$ for $\tau > 0$ sufficiently small. Since we know the choice of player II between time t and time $t + \tau$, one can hence evaluate $y_2(t + \tau)$ as

$$y_2(t + \tau) = \frac{t y_2(t)}{t + \tau}. \tag{3}$$

This can be written as $\frac{y_2(t+\tau) - y_2(t)}{\tau} = -y_2(t)$.

Bet letting τ converge to 0, we obtain $y_2'(t) = \frac{y_2(t)}{t}$.

In a similar way, we obtain $x_2'(t) = \frac{1 - x_2(t)}{t}$.

The points that satisfy these two equations are on a straight line that starts from $(x_2(t), y_2(t))$ and that joins point $(1, 0)$. A similar study on zones B, C, and D of the left part of Figure 5 shows that the dynamic must be the one depicted

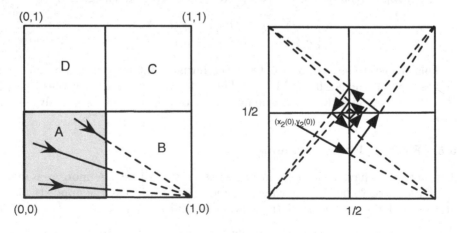

Fig. 5. Convergence towards a mixed equilibrium

on the right part of Figure 5. It converges towards the mixed Nash equilibrium of the game. Once again, the collective dynamic converges towards the rational equilibrium. Unfortunately, once again, this is not the case for all the games: one can easily consider games where trajectories do not converge, or with limit cycles [8].

5.6   Evolutionary Game Theory Models

Evolutionary game theory is another way to associate dynamics to games.

Evolutionary game theory is born from the book from Maynard Smith [21].

To illustrate how, to a game, can be associated a biological dynamic, let's take the fictive example of a population of individuals from [8]. Binmore chooses to call these individuals *dodos*.

The day of a dodo lasts a fraction τ of a year. There are n types of dodos: the dodos that play action 1, the dodos that play action 2, ..., and the dodos that play action n. Babies of a dodo of type i are always of type i.

We are interested in the proportion $x_i(t)$ of dodos that play action i. We have of course $\sum_{i=1}^{n} x_i(t) = 1$.

At the end of each day, the dodos fight pairwise. The outcome of a fight has some influence on the fecundity of involved participants. One reads on a matrix A $n \times n$ at entry $a_{i,j}$ the birth rate of a given dodo, if it is of type i and if he fights again an individual of type j: his expected number of babies at next day is given by $\tau a_{i,j}$.

How many babies a dodo of type i can expect to have at next day? The answer is

$$\sum_{j=1}^{n} x_j(t)\tau a_{i,j} = (A\mathbf{x})_i \tau.$$

Indeed, since the pairing for the fights on the evening between dodos are chosen at random and uniformly among the population, in expectation its birth rate is given by previous expression.

The number of dodos of type i in the next morning is hence

$$N x_i(t)(1 + (A\mathbf{x})_i \tau).$$

Mortality being not a function of the type of dodos, the next day, the fraction of dodos of type i will be given by

$$x_i(t + \tau) = \frac{N x_i(t)(1 + (A\mathbf{x})_i \tau)}{N x_1(t)(1 + (A\mathbf{x})_1 \tau) + \cdots + N x_n(t)(1 + (A\mathbf{x})_n \tau)}.$$

Hence

$$x_i(t + \tau) = \frac{x_i(t)(1 + (A\mathbf{x})_i \tau)}{1 + \mathbf{x}^T A \mathbf{x} \tau}.$$

where $\mathbf{x}^T A \mathbf{x} \tau$ can be interpreted as the expected number of birth for a dodo in a day.

This can be rewritten as

$$\frac{x_i(t + \tau) - x_i(t)}{\tau} = x_i(t)\frac{(Ax)_i - \mathbf{x}^T A \mathbf{x}}{1 + \mathbf{x}^T A \mathbf{x}\tau}.$$

By taking limit when τ goes to 0, we obtain

$$x_i' = x_i((Ax)_i - \mathbf{x}^t A \mathbf{x}).$$

This is what is called *replicator dynamic*. Such an equation models the fact that individuals whose score (fitness) given by matrix A is above mean score (fitness) have tendency to reproduce, whereas those that have a score under the mean score have tendency to disappear.

Of course the model about dodos is relatively ad hoc, but many situations and models give rise to same dynamics: see e.g. [21].

Evolutionary game theory aims at studying the behaviors of such dynamics in function of matrix A.

It has its own notions of equilibria, motivated by the stability of underlying dynamical systems, such as the notion of evolutionary stable equilibrium. An evolutionary stable equilibrium is a particular Nash equilibrium. It makes it possible to link the notions of equilibria for the game given by A to the notions of stability for the corresponding dynamical system.

Actually, it does not only consider replicator dynamics, but other dynamics such as imitation dynamics, best response dynamics, and so on..., with in all dynamics the idea that individuals with highest score reproduce faster than others. Refer to [21], [28], [18] for presentations.

References

1. Angluin, D., Aspnes, J., Chan, M., Fischer, M.J., Jiang, H., Peralta, R.: Stably computable properties of network graphs. In: Prasanna, V.K., Iyengar, S., Spirakis, P.G., Welsh, M. (eds.) DCOSS 2005. LNCS, vol. 3560, pp. 63–74. Springer, Heidelberg (2005)
2. Angluin, D., Aspnes, J., Diamadi, Z., Fischer, M.J., Peralta, R.: Computation in networks of passively mobile finite-state sensors. In: Twenty-Third ACM Symposium on Principles of Distributed Computing, July 2004, pp. 290–299. ACM Press, New York (2004)
3. Angluin, D., Aspnes, J., Eisenstat, D.: Fast computation by population protocols with a leader. In: Dolev, S. (ed.) DISC 2006. LNCS, vol. 4167, Springer, Heidelberg (2006)
4. Angluin, D., Aspnes, J., Eisenstat, D.: Stably computable predicates are semilinear. In: PODC '06: Proceedings of the twenty-fifth annual ACM symposium on Principles of distributed computing, New York, NY, USA, pp. 292–299. ACM Press, New York (2006)
5. Angluin, D., Aspnes, J., Fischer, M.J., Jiang, H.: Self-stabilizing population protocols. In: Anderson, J.H., Prencipe, G., Wattenhofer, R. (eds.) OPODIS 2005. LNCS, vol. 3974, pp. 79–90. Springer, Heidelberg (2006)
6. Artobolevskii, I.I.: Mechanisms for the generation of plane curves. Macmillan, New York (1964) (Translated by Wills, R.D., Johnson, W.)

7. Axelrod, R.M.: The Evolution of Cooperation. Basic Books (1984)
8. Binmore, K.: Jeux et Théorie des jeux. DeBoeck Université, Paris-Bruxelles (1999) (Translated from "Fun and Games: a text on game theory" by Bismans, F., Damaso, E.)
9. Bournez, O.: Modéles Continus. Calculs. Algorithmique Distribuée. Habilitationá diriger les recherches, Institut National Polytechnique de Lorraine (Décembre 7, 2006)
10. Brémaud, P.: Markov Chains, Gibbs Fields, Monte Carlo Simulation, and Queues. Springer, New York (2001)
11. Bush, V.: The differential analyser. Journal of the Franklin Institute 212(4), 447–488 (1931)
12. Dyer, M.E., Goldberg, L.A., Greenhill, C.S., Istrate, G., Jerrum, M.: Convergence of the iterated prisoner's dilemma game. Combinatorics, Probability & Computing 11(2) (2002)
13. Fribourg, L., Messika, S., Picaronny, C.: Coupling and self-stabilization. In: Guerraoui, R. (ed.) DISC 2004. LNCS, vol. 3274, pp. 201–215. Springer, Heidelberg (2004)
14. Graça, D.: Computability with Polynomial Differential Equations. PhD thesis, Instituto Superior Técnico (2007)
15. Graça, D.S.: Some recent developments on Shannon's general purpose analog computer. Mathematical Logic Quarterly 50(4-5), 473–485 (2004)
16. Graça, D.S., Costa, J.F.: Analog computers and recursive functions over the reals. Journal of Complexity 19(5), 644–664 (2003)
17. Hirsch, M.W., Smale, S., Devaney, R.: Differential Equations, Dynamical Systems, and an Introduction to Chaos. Elsevier Academic Press, Amsterdam (2003)
18. Hofbauer, J., Sigmund, K.: Evolutionary game dynamics. Bulletin of the American Mathematical Society 4, 479–519 (2003)
19. Kempe, A.B.: On a general method of describing plane curves of the n–th degree by linkwork. Proceedings of the London Mathematical Society 7, 213–216 (1876)
20. Lipshitz, L., Rubel, L.A.: A differentially algebraic replacement theorem, and analog computability. Proceedings of the American Mathematical Society 99(2), 367–372 (1987)
21. Maynard-Smith, J.: Evolution and the Theory of Games. Cambridge University Press, Cambridge (1981)
22. Murray, J.D.: Mathematical biology. I: An introduction. In: Biomathematics, 3rd edn., vol. 17, Springer, Heidelberg (2002)
23. Nash, J.F.: Equilibrium points in n-person games. Proc. of the National Academy of Sciences 36, 48–49 (1950)
24. Osbourne, Rubinstein: A Course in Game Theory. MIT Press, Cambridge (1994)
25. Pour-El, M.B.: Abstract computability and its relation to the general purpose analog computer (some connections between logic, differential equations and analog computers). Transactions of the American Mathematical Society 199, 1–28 (1974)
26. Shannon, C.E.: Mathematical theory of the differential analyser. Journal of Mathematics and Physics MIT 20, 337–354 (1941)
27. Svoboda, A.: Computing Mechanisms and Linkages. McGraw Hill (1948) (Dover reprint 1965)
28. Weibull, J.W.: Evolutionary Game Theory. MIT Press, Cambridge (1995)

Universality, Reducibility, and Completeness

Mark Burgin

Department of Computer Science,
University of California, Los Angeles
Los Angeles, California 90095, USA
mburgin@math.ucla.edu

Abstract. Relations between such concepts as reducibility, universality, hardness, completeness, and deductibility are studied. The aim is to build a flexible and comprehensive theoretical foundations for different techniques and ideas used in computer science. It is demonstrated that: concepts of universality of algorithms and classes of algorithms are based on the construction of reduction of algorithms; concepts of hardness and completeness of problems are based on the construction of reduction of problems; all considered concepts of reduction, as well as deduction in logic are kinds of reduction of abstract properties. The Church-Turing Thesis, which states universality of the class of all Turing machines, is considered in a mathematical setting as a theorem proved under definite conditions.

Keywords: universal, reducibility, computability, algorithm, problem completeness, problem hardness, computing power.

1 Introduction

Reducibility is a powerful technique of problem solving. Psychologists found that reducibility is at the core of human comprehension. People recognize things only when they are able to reduce them to known patterns. Although this approach works well in many situations, in cases of encountering something essentially new, original, and innovative, reducibility becomes an obstacle that hinders correct comprehension and causes serious mistakes. A notorious example of this is the situation with the famous Church-Turing Thesis. The essence of the Thesis is a possibility to reduce (model) any algorithm to (by) a Turing machine. Overcoming this absolute reducibility and consequent i refutation of the Church-Turing Thesis brought researchers to the rich universe of superrecursive algorithms [12,13].

Reducibility is often used in mathematics and computer science to solve different problems or to show that these problems are unsolvable. For instance, the general formula for the solution of a cubic equation was found by reduction of the general cubic equation to one in which the second-degree term was absent [16]. In the theory of differential equations, the Cauchy problem for an arbitrary linear system of differential equations is reduced to Cauchy problem for a linear system of first order differential equations.

J. Durand-Lose and M. Margenstern (Eds.): MCU 2007, LNCS 4664, pp. 24–38, 2007.

In a similar way, undecidability of the problem whether a language of a Turing machine is finite is proved by a reduction of the halting problem for Turing machines to this problem. By this technique, undecidability of the following problems is also proved:

if the language of a Turing machine is empty;

if the language of a Turing machine is contains all words in a given alphabet;

if a Turing machine computes a total function.

Reduction is used to prove the very important Rice theorem [19] and its axiomatic version [14].

Reducibility is at the core of some basic concepts in complexity theory, such as NP-hard and NP-complete problems, K-completeness for an arbitrary class K of algorithms and some other concepts.

At the same time, universality, universal automata and algorithms play an important role in computer science and technology. As it is written in [4], "A pillar of the classical theory of computation is the existence of a universal Turing machine, a machine that can compute any (recursively, M.B.) computable function. This theoretical construct foretold and provides a foundation for the modern general-purpose computer." Any universal Turing machine determines what is recursively computable, acceptable or decidable. In addition, the whole theory of Kolmogorov complexity is based on the concept of universal Turing machine. Moreover, computer technology also owes a lot to universal Turing machines. The structure of a universal Turing machine served as a model for the famous von Neumann architecture for a general-purpose computer. This architecture has determined for decades how computers have been built. Now an important property of programming languages is Turing completeness, which means a possibility to write a program that simulates a universal Turing machine in this language. Parallel to this, the Universality Axiom AU, which demands existence of a universal algorithm, is one of the basic axioms in the axiomatic theory of algorithms [14].

In this paper, we study relations between such concepts as reducibility, universality, hardness, completeness, and deductibility. In Section 2, going after Introduction, we introduce several types of reducibility for algorithms and automata and demonstrate how reducibility determines universality of algorithms and automata. In Section 3, our main concern are universal classes of algorithms and automata in the context of the Church-Turing Thesis. The topic of Section 4 is completeness and hardness of computational problems. Section 5 explicates relations between those kinds of reducibilities that are studied in previous sections and reduction of abstract properties.

2 Universality of Algorithms and Reducibility

An algorithm provides a recipe to solve a given problem. For simplicity, it is possible to assume that an algorithm consists of a finite number of rules, each having well defined and realizable meaning. Often algorithms that have states, such as Turing machines or finite automata, are considered.

Not to be limited by a definite model of algorithms, in this section, we treat algorithms in the context of the axiomatic theory of algorithms [14].

Let **K** be a class of automata/algorithms that take inputs from a set X and give outputs that belong to a set Y. There are two principal axioms that characterize algorithms, in general, and deterministic algorithms, in particular.

Computation Postulate (PCM). Any algorithm A from **K** determines a binary relation r_A in the direct product $X \times Y$ of all its inputs X_A and all its outputs Y_A.

We remind that the set X_A is called the *domain* of A and the set Y_A is called the *codomain* of A. If $x \in X$ and A is an algorithm from **K**, then $A(x)$ denotes the result of application of A to x.

However, in many cases, it is preferable to have such algorithms that for each input give only one result. These algorithms are called deterministic and are characterized by the following axiom.

Deterministic Computation Postulate (PDC). Any algorithm A from **K** determines a function f_A from X into Y.

Informally it means that given some input, A always produces the same result.

Remark 1. Functions may be partial and total. The latter are defined for all elements of X.

Examples of classes that compute relation and not a function are: non-deterministic computing finite automata, algorithms for multiple computations [8], and interactive algorithms [18].

We remind that a relation r in the direct product $X \times Y$ is called *computable* in **K** if $r = r_A$ for some algorithm A from **K**. In particular, a function f from X into Y is called computable in **K** if $f = f_A$ for some algorithm A from **K**.

All algorithms are divided into three big classes [13]: *subrecursive*, *recursive*, and *super-recursive*. Algorithms and automata that have the same computing/accepting power (cf., [14]) as Turing machines are called *recursive*. Examples are partial recursive functions or random access machines.

Algorithms and automata that are weaker than Turing machines, *i.e.*, that can compute less functions, are called *subrecursive*. Examples are finite automata, context free grammars or push-down automata.

Algorithms and automata that are more powerful than Turing machines are called *super-recursive*. Examples are inductive Turing machines, Turing machines with oracles or finite-dimensional machines over the field of real numbers [4].

Let us consider:

- an algorithm A that takes inputs from the set X and gives outputs that belong to a set Z,
- an algorithm B that takes inputs from Y and gives outputs that belong to Z,
- an algorithm C that takes inputs from X and gives outputs that belong to Y,
- a class **R** of automata/algorithms that take inputs from X and give outputs that belong to a set Y,

– a class of automata/algorithms **Q** that take inputs from Y and give outputs that belong to Z.

Definition 1. *An algorithm A is* **left R-reducible** *(right **Q**-reducible or* (**R**,**Q**)*-reducible) to an algorithm B if there is an algorithm D from **R** (correspondingly, an algorithm H from **Q** or an algorithm D from **R** and an algorithm H from Q) such that for any element $x \in X$, we have $A(x) = B(D(x))$ (correspondingly, $A(x) = H(B(x))$ or $A(x) = H(B(D(x)))$), or $r_A = r_{D \circ} r_B$ (correspondingly, $r_A = r_{B \circ} r_H$ or $r_A = r_{D \circ} r_{B \circ} r_H$).*

Left **R**-reducibility of A to B is denoted by $A \leq_{\mathbf{R}} B$, and right **Q**-reducibility of A to B is denoted by $A \leq^{\mathbf{Q}} B$, and (**R**,**Q**)-reducibility of A to B is denoted by $A \leq^{\mathbf{Q}}_{\mathbf{R}} B$.

Remark 2. It is possible to take classes of functions or binary relations as **R** and **Q** and use them to define reducibility of an algorithm A to an algorithm B.

Lemma 1. *If an algorithm A is left (right) **R**-reducible to an algorithm B and $\mathbf{R} \subseteq \mathbf{H}$, then A is left (correspondingly, right) **H**-reducible to B.*

Let us consider reducibility for some popular classes of algorithms, the class of all Turing machines **T**.

Theorem 1. *If a Turing machine B defines the total function f_B that is a projection(injection), then any Turing machine A is left **T**-reducible(right **T**-reducible) to B.*

Many concepts in recursion theory and theory of algorithms are special kinds of reductions. At first, we consider such property as universality. We know that some classes of algorithms have universal algorithms, such as universal Turing machines, universal inductive Turing machines, universal cellular automata, etc. Reducibility allows us to define universality. As reducibility is a relative property, it defines several types of universality.

To build a general concept, let us consider universal Turing machines. The well known definition tells us that a Turing machine U is universal if given a description $\mathbf{c}(T)$ of a Turing machine T and some input data x for it, then the machine U gives the same result as gives T working with the input x, and U does not give the result when T does not give the result for input x.

We see that the construction of universal for the class **K** automata and algorithms is usually based on some codification (symbolic description) $\mathbf{c} \colon \mathbf{K} \mapsto X$ of all automata/algorithms in **K**.

Definition 2. *An automaton/algorithm U is universal for the class **K** if there is a codification $\mathbf{c} \colon \mathbf{K} \mapsto X$ such that any automaton/algorithm A from **K** is left $\mathbf{c}$-reducible to U.*

Examples of universal automata are universal Turing machines, universal cellular automata [3], universal partial prefix functions [21] universal inductive Turing machines, universal limit Turing machines [11], and universal functions in the sense of [22].

A more general concept is **R**-universality.

Definition 3. *An automaton/algorithm U is* **R**-*universal for the class* **K** *if there is an automaton/algorithm C from* **R** *such that any automaton/algorithm A from* **K** *is left C-reducible to U.*

Lemma 2. *If an algorithm A is universal for the class* **K** *and* **H** ⊆ **K**, *then A is universal for the class* **H**.

Universal algorithms for the class **K** does not necessary belong to **K** as the following result shows.

Theorem 2. *There is no primitive recursive function universal for the class* **PRR** *of recursive recursive functions, but there is a recursive function universal for the class* **PRR**.

As Lemma 2 implies, the same is true for Turing machines, that is, any universal Turing machine is universal for the class **TT** of Turing machines that compute total functions, but universal Turing machines do not belong to **TT** and this class does not have a universal algorithm. In a similar way, any inductive Turing machine is universal for the class **ITT** of inductive Turing machines that compute total functions, but universal inductive Turing machines do not belong to **ITT** and this class does not have a universal algorithm.

There is an even more general concept of universality.

Definition 4. *An automaton/algorithm U is* **weakly R-universal** *for the class* **K** *if any automaton/algorithm A from* **K** *is left* **R**-*reducible to U.*

Theorem 1 implies the following result.

Corollary 1. *Any Turing machine B that defines the total function* f_B *is weakly* **T**-*universal for the class* **T**.

A stronger type of reducibility is compositional reducibility of algorithms and automata. To describe it, we need to formalize the notion of equivalence of algorithms.

Definition 5. *Two algorithms A and B are called* **functionally (linguistically) equivalent (with respect to acceptability** *or* **decidability)** *if they compute the same function* f_A *or relation* r_A *(accept or decide the same language* L_A*).*

Let X_A and X_B be the domains and Y the range of algorithms A and B, correspondingly, and $\mathbf{1}_X$ is the identity mapping of X.

Proposition 1. *a) Algorithms A and B are functionally equivalent if and only if each of them is left* $\mathbf{1}_X$-*reducible to the other one. b) Algorithms A and B are linguistically equivalent if and only if there are mappings* $g_A : X_A \mapsto X_B$ *and* $g_B : X_B \mapsto X_A$ *such that A is* $(g_A, \mathbf{1}_Y)$-*reducible to B and B is* $(g_B, \mathbf{1}_Y)$-*reducible to A.*

Example 1. In the theory of finite automata, linguistic equivalence means that two finite automata accept the same language [19]. This relation is used frequently to obtain different properties of finite automata. The same is true for the theory of pushdown automata.

Let us consider some system **P** of schemas for algorithm/automata composition. Examples of composition schemas are: sequential composition, parallel composition, compositions that are used in programming languages, such as IF ... DO ... ELSE ... and DO ... WHILE .... The system **P** allows us to define compositional reducibility of algorithms and automata.

Definition 6. *An algorithm A is* **P-reducible** *to an algorithm B if applying schemas from* **P***, it is possible to obtain an algorithm D that is functionally equivalent to A. The algorithm D is called a* **compositional reduction** *of A.*

In this context, right and left reducibilities are compositional reducibilities defined by the schema of sequential composition.

In turn, compositional reducibility is a kind of operational reducibility.

Let **R** be a class of automata/algorithms and B an automaton/algorithm. Then **R**[B] denotes the class of automata/algorithms that use B as an elementary operation.

Definition 7. *An algorithm A is* **operationally reducible** *to an algorithm B in* **R** *if there is an algorithm D in* **R**[B] *that is functionally equivalent to A. The algorithm D is called an* **operational reduction** *of A.*

It is possible to formalize operational reducibility using algorithms with oracles, *i.e.*, algorithms that have a possibility to get data from some device called oracle. This oracle can give, for example, values of some function or inform whether some element belongs to a given set. In case of **R** = **T** and set reducibility by Turing machines with oracles, it gives the well know concept of Turing reducibility [24].

Proposition 2. *If algorithm A is* **P***-reducible to an algorithm B and* **R** *is a class of automata/algorithms closed with respect to schemas from* **P***, then A is operationally reducible to B in* **R***.*

In automata/algorithms that are compositional or operational reductions of an automaton (program/algorithm) A is **P**-reducible to an automaton (program/algorithm) B, the automaton/algorithm B becomes an imbedded device (a subprogram). Correspondingly, in an operational reduction, automata from **R** form the system in which B is imbedded, while in an compositional reduction, automata from **R** are used to build the system in which B is imbedded.

Concepts of compositional and operational reducibilities give corresponding concepts of universality.

Definition 8. *An automaton/algorithm U is* **compositionally P-universal** *(***operationally universal in R***) for the class* **K** *if any automaton/algorithm A from* **K** *is reducible to U in* **R***.*

Universal gates in Boolean logic are examples of compositionally universal algorithms. A gate is called universal if all other types of Boolean logic gates (i.e., AND, OR, NOT, XOR, XNOR) can be created from a suitable network of this gate. NAND and NOR logic gates are such universal gates.

Universal partially recursive functions [22] are examples of operationally universal algorithms. At the same time, there is a wider class of universal functions. A function $f: \mathbf{N} \mapsto \mathbf{N}$ is called a function of big extension if for any number n from $\mathbf{N}$, its inverse image $f^{-1}(n)$ is infinite.

Theorem 3. [23] *Any primitive recursive function f of big extension is operationally M-universal for the class $\mathbf{PR}$ of all partial recursive functions where M consists of two schemas: minimization and superposition.*

3 Universality of Classes of Algorithms, Models of Computation, and Reducibility

From universality of individual algorithms, we go to universality of classes and models of algorithms. Such universality is also based on the construction of reduction and computing power of algorithms. To understand what algorithms can do and what they cannot is very important not only for theory but also for the practice of information processing. Different researchers discussed these problems (cf., for example, [2,12,20,25,27]). One of the pillars of contemporary computer science is the Church-Turing Thesis (**CTT**) that gives boundaries of computer power. In theoretical research and practical development, it is essential to compare power of different algorithms, computational schemas, programming systems, programming languages, computers, and network devices.

Informally, a class of algorithms A (is weaker than or equivalent to) has computing power less than or equal to computing power of a class of algorithms B when algorithms from B can compute everything that algorithms from A can compute.

Remark 3. Any mathematical or programming model of algorithms defines some class of algorithms. Thus, comparing classes corresponding to models, we are able to compare power of these models.

There are different formalizations of computing power comparison. Boker and Dershowitz [6] give the following definition.

Definition 9. *A system of algorithms (or in their terminology, computational model) $\mathbf{B}$ is (**computationally**), at least, as powerful as a system of algorithms (model) $\mathbf{A}$ if there is a bijective mapping π of the domain of $\mathbf{B}$ onto the domain of $\mathbf{A}$ such that the corresponding image of any function computed by some algorithm in $\mathbf{A}$ is a function computed by some algorithm in $\mathbf{B}$. It is denoted by $\mathbf{A} \preceq \mathbf{B}$.*

In the context of this paper, it means that algorithms from $\mathbf{A}$ can be $(i\pi,\pi^{-1})$-reduced to algorithms from $\mathbf{B}$.

Boker and Dershowitz also study other types of techniques for comparing algorithms and classes of algorithms [5,7].

Another approach of computing power comparison is suggested in [14].

Definition 10. *A class of algorithms* **A** *has* **less or equal functional computing power** *than (is* **functionally weaker than or equivalent to***) a class of algorithms* **B** *when algorithms from* **B** *can compute any function that algorithms from* **A** *can compute.*

Informally it means that algorithms from **A** can be functionally reduced to algorithms from **B**.

Definition 11. *Two classes of algorithms are* **functionally equivalent** *(or simply,* **equivalent***) if they compute the same class of functions, or relations for non-deterministic algorithms.*

One of the most illustrious problems at the turn of the 21st century is whether the classes **P** of all problems that have a deterministic polynomial time solution and **NP** of all problems that have a nondeterministic polynomial time solution are functionally equivalent. Formally, it is denoted by "**P** = **NP** ?". This problem is equivalent to the problem whether the classes **PT** of all deterministic Turing machines that solve problems in a polynomial time and **NTP** of all nondeterministic Turing machines that solve problems in a polynomial time are functionally equivalent.

Let us consider a class **R** of automata/algorithms and a family **F** of classes of automata/algorithms.

Definition 12. *The class* **R** *of automata/algorithms is called* **universal** *for the family* **F** *if for any automaton/algorithm A that belongs to a class from* **F***, there is an automaton/algorithm C from* **R** *equivalent to A.*

For a long time, it was assumed that the following classes are universal for family of arbitrary classes of algorithms: the class **T** of all Turing machines, class **PR** of all partial recursive functions, class **CA** of all cellular automata and some others. This was, in essence, the statement of the Church-Turing Thesis (**CTT**). As the notion of algorithm is informal, **CTT** has been considered as physical law that is impossible to prove by mathematical means. Some of researchers suggested that it is necessary to prove **CTT** under some natural assumptions. Recently, the situation with **CTT** has been mostly clarified. At first, it was demonstrated that there are classes of algorithms more powerful than **T** [12,13], then Boker and Dershowitz [6] obtained a very important result proving **CTT** for a comprehensible family of state transition machine classes and models of computation.

Definition 13. *The class* **R** *of automata/algorithms is called* **strongly universal** *for the family* **F** *if for any class* **K** *from* **F***, we have* **K** $\preceq$ **R**.

Let a family **R** of classes of automata/algorithms satisfies the following axioms.

Axiom BD1 (Sequential Time). Any computational procedure can be viewed as a collection of states, a sub-collection of initial states and a transition function from state to state.

Actually, it is possible to consider only one initial state.

Axiom BD2a (Abstract State). All states are first-order structures with the same vocabulary.

Axiom BD2b (Input-Output). There are input In and output Out functions on states.

Axiom BD2c (Closure). Procedures are closed with respect to isomorphisms of states.

Axiom BD2d (Transition). The transition function preserves domains and isomorphisms of states.

Axiom BD3 (Bounded Exploration). There is a finite bound on the number of vocabulary terms that affect the transition function.

Axiom BD4 (Initial Data). The initial state consists of an infinite base structure and an almost constant structure.

In this model, algorithms/automata are called procedures and a computational model is identified with a class of procedures. A run of a procedure gives a result by means of the output function Out if and only if this run is finite or is stabilizing.

Theorem 4. (Boker and Dershowitz [6]) *The class* **T** *of all Turing machines is strongly universal for the family* **R**.

It is possible to extend this result to the realm of superrecursive algorithms.

Let a family **SR** of classes of automata/algorithms satisfy Axioms BD1, BD2b, BD2c, BD2d, BD3, BD4, and the following modification of the Axioms BD2a.

Axiom SR2a (Abstract State). All states are direct products of two first-order structures with the same vocabulary.

This allows us to change the definition of procedure convergence and obtaining the result in the model of Boker and Dershowitz [6]. First, the result is defined on the second projections of states. Second, a run of a procedure gives a result by means of the output function Out if and only if this run is finite or is stabilizing on the second projections of its states.

Theorem 5. *The class* **IT** *of all inductive Turing machines is universal for the family* **SR**.

In Theorems 4 and 5, algorithms are characterized by simple operations and consequently, universality of the classes **T** and **IT** is characterized from below: they give the upper bounds (supremum) of computability that uses those simple operations. At the same time, it is possible to characterize universality of the classes **T** and **IT** from above (as an infinum), taking such algorithmic constructions as transrecursive operators, which go much beyond algorithms.

Let **A** be a class of algorithms. A sequence $sc\ Q = \{A_i \in \mathbf{A}; i = 1, 2, 3, \ldots\}$ is called a schema of a transrecursive operator Q. A transrecursive operator is defined on a set X and takes value in a topological space Y. Given an element x from X as input, the transrecusive operator Q produces a sequence $\mathrm{run}Q(x) = \{a_i; i = 1, 2, 3, \ldots\}$ where $a_i = A_i(x)$ when $A_i(x)$ is defined and $a_i = *$ when $A_i(x)$ is not defined. The result of the run $\mathrm{run}Q(x)$ is defined only when a finite number of $A_i(x)$ are not defined and $\mathrm{run}Q(x)$ converges in the topological space Y. The result of the run $\mathrm{run}Q(x)$ is equal to the limit $\lim \mathrm{run}Q(x)$.

Definition 14. *A transrecusive operator Q is called* **constructive** *if its schema is constructed (computed) by a recursive algorithm, e.g., by a Turing machine.*

Theorem 6. (Burgin and and Borodyanskii [15]) *The class* **IT** *of all inductive Turing machines is universal for any family* **TR** *of classes of constructive transrecursive operators.*

If we add one more condition, the class T of all Turing machines becomes universal.

Definition 15. *A transrecusive operator Q is called* **(recursively)** *halting if all its converging runs are finite (and a recursive algorithm regulates the lengths of all its runs).*

Theorem 7. *The class* **T** *of all Turing machines is strongly universal for the family* **FR** *of classes of constructive recursively halting transrecursive operators.*

4   Completeness of Problems and Reducibility

Computers are made and programs are written to solve different problems. That is why, it is natural to look at relations between reducibility and universality in the realm of problems. The first thing that we can find is that universality there has a different name, or actually, two names - completeness and hardness. We start with the most general definition of these concepts.

In a general sense, one problem is reducible to another if a method of solving the second problem yields a method for solving the first. Different kinds of problem reducibilities (one-one reducibility, many-one reducibility, truth-table reducibilities and Turing reducibility) are studied in [24] where sets are used to represent problems and reducibility is considered as relation between sets of integers.

Although there are reductions of general problems to decidability of sets, these reductions can hide essential properties of problems and even change their solvability. There are problems in which solvability and/or efficiency of solutions depend on the initial data representation. That is why here we consider algorithmic problems, solutions to which are given by algorithms or by algorithmic schemas.

Let E be some schema of reduction of algorithms.

Definition 16. *A problem q is* E-**reducible** *to a problem p if there is an algorithm B that solves problem p such that some algorithm A that solves problem q is E-reducible to the algorithm B.*

If **K** is a class of algorithmic problems, and **Q** is a class of algorithms, complete and hard problems for the class **K** relative to the class **Q** are naturally introduced. It is possible to define the class **Q** as a complexity class. For example, **Q** is the class of all algorithms the computational complexity measure **Fc** [13] of which is bounded by a function f or by some function from a class of functions **F**. It gives us the following concepts.

Definition 17. *A problem p is called hard for the class **K** relative to the class **Q** (with respect to the function f or to the class **F**) if any problem from **K** can be reduced to the problem p by some algorithms from **Q** (reduced to the problem p with complexity **Fc** less than or equal to f or less than or equal to some function from **F**, respectively).*

Definition 18. *A problem p from the class **K** is called complete for the class **K** (relative to the class **Q**) if any problem from **K** can be reduced to the problem p by some algorithms from **K** (from **Q**).*

For example, the following problems are complete in the class **NP** of all problems that have a nondeterministic polynomial time solution (**NP**-complete problems): the Traveling Salesman Problem, Satisfiability Problem, Hamiltonian Circuit Problem, Independent Set Problem, Knapsack Problem, Clique Problem, Node Cover Problem, and Coloring Problem.

Definition 19. *A problem p from the class **K** is called complete for the class **K** with respect to the function f (to the class **F**) and the measure **Fc** if any problem from K can be reduced to the problem p with complexity **Fc** less than or equal to f (to some function from **F**).*

In other words, complete problems for a class are hard problems that belong to the same class.

Proposition 3. *Hardness (completeness) with respect to function (to a class of functions) can be reduced to hardness (respectively, completeness) relative to a class of algorithms.*

The concept of completeness has two parameters. It depends on the type of reducibility used, and the class **Q** of algorithms used for reductions. For instance, there are two types of **NP**-completeness: Cook-completeness and Karp-completeness [19]. Cook-completeness uses operational reduction, while Karp-completeness uses left reduction.

Two following results demonstrate how reduction depends on algorithms used for reduction.

Theorem 8. *Deciding if a Turing machine computes a total function can be reduced by inductive Turing machines of the first order to the halting problem, but cannot be reduced by Turing machines to the halting problem.*

Let f be some function on words in some alphabet. It is possible to consider the classes **PTf** of all deterministic Turing machines with the advice f that solve problems in a polynomial time and **NTPf** of all nondeterministic Turing machines with the advice f that solve problems in a polynomial time are functionally equivalent.

Theorem 9. (Baker, Gill, and Solovey, [1]) *There is an advice f such that any machine from $\mathbf{NTP}_f$ can be reduced in deterministic polynomial time to a machine from $\mathbf{PT}_f$ and there is an advice g such that there are machines in $\mathbf{NTP}_g$ that cannot be reduced in deterministic polynomial time to a machine from $\mathbf{PT}_g$.*

5   Reduction of Properties and Deduction of Theorems

Reducibility of algorithms and problems is a special kind of reducibility of abstract properties [10].

Definition 20. *An abstract property P is a triad of the form $P = (U, p, L)$ where the property P is defined on objects from a universe U and takes value in a partially ordered set L called the scale of the property P, while $p: U \mapsto L$ is a partial function.*

Example 2. Let take as U the set of all people. Then we can consider such properties as age, height, and weight. It is possible to represent age by the abstract property $Age = (U, age, T)$ where T is the set of natural numbers and the function $age: U \mapsto T$ corresponds to each individual the number of years that passed from her/his birth. In a similar way, it is possible to represent height and weight by the abstract properties $Height = (U, height, R^{++})$ and $Weight = (U, weight, R^{++})$ where R^{++} is the set of all positive real numbers and the functions $height: U \mapsto R^{++}$ and $weight: U \mapsto R^{++}$ relate to each individual her/his height and weight, correspondingly.

Functions that algorithms compute are abstract properties. Languages that algorithms accept or decide can be determined by their characteristic (membership) functions.

Informally, reduction of a property P_1 to a property P_2 means that knowing values of the property P_2 , we can find values of the property P_1 . This idea is formalized in the following way.

Let us consider two universes U_1 and U_2 and two properties $P_1 = (U_1, p_1, L_1)$ and $P_2 = (U_2, p_2, L_2)$. We can build the following sets and mappings:

$U_2^* = \cup_{n=1}^{\infty} U_2^n$ where U_2^n is the n-th direct power of U_2;
$L_2^* = \cup_{n=1}^{\infty} L_2^n$ where L_2^n is the n-th direct power of L_2;
$1_{U_1} : U_1 \mapsto U_1$ is the identical mapping of U_1;

if $p_2 : U_2 \mapsto L_2$ is a partial mapping, then $p_2^*: U_2^* \mapsto L_2^*$ is a partial mapping such that the restriction of p_2^* on the set L_2^n is equal to p_2^n.

Definition 21. *A property $P_1 = (U_1, p_1, L_1)$ is reduced to a property $P_2 = (U_2, p_2, L_2)$ if there is there are mappings $g: U_1 \mapsto U_2^*$ and $h: L_2^* \times U_1 \mapsto L_1$ where h preserves the partial order in L_2 such that $p_1 = h \circ (p_2 * \times 1_{U_1}) \circ (g \times 1_{U_1})$.*

Example 3. If we take such properties as the weight P_1 of an individual in kilograms and the weight P_2 of an individual in pounds, then P_1 is reducible to P_2 and P_2 is reducible to P_1.

Reduction of abstract properties studied in [10] is a special case the construction introduced in Definition 21. This special case corresponds to the right reduction of algorithms. General reduction of abstract properties allows us to represent all kinds of reduction of algorithms. Indeed, any partial function in general and any partial function $f\colon X^* \mapsto X^*$ on words in an alphabet X, in particular, is some abstract property on these words. Thus, any deterministic algorithm/automaton determines, according to the PDC postulate, some property on X^*. Now let us consider, for example, operational reduction for deterministic algorithms with finite utilization of embedded algorithm (cf. Section 2). This is the case when we have two algorithms A and B, a class of algorithms $\mathbf{R}$ and B is used as an elementary operation in algorithms from $\mathbf{R}[B]$. As it was mentioned, it is possible to substitute the algorithm B as an operation in algorithms from $\mathbf{R}[B]$ by the operation of asking an oracle O_B, which given some input z, gives the result $B(z)$ as its answer.

Thus, if the algorithm A is operationally reduced to B in $\mathbf{R}$, there is an algorithm D in $\mathbf{R}[B]$ that is functionally equivalent to A, *i.e.*, there are algorithms $W, V \in \mathbf{R}$ such that $A(x) = W(D(V(x)))$ and D uses B only finite number of times. Consequently, there are elements x_1, x_2, ..., x_n such that D in its computation with the input $V(x)$ uses only outputs $B(x_1)$, $B(x_2)$, ..., $B(x_n)$ of the algorithm B. Then we define $g(x) = (x_1, x_2, \ldots, x - n)$ and $h(B(x_1), B(x_2), \ldots, B(x_n), x) = W(D(B(x_1), B(x_2), \ldots, B(x_n), V(x)))$. As a result, we obtain a reduction of the property $P_1 = (X^*, f_A, X^*)$ to a property $P2 = (X^*, f_B, X^*)$. This reduction completely represents reduction of the algorithm A to the algorithm B.

Reduction of properties also provides a new perspective on logic. We know that axioms and theorems of formal theories define properties of objects in models of these theories [17]. Usually axioms define simple properties and theorems define much more complex properties. These properties are binary, that is, an object either have this property or does not have it.

Proof of a theorem is a reduction of the property represented by this theorem to the properties represented by axioms. Usually, it is a left $\mathbf{D}$-reduction where $\mathbf{D}$ is the class of all logical deductions. Thus, deduction becomes a kind of reduction.

6   Conclusion

In this paper, we explicated relations between such concepts as reducibility, universality, hardness, completeness, and deductibility. It is demonstrated that: concepts of universality of algorithms and classes of algorithms are based on the construction of reduction of algorithms; concepts of hardness and completeness of problems are based on the construction of reduction of problems; all considered concepts of reduction and deduction in logic are kinds of reduction of abstract properties.

It would be also interesting to study connections between the construction of reduction and concepts of universality in algebra (e.g., universal algebra), topology (e.g., universal fibration), theory of categories (e.g., universal map), and other mathematical fields.

The author is grateful to Maurice Margenstern for useful remarks and advice.

References

1. Baker, T., Gill, J., Solovey, R.: Relativizations of the **P** =? **NP** question. SIAM Journal of Computing 4, 431–442 (1975)
2. Bennett, C.N., Landauer, R.: On Fundamental Physical Limits of Computation. Scientific American 7, 48–56 (1985)
3. Berlekamp, E.R., Conway, J.H., Guy, R.K.: Winning Ways for Your Mathematical Plays. Academic Press, London (1982)
4. Blum, L., Cucker, F., Shub, M., Smale, S.: Complexity of Real Computation. Springer, New York (1998)
5. Boker, U.: Comparing Computational Power. PhD thesis, Tel-Aviv University (2004)
6. Boker, U., Dershowitz, N.: A Formalization of the Church-Turing Thesis for State-Transition Models, `http://www.cs.tau.ac.il/`
7. Boker, U., Dershowitz, N.: How to Compare the Power of Computational Models. In: Cooper, S.B., Löwe, B., Torenvliet, L. (eds.) CiE 2005. LNCS, vol. 3526, pp. 54–64. Springer, Heidelberg (2005)
8. Burgin, M.: Multiple computations and Kolmogorov complexity for such processes (translated from Russian). Notices of the Academy of Sciences of the USSR 269(4), 793–797 (1983)
9. Burgin, M.: Composition of operators in a multidimensional structured model of parallel computations and systems (translated from Russian). Cybernetics and System Analysis 19(3), 340–350 (1984)
10. Burgin, M.: Abstract Theory of Properties and Sociological Scaling (in Russian). In: Expert Evaluation in Sociological Studies. Kiev, pp. 243–264 (1990)
11. Burgin, M.: Universal limit Turing machines (translated from Russian). Notices of the Russian Academy of Sciences 325(4), 654–658 (1992)
12. Burgin, M.: How We Know What Technology Can Do. Communications of the ACM 44(11), 82–88 (2001)
13. Burgin, M.: Superrecursive Algorithms. Springer, New York (2005)
14. Burgin, M.: Measuring Power of Algorithms, Programs, and Automata. In: Shannon, S. (ed.) Artificial Intelligence and Computer Science, pp. 1–61. Nova Science Publishers, New York (2005)
15. Burgin, M.S., Borodyanskii, Y.M.: Alphabetic Operators and Algorithms. Cybernetics and System Analysis 29(3), 42–57 (1993)
16. Burton, D.M.: The History of Mathematics. McGrow Hill Co., New York (1997)
17. Dreyfus, H.L.: What Computers Can't Do - The Limits of Artificial Intelligence. Harper and Row (1979)
18. Eberbach, E., Goldin, D., Wegner, P.: Turing's Ideas and Models of Computation. In: Teuscher, C. (ed.) Alan Turing: Life and Legacy of a Great Thinker, pp. 159–194. Springer, Heidelberg (2004)
19. Hopcroft, J.E., Motwani, R., Ullman, J.D.: Introduction to Automata Theory, Languages, and Computation. Addison Wesley, Boston, San Francisco, New York (2001)

20. Lewis, J.P.: Limits to Software Estimation. Software Engineering Notes 26(4), 54–59 (2001)
21. Li, M., Vitanyi, P.: An Introduction to Kolmogorov Complexity and its Applications. Springer, New York (1997)
22. Malcev, A.I.: Algorithms and Recursive Functions (in Russian), Nauka, Moscow (1965)
23. Markov, A.A.: Theory of Algorithms (in Russian). Transactions of the Mathematical Institute of the Academy of Sciences of the USSR 42 (1954)
24. Rogers, H.: Theory of Recursive Functions and Effective Computability. MIT Press, Cambridge Massachusetts (1987)
25. Rubel, L.A.: Some Mathematical Limitations of the General-Purpose Analog Computer. Advances in Applied Mathematics 9, 22–34 (1988)
26. Shoenfield, J.R.: Mathematical Logic. Addison-Wesley, Reading, Mass (1967)
27. Turing, A.M.: Can digital computers think? In: Machine Intelligence, vol. 15, Oxford University Press, Oxford (1951, 1999)

Using Approximation to Relate Computational Classes over the Reals

Manuel L. Campagnolo[1] and Kerry Ojakian[2]

[1] DM/ISA, Lisbon University of Technology and SQIG/IT Lisbon
mlc@math.isa.utl.pt
[2] SQIG/IT Lisbon and IST, Portugal
ojakian@math.ist.utl.pt

Abstract. We use our method of approximation to relate various classes of computable functions over the reals. In particular, we compare *Computable Analysis* to the two analog models, the *General Purpose Analog Computer* and *Real Recursive Functions*. There are a number of existing results in the literature showing that the different models correspond exactly. We show how these exact correspondences can be broken down into a two step process of *approximation and completion*. We show that the method of approximation has further application in relating classes of functions, exploiting the transitive nature of the approximation relation. This work builds on our earlier work with our method of approximation, giving more evidence of the breadth of its applicability.

1   Introduction

In short, the goal of this paper is to relate various computational models over the reals, using our notion of *approximation* as a unifying tool and language. *Computable Analysis* (originating with Grzegorczyk [13]) is a model of computation in which the data consists of the real numbers and the computation proceeds in discrete time steps. From this point of view, a function is considered computable if (*roughly*) from approximations for the inputs we can compute (using, for example, a typical discrete Turing Machine) approximations for the outputs. Various models of *analog computation* also compute on the real numbers, but the computation can instead be argued to proceed in an analog manner. We will consider two analog models, Shannon's *General Purpose Analog Computer* (GPAC) [20] and Moore's *Real Recursive Functions* [16] (with some problems corrected by Costa and Mycka in [17] and [18]). The GPAC is an analog circuit model, which by the work of Graça and Costa [11] is equivalent to certain dynamical systems. The Real Recursive Functions are given by a function algebra in which the typical discrete operations of recursion are replaced by operations which yield the solution of a differential equation. Bournez and Hainry ([1], [2]) have related various classes of Computable Analysis and Real Recursive Functions; we have expanded upon their work in [8] and [7]. Bournez, Campagnolo, Graça, and Hainry [19] have related Computable Analysis to the GPAC. We will

J. Durand-Lose and M. Margenstern (Eds.): MCU 2007, LNCS 4664, pp. 39–61, 2007.
© Springer-Verlag Berlin Heidelberg 2007

use our method of approximation to provide a unified view of these results and show how this approach can facilitate the technical development.

The motivation for characterizing the functions of Computable Analysis can be seen as twofold. On the one hand this work can be seen as a kind of search for a Church-Turing thesis in the context of real computation. For computation on the natural numbers there is an agreed upon notion of what it means to be *computable*, bolstered by the impressive fact that a number of different models of computation (e.g. Turing Machines, recursive functions, while programs, etc) yield the same set of functions. There are various models of computation over the reals, but many lack that kind of correspondence. In the work surveyed here the authors have developed exact correspondences within real computation by modifying existing models in reasonable ways. Developing these correspondences should be an important step towards some kind of a Church-Turing thesis for real computation. Another motivation for finding these correspondences is the possibility of shedding light on the questions of classic complexity theory. In particular, the complexity class separations (such as the classic P versus NP question) for the naturals correspond to the analogous questions in Computable Analysis. Thus, interesting and useful correspondences to Computable Analysis could allow the use of different tools to attack these questions; for example, perhaps the P versus NP question would be reduced to a question about differential equations, allowing new tools to come into play. This latter line of thought is the motivation behind the work of Costa and Mycka [9], which discusses the equivalence of an analytic condition to $P = NP$.

In section 3 we show how the various results (i.e. relating Computable Analysis, the GPAC, and Real Recursive Functions) all fit into a similar two step pattern we call *approximation and completion*. To get the rough idea, suppose $\mathcal{F}$ is the class of functions arising from one model, say Computable Analysis, and $\mathcal{H}$ is the class of functions of another model, say the GPAC, and the goal is to show that $\mathcal{F} = \mathcal{H}$. The classes happen to be defined in such a way that we can isolate subclasses $\mathcal{F}' \subseteq \mathcal{F}$ and $\mathcal{H}' \subseteq \mathcal{H}$, such that $\mathcal{F} = (\mathcal{F}')^*$ and $\mathcal{H} = (\mathcal{H}')^*$, where we use the star superscript to indicate some kind of "completion" operation. The approximation step involves showing, roughly, that $\mathcal{F}' \approx^{\mathcal{E}} \mathcal{H}'$, which means that for any function in one class, there is a function in the other one that approximates it with an accuracy dictated by $\mathcal{E}$ ($\mathcal{E}$ is some set of functions used to measure the accuracy). The completion step requires showing that from the approximate equality $\mathcal{F}' \approx^{\mathcal{E}} \mathcal{H}'$ we can derive the genuine equality $(\mathcal{F}')^* = (\mathcal{H}')^*$, i.e. $\mathcal{F} = \mathcal{H}$. On the technical side, this way of phrasing the problem allows us to bring in our tools involving the method of approximation. On the more philosophical side, we believe the approximation and completion approach makes important issues concerning these results more explicit. In our discussion on future work, in section 5, we discuss questions this raises.

In section 4, we show how approximations can be used to facilitate the technical work of relating different classes of functions. Supposing we are interested in the claim $\mathcal{F} \approx^{\mathcal{E}} \mathcal{H}$, the transitive property of the approximation relation can facilitate the proof. Rather than attempting to show the claim directly, which could become cumbersome, we can develop an intermediary class $\mathcal{G}$ and break the task down into two subtasks $\mathcal{F} \approx^{\mathcal{E}} \mathcal{G}$ and $\mathcal{G} \approx^{\mathcal{E}} \mathcal{H}$. In particular, we will show how this facilitates the elimination of non-analytic functions from models of computation, while maintaining the desired properties.

In section 2 we give a streamlined account of the notion of approximation and related concepts (the details are worked out in our papers [8] and [7], the latter one providing an improved development). In section 5 we discuss ideas for future work.

2   Technical Preliminaries

We provide an outline of the technical development from [8] and [7], where we consider the latter paper to be the improved version, and the one we will generally cite here. We start by discussing the approximation relation and then discuss its connections to function algebras.

2.1   Approximation

To develop formally the definition of approximation we will need to be able to talk about functions and their arguments in a precise way. Unless otherwise stated, a function has a finite number of real arguments and a single real number as an output. We let

$$\mathsf{Var} = \{x_i \mid i \in \mathbb{N}\}$$

be the **set of variables**. A function is always associated with a *finite set* of such variables and the values of the functions result from assigning elements of $\mathbb{R}$ to its variables. For convenience, we will use any lower case letters to refer to variables, and to refer to a finite set of variables we will put a bar over the letter (e.g. x refers to a variable and $\bar{x}$ refers to a *possibly empty* finite subset of Var); we also use lower case letters to refer to real numbers. When we write a function f as $f(\bar{x})$ we mean that the set of variables associated to f is exactly the set $\bar{x}$ (i.e. no more variables and no less). When we write variables or sets of variables as a list separated by commas, such as $\bar{x}, \bar{y}$, we intend that the variables are all distinct. If we have lists of variables or numbers $\bar{a}$ and $\bar{b}$, the same lengths as $\bar{x}$ and $\bar{y}$, respectively, then by $f(\bar{a}, \bar{b})$ we mean the value of f when the variables $\bar{x}, \bar{y}$ are assigned to $\bar{a}, \bar{b}$ in order (though the elements in a set do not have an order, we can always think of a set of variables as ordered by its indices). In fact, given a function $f(\bar{x})$ with domain X, we often write $\bar{x} \in X$ to mean that the variables of $\bar{x}$ should be assigned arbitrarily in X. We will often speak of a set of functions without explicitly discussing its variables; we always assume that every function in a set of functions exists in all its "instantiations" with variables, e.g. the function "$x + y$" occurring among a set of functions refers to: $x_0 + x_1, x_1 + x_0, x_1 + x_1, x_0 + x_2$, etc. The key point is that given two functions, the notion of variables allows us to associate the arguments of the functions in any way we wish. Any classes of functions we work with will be sufficiently strong that we can freely manipulate variables in typical ways.

We will now define the approximation notion between classes of functions, building on the notion of approximation between two single functions.

Definition 1. *Given a function $f(x_1, \ldots, x_k)$ we let $\mathsf{domain}(f) \subseteq \mathbb{R}^k$ refer to its domain.*

Definition 2. *If $X \subseteq \mathbb{R}^k$ and $Y \subseteq \mathbb{R}^{k+r}$, we say $X \sqsubseteq Y$ if for every $\bar{x} \in X$, there is a $\bar{y} \in \mathbb{R}^r$ such that $\bar{x}, \bar{y} \in Y$.*

Definition 3. *Suppose $f(\bar{x})$, $h(\bar{y})$, and $\varepsilon(\bar{u})$ are functions such that $\bar{x}, \bar{u} \subseteq \bar{y}$. Suppose also that $\mathsf{domain}(f) \subseteq \mathsf{domain}(h)$. We say*

$$f \preceq^\varepsilon h,$$

if for any assignment to the variables $\bar{y}$ (which induces assignments on its subsets $\bar{x}, \bar{u}$) such that $\bar{x} \in \mathsf{domain}(f)$, the function ε is defined at $\bar{u}$ and the following holds:

$$|f(\bar{x}) - h(\bar{y})| \le \varepsilon(\bar{u}).$$

In the above definition we tend to think of the variables $\bar{y}$ as converging to infinity, motivating the following definition.

Definition 4. *A function $f(\bar{x}, \bar{y})$ **has unbounded domain in** $\bar{y}$ if for any $\bar{x} \in \mathbb{R}$, the set $\{\bar{y} \mid (\bar{x}, \bar{y}) \in \mathsf{domain}(f), \bar{y} > 0\}$ is either empty or unbounded.*

An important point in the relationship of the function and the function approximating it, is the structure of the variables, formalized in the following definition.

Definition 5. *Let $\mathcal{P}(\mathsf{Var})$ be the set of finite subsets of Var. We call a function $\flat : \mathcal{P}(\mathsf{Var}) \to \mathcal{P}(\mathsf{Var}) \times \mathcal{P}(\mathsf{Var})$ a **structure function**, and let $\flat_1$ refer to its first component and $\flat_2$ to its second.*

Now we define two notions of approximation between classes of functions, say $\mathcal{A}$ and $\mathcal{B}$, so that roughly, we write $\mathcal{A} \preceq \mathcal{B}$ to mean that for any function in $\mathcal{A}$, there is a function in $\mathcal{B}$ that "approximates" it. The approximation relation will be defined relative to a class of functions $\mathcal{E}$ that measures the accuracy of the approximation. The definition will also use a set of structure functions S which are used to enforce certain relationships between the variables of the function being approximated and the function approximating it (for example, sometimes we will want to force the approximating function to have "parameter variables" and at other times we want to forbid this).

Definition 6. *Let $\mathcal{A}$, $\mathcal{B}$, and $\mathcal{E}$ be non-empty classes of functions Let S be a non-empty set of structure functions.*

- *We write*
  $$\mathcal{A} \preceq_{\mathsf{S}}^{\forall \varepsilon} \mathcal{B}$$
  to mean that $\forall f(\bar{x}) \in \mathcal{A}$, $\forall \flat \in \mathsf{S}$, $\forall \varepsilon \in \mathcal{E}$ (with variables $\flat_1(\bar{x})$), $\exists h \in \mathcal{B}$ (with variables $\flat_2(\bar{x})$), such that $f \preceq^\varepsilon h$, where ε and h have unbounded domain in their variables other than $\bar{x}$.

– *We write*
$$\mathcal{A} \preceq_S^{\exists}{}^{\mathcal{E}} \mathcal{B}$$
to mean the same thing as $\mathcal{A} \preceq_S^{\forall}{}^{\mathcal{E}} \mathcal{B}$, *except that the second and third universal quantifiers* (∀) *are replaced by existential quantifiers* (∃).

To obtain "approximations with no error," we will use the following set of functions:

Zero is the set of all functions $f(x_1, \ldots, x_k)$, for any arity $k \in \mathbb{N}$, such that $\mathrm{domain}(f) = \mathbb{R}^k$ and its value is zero everywhere.

We will be interested in the following sets of structure functions.

– We let the minus sign ("−") refer to the following singleton set of structure functions:
   On input $\bar{x}$ it outputs $(\bar{x}, \bar{x})$.
   Thus to write $\mathcal{A} \preceq_-^{\forall}{}^{\text{Zero}} \mathcal{B}$ means that for any function in $\mathcal{A}$ there is a function in $\mathcal{B}$, possibly with an extended domain, so that on their common domain they are equal (i.e. the "approximation" must have no error).
– We let the plus sign ("+") refer to the following set of structure functions given by taking all the functions of the following form:
   On input $\bar{x}$ it outputs $(\bar{x} \cup \bar{y}, \bar{x} \cup \bar{y})$, where $\bar{y}$ is a disjoint and possibly empty finite subset of variables.
– We let $\wp$ refer to the following set of structure functions given by taking all the functions of the following form:
   On input $\bar{x}$ it outputs $(\bar{u} \cup \bar{y}, \bar{x} \cup \bar{y})$, for any *non-empty* $\bar{y}$ disjoint from $\bar{x}$ and any $\bar{u} \subseteq \bar{x}$ ($\bar{u}$ may be empty).

Thus the "−" approximation does not allow "parameter" variables, the $\wp$ approximation requires some "parameter" variables, and the + approximation allows "parameter" variables, but does not require them. The following lemma follow immediately from the definitions.

Lemma 1. $\mathcal{A} \preceq_+^{\forall \mathcal{E}} \mathcal{B}$ *implies* $\mathcal{A} \preceq_\wp^{\exists \mathcal{E}} \mathcal{B}$

The stronger definition (i.e. "$\preceq_+$") is useful for the involved technical work with approximating, as done in [7], but ultimately, a weaker kind of approximation (i.e. "$\preceq_\wp^{\exists}$") often suffices for our purposes; in particular, a weaker notion satisfies lemma 5. However the stronger notion has other important properties, such as satisfying lemma 3 and satisfying *transitivity* (lemma 2). It will be useful to list a number of conventions regarding the approximation notation.

1. If the quantifier is missing in the superscript we assume it is ∀.
2. If the subscript is missing we assume it is "−".
3. If $\mathcal{E}$ is missing, we assume $\mathcal{E} = $ Zero.

Thus for example, $\mathcal{A} \preceq \mathcal{B}$ abbreviates $\mathcal{A} \preceq_-^{\forall \text{Zero}} \mathcal{B}$.
   We recall the definition of "bounding class" (we use our older definition from [8]). A number of technical aspects of the definition are not used in this paper, but are important for some of the results that are referenced.

Definition 7. *For a function $f(y, \bar{x})$, we say it **converges uniformly to infinity in y** if for every $n > 0$ there is $m_0 > 0$ such that for any $m, \bar{x} \in domain(f)$, $m \geq m_0$, we have $f(m, \bar{x}) \geq n$.*

Definition 8. *A class of functions $\mathcal{B}$ is a **bounding class** if it has the following properties:*

1. *There is an $f \in \mathcal{B}$ such that $f \geq 1$.*
2. *$f(\bar{x}) \in \mathcal{B}$ implies the value of $f(\bar{x}) > 0$.*
3. *For $f(\bar{x}; t) \in \mathcal{B}$, $f(\bar{x}; t) = f(\bar{x}; -t)$, for any variable t.*
4. *$f \in \mathcal{B}$ implies f is increasing.*
5. *$f \in \mathcal{B}$ converges uniformly to infinity in any of its variables.*
6. *If $f(\bar{x}) \in \mathcal{B}$ and $\bar{y}$ are variables disjoint from $\bar{x}$, then there is $f^*(\bar{x}, \bar{y}) \in \mathcal{B}$ such that $f(\bar{x}) \leq f^*(\bar{x}, \bar{y})$.*
7. *If $f, g \in \mathcal{B}$, then there are $h_1, h_2, h_3 \in \mathcal{B}$ such that $f + g \leq h_1$, $f \circ g \leq h_2$, and $f * g \leq h_3$*

An example of a bounding class is the following set of functions that grow like a tower of exponentials; it will be useful for our work with the elementary functions.

Definition 9. *Let $\exp^{[n]}(z)$ be defined by $\exp^{[0]}(z) = z$ and $\exp^{[n+1]}(z) = \exp^{[n]}(\exp(z))$ for $n \in \mathbb{N}$ and $z \in \mathbb{R}$. Let $\mathcal{T}$ be the bounding class*

$$\mathcal{T} = \{\exp^{[n]}(|x_1| + \cdots + |x_k|) \mid k, n \in \mathbb{N}\}.$$

We will form "error classes" by taking the reciprocal of a bounding class, i.e. for a set of functions $\mathcal{F}$, $1/\mathcal{F} = \{1/f \mid f \in \mathcal{F}\}$. The following lemma indicates that the a form of the approximation relation is transitive.

Lemma 2. *Suppose $\mathcal{A}$, $\mathcal{B}$, and $\mathcal{C}$ are classes of functions, and $\mathcal{D}$ is a bounding class. If $\mathcal{A} \preceq^{1/\mathcal{D}}_+ \mathcal{B} \preceq^{1/\mathcal{D}}_+ \mathcal{C}$ then $\mathcal{A} \preceq^{1/\mathcal{D}}_+ \mathcal{C}$.*

A useful shorthand is the following "approximate equality."

Definition 10. *We write $\mathcal{A} \approx^{\mathcal{E}}_S \mathcal{B}$ to mean that both $\mathcal{A} \preceq^{\mathcal{E}}_S \mathcal{B}$ and $\mathcal{B} \preceq^{\mathcal{E}}_S \mathcal{A}$ hold.*

Another important kind of relationship between classes of functions will be that of one class dominating another.

Definition 11. *Suppose $\mathcal{A}$ and $\mathcal{B}$ are classes of functions. We write $\mathcal{A} \leq \mathcal{B}$ if for every function $f(\bar{x}) \in \mathcal{A}$ there is a function $h(\bar{x}) \in \mathcal{B}$ such that $domain(f) \subseteq domain(h)$, and $|f(\bar{x})| \leq h(\bar{x})$ for all $\bar{x} \in domain(f)$.*

The growth rate of a class of functions turns out to be a significant issue. In fact for two bounding classes $\mathcal{B}_1$ and $\mathcal{B}_2$, if both $\mathcal{B}_1 \leq \mathcal{B}_2$ and $\mathcal{B}_2 \leq \mathcal{B}_1$ (*not* the same as $\mathcal{B}_1 = \mathcal{B}_2$), then they can typically be interchanged without effecting our results.

2.2   Function Algebras

We will use function algebras to define most of our classes of functions. They are defined by giving some basic functions and closing the class under operations on functions.

Definition 12. *Suppose $\mathcal{A}$ is a class of functions. An **operation with domain** $\mathcal{A}$ is a function which takes as input some functions in $\mathcal{A}$, and outputs a single function.*

Definition 13. *Suppose $\mathcal{B}$ is a set of functions (called **basic** functions), and $\mathcal{O}$ is a set of operations. Then $FA[\mathcal{B}; \mathcal{O}]$ is called a **function algebra**, and it denotes the smallest set of functions containing $\mathcal{B}$ and closed under the operations in $\mathcal{O}$. For ease of readability, we often list the elements of $\mathcal{B}$ or $\mathcal{O}$ simply as a list separated by commas.*

One consequence of this definition is that if the set of basic functions have some property which is preserved under the operations, then all functions in the algebra will satisfy it. For $k \in \mathbb{N}$, by $\mathcal{C}^k$ we mean the $k-$times continuously differentiable functions on $\mathbb{R}$. We give an example of a function algebra that only contains $\mathcal{C}^2$ functions. It will use the operation of obtaining a solution to a linear differential equation.

Definition 14. *LI is the operation which takes as input functions:*

$$g_1(\bar{x}), \ldots, g_n(\bar{x}), s_{11}(y, \bar{x}), \ldots, s_{nn}(y, \bar{x}),$$

and returns $h_1(y, \bar{x})$ where we have the following defining equations:

$$h_1(0, \bar{x}) = g_1(\bar{x})$$
$$\vdots$$
$$h_n(0, \bar{x}) = g_n(\bar{x})$$

$$\tfrac{\partial}{\partial y} h_1(y, \bar{x}) = s_{11}(y, \bar{x}) h_1(y, \bar{x}) + \ldots + s_{1n}(y, \bar{x}) h_n(y, \bar{x})$$
$$\vdots$$
$$\tfrac{\partial}{\partial y} h_n(y, \bar{x}) = s_{n1}(y, \bar{x}) h_1(y, \bar{x}) + \ldots + s_{nn}(y, \bar{x}) h_n(y, \bar{x})$$

Note that technically LI is not an operation in our sense because it does not have a fixed arity; we can simply view it as a convenient way to refer to a set of operations, each having a fixed arity. Note that an aspect of the operation is to choose the variable y with respect to which we differentiate; we avoid this technical point for this operation and for others. The basic functions will include a function θ_3, where for any $k \in \mathbb{N}$ ($k > 0$), $\theta_k(x) = \begin{cases} 0, & x < 0; \\ x^k, & x \geq 0. \end{cases}$, a $\mathcal{C}^{k-1}$ version of the discontinuous function which indicates whether a number is to the left or right of zero. We will also include some constants such as π, as well as the set of *projection functions* which we denote by P. By comp we mean the operation of composition.

Definition 15. *Let $\mathcal{L}$ abbreviate $FA[0, 1, -1, \pi, \theta_3, P; comp, LI]$.*

To compare function algebras it will be useful to talk about a class of functions, $\mathcal{B}$, approximating an operation; intuitively this means that if any functions are approximated by $\mathcal{B}$ then applying the operation maintains this approximation by $\mathcal{B}$.

Definition 16. *Suppose op is an arity k operation with domain $\mathcal{A}$, and $\mathcal{B}$ is a class of functions. We write $op \preceq^{\mathcal{E}}_+ \mathcal{B}$ to mean:*

For any $f_1, \ldots, f_k \in \mathcal{A}$, if $f_i \preceq^{\mathcal{E}}_+ \mathcal{B}$ ($i = 1 \ldots k$) then $op(f_1, \ldots, f_k) \preceq^{\mathcal{E}}_+ \mathcal{B}$

The following is an easy but repeatedly used lemma.

Lemma 3. *Suppose $\mathcal{B}_1$ and $\mathcal{B}_2$ are classes of functions and $\mathcal{O}_1$ and $\mathcal{O}_2$ are sets of operations.*

If $\mathcal{B}_1 \preceq^{\mathcal{E}}_+ FA[\mathcal{B}_2; \mathcal{O}_2]$ and $op \preceq^{\mathcal{E}}_+ FA[\mathcal{B}_2; \mathcal{O}_2]$ holds for every $op \in \mathcal{O}_1$ then $FA[\mathcal{B}_1; \mathcal{O}_1] \preceq^{\mathcal{E}}_+ FA[\mathcal{B}_2; \mathcal{O}_2]$.

We will now recall how composition can be approximated in a general way, using the concept of modulus functions (recalling the definition from [7], for technical reasons, in this paper, we add a few requirements).

Definition 17

- $|\bar{b} - \bar{a}|$ *abbreviates* $|b_1 - a_1| + \ldots + |b_n - a_n|$.
- *Suppose $f(\bar{x})$ and $m(\bar{x}, z)$ are functions such that $domain(f) \subseteq domain(m)$. Then m is a **modulus** for f if m is increasing, has unbounded domain in z, and:*

    For all $\bar{x} \in domain(f)$ and $z > 0$ such that $\bar{x}, z \in domain(m)$, we have that $|\bar{x} - \bar{y}| \leq m(\bar{x}, z)$ implies $|f(\bar{x}) - f(\bar{y})| \leq 1/z$, for all $\bar{y} \in domain(f)$.

- *A class of functions $\mathcal{M}$ is a modulus for the class of functions $\mathcal{F}$ if for any $f \in \mathcal{F}$, there is $m \in \mathcal{M}$ such that m is a modulus for f.*

It will be useful here and later to define the notion of restricting a function (whether a real function or even in the case where the function is an operation).

Definition 18. *If f is any function, say with domain $\mathcal{A}$, and $\mathcal{B}$ is a set, we write $f_{|\mathcal{B}}$ to indicate the function f with its domain restricted to $\mathcal{A} \cap \mathcal{B}$.*

Lemma 4. *(see [7]) Let $\mathcal{H}$ and $\mathcal{F}$ be a classes of functions closed under composition and let $\mathcal{B}$ be a bounding class.*

If $\mathcal{H} \leq \mathcal{B}$ and $\mathcal{H}$ has a $1/\mathcal{B}$ modulus then $comp_{|\mathcal{H}} \preceq^{1/\mathcal{B}}_+ \mathcal{F}$.

3   Characterizing Computable Analysis

We will begin by introducing the technical framework and then discuss our general approach to characterizing the classes of computable analysis via the two step pattern of *approximation and completion*. We will use standard notions from Computable Analysis, as described in Ko [14] and Weihrauch [21], though following more closely the former. For the most part Ko restricts his attention to functions defined on a finite interval, while we consider functions defined on all of $\mathbb{R}$. Thus in this work, a number of notions will depend on both the input value to the function, as well as the usual accuracy parameter (as in, for example, the case of the modulus functions).

By $\mathbf{C}(\mathbb{R})$ we mean the *total* $\mathbb{R}$−functions $f(\overline{x})$ which can be computed to accuracy $1/n$ ($n \geq 1$). The real input $\overline{x}$ is given by an oracle which gives $\overline{x}$ to any demanded precision as a dyadic rational; the precision $1/n$ is given by putting n on the input tape (we call this the **accuracy input**). Note that we use the approximation of the form $1/n$ rather than $1/2^n$, since for the classes we work with are sufficiently strong that such distinctions have no effect.

We now consider the process of approximation and completion. We will use the approximation as defined in the previous section, as a first step in this process. For the second step, the completion, all the results will use some kind of limit operation, which will be defined relative to a class of suitable functions (the idea of using a limit operation goes back to work from Costa and Mycka, see [17] and [18]).

Definition 19. *We say a class of functions $\mathcal{E}$ **converges to** 0 if any function in $\mathcal{E}$ converges to 0 as any of its arguments (which has unbounded definition) converges to $+\infty$.*

A useful class that converges to 0 is $1/\mathcal{ID}$, where $\mathcal{ID}$ is the set of unary identity functions, one for each variable (i.e. $1/\mathcal{ID} = \{\frac{1}{x_0}, \frac{1}{x_1}, \frac{1}{x_2}, \ldots\}$). The limit definition follows our older paper [8].

Definition 20. *Suppose $\mathcal{E}$ is a class of functions that converges to 0. $\mathcal{E} - \mathsf{LIM}$ is the operation which takes a function $f(t, \overline{x})$ and returns $F(\overline{x}) = \lim_{t \to \infty} f(t, \overline{x})$ if the limit exists and there is a function $\alpha(t, \overline{x}) \in \mathcal{E}$ such that $F \preceq^\alpha f$, for positive t.*

If we write LIM without a prefix, we mean $1/\mathcal{ID}-\mathsf{LIM}$.

By $\mathcal{F}(\mathsf{op})$, for a class of functions $\mathcal{F}$ and an operation op, we mean the set of functions $\mathcal{F}$ together with those that result from a *single* application of op to a function in $\mathcal{F}$. The next proposition points out how a sufficiently good approximation leads to a kind of containment when limits are added.

Lemma 5. *Suppose $\mathcal{A}$ and $\mathcal{B}$ are classes of functions and $\mathcal{E}$ is a class of functions that converges to 0. Then $\mathcal{A} \preceq_{\wp}^{\exists \mathcal{E}} \mathcal{B}$ implies $\mathcal{A} \preceq \mathcal{B}(\mathcal{E}-\mathsf{LIM})$*

The approach of approximation and completion highlights some interesting issues. In making the process of completion more distinct, we raise the question of considering the range of techniques that might be employed to complete a class. Going even further, this raises the question of eliminating completion from the characterizations of Computable Analysis. Given that Computable Analysis is defined via an implicit completion process (made explicit in proposition 4), it is not surprising that its characterizations can all be shown to employ completion in an explicit manner. Thus, to characterize Computable Analysis without the use of a completion process would be more of a surprise and provide a more distinctly alternative model of computation. We expand upon these thoughts in section 5. In the ensuing subsections we work out the approximation and completion approach for particular cases: The elementary Real Recursive Functions in part 3.1, Computable Analysis in part 3.2, the computable Real Recursive Functions in part 3.3, and the GPAC in part 3.4.

3.1   Elementary Computability

In this section we recall our work ([8], [7]) concerning elementary computability, which extended the work of [1]. By $\mathbf{E}(\mathbb{R})$ we mean the same class as $\mathbf{C}(\mathbb{R})$, except that for real input x and accuracy input n, the computation time is restricted to elementary time. A fundamental point in this development is the following approximation theorem (from [7], though stated there with a different, though "equivalent" bounding class).

Proposition 1. $\mathbf{E}(\mathbb{R}) \approx_+^{1/\mathcal{T}} \mathcal{L}$

To obtain a class of functions which actually equals $\mathbf{E}(\mathbb{R})$ we will add various kinds of limit operations to $\mathcal{L}$. The following is a limit operation that resembles LIM$_\omega$ (definition 8 from [1]).

Definition 21. *dLIM is the operation which takes a function $f(t, \bar{x})$ and if $|\frac{\partial}{\partial t} f| \leq 1/2^t$ for $t \geq 1$, it returns $F(\bar{x}) = \lim_{t \to \infty} f(t, \bar{x})$.*

Note that the derivative condition guarantees the existence of the limit. Our main result from [7] is the following.

Proposition 2. $\mathbf{E}(\mathbb{R}) = \mathcal{L}(LIM) = \mathcal{L}(dLIM)$

Proof. By proposition 1 we know $\mathbf{E}(\mathbb{R}) \approx_+^{1/\mathcal{T}} \mathcal{L}$, which implies $\mathbf{E}(\mathbb{R}) \approx_\varphi^{\exists \, 1/\mathcal{ID}} \mathcal{L}$. Thus by lemma 5 we can conclude $\mathbf{E}(\mathbb{R})(LIM) \approx \mathbf{E}(\mathbb{R})$, and since we are dealing with total functions, $\mathbf{E}(\mathbb{R}) = \mathcal{L}(LIM)$. The part on dLIM follows from our work in [7].

Thus the result characterizing $\mathbf{E}(\mathbb{R})$ can be stated as an approximation (proposition 1) and completion (proposition 2), for two different kinds of completion processes.

3.2   Rephrasing Computable Analysis

We will show how the functions of computable analysis can be defined by an approximation and completion. We use a class of functions defined on the rationals. A $\mathbb{Q}$−function $f(x)$ is in $\mathbf{C}(\mathbb{Q})$ if there is a computable function on $\mathbb{N}$ that computes it in the following sense: On input $x = (-1)^k (p/q) \in \mathbb{Q}$ (p/q in lowest terms and $k = 0$ or 1) the machine is given the triple (p, q, k), and it computes a triple (a, b, s) such that $f(x) = (-1)^s(a/b)$; for a sequence of inputs $\overline{x}$ we use a sequence of triples. Note that $\mathbf{C}(\mathbb{R})$ contains only continuous functions, while $\mathbf{C}(\mathbb{Q})$ contains discontinuous functions.

Definition 22. *Consider the $\mathbb{Q}$−functions from $\mathbf{C}(\mathbb{Q})$ that have a computable modulus function (so they are all continuous). Let ModRec be the unique continuous extensions of these functions to $\mathbb{R}$.*

Now we make an observation that is similar to corollary 2.14 of Ko [14].

Proposition 3. $\mathbf{C}(\mathbb{R}) \approx_{\wp}^{1/\mathcal{ID}}$ ModRec

The proof is basically identical to that of [7], lemma 6.7, except that here we consider computable rather than elementary functions, and only care about a $1/\mathcal{ID}$ approximation. From proposition 3 and the fact that $\mathbf{C}(\mathbb{R})$ is closed under LIM, lemma 5 yields the following.

Proposition 4. $\mathbf{C}(\mathbb{R}) = $ ModRec(LIM)

Definition 23. *Consider the $\mathbb{Q}$−functions from $\mathbf{C}(\mathbb{Q})$ that are continuous. Let CtnRec be the unique continuous extensions of these functions to $\mathbb{R}$.*

Question 1. *Is the following true: $\mathbf{C}(\mathbb{R}) = $ CtnRec(LIM)?*

If the answer to the question is *yes*, then we have an interesting characterization of $\mathbf{C}(\mathbb{R})$: Starting with $\mathbf{E}(\mathbb{Q})$, a *discrete* class making no reference to approximation or oracle inputs, we restrict it in a necessary way in order to equal $\mathbf{C}(\mathbb{R})$ (i.e. being continuous) and this turns out to be sufficient. However, a negative answer seems reasonable, in which case there is a continuous function defined via a computable function, whose modulus is *not* computably bounded, which would be an interesting negative result.

3.3 A Function Algebra for the Computable Functions over the Reals

We recall that Bournez and Hainry [2] find a function algebra characterizing the $\mathcal{C}^2$ functions of $\mathbf{C}(\mathbb{R})$. For their results they define an operation CLI which is similar to LI except that it receives an extra input function and requires the result of the operation to be bounded by this function. They also define a restricted root-finding operation called UMU (see [2] for details on these operations). Both here and later, we will need to restrict classes of functions in various ways.

Definition 24. *Suppose $\mathcal{S}$ is a set which contains finite lists of the form $(X_1, \ldots, X_k)$, where $X_i \subseteq \mathbb{R}$. For a class of functions $\mathcal{F}$, we let*

$$\mathcal{F}_{\mathcal{S}} = \{f(x_1, \ldots, x_k)_{|X_1 \times \ldots \times X_k} \mid f \in \mathcal{F} \text{ and } (X_1, \ldots, X_k) \in \mathcal{S}\}.$$

In this section we will be interested in the following set of lists:

$$\mathcal{R} = \{([a_1, b_1], \ldots, [a_k, b_k]) \mid k \in \mathbb{N}, \ a_i, b_i \in \mathbb{Q} \text{ such that } 0 \in [a_i, b_i]\},$$

They then prove (though restated here) as theorem 7.1 in [2]:

For $\mathcal{C}^2$ functions

$$\mathbf{C}(\mathbb{R})_{|\mathcal{R}} \approx \mathsf{FA}[0, 1, \theta_3, \mathsf{P}; \mathsf{comp}, \mathsf{CLI}, \mathsf{UMU}, \mathsf{LIM}_\omega]_{|\mathcal{R}}$$

Note that we have used an approximate equality in the above claim; recalling the definition, this means that for a function from either class there is one that *extends* it in the other class. Though the essential aspects of the proofs in [2] seem sound, there are some ambiguities. We restrict our statement of their theorem in two ways. First, we have stated it with reference to the set $\mathcal{R}$, rather than with reference to all compact domains (which appears to be more in line with their work, namely lemma 7.4 of [2]). Second, by stating it as an approximate equality, rather than an equality, we are not requiring that the domains of corresponding functions be identical. To get an actual equality (requiring equal functions to also have equal domains) would require restricting $\mathbf{C}(\mathbb{R})$ to having exactly the domains that can be achieved with functions from $\mathsf{FA}[0, 1, \theta_3, \mathsf{P}; \mathsf{comp}, \mathsf{CLI}, \mathsf{UMU}, \mathsf{LIM}_\omega]$. This leads to a question of interest here and generally for function algebras containing partial functions.

Question 2. *Can we provide a nice characterization of the following set:*

$$\{Domain(f) \mid f \in \mathsf{FA}[0, 1, \theta_3, \mathsf{P}; \mathsf{comp}, \mathsf{CLI}, \mathsf{UMU}, \mathsf{LIM}_\omega]\}.$$

Now we consider formulating their result as an approximation and completion. From proposition 7.1 and an inspection of the proofs of lemmas 7.4 and 7.5 of [2], we can restate the core of their results as follows.

Proposition 5. *For $\mathcal{C}^2$ functions the following holds:*

- $\mathsf{FA}[0, 1, \theta_3, \mathsf{P}; \mathsf{comp}, \mathsf{CLI}, \mathsf{UMU}] \preceq \mathbf{C}(\mathbb{R})$
- $\mathbf{C}(\mathbb{R})_{|\mathcal{R}} \preceq_\wp^{1/\mathcal{ID}} \mathsf{FA}[0, 1, \theta_3, \mathsf{P}; \mathsf{comp}, \mathsf{CLI}, \mathsf{UMU}]$

Applying lemma 5 and using the fact that $\mathbf{C}(\mathbb{R})$ is closed under LIM, we can conclude the following.

Proposition 6

- $\mathsf{FA}[0, 1, \theta_3, \mathsf{P}; \mathsf{comp}, \mathsf{CLI}, \mathsf{UMU}](LIM) \preceq \mathbf{C}(\mathbb{R})$
- $\mathbf{C}(\mathbb{R})_{|\mathcal{R}} \preceq \mathsf{FA}[0, 1, \theta_3, \mathsf{P}; \mathsf{comp}, \mathsf{CLI}, \mathsf{UMU}](LIM)$

We can state the above result as an approximate equality, and using our work from [7], we can include dLIM, as an equivalent completion process.

Proposition 7. *For $\mathcal{C}^2$ functions:*

$$\mathbf{C}(\mathbb{R})_{|\mathcal{R}} \approx \mathsf{FA}[0, 1, \theta_3, \mathsf{P}; \mathsf{comp}, \mathsf{CLI}, \mathsf{UMU}](LIM)_{|\mathcal{R}}$$
$$= \mathsf{FA}[0, 1, \theta_3, \mathsf{P}; \mathsf{comp}, \mathsf{CLI}, \mathsf{UMU}](dLIM)_{|\mathcal{R}}$$

Thus their result can be stated as an approximation and completion. Furthermore, following the form of our proof for $\mathcal{L}$ in [7], the following should be true (i.e. without a restriction to C^2 functions), using our *method of lifting*.

Conjecture 1. *For total functions:*

$$\mathbf{C}(\mathbb{R}) = FA[0, 1, \theta_3, P; \text{comp}, CLI, UMU](LIM)$$
$$= FA[0, 1, \theta_3, P; \text{comp}, CLI, UMU](dLIM)$$

3.4   GPAC Computability

We begin by considering the result from [19], which shows how to characterize $\mathbf{C}(\mathbb{R})$ by a kind of circuit model. We discuss their result and how to phrase it as an approximation and completion. We then discuss some short-comings of the result, which suggests a series of questions. The General Purpose Analog Computer (GPAC) is an analog circuit model of computation, which by the work of Graça and Costa [11] can be characterized as the solution of a system of polynomial differential equations (the solutions of such a system are called the GPAC or GPAC−**generable** functions). In [19], they build upon the definition of GPAC−*generability* to define a notion they call GPAC−**computable**, which adds a mechanism of "converging computation" to the model. We recall the definition from that paper with the modification that we only consider the interval $[0, 1]$ (just for notational convenience, as treating a general interval $[a, b]$ is about the same).

Definition 25. *[19] A function $f : [0, 1] \to \mathbb{R}$ is GPAC−computable iff there exists some computable polynomials $p : \mathbb{R}^{n+1} \to \mathbb{R}^n$, $p_0 : \mathbb{R} \to \mathbb{R}$, and $n - 1$ computable real values $\alpha_1, ..., \alpha_{n-1}$ such that:*

1. *$(y_1, ..., y_n)$ is the solution of Cauchy problem $y' = p(y, t)$ with initial condition $(\alpha_1, ..., \alpha_{n-1}, p_0(x))$ set at time $t_0 = 0$*
2. *There are $i, j \in \{1, ..., n\}$ such that $\lim_{t \to \infty} y_j(t) = 0$ and $|f(x) - y_i(t)| \leq y_j(t)$ for all $x \in [0, 1]$ and all $t \in [0, +\infty)$.*[1]

They then show in [19] (theorem 17) that (recalling definition 24, in this section we use sets of lists which just contain one element and simply list that element):

$$\mathbf{C}(\mathbb{R})_{|[0,1]} = \text{GPAC−computable}.$$

To put the problem into our language, we will define an operation which takes a list of polynomials and a list of initial conditions and returns the first component of the resulting system of polynomial differential equations.

Definition 26. *Let PI be the operation which takes as input some polynomials*

$$P_0(x),\ P_1(u_1, \ldots, u_n, t),\ \ldots,\ P_n(u_1, \ldots, u_n, t),$$

---

[1] We assume that $y(t)$ is defined for all $t \geq 0$. This condition is not necessarily satisfied for all polynomial ODEs, and we restrict our attention only to ODEs satisfying this condition.

and some initial conditions: $\alpha_1, \ldots, \alpha_{n-1} \in \mathbb{R}$. *Consider the following initial value problem:*

$$\frac{\partial}{\partial t} y_1(t, x) = P_1(y_1, \ldots, y_n, t)$$

$$\vdots$$

$$\frac{\partial}{\partial t} y_n(t, x) = P_n(y_1, \ldots, y_n, t)$$
$$y_1(0, x) = \alpha_1$$

$$\vdots$$

$$y_{n-1}(0, x) = \alpha_{n-1}$$
$$y_n(0, x) = P_0(x)$$

and return $y_1(t, x)$ *if it is defined for all* $0 \le x \le 1$ *and* $t \ge 0$.

We define a version of GPAC−generability, relative to a set of real numbers.

Definition 27. *For a set* $X \subseteq \mathbb{R}$, *let* GPAC$_X$ *be the set of functions that can be created by PI using polynomials with coefficients from* X *and initial conditions from* X.

Definition 28. *For* $X \subseteq \mathbb{R}$, *let* $\mathcal{GE}_X$ *be the set of functions* $y(t, x)$ *in* GPAC$_X$ *such that for any* x, $y(t, x) \to 0$ *as* $t \to \infty$.

Now, if we let $\mathcal{CR}$ be the set of computable real numbers, then

$$\text{GPAC−computable} = \text{GPAC}_{\mathcal{CR}}(\mathcal{GE}_{\mathcal{CR}}\text{−LIM}).$$

Note that this uses the observation that for a polynomial, being computable is the same as having computable coefficients. This way of talking about GPAC− computability has the advantage of making the concept of limits a separate and distinct idea, thus allowing us to state the approximation claim (a significant claim, which is basically a restatement of much of the work from [19]).

Proposition 8. $\mathbf{C}(\mathbb{R})_{|[0,1]} \preceq_\wp^{\exists \mathcal{GE}_{\mathcal{CR}}} \text{GPAC}_{\mathcal{CR}} \subseteq \mathbf{C}(\mathbb{R})_{|[0,1],[0,\infty)}$

In the previous proposition, the inclusion follows immediately from theorem 24 of [19] (a theorem in fact restating a result from [12]). The approximation follows from theorem 17 of [19] and the definitions; if $f(x) \in \mathbf{C}(\mathbb{R})_{|[0,1]}$ then by theorem 17, $f(x)$ is GPAC−computable, which in our terminology implies the approximation (it should be possible to extract a more direct proof from [19], using the proof of theorem 18 and the latter part of section 5).

The following shows essentially that $\mathbf{C}(\mathbb{R})$ is closed under limits.

Lemma 6. $\mathbf{C}(\mathbb{R})_{|[0,1],[0,\infty)}(\mathcal{GE}_{\mathcal{CR}}\text{−LIM}) \subseteq \mathbf{C}(\mathbb{R})_{|[0,1]}$

Proof. Suppose $f(x, t) \in \mathbf{C}(\mathbb{R})_{|[0,1],[0,\infty)}$ and $y(x, t) \in \mathcal{GE}_{\mathcal{CR}}$, and suppose $g(x) = \lim_{t \to \infty} f(x, t)$, such that $g \preceq^y f$. We need to show that $g \in \mathbf{C}(\mathbb{R})_{|[0,1]}$, that is on input $x \in [0, 1]$, and accuracy input $n \in \mathbb{N}$, we need to compute $g(x)$ to accuracy $1/n$. We just need to compute $f(x, t)$ for a large enough t, and to find such a t we just follow the algorithm of [19], at the end of section 6.

Proposition 9. $\mathbf{C}(\mathbb{R})_{[0,1]} = GPAC_{\mathcal{CR}}(\mathcal{GE}_{\mathcal{CR}}-LIM)$

Proof. Using lemma 6 and proposition 8, together with lemma 5, we can conclude:

$$\mathbf{C}(\mathbb{R})_{|[0,1]} \subseteq GPAC_{\mathcal{CR}}(\mathcal{GE}_{\mathcal{CR}}-LIM)$$
$$\subseteq \mathbf{C}(\mathbb{R})_{|[0,1],[0,\infty)}(\mathcal{GE}_{\mathcal{CR}}-LIM)$$
$$\subseteq \mathbf{C}(\mathbb{R})_{|[0,1]}$$

Now we consider some short-comings of the result. This result fits into a series of results which characterize computable analysis in a manner that is different and distinct from it. The result of [19] only does this to an extent, because it includes notions from computable analysis in the definition of GPAC−computability. Or stated in terms of the $GPAC_X$, the approximation and completion results use the fact that $X = \mathcal{CR}$, the computable reals. Thus a very natural question is to consider if the result of [19] can be modified so that it holds for a notion of GPAC computability that is distinct from computable analysis. In our notation, this amounts to the following question:

Question 3. *Does there exist a nice set $X \subseteq \mathbb{R}$, defined without computable analysis, such that:*

$$\mathbf{C}(\mathbb{R})_{|[0,1]} = GPAC_X(\mathcal{GE}_X-LIM)?$$

Phrasing the result as an approximation and completion, emphasizes the exact completion process used, in this case $\mathcal{GE}_X-LIM$. Thus a refinement of the above question would be to consider a more natural limit operation $\mathcal{E}-LIM$, for some nicer $\mathcal{E}$ such as $1/\mathcal{ID}$. To answer the previous question (say, with a nicer $\mathcal{E}$), following the approach above, first we would show an approximation:

$$\mathbf{C}(\mathbb{R})_{|[0,1]} \preceq_{\wp}^{\exists \mathcal{E}} GPAC_X \subseteq \mathbf{C}(\mathbb{R})_{|[0,1],[0,\infty)}.$$

Since we are thinking of $X \subseteq \mathcal{CR}$, the inclusion is immediate, and the work involved is to show the approximation, which, if true, by lemma 5 would answer the question affirmatively.

We hope that we can use our methods to facilitate answering these questions. Note that $GPAC_X = X(\mathsf{PI})$, which is probably not the same as $FA[X; \mathsf{PI}]$; recall that the first notation indicates that PI can be applied once with coefficients from X, while the latter function algebra allows repeated use of PI. To bring our methods into play, we would like to be able to discuss the GPAC as a function algebra. This motivates the following question.

Question 4. *Is there an operation PI^* which is similar to PI, but has the property that for $X \subseteq \mathbb{R}$, $X(\mathsf{PI}^*) = FA[X; \mathsf{PI}^*]$, or at least $X(\mathsf{PI}^*) \approx_+^{\mathcal{E}} FA[X; \mathsf{PI}^*]$, for a suitable $\mathcal{E}$?*

We could refer to $X(\mathsf{PI}^*)$ by $GPAC_X^*$. If we found such an operation PI^*, then showing $\mathbf{C}(\mathbb{R}) = GPAC_X^*(\mathcal{E}-LIM)$ could be reduced to showing $\mathbf{C}(\mathbb{R}) \preceq_+^{\mathcal{E}}$

FA[X; PI*], perhaps with the domains of the functions of $\mathbf{C}(\mathbb{R})$ restricted in some way. Now we could employ a strategy that we will use in the next section. We could consider the intermediary class FA[$\mathcal{CR}$; PI*] and then due to transitivity, break down the goal into the two subgoals:

1. $\mathbf{C}(\mathbb{R}) \preceq_+^{\mathcal{E}}$ FA[$\mathcal{CR}$; PI*], and
2. FA[$\mathcal{CR}$; PI*] $\preceq_+^{\mathcal{E}}$ FA[X; PI*]

We expect the first subgoal to proceed as in [19]. Furthermore, we expect that PI* has been defined so that PI* $\preceq_+^{\mathcal{E}}$ FA[X; PI*], thus by lemma 3, we can reduce the second subgoal to $\mathcal{CR} \preceq_+^{\mathcal{E}}$ FA[X; PI*], or in words:

> Starting with coefficients from X and applying polynomial differential equations, can we approximate all the computable reals?

4   Making Classes Analytic

In the previous section we discussed some connections between Computable Analysis and analog models like the Real Recursive Functions and the GPAC. These models are claimed to be closely related to classical physics, where initial value problems play a prominent role. As pointed out in [10], models of natural phenomena arising from classical physics typically involve differential equations with analytic solutions. However, the function algebras considered in sections 3.1 and 3.3 do not satisfy this condition since they include the function θ_3 which is not analytic. The role of θ_3 is crucial in the proofs of the results stated in sections 3.1 and 3.3, since it allows us to define continuous "clocks" and simulate the discrete dynamics of Turing Machines. This is done using a technique first applied in [3] and refined in the context of function algebras on the reals in [5] and [6]. In this section we apply the method of approximation to show that θ_3 can be removed from the function algebra $\mathcal{L}$ (we also remove the constant π), obtaining therefore an analytic characterization we denote by $\mathcal{L}^a$ of the elementary computable functions. The basic technical point we use here is the fact that the approximation relation is transitive, which allows us to define an intermediary class of functions for convenience and then dispense with it in the end. For example, in relating $\mathbf{E}(\mathbb{R})$ and $\mathcal{L}^a$, we use $\mathcal{L}$ as a convenient intermediary class (convenient because it has the non-analytic function θ_3 which makes technical work easier).

Formally, we define the class

$$\mathcal{L}^a = \mathsf{FA}[0, 1, -1, \mathsf{P}; \mathsf{comp}, \mathsf{LI}],$$

which only contains analytic functions. As pointed out in [6], if the input functions to the operation LI are total, then the operation defines a new total function whose bound is exponential in terms of the bound on the input functions, allowing us to conclude the following.

Lemma 7. *All functions in $\mathcal{L}$ and $\mathcal{L}^{\mathrm{a}}$ are total. Furthermore, $\mathcal{L}, \mathcal{L}^{\mathrm{a}} \leq \mathcal{T}$.*

We claim that $\mathcal{L} \approx_+^{1/\mathcal{T}} \mathcal{L}^{\mathrm{a}}$. We just need to show that $\mathcal{L} \preceq_+^{1/\mathcal{T}} \mathcal{L}^{\mathrm{a}}$ since the other direction is trivial. We show how $\mathcal{L}^{\mathrm{a}}$ can approximate θ_3 and π and the operations of $\mathcal{L}$.

Lemma 8. $\theta_3, \pi \preceq_+^{1/\mathcal{T}} \mathcal{L}^{\mathrm{a}}$.

Proof. Let $\alpha(x, z) \in \mathcal{T}$. Consider the well known function $y(t) = e^{-t^2}$ defined in $\mathcal{L}^{\mathrm{a}}$ by $y' = -2ty$ and $y(0) = 1$ which satisfies $\int_{-\infty}^{+\infty} y(t)dt = \sqrt{\pi}$. Therefore, $c_1(x) = 2 \int_0^x y(t)dt$ gives an approximation of $\sqrt{\pi}$ in $\mathcal{L}^{\mathrm{a}}$ with error smaller than e^{-x^2}. Squaring that function gives an approximation of π. Given c_1, we can also obtain an approximation $c_2(x)$ of $\frac{1}{\sqrt{\pi}}$ in $\mathcal{L}^{\mathrm{a}}$ since it contains a function that approximates $\frac{1}{x}$ over $\mathbb{R}^+$ as noticed in Remark 6 of [1].

Now, take the indefinite integral $F(x) = \int_0^x y(t)dt$, which is a strictly increasing function such that $\lim_{x \to -\infty} F(x) = -\frac{\sqrt{\pi}}{2}$ and $\lim_{x \to +\infty} F(x) = \frac{\sqrt{\pi}}{2}$. Define the analytic function $H(x, u) = c_2(u)F(xu) + \frac{1}{2}$ which is therefore in $\mathcal{L}^{\mathrm{a}}$ (H stands for an approximation of the Heaviside function). Finally, there is a $u \in \mathcal{L}^{\mathrm{a}}$ such that $\theta^{\mathrm{a}}(x, z) = H(x, u(x, z)) x^3$ is the desired approximation of θ_3, i.e. $|\theta^{\mathrm{a}}(x, z) - \theta_3(x)| < \frac{1}{\alpha(x,z)}$. To see that this is true, notice that u can be chosen sufficiently larger than any $\alpha \in \mathcal{T}$.

To approximate the operations we follow a more general approach than necessary, since we believe it may be more generally applicable (discussed at the end of the section). The goal is to show for any operations op in the algebra that replacing a set of functions $f_1, \ldots, f_k$ by their approximations $f_1^*, \ldots, f_k^*$, still defines an approximation $h^* = \mathsf{op}(f_1^*, \ldots, f_k^*)$ of $h = \mathsf{op}(f_1, \ldots, f_k)$. To achieve this we have to understand how far apart h^* and h are when their arguments vary. Toward this end we define the notion of Lipschitz functions.

Definition 29

- *Let f be a function on n arguments, and L a function on $2n$ arguments. f is $L-Lipschitz$ if $domain(f) \times domain(f) \subseteq domain(L)$, and $|f(\bar{b}) - f(\bar{a})| \leq L(\bar{b}, \bar{a})|\bar{b} - \bar{a}|$ for all $\bar{a}$ and $\bar{b}$ in the domain of f.*
- *A class of functions $\mathcal{F}$ is $\mathcal{B}-Lipschitz$ if for every f in $\mathcal{F}$ there is an L in $\mathcal{B}$ such that f is $L-Lipschitz$.*

A given f trivially admits the Lipschitz function $|f(\bar{b}) - f(\bar{a})|/|\bar{b} - \bar{a}|$. However, this cannot always be defined (for instance $\mathcal{L}$ is not closed under division). Moreover, we will be interested in *increasing* Lipschitz functions. To show that classes have increasing Lipschitz functions we can use derivative bounds.

Definition 30. *Let $\mathcal{F}$ be a class of differentiable functions. Then*

$$\mathcal{F}' = \{ \frac{\partial}{\partial x_i} f(x_1, \ldots, x_k) \mid f \in \mathcal{F} \}.$$

Lemma 9. *If $\mathcal{F}$ is a class of functions such that $\mathcal{F}' \leq \mathcal{B}$, where $\mathcal{B}$ is a bounding class, then $\mathcal{F}$ is $\mathcal{B}-Lipschitz$.*

Proof. Let $h(x_1, \ldots, x_n)$ be in $\mathcal{F}$. To find a Lipschitz function, consider:

$$
\begin{aligned}
|h(\bar{b}) - h(\bar{a})| \leq \ &|h(b_1, b_2, \ldots, b_n) - h(a_1, b_2, \ldots, b_n)| \\
&+ |h(a_1, b_2, \ldots, b_n) - h(a_1, a_2, b_3 \ldots, b_n)| \\
&\vdots \\
&+ |h(a_1, \ldots, a_{n-1}, b_n) - h(a_1, \ldots, a_n)|
\end{aligned}
$$

Consider the first term $|h(b_1, b_2, \ldots, b_n) - h(a_1, b_2, \ldots, b_n)|$. Consider the function $\frac{\partial}{\partial x_1} h(x_1, x_2, \ldots, x_n) \in \mathcal{F}'$ and let $\beta(x_1, \ldots, x_n) \in \mathcal{B}$ such that β dominates it. Let $L_1(\bar{b}; \bar{a}) = \beta(|a_1| + |b_1|, b_2, \ldots, b_n)$, which is dominated by a function in $\mathcal{B}$ (which for convenience we also call L_1). Since β is increasing and $|a_1|, |b_1| \leq |a_1| + |b_1|$, L_1 dominates the derivative $\frac{\partial}{\partial x_1} h(x_1, b_2, \ldots, b_n)$ for all x_1 on the interval between a_1 and b_1, and so we have:

$$
\begin{aligned}
&|h(b_1, b_2, \ldots, b_n) - h(a_1, b_2, \ldots, b_n)| \leq \\
&|(h(a_1, b_2, \ldots, b_n) + |b_1 - a_1| L_1(\bar{b}; \bar{a})) - h(a_1, b_2, \ldots, b_n)| = L_1(\bar{b}; \bar{a}) |b_1 - a_1|.
\end{aligned}
$$

We obtain $L_2(\bar{b}; \bar{a}), \ldots, L_n(\bar{b}; \bar{a})$ for all the terms and we bound the sum by something in $\mathcal{B}$, yielding our Lipschitz function.

For instance, Proposition 4.3 of [6] gives bounds on the derivatives of functions in $\mathcal{L}$. The same bounds apply to $\mathcal{L}^{\mathrm{a}}$. By lemmas 9 and 7 this implies that $\mathcal{L}$ and $\mathcal{L}^{\mathrm{a}}$ are $\mathcal{T}-Lipschitz$. In our notation this gives the following lemma.

Lemma 10. $\mathcal{L}', (\mathcal{L}^{\mathrm{a}})' \leq \mathcal{T}$. *Moreover, $\mathcal{L}$ and $\mathcal{L}^{\mathrm{a}}$ are $\mathcal{T}-Lipschitz$.*

This permits us to establish a bound on the distance of the solutions of two different initial value problems. In our case we are interested in comparing initial value problems defined with a function and its approximation.

Lemma 11. *(Gronwall-type inequality) Let $f(t, y)$ and $f^*(t, y, \alpha)$ be total C^1 functions with domain $\mathbb{R}$ such that $f \preceq_{+}^{1/\alpha} f^*$. Let $y(t)$ and $y^*(t, \alpha)$ be the solutions of the following initial value problems:*

$$
y(t_0) = a, \ \tfrac{d}{dt} y(t) = f(t, y) \qquad and \qquad y^*(t_0) = a^*, \ \tfrac{\partial}{\partial t} y^*(t, \alpha) = f^*(t, y^*, \alpha)
$$

If f is $\beta-Lipschitz$, and we let $\int^x \beta$ abbreviate $\int_{t_0}^x \beta(u, u, y(u), y^*(u, \alpha)) \, du$, then where defined we have:

$$
|y(t) - y^*(t, \alpha)| \leq e^{\int^t \beta} \left(|a - a^*| + \int_{t_0}^t \frac{e^{-\int^s \beta}}{\alpha} ds \right)
$$

Proof. The hypothesis lead to the inequalities (the first inequality follows from y and y^* being C^1; for ease of readability we sometimes drop the arguments to these functions.).

$$\frac{\partial}{\partial t}|y(t) - y^*(t,\alpha)| \leq |\frac{d}{dt}y(t) - \frac{\partial}{\partial t}y^*(t,\alpha)|$$
$$= |f(t,y) - f^*(t,y^*,\alpha)|$$
$$\leq |f(t,y) - f(t,y^*)| + |f(t,y^*) - f^*(t,y^*,\alpha)|$$
$$\leq \beta(t,t,y,y^*)|y - y^*| + \frac{1}{\alpha}.$$

The inequality above implies that

$$\frac{\partial}{\partial t}|y(t) - y^*(t,\alpha)| - \beta(t,t,y,y^*)|y(t) - y^*(t,\alpha)| \leq \frac{1}{\alpha}.$$

Multiplication by the integrating factor $e^{-\int^t \beta}$ yields

$$\frac{\partial}{\partial t}(e^{-\int^t \beta}|y(t) - y^*(t,\alpha)|) \leq \frac{e^{-\int^t \beta}}{\alpha}.$$

Integrating this from t_0 to t gives

$$e^{-\int^t \beta}|y(t) - y^*(t,\alpha)| - |a - a^*| \leq \int_{t_0}^t \frac{e^{-\int^s \beta}}{\alpha}ds,$$

which finally leads to the claimed bound.

Lemma 12. $Ll_{|\mathcal{L}} \preceq_+^{1/T} \mathcal{L}^{\mathbf{a}}.$

Proof. Let h be the solution of the linear initial value problem $h(\bar{x},0) = g(\bar{x})$ and $\frac{\partial}{\partial t}h(\bar{x},t) = s(\bar{x},t)\,h(\bar{x},t)$, where $g, s \in \mathcal{L}$. Let $g^*, s^* \in \mathcal{L}^{\mathbf{a}}$ be approximations of g and s. We claim that the solution h^* of the linear initial value problem $h^*(\bar{x},0,\alpha) = g^*(\bar{x},\alpha)$ and $\frac{\partial}{\partial t}h^*(\bar{x},t,\alpha) = s^*(\bar{x},t,\alpha)\,h^*(\bar{x},t,\alpha)$ can be made arbitrarily close to h in $\mathcal{L}^{\mathbf{a}}$. More precisely, we claim that there is a $H(\bar{x},t,z) = h^*(\bar{x},t,\alpha(t,z)) \in \mathcal{L}^{\mathbf{a}}$ such that $|h(\bar{x},t) - H(\bar{x},t,z)| \leq 1/z$.

To show this, and since all functions in $\mathcal{L}$ and $\mathcal{L}^{\mathbf{a}}$ are total and C^1, we apply lemma 11 where f in the lemma is now the product $h\,s$ and the initial condition in the lemma is now $a = g(\bar{x})$. By lemma 10 there is a $\beta \in \mathcal{T}$ such that f is β-Lipschitz. We want to get rid of the dependence of $\int^x \beta$ on α so we can freely bound $|h - h^*|$ adjusting α. By hypothesis $f \preceq_+^{1/\alpha} f^*$ which means that $f^*(t,y,\alpha) < f(t,y) + 1 \leq \exp(f(t,y))$ for all α. Likewise, the initial conditions in the lemma satisfy $a^* < a + 1$. Consider the initial value problem $\frac{\partial}{\partial t}y^+(t) = \exp(f(t,y^+))$ and $y^+(t_0) = a + 1$. The solution $y^+(t)$ exists in $\mathcal{L}$, is increasing, and bounds $y^*(t,\alpha)$ for all α. Now, $\int^t \beta$ can be bounded by $\phi(t) = \int_{t_0}^t \beta(u,u,y(u),y^+(u))\,du$ and this is bounded in $\mathcal{T}$. Moreover, $\int_{t_0}^t e^{-\int^s \beta}ds$ is bounded by some constant K for β large enough. For the initial condition, we suppose that $|a - a^*| < |a - a^+| \leq 1/\alpha$.

Therefore, the right hand side in the inequality in lemma 11 can be bounded by $\exp(\phi(t))(1 + K)/\alpha$. Therefore, choosing $\alpha(t,z) \in \mathcal{T}$ sufficiently large we can guarantee that $|y(t) - y^*(t,\alpha)| \leq 1/z$. This function $y^*(t,\alpha(t,z))$ corresponds to the desired approximation H mentioned earlier in the proof.

To conclude with our goal, we only have to show that the approximation also holds for composition. To be able to use lemma 4 we have to show that $\mathcal{L}$ has an appropriate modulus. The following lemma shows that this is a direct consequence of $\mathcal{L}$ being $\mathcal{T}$−Lipschitz.

Lemma 13. *Suppose $\mathcal{B}$ is a bounding class and $\mathcal{F}$ is class of functions that is $\mathcal{B}$−Lipschitz. Then $\mathcal{F}$ has a $1/\mathcal{B}$−modulus.*

Proof. Let $f(\bar{x}) \in \mathcal{F}$ and $L(\bar{x}, \bar{y}) \in \mathcal{B}$ be such that $|f(\bar{x}) - f(\bar{y})| \leq L(\bar{x}, \bar{y})|\bar{x} - \bar{y}|$; recall that L is increasing. Let $m(\bar{x}, z) \in \mathcal{B}$ be a function that dominates $L(\bar{x}, \bar{x} + 1)z + 1$, and suppose $|\bar{x} - \bar{y}| \leq 1/m(\bar{x}, z)$. First note that this implies that $\bar{y} \leq \bar{x} + 1$, and thus $|\bar{x} - \bar{y}| \leq 1/m(\bar{x}, z)$ further implies:

$$|f(\bar{x}) - f(\bar{y})| \leq L(\bar{x}, \bar{y})\frac{1}{m(\bar{x}, z)}$$

$$\leq L(\bar{x}, \bar{x} + 1)\frac{1}{L(\bar{x}, \bar{x} + 1)z + 1}$$

$$\leq \frac{1}{z}$$

Proposition 10. $\mathcal{L} \approx_{+}^{1/T} \mathcal{L}^{\mathrm{a}}$

Proof. $\mathcal{L}^{\mathrm{a}} \preceq_{+}^{1/T} \mathcal{L}$ is immediate, so we consider the approximation $\mathcal{L} \preceq_{+}^{1/T} \mathcal{L}^{\mathrm{a}}$. By lemma 8, we can approximate all the basic functions of $\mathcal{L}$. Since $\mathcal{L}$ is $\mathcal{T}$−Lipschitz, it has, by lemma 13, a $1/\mathcal{T}$ modulus, and thus we apply lemma 4 to obtain $\mathrm{comp}_{|\mathcal{L}} \preceq_{+}^{1/T} \mathcal{L}^{\mathrm{a}}$. By lemma 12, $\mathrm{LI}_{|\mathcal{L}} \preceq_{+}^{1/T} \mathcal{L}^{\mathrm{a}}$. Finally, we apply lemma 3 to conclude the proof.

Proposition 1, together with transitivity obtains the following approximation for $\mathbf{E}(\mathbb{R})$ with analytic functions.

Proposition 11. $\mathbf{E}(\mathbb{R}) \approx_{+}^{1/T} \mathcal{L}^{\mathrm{a}}$

As a result we get an improved characterization of the elementary computable functions, applying lemma 5 (and obtaining exact equality because we are dealing with total functions).

Proposition 12. $\mathbf{E}(\mathbb{R}) = \mathcal{L}^{\mathrm{a}}(LIM)$

We consider now the following generalization of LI where the initial value problem is not required to be linear.

Definition 31. *I is the operation which takes input functions $f_1(\bar{x}), \ldots, f_k(\bar{x})$ and $g_1(\bar{x}, t, y), \ldots, g_k(\bar{x}, t, y)$ of appropriate arities and returns h_1 which is defined by the equations*

$$h_1(\bar{x}, t_0) = f_1(\bar{x})$$

$$\cdots$$

$$h_k(\bar{x}, t_0) = f_k(\bar{x})$$
$$\tfrac{\partial}{\partial t}h_1(\bar{x}, t) = g_1(\bar{x}, t, \bar{h})$$

$$\cdots$$

$$\tfrac{\partial}{\partial t}h_k(\bar{x}, t) = g_k(\bar{x}, t, \bar{h}).$$

We will write this as $h = I(f, g)$. Replacing LI by I in $\mathcal{L}$ and $\mathcal{L}^a$ lead to the following classes.

Definition 32

- Let $\mathcal{G}$ be $FA[0, 1, -1, \theta_3, P; comp, I]$.
- Let $\mathcal{G}^a$ be $FA[0, 1, -1, P; comp, I]$.

The class $\mathcal{G}$ was investigated in [4] and shown to be closed under an iteration operation, thus allowing Turing Machines to be simulated. It would be interesting to show that the class of analytic functions $\mathcal{G}^a$ could do the same. In fact, related work has already been carried out. In [15] it was shown that analytic maps over unbounded domains can simulate the *transition function* of any Turing Machine, while only recently (by [10]) was it shown that the *iterations* of those transition functions can also be simulated with analytic flows over unbounded domains. These results motivate the search for an approximation between $\mathcal{G}$ and $\mathcal{G}^a$.

Unlike the case of the elementary functions, there does not appear to be a convenient bounding class like $\mathcal{T}$. However, there is a generic way to create bounding functions that correspond to a given class of functions, by choosing out the right functions from the class.

Definition 33. *Given a class of functions $\mathcal{F}$, let $bd\mathcal{F}$ be the functions in $\mathcal{F}$ that satisfy properties 2 through 5 of the definition of bounding class.*

Lemma 14. *If $\mathcal{F}$ is closed under addition, multiplication, and composition, contains a function $f \geq 1$ and satisfies property 6 of bounding classes, then $bd\mathcal{F}$ is a bounding class.*

Definition 34. *We write $A \preceq_+^\vee B$ to mean $A \preceq_+^{\vee \frac{1}{bd\mathcal{B}}} B$.*

Question 5. *Does the approximation $\mathcal{G} \approx_+^\vee \mathcal{G}^a$ hold?*

We could try to prove this using the approach we described for $\mathcal{L}$. However, some difficulties need to be overcome. Firstly, it is not clear if given approximations f^* and g^* of f and g, $h = I(f, g)$ and $h^* = I(f^*, g^*)$ have the same domains. An additional difficulty is to show that the associated bounding classes are "appropriate," amounting to the question of whether or not $bd\mathcal{G} \leq bd\mathcal{G}^a$.

5   Future Work

We make the informal claim that the method of approximation provides a useful way to organize and think about the relationships between various computational classes. It both facilitates the technical work and suggests ideas. In particular we consider the idea of approximation and completion and some issues raised by organizing the work in this manner. We have seen how the various ways to characterize Computable Analysis all fit into this two step process of approximation and completion. One advantage of this is approach is to emphasize that the fundamental point of the various characterizations is to find an approximation. It also helps from a technical point of view, separating the proofs into two steps, where the approximation step can be facilitated by the various tools developed for this method. Furthermore, by separating out the notion of completion as a distinct step, we have seen that in some cases, different kinds of completions are equivalent. This raises the question of considering more broadly the ways that a class of functions can be completed. To date, the method of choice has been to use limits, but we could also consider search operators, given the result of Mycka [17], showing that in a certain context with Real Recursive Functions, limits and zero-finding are equivalent.

Question 6. *What other manners of "completion" are interesting and useful in relating computational classes to Computable Analysis?*

A related line of thought, alluded to earlier, is to consider the elimination of the completion step.

Question 7. *Are there characterizations of Computable Analysis, which naturally capture all of its functions, without a completion operation?*

This would be especially interesting in light of the fact that the very definition of Computable Analysis is tied up with a notion of completion. Already this is apparent in the standard definitions of Computable Analysis as a computable process which gets increasingly closer to the result, only finished as the accuracy parameter converges to infinity (proposition 4 points out exactly how to put the limit into the definition). Thus, to find an alternative model with no apparent completion step would provide a more genuinely distinct way of conceiving of Computable Analysis. This would seem to be interesting from two points of view. It would seem to be a very useful kind of result in understanding a Church-Turing thesis for real computation (recalling the discussion of the introduction). Furthermore, recall that in the introduction we considered the project of using the correspondences to Computable Analysis as a way to bring in the methods of analysis to the questions of classic complexity theory. A model of computation which is more different and does not employ completion could be more useful in this vein.

Acknowledgements

This work was partially supported by *Fundação para a Ciência e a Tecnologia* and EU FEDER POCTI/POCI, namely, via CLC, project ConTComp POCTI / MAT / 45978 / 2002, and grant SFRH / BPD / 16936 / 2004.

References

1. Bournez, O., Hainry, E.: Elementarily computable functions over the real numbers and R-sub-recursive functions. Theoretical Computer Science 348(2–3), 130–147 (2005)
2. Bournez, O., Hainry, E.: Recursive analysis characterized as a class of real recursive functions. Fundamenta Informaticae 74(4), 409–433 (2006)

3. Branicky, M.S.: Universal computation and other capabilities of hybrid and continuous dynamical systems. Theoretical Computer Science 138(1), 67–100 (1995)
4. Campagnolo, M.L.: Computational complexity of real valued recursive functions and analog circuits. PhD thesis, IST, Universidade Técnica de Lisboa (2001)
5. Campagnolo, M.L., Moore, C., Costa, J.F.: Iteration, inequalities, and differentiability in analog computers. Journal of Complexity 16(4), 642–660 (2000)
6. Campagnolo, M.L., Moore, C., Costa, J.F.: An analog characterization of the Grzegorczyk hierarchy. Journal of Complexity 18(4), 100–977 (2002)
7. Campagnolo, M.L., Ojakian, K.: The elementary computable functions over the real numbers: Applying two new techniques (submitted)
8. Campagnolo, M.L., Ojakian, K.: The methods of approximation and lifting in real computation. In: Cenzer, D., Dillhage, R., Grubba, T., Weihrauch, K. (eds.) Proceedings of the Third International Conference on Computability and Complexity in Analysis, CCA 2006, Gainesville, Florida, USA, November 1–5, 2006. Electronic Notes in Theoretical Computer Science, vol. 167, Elsevier, Amsterdam (2007)
9. Costa, J.F., Mycka, J.: The $P \neq NP$ conjecture in the context of real and complex analysis. Journal of Complexity 22(2), 287–303 (2006)
10. Graça, D.S., Campagnolo, M.L., Buescu, J.: Computability with polynomial differential equations. Advances in Applied Mathematics (to appear, 2007)
11. Graça, D.S., Costa, J.F.: Analog computers and recursive functions over the reals. Journal of Complexity 19(5), 644–664 (2003)
12. Graça, D.S., Zhong, N., Buescu, J.: Computability, noncomputability and undecidability of maximal intervals of IVPs. Transactions of the American Mathematical Society (to appear, 2007)
13. Grzegorczyk, A.: Computable functionals. Fundamenta Mathematicae 42, 168–202 (1955)
14. Ko, K.-I.: Complexity Theory of Real Functions. Birkhaüser (1991)
15. Koiran, P., Moore, C.: Closed-form analytic maps in one and two dimensions can simulate universal Turing machines. Theoretical Computer Science 210(1), 217–223 (1999)
16. Moore, C.: Recursion theory on the reals and continuous-time computation. Theoretical Computer Science 162, 23–44 (1996)
17. Mycka, J.: μ-recursion and infinite limits. Theoretical Computer Science 302, 123–133 (2003)
18. Mycka, J., Costa, J.F.: Real recursive functions and their hierarchy. Journal of Complexity 20(6), 835–857 (2004)
19. Graça, D.S., Bournez, O., Campagnolo, M.L., Hainry, E.: Polynomial differential equations compute all real computable functions on computable compact intervals. Journal of Complexity (2007), doi:10.1016/j.jco.2006.12.005
20. Shannon, C.E.: Mathematical theory of the differential analyzer. J. Math. Phys. MIT 20, 337–354 (1941)
21. Weihrauch, K.: Computable Analysis: An Introduction. Springer, Heidelberg (2000)

A Survey of Infinite Time Turing Machines*

Joel David Hamkins**

The City University of New York
jdh.hamkins.org

Infinite time Turing machines extend the operation of ordinary Turing machines into transfinite ordinal time, thereby providing a natural model of infinitary computability, with robust notions of computability and decidability on the reals, while remaining close to classical concepts of computability. Here, I survey the theory of infinite time Turing machines and recent developments. These include the rise of infinite time complexity theory, the introduction of infinite time computable model theory, the study of the infinite time analogue of Borel equivalence relation theory, and the introduction of new ordinal computational models. The study of infinite time Turing machines increasingly relies on the interaction of methods from set theory, descriptive set theory and computability theory.

There is no claim or expectation here for the machines to be physically realized or for the algorithms ever to be carried out by an actual computing device, even in principle. Rather, the point is to analyze what in principle is *mathematically* possible with infinitary computation, rather than what is physically possible, and to mount a mathematical investigation of the resulting structures and hierarchies, making use of insights arising from the computational paradigm.

Infinite time Turing machines were first considered by Hamkins and Kidder in 1989, with the principal introduction provided by Hamkins and Lewis [HL00]. The theory has now been extended by many others, including Philip Welch, Benedikt Löwe, Daniel Seabold, Ralf Schindler, Vinay Deolalikar, Russell Miller, Steve Warner, Giacomo Lenzi, Erich Monteleone, Peter Koepke and others. Numerous precursors to the theory include Blum-Shub-Smale machines (1980s), Büchi machines (1960s) and accompanying developments, Barry Burd's model of Turing machines with "blurs" at limits (1970s), the extensive development of α-recursion and E-recursion theory, a part of higher recursion theory (since the 1970s), Jack Copeland's accelerated Turing machines (1990s), Ryan Bissell-Siders' ordinal machines (1990s), and more recently, Peter Koepke's ordinal Turing machines and ordinal register machines (2000s). The expanding literature involving infinite time Turing machines includes [HL00], [Wel99], [Wel00a],

---

* Math Subject Codes: 03D30, 03D60, 03E15. Keywords: infinite time Turing machines, infinitary computability, ordinal computation. This article is adapted from an abstract of the same title written for the Bonn International Workshop on Ordinal Computation (BIWOC) 2007.

** The author's research has been supported in part by grants from the Research Foundation of CUNY and by grants from the Netherlands Organization for Scientific Research (NWO). The author is also grateful to the University of Amsterdam ILLC for the support of a Visiting Professorship during his 2007 sabbatical from CUNY.

J. Durand-Lose and M. Margenstern (Eds.): MCU 2007, LNCS 4664, pp. 62–71, 2007.
© Springer-Verlag Berlin Heidelberg 2007

[Wel00b], [Lö1], [HS01], [HL02], [Sch03], [HW03], [Ham02], [Ham04], [LM04], [DHS05], [HMSW07], [Ham05], [Wel], [Wel05], [Koe05] and others.

1 A Brief Review of Infinite Time Turing Machines

Let us quickly review the basic operation of the machines and some key concepts. An infinite time Turing machine has the same hardware as its classical finite time counterpart, with a head moving on a semi-infinite paper tape, writing 0s and 1s in accordance with the rigid instructions of a finite program having finitely many states. For convenience, we have used a three tape model, with separate tapes for input, scratch work and output. At successor stages of computation,

		q						
input:	1	1	0	0	1	1	1	1	...
scratch:	0	1	1	1	1	1	0	0	...
output:	0	0	1	0	1	0	1	1	...

the machine operates in exactly the classical manner, according to the program instructions. The new part of the computational behavior comes at limit ordinal stages. At any limit stage ξ, the machine is placed into the special *limit* state, one of the distinguished states alongside the *start* and *halt* states; the head is reset to the left-most cell; and the tape is updated by placing in each cell the lim sup of the values previously displayed in that cell. This completely specifies the configuration of the machine at stage ξ, and the computation may continue to stage $\xi+1$ and so on. Output is given only when the machine explicitly attains the *halt* state, and computation ceases when this occurs.

Since there is plenty of time for the machines to write out and inspect infinite binary strings, the natural context for input and output to the machines is Cantor space 2^ω, which I shall denote by $\mathbb{R}$ and refer to as the reals. The machines therefore provide an infinitary notion of computability on the reals. Program p computes the partial function $\varphi_p : \mathbb{R} \to \mathbb{R}$, defined by $\varphi_p(x) = y$ if program p on input x yields output y. A subset $A \subseteq \mathbb{R}$ is *infinite time decidable* if its characteristic function is infinite time computable. The set A is *infinite time semi-decidable* if the constant function $1 \upharpoonright A$ is computable. This is equivalent to A being the domain of an infinite time computable function (but not necessarily equivalent to A being the range of such a function). Initial results in [HL00] show that the arithmetic sets are exactly those that are decidable in time uniformly less than ω^2 and the hyperarithmetic sets are those that are decidable in time less than some recursive ordinal. Every Π_1^1 set is decidable, and the class of decidable sets is contained in Δ_2^1.

An easy cofinality argument establishes that every computation either halts or repeats by some countable ordinal stage. An ordinal α is *clockable* if there is a computation $\varphi_p(0)$ halting on exactly the αth step. A real x is *writable* if it is the output of a computation $\varphi_p(0)$, and an ordinal is writable if it is coded by such a real. There are of course only countably many clockable and writable ordinals, because there are only countably many programs. Both the clockable and writable ordinals extend through all the recursive ordinals and far beyond; their supremum is recursively inaccessible and more. While the writable ordinals form an initial segment of the ordinals, there are gaps in the clockable ordinals, intervals of non-clockable ordinals below the supremum of the clockable ordinals. The gap structure itself becomes quite complicated, with limits of gaps sometimes being gaps and so on, and ultimately it exhibits the same complexity as the infinite time version of the halting problem. Nevertheless, [Wel00b] established that the supremum of the clockable and writable ordinals is the same. A real x is *eventually writable* if there is a computation $\varphi_p(0)$ for which x appears on the output tape from some point on (even if the computation does not halt), and x is *accidentally writable* if it appears on any of the tapes at any stage during a computation $\varphi_p(0)$. By coding ordinals with reals, we obtain the notions of eventually and accidentally writable ordinals. If λ is the supremum of the clockable or writable ordinals, ζ is the supremum of the eventually writable ordinals and Σ is the supremum of the accidentally writable ordinals, then [HL00] establishes $\lambda < \zeta < \Sigma$. Welch [Wel00a] showed that $L_\lambda \prec_{\Sigma_1} L_\zeta \prec_{\Sigma_2} L_\Sigma$, and furthermore, these ordinals are characterized as the least example of this pattern.

Many of the fundamental constructions of classical finite time computability theory carry over to the infinite time context. For example, one can prove the infinite time analogues of the *smn*-theorem, the Recursion theorem and the undecidability of the infinite time halting problem, by essentially the classical arguments. Some other classical facts, however, do not directly generalize. For example, it is not true in the infinite time context that if the graph of a function f is semi-decidable, then the function is computable. This is a consequence of the following:

Theorem 1 (Lost Melody Theorem). *There is a real c such that $\{c\}$ is infinite time decidable, but c is not writable.*

The real c is like the lost melody that you can recognize yes-or-no when someone sings it to you, but which you cannot sing on your own; it is a real that exhibits sufficient internal structure that $\{c\}$ is decidable, but is too complicated itself to be writable. If $f(x) = c$ is the function with constant value c, then f is not computable because c is not writable, but the graph is decidable, because we can recognize whether a pair has the form (x, c).

The infinite time analogue of the halting problem breaks into lightface and boldface versions, $h = \{p \mid \varphi_p(p) \downarrow\}$ and $H = \{(p, x) \mid \varphi_p(x) \downarrow\}$, respectively. These are both semi-decidable and not decidable, but in the infintary context, they are not computably equivalent.

There are two natural sorts of oracles to be used in oracle computations. First, one can use any real as an oracle in exactly the classical manner, by adjoining an oracle tape on which the values of that real are written out. Second, one naturally wants somehow to use a *set* of reals as oracle; but we cannot expect in general to write such a set out on the tape (perhaps it is even uncountable). Instead, the oracle tape is initially empty, and during the computation the machine may freely write on this tape. Whenever the algorithm calls for it, the machine may make a membership query about whether the real currently written on the oracle tape is a member of the oracle or not. Thus, the machine is able to know of any real that it can produce, whether the real is in the oracle set or not.

The result is a notion of relative computabiliy $\varphi_p^A(x)$, a notion of reduction $A <_\infty B$ and a notion of equivalence $A \equiv_\infty B$, with a rich theory of the infinite time Turing degrees. For any set A, we have the lightface jump $A^\triangledown$ and the boldface jump $A^\blacktriangledown$, corresponding to the two halting problems. One can show $A <_\infty A^\triangledown <_\infty A^\blacktriangledown$, as well as $A^{\triangledown\blacktriangledown} \equiv_\infty A^\blacktriangledown$ and a great number of other interesting interactions. In [HL02], we settled the infinite time analogue of Post's problem, the question of whether there are intermediate semi-decidable degrees between 0 and the jump $0^\triangledown$. The answer cuts both ways:

Theorem 2. *The infinite time analogue of Post's problem has both affirmative and negative solutions.*

1. *There are no reals z with $0 <_\infty z <_\infty 0^\triangledown$.*
2. *There are sets of reals A with $0 <_\infty A <_\infty 0^\triangledown$. Indeed, there are incomparable semi-decidable sets of reals $A \perp_\infty B$.*

In other work, Welch [Wel99] found minimality in the infinite time Turing degrees. Hamkins and Seabold [HS01] analyzed one-tape versus multi-tape infinite time Turing machines, and Benedikt Löwe [LÖ1] observed the connection between infinite time Turing machines and revision theories of truth.

2   A Survey of Recent Developments

Let me now discuss some of the recent developments in the theory of infinite time Turing machines, including the rise of infinite time complexity theory, the introduction of infinite time computable model theory, the beginnings of infinite time computable equivalence relation theory and the introduction of new related models of ordinal computation.

2.1   Infinite Time Complexity Theory

Ralf Schindler [Sch03] initiated the study of infinite time complexity theory by solving the infinite time Turing machine analogue of the P versus NP question. To define the polynomial class P in the infinite time context, Schindler observed simply that all reals have length ω and the polynomial functions of ω are bounded by those of the form ω^n. Thus, he defined that a set $A \subseteq \mathbb{R}$ is in P if there is a program p and a natural number n such that p decides A and halts on all inputs in time before ω^n. The set A is in NP if there is a program p and a natural number n such that $x \in A$ if and only if there is y such that p accepts (x, y), and p halts on all inputs in time less than ω^n. Schindler proved P $\neq$ NP for infinite time Turing machines in [Sch03], using methods from descriptive set theory to analyze the complexity of the classes P and NP. This has now been generalized in joint work [DHS05] to the following, where the class co-NP consists of the complements of sets in NP.

Theorem 3. $P \neq NP \cap co\text{-}NP$ *for infinite time Turing machines.*

Some of the structural reasons behind $P \neq NP \cap co\text{-}NP$ are revealed by placing the classes P and NP within a larger hierarchy of complexity classes P_α and NP_α using computations of size bounded below α. We proved, for example, that the classes NP_α are identical for $\omega + 2 \leq \alpha \leq \omega_1^{CK}$, but nevertheless, $P_{\alpha+1} \subsetneq P_{\alpha+2}$ for any clockable limit ordinal α. It follows, since the P_α are steadily increasing while the classes $NP_\alpha \cap co\text{-}NP_\alpha$ remain the same, that $P_\alpha \subsetneq NP_\alpha \cap co\text{-}NP_\alpha$ for any ordinal α with $\omega + 2 \leq \alpha < \omega_1^{CK}$. Thus, $P \neq NP \cap co\text{-}NP$. Nevertheless, we attain equality at the supremum ω_1^{CK} with

$$P_{\omega_1^{CK}} = NP_{\omega_1^{CK}} \cap co\text{-}NP_{\omega_1^{CK}}.$$

In fact, this is an instance of the equality $\Delta_1^1 = \Sigma_1^1 \cap \Pi_1^1$.

This same pattern of inequality $P_\alpha \subsetneq NP_\alpha \cap co\text{-}NP_\alpha$ is mirrored higher in the hierarchy, whenever α lies strictly within a contiguous block of clockable ordinals, with the corresponding $P_\beta = NP_\beta \cap co\text{-}NP_\beta$ for any β that begins a gap in the clockable ordinals. In addition, the question is settled in [DHS05] for the other complexity classes P^+, P^{++} and P^f. Benedikt Löwe has introduced analogues of PSPACE.

2.2   Infinite Time Computable Model Theory

Computable model theory is model theory with a view to the computability of the structures and theories that arise. Infinite time computable model theory carries out this program with the notion of infinite time computability provided by infinite time Turing machines. The classical theory began decades ago with such topics as computable completeness (Does every decidable theory have a decidable model?) and computable categoricity (Does every isomorphic pair of computable models have a computable isomorphism?), and the field has now matured into a sophisticated analysis of the complexity spectrum of countable models and theories.

The motivation for a broader context is that, while classical computable model theory is necessarily limited to countable models and theories, the infinitary computability context allows for uncountable models and theories, built on the reals. Many of the computational constructions in computable model theory generalize from structures built on $\mathbb{N}$, using finite time computability, to structures built on $\mathbb{R}$, using infinite time computability. The uncountable context opens up new questions, such as the infinitary computable Löwenheim-Skolem Theorem, which have no finite time analogue. Several of the most natural questions turn out to be independent of ZFC.

In joint work [HMSW07], we defined that a model $\mathcal{A} = \langle A, \ldots \rangle$ is infinite time *computable* if $A \subseteq \mathbb{R}$ is decidable and all functions, relations and constants are uniformly infinite time computable from their Gödel codes and input. The structure $\mathcal{A}$ is *decidable* if one can compute whether $\mathcal{A} \models \varphi[\bar{a}]$ given $\ulcorner\varphi\urcorner$ and $\bar{a}$. A theory T is infinite time *decidable* if the relation $T \vdash \varphi$ is computable in $\ulcorner\varphi\urcorner$. Because we want to treat uncountable languages, the natural context for Gödel codes is $\mathbb{R}$ rather than $\mathbb{N}$.

The initial question, of course, is the infinite time computable analogue of the Completeness Theorem: Does every consistent decidable theory have a decidable model? The answer turns out to be independent of ZFC.

Theorem 4 ([HMSW07]). *The infinite time computable analogue of the Completeness Theorem is independent of ZFC. Specifically:*

1. *If $V = L$, then every consistent infinite time decidable theory has an infinite time decidable model, in a computable translation of the language.*
2. *It is relatively consistent with ZFC that there is an infinite time decidable theory, in a computably presented language, having no infinite time computable or decidable model in any translation of the language.*

The proof of (1) uses the concept of a *well-presented* language $\mathcal{L}$, for which there is an enumeration of the symbols $\langle s_\alpha \mid \alpha < \delta \rangle$ such that from any $\ulcorner s_\alpha \urcorner$ one can uniformly compute a code for the prior symbols $\langle \ulcorner s_\beta \urcorner \mid \beta \le \alpha \rangle$. One can show that every consistent decidable theory in a well-presented language has a decidable model, and if $V = L$, then every computable language has a well presented computable translation. For (2), one uses the theory T extending the atomic diagram of $\langle WO, \equiv \rangle$ while asserting that f is a choice function on the $\equiv$ classes. This is a decidable theory, but for any computable model $\mathcal{A} = \langle A, \equiv, f \rangle$ of T, the set $\{ f(c_u) \mid u \in WO \}$ is Σ_2^1 and has cardinality ω_1. It is known to be consistent with ZFC that no Σ_2^1 set has size ω_1.

For the infinite time analogues of the Löwenheim-Skolem Theorem, we proved for the upward version that every well presented infinite time decidable model has a proper elementary extension with a decidable presentation, and for the downward version, every well presented uncountable decidable model has a countable decidable elementary substructure. There are strong counterexamples to a full direct generalization of the Löwenheim-Skolem theorem, however, because [HMSW07] provides a computable structure $\langle \mathbb{R}, U \rangle$ on the entire set of reals, which has no proper computable elementary substructure.

Some of the most interesting work involves computable quotients. A structure has an infinite time computable *presentation* if it is isomorphic to a computable structure, and has a computable *quotient presentation* if it is isomorphic to the quotient of a computable structure by a computable equivalence relation (a congruence). For structures on $\mathbb{N}$, in either the finite or infinite time context, these notions are equivalent, because one can computably find the least element of any equivalence class. For structures on $\mathbb{R}$, however, computing such distinguished elements of every equivalence class is not always possible.

Question 5. Does every structure with an infinite time computable quotient presentation have an infinite time computable presentation?

In the finite time theory, or for structures on $\mathbb{N}$, the answer of course is Yes. But in the full infinite time context for structures on $\mathbb{R}$, the answer depends on the set theoretic background.

Theorem 6. *The answer to Question 5 is independent of* ZFC. *Specifically,*

1. *It is relatively consistent with* ZFC *that every structure with an infinite time computable quotient presentation has an infinite time computable presentation.*
2. *It is relatively consistent with* ZFC *that there is a structure having an infinite time computable quotient presentation, but no infinite time computable presentation.*

Let me briefly sketch some of the ideas appearing in the proof. In order to construct an infinite time computable presentation of a structure, given a computable quotient presentation, we'd like somehow to select a representative from each equivalence class, in a computably effective manner, and build a structure on these representatives. Under the set theoretic assumption $V = L$, we can attach to the L-least member of each equivalence class an escort real that is powerful enough to reveal that it is the L-least member of its class, and build a computable presentation out of these escorted pairs of reals. (In particular, the new presentation is not built out of mere representatives from the original class, since these reals may be too weak; they need the help of their escorts.) Thus, if $V = L$, then every structure with a computable quotient presentation has a computable presentation. On the other side of the independence, we prove statement 2 by the method of forcing. The structure $\langle \omega_1, < \rangle$ always has a computable quotient presentation built from reals coding well orders, but there are forcing extensions in which no infinite time computable set has size ω_1, on descriptive set theoretic grounds. In these extensions, therefore, $\langle \omega_1, < \rangle$ has a computable quotient presentation, but no computable presentation.

2.3   Infinite Time Computable Equivalence Relation Theory

Recently, Sam Coskey and I have introduced the infinite time analogue of Borel equivalence relation theory and reductions. The idea of the classical Borel theory is to provide a structural analysis of the relative complexity of canonical equivalence relations on the reals (or more generally, Polish spaces) by comparing them under many-one Borel reducibility. Since Borel functions are all infinite time computable from their real parameters, it is a slight generalization of this theory to consider infinite time computable reductions. Thus, for any two equivalence relations E and F on $\mathbb{R}$, we say that E computably reduces to F, written $E \leq_c F$, if there is an infinite time computable function f (freely allowing real parameters) such that $x \, E \, y \longleftrightarrow f(x) \, F \, f(y)$. A slightly more generous notion of reduction is $E \leq_{sc} F$ if there is a semi-computable function $f : \mathbb{R} \to \mathbb{R}$, that is, a function whose graph is infinite time decidable (in a real parameter), such that $x \, E \, y \longleftrightarrow f(x) \, F \, f(y)$. An intriguing threshold phenomenon suggests that the distinction between computable reductions and semi-computable reductions is near a critical boundary.

To explain, let me first mention that there are an enormous number of natural equivalence relations on the reals to which this reduction theory applies, including all the Borel relations that have been studied in the classical theory. All the positive Borel reductions, of course, carry over to the infinite time context because all Borel functions are infinite time computable from their real parameters. Furthermore, many of the classical non-reductions in the Borel theory actually establish the lack of an infinite time computable reduction, because they often establish the lack of a measurable reduction, and all infinite time computable functions are measurable. In this way, the infinite time computable reduction theory is tightly interwoven into the classical Borel theory. Sample theorems include:

Theorem 7

1. E_0 and $\equiv_{SET}$ do not computably reduce to $=$.
2. $\equiv_{WO}$ and $\equiv_{SET}$ computably reduce to $\equiv_{HC}$.
3. $\equiv_{HC}$ and $\equiv_{SET}$ do not computably reduce to $\equiv_{WO}$.
4. $\equiv_{ck}$ and $\equiv_{WO}$ are computably bi-reducible.

Interestingly, we know that it is consistent that the semi-computable reduction theory completely collapses.

Theorem 8. *If $V = L$, then every infinite time computable equivalence relation E on $\mathbb{R}$ semi-computably reduces to the equality relation.*

In this sense, under $V = L$ every computable relation is semi-computably smooth. The proof uses the ideas of Theorem 6, and as in that argument, the reduction functions are not selectors for the relation.

One should not construe this theorem to suggest that the semi-computable reduction relation is trivial, however, since under other set theoretic hypotheses inconsistent with $V = L$, such as a mild determinacy assumption, every semi-computable function is measurable. In this case the semi-computable degrees are definitely not collapsed in this way.

2.4   New Models of Ordinal Computation

Lastly, let me briefly discuss some new models of ordinal computation. Peter Koepke [Koe05] introduced the *Ordinal Turing Machines*, which generalize the infinite time Turing machines by extending the tape to transfinite ordinal length. The limit rules are accordingly adjusted so that the machine can make use of this extra space. Specifically, rather than using a special *limit* state, the ordinal Turing machines simply have a fixed order on their (finitely many) states, and at any limit stage, the state is defined to be the lim inf of the prior states. The head position is then defined to be the lim inf of the head positions when the machine was previously in that resulting limit state. For uniformity, then, Koepke defines that the cells of the tape use the lim inf of the prior cell values (rather than lim sup as with the infinite time Turing machines). If the head moves left from a cell at a limit position, then it appears all the way to the left on the first cell.

These machines therefore provide a model of computation for functions on the ordinals, and notions of decidability for classes of ordinals. The main theorem is that the power of these machines is essentially the same as that of Gödel's constructible universe.

Theorem 9 (Koepke). *The sets of ordinals that are ordinal Turing machine decidable, with finitely many ordinal parameters, are exactly the sets of ordinals in Gödel's constructible universe L.*

Koepke and Siders [KS06] introduced another highly interesting model, the ordinal register machines. These machines generalize ordinary register machines to ordinal values and ordinal time. Thus, the machines have finitely many registers, each capable of holding one ordinal. The (finite) program is allowed to copy the contents of one register to another, to increment a register by 1, to zero out a register, and to branch depending on whether one register is larger than another. At limit stages, the contents of the registers are simply the lim inf of the previous contents, and the program line is the lim inf of the previously executed lines. Despite the apparently weak power of these machines, Koepke and Siders have proved that they are fully as powerful as the ordinal Turing machines, in terms of the sets of ordinals they can decide.

Theorem 10 (Koepke, Siders). *The ordinal register machine computable sets of ordinals, with finitely many ordinal parameters, are exactly the sets of ordinals in Gödel's constructible universe L.*

The most recent work of Koepke shows that both the ordinal Turing machines and the ordinal register machines, when restricted to computations of time length α, for an admissible ordinal α, give rise exactly to the intensely-studied computability theory of α-recursion theory, known for example from [Sac90].

References

[DHS05]   Deolalikar, V., Hamkins, J.D., Schindler, R.-D.: $P \neq NP \cap$ co-NP for infinite time turing machines. Journal of Logic and Computation 15(5), 577–592 (2005)

[Ham02]   Hamkins, J.D.: Infinite time turing machines. Minds and Machines 12(4), 521–539 (2002) (special issue devoted to hypercomputation)

[Ham04]   Hamkins, J.D.: Supertask computation. In: Piwinger, B., Löwe, B., Räsch, T. (eds.) Classical and New Paradigms of Computation and their Complexity Hierarchies. Trends in Logic, vol. 23, pp. 141–158. Kluwer Academic Publishers, Dordrecht (2004)

[Ham05]   Hamkins, J.D.: Infinitary computability with infinite time Turing machines. In: Cooper, S.B., Löwe, B., Torenvliet, L. (eds.) CiE 2005. LNCS, vol. 3526, Springer, Heidelberg (2005)

[HL00]   Hamkins, J.D., Lewis, A.: Infinite time Turing machines. J. Symbolic Logic 65(2), 567–604 (2000)

[HL02]   Hamkins, J.D., Lewis, A.: Post's problem for supertasks has both positive and negative solutions. Archive for Mathematical Logic 41(6), 507–523 (2002)

[HMSW07]   Hamkins, J.D., Miller, R., Seabold, D., Warner, S.: Infinite time computable model theory. In: Cooper, S.B., Löwe, B., Sorbi, A. (eds.) New Computational Paradigms: Changing Conceptions of What is Computable, Springer, Heidelberg (2007)

[HS01]   Hamkins, J.D., Seabold, D.: Infinite time Turing machines with only one
            tape. Mathematical Logic Quarterly 47(2), 271–287 (2001)
[HW03]   Hamkins, J.D., Welch, P.: $P^f \neq NP^f$ for almost all f. Mathematical
            Logic Quarterly 49(5), 536–540 (2003)
[Koe05]   Koepke, P.: Turing computations on ordinals. Bulletin of Symbolic
            Logic 11(3), 377–397 (2005)
[KS06]   Koepke, P., Siders, R.: Register computations on ordinals. Archive for
            Mathematical Logic (submitted)
[Lö01]   Löwe, B.: Revision sequences and computers with an infinite amount of
            time. Logic Comput. 11(1), 25–40 (2001)
[LM04]   Lenzi, G., Monteleone, E.: On fixpoint arithmetic and infinite time turing
            machines. Information Processing Letters 91(3), 121–128 (2004)
[Sac90]   Sacks, G.E.: Higher Recursion Theory. Perspectives in Mathematical
            Logic. Springer, Heidelberg (1990)
[Sch03]   Schindler, R.-D.: P $\neq$ NP for infinite time Turing machines. Monatshefte
            für Mathematik 139(4), 335–340 (2003)
[Wel]   Welch, P.: On a question of Deolalikar, Hamkins and Schindler, available
            on the author's web page at
            http://www2.maths.bris.ac.uk/$\sim$mapdw/dhs.ps
[Wel99]   Welch, P.: Friedman's trick: Minimality arguments in the infinite time
            Turing degrees. In: "Sets and Proofs", Proceedings ASL Logic Collo-
            quium, vol. 258, pp. 425–436 (1999)
[Wel00a]   Welch, P.: Eventually infinite time Turing machine degrees: Infinite time
            decidable reals. Journal of Symbolic Logic 65(3), 1193–1203 (2000)
[Wel00b]   Welch, P.: The lengths of infinite time Turing machine computations.
            Bulletin of the London Mathematical Society 32(2), 129–136 (2000)
[Wel05]   Welch, P.: The transfinite action of 1 tape Turing machines. In: Cooper,
            S.B., Löwe, B., Torenvliet, L. (eds.) CiE 2005. LNCS, vol. 3526, Springer,
            Heidelberg (2005)

The Tiling Problem Revisited
(Extended Abstract)

Jarkko Kari*

Department of Mathematics, FIN-20014 University of Turku, Finland
jkari@utu.fi

Abstract. We give a new proof for the undecidability of the tiling problem. Then we show how the proof can be modified to demonstrate the undecidability of the tiling problem on the hyperbolic plane, thus answering an open problem posed by R.M.Robinson 1971 [6].

1 Introduction

A *Wang tile* is a unit square tile with colored edges. Tiles are placed on the plane edge-to-edge, under the matching constraint that abutting edges must have the same color. Tiles are used in the given orientation, without rotating. If T is a finite set of Wang tiles, a tiling of the plane is a covering $t : \mathbb{Z}^2 \longrightarrow T$ of the plane by copies of the tiles in such a way that the color constraint is satisfied everywhere.

The *tiling problem* (also known as the domino problem) is the decision problem that asks whether a given finite tile set T admits at least one valid tiling $t : \mathbb{Z}^2 \longrightarrow T$. This problem was proved undecidable by R.Berger in 1966 [1]. Later, a simplified proof was given by R.M.Robinson [6]. Both proofs rely on an explicit construction of an *aperiodic* tile set. Set T is called aperiodic if it admits some valid tiling of the plane, but it does not admit a valid periodic tiling, i.e. a tiling that is invariant under some translation. Note that existence of such aperiodic sets is not obvious, and in fact it was conjectured prior to Berger's work that they do not exist. If aperiodic sets did not exist, then the tiling problem would be decidable as one can simply try tilings of larger and larger rectangles until either (1) a rectangle is found that can no longer be tiled, or (2) a tiling of a rectangle is found that can be repeated periodically. Only aperiodic tile sets fail to reach either (1) or (2).

Note that Wang tiles are an abstraction of geometric tiles. Indeed, by using suitable "bumps" and "dents" on the sides to represent different colors, one can effectively replace any set of Wang tiles by a set of geometric tiles (all polygons with rational coordinates) such that the geometric tiles admit a tiling (a non-overlapping covering of the plane) if and only if the Wang tiles admit a tiling. Hence undecidability of the tiling problem by geometric tiles follows from Berger's result.

---

* Research supported by the Academy of Finland grant 54102.

J. Durand-Lose and M. Margenstern (Eds.): MCU 2007, LNCS 4664, pp. 72–79, 2007.

In this work we present a new proof for the undecidability of the tiling problem. The proof is rather different from the earlier proofs. A particularly nice feature of our proof is the fact that it is purely combinatorial: the role of Euclidean geometry is minimal. As a consequence the method generalizes easily to tilings in other lattices as well. In particular, we show that the tiling problem is undecidable in the hyperbolic plane. This resolves an open question asked already by Robinson in 1971 [6], and discussed by him in more details in 1978 [7]. In particular, Robinson proved the undecidability of the origin constrained tiling problem in the hyperbolic plane. This is the easier question where one asks the existence of a valid tiling that contains a copy of a fixed seed tile. We mention that there is a concurrent, independent and unpublished approach by M.Margenstern to the tiling problem in the hyperbolic plane [5].

2 Mortality Problems of Turing Machines and Piecewise Affine Maps

Our proof is based on a reduction from the *mortality problem* of Turing machines. In this question we are given a deterministic Turing machine with a halting state, and the problem is to determine if there exists a non-halting configuration, that is, a configuration of the Turing machine that never evolves into the halting state. Such configuration is called immortal. Note that the Turing machine operates on an infinite tape, and configurations may contain infinitely many non-blank symbols.

Mortality problem of Turing machines. Does a given Turing machine have an immortal configuration ?

The mortality problem was proved undecidable by P.K.Hooper in 1966 [3], the same year that Berger proved his result. The two results have similar flavor, but proofs are independent in the sense that they do not rely on each other in either direction. Note an analogy to aperiodic tile sets: Hooper's result means that there must exist aperiodic Turing machines, that is, Turing machines that have immortal configurations but no immortal configuration repeats itself periodically. Our present proof establishes another connection between Hooper's and Berger's results since we reduce the mortality problem to the tiling problem.

We first consider dynamical systems determined by piecewise affine transformations of the plane. There exists a well known technique to simulate Turing machines by such transformations. The idea is to encode Turing machine configurations as two real numbers $(l, r) \in \mathbb{R}^2$, encoding the left and the right halves of the infinite tape, respectively. The integer parts of l and r uniquely determine the next rule of the Turing machine to be used.

For each transition rule of the Turing machine we effectively associate a rational affine transformation of $\mathbb{R}^2$ that simulates that transition. In this fashion any deterministic Turing machine is converted into a system of finitely many rational affine transformations $f_1, f_2, \ldots, f_n$ of $\mathbb{R}^2$ and corresponding disjoint unit squares $U_1, U_2, \ldots, U_n$ with integer corners. Squares U_i serve as domains for the affine maps: the affine transformation f_i is applied when (l, r) is in the unit square U_i. Together the transformations define a partial function $f : \mathbb{R}^2 \longrightarrow \mathbb{R}^2$ whose domain is $U = U_1 \cup U_2 \cup \ldots \cup U_n$, and whose operation is

$$x \mapsto f_i(x) \text{ for } x \in U_i.$$

Point $x \in \mathbb{R}^2$ is called immortal if for every $i = 0, 1, 2, \ldots$ the value $f^i(x)$ is in the domain U. In other words, we can continuously apply the given affine transformations and the point we obtain always belongs to one of the given unit squares U_i.

The reduction from Turing machines to piecewise affine transformations preserves immortality: the Turing machine has an immortal configuration if and only if the corresponding system of affine maps has an immortal starting point. Hence we conclude from Hooper's result that the following immortality question is undecidable:

Mortality problem of piecewise affine maps. Does a given system of rational affine transformations $f_1, f_2, \ldots, f_n$ of the plane and disjoint unit squares $U_1, U_2, \ldots, U_n$ with integer corners have an immortal starting point ?

3   Reduction into the Euclidean Tiling Problem

Next the mortality question of piecewise affine maps is reduced into the tiling problem of Wang tiles. The idea is very similar to a construction of an aperiodic Wang tile set presented in [4]. In [4] a tile set was given such that every valid tiling is forced to simulate an infinite orbit according to the one-dimensional piecewise linear function $f : [\frac{1}{2}, 2] \longrightarrow [\frac{1}{2}, 2]$ where

$$f(x) = \begin{cases} 2x, & \text{if } x \leq 1, \text{ and} \\ \frac{2}{3}x, & \text{if } x > 1. \end{cases}$$

Function f has no periodic orbits so the corresponding tile set is aperiodic.

The construction needs to be generalized in two ways: (1) instead of linear maps we need to allow more general affine maps, and (2) instead of $\mathbb{R}$ the maps are now over $\mathbb{R}^2$. Fortunately both generalizations are very natural and work without any complications.

The colors of our Wang tiles are elements of $\mathbb{R}^2$. Let $f : \mathbb{R}^2 \longrightarrow \mathbb{R}^2$ be an affine function. We say that tile

computes function f if

$$f(n) + w = s + e.$$

(The "input" n comes from north, and $f(n)$ is computed. A "carry in" w from the west is added, and the result is split between the "output" s to the south and the "carry out" e to the east.)

Suppose we have a correctly tiled horizontal segment of length n where all tiles compute the same f.

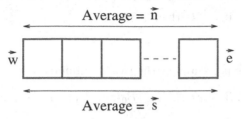

It easily follows that

$$f(n) + \frac{1}{n}w = s + \frac{1}{n}e,$$

where n and s are the averages of the top and the bottom labels. As the segment is made longer, the effect of the carry in and out labels w and e vanish. In the limit, if we have an infinite row of tiles, the average of the input labels (if it exists!) is mapped by f to the average of the output labels.

Consider now a given system of affine maps f_i and unit squares U_i. For each i we construct a set T_i of Wang tiles that compute function f_i and whose top edge labels n are in U_i. An additional label i on the vertical edges makes sure that tiles of different sets T_i and T_j cannot be mixed on any horizontal row of tiles. Let

$$T = \bigcup_i T_i.$$

If T admits a valid tiling then the system of affine maps has an immortal point. Namely, consider any horizontal row in a valid tiling. The top labels belong to a compact and convex set U_i. Hence there is $x \in U_i$ that is the limit of the top label averages over a sequence of segments of increasing length. Then $f_i(x)$ is the limit of the bottom label averages over the same sequence of segments. But the bottom labels of a row are the same as the top labels of the next row below, so $f_i(x)$ is the limit of top label averages of the next row. The reasoning is repeated for the next row, and for all rows below. We see that x starts an infinite orbit of the affine maps, so it is an immortal point.

We still have to detail how to choose the tiles so that any immortal orbit of the affine maps corresponds to a valid tiling. Consider a unit square

$$U = [n, n+1] \times [m, m+1]$$

where $n, m \in \mathbb{Z}$. Elements of

$$\mathrm{Cor}(U) = \{(n, m), (n, m+1), (n+1, m), (n+1, m+1)\}$$

are the *corners* of U. For any $x \in \mathbb{R}^2$ and $k \in \mathbb{Z}$ denote

$$A_k(x) = \lfloor kx \rfloor$$

where the floor is taken for each coordinate separately:

$$\lfloor (x, y) \rfloor = (\lfloor x \rfloor, \lfloor y \rfloor).$$

Denote

$$B_k(\boldsymbol{x}) = A_k(\boldsymbol{x}) - A_{k-1}(\boldsymbol{x}) = \lfloor k\boldsymbol{x} \rfloor - \lfloor (k-1)\boldsymbol{x} \rfloor.$$

It easily follows that if $\boldsymbol{x} \in U$ then

$$B_k(\boldsymbol{x}) \in \mathrm{Cor}(U).$$

Vector $\boldsymbol{x}$ will be represented as the two-way infinite sequence

$$\ldots B_{-2}(\boldsymbol{x}), B_{-1}(\boldsymbol{x}), B_0(\boldsymbol{x}), B_1(\boldsymbol{x}), B_2(\boldsymbol{x}), \ldots$$

of corners. It is the *balanced representation* of $\boldsymbol{x}$, or the sturmian representation of $\boldsymbol{x}$. Note that both coordinate sequences are sturmian.

The tile set corresponding to a rational affine map

$$f_i(\boldsymbol{x}) = M\boldsymbol{x} + \boldsymbol{b}$$

and its domain square U_i consists of all tiles

$$B_k(\boldsymbol{x})$$

$$\begin{array}{c} f_i(A_{k-1}(\boldsymbol{x})) \\ -A_{k-1}(f_i(\boldsymbol{x})) \\ +(k-1)\boldsymbol{b} \end{array} \qquad \boxed{} \qquad \begin{array}{c} f_i(A_k(\boldsymbol{x})) \\ -A_k(f_i(\boldsymbol{x})) \\ +k\boldsymbol{b} \end{array}$$

$$B_k(f_i(\boldsymbol{x}))$$

where $k \in \mathbb{Z}$ and $\boldsymbol{x} \in U_i$. Observe the following facts:

(1) For fixed $\boldsymbol{x} \in U_i$ the tiles for consecutive $k \in \mathbb{Z}$ match in the vertical edges so that a horizontal row can be formed whose top and bottom labels read the balanced representations of $\boldsymbol{x}$ and $f_i(\boldsymbol{x})$, respectively.

(2) A direct calculation shows that the tile above computes function f_i, that is,

$$f_i(\boldsymbol{n}) + \boldsymbol{w} = \boldsymbol{s} + \boldsymbol{e}.$$

(3) Because f_i is rational, there are only finitely many tiles constructed, even though there are infinitely many $k \in \mathbb{Z}$ and $\boldsymbol{x} \in U_i$. Moreover, the tiles can be effectively constructed.

Now it is clear that if the given system of affine maps has an immortal point $\boldsymbol{x}$ then a valid tiling exists where the labels of consecutive horizontal rows read the balanced representations of the consecutive points of the orbit for $\boldsymbol{x}$. We conclude that the tile set we constructed admits a tiling of the plane if and only if the given system of affine maps is immortal. Undecidability of the tiling problem follows from the undecidability of the immortality problem that we established in Section 2.

4 Reduction into the Tiling Problem on the Hyperbolic Plane

The method of the previous section works just as well in the hyperbolic plane. Instead of Wang tiles we use hyperbolic pentagons that in the half-plane model of hyperbolic geometry are copies of

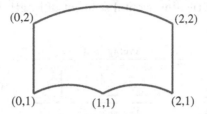

Note that all five edges are straight line segments. These tiles admit valid tilings of the hyperbolic plane in uncountably many different ways

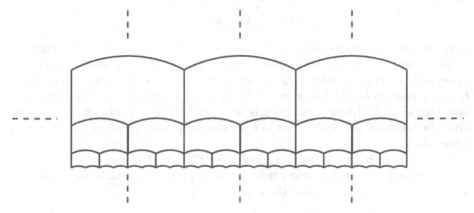

In these tilings the tiles form infinite "horizontal rows" in such a way that each tile has two adjacent tiles in the next row "below".

In the following these hyperbolic pentagons are used instead of the Euclidean square shaped Wang tiles. The five edges will be colored, and in a valid tiling abutting edges of adjacent tiles must match. This is an abstraction – analogous to Wang tiles in the Euclidean plane – that can be transformed into hyperbolic geometric shapes using bumps and dents.

Exactly as in the Euclidean case we color the edges by vectors $x \in \mathbb{R}^2$. We say that pentagon

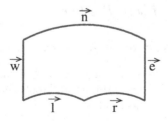

computes the affine transformation $f : \mathbb{R}^2 \longrightarrow \mathbb{R}^2$ if

$$f(\boldsymbol{n}) + \boldsymbol{w} = \frac{\boldsymbol{l} + \boldsymbol{r}}{2} + \boldsymbol{e}.$$

Note that the difference to Euclidean Wang tiles is the fact that the "output" is now divided between $\boldsymbol{l}$ and $\boldsymbol{r}$.

Consider a correctly tiled horizontal segment of length n where all tiles compute the same f.

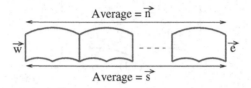

Clearly we have

$$f(\boldsymbol{n}) + \frac{1}{n}\boldsymbol{w} = \boldsymbol{s} + \frac{1}{n}\boldsymbol{e},$$

where $\boldsymbol{n}$ and $\boldsymbol{s}$ are the averages of the top and the bottom labels on the segment.

Analogously to the Euclidean case, given a system of affine maps f_i and unit squares U_i, we construct for each i a set T_i of pentagons that compute function f_i and whose top edge labels $\boldsymbol{n}$ are in U_i. It follows, exactly as in the Euclidean case, that if a valid tiling of the hyperbolic plane with such pentagons exists then from the labels of horizontal rows one obtains an infinite orbit in the system of affine maps.

We still have to detail how to choose the tiles so that the converse is also true: if an immortal point exists then its orbit provides a valid tiling. The tile set corresponding to a rational affine map

$$f_i(\boldsymbol{x}) = M\boldsymbol{x} + \boldsymbol{b}$$

and its domain square U_i consists of all tiles

$$
\begin{array}{cc}
& B_k(\boldsymbol{x}) \\
\begin{array}{c} f_i(A_{k-1}(\boldsymbol{x})) \\ -\frac{1}{2}A_{2(k-1)}(f_i(\boldsymbol{x})) \\ +(k-1)\boldsymbol{b} \end{array} & \qquad\qquad \begin{array}{c} f_i(A_k(\boldsymbol{x})) \\ -\frac{1}{2}A_{2k}(f_i(\boldsymbol{x})) \\ +k\boldsymbol{b} \end{array} \\
& B_{2k-1}(f_i(\boldsymbol{x})) \quad B_{2k}(f_i(\boldsymbol{x}))
\end{array}
$$

where $k \in \mathbb{Z}$ and $\boldsymbol{x} \in U_i$. Now we can reason exactly as in the Euclidean case:

(1) For fixed $\boldsymbol{x} \in U_i$ the tiles for consecutive $k \in \mathbb{Z}$ match so that a horizontal row can be formed whose top and bottom labels read the balanced representations of $\boldsymbol{x}$ and $f_i(\boldsymbol{x})$, respectively.

(2) A direct calculation shows that the tile computes function f_i:

$$f_i(n) + w = \frac{l + r}{2} + e.$$

(3) There are only finitely many pentagons constructed (because f_i is rational), and they can be formed effectively.

The tiles constructed admit a valid tiling of the hyperbolic plane if and only if the corresponding system of affine maps has an immortal point. So we have proved

Theorem. The tiling problem is undecidable in the hyperbolic plane.

References

1. Berger, R.: Undecidability of the Domino Problem. Memoirs of the American Mathematical Society 66, 72 (1966)
2. Goodman-Strauss, C.: A strongly aperiodic set of tiles in the hyperbolic plane. Inventiones Mathematicae 159, 119–132 (2005)
3. Hooper, P.K.: The undecidability of the Turing machine immortality problem. The Journal of Symbolic Logic 31, 219–234 (1966)
4. Kari, J.: A small aperiodic set of Wang tiles. Discrete Mathematics 160, 259–264 (1996)
5. Margenstern, M.: About the domino problem in the hyperbolic plane, a new solution. Manuscript, pp. 109 (2007), available at: http://www.lita.univ-metz.fr/~margens/ and also see arXiv:cs/0701096, same title, p. 60
6. Robinson, R.M.: Undecidability and nonperiodicity for tilings of the plane. Inventiones Mathematicae 12, 177–209 (1971)
7. Robinson, R.M.: Undecidable tiling problems in the hyperbolic plane. Inventiones Mathematicae 44, 259–264 (1978)

Decision Versus Evaluation
in Algebraic Complexity

Pascal Koiran

LIP*, École Normale Supérieure de Lyon
Pascal.Koiran@ens-lyon.fr

Abstract. This is a survey of some of my joint work with Sylvain Périfel. It is focused on transfer theorems that connect boolean complexity to algebraic complexity in the Valiant and Blum-Shub-Smale models.

Keywords: computational complexity, algebraic complexity, Blum-Shub-Smale model, Valiant's model.

1 Introduction

The goal of this note is to highlight some developments in algebraic complexity theory that have occured since my previous survey [11] was written. The scope of the present note is much narrower since I will only attempt to present some of my joint work with Sylvain Périfel.

The survey [11] contained an introduction to the Blum-Shub-Smale theory of computation in rings [3,2] and its extension to "arbitrary" structures by Poizat [23]; a presentation of some then-recent results, including the transfer theorems for the "P=NP ?" problem over the reals with addition and order [8,9]; and some suggestions of future research directions as well as a few concrete steps in those directions. The main message of the paper was that in order to study the "$P_M = NP_M$?" problem in a structure M, it is essential to find out whether NP_M problems can be solved by polynomial depth computation trees. Indeed, we know that $P_M \neq NP_M$ if there exists some problem X in NP_M that cannot be solved by polynomial depth computation trees. This follows from the fact that computation trees are always at least as powerful as circuits: if problem X cannot be solved by polynomial depth computation trees then it cannot be solved by polynomial size circuits. On the other hand, if all NP_M problems can be solved by polynomial depth computation trees it may be possible to obtain a transfer theorem for the "$P_M = NP_M$?" problem. It turns out that the structure M of the real numbers with addition and equality complies with the first branch of this "computation tree alternative". Indeed, it has been known for a long time that this structure satisfies $P_M \neq NP_M$ [19]. By contrast, it is known that for the structure of the real numbers with addition and order all NP_M problems can be solved by polynomial depth computation trees. This follows from results of computational geometry due Meiser [20] and Meyer auf

---

* UMR 5668 ENS Lyon, CNRS, UCBL, INRIA.

J. Durand-Lose and M. Margenstern (Eds.): MCU 2007, LNCS 4664, pp. 80–89, 2007.

der Heide [21,22]. Those results are instrumental in the proof of our transfer theorems [8,9], which show that the "P = NP ?" problem in that structure is equivalent to the classical "P = NP ?" problem[1]. For the ordered field of the real numbers, the "$P_\mathbb{R} = NP_\mathbb{R}$?" problem is still open but the following result was established in [11].

Theorem 1. *If* $NP_\mathbb{R}$ *problems can be solved by constant-free computation trees of polynomial depth, we have the following transfer theorem:* P = PSPACE *implies* $P_\mathbb{R} = NP_\mathbb{R}$.

It is still not known whether the hypothesis that $NP_\mathbb{R}$ problems can be solved by computation trees of polynomial depth holds true, and my guess is that it doesn't[2]. Nevertheless, we recently managed to make some progress on these questions by bringing in a new ingredient, namely, Valiant's own algebraic version of the "P = NP?" problem [25,26,4]. In Valiant's framework one studies the complexity of evaluating polynomials rather than the complexity of decision problems as in the boolean or Blum-Shub-Smale frameworks. In [14] and [13] we showed that a collapse of complexity classes in Valiant's framework implies $P_\mathbb{R} = NP_\mathbb{R}$ and $P_\mathbb{C} = NP_\mathbb{C}$. These results and some relevant background are presented in the remainder of this paper.

2 The Blum-Shub-Smale Model

Although the original definitions of Blum, Shub and Smale [3,2] are in terms of uniform machines, we will follow [23] by using families of algebraic circuits to recognize languages over a field K, that is, subsets of $K^\infty = \bigcup_{n \geq 0} K^n$. The ordinary (boolean) theory of computation is recovered by choosing for K the two-element field $\mathbb{Z}/2\mathbb{Z}$. A similar circuit model was defined by von zur Gathen [28] (see also [1], section 4.1).

An algebraic circuit is a directed acyclic graph whose vertices, called gates, have indegree 0, 1 or 2. An input gate is a vertex of indegree 0. An output gate is a gate of outdegree 0. We assume that there is only one such gate in the circuit. Gates of indegree 2 are labelled by a symbol from the set $\{+, -, \times\}$. Gates of indegree 1, called test gates, are labelled "= 0?" if K is unordered (e.g., if $K = \mathbb{C}$), or "≤ 0?" if K is ordered (e.g., if $K = \mathbb{R}$). The size of a circuit C, in symbols $|C|$, is the number of vertices of the graph.

A circuit with n input gates computes a function from K^n to K. On input $\bar{u} \in K^n$ the value returned by the circuit is by definition equal to the value of its

---

[1] Strictly speaking, equivalence to the classical problem only holds true in the constant-free version of the Blum-Shub-Smale model; in the full-fledged model arbitrary real constants are allowed, and we have proved equivalence to the non-uniform problem "P/poly = NP/poly ?".

[2] I will be proved right once since we made the opposite conjecture in [8]. Even for the linear programming problem (feasibility of sytems of linear inequalities), it seems that the answer to this question is not known.

output gate. The value of a gate is defined in the usual way. Namely, the value of input gate number i is equal to the i-th input u_i. The value of other gates is then defined recursively: it is the sum of the values of its entries for a $+$-gate, their difference for a $-$-gate, their product for a $\times$-gate. If K is unordered, the value taken by a test gate is 1 if the value of its entry is equal to 0, and 0 otherwise. If K is ordered, the value taken by a test gate is 1 if the value of its entry is ≤ 0 and 1 otherwise. We assume without loss of generality that the output is a test gate. The value returned by the circuit is therefore 0 or 1.

The class P_K is the set of languages $L \subseteq K^\infty$ such that there exists a tuple $\bar{a} \in \mathbb{R}^p$ (independent of n) and a P-uniform family of polynomial-size circuits (C_n) satisfying the following condition: C_n has exactly $n + p$ inputs, and for any $\bar{x} \in \mathbb{R}^n$, $\bar{x} \in L \Leftrightarrow C_n(\bar{x}, \bar{a}) = 1$. The P-uniformity condition means that C_n can be built in time polynomial in n by an ordinary (discrete) Turing machine. Note that $\bar{a}$ plays the role of the machine constants of [2,3].

As in [6], we define the class PAR_K as the set of languages over K recognized by a PSPACE-uniform family of algebraic circuits of polynomial depth (and possibly exponential size). The same tuple of constants $\bar{a}$ is used for every input size n, as in the definition of P_K. Note at last that we could also define similar classes without the constants $\bar{a}$. We will use the superscript 0 to denote these constant-free classes, for instance P_K^0 and PAR_K^0.

3   Valiant's Model

In Valiant's model, one computes polynomials instead of recognizing languages. We thus use arithmetic circuits instead of algebraic circuits. A book-length treatment of this topic can be found in [4].

An arithmetic circuit is the same as an algebraic circuit but test gates are not allowed. That is to say we have indeterminates $x_1, \ldots, x_{u(n)}$ as input together with arbitrary constants of K; there are $+$, $-$ and $\times$-gates, and we therefore compute multivariate polynomials.

The polynomial computed by an arithmetic circuit is defined in the usual way by the polynomial computed by its output gate. Thus a family (C_n) of arithmetic circuits computes a family (f_n) of polynomials, $f_n \in K[x_1, \ldots, x_{u(n)}]$. The class VP_{nb} defined in [17,18] is the set of families (f_n) of polynomials computed by a family (C_n) of polynomial-size arithmetic circuits, i.e., C_n computes f_n and there exists a polynomial $p(n)$ such that $|C_n| \leq p(n)$ for all n. We will assume without loss of generality that the number $u(n)$ of variables is bounded by a polynomial function of n. The subscript "nb" indicates that there is no bound on the degree of the polynomial, in contrast with the original class VP of Valiant where a polynomial bound on the degree of the polynomial computed by the circuit is required. Note that these definitions are nonuniform. The class uniform VP_{nb} is obtained by adding a condition of polynomial-time uniformity on the circuit family, as in Section 2.

The class VNP is the set of families of polynomials defined by an exponential sum of VP families. More precisely, $(f_n(\bar{x})) \in$ VNP if there exists $(g_n(\bar{x}, \bar{y})) \in$ VP and a polynomial p such that $|\bar{y}| = p(n)$ and $f_n(\bar{x}) = \sum_{\bar{\epsilon} \in \{0,1\}^{p(n)}} g_n(\bar{x}, \bar{\epsilon})$.

We can also forbid constants from our arithmetic circuits in unbounded-degree classes, and define constant-free classes. The only constant allowed is 1 (in order to allow the computation of constant polynomials). As for classes of decision problems, we will use the superscript 0 to indicate the absence of constant: for instance, we will write VP_{nb}^0 (for bounded-degree classes, we are to be more careful; see [17]).

In order to state our transfer theorems it is convenient to define a new class, called VPSPACE. We will only do this for fields of characteristic 0 since those are the only fields that we consider in the remainder of this note (the extension to fields of positive characteristic is straightforward). Roughly speaking, a family of polynomials is in VPSPACE if its coefficients can be computed in polynomial space. We first define formally the notion of coefficient function. If α is a tuple $(\alpha_1, \ldots, \alpha_{u(n)})$, we denote by $\bar{x}^\alpha$ the monomial $x_1^{\alpha_1} \cdots x_{u(n)}^{\alpha_{u(n)}}$.

Definition 1. *Let* (f_n) *be a family of multivariate polynomials with integer coefficients. The coefficient function of* (f_n) *is the function* a *whose value on input* (n, α, i) *is the* i-*th bit* $a(n, \alpha, i)$ *of the coefficient of the monomial* $\bar{x}^\alpha$ *in* f_n. *Furthermore,* $a(n, \alpha, 0)$ *is the sign of the coefficient of the monomial* $\bar{x}^\alpha$. *Thus* f_n *can be written as*

$$f_n(\bar{x}) = \sum_\alpha \left((-1)^{a(n,\alpha,0)} \sum_{i \geq 1} a(n, \alpha, i) 2^{i-1} \bar{x}^\alpha \right).$$

The coefficient function is a function $a : \{0,1\}^* \to \{0,1\}$ and can therefore be viewed as a language. This allows us to speak of the complexity of the coefficient function.

Definition 2. *The class* uniform VPSPACE^0 *is the set of all families* (f_n) *of multivariate polynomials* $f_n \in K[x_1, \ldots, x_{u(n)}]$ *satisfying the following requirements:*

1. *the number* $u(n)$ *of variables is polynomially bounded;*
2. *the polynomials* f_n *have integer coefficients;*
3. *the size of the coefficients of* f_n *is bounded by* $2^{p(n)}$ *for some polynomial* p;
4. *the degree of* f_n *is bounded by* $2^{p(n)}$ *for some polynomial* p;
5. *the coefficient function of* (f_n) *is in PSPACE.*

We have chosen to define first uniform VPSPACE^0, a uniform class without constants, because this is the main object of study in this paper. In keeping with the tradition set by Valiant, however, the class VPSPACE defined in Section 6, is nonuniform and allows for arbitrary constants. In [12] we have also defined a class VIIP, which sits in between VP_{nb} and VPSPACE.

4   The Transfer Theorems

One difficulty springs to mind immediately when one tries to establish transfer theorems between Valiant's model and the Blum-Shub-Smale model: the former model is highly non uniform (there is no uniformity requirement on circuit families, and arbitrary constants are allowed), whereas the latter model is much more uniform (the availability of arbitrary constants may still be a source of non-uniformity, especially in the real case). I believe that these discrepancies are mostly historical accidents. That is, there is nothing special about evaluation problems that makes them more suitable for non-uniform models, and there is nothing special about decision problems that makes them more suitable for uniform models. One should therefore feel free to modify the Valiant and Blum-Shub-Smale conventions in order to facilitate comparisons. This is just what we do in the following theorem, where we work in the most uniform setting: our circuit families are uniform and constant-free. It is possible to state (and prove!) variations of this theorem for other uniformity conventions.

Theorem 2. *If* uniform VPSPACE^0 = uniform VP^0_{nb} *then* $\text{PAR}^0_{\mathbb{R}} = \text{P}^0_{\mathbb{R}}$ *and* $\text{PAR}^0_{\mathbb{C}} = \text{P}^0_{\mathbb{C}}$.

The real case of this theorem is established in [14], and the complex case in [13]. In principle, the definitions of Valiant's classes are relative to a given field K. Note however that we work with constant-free circuits in this theorem, and our two fields $\mathbb{R}$ and $\mathbb{C}$ are both of characteristic 0. There is therefore actually only one class uniform VP^0_{nb} to consider, and likewise there is only one class uniform VPSPACE^0. It is therefore really the same hypothesis that implies the two collapses $\text{PAR}^0_{\mathbb{R}} = \text{P}^0_{\mathbb{R}}$ and $\text{PAR}^0_{\mathbb{C}} = \text{P}^0_{\mathbb{C}}$.

Note that for any field K, the collapse of the constant-free class PAR^0_K to P^0_K implies the collapse of PAR_K to P_K: just replace constants by new variables in order to transform a PAR_K problem into a PAR^0_K problem, and then replace these variables by their original values in order to transform a P^0_K problem into a P_K problem. Moreover, for $K = \mathbb{R}$ or $K = \mathbb{C}$ the collapse of PAR_K to P_K implies the collapse of NP_K to P_K since $\text{P}_K \subseteq \text{NP}_K \subseteq \text{PAR}_K$ [2].

It would be interesting to find out whether a converse to Theorem 2 can be established. Results of this type have already been established by Bürgisser [5] and Lickteig [15,16]. For instance, Bürgisser ([5], Corollary 4.5) has shown that if $\text{P}_{\mathbb{R}} = \text{PAR}_{\mathbb{R}}$, VNP families are "easy to approximate".

5   A Proof Sketch

In this section we assume that $K = \mathbb{R}$ or $K = \mathbb{C}$. In both cases, the proof of Theorem 2 builds on the fact that PAR_K problems can be solved by families of branching trees of polynomial depth. This result is established in [10] in the real case, and in [11] in the complex case. At any internal node v of such a tree, one tests the sign that an *arbitrary* polynomial P_v takes on the input $x \in K^n$. As usual, testing the sign means testing whether $P_v(x) = 0$ when $K = \mathbb{C}$, or whether $P_v(x)$ is < 0, > 0 or equal to 0 when $K = \mathbb{R}$. The leaves of the tree are labeled by *Accept* or *Reject*.

The constructions of [10] and [11] exploit the geometric structure of PAR_K problems. For any problem $A \in \text{PAR}_K$, the restriction $A \cap K^n$ of A to n-dimensional inputs is a union of cells of an arrangement of a finite set of hypersurfaces. These hypersurfaces are defined by the polynomials whose sign is tested at the test gates of the circuit recognizing $A \in K^n$. Their degree is bounded by a singly exponential function of n (because our circuits have polynomial depth), and it turns out that their number is also bounded by a singly exponential function of n. By definition, two points $x, y \in K^n$ are in the same cell if for any such polynomial P occuring in the arrangement, $P(x)$ and $P(y)$ have the the same sign (where the sign is defined as above). Nonempty cells form a partition of the input space K^n. To decide whether an input $x \in K^n$ should be accepted, it is therefore sufficient to locate x in the arrangement, that is, to find to which cell it belongs. It is shown in [10] that point location in an arrangement of real hypersurfaces can be performed by branching trees of depth $O(\log N)$, where N is the number of nonempty cells. The bound established in [11] for the complex case (or in fact for any unordered field) is $O(n \log N)$. It follows from standard bounds in effective algebraic geometry that N is bounded by a singly exponential function of n. We have therefore obtained the desired polynomial bound on the branching complexity of PAR_K problems.

The reader may have noticed a difference between branching trees and the computation trees mentioned in the introduction: in the branching tree model, the cost of polynomial evaluation is completely ignored. This model is therefore rather unrealistic, at least for the purpose of proving upper bounds (lower bounds can be found in [24,27]). To obtain a more realistic model, one should take the cost of evaluating the polynomials P_v into account. Not surprisingly, this is where Valiant's model comes into the picture. Namely, an analysis of the constructions of [10] and [11] shows that the polynomials P_v can be computed by (uniform, constant free) VPSPACE families. In fact, the analysis reveals that theses two constructions can be implemented by polynomial size arithmetic circuits augmented with special "help gates" that can test the sign of VPSPACE families. Theorem 2 follows immediately from this observation.

In the above proof sketch we have tried as much as possible to handle simultaneously the real and complex fields. We now fill in some of the details that are specific to each field, beginning with the branching tree construction for the point location problem.

5.1   The Real Case

Point location also plays an important role in the transfer theorems of [8,9]; these two papers deal with arrangements of hyperplanes rather than hypersurfaces since the underlying computation model is multiplication-free. In fact, these transfer theorems can be viewed as effective versions of the constructions of Meiser [20] and Meyer auf der Heide [21,22]. Meiser's point location algorithm especially looks at first sight like a good candidate for a generalization to hypersurfaces. It relies in particular on an efficient algorithm for dividing convex polyhedra into unions of simplexes. In order to generalize to arrangements of hypersurfaces, why not divide semi-algebraic sets into unions of "simple" semi-algebraic sets? Unfortunately, we do not know how to do that efficiently. It turns out that Grigoriev's solution [10] is very different, and has a more combinatorial character. The key combinatorial lemma, also established in [10], is as follows.

Lemma 1. *Let* $u_1, \ldots, u_m$ *be pairwise distinct vectors of* $(\mathbb{Z}/2\mathbb{Z})^k$. *If* $m \geq 6$ *there exists a vector* $v \in (\mathbb{Z}/2\mathbb{Z})^k$ *such that*

$$m/3 \leq |\{1 \leq i \leq m; \ \langle v, u_i \rangle = 0\}| \leq 2m/3.$$

In the application to point location, k should be viewed as the number of hyper-surfaces in the arrangement, and m as the number of satisfiable sign conditions. By "sign condition", we mean here a system of polynomial inequalities of the form $f_i < 0$ or $f_i > 0$, where the f_i are the polynomials defining the hypersur-faces of the arrangement (conditions of the form $f_i = 0$ are handled in a different way). Lemma 1 is used to perform a kind of binary search among sign conditions (see [10] for details). In order to obtain a constructive version of Grigoriev's re-sult, one needs a constructive version of this lemma. Unfortunately, the original proof is highly nonconstructive since it is a proof of contradiction. A very dif-ferent proof, based on a probabilistic argument, was given in [7]. Instead of the $[m/3, 2m/3]$ range of Lemma 1, this proof yields the smaller and almost opti-mal range $[m/2 - \sqrt{m}/2, m/2 + \sqrt{m}/2]$. A probabilistic algorithm (just choose v at random) follows by relaxing slightly these bounds. More importantly for the application to Theorem 2, a deterministic algorithm running in logarithmic space can be obtained by derandomizing the probabilistic algorithm (or more precisely, the probabilistic proof). Note that in the application to Theorem 2, "logarithmic space" should be viewed as "polynomial space" since the the num-ber of hypersurfaces (k) and of satisfiable sign conditions (m) can be exponential in the input dimension n. Our derandomization technique is reminiscent of the proof that bounded-error probabilistic algorithms can be efficiently simulated by boolean circuit families (i.e., BPP $\subseteq$ P/poly). Namely, for each k and m we build in logarithmic space a list of vectors which is guaranteed to contain a suit-able vector v for every possible input. Then we find a suitable v in this list by an exhaustive search, which can also be implemented in logarithmic space. Of course, one major difference with the proof that BPP $\subseteq$ P/poly is that making that proof constructive remains a major open problem.

5.2   The Complex Case

The complex case is in a way simpler than the real case because we do not have to distinguish between positive and negative inputs. As a result, we do not need anything like Lemma 1. On the other hand, the complex case looks more difficult because we cannot use as in [10] the standard "sum of squares" trick to decide whether a point belong to an algebraic set.

One important ingredient in the $O(n \log N)$ branching complexity bound of [11] is the well-known fact that any algebraic subset of $\mathbb{C}^n$ (defined by some number k of polynomial equations) can be defined by only $n+1$ equations (this is actually where the factor "n" in the $O(n \log N)$ bound comes from). The $n+1$ equations can be obtained by taking "generic" linear combinations of the k original equations. The constructive version of this proof obtained in [13] replaces the generic coefficients in these linear combinations by sufficiently fast growing sequences of integers. This is by no means a new method in algebraic complexity, but one must perhaps work harder than usual to keep the size of these integers under control (see [13] for details).

6   On the Hypothesis That VPSPACE Families Have Small Circuits

There are actually several version of this hypothesis, depending on uniformity conditions and the role of constants. As pointed in section 4 the hypothesis uniform $\mathrm{VPSPACE}^0 =$ uniform $\mathrm{VP}_{\mathrm{nb}}^0$ in Theorem 2 is the most uniform, hence the strongest. We define below two increasingly nonuniform classes, $\mathrm{VPSPACE}^0$ and VPSPACE. The only difference between $\mathrm{VPSPACE}^0$ and uniform $\mathrm{VPSPACE}^0$ is the nonuniformity of the coefficient function; VPSPACE is even more nonuniform since arbitrary constants are allowed.

Definition 3. *The class* $\mathrm{VPSPACE}^0$ *is the set of all families* (f_n) *of multivariate polynomials* $f_n \in K[x_1, \dots, x_{u(n)}]$ *satisfying the following requirements:*

1. *the number* $u(n)$ *of variables is polynomially bounded;*
2. *the polynomials* f_n *have integer coefficients;*
3. *the size of the coefficients of* f_n *is bounded by* $2^{p(n)}$ *for some polynomial* p;
4. *the degree of* f_n *is bounded by* $2^{p(n)}$ *for some polynomial* p;
5. *the coefficient function of* (f_n) *is in* PSPACE/poly.

Now, the class VPSPACE *is the set of all families* $(f_n(\bar{x}))$ *of multivariate polynomials* $f_n \in K[x_1, \dots, x_{u(n)}]$ *such that there exist a family* $(g_n(\bar{x}, \bar{y}))$ *in* $\mathrm{VPSPACE}^0$ *together with a family of tuples of constants* $(\bar{a}^{(n)})$ *satisfying for all* n:

$$f_n(\bar{x}) = g_n(\bar{x}, \bar{a}^{(n)}).$$

One could consider up to 6 different versions of the class VPSPACE since there are 2 possible choices for the coefficient function (uniform or nonuniform) and 3 possible choices for constants (no constants, arbitrary constants as in Valiant's original definitions, or the intermediate Blum-Shub-Smale convention in which the same tuple of constants is used for every input size). Some of these classes are in fact equal since nonuniformity comes for free when arbitrary constants are available. We have shown in [14] that the weakest hypothesis, namely, $\mathrm{VP}_{\mathrm{nb}} =$ VPSPACE, already has strong consequences:

Proposition 1. *Under the generalized Riemann hypothesis (GRH),*

$$VP_{nb} = VPSPACE \iff [P/poly = PSPACE/poly \text{ and } VP = VNP].$$

Moreover, the implication from right to left holds even without GRH.

One advantage of working with these nonuniform classes is therefore that there is after all no need to introduce the new class VPSPACE: since we have an equivalence in Proposition 1, the hypothesis can be formulated using only the familiar classes   P/poly,   PSPACE/poly,   VP   and   VNP.   The   hypothesis uniform $VPSPACE^0$ = uniform VP_{nb}^0 has an even more dire consequence:

Proposition 2

$$\text{uniform } VPSPACE^0 = \text{uniform } VP_{nb}^0 \implies PSPACE = \text{P-uniform NC}.$$

The separation "PSPACE $\neq$ P-uniform NC" is extremely plausible, but to the best of my knowledge remains a conjecture (by contrast, PSPACE can be separated from logspace-uniform NC thanks to the space hierarchy theorem).

References

1. Allender, E.: Arithmetic circuits and counting complexity classes. In: Krajicek, J. (ed.) Complexity of Computations and Proofs, Quaderni di Matematica. Seconda Universita di Napoli, vol. 13, pp. 2–15 (2004)
2. Blum, L., Cucker, F., Shub, M., Smale, S.: Complexity and Real Computation. Springer, Heidelberg (1998)
3. Blum, L., Shub, M., Smale, S.: On a theory of computation and complexity over the real numbers: NP-completeness, recursive functions and universal machines. Bulletin of the American Mathematical Society 21(1), 1–46 (1989)
4. Bürgisser, P.: Completeness and Reduction in Algebraic Complexity Theory. Algorithms and Computation in Mathematics, vol. 7. Springer, Heidelberg (2000)
5. Bürgisser, P.: The complexity of factors of multivariate polynomials. Foundations of Computational Mathematics 4(4), 369–396 (2004)
6. Chapuis, O., Koiran, P.: Saturation and stability in the theory of computation over the reals. Annals of Pure and Applied Logic 99, 1–49 (1999)
7. Charbit, P., Jeandel, E., Koiran, P., Périfel, S., Thomassé, S.: Finding a vector orthogonal to roughly half a collection of vectors. Journal of Complexity (to appear, 2007)
8. Fournier, H., Koiran, P.: Are lower bounds easier over the reals? In: Proc. 30th ACM Symposium on Theory of Computing, pp. 507–513. ACM Press, New York (1998)
9. Fournier, H., Koiran, P.: Lower bounds are not easier over the reals: Inside PH. In: Welzl, E., Montanari, U., Rolim, J.D.P. (eds.) ICALP 2000. LNCS, vol. 1853, pp. 832–843. Springer, Heidelberg (2000)
10. Grigoriev, D.: Topological complexity of the range searching. Journal of Complexity 16, 50–53 (2000)
11. Koiran, P.: Circuits versus trees in algebraic complexity. In: Reichel, H., Tison, S. (eds.) STACS 2000. LNCS, vol. 1770, pp. 35–52. Springer, Heidelberg (2000)

12. Koiran, P., Périfel, S.: Valiant's model: from exponential sums to exponential products. In: Královič, R., Urzyczyn, P. (eds.) MFCS 2006. LNCS, vol. 4162, pp. 596–607. Springer, Heidelberg (2006)
13. Koiran, P., Périfel, S.: VPSACE and a transfer theorem over the complex field (2007), available from http://perso.ens-lyon.fr/pascal.koiran
14. Koiran, P., Périfel, S.: VPSACE and a transfer theorem over the reals. In: Thomas, W., Weil, P. (eds.) STACS 2007. LNCS, vol. 4393, pp. 417–428. Springer, Heidelberg (2007), long version: http://prunel.ccsd.cnrs.fr/ensl-00103018
15. Lickteig, T.: Testing polynomials for zero. Internal report, Universität Tübingen (1988)
16. Lickteig, T.: On semialgebraic decision complexity. Technical Report TR-90-52, International Computer Science Institute, Berkeley, Habilitationsschrift, Universität Tübingen (1990)
17. Malod, G.: Polynômes et coefficients. PhD thesis, Université Claude Bernard - Lyon 1 (2003)
18. Malod, G.: The complexity of polynomials and their coefficient functions. In: Proc. 22nd IEEE Conference on Computational Complexity, IEEE Computer Society Press, Los Alamitos (2007)
19. Meer, K.: A note on a $P{\neq}NP$ result for a restricted class of real machines. Journal of Complexity 8, 451–453 (1992)
20. Meiser, S.: Point location in arrangements of hyperplanes. Information and Computation 106(2), 286–303 (1993)
21. Meyer auf der Heide, F.: A polynomial linear search algorithm for the n-dimensional knapsack problem. Journal of the ACM 31(3), 668–676 (1984)
22. Meyer auf der Heide, F.: Fast algorithms for n-dimensional restrictions of hard problems. Journal of the ACM 35(3), 740–747 (1988)
23. Poizat, B.: Les Petits Cailloux. Nur Al-Mantiq Wal-Ma'rifah. vol. 3, Aléas, Lyon (1995)
24. Smale, S.: On the topology of algorithms. I. Journal of Complexity 3, 81–89 (1987)
25. Valiant, L.G.: Completeness classes in algebra. In: Proc. 11th ACM Symposium on Theory of Computing, pp. 249–261. ACM Press, New York (1979)
26. Valiant, L.G.: Reducibility by algebraic projections. In: Logic and Algorithmic (an International Symposium held in honour of Ernst Specker). Monographie n° 30 de L'Enseignement Mathématique, pp. 365–380 (1982)
27. Vassiliev, V.A.: On decision trees for orthants. Information Processing Letters 62(5), 265–268 (1997)
28. von zur Gathen, J.: Parallel linear algebra. In: Reif, J. (ed.) Synthesis of Parallel Algorithms, pp. 573–617. Morgan Kaufmann, San Francisco (1993)

A Universal Reversible Turing Machine

Kenichi Morita and Yoshikazu Yamaguchi

Hiroshima University, Graduate School of Engineering,
Higashi-Hiroshima, 739-8527, Japan

Abstract. A reversible Turing machines is a computing model with a "backward deterministic" property, which is closely related to physical reversibility. In this paper, we study the problem of finding a small universal reversible Turing machine (URTM). As a result, we obtained a 17-state 5-symbol URTM in the quintuple form that can simulate any cyclic tag system.

Keywords: reversible computing, universal Turing machine, cyclic tag system.

1 Introduction

Reversible computing is a paradigm of computing closely related to physical reversibility. Since reversibility is one of the fundamental microscopic physical laws of Nature, it is very important to investigate how computation can be carried out efficiently in a system having such a property. This is because the size of future computing devices will surely become nanoscale ones.

A reversible Turing machine (RTM) is a typical model in reversible computing. Bennett [2] proved computation-universality of RTMs. Particularly, he showed that for any (irreversible) TM, there is an RTM that simulates the former without producing garbage information. RTMs also have close connection to other models of reversible computing. In fact, RTMs can be simulated (or implemented) by the following models in a garbage-less manner.

- Reversible logic circuits
- Reversible cellular automata
- Reversible physical models

Reversible logic elements and circuits were first studied by Toffoli [15,16] and Fredkin and Toffoli [5]. A Fredkin gate [5] is a universal reversible logic gate from which any RTM can be constructed. A rotary element (RE) is another universal reversible logic element proposed by Morita [10]. An RE has one-bit memory and its operation is very simple as in Fig. 1. It was shown that any RTM can be constructed by using only REs [10]. Fig. 2 gives an example.

It is also possible to embed RTMs in reversible cellular automata (RCAs). A direct simulation method of an RTM by a one-dimensional RCA was given by Morita and Harao [9] (the number of states of the RCA depends on the simulated RTM). On the other hand, if we use two-dimensional RCAs, it is

J. Durand-Lose and M. Margenstern (Eds.): MCU 2007, LNCS 4664, pp. 90–98, 2007.

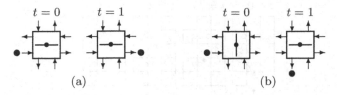

Fig. 1. Operations of a rotary element (RE): (a) the parallel case (i.e., the coming direction of a particle is parallel to the rotating bar), and (b) the orthogonal case

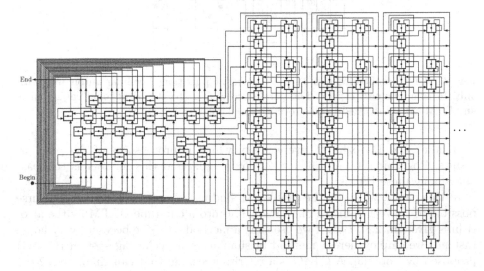

Fig. 2. An example of an RTM composed only of REs [10]

possible to simulate any RTM by a single RCA with very simple local transition function. So far, various models of such universal two-dimesional RCAs have been proposed. Fig. 3 shows one of these RCAs in which an RE can be embedded, and hence any RTM can be realized in it [11].

Furthermore, there is a reversible physical model of computation. A billiard-ball model (BBM) by Fredkin and Toffoli [5] is an interesting model of such a kind, although it works only in an ideal situation. In a BBM, an RE as well as a Fredkin gate can be realized, and hence any RTM can be embedded in this reversible physical system.

Since RTMs plays a key role in the theory of reversible computing, finding small universal reversible Turing machines (URTMs) is an important problem. In the case of a classical (i.e., irreversible) universal Turing machine (UTM), many kinds of very small UTMs have been given so far. Minsky [7] constructed a UTM(7,4) that can simulate any 2-tag system, where UTM(m, n) stands for an m-state n-symbol UTM. Rogozhin [13] presented a UTM(24,2), a UTM(10,3), a UTM(7,4), a UTM(5,5), a UTM(4,6), a UTM(3,10), and a UTM(2,18). Later, a UTM(22,2) by Rogozhin [14], a UTM(19,2) by Baiocchi [1], and a UTM(3,9)

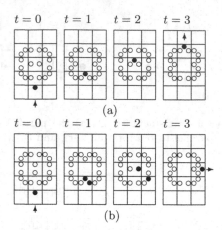

Fig. 3. An RE embedded in a 3^4-state reversible partitioned cellular automaton with only 10 rule schemes [11]: (a) The parallel case, and (b) the orthogonal case. Hence, any RTM can be realized in this reversible cellular space.

by Kudlek and Rogozhin [6] were given, which improve some of the previous results. Rogozhin's UTM(4,6) has 22 commands, and this number is the least one among these UTMs.

In this paper, we study the problem of finding a small URTM. It is of course possible to convert a known one-tape UTM into a one-tape URTM by the algorithms given in [2,8]. But, if we use such a method, the size becomes very large. Instead, we employ here a method of simulating a cyclic tag system (CTAG) proposed by Cook [3]. A CTAG is a rewriting system that can simulate a 2-tag system, hence it is universal. Since a CTAG is very simple, it is useful to show universality of other systems. Cook proved universality of the elementary cellular automaton rule 110 by this. In [12], it is used to construct universal RCAs with small number of states. A CTAG is also used to derive time complexity results on UTMs [4].

We give here a URTM(17,5) that can simulate any given CTAG. It has 67 commands, and the product of the numbers of the states and symbols is 85.

2   Preliminaries

2.1   Reversible Turing Machines (RTMs)

When Bennett [2] first introduced an RTM, it was defined in a quadruple form. This is because an "inverse" Turing machine for a given RTM can be defined easily if a quadruple formalization is used. However, we also need a quintuple formalization, because most classical UTMs are given in the quintuple form. Here, we first give a definition of an RTM in the quadruple form according to Bennett [2], and then that of an RTM in the quintuple form.

Definition 1. *A one-tape Turing machine in the quadruple form is defined by*

$$T_4 = (Q, S, q_0, q_f, s_0, \delta),$$

where Q is a non-empty finite set of states, S is a non-empty finite set of symbols, q_0 is an initial state ($q_0 \in Q$), q_f is a final (halting) state ($q_f \in Q$), s_0 is a special blank symbol ($s_0 \in S$). (Note that, in the construction of a UTM, the final state is usualy omitted from the state set S.) δ is a move relation, which is a subset of $(Q \times S \times S \times Q) \cup (Q \times \{/\} \times \{-, 0, +\} \times Q)$. Each element of δ is a quadruple, and either of the form $[p, s, s', q] \in (Q \times S \times S \times Q)$ or $[p, /, d, q] \in (Q \times \{/\} \times \{-, 0, +\} \times Q)$. The symbols "$-$", "$0$", and "$+$" stand for "left-shift", "zero-shift", and "right-shift", respectively. $[p, s, s', q]$ means if T_4 reads the symbol s in the state p, then write s' and go to the state q. $[p, /, d, q]$ means if T_4 is in p, then shift the head to the direction d and go to the state q.

Determinism of T_4 can be defined as usual, hence we omit its definition. (Note that, in what follows, we consider only deterministic Turing machines.) Its reversibility is defined as follows. T_4 is called a reversible Turing machine *(RTM) iff the following condition holds for any pair of distinct quadruples $[p_1, b_1, c_1, q_1]$ and $[p_2, b_2, c_2, q_2]$ in δ.*

$$\text{If } q_1 = q_2, \text{ then } b_1 \neq / \ \wedge \ b_2 \neq / \ \wedge \ c_1 \neq c_2.$$

Definition 2. *A one-tape Turing machine in the quintuple form is defined by*

$$T_5 = (Q, S, q_0, q_f, s_0, \delta),$$

where Q, S, q_0, q_f, s_0 are the same as in Definition 1. δ is a move relation, which is a subset of $(Q \times S \times S \times \{-, 0, +\} \times Q)$. Each element of δ is a quintuple of the form $[p, s, s', d, q]$. It means if T_5 reads the symbol s in the state p, then write s', shift the head to the direction d, and go to the state q.

Again, determinism of T_5 can be defined as usual. We say T_5 is reversible iff the following condition holds for any pair of distinct quintuples $[p_1, s_1, s_1', d_1, q_1]$ and $[p_2, s_2, s_2', d_2, q_2]$ in δ.

$$\text{If } q_1 = q_2, \text{ then } s_1' \neq s_2' \ \wedge \ d_1 = d_2.$$

Proposition 1. *For any RTM T_5 in the quintuple form, there is an RTM T_4 in the quadruple form that simulates each step of the former in two steps.*

Proof. For $T_5 = (Q, S, q_0, q_f, s_0, \delta)$, we define $T_4 = (Q', S, q_0, q_f, s_0, \delta')$ as follows. Let $Q' = Q \cup \{q' \mid q \in Q\}$. The set δ' is given by the next procedure.

First, set the initial value of δ' to the empty set. Next, for each $q \in Q$ do the following operation. Let $[p_1, s_1, s_1', d_1, q], [p_1, s_2, s_2', d_2, q], \cdots, [p_m, s_m, s_m', d_m, q]$ be all the quintuples in δ whose fifth element is q. Note that $d_1 = d_2 = \cdots = d_m$ holds, and $s_1', s_2', \cdots, s_m'$ are pair-wise distinct, because T_5 is reversible. Then, include the $m+1$ quadruples $[p_1, s_1, s_1', q'], [p_1, s_2, s_2', q'], \cdots, [p_m, s_m, s_m', q']$, and $[q', /, d_1, q]$ in δ'.

It is easy to see that T_4 has the required property. □

By Proposition 1, we see the definition of an RTM in the quintuple form is compatible with that in the quadruple form.

The converse of Proposition 1, i.e., converting an RTM in the quadruple form to an RTM in the quintuple form, is very easy if we construct the latter RTM so that it simulates each quadruple by a single quintuple. It is also possible to simulate a consecutive pair of read/write and shift quadruples by one quintuple, and thus we can reduce the numbers of states and quintuples.

2.2   Cyclic Tag Systems (CTAGs)

A cyclic tag system (CTAG) is a very simple string rewriting system proposed by Cook [3]. He showed that a CTAG can simulate a 2-tag system, hence it is universal.

In the original definition of a CTAG in [3], the notion of halting was not defined explicitly. In fact, it never halts unless a rewritten string becomes the empty string ε. In [12], a modified definition of a CTAG with the halting property was introduced. Here, we employ the latter definition, because we want to construct a URTM that gives a value of a recursive function when it halts.

Definition 3. *A* cyclic tag system *(CTAG) is defined by*

$$C = (k, \{Y, N\}, (\text{halt}, p_1, \cdots, p_{k-1})),$$

where k $(k = 1, 2, \cdots)$ is the length of a cycle (i.e., period), $\{Y, N\}$ is the (fixed) alphabet, and $(p_1, \cdots, p_{k-1}) \in (\{Y, N\}^*)^{k-1}$ is a $(k-1)$-tuple of production rules. A pair (v, m) is called an instantaneous *description (ID) of C, where $v \in \{Y, N\}^*$ and $m \in \{0, \cdots, k-1\}$. m is called a* phase *of the ID. A* halting ID *is an ID of the form $(Yv, 0)$ $(v \in \{Y, N\}^*)$. The transition relation $\Rightarrow$ is defined as follows. For any $(v, m), (v', m') \in \{Y, N\}^* \times \{0, \cdots, k-1\}$,*

$$(Yv, m) \Rightarrow (v', m') \quad \textit{iff} \quad [m \neq 0] \wedge [m' = m + 1 \bmod k] \wedge [v' = vp_m],$$
$$(Nv, m) \Rightarrow (v', m') \quad \textit{iff} \quad [m' = m + 1 \bmod k] \wedge [v' = v].$$

A sequence of IDs $((v_0, m_0), \cdots, (v_n, m_n))$ is called a complete computation *starting from $v \in \{Y, N\}^*$ iff $(v_0, m_0) = (v, 0)$, $(v_i, m_i) \Rightarrow (v_{i+1}, m_{i+1})$ $(i = 0, 1, \cdots, n-1)$, and (v_n, m_n) is a halting ID.*

The following example shows that a 2-tag system with the halting property is properly simulated by a CTAG. (Note that the coding and rewriting methods employed in the following CTAG is the same as in [3]. Only the handling method of halting is different.)

Example 1. Let $T_1 = (2, \{a_0, a_1, a_2\}, \{a_0 : \text{halt}, \ a_1 \to a_2, \ a_2 \to a_0a_1\})$ be a 2-tag system (see [7] or [13] for the detail of a 2-tag system). T_1 is simulated by the following CTAG: $C_1 = (6, \{Y, N\}, (\text{halt}, NNY, YNN\,NYN, \varepsilon, \varepsilon, \varepsilon))$, where a_0, a_1, and a_2 in T_1 are coded by YNN, NYN, and NNY in C_1.

A computation $a_2a_1 \Rightarrow a_0a_1$ in T_1 is simulated by the following complete computation in C_1: $(NNY\,NYN, 0) \Rightarrow (NY\,NYN, 1) \Rightarrow (Y\,NYN, 2) \Rightarrow (NYN\,YNN\,NYN, 3) \Rightarrow (YN\,YNN\,NYN, 4) \Rightarrow (N\,YNN\,NYN, 5) \Rightarrow (YNN\,NYN, 0)$.

3   A 17-State 5-Symbol URTM

We give a URTM(17,5) $T_{17,5}$ in the quintuple form that simulates any CTAG as follows:

$$T_{17,5} = (\{q_0, \cdots, q_{16}\}, \{b, Y, N, *, \$\}, q_0, b, \delta),$$

where the set δ of quintuples is shown in Table 1.

Table 1. The set of quintuples of the URTM $T_{17,5}$

	b	Y	N	$*$	$\$$
q_0	$\$-q_2$	$\$-q_1$	$b-q_{13}$		
q_1	halt	$Y-q_1$	$N-q_1$	$*+q_0$	$b-q_1$
q_2	$*-q_3$	$Y-q_2$	$N-q_2$	$*-q_2$	null
q_3	$b+q_{12}$	$b+q_4$	$b+q_7$	$b+q_{10}$	
q_4	$Y+q_5$	$Y+q_4$	$N+q_4$	$*+q_4$	$\$+q_4$
q_5	$b-q_6$				
q_6	$Y-q_3$	$Y-q_6$	$N-q_6$	$*-q_6$	$\$-q_6$
q_7	$N+q_8$	$Y+q_7$	$N+q_7$	$*+q_7$	$\$+q_7$
q_8	$b-q_9$				
q_9	$N-q_3$	$Y-q_9$	$N-q_9$	$*-q_9$	$\$-q_9$
q_{10}		$Y+q_{10}$	$N+q_{10}$	$*+q_{10}$	$\$+q_{11}$
q_{11}		$Y+q_{11}$	$N+q_{11}$	$*+q_{11}$	$Y+q_0$
q_{12}		$Y+q_{12}$	$N+q_{12}$	$*+q_{12}$	$\$-q_3$
q_{13}	$*-q_{14}$	$Y-q_{13}$	$N-q_{13}$	$*-q_{13}$	$\$-q_{13}$
q_{14}	$b+q_{16}$	$Y-q_{14}$	$N-q_{14}$	$b+q_{15}$	
q_{15}	$N+q_0$	$Y+q_{15}$	$N+q_{15}$	$*+q_{15}$	$\$+q_{15}$
q_{16}		$Y+q_{16}$	$N+q_{16}$	$*+q_{16}$	$\$-q_{14}$

There are 67 quintuples in total. If a CTAG halts with a halting ID, then $T_{17,5}$ halts in the state q_1. If the string becomes an empty string, then it halts in the state q_2. In Table 1, it is indicated by "null".

Fig. 4 shows how the CTAG C_1 with the initial string $NNYNYN$ in Example 1 is simulated by the URTM $T_{17,5}$. On the tape of the URTM, the production rules (halt, NNY, $YNN\,NYN$, $\varepsilon, \varepsilon, \varepsilon$) of C_1 are expressed by the reversal sequence over $\{Y, N, *\}$, i.e., $*\,*\,*NYNNNY*YNN**$, where $*$ is used as a delimiter between rules, and "halt" is represented by the empty string. Note that in the initial tape of $T_{17,5}$ $(t = 0)$, the rightmost $*$ is replaced by b. This indicates that the phase is 0. In general, if the phase is $i - 1$, then the i-th $*$ from the right is replaced by b. This symbol b is called a "phase marker." On the other hand, the given initial string for C_1 is placed to the right of the rules, where $\$$ is used as a delimiter.

One step of a rewriting process of a CTAG is simulated by $T_{17,5}$ as follows. At first, the first symbol of a rewritten string is read by the state q_0 of $T_{17,5}$. If the symbol is Y (N, respectively), then $T_{17,5}$ becomes in the state q_1 (q_{13}).

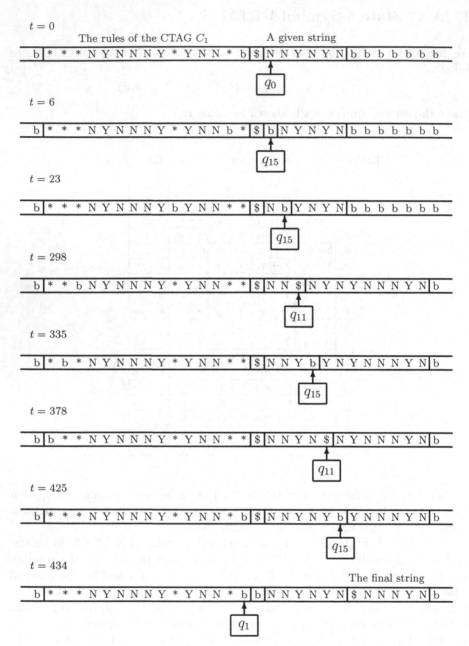

Fig. 4. Simulating the CTAG C_1 in Example 1 by the URTM $T_{17,5}$. The IDs in the complete computation $(NNY\ NYN,\ 0)\ \Rightarrow\ (NY\ NYN,\ 1)\ \Rightarrow\ (Y\ NYN,\ 2)\ \Rightarrow$ $(NYN\ YNN\ NYN,\ 3)\ \Rightarrow\ (YN\ YNN\ NYN,\ 4)\ \Rightarrow\ (N\ YNN\ NYN,\ 5)\ \Rightarrow$ $(YNN\ NYN,\ 0)$ of C_1 appear in the computational configurations of $T_{17,5}$ at $t = 0, 6, 23, 298, 335, 378$ and 425, respectively. The symbol \$ in the final string ($t = 434$) should be regarded as Y.

(1) The case that the leftmost symbol is Y.

$T_{17,5}$ checks if the phase is 0 by using the state q_1. If it is the case, it halts in the state q_1. Otherwise, it moves to the left to find the phase marker b using q_2.

$T_{17,5}$ reads each symbol of the i-th rule of the CTAG in the state q_3. If it is Y (N, respectively), it appends this symbol at the end of the string, and returns back to this position by using the states q_4, q_5 and q_6 (q_7, q_8 and q_9). If it reads $*$, which means that the application of the rule is completed, then it puts the phase marker there, and goes back to the first symbol of the rewritten string using the states q_{10} and q_{11}. If it reads b, which means the end of a cycle, it moves the phase marker b to the rightmost $*$ using the states q_{12} and q_3, and then goes back to the first symbol of the string by q_{10} and q_{11}.

(2) The case that the leftmost symbol is N.

$T_{17,5}$ moves leftward to find the phase marker in q_{13}, and shifts it to the next position by q_{14} (if it detects the end of a cycle, it shifts the phase marker to the first position by q_{16}). Then, it goes back to the first symbol of the string by q_{15}.

It is easy to see that $T_{17,5}$ is reversible by checking the set of quintuples shown in Table 1 according to the definition of an RTM. Intuitively, its reversibility is guaranteed from the fact that no information is erased in the whole simulation process. Furthermore, every branch of the program caused by reading the symbol Y or N is "merged reversibly" by writing the original symbol. For example, the states q_{11} and q_{15} transit to the same state q_0 by writing Y and N, respectively, using the quintuples $[q_{11}, \$, Y, +, q_0]$ and $[q_{15}, b, N, +, q_0]$.

4   Concluding Remarks

In this paper, we studied the problem of finding a small universal reversible Turing machine (URTM). Here, we constructed a 17-state 5-symbol URTM $T_{17,5}$ that can simulate any cyclic tag system (CTAG). The product of the numbers of states and symbols is 85. As far as we tried, it was easier to simulate a CTAG by a URTM than to simulate a classical 2-tag system. But, it is not known whether there is a small URTM that simulates any 2-tag system directly.

Though the URTM $T_{17,5}$ is relatively small, it has many open entry boxes (i.e., undefined quintuples) as seen in Table 1. But, because of the reversibility constraint, it is difficult to reduce the number of states of $T_{17,5}$. For example, the states q_5 and q_{10} of $T_{17,5}$ cannot be merged into one state since there are quintuples $[q_4, b, Y, +, q_5]$ and $[q_{10}, Y, Y, +, q_{10}]$. However, we think it will be possible to reduce the size of a URTM much more by using a new method. Hence, this study is a start point of finding very small URTMs.

Acknowledgement. The authors express their thanks to Dr. Chuzo Iwamoto and Dr. Katsunobu Imai of Hiroshima University for their helpful discussions and useful comments. This work was supported in part by Grant-in-Aid for Scientific Research (C) No. 16500012 from JSPS.

References

1. Baiocchi, C.: Three small universal Turing machines. In: Margenstern, M., Rogozhin, Y. (eds.) MCU 2001. LNCS, vol. 2055, pp. 1–10. Springer, Heidelberg (2001)
2. Bennett, C.H.: Logical reversibility of computation. IBM J. Res. Dev. 17, 525–532 (1973)
3. Cook, M.: Universality in elementary cellular automata. Complex Systems 15, 1–40 (2004)
4. Woods, D., Neary, T.: On the time complexity of 2-tag systems and small universal Turing machines. In: Proc. of 47th Symposium on Foundations of Computer Science (FOCS), pp. 439–446 (2006)
5. Fredkin, E., Toffoli, T.: Conservative logic. Int. J. Theoret. Phys. 21, 219–253 (1982)
6. Kudlek, M., Rogozhin, Y.: A universal Turing machine with 3 states and 9 symbols. In: Kuich, W., Rozenberg, G., Salomaa, A. (eds.) DLT 2001. LNCS, vol. 2295, pp. 311–318. Springer, Heidelberg (2002)
7. Minsky, M.L.: Computation: Finite and Infinite Machines. Prentice-Hall, Englewood Cliffs (1967)
8. Morita, K., Shirasaki, A., Gono, Y.: A 1-tape 2-symbol reversible Turing machine. Trans. IEICE Japan E-72, 223–228 (1989)
9. Morita, K., Harao, M.: Computation universality of one-dimensional reversible (injective) cellular automata. Trans. IEICE Japan E-72, 758–762 (1989)
10. Morita, K.: A simple universal logic element and cellular automata for reversible computing. In: Margenstern, M., Rogozhin, Y. (eds.) MCU 2001. LNCS, vol. 2055, pp. 102–113. Springer, Heidelberg (2001)
11. Morita, K., Ogiro, T.: Simple universal reversible cellular automata in which reversible logic elements can be embedded. IEICE Trans. on Information and Systems E87-D, 650–656 (2004)
12. Morita, K.: Simple universal one-dimensional reversible cellular automata. Journal of Cellular Automata (in press)
13. Rogozhin, Y.: Small universal Turing machines. Theoretical Computer Science 168, 215–240 (1996)
14. Rogozhin, Y.: A universal Turing machine with 22 states and 2 symbols. Romanian J. Inform. Sci. Technol. 1, 259–265 (1998)
15. Toffoli, T.: Reversible computing. In: de Bakker, J.W., van Leeuwen, J. (eds.) Automata, Languages and Programming. LNCS, vol. 85, pp. 632–644. Springer, Heidelberg (1980)
16. Toffoli, T.: Bicontinuous extensions of invertible combinatorial functions. Mathematical Systems Theory 14, 12–23 (1981)

P Systems and Picture Languages

K.G. Subramanian

School of Mathematical Sciences, Universiti Sains Malaysia,
11800 Penang, Malaysia
kgsmani1948@yahoo.com

Abstract. Array-rewriting P systems were introduced in [2] linking the two areas of membrane computing and picture grammars. Subsequently a variety of P systems with array objects and different kinds of rewriting has been introduced. Here we discuss a few prominent systems among these, point out their features and indicate possible problems for future study.

1 Introduction

In the area of membrane computing, a new computability model, was introduced by Păun [8] which is inspired by the structure and functioning of living cells. This is now called P system in honour of its originator. P systems have proved to be a rich frame work to obtain universality results and study many computational problems. The basic model processes multi-sets of objects in the regions that are defined by a hierarchical arrangement of membranes, by evolution rules associated with the regions. One of the branches of membrane computing is Rewriting P systems in which objects in the membranes are described by strings and these strings are processed by rewriting rules or other string manipulating operations. Universality results have been obtained for a variety of rewriting P systems with string objects and string rewriting rules.

Recently, these P systems were extended to array objects and array rewriting rules for describing picture languages in [2] by introducing array-rewriting P systems and thus linking the two areas of membrane computing and picture grammars. Subsequently a number of P systems with array objects and different kinds of rewriting has been introduced. We discuss a few prominent systems [2,14] among these and point out their salient features. We also indicate possible directions of study in this area.

2 Basic Definitions

We refer to [10] for unexplained concepts of formal language theory and to [4,9] for array languages and array grammars. We will also use the intuitive pictorial representation for arrays.

An alphabet V is a finite set of symbols. A word or string w over V is a sequence of symbols from V. The set of all words, including the empty word λ with no symbols, is denoted by V^* and $V^+ = V^* - \lambda$.

J. Durand-Lose and M. Margenstern (Eds.): MCU 2007, LNCS 4664, pp. 99–109, 2007.

The arrays we consider consist of finitely many symbols from a specified alphabet V placed in the points of the plane. The points of the plane not marked with elements of V are assumed to have the *blank symbol* $\# \notin V$. In order to specify an array, it is sufficient to specify the *pixels* v of nonblank points, together with their associated symbols from V. Whenever possible, we will pictorially represent the arrays, indicating their non-blank pixels. Also we take into account only the relative positions of non-blank pixels in the array. For example, the L-shaped angle with equal arms from Figure 1 is formally given by

$$\{((0,0),m),\ ((1,0),c),\ (2,0),u),\ ((3,0),0),\ ((4,0),7),$$
$$((0,1),c),\ ((0,2),u),\ ((0,3),0),\ ((0,4),7)\}$$

$$\begin{array}{ccccc} 7 & & & & \\ 0 & & & & \\ u & & & & \\ c & & & & \\ m & c & u & 0 & 7 \end{array}$$

Fig. 1. L-shaped angle with equal arms

We denote by V^{+2} the set of all two-dimensional non-empty finite arrays over V. The empty array is denoted by λ, and then the set of all arrays over V is $V^{*2} = V^{+2} \cup \{\lambda\}$. Any subset of V^{*2} is called an *array language*.

An *array production* p over V is of the form $p : \mathcal{A} \longrightarrow \mathcal{B}$ where $\mathcal{A}$ and $\mathcal{B}$ are arrays over V. For two arrays $\mathcal{C}, \mathcal{D}$ over V and a production p as above, we write $\mathcal{C} \Longrightarrow_p \mathcal{D}$ if $\mathcal{D}$ can be obtained by replacing a subarray of $\mathcal{C}$ identical to $\mathcal{A}$ with $\mathcal{B}$. The reflexive and transitive closure of the relation $\Longrightarrow$ is denoted by $\Longrightarrow^*$.

An array production $p = (W, \mathcal{A}, \mathcal{B})$ is called:

1. *monotonic*, if the symbol positions of $\mathcal{A}$ are all contained in $\mathcal{B}$;
2. *#-context-free*, if there is exactly one nonblank symbol in $\mathcal{A}$;
3. *context-free*, if it is both monotonic and #-context-free.

The array grammars we consider here are direct extensions of string grammars to two dimensional pictures [3,9,15,16].

A Chomsky-like array grammar is a construct $G = (N, T, \#, \{((0,0),S)\}, P)$, where N, T are disjoint alphabets of nonterminal symbols and of terminal symbols, respectively, $\# \notin N \cup T$ is the blank symbol, $S \in N$, and P is a finite set of array rewriting rules $\mathcal{A} \longrightarrow \mathcal{B}$ such that at least one pixel of $\mathcal{A}$ is marked with an element of N; usually, the *axiom array* $\{((0,0),S)\}$ will be simply written as S.

An array grammar is monotonic, #-context-free, or context-free if all its rules are of these types; clearly, in the case of #-context-free and context-free grammars, there is a unique non-blank pixel in the left hand array of each rule, marked with a nonterminal. *Regular* array grammar rules are defined as one of the following forms: $A\ \# \longrightarrow a\ B$, $\#\ A \longrightarrow B\ a$, $\begin{array}{c}\# \\ A\end{array} \longrightarrow \begin{array}{c}B \\ a\end{array}$, $\begin{array}{c}A \\ \#\end{array} \longrightarrow \begin{array}{c}a \\ B\end{array}$, $A \longrightarrow a$, where A, B are nonterminals and a is a terminal.

The array language generated by G is

$$L(G) = \{\mathcal{A} \in T^{*2} \mid \{((0,0), S)\} \Longrightarrow^* \mathcal{A}\}.$$

The families of array languages generated by arbitrary, monotonic, #-context-free, context-free, and regular array grammars are denoted by $ARE, AMON,$ $A\#CF, ACF, AREG$ respectively. The following strict inclusions are known: $AREG \subset ACF \subset AMON \subset ARE, ACF \subset A\#CF \subset ARE$.

The definition of a *matrix array grammar [2]* is the obvious extension from the string case. Such a grammar is a construct $G = (N, T, \#, S, M)$, where N is the nonterminal alphabet, T is the terminal alphabet, # is the blank symbol, S is the start symbol marking the unique pixel of a start array, and M is a finite set of matrices (that is, finite ordered sequences) of array productions. The grammar is regular, context-free or #-context-free, depending on whether all the rules in its matrices are of these types, respectively. As in the string case, the rules of a matrix are applied one by one, in the order they appear in the matrix. The array language generated by a n array matrix grammar G is denoted by $AL(G)$.

Theorem 2.1. *[2] Each array language from ARE can be generated by a #-context-free matrix array grammar. Context-free matrix array grammars are strictly less powerful.*

3   Array-Rewriting P Systems

We first informally describe the basic model of a rewriting string-objects P system [8]. A rewriting rule used in a string-objects P system is of the form $X \longrightarrow u(tar)$, where $X \longrightarrow u$ is a context-free rule and $tar \in \{here, out, in\}$ is a target indication, indicating the region where the string which is result of the rewriting should be sent in the next step. *here* means that the result remains in the same region where the rule was applied, *out* means that the string has to be sent to the region immediately surrounding the region where it has been produced, and *in* means that the string should be sent to one of the direct inner membranes, if any exists. A string can leave the system when a command *out* is encountered and this can happen when it is produced in the external or skin membrane of a system. Each string is processed by at most one rule at a time; if any rule can be used, then one of them, nondeterministically chosen, is used; if no rule can rewrite a string, then it remains unchanged. All strings, from all regions, are rewritten at the same time. A sequence of such steps is called a computation. A computation yields a result only if it halts and a configuration of the system is reached where no further rule can be applied. The result of a computation is the set of strings collected in a specified elementary membrane in the halting configuration.

We pass on to describe the main object of our discussion, the *array P systems* introduced in [2].

The extension from string-objects P systems to array-objects P systems is immediate: in the compartments of a membrane structure we place arrays, which evolve by means of array rewriting rules; in each step of a computation one rule (at most) is applied to each array and the resulting array remains in the same membrane, exits it, or enters a directly lower membrane, depending on the target indication associated with the applied rule. The arrays present in a specified membrane at the end of a halting computation constitute the result of the computation.

In order to also extend from strings to arrays the universality results known for string P systems it is necessary to prove a binary normal form for array matrix grammars. This is accomplished here in two different forms in [2], one for erasing and one for non-erasing array matrix grammars. Because erasing array matrix grammars are known to be universal, equivalent in power with arbitrary array grammars, we obtain the universality of array P systems.

An array-rewriting P system (of degree $m \geq 1$)[2] is a construct

$$\Pi = (N, T, \#, \mu, F_1, \ldots, F_m, R_1, \ldots, R_m, i_o),$$

where: V is the total alphabet, $T \subseteq V$ is the terminal alphabet, $\#$ is the blank symbol, μ is a membrane structure with m membranes labelled in a one-to-one way with $1, 2, \ldots, m$, $F_1, \ldots, F_m$ are finite sets of arrays over V associated with the m regions of μ, $R_1, \ldots, R_m$ are finite sets of array rewriting rules over V associated with the m regions of μ; the rules have attached targets *here, out, in* (in general, *here* is omitted), hence they are of the form $\mathcal{A} \to \mathcal{B}(tar)$; finally, i_o is the label of an elementary membrane of μ (the output membrane).

A computation in an array P system is defined in the same way as in a string rewriting P system with the successful computations being the halting ones: each array, from each region of the system, which can be rewritten by a rule associated with that region (membrane), should be rewritten; this means that one rule is applied (the rewriting is sequential at the level of arrays); the array obtained by rewriting is placed in the region indicated by the target associated with the used rule (*here* means that the array remains in the same region, *out* means that the array exit the current membrane – thus, if the rewriting was done in the skin membrane, then it can exit the system; arrays leaving the system are "lost" in the environment), and *in* means that the array is immediately sent to one of the directly lower membranes, nondeterministically chosen if several exist there; if no internal membrane exists, then a rule with the target indication *in* cannot be used). A computation is successful only if it stops, a configuration is reached where no rule can be applied to the existing arrays. The result of an halting computation consists of the arrays composed only of symbols from T placed in the membrane with label i_o in the halting configuration. The set of all such arrays computed (we also say *generated*) by a system Π is denoted by $AL(\Pi)$.

The family of all array languages $AL(\Pi)$ generated by systems Π as above, with at most m membranes, with rules of type $\alpha \in \{REG, CF, \#CF\}$ is denoted by $EAP_m(\alpha)$; if non-extended systems are considered (that is, we have $V = T$;

in such a case we ignore the condition to have at least one nonterminal pixel in the left hand side of rules), then we write $AP_m(\alpha)$.

Example1. [2] Consider the non-extended context-free system $\Pi_1 \quad = $
$(\{a\}, \{a\}, \#, [_1[_2[_3]_3]_2]_1, \left\{ \begin{matrix} a \\ a \end{matrix} \right\}, \emptyset, \emptyset, R_1, R_2, R_3, 3),$

$$R_1 = \{ \begin{matrix} \# \\ \# \ a \end{matrix} \to \begin{matrix} a \\ \# \ a \end{matrix} (in)\},$$

$$R_2 = \{ \begin{matrix} a \ \# \\ \# \end{matrix} \to \begin{matrix} a \ a \\ \# \end{matrix} (out), \begin{matrix} a \ \# \ \# \\ \# \end{matrix} \to \begin{matrix} a \ a \ a \\ \# \end{matrix} (in)\},$$

$$R_3 = \emptyset.$$

Starting from the only array initially present in region 1, the two arms of an L-shaped angle are grown step by step, with one pixel grown in the upper arm of L in the skin membrane and with one pixel, to the right in membrane 2; at any moment, from membrane 2 we can send the array to membrane 3 (at that step two pixels are added to the horizontal arm) and the computation stops. Thus, $AL(\Pi_1)$ consists of all L-shaped angles with equal arms, each arm being of length at least three.

We now state the main result of this array P system.

Theorem 3.1. [2] $ARE = AP_4(\#CF)$.

The proof of this assertion is done in a similar way as proving the fact that each string matrix grammar can be simulated by a string P system with four membranes [8].

We state an auxiliary result.

Lemma 3.1. [2] *Given a matrix array context-free grammar in the binary normal form, an equivalent non-extended context-free array P system can be constructed, of degree 4.*

4   BPG Array P System

Adapting the techniques of formal string language theory, various types of picture or array grammars have been introduced and investigated [9,12,11]. Puzzle grammars introduced in [7] are array generating two-dimensional grammars motivated by the problem of tiling the plane. A subclass called basic puzzle grammars was introduced in [13].

We now recall the definition of basic puzzle grammars introduced in [13]. These grammars constitute a special class of puzzle grammars defined in [7] for generation of arrays non-rectangular or rectangular.

A basic puzzle grammar (BPG) [13] is a structure $G = (N, T, R, S)$ where N and T are finite sets of symbols; $N \cap T = \emptyset$; Elements of N are called nonterminals and elements of T, terminals; $S \in N$ is the start symbol or the axiom; R consists of rules of the following forms:

$$A \longrightarrow \widehat{a}\, B \ , \quad A \longrightarrow a\, \widehat{B} \ , \quad A \longrightarrow B\, \widehat{a} \ , \quad A \longrightarrow \widehat{B}\, a \ ,$$

$$A \longrightarrow \frac{\widehat{a}}{B} \ , \quad A \longrightarrow \frac{a}{\widehat{B}} \ , \quad A \longrightarrow \frac{B}{\widehat{a}} \ , \quad A \longrightarrow \frac{\widehat{B}}{a} \ , \quad A \longrightarrow \widehat{a}$$

where $A, B \in N$ and $a \in T$. We may omit the circle in the rule with a single a on the right side.

Derivations begin with S written in a unit cell in the two-dimensional plane, with all the other cells containing the blank symbol #, not in $N \cup T$. In a derivation step, denoted $\Rightarrow$, a non-terminal A in a cell is replaced by the right-hand member of a rule whose left-hand side is A. In this replacement, the circled symbol of the right-hand side of the rule used, occupies the cell of the replaced symbol and the non-circled symbol of the right side occupies the cell to the right or the left or above or below the cell of the replaced symbol depending on the type of rule used. The replacement is possible only if the cell to be filled in by the non-circled symbol contains a blank symbol.

The basic puzzle language (BPL) generated by the BPG G, denoted $L(G)$, is the set of connected finite arrays over T, derivable in one or more steps from the axiom. We denote the family of BPL by $L(BPL)$.

We denote by $L(RAL)$ the family of the regular array languages (RAL) generated by $RAGs$. It is known [13] that $L(RAL) \subset L(BPL)$.

A BPG array P System of degree $m (\geq 1)$ [14] is a construct $\Pi = (V, T, \#, \mu, F_1, \cdots, F_m, R_1, \cdots, R_m, i_0)$, where V is the total alphabet, $T \subseteq V$ is the terminal alphabet, # is the blank symbol, μ is a membrane structure with m membranes labeled in a one-to-one way with $1, 2, \cdots, m$; $F_1, \cdots, F_m$ are finite sets of arrays over V initially associated with the m regions of μ; $R_1, \cdots, R_m$ are finite sets of BPG rules over $V \cup T$ associated with the m regions of μ; the rules have attached targets, *here, out, in* (in general, *here* is omitted); finally, i_o is the label of an elementary membrane of μ (the output membrane).

A computation in a BPG array P system is defined in the same way as in a string rewriting P system [8] with the successful computations being the halting ones; each array from each region of the system, which can be rewritten by a rule associated with that region (membrane), should be rewritten; this means that one rule is applied (the rewriting is sequential at the level of arrays); The array obtained by rewriting is placed in the region indicated by the target associated with the rule used; *"here"* means that the array remains in the same region, *"out"* means that the array exits the current membrane - thus, if the rewriting was done in the skin membrane, then it can exit the system; arrays leaving the system are "lost" in the environment, and *"in"* means that the array is immediately sent to one of the directly lower membranes, non-deterministically chosen if several exist (if no internal membrane exists, then a rule with the target indication *in* cannot be used).

A computation is successful only if it stops; a configuration is reached where no rule can be applied to the existing arrays. The result of a halting computation consists of the arrays composed only of symbols from T placed in the membrane with label i_o in the halting configuration.

The set of all such arrays computed (we also say generated) by a system Π is denoted by $AL(\Pi)$. The family of all array languages $AL(\Pi)$ generated by systems Π as above, with at most m membranes, is denoted by $EAP_m(BPG)$. The regular array rewriting (REGA) rules are also BPG rules. So when REGA rules alone are used in the regions, we call the family as $EAP_m(REGA)$.

By definition it follows that

1. $EAP_m(X) \subseteq EAP_{m+1}(X)\ for X \in \{REGA, BPG\}$
2. $EAP_m(REGA) \subseteq EAP_m(BPG)$

Theorem 4.1. *[14] (i)* $L(RAL) \subset EAP_1(REGA)$
(ii) $L(BPL) \subset EAP_1(BPG)$
(iii) $EAP_1(REGA) \subset EAP_1(BPG)$
(iv) $EAP_1(REGA) \subset EAP_2(REGA)$
(v) $EAP_1(BPG) \subset EAP_2(BPG)$
(vi) $EAP_2(REGA) \subset EAP_2(BPG)$

5   Array Rewriting Parallel P Systems

The well-known biologically motivated Lindenmayer systems [5] have been extensively studied establishing deep results during the past several years. Incorporating the developmental type of generation used in L-systems into arrays, a very general model called $ECTLA$ system was proposed by [11]. This study is one among the several models for picture generation introduced and explored in the literature, falling under the area of syntactic techniques for Pattern Recognition and Image Analysis. A new class of array P system called Array Rewriting Parallel P Systems (APPS), was introduced in [14] generating pictures of rectangular arrays. These systems have tables of rules as in $ECTLA$ systems and rectangular arrays as objects in the membranes.

A rectangular $m \times n$ array M over V is of the form

$$M = \begin{matrix} a_{11} & \cdots & a_{1n} \\ \vdots & \ddots & \vdots \\ a_{m1} & \cdots & a_{mn} \end{matrix}$$

where each $a_{ij} \in V, 1 \le i \le m,\ 1 \le j \le n$. The set of all arrays over V is denoted by V^{**}, which includes the empty array.

We first recall the notion of Extended Controlled Table L array systems introduced in [11].

An Extended, controlled table $0L-$ array grammar ($ECT0LA$) [11] is a $5-$tuple $G = (V, T, \wp, C, S, \#)$ where
◇ V is a finite nonempty set (the alphabet of G);
◇ $T \subseteq V$ is the terminal or target alphabet of G;

◇ $\wp$ is a finite set of tables, $\{P_1, P_2, \ldots, P_k\}$, and each P_i, $i = 1, \ldots, k$, is a left, right, up, or down table consisting respectively, of a finite set of left, right, up, or down rules only. The rules within a table are context-free in nature but all right hand sides of rules within the same table are of the same length;

◇ C is a control language over $\wp$; and $S \notin V$ is the start matrix.

   # is an element not in V (the marker of G).

In particular,

(1) if $V = T$ and S is a matrix M_0 (the axiom), G is a controlled table $L-$ array grammar;

(2) if $C = \wp^*$, then there is no control and the order of applications of the tables is arbitrary; G is then an extended table $L-$ array grammar. We shall refer to this as context-free (or $0L$) table array grammar.

Let $G = (V, T, \wp, C, S, \#)$ be an $ECT0LA$ grammar. Let

$$M_1 = \begin{matrix} a_{11} & \cdots & a_{1n-1} & a_{1n} \\ \vdots & \ddots & & \vdots \\ a_{m1} & \cdots & a_{mn-1} & a_{mn} \end{matrix} \ , \qquad M_2 = \begin{matrix} a_{11} & \cdots & a_{1n-1} & \omega_{1n} \\ \vdots & \ddots & & \vdots \\ a_{m1} & \cdots & a_{mn-1} & \omega_{mn} \end{matrix}$$

with a_{ij} in V and ω_{in} in V^+, $i = 1, \ldots, m$, $j = 1, \ldots, n$. We say that M_1 directly derives M_2 (by a right table R in $\wp$) denoted $M_1 \Rightarrow^R M_2$ if M_2 is obtained by applying in parallel the rules in a right table to all the symbols in the rightmost column of M_1. Similarly we define $\Rightarrow^L, \Rightarrow^U, \Rightarrow^D$ corresponding to a left, up, or down table. We write $M_1 \Rightarrow M_2$ if either $M_1 \Rightarrow^R M_2$, or $M_1 \Rightarrow^L M_2$, or $M_1 \Rightarrow^U M_2$, or $M_1 \Rightarrow^D M_2$. We write $M_0 \Rightarrow^* M$ iff there exists a sequence of derivations $M_0 \Rightarrow^{P_{i1}} M1 \Rightarrow^{P_{i2}} \cdots \Rightarrow^{P_{in}} M_n = M$, such that $P_{i1} P_{i2} \cdots P_{in} \in C$. If necessary, we may use the symbols l, r, u and d above the $\Rightarrow$, to indicate that it represents a left , right, up and down derivation step respectively.

A set $\mathcal{M}(G)$ of arrays is called an extended controlled table $0L$ array language ($ECT0LAL$) iff there exists an extended controlled table $0L$ array grammar $G(ECT0LAG)$ such that $\mathcal{M}(G) = \{M/S \Rightarrow^* M, M \in T^{++}\}$.

We now take the objects in the array-rewriting P System [2] as rectangular arrays instead of any array (rectangular or non- rectangular). Also we take tables of context free rules of the form $a \rightarrow \alpha$, $\alpha \in V^*$ in the regions of the P system. We call the resulting array P system as Array - rewriting Parallel P system ($APPS$).

An Array - rewriting Parallel P system ($APPS$)[14] is a construct
$\Pi_1 = (V, T, \#, \mu, F_1, \cdots, F_m, R_1, \cdots, R_m, i_0)$, where

◇ V is the total alphabet, $T \subseteq V$ the terminal alphabet.

◇ μ is a membrane structure with m membranes labelled in a one to one way with $1, 2, , m$.

◇ $F_1, \cdots, F_m$ are finite sets of rectangular arrays over V associated with the m regions of μ.

⋄ $R_1, \cdots, R_m$ are finite sets of tables of context free rules over V of the form $a \rightarrow \alpha$, $a \in V$, $\alpha \in V^*$ and all $\alpha's$ have the same length in a table associated with m regions of μ.

⋄   the tables have attached targets *here, out, in*

⋄ i_0 is the label of an elementary membrane of μ (output membrane).

When a set T is distinguished, we speak about an extended P system, when $V = T$ we have a non-extended system.

A computation in an array-rewriting parallel P system is defined analogous to a string rewriting P system with the successful computations being the halting ones: each rectangular array, from each region of the system, which can be rewritten by a table of rules associated with that region (membrane), should be rewritten and the rewriting is as in an ECT0LA grammar; when a table is applied, the rectangular array obtained by rewriting is placed in the region indicated by the target associated with the table used; (*here* means that the array remains in the same region, *out* means that the array exits the current membrane - thus , if the rewriting was done in the skin membrane, then it can exit the system ; arrays leaving the system are "lost " in the environment, and *in* means that the array is immediately sent to one of the directly lower membranes, nondeterministically chosen if several exist. If no internal membrane exists, then a rule with the target indication *in* cannot be used).

A computation is successful only if it stops, a configuration is reached where no table can be applied to the existing rectangular arrays. The result of a halting computation consist of the arrays composed only of symbols from T placed in the membrane with label i_0 in the halting configuration. The set of all such arrays computed by a system Π is denoted by $RAL(\Pi)$. The family of all array languages $RAL(\Pi)$ generated by systems Π as above, with at most m membranes, is denoted by RAP_m; if non- extended systems are considered, then we write $REAP_m$. We now state the results [14] relating to these systems.

5.1   Theorem

(*i*) $RAP_m \subseteq RAP_{m+1}$ for $m \geq 1$.

(*ii*) $REAP_m \subseteq REAP_{m+1}$ for $m \geq 1$.

(*iii*) $RAP_m \subseteq REAP_m$ for $m \geq 1$.

5.2   Theorem

(*i*) The family of array languages generated by Tabled L array systems is included in RAP_1

(*ii*) The family of array languages generated by Extended Tabled L array systems is included in $REAP_1$

(*iii*) The family of array languages generated by Tabled L array systems is properly included in RAP_3

(*iv*) The family of array languages generated by Extended Tabled L array systems is properly included in $REAP_3$

5.3 Theorem

The family of array languages generated by Regular controlled Tabled L array systems and context free Tabled L array systems intersects the family of array languages generated by array-rewriting parallel P systems.

6 Conclusion

The matrix array grammars with context-free rules are not more powerful than array-rewriting P systems [2] with context-free rules. The following problems thus remain open: Can any array P system with context-free rules be simulated by a matrix array grammar with context-free rules ? What is the power of array P systems with regular rules?

Among several variations of P systems, with string-objects and string-processing rules, conditional communication is a feature introduced in [1]. Incorporating the feature of conditional communication in array-rewriting P systems of [2] array-rewriting P system with conditional communication, has been introduced in [6]. This system can generate all solid rectangles and all solid squares over a single letter which is not possible in [2]. It will be interesting to examine the power of these systems.

Acknowledgement. The author is grateful to Prof. Dr Rosihan M. Ali for his interest and academic support and to Universiti Sains Malaysia for their financial support.

References

1. Bottoni, P., Labella, A., Martin-vide, C., Păun, G.: Rewriting P Systems with Conditional Communication. In: Brauer, W., Ehrig, H., Karhumäki, J., Salomaa, A. (eds.) Formal and Natural Computing. LNCS, vol. 2300, pp. 325–353. Springer, Heidelberg (2002)
2. Ceterchi, R., Mutyam, M., Paun, G., Subramanian, K.G.: Array - rewriting P systems. Natural Computing 2, 229–249 (2003)
3. Cook, C.R., Wang, P.S.-P.: A Chomsky hierarchy of isotonic array grammars and languages. Computer Graphics and Image Processing 8, 144–152 (1978)
4. Freund, R.: Array Grammars, Technical Rep. 15/00, Research Group on Mathematical Linguistics, Rovira i Virgili University, Tarragona, 164 pages (2000)
5. Herman, G., Rozenberg, G.: Developmental Systems and languages. North - Holland, Amsterdam (1975)
6. Hemalatha, S., Dersanambika, K.S., Subramanian, K.G., SriHariNagore, C.: Array-Rewriting P systems with Conditional Communication. Paper presented at IIT, Madras (2006)
7. Nivat, M., Saoudi, A., Subramanian, K.G., Siromoney, R., Dare, V.R.: Puzzle Grammars and Context-free Array Grammars. Int. Journal of Pattern Recognition and Artificial Intelligence 5, 663–676 (1991)

8. Păun, G.: Computing with Membranes: An Introduction. Springer, Heidelberg (2002)
9. Rosenfeld, A.: Picture Languages. Academic Press, Reading, MA (1979)
10. Salomaa, A.: Formal Languages. Academic Press, New York (1973)
11. Siromoney, R., Siromoney, G.: Extended Controlled Tabled L- arrays. Information and Control 35(2), 119–138 (1977)
12. Siromoney, G., Siromoney, R., Krithivasan, K.: Abstract families of Matrice and Picture languages. Computer Graphics and Image Processing 1, 234–307 (1972)
13. Subramanian, K.G., Siromoney, R., Dare, V.R., Saoudi, A.: Basic Puzzle Languages. Int. Journal of Pattern Recognition and Artificial Intelligence 9, 763–775 (1995)
14. Subramanian, K.G., Saravanan, R., Geethalakshmi, M., Helenchandra, P., Margenstern, M.: P Systems with array objects and array rewriting rules. In: Proceedings of Bio-inspired Computing: Theory and Applications, China (2006)
15. Wang, P.S.-P.: Some new results on isotonic array grammars. Information Processing Letters 10, 129–131 (1980)
16. Yamamoto, Y., Morita, K., Sugata, K.: Context-sensitivity of two-dimensional regular array grammars. In: Wang, P.S.-P. (ed.) Array Grammars, Patterns and Recognizers. WSP Series in Computer Science, vol. 18, pp. 17–41. World Scientific Publ., Singapore (1989)

Partial Halting in P Systems Using Membrane Rules with Permitting Contexts

Artiom Alhazov[1], Rudolf Freund[2], Marion Oswald[2], and Sergey Verlan[3]

[1] Department of Information Technologies, Abo Akademi University
Turku Center for Computer Science, FIN-20520 Turku, Finland
and
Institute of Mathematics and Computer Science
Academy of Sciences of Moldova
Str. Academiei 5, Chişinău, MD-2028, Moldova
aalhazov@abo.fi, aartiom@math.md
[2] Faculty of Informatics, Vienna University of Technology
Favoritenstr. 9, 1040 Vienna, Austria
{rudi,marion}@emcc.at
[3] LACL, Département Informatique, UFR Sciences et Technologie
Université Paris XII, 61, av. Général de Gaulle, 94010 Créteil, France
verlanuniv-paris12.fr

Abstract. We consider a new variant of the halting condition in P systems, i.e., a computation in a P system is already called halting if not for all membranes a rule is applicable anymore at the same time, whereas usually a computation is called halting if no rule is applicable anymore in the whole system. This new variant of partial halting is especially investigated for several variants of P systems using membrane rules with permitting contexts and working in different derivation modes.

Keywords: computational completeness, halting, minimal parallelism, P systems, permitting context.

1 Introduction

In the first papers of Gheorghe Păun (e.g., see [17], [10]) introducing membrane computing, membrane systems were introduced as systems with a hierarchical (tree-like) structure and the rules being applied in a maximally parallel manner; the results were taken as the contents of a specified output membrane in the final configurations of halting computations, i.e., at the end of computations to which no rule was applicable anymore. In this paper, we continue the investigation of the new variant of halting – *partial halting* –, first introduced [12], i.e., we consider a computation to halt as soon as no multiset of rules containing at least one rule from each set of rules assigned to the membranes is applicable anymore (*partial halting*), which reflects the idea that a (biological) system only stays alive as long as all its main components are still able to evolve in parallel.

Moreover, we especially also consider the derivation mode of minimal parallelism (e.g., see [8]), i.e., for each membrane, at least one rule – if possible – has

J. Durand-Lose and M. Margenstern (Eds.): MCU 2007, LNCS 4664, pp. 110–121, 2007.

to be applied, but it is not required to use a maximal multiset of rules. Finally, in the asynchronous derivation mode an arbitrary number of rules can be applied in parallel, and in the sequential derivation mode exactly one rule has to be applied in each computation step.

In the following, we elaborate some general results for the new stopping mode of partial halting and in more detail investigate P systems using membrane rules with permitting contexts such as antiport P systems and evolution/communication P systems together with partial halting and with the different derivation modes, especially for the newly introduced variant of minimal parallelism. Above all we prove that P systems using membrane rules with permitting contexts together with partial halting can only generate semilinear sets of non-negative integers.

2 Definitions

In this section, we first recall some basic notions and notations and then give precise definitions for matrix grammars, register machines, and a general model of P systems using membrane rules with permitting contexts as they are considered in this paper; moreover, we show how several well-known models of P systems (P systems with symport/antiport rules, evolution/communication P systems) can be interpreted as special variants of this general model.

2.1 Preliminaries

For the basic elements of formal language theory needed in the following, we refer to [9] and [21]. We just list a few notions and notations: $\mathbb{N}$ denotes the set of non-negative integers. V^* is the free monoid generated by the alphabet V under the operation of concatenation and the empty string, denoted by λ, as unit element; by NRE and $NREG$ we denote the family of recursively enumerable sets and regular sets of non-negative integers, respectively.

Let $V = \{a_1, ..., a_n\}$ be an arbitrary alphabet; the number of occurrences of a symbol a_i in x is denoted by $|x|_{a_i}$; the *Parikh vector* associated with a string $x \in V^*$ with respect to $(a_1, ..., a_n)$ is $\left(|x|_{a_1}, ..., |x|_{a_n}\right)$. The *Parikh image* of a language $L \subseteq V^*$ with respect to $(a_1, ..., a_n)$ is the set of all Parikh vectors of strings in L. For a family of languages F, the family of Parikh images of languages in F is denoted by PsF. A (finite) multiset $\langle m_1, a_1 \rangle ... \langle m_n, a_n \rangle$ with $m_i \in \mathbb{N}$, $1 \le i \le n$, can be represented by any string x the Parikh vector of which with respect to $(a_1, ..., a_n)$ is $(m_1, ..., m_n)$.

The family of recursively enumerable languages is denoted by RE, the family of context-free and regular languages by CF and REG, respectively. The corresponding families of languages over a k-letter alphabet are denoted by $X(k)$, $X \in \{RE, CF, REG\}$; for $k = 1$ we obtain $PsX(1) = NX$ and, moreover, $NREG = NCF$.

2.2 Matrix Grammars

A context-free *matrix grammar* (without appearance checking) is a construct
$G = (N, T, S, M)$ where N and T are sets of *non-terminal* and *terminal symbols*,
respectively, with $N \cap T = \emptyset$, $S \in N$ is the *start symbol*, M is a finite set of
matrices, $M = \{m_i \mid 1 \le i \le n\}$, where the matrices m_i are sequences of the form
$m_i = (m_{i,1}, \ldots, m_{i,n_i})$, $n_i \ge 1$, $1 \le i \le n$, and the $m_{i,j}$, $1 \le j \le n_i$, $1 \le i \le n$,
are context-free productions over (N, T). For $m_i = (m_{i,1}, \ldots, m_{i,n_i})$ and $v, w \in$
$(N \cup T)^*$ we define $v \Longrightarrow_{m_i} w$ if and only if there are $w_0, w_1, \ldots, w_{n_i} \in (N \cup T)^*$
such that $w_0 = v$, $w_{n_i} = w$, and for each $j, 1 \le j \le n_i$, w_j is the result of the
application of $m_{i,j}$ to w_{j-1}. The language generated by G is

$$L(G) = \{w \in T^* \mid S \Longrightarrow_{m_{i_1}} w_1 \ldots \Longrightarrow_{m_{i_k}} w_k, \; w_k = w,$$
$$w_j \in (N \cup T)^*, \; m_{i_j} \in M \text{ for } 1 \le j \le k, k \ge 1\}.$$

The family of languages generated by matrix grammars without appearance
checking (over a one-letter alphabet) is denoted by MAT^λ ($MAT^\lambda(1)$). It is
known that $CF \subset MAT^\lambda \subset RE$ as well as $PsCF \subset PsMAT^\lambda \subset PsRE$, and
especially $NREG = NCF = PsMAT^\lambda(1) \subset NRE$. For further details about
matrix grammars we refer to [9] and to [21].

2.3 Register Machines

An *n-register machine* is a construct $M = (n, B, P, l_0, l_h)$, where n is the number
of registers, B is a set of labels for injectively labelling the instructions in P,
l_0 is the initial/start label, and l_h is the final label. The instructions are of the
following forms:

- $p : (A(r), q, s)$ (ADD instruction)
  Add 1 to the contents of register r and proceed to one of the instructions
  (labelled with) q and s.
- $p : (S(r), q, s)$ (SUB instruction)
  If register r is not empty, then subtract 1 from its contents and go to in-
  struction q, otherwise proceed to instruction s.
- $l_h : halt$ (HALT instruction)
  Stop the machine. The final label l_h is only assigned to this instruction.

A (non-deterministic) register machine M is said to generate a vector
$(s_1, \ldots, s_\beta)$ of natural numbers if, starting with the instruction with label l_0
and all registers containing the number 0, the machine stops (it reaches the instruction $l_h : halt$) with the first β registers containing the numbers $s_1, \ldots, s_\beta$
(and all other registers being empty).

Without loss of generality, in the succeeding proofs we will assume that in
each ADD instruction $p : (A(r), q, s) \in P$ and in each SUB instruction $p :$
$(S(r), q, s) \in P$ the labels p, q, s are mutually distinct (for a proof see [14]).

The register machines are known to be computationally complete, equal in
power to (non-deterministic) Turing machines: they generate exactly the sets
of vectors of non-negative integers which can be generated by Turing machines,
i.e., the family $PsRE$. The following result is well known (e.g., see [15], [11]):

Proposition 1. *For any recursively enumerable set $L \subseteq \mathbb{N}^\beta$ of vectors of non-negative integers there exists a non-deterministic $(\beta + 2)$-register machine M generating L in such a way that, when starting with all registers 1 to $\beta + 2$ being empty, M non-deterministically computes and halts with n_i in registers i, $1 \leq i \leq \beta$, and registers $\beta+1$ and $\beta+2$ being empty if and only if $(n_1, ..., n_\beta) \in L$. Moreover, the registers 1 to β are never decremented.*

2.4   A General Model of P Systems with Permitting Contexts

We now introduce a general model of P systems with permitting contexts covering the most important models of communication P systems as well as evolution/communication P systems. For the state of the art in the P systems area, we refer to the P systems web page [23].

A *P system (of degree d, $d \geq 1$) with permitting contexts* (in the following also called P system for short) is a construct

$$\Pi = (V, T, E, \mu, w_1, \ldots, w_d, R_1, \ldots, R_d, i_o) \text{ where}$$

1. V is an alphabet; its elements are called *objects*;
2. $T \subseteq V$ is an alphabet of *terminal objects*;
3. $E \subseteq V$ is the set of objects occurring in an unbounded number in the environment;
4. μ is a *membrane structure* consisting of d membranes (usually labelled with i and represented by corresponding brackets $[_i$ and $]_i$, $1 \leq i \leq d$);
5. w_i, $1 \leq i \leq d$, are strings over V associated with the regions $1, 2, \ldots, d$ of μ; they represent multisets of objects initially present in the regions of μ;
6. R_i, $1 \leq i \leq d$, are finite sets of *membrane rules with permitting contexts* over V associated with the membranes $1, 2, \ldots, d$ of μ; these evolution rules in R_i are of the form ${}^{u}_{w}[{}^{x}_{z} \to {}^{v}_{w}[{}^{y}_{z}$, where $w, z \in V^*$ are the contexts in the region outside membrane i and inside membrane i, respectively, u outside membrane i is replaced by v and x inside membrane i is replaced by y;
7. i_o, $1 \leq i_o \leq d$, specifies the *output* membrane of Π.

The rule ${}^{u}_{w}[{}^{x}_{z} \to {}^{v}_{w}[{}^{y}_{z}$ from R_i is applicable if and only if the multiset uw occurs in the region outside membrane i (in the following also denoted by $\hat{i}$) and the multiset xz occurs in the region inside membrane i. The application of this rule results in subtracting the multiset identified by u from the multiset in $\hat{i}$ and adding v instead as well as subtracting x and adding y in the region inside membrane i. Instead of writing ${}^{u}_{w}[{}^{x}_{z} \to {}^{v}_{w}[{}^{y}_{z} \in R_i$ we can also write ${}^{u}_{w}[_i {}^{x}_{z} \to {}^{v}_{w}[_i {}^{y}_{z}$ and in this way collect all rules from the R_i, $1 \leq i \leq d$, in one single set of rules $R = \{ {}^{u}_{w}[_i {}^{x}_{z} \to {}^{v}_{w}[_i {}^{y}_{z} \mid {}^{u}_{w}[{}^{x}_{z} \to {}^{v}_{w}[{}^{y}_{z} \in R_i \}$. The membrane structure and the multisets represented by w_i, $1 \leq i \leq d$, in Π constitute the *initial configuration* of the system.

In the *maximally parallel derivation mode*, a transition from one configuration to another one is obtained by the application of a maximal multiset of rules, i.e., no additional rules could be applied anymore. The system continues maximally parallel derivation steps until there remain no applicable rules in any region of

Π; then the system halts (*total halting*). We consider the number of objects from T contained in the output membrane i_o at the moment when the system halts as the *result* of the underlying computation of Π yielding a vector of non-negative integers for the numbers of terminal symbols in the output membrane i_0; observe that here we do not count the non-terminal objects present in the output membrane. The set of results of all halting computations possible in Π is denoted by $Ps(\Pi)$, respectively. Below, we shall consider variants of P systems using only rules of very restricted types α. The family of all sets of vectors of non-negative integers computable by P systems with d membranes and using rules of type α is denoted by $Ps_gOP_d(\alpha, max, H)$.

When using the *minimally parallel derivation mode (min)*, in each derivation step we choose a multiset of rules from the R_i, $1 \le i \le d$, in such way that this chosen multiset includes at least one rule from every set of rules containing applicable rules. In the *asynchronous (asyn)* and the *sequential derivation mode (sequ)*, in each derivation step we apply an arbitrary number of rules/ exactly one rule, respectively. The corresponding families of sets of vectors of non-negative integers generated by P systems with d membranes and using rules of type α are denoted by $Ps_gOP_d(\alpha, X, H)$, $X \in \{min, asyn, sequ\}$.

If instead of the total halting we take *partial halting*, i.e., computations halting as soon as no multiset of rules containing at least one rule from each set of rules assigned to the membranes is applicable anymore, the corresponding families are denoted by $Ps_gOP_d(\alpha, X, h)$, $X \in \{max, min, asyn, sequ\}$.

All these variants of P systems can also be considered as accepting devices, the input being given as the numbers of objects in the distinguished membrane i_0. The corresponding families of sets of vectors of non-negative integers accepted by P systems with d membranes and using rules of type α are denoted by $Ps_aOP_d(\alpha, X, Y)$, $X \in \{max, min, asyn, sequ\}$, $Y \in \{H, h\}$. In this case, it also makes sense to consider deterministic P systems, i.e., systems where for each configuration obtained in this system we can derive at most one configuration. The corresponding families are denoted by $DPs_aOP_d(\alpha, X, Y)$.

If we only count the number of terminal objects and do not distinguish between different (terminal) objects, in all the definitions given above, we replace Ps by N. When the parameter d is not bounded, it is replaced by $*$.

In the following, we now consider several restricted variants of membrane rules with permitting contexts well known from the literature.

P systems with symport/antiport rules. For definitions and results concerning P systems with symport/antiport rules, we refer to the original paper [16] as well as to the overview given in [20]. An *antiport rule* is a rule of the form $^u[^x \rightarrow {}^x[^u$ usually written as $(x, out; u, in)$, $ux \ne \lambda$. A *symport rule* is of the form $[^x \rightarrow {}^x[$ or $^u[\rightarrow [^u$ usually written as (x, out), $x \ne \lambda$, or (u, in), $u \ne \lambda$, respectively.

The weight of the antiport rule $(x, out; u, in)$ is defined as $\max\{|x|, |u|\}$. Using only antiport rules with weight k induces the type α usually written as $anti_k$. The weight of a symport rule (x, out) or (u, in) is defined as $|x|$ or $|u|$, respectively. Using only symport rules with weight k induces the type α usually written as

sym_k. If only antiport rules $(x, out; u, in)$ of weight ≤ 2 and with $|x| + |u| \leq 3$ as well as symport rules of weight 1 are used, we shall write $anti_{2'}$.

P systems with conditional uniport rules. A *conditional uniport rule* is a rule of one of the forms ${}^{ab}[\rightarrow {}^{b}[{}^{a}$, $[{}^{ab} \rightarrow {}^{a}[{}^{b}$, ${}^{a}[{}^{b} \rightarrow [{}^{ab}$, ${}^{b}[{}^{a} \rightarrow {}^{ab}[$, with $a, b \in V$; in every case, the object a is moved across the membrane, whereas the object b stays where it is. Using only rules of that kind induces the type $uni_{1,1}$. Conditional uniport rules were first considered in [22] for the case of tissue P systems, showing computational completeness with maximal parallelism and total halting (using 24 cells).

P systems with boundary rules and evolution/communication P systems. In P systems with boundary rules as defined in [5], evolution rules as well as communication rules with permitting contexts are considered. Usually, we only consider evolution rules that are non-cooperative, i.e., of the form $a \rightarrow v$ with $a \in V$ and $v \in V^*$; a rule $a \rightarrow v \in R_i$ corresponds to $[{}^{a} \rightarrow [{}^{v} \in R_i$ in our general notation. The communication rules are symport or antiport rules with permitting contexts, i.e., of the form ${}_{w}^{u}[{}_{z}^{x} \rightarrow {}_{w}^{x}[{}_{z}^{u}$. In [6], boundary rules of the form ${}^{u}[{}^{x} \rightarrow {}^{v}[{}^{y}$ are considered, i.e., rewriting on both sides of the membrane. In evolution/communication P systems as introduced in [7], we allow non-cooperative evolution rules as well as antiport (of weight k) and symport rules (of weight l), and we denote this type of rules by $(ncoo, anti_k, sym_l)$.

3 Results

After recalling some general results for the new variant of *partial halting* already established in [12], which immediately yield comparable computational completeness results in the case of antiport P systems for total and partial halting, we prove that working in the asynchronous or in the sequential derivation mode we can only obtain Parikh sets of matrix languages (regular sets of non-negative integers) with partial halting as with total halting. Moreover, antiport P systems working in the minimally parallel derivation mode with partial halting only yield Parikh sets of matrix languages (regular sets), too.

3.1 General Observations

Looking carefully into the definitions of the derivation modes as well as the halting modes explained above, we observe the following general results already established in [12]:

Theorem 1. *Any variant of P systems yielding a family of sets of non-negative integers F when working in the derivation mode X, $X \in \{max, min, asyn, sequ\}$, with only one set of rules assigned to a single membrane and stopping with total halting yields the same family F when working in the derivation mode X with only one set of rules assigned to a single membrane when stopping with partial halting, too.*

Theorem 2. *Any variant of P systems yielding a family of sets of non-negative integers F when working in the derivation mode X, X ∈ {asyn, sequ}, with only one set of rules assigned to a single membrane and stopping with total or partial halting, respectively, yields the same family F when working in the minimally parallel derivation mode and stopping with the corresponding halting mode, too.*

For any P system using rules of type α, with a derivation mode X, $X \in \{min, asyn, sequ\}$, and partial halting, we only get Parikh sets of matrix languages (regular sets of non-negative integers):

Theorem 3. *For every $X \in \{min, asyn, sequ\}$,*
$$Ps_gOP_* (\alpha, X, h) \subseteq PsMAT^\lambda \text{ and } N_gOP_* (\alpha, X, h) \subseteq NREG.$$

Proof. We only prove $Ps_gOP_* (\alpha, X, h) \subseteq PsMAT^\lambda$; the second inequality $N_gOP_* (\alpha, X, h) \subseteq NREG$ is a direct consequence of the first one, having in mind that $NREG = PsMAT^\lambda (1)$. Hence, let us start with a P system $\Pi = (V, T, E, \mu, w_1, \ldots, w_d, R_1, \ldots, R_d, i_o)$ using rules of a specific type α, working with the derivation mode X. The stopping condition h – partial halting – then guarantees that in order to continue a derivation there must exist a sequence of rules $\langle r_1, \ldots, r_d \rangle$ with $r_i \in R_i$, $1 \leq i \leq d$, such that all these rules are applicable in parallel. We now consider all functions δ with $\delta (i, r) \in \{0, 1\}$ and $\delta (i, r) = 1$ if and only if the rule $r \in R_i$, $1 \leq i \leq d$, is assumed to be applicable to the current sentential form in a matrix grammar $G_M = (V_M, \overline{T}, S, M)$ generating representations of all possible configurations computable in the given P system Π with the representation of an object a in membrane i as (i, a). We start with the matrix $(S \to Kh (w))$ where $h (w)$ is a representation of the initial configuration. A derivation step in Π then is simulated in G_M as follows:

(i)   We non-deterministically choose some δ as described above and use the matrix $(K \to K (\delta))$. Afterwards, we use the matrix $(K (\delta) \to K' (\delta), s_1, \ldots, s_m)$ where each subsequence s_j, $1 \leq j \leq m$, checks the applicability of a rule $r \in R_i$ with $\delta (i, r) = 1$. For checking the applicability of $\begin{smallmatrix} u \\ w \end{smallmatrix} \begin{bmatrix} x \\ z \end{bmatrix} \to \begin{smallmatrix} v \\ w \end{smallmatrix} \begin{bmatrix} y \\ z \end{bmatrix} \in R_i$, we have to check for the appearance of uw in membrane $\hat{i}$ (the outer region of membrane i) and for the appearance of xz in the (inner) region of membrane i. This can be done by the subsequence $((\hat{i}, uw) \to (\hat{i}, \overline{uw}), (\hat{i}, \overline{uw}) \to (\hat{i}, uw), (i, xz) \to (i, \overline{xz}), (i, \overline{xz}) \to (i, xz))$, where $(i, v) \to (i, \overline{v})$, for $v = v_1 \ldots v_h$, $v_j \in V$, $1 \leq j \leq h$, $h \geq 0$, is a shortcut for the sequence $((i, v_1) \to (i, \overline{v_1}), \ldots, (i, v_h) \to (i, \overline{v_h}))$ etc.

(ii)   After that, we non-deterministically guess a sequence of rules $\langle r_1, \ldots, r_d \rangle$ with $r_i \in R_i$, $r_i = \begin{smallmatrix} u(i) \\ w(i) \end{smallmatrix} \begin{bmatrix} x(i) \\ z(i) \end{bmatrix} \to \begin{smallmatrix} v(i) \\ w(i) \end{smallmatrix} \begin{bmatrix} y(i) \\ z(i) \end{bmatrix}$, and $\delta (i, r_i) = 1$, $1 \leq i \leq d$, such that all these rules are applicable in parallel. This can be checked by the corresponding matrix $(K' (\delta) \to K'' (\delta), t_1, \ldots, t_d, t'_1, \ldots, t'_d)$ with the subsequences t_i, t'_i, $1 \leq i \leq d$, being defined (in the shortcut notation as above) by $t_i = \left((\hat{i}, u(i)) \to \left(\hat{i}, \overline{u(i)} \right), (i, x(i)) \to \left(i, \overline{x(i)} \right) \right)$ and $t'_1 = \left(\left(\hat{i}, \overline{u(i)} \right) \to (\hat{i}, u(i)), \left(i, \overline{x(i)} \right) \to (i, x(i)) \right)$. Observe that only the objects in

$u\,(i)$ and $x\,(i)$ are assigned to the rule r_i, whereas the permitting contexts $w\,(i)$ and $z\,(i)$ may be contexts for another rule or be affected themselves by another rule, and, moreover, that the applicability of the rules themselves has already been checked in (i).

(iii)   Finally, we take different matrices depending on the derivation mode:

In the *sequential derivation mode*, we only have to take all possible matrices simulating the application of one rule ${}^u_w[{}^x_z \rightarrow {}^v_w[{}^y_z \in R_i$ with $\delta\,(i,r) = 1$: $(K''\,(\delta) \rightarrow K h_{\hat{\imath}}\,(v)\,h_i\,(y)\,,(\hat{\imath},u) \rightarrow \lambda,(i,x) \rightarrow \lambda)$, where the morphisms h_j are defined by $h_j\,(a) = (j,a)$, $0 \le j \le d$, $a \in V$, except $h_0\,(a) = \lambda$ for $a \in E$.

In the *asynchronous derivation mode*, we have to allow an arbitrary number of rules to be applied in parallel; we simulate the application of rules sequentially, priming the results such that they cannot be used immediately. Finally, if for the current derivation step, the application of no further rule is intended, we can deprime the result symbols to be available for the simulation of the next derivation step. In sum, we use the matrices $(K''\,(\delta) \rightarrow K'''\,(\delta))$, $(K'''\,(\delta) \rightarrow K'''\,(\delta)\,h'_{\hat{\imath}}\,(v)\,h'_i\,(y)\,,(\hat{\imath},u) \rightarrow \lambda,(i,x) \rightarrow \lambda)$ – where the morphisms h'_j are defined by $h'_j\,(a) = (j,a')$, $0 \le j \le d$, $a \in V$, except $h'_0\,(a) = \lambda$ for $a \in E$ – for every rule ${}^u_w[{}^x_z \rightarrow {}^v_w[{}^y_z \in R_i$ with $\delta\,(i,r) = 1$, as well as $(K'''\,(\delta) \rightarrow \overline{K}\,(\delta))$, $(\overline{K}\,(\delta) \rightarrow \overline{K}\,(\delta)\,,(j,a') \rightarrow (j,a))$, $0 \le j \le d$, $a \in V$, and finally $(\overline{K}\,(\delta) \rightarrow K)$.

For the *minimally parallel mode*, instead of $(K''\,(\delta) \rightarrow K'''\,(\delta))$ as in 2, we simulate the application of a sequence of rules $\langle r_1,\ldots,r_d \rangle$ with $r_i = {}^{u(i)}_{w(i)}[{}^{x(i)}_{z(i)} \rightarrow {}^{v(i)}_{w(i)}[{}^{y(i)}_{z(i)}$, $r_i \in R_i$, $1 \le i \le d$, and $\delta\,(i,r_i) = 1$ such that all these rules are applicable in parallel, which is accomplished by the matrix $\Big(K''\,(\delta) \rightarrow K'''\,(\delta)\,h'_{\hat{1}}\,(v)\,h'_1\,(y)\,...h'_{\hat{d}}\,(v)\,h'_d\,(y)\,,$

$(\hat{1},u\,(1)) \rightarrow \lambda,(1,x\,(1)) \rightarrow \lambda,...,\Big(\hat{d},u\,(d)\Big) \rightarrow \lambda,(d,x\,(d)) \rightarrow \lambda\Big)$.

As a technical detail we have to mention that it does not matter whether all the primed symbols are deprimed again, this would just make them unavailable during the next steps. Any sentential form containing primed symbols is considered to be non-terminal, hence, it cannot contribute to $L\,(G_M)$. Moreover, every symbol $e \in E$ from the environment being available there in an unbounded number neither needs to be checked for appearance in $\hat{1}$ ($= 0$) nor to be generated/eliminated or primed/deprimed, i.e., rules like $(0,e) \rightarrow \lambda$, $(0,e) \rightarrow (0,\overline{e})$, $(0,\overline{e}) \rightarrow (0,e)$ have to be omitted.

Finally, we may stop the simulation of computation steps of Π and use the matrices $(K \rightarrow F)$, $(F \rightarrow F,(i,a) \rightarrow (i,\overline{a}))$ for every object a and every membrane i, and the final matrix $(F \rightarrow \lambda)$ for generating a terminal string of G_M.

Now, we have to extract the representations of final configurations from $L\,(G_M)$: For every possibility of choosing a sequence of rules $\langle r_1,\ldots,r_d \rangle$ with $r_i \in R_i$, $1 \le i \le d$, such that all these rules are applicable in parallel, we construct a regular set checking for the applicability of this sequence in any possible representation of configurations of Π; then we take the union of all these regular sets and take its complement thus obtaining a regular set R. In $L\,(G_M) \cap R$ we then find at least one representation for every final configuration of computations in Π, but no representation of a non-final configuration.

Finally, let g be a projection with $g\left((i,\overline{a})\right) = \lambda$ for every $i \neq i_0$ as well as $g\left((i_0,\overline{a})\right) = \lambda$ for $a \in V \smallsetminus T$ and $g\left((i_0,\overline{a})\right) = a$ for $a \in T$. Due to the closure properties of MAT^λ, we obtain $Ps\left(g\left(L\left(G_M\right) \cap R\right)\right) = Ps\left(\Pi\right) \in PsMAT^\lambda$. □

3.2   Results for Symport/Antiport Systems

The following results are well known (e.g., see [18]; for an overview of actual results also see [20]):

Theorem 4. $Ps_gOP_1\left(anti_{2'}, max, H\right) = DPs_aOP_1\left(anti_{2'}, max, H\right) = PsRE.$

Theorem 5. *For every* $X \in \{asyn, sequ\}$,
$\quad Ps_gOP_*\left(anti_*, X, H\right) = Ps_gOP_1\left(anti_{2'}, X, H\right) = PsMAT^\lambda$ *and*
$\quad N_gOP_*\left(anti_*, X, H\right) = N_gOP_1\left(anti_{2'}, X, H\right) = NREG.$

Recently, $N_gOP_3\left(anti_2, min, H\right) = NRE$ was shown in [8]; we shall improve this result by showing that only two membranes are needed:

Theorem 6. $Ps_gOP_2\left(anti_{2'}, min, H\right) = PsRE.$

Proof. We only give a sketch of the proof, because the basic ideas are the same as in the usual proofs showing computational completeness for antiport P systems. Now let $M = (n, B, P, l_0, l_h)$ be a register machine generating an output vector of dimension k ($\leq n$); then we construct the P system

$$
\begin{aligned}
\Pi \quad &= \left(V, T, V, [_1 [_2 \ ]_2]_1, l_0, ZX, R_1, R_2, 2\right), \\
V \quad &= \{p, p', p'', p''', \tilde{p}, \tilde{p}', \tilde{p}'', \bar{p}, \bar{p}', \bar{p}'' \mid p \in B\} \\
&\quad \cup \{X, Y, Z, Z'\} \cup \{A_i \mid 1 \leq i \leq n\}, \\
T \quad &= \{A_i \mid 1 \leq i \leq k\}, \\
R_1 \quad &= R_{1,A} \cup R_{1,S} \cup R_{1,F}, \\
R_{1,A} &= \{(p, out; A_r q, in), (p, out; A_r s, in) \mid p : (A\left(r\right), q, s) \in P\}, \\
R_{1,S} &= \{(p, out; p'p'', in), (p''A_r, out; p''', in), (p''X, out; \bar{p}, in), \\
&\qquad (p'''X, out; \tilde{p}, in), (\tilde{p}, out; \tilde{p}'X, in), (\tilde{p}', out; \tilde{p}''Y, in), \\
&\qquad (\tilde{p}'', out; s, in), (\tilde{p}, out; \tilde{p}'X, in), (\tilde{p}', out; \tilde{p}''Y, in), \\
&\qquad (\tilde{p}'', out; q, in) \mid p : (S\left(r\right), q, s) \in P\}, \\
R_{1,F} &= \{(p'Y, out; Z', in) \mid p \in B \smallsetminus \{l_h\}\} \cup \{(Z', out), (ZX, out; Z', in)\}, \\
R_2 \quad &= R_{2,A} \cup R_{2,S} \cup R_{2,F}, \\
R_{2,A} &= \{(A_i, in) \mid 1 \leq i \leq k\}, \\
R_{2,S} &= \{(X, out; p', in) \mid p \in B \smallsetminus \{l_h\}\} \cup \{(Z, out; XY, in), (Z, in)\}, \\
R_{2,F} &= \{(p'Y, out; l_h, in) \mid p \in B \smallsetminus \{l_h\}\} \cup \{(ZX, out; l_h, in), (l_h, out)\}.
\end{aligned}
$$

An ADD instruction $p : (A\left(r\right), q, s) \in P$ is simulated by using one of the rules $(p, out; A_r q, in)$, $(p, out; A_r s, in)$ assigned to membrane 1; in case r is an output register, the terminal symbol A_r is moved into the output region 2 by using (A_r, in) from R_2. A SUB instruction $p : (S\left(r\right), q, s) \in P$ is simulated by using the rules from $R_{1,S}$ and $R_{2,S}$ in parallel. The final procedure in Π starts when the final label l_h appears; as the number of symbols p' equals the number of symbols Y as they have been introduced when simulating a SUB instruction, we finally eliminate pairs $p'Y$ from the system using the rules from $R_{1,F}$ and $R_{2,F}$ until finally only l_h remains in the skin membrane and the desired output is found in the second membrane region, without any additional symbols remaining there anymore.

$$\square$$

The general result in Theorem 1 and the special result in Theorem 4 immediately yield the following one:

Corollary 1. $Ps_gOP_1\left(anti_{2'}, max, h\right) = DPs_aOP_1\left(anti_{2'}, max, h\right) = PsRE.$

With the other derivation modes and partial halting, we only get Parikh sets of matrix languages (regular sets of non-negative integers), which is an immediate consequence of Theorem 3:

Corollary 2. *For every* $X \in \{min, asyn, sequ\}$,
$$Ps_gOP_*\left(anti_*, X, h\right) = Ps_gOP_1\left(anti_{2'}, X, h\right) = PsMAT^\lambda \quad \text{and}$$
$$N_gOP_*\left(anti_*, X, h\right) = N_gOP_1\left(anti_{2'}, X, h\right) = NREG.$$

For symport rules, the following result is known (e.g., see [20]):

Theorem 7. $Ps_gOP_2\left(sym_2, max, H\right) = Ps_aOP_2\left(sym_2, max, H\right) = PsRE.$

In [4] we show that computational completeness can also be obtained with minimal parallelism and total halting, whereas as a direct consequence of Theorem 3, we only get Parikh sets of matrix languages (regular sets of non-negative integers) with partial halting:

Theorem 8. $Ps_gOP_2\left(sym_3, min, H\right) = PsRE.$

Corollary 3. *For every* $X \in \{min, asyn, sequ\}$,
$$Ps_gOP_*\left(sym_*, X, h\right) = PsMAT^\lambda \quad and \quad N_gOP_*\left(sym_*, X, h\right) = NREG.$$

3.3   Results for P Systems with Conditional Uniport Rules

Using only conditional uniport rules of type $uni_{1,1}$, we again obtain computational completeness, even with the minimally parallel derivation mode, together with total halting (a proof for this result can be found in [4]), whereas, as a direct consequence of Theorem 3, with partial halting we only get Parikh sets of matrix languages (regularsets of non-negative integers) with the minimally parallel derivation mode.

Theorem 9. $Ps_gOP_{13}\left(uni_{1,1}, X, H\right) = PsRE$, *for every* $X \in \{min, max\}$.

3.4   Results for Evolution/Communication P Systems

For evolution/communication P systems, the constructions from [2], Theorems 1 and 2, and from [3], Theorems 4.3.1 and 4.3.2, already show the computational completeness, using two membranes, for the minimally parallel setup (when working in the maximally parallel way, the system never applies simultaneously more than one rule from the same set of rules assigned to a membrane):

Corollary 4. $Ps_gOP_2\left((ncoo, anti_1, sym_1), X, H\right) = PsRE, \ X \in \{min, max\}.$

We can extend these results by showing that *deterministic* evolution-communication P systems with non-cooperative evolution rules and communication rules of weight one (also see [1]) are computationally complete, using three membranes (for a proof, see [4]).

Theorem 10. *For* $X \in \{min, max\}$,
$DPs_aOP_3((ncoo, sym_1, anti_1), X, H) = PsRE$.

4 Conclusion

In this paper, we have investigated a new variant of halting – we call it *partial halting* – in membrane systems where all membranes are required to allow for the application of a rule at the same time in order to keep a computation alive. Obviously, for systems with only one membrane this way of halting is equivalent with the original one where a system halts if and only if no rule is applicable anymore in the whole system – we also call this *total halting*. Besides this general result, we also have shown that P systems working in the minimally parallel mode, the asynchronous or the sequential derivation mode and with partial halting can only generate Parikh sets of matrix languages/regular sets, the same what we obtain with the sequential and the asynchronous derivation mode and total halting.

Comparing the results for total and partial halting for the minimally parallel derivation mode elaborated above, we realize that for any of the specific restricted variants α of P systems with permitting contexts we have

$$Ps_gOP_* (\alpha, min, h) \subseteq PsMAT^\lambda \subsetneqq PsRE = Ps_gOP_* (\alpha, min, H) \text{ and}$$
$$N_gOP_* (\alpha, min, h) = NREG \subsetneqq NRE = N_gOP_* (\alpha, min, H),$$

i.e., in the case of the minimally parallel derivation mode the halting condition – *total* in contrast to *partial* halting – makes the difference. Intuitively speaking, the requirement for a computation to continue only if for every membrane a rule is applicable, together with the minimally parallel derivation mode means that we do not have the possibility of appearance checking and therefore cannot simulate the zero test for register machines, hence, we cannot obtain computational completeness. In the future, the new variant of partial halting should also be investigated for other variants of P systems working in the different derivation modes, with multisets of objects, but also with strings, arrays, etc.

Acknowledgements. Artiom Alhazov gratefully acknowledges support by the Academy of Finland, project 203667; he also acknowledges the project 06.411.03.04P from the Supreme Council for Science and Technological Development of the Academy of Sciences of Moldova. The work of Marion Oswald was supported by FWF-project T225-N04. 2006.

References

1. Alhazov, A.: On determinism of evolution-communication P systems. Journal of Universal Computer Science 10(5), 502–508 (2004)
2. Alhazov, A.: Number of protons/bi-stable catalysts and membranes in P systems. In: Freund, R., Păun, G., Rozenberg, G., Salomaa, A. (eds.) WMC 2005. LNCS, vol. 3850, pp. 79–95. Springer, Heidelberg (2006)

3. Alhazov, A.: Communication in Membrane Systems with Symbol Objects, Ph.D. Thesis, Tarragona, Spain (2006)
4. Alhazov, A., Freund, R., Oswald, M., Verlan, S.: Partial versus total halting in P systems. In: Proc. Fifth Brainstorming Week on Membrane Computing, Sevilla (to appear, 2007)
5. Bernardini, F., Manca, V.: P systems with boundary rules. In: Păun, G., Rozenberg, G., Salomaa, A., Zandron, C. (eds.) Membrane Computing. LNCS, vol. 2597, pp. 107–118. Springer, Heidelberg (2003)
6. Bernardini, F., Romero-Campero, F.J., Gheorghe, M., Pérez-Jiménez, M.J., Margenstern, M., Verlan, S., Krasnogor, N.: On P systems with bounded parallelism. In: Ciobanu, G., Păun, G. (eds.) Pre-Proc. of First International Workshop on Theory and Application of P Systems, Timisoara, Romania, September 26–27, 2005, pp. 31–36 (2005)
7. Cavaliere, M.: Evolution-communication P systems. In: Păun, G., Rozenberg, G., Salomaa, A., Zandron, C. (eds.) Membrane Computing. LNCS, vol. 2597, pp. 134–145. Springer, Heidelberg (2003)
8. Ciobanu, G., Pan, L., Păun, G., Pérez-Jiménez, M.J.: P systems with minimal parallelism (accepted for TCS)
9. Dassow, J., Păun, G.: Regulated Rewriting in Formal Language Theory. Springer, Heidelberg (1989)
10. Dassow, J., Păun, G.: On the power of membrane computing. Journal of Universal Computer Science 5(2), 33–49 (1999)
11. Freund, R., Oswald, M.: P Systems with activated/prohibited membrane channels. In: Păun, G., Rozenberg, G., Salomaa, A., Zandron, C. (eds.) Membrane Computing. LNCS, vol. 2597, pp. 261–268. Springer, Heidelberg (2003)
12. Freund, R., Oswald, M.: P systems with partial halting (accepted, 2007)
13. Freund, R., Păun, G., Rozenberg, G., Salomaa, A. (eds.): WMC 2005. LNCS, vol. 3850. Springer, Heidelberg (2006)
14. Freund, R., Păun, G., Pérez-Jiménez, M.J.: Tissue-like P systems with channel states. Theoretical Computer Science 330, 101–116 (2005)
15. Minsky, M.L.: Computation: Finite and Infinite Machines. Prentice Hall, Englewood Cliffs, New Jersey, USA (1967)
16. Păun, A., Păun, G.: The power of communication: P systems with symport/ antiport. New Generation Computing 20(3), 295–306 (2002)
17. Păun, G.: Computing with membranes. J. of Computer and System Sciences 61(1), 108–143 (2000) and TUCS Research Report 208 (1998) http://www.tucs.fi
18. Păun, G.: Membrane Computing. An Introduction. Springer, Berlin (2002)
19. Păun, G., Rozenberg, G., Salomaa, A., Zandron, C. (eds.): Membrane Computing. LNCS, vol. 2597. Springer, Heidelberg (2003)
20. Rogozhin, Y., Alhazov, A., Freund, R.: Computational power of symport/antiport: history, advances, and open problems. In: Freund, R., Păun, G., Rozenberg, G., Salomaa, A. (eds.) WMC 2005. LNCS, vol. 3850, pp. 1–30. Springer, Heidelberg (2006)
21. Rozenberg, G., Salomaa, A. (eds.): Handbook of Formal Languages, 3 volumes. Springer, Berlin (1997)
22. Verlan, S., Bernardini, F., Gheorghe, M., Margenstern, M.: On communication in tissue P systems: conditional uniport. In: Hoogeboom, H.J., Păun, G., Rozenberg, G., Salomaa, A. (eds.) WMC 2006. LNCS, vol. 4361, pp. 507–521. Springer, Heidelberg (2006)
23. The P Systems Web Page, http://psystems.disco.unimib.it

Uniform Solution of QSAT Using Polarizationless Active Membranes[*]

Artiom Alhazov[1,2] and Mario J. Pérez-Jiménez[3]

[1] Department of Information Technologies, Åbo Akademi University
Turku Center for Computer Science, FIN-20520 Turku, Finland
aalhazov@abo.fi
[2] Institute of Mathematics and Computer Science, Academy of Sciences of Moldova
Str. Academiei 5, Chişinău, MD-2028, Moldova
artiom@math.md
[3] Research Group on Natural Computing
Department of Computer Science and Artificial Intelligence, University of Sevilla
Avda. Reina Mercedes s/n, 41012 Sevilla, Spain
marper@us.es

Abstract. It is known that the satisfiability problem (SAT) can be solved with a semi-uniform family of deterministic polarizationless P systems with active membranes with non–elementary membrane division. We present a double improvement of this result by showing that the satisfiability of a *quantified* Boolean formula (QSAT) can be solved by a *uniform* family of P systems of the same kind.

1 Introduction

A particularly interesting model of membrane systems are the systems with active membranes, see [10], where membrane division can be used in order to solve computationally hard problems in polynomial or even linear time, by a space–time trade-off. The description of rules in this model involves membranes and objects; the typical types of rules are (a) object evolution, $(b), (c)$ object communication, (d) membrane dissolution, $(e), (f)$ membrane division. Since membrane systems are an abstraction of living cells, the membranes are arranged hierarchically, yielding a tree structure. A membrane is called elementary if it is a leaf of this tree, i.e., if it does not contain other membranes.

The first efficient *semi–uniform solution* to SAT was given by Gh. Păun in [10], using division for non–elementary membranes and three electrical charges. This result was improved by Gh. Păun, Y. Suzuki, H. Tanaka, and T. Yokomori in [11] using only division for elementary membranes (in that paper also a semi–uniform solution to *HPP* using membrane creation is presented).

[*] The first author gratefully acknowledges the support by Academy of Finland, project 203667, and by the Supreme Council for Science and Technological Development of the Academy of Sciences of Moldova, project 06.411.03.04P. The second author wishes to acknowledge the support of the project TIN2005-09345-C04-01 of the Ministerio de Educación y Ciencia of Spain, cofinanced by FEDER funds.

J. Durand-Lose and M. Margenstern (Eds.): MCU 2007, LNCS 4664, pp. 122–133, 2007.
© Springer-Verlag Berlin Heidelberg 2007

P. Sosík in [19] provides an efficient *semi–uniform solution* to QSAT (quantified satisfiability problem), a well known **PSPACE**–complete problem, in the framework of P systems with active membranes but using cell division rules for non–elementary membranes. A *uniform solution* for QSAT was presented in [1], while a *semi–uniform* **polarizationless** *solution* for SAT was presented in [3].

Different efficient *uniform solutions* have been obtained in the framework of recognizer P systems with active membranes, with polarizations and only using division rules for elementary membranes ([14], [13], [5], [17], [2], [15], and [18]). Nevertheless, the polynomial complexity class associated with recognizer P systems with active membranes and with polarizations does not seem precise enough to describe classical complexity classes below **PSPACE**. Therefore, it is challenging to investigate weaker variants of membrane systems able to characterize classical complexity classes.

This is a final version of [4]. Here we work with a variant of these membrane systems that do not use polarizations. With this model, dissolution rules have been shown in [6] to provide a borderline between efficiency and non–efficiency.

In the next section some preliminary ideas about recognizer membrane systems and polynomial complexity classes are introduced. In Section 3 we present a *uniform* and polynomial solution of the *quantified satisfiability* problem by a family of recognizer P systems with active membranes, without polarization, permitting dissolution rules and division for both elementary and non–elementary membranes. Conclusions and some final remarks are given in Section 4.

2   Preliminaries

Membrane computing is a recent branch of natural computing initiated by Gh. Păun in [9]. The devices of this model, called P systems, provide distributed parallel and non–deterministic computing models.

In short, one abstracts computing models from the structure and the functioning of living cells, as well as from the organization of cell in tissues, organs, and other higher order structures. The main components of such a model are a cell-like *membrane structure*, in the *compartments* of which one places *multisets of symbol-objects* which evolve in a synchronous maximally parallel manner according to given *evolution rules*, also associated with the membranes.

Definition 1. *A P system with external output, Π, is a tuple*

$$\Pi = \big(\Gamma, H, \mu, \mathcal{M}_1, \ldots, \mathcal{M}_p, R\big), \text{ where:}$$
- *Γ is the working alphabet of the system whose elements are called objects.*
- *H is an alphabet whose elements are called labels.*
- *μ is a membrane structure (a rooted tree) consisting of p membranes injectively labelled by elements of H.*
- *$\mathcal{M}_i$, $1 \leq i \leq p$, is an initial multiset over Γ associated with membrane i.*
- *R are rules defining the behavior of objects from Γ and membranes from H.*

The *semantics* of P systems is defined through a non–deterministic and synchronous model (a global clock is assumed) as follows:

- A *configuration* of a membrane system consists of a membrane structure and a family of multisets of objects associated with each region of the structure.
- In each time unit we can transform a given configuration in another configuration by applying the evolution rules to the objects placed inside the regions of the configurations, in a non–deterministic, maximally parallel manner, thus defining the *transitions* between the configurations.
- A *computation* of the system is a (finite or infinite) sequence of configurations according to the transition relation.
- A computation which reaches a configuration where no more rules can be applied to the existing objects, is called a *halting computation*.
- The result of a halting computation is defined through the contents of the environment in the final configuration.

Let us recall that a decision problem X is a pair (I_X, θ_X) where I_X is a language over a finite alphabet (whose elements are called *instances*) and θ_X is a total Boolean function over I_X. In order to solve this kind of problems, we consider P systems as *recognizer languages* devices.

Definition 2. *A recognizer P system is a P system with external output such that: (a) the working alphabet contains two distinguished elements* yes *and* no; *(b) all computations halt; and (c) if* C *is a computation of the system, then either object* yes *or object* no *(but not both) must have been released into the environment, and only in the last step of the computation.*

In recognizer P systems, we say that a computation C is an *accepting computation* (resp. *rejecting computation*) if the object *yes* (resp. *no*) appears in the environment associated with the corresponding halting configuration of C.

Definition 3. *Let* $X = (I_X, \theta_X)$ *be a decision problem. We say that* X *is solvable in polynomial time by a (countable) family* $\mathcal{R}$ *of recognizer membrane systems* $\Pi = (\Pi(u))_{u \in I_X}$, *denoted by* $X \in \mathbf{PMC}^*_{\mathcal{R}}$, *if the following is true.*

- *The family* Π *is polynomially uniform by Turing machines, that is, there exists a deterministic Turing machine working in polynomial time which constructs the system* $\Pi(u)$ *from the instance* $u \in I_X$.
- *The family* Π *is polynomially bounded: for some polynomial function* $p(n)$ *each* $u \in I_X$, *all computations of* $\Pi(u)$ *halt in, at most,* $p(|u|)$ *steps.*
- *The family* Π *is sound with regard to* X: *for each instance of the problem* $u \in I_X$ *such that there exists an accepting computation of* $\Pi(u)$, $\theta_X(u) = 1$.
- *The family* Π *is complete with regard to* X: *for each instance of the problem* $u \in I_X$ *such that* $\theta_X(u) = 1$, *every computation of* $\Pi(u)$ *is accepting.*

We say that the family Π is a *semi–uniform solution* of the problem X.

A direct consequence of working with recognizer membrane systems is that the complexity classes $\mathbf{PMC}^*_{\mathcal{R}}$ are closed under complement. Moreover, these complexity classes are closed under polynomial time reduction, see [12].

Now, we deal with recognizer membrane systems *with an input membrane* solving decision problems in a *uniform* way in the following sense: all instances of a decision problem with the same *size* (according to a previously fixed polynomial time computable criterion) are processed by the same system, on which an appropriate input, representing the specific instance, is supplied.

Definition 4. *A P system with an input membrane is a tuple* (Π, Σ, i_Π), *where: (a)* Π *is a P system with external output, with working alphabet* Γ, *with p membranes labelled with* $1, \ldots, p$, *and initial multisets* $\mathcal{M}_1, \ldots, \mathcal{M}_p$ *associated with them; (b)* Σ *is an (input) alphabet strictly contained in* Γ *and the initial multisets are over* $\Gamma - \Sigma$; *(c)* i_Π *is the label of a distinguished (input) membrane.*

If m is a multiset over the input alphabet Σ, then the *initial configuration of the P system* (Π, Σ, i_Π) *with an input* m is $(\mu, \mathcal{M}_1, \ldots, \mathcal{M}_{i_\Pi} \cup m, \ldots, \mathcal{M}_p)$.

Definition 5. *Let* $X = (I_X, \theta_X)$ *be a decision problem. We say that* X *is solvable in polynomial time by a family* $\Pi = (\Pi(n))_{n \in \mathbb{N}}$ *of recognizer membrane systems with an input membrane, and we denote it by* $X \in \mathbf{PMC}_\mathcal{R}$, *if*

- *The family* Π *is polynomially uniform by TM: some deterministic TM constructs in polynomial time the system* $\Pi(n)$ *from* $n \in \mathbb{N}$.
- *There exists a pair* (cod, s) *of polynomial-time computable functions whose domain is* I_X, *such that for each* $u \in I_X$, $s(u)$ *is a natural number and* $cod(u)$ *is an input multiset of the system* $\Pi(s(u))$, *verifying the following:*
- *The family* Π *is polynomially bounded with regard* (X, cod, s); *that is, there exists a polynomial function* $p(n)$ *such that for each* $u \in I_X$ *every computation of the system* $\Pi(s(u))$ *with input* $cod(u)$ *halts in at most* $p(|u|)$ *steps.*
- *The family* Π *is sound with regard to* (X, cod, s); *that is, for each instance of the problem* $u \in I_X$ *such that there exists an accepting computation of* $\Pi(s(u))$ *with input* $cod(u)$, *we have* $\theta_X(u) = 1$.
- *The family* Π *is complete with regard to* (X, cod, s); *that is, for each instance of the problem* $u \in I_X$ *such that* $\theta_X(u) \doteq 1$, *every computation of* $\Pi(s(u))$ *with input* $cod(u)$ *is an accepting one.*

We say that the family Π is a *uniform solution* to the problem X. The complexity classes $\mathbf{PMC}_\mathcal{R}$ are closed under complement and closed under polynomial time reduction, in the classical sense, see [12].

Notice that if Π is a family of recognizer P systems solving a decision problem X in polynomial time and in a *uniform* way, then it provides a polynomial time solution of X in a *semi–uniform* way. Therefore, $\mathbf{PMC}_\mathcal{R} \subseteq \mathbf{PMC}_\mathcal{R}^*$.

2.1   P Systems with Polarizationless Active Membranes

Definition 6. *A P system with active membranes and without polarizations is a P system with* Γ *as working alphabet, with* H *as the finite set of labels for membranes, and where the rules are of the following forms:*

(a_0) $[a \rightarrow u]_h$ *for* $h \in H$, $a \in \Gamma$, $u \in \Gamma^*$. *These are object evolution rules. An object* $a \in \Gamma$ *in a membrane labelled by* h *evolves to a string* $u \in \Gamma^*$.

(b_0) $a[\ ]_h \to [b]_h$ *for* $h \in H$, $a, b \in \Gamma$. *These are send–in communication rules. An object from the region immediately outside a membrane labelled by h is introduced in this membrane, possibly transformed into another object.*

(c_0) $[a]_h \to b[\ ]_h$ *for* $h \in H$, $a, b \in \Gamma$. *These are send–out communication rules. An object is sent out from membrane labelled by h to the region immediately outside, possibly transformed into another object.*

(d_0) $[a]_h \to b$ *for* $h \in H$, $a, b \in \Gamma$. *These are dissolution rules. A membrane labelled by h (not skin) is dissolved in reaction with an object.*

(e_0) $[a]_h \to [b]_h\,[c]_h$ *for* $h \in H$, $a, b, c \in \Gamma$. *These are division rules for elementary membranes. An elementary membrane can be divided into two membranes with the same label, possibly transforming some objects.*

(f_0) $[\,[\ ]_{h_1}[\ ]_{h_2}]_{h_0} \to [\,[\ ]_{h_1}]_{h_0}\,[\,[\ ]_{h_2}]_{h_0}$, *where h_0, h_1, h_2 are labels. These are division rules for non–elementary membranes. If the membrane with label h_0 contains other membranes than those with labels h_1, h_2, these membranes and their contents are duplicated and placed in both new copies of the membrane h_0; all membranes and objects placed inside membranes h_1, h_2, as well as the objects from membrane h_0 placed outside membranes h_1 and h_2, are reproduced in the new copies of membrane h_0.*

These rules are applied according to the following principles:

- All the rules are applied in parallel and in a maximal manner. In one step, one object of a membrane can be used by only one rule (chosen non–deterministically), but any object which can evolve, must evolve.
- If at the same time a membrane labelled with h is divided by a rule of type (e_0) or (f_0) and there are objects in this membrane which evolve by means of rules of type (a_0), then we suppose that first the evolution rules of type (a_0) are used, and then the division is produced. The process takes one step.
- The rules for membranes h are used for all copies of this membrane. At one step, a membrane can be the subject of *only one* rule of types (b_0)–(f_0).

We denote by $\mathcal{AM}^0(\alpha, \beta)$, where $\alpha \in \{-d, +d\}$ and $\beta \in \{-ne, +ne\}$, the class of all recognizer P systems with polarizationless active membranes such that: $-d$ forbids rules (d_0), and $-ne$ forbids rules (f_0).

Proposition 1. *For each $\alpha \in \{-d, +d\}$ and $\beta \in \{-ne, +ne\}$ we have:*

(1) $\mathbf{PMC}_{\mathcal{AM}^0(\alpha,\beta)} \subseteq \mathbf{PMC}^*_{\mathcal{AM}^0(\alpha,\beta)}$.
(2) $\mathbf{PMC}_{\mathcal{AM}^0(\alpha,-ne)} \subseteq \mathbf{PMC}_{\mathcal{AM}^0(\alpha,+ne)}$.
(3) $\mathbf{PMC}^*_{\mathcal{AM}^0(\alpha,-ne)} \subseteq \mathbf{PMC}^*_{\mathcal{AM}^0(\alpha,+ne)}$.
(4) $\mathbf{PMC}_{\mathcal{AM}^0(-d,\beta)} \subseteq \mathbf{PMC}_{\mathcal{AM}^0(+d,\beta)}$.
(5) $\mathbf{PMC}^*_{\mathcal{AM}^0(-d,\beta)} \subseteq \mathbf{PMC}^*_{\mathcal{AM}^0(+d,\beta)}$.

A conjecture known in the membrane computing area under the name of the P–conjecture (proposed by Gh. Păun in 2005) is that $\mathbf{P} = \mathbf{PMC}_{\mathcal{AM}^0(+d,-ne)}$.

In [6] one obtains some partial answers of that conjecture. Specifically, in the framework of recognizer P systems with membrane division but without using polarizations a surprising role of the dissolution rules is shown, as it makes the difference between efficiency and non–efficiency for P systems with membrane division and without polarization.

Theorem 1. *The following statements hold:*

(1) $\mathbf{P} = \mathbf{PMC}_{\mathcal{AM}^0(-d,\beta)} = \mathbf{PMC}^*_{\mathcal{AM}^0(-d,\beta)}$, *for each* $\beta \in \{-ne, +ne\}$.

(2) $\mathbf{NP} \subseteq \mathbf{PMC}^*_{\mathcal{AM}^0(+d,+ne)}$.

3 A Uniform Solution of QSAT

In this section we extend the result (2) from Theorem 1, providing an uniform and linear time solution of QSAT (*quantified satisfiability*) problem, through a family of recognizer P systems using polarizationless active membranes, dissolution rules and division for elementary and non–elementary membranes.

Given a Boolean formula $\varphi(x_1, \ldots, x_n)$ in conjunctive normal form, with Boolean variables $x_1, \ldots, x_n$, the sentence $\varphi^* = \exists x_1 \forall x_2 \ldots Q_n x_n \varphi(x_1, \ldots, x_n)$ (where Q_n is $\exists$ if n is odd, and Q_n is $\forall$ otherwise) is said to be the (existential) *fully quantified* formula associated with $\varphi(x_1, \ldots, x_n)$. Recall that a sentence is a Boolean formula in which every variable is in scope of a quantifier.

We say that φ^* is satisfiable if for each truth assignment, σ, over $\{i : 1 \leq i \leq n \wedge i \text{ even}\}$ there is an extension σ^* of σ over $\{1, \ldots, n\}$ such that the value of x_i only depends on the values of x_j, $1 \leq j < i$, verifying $\sigma^*(\varphi(x_1, \ldots, x_n)) = 1$.

The QSAT problem is the following one: *Given the (existential) fully quantified formula* φ^* *associated with a Boolean formula* $\varphi(x_1, \ldots, x_n)$ *in conjunctive normal form, determine whether or not* φ^* *is satisfiable.*

It is well known that QSAT is a **PSPACE**–complete problem [8].

Theorem 2. $\text{QSAT} \in \mathbf{PMC}_{\mathcal{AM}^0(+d,+ne)}$.

Proof. The solution proposed follows a brute force approach, in the framework of recognizer P systems with polarizationless active membranes where dissolution rules, and division for elementary and non–elementary membranes are permitted. The solution consists in the following stages:

- *Generation Stage*: using membrane division for elementary and non–elementary membranes, all truth assignments for the variables associated with the Boolean formula are produced.
- *Assignments stage*: in a special membrane we encode the clauses that are satisfied for each truth assignment.
- *Checking Stage*: we determine what truth assignments make the Boolean formula evaluate to true.
- *Quantifier Stage*: the universal and existential gates of the fully quantified formula are simulated and its satisfiability is encoded by a special object in a suitable membrane.
- *Output Stage*: The systems sends out to the environment the right answer according to the result of the previous stage.

Let us consider a propositional formula in the conjunctive normal form:

$$\varphi = C_1 \wedge \cdots \wedge C_m,$$
$$C_i = y_{i,1} \vee \cdots \vee y_{i,l_i}, \ 1 \leq i \leq m, \text{ where}$$
$$y_{i,k} \in \{x_j, \neg x_j \mid 1 \leq j \leq n\}, \ 1 \leq i \leq m, 1 \leq k \leq l_i.$$

We consider a normal form for QSAT: the number of variables is even ($n = 2n'$) and the quantified formula is $\varphi^* = \exists x_1 \forall x_2 \cdots \exists x_{n-1} \forall x_n \; \varphi(x_1, \ldots, x_n)$.

Let us consider the (polynomial time computable and bijective) pair function from $\mathbb{N}^2$ onto $\mathbb{N}$ defined by $\langle n, m \rangle = ((n+m)(n+m+1)/2) + n$. Depending on numbers m (of clauses) and n (of variables), we will consider a system $(\Pi(\langle n, m \rangle), \Sigma(\langle n, m \rangle), i_0)$, where $i_0 = 0$ is the input region and $\Sigma(\langle n, m \rangle) = \{v_{i,j}, v'_{i,j} \mid 1 \le i \le m, \; 1 \le j \le n\}$ is the input alphabet.

The problem instance φ will be encoded in the P system by a multiset containing one copy of each symbol from sets $X, X' \subseteq \Sigma(\langle n, m \rangle)$, corresponding to the clause-variable pairs such that the clause is satisfied by *true* and *false* assignment of the variable, defined below. We now construct the P system

$$X_\varphi = \{v_{i,j} \mid x_j \in \{y_{i,k} \mid 1 \le k \le l_i\}, 1 \le i \le m, \; 1 \le j \le n\},$$
$$X'_\varphi = \{v'_{i,j} \mid \neg x_j \in \{y_{i,k} \mid 1 \le k \le l_i\}, 1 \le i \le m, \; 1 \le j \le n\}.$$
$$\Pi(\langle n, m \rangle) = (O, H, \mu, w_0, \cdots, w_{m+5n+3}, R), \text{ with}$$
$$O = \Sigma(\langle n, m \rangle) \cup \{u_{i,j}, u'_{i,j} \mid 1 \le i \le m, \; 1 \le j \le n\}$$
$$\cup \{d_i \mid 0 \le i \le 2m + 7n + 2\} \cup \{a_i, t_i, f_i \mid 1 \le i \le n\}$$
$$\cup \{c_i \mid 1 \le i \le m\} \cup \{t, f, z, z', T, T', \text{yes}, \text{no}\},$$
$$\mu = [\, [\, \cdots [\, [\;]_0\,]_1 \cdots\;]_{m+5n+2}\,]_{m+5n+3},$$
$$w_0 = w_{m+5n+1} = d_0,$$
$$w_{m+2n+3i} = d_{m+5n}, \; 1 \le i \le n,$$
$$w_i = \lambda, i \notin \{0, m+5n+1\} \cup \{m+2n+3i \mid 1 \le i \le n\},$$
$$H = \{0, \cdots, m+5n+3\},$$

and the following rules (we also explain their use):

Generation stage
G1 $[\; d_{3i} \rightarrow a_{i+1} d_{3i+1} \;]_0,$
$[\; d_{3i+1} \rightarrow d_{3i+2} \;]_0,$
$[\; d_{3i+2} \rightarrow d_{3i+3} \;]_0, \; 0 \le i < n.$
$[\; d_{3n+i} \rightarrow d_{3n+i+1} \;]_0, \; 0 \le i < m+2n.$

We count to $m + 5n$, which is the time needed for producing all 2^n truth assignments for the n variables, as well as membrane sub-structures which will examine the truth value of formula φ for each of these truth assignments; this counting is done in the central membrane; moreover during steps $3i - 2, 1 \le i \le n$, symbols $a_1, \cdots, a_n$ are subsequently produced.

G2 $[\; a_i \;]_0 \rightarrow [\; t_i \;]_0 [\; f_i \;]_0, \; 1 \le i \le n.$

In membrane 0, we subsequently choose each variable $x_i, 1 \le i \le n$, and both values *true* and *false* are associated with it, in form of objects t_i and f_i, which are separated in two membranes with label 0. The division of membrane 0 is triggered by the objects a_i, which are introduced by the first rule from group G1 in steps $3i - 2, 1 \le i \le n$; this is important in interleaving the use of these

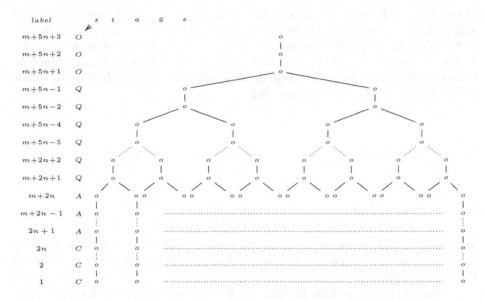

Fig. 1. The membrane structure of the system Π after $m + 5n$ steps

rules (hence the division of membrane 0) with the use of the rules of group G4, for dividing membranes placed above membrane 0.

G3 $[\, d_j \to d_{j-1} \,]_{m+2n+3i}$, $1 \le j \le m + 5n - 2$, $1 \le i \le n$,
$[\, d_0 \,]_{m+2n+3i} \to z'$, $1 \le i \le n$.

After $m + 5n$ steps, dissolution rule is applied to membranes $m + 2n + 3i$.

G4 $[\, [\ ]_i [\ ]_i \,]_{i+1} \to [\, [\ ]_i \,]_{i+1} [\, [\ ]_i \,]_{i+1}$, $0 \le i < m + 5n$.

These are division rules for membranes with label $0, 1, \cdots, m+5n$, to be used for the central membrane 0 in steps which follow the use of the first rule of type G1. The division of a membrane with label 1 is then propagated from lower levels to upper levels of the membrane structure and the membranes are continuously divided. The membrane division stops at the level where a membrane $m+2n+3i$ has been already dissolved by a rule from group G3. This results in the structure as shown in Fig. 1 after $m + 5n$ steps.

G5 $[\, d_{m+5n} \,]_0 \to T$.

After $m + 5n$ steps, each copy of membrane with label 0 is dissolved and the contents is released into the surrounding membrane, which is labeled with 1.

Assignments stage
A1 $[\, t_i \to t' \,]_{2i-1}$,
$[\, t' \,]_{2i-1} \to z$,
$[\, f_i \,]_{2i-1} \to f'$,
$[\, f' \to z \,]_{2i}$,
$[\, z \,]_{2i} \to z'$, $1 \le i \le n$.

Depending on the variable assignments, we need to determine what clauses are satisfied. For a variable x_i, this is done in membranes $2i - 1$ and $2i$. The objects encoding the problem propagate through the membrane structure: object t_i dissolves membrane $2i - 1$ after one step, and then it dissolves membrane $2i$ immediately, while object f_i dissolves membrane $2i - 1$ immediately, and then it dissolves membrane $2i$ after one step.

A2 $[\ v_{i,j} \to u_{i,j}\ ]_{2i-1}$,
$[\ v'_{i,j} \to u'_{i,j}\ ]_{2i-1}$, $1 \le i \le n, 1 \le j \le m$.

Once in membrane $2i - 1$, objects $v_{i,j}$ and $v'_{i,j}$ wait for one step.

A3 $[\ u'_{i,j} \to \lambda\ ]_{2i-1}$,
$[\ u_{i,j} \to c_i\ ]_{2i-1}$,
$[\ u_{i,j} \to \lambda\ ]_{2i}$,
$[\ u'_{i,j} \to c_i\ ]_{2i}$, $1 \le i \le n, 1 \le j \le m$.

If membrane $2i-1$ is not in the meantime, then the objects encoding the instance of SAT evolve according to the true value of x_i, otherwise, they evolve according to the false value of x_i.

At the end of this routine (it takes $3n$ steps), a membrane with label $2n + 1$ which contains all the symbols $c_1, \cdots, c_m$, corresponds to the truth assignment satisfying all clauses, hence it satisfies formula φ, and vice-versa.

Checking stage
C1 $[\ c_i\ ]_{2n+i} \to c_i$, $1 \le i \le m$.

A membrane with label $2n+i$, $1 \le i \le m$, is dissolved if and only if c_i appears in it (i.e., clause C_i is satisfied by the current truth assignment); if this is the case, the truth assignment associated with the membrane is released in the surrounding membrane. Otherwise, the truth assignment remains blocked in membrane $2n+i$ and never used at the next steps by the membranes placed above.

C2 $[\ T\ ]_{m+2n+1} \to T$.

The fact the object T appears in the membrane with the label $m + 2n + 1$ means that there is a truth assignment which satisfies the formula φ. In this case, the membrane with label $m + 2n + 1$ is dissolved and the contents are released into the membrane with label $m + 2n + 2$. Otherwise, the formula is not satisfiable, and the membrane with label $m + 2n + 1$ will not dissolve.

Quantifier stage
Q1 $[\ T\ ]_{m+2n+6i+1} \to T'$,
$[\ T\ ]_{m+2n+6i+2} \to T$,
$[\ T' \to \lambda\ ]_{m+2n+6i+2}$, $1 \le 2i \le m$.

The universal gate of the formula is simulated by dissolution of two membranes: this happens if and only if two copies of T are present. One copy dissolves membrane $m+2n+6i+1$ and is erased while the other copy dissolves membrane $m+2n+6i+2$ and sends one copy of T outside; otherwise the computation in this gate stops without sending any object out. Recall that membrane $m+2n+6i+3$ has been erased by rule from group G3.

Q2 $[\,T\,]_{m+2n+6i+4} \rightarrow T'$,
$[\,T'\,]_{m+2n+6i+5} \rightarrow T$,
$[\,T \rightarrow \lambda\,]_{m+2n+6i+5}$, $1 \leq 2i \leq m$.

The existential gate of the formula is simulated by dissolution of two membranes: this happens if and only at least one copy of T is present. One copy dissolves membrane $m + 2n + 6i + 4$ and then it also dissolves membrane $m + 2n + 6i + 2$, (thus sending one copy of T outside) while the other copy (if exists) is erased; if no copy of T is present, no rule is applied, so the gate sends nothing outside. Recall that membrane $m + 2n + 6i + 6$ has been erased by rule from group G3.

Q3 $[\,d_i \rightarrow d_{i+1}\,]_{m+5n+1}$, $0 \leq i \leq 2m + 8n + 1$.

At the same time as the membrane with label $m + 5n + 1$ is dissolved (at step $2m + 8n + 1$), the object $d_{2m+8n+1}$ evolves to $d_{2m+8n+2}$, and then released to the membrane with label $m + 5n + 2$.

Output stage
O1 $[\,d_{2m+8n+2}\,]_{m+5n+2} \rightarrow$ **yes**.
O2 $[\,a\,]_{m+8n+3} \rightarrow [\,\,]_{m+5n+3} a$, $a \in \{$**yes**, **no**$\}$.

In the next two steps, the object **yes** is produced, and sent to the environment.

O3 $[\,d_{2m+8n+2}\,]_{m+5n+1} \rightarrow$ **no**.
O4 $[\,$**no**$\,]_{m+5n+2} \rightarrow$ **no**.

If the formula is not satisfiable, then the object $d_{2m+8n+1}$ remains in the membrane with label $m + 5n + 1$, which produces the object *no*, ejecting it into the membrane with label $m + 5n + 2$, then into the membrane with label $m + 5n + 3$, finally into the environment.

Therefore, in $2m + 8n + 3$ the system halts and sends into the environment one of the objects **yes**, **no**, indicating whether or not the formula φ^* is satisfiable.

It is easy to see that the system Π can be constructed in a polynomial time starting from numbers m, n, and this concludes the proof.[1]   □

This result can be contrasted to the result from [1] in the following way: we used membrane dissolution instead of polarization. One of the techniques used to achieve this goal is: instead of modifying the (polarization of the) membrane and checking it later, we use two membranes and control the time when the inner membrane is dissolved. In this case checking the membrane polarization is replaced by checking whether it exists, i.e., checking the membrane label.

This is used in the Assignments stage (truth-value objects influence the input objects, rules A1 and A3). In the Checking stage the dissolution picks one object

---

[1] The systems constructed above are deterministic.

It is possible to speed up the system; the present construction is made for an easier explanation: the stages do not overlap in time.

The only rules of type (c_0) in the system are O2, executed in the last step. Hence, these rules are not important for deciding whether φ^* is satisfied; they are only needed to send the answer out of the skin membrane.

c_i, performing the "if" behavior. In the Output stage the dissolution makes it possible to send exactly one of objects yes and no out. in the Quantifier stage OR and AND are implemented by counting until one or two by dissolution.

Another way the dissolution is used in the construction is to stop (by rules G3) the propagation of the non-elementary division (rules G4) from the elementary membranes outwards, to obtain the structure on Figure 1, because the rule is more restricted then in the case with polarizations.

The dissolution is crucial here since, after membrane polarizations have been removed, it remained the only way the objects can influence the behavior of other objects; otherwise the behavior of each object is easily decidable, see [6]. From Theorem 2, since the complexity class $\mathbf{PMC}_{\mathcal{AM}^0(+d,+ne)}$ is closed under polynomial time reductions, we have the following result.

Corollary 1. $\mathbf{PSPACE} \subseteq \mathbf{PMC}_{\mathcal{AM}^0(+d,+ne)}$.

4 Conclusions

The framework of recognizer P systems with active membranes and with three electrical charges does not seem precise enough to describe classical complexity classes below **PSPACE**. In [6], [7] one has considered weaker variants of these P systems removing polarizations but keeping other usual ingredients associated with active membranes (no cooperation, no priorities, and without changing the labels of membranes). In [6] one shows that in the above framework but without using dissolution rules, it is possible to solve in polynomial time only decision problems which are tractable in the standard sense. Moreover, if we consider membrane dissolution rules then we can solve **NP**–complete problems in polynomial time and in a semi–uniform way and using division for elementary and non–elementary membranes, see [3] and [6].

In this paper we give a polynomial time and uniform solution of QSAT, a well-known **PSPACE**–complete problem, through a family of recognizer P systems using polarizationless active membranes, dissolution rules and division for elementary and non–elementary membranes. It remain as an open question if the division for non–elementary membranes can be removed. Our result thus presents an interesting counterpart of the result from [1], compared to which the polarizations have been replaced by membrane dissolution.

References

1. Alhazov, A., Martín-Vide, C., Pan, L.: Solving a PSPACE-complete problem by P systems with restricted active membranes. Fundamenta Informaticae 58(2), 67–77 (2003)
2. Alhazov, A., Martín–Vide, C., Pan, L.: Solving graph problems by P systems with restricted elementary active membranes. In: Jonoska, N., Păun, G., Rozenberg, G. (eds.) Aspects of Molecular Computing. LNCS, vol. 2950, pp. 1–22. Springer, Heidelberg (2003)
3. Alhazov, A., Pan, L., Păun, G.: Trading Polarizations for Labels in P Systems with Active Membranes. Acta Informaticae 41(2-3), 111–144 (2004)

4. Alhazov, A., Pérez-Jiménez, M.J.: Uniform Solution to QSAT Using Polarizationless Active Membranes. In: Gutiérrez-Naranjo, M.A., Păun, G., Riscos-Núñez, A., Romero-Campero, F.J. (eds.) Fourth Brainstorming Week on Membrane Computing, Sevilla, vol. I, pp. 29–40. Fénix Editora (2006)
5. Gutiérrez-Naranjo, M.A., Pérez-Jiménez, M.J., Riscos-Núñez, A.: A fast P system for finding a balanced 2-partition. Soft Computing 9(9), 673–678 (2005)
6. Gutiérrez-Naranjo, M.A., Pérez-Jiménez, M.J., Riscos-Núñez, A., Romero-Campero, F.J.: On the power of dissolution in P systems with active membranes. In: Freund, R., Păun, G., Rozenberg, G., Salomaa, A. (eds.) WMC 2005. LNCS, vol. 3850, pp. 224–240. Springer, Heidelberg (2006)
7. Gutiérrez-Naranjo, M.A., Pérez-Jiménez, M.J., Riscos-Núñez, A., Romero-Campero, F.J.: P systems with active membranes, without polarizations and without dissolution: A characterization of P. In: Calude, C.S., Dinneen, M.J., Păun, G., Pérez-Jiménez, M.J., Rozenberg, G. (eds.) UC 2005. LNCS, vol. 3699, pp. 105–116. Springer, Heidelberg (2005)
8. Papadimitriou, C.H.: Computational Complexity. Addison–Wesley, Reading (1995)
9. Păun, G.: Computing with membranes. Journal of Computer and System Sciences 61(1), 108–143 (2000)
10. Păun, G.: P systems with active membranes: Attacking NP–complete problems. Journal of Automata, Languages and Combinatorics 6(1), 75–90 (2001)
11. Păun, G., Suzuki, Y., Tanaka, H., Yokomori, T.: On the power of membrane division in P systems. Theoretical Computer Science 324(1), 61–85 (2004)
12. Pérez–Jiménez, M.J.: An approach to computational complexity in Membrane Computing. In: Mauri, G., Păun, G., Pérez-Jiménez, M.J., Rozenberg, G., Salomaa, A. (eds.) WMC 2004. LNCS, vol. 3365, pp. 85–109. Springer, Heidelberg (2005)
13. Pérez-Jiménez, M.J., Riscos-Núñez, A.: Solving the Subset-Sum problem by active membranes. New Generation Computing 23(4), 367–384 (2005)
14. Pérez-Jiménez, M.J., Riscos-Núñez, A.: A linear–time solution to the Knapsack problem using P systems with active membranes. In: Martín-Vide, C., Mauri, G., Păun, G., Rozenberg, G., Salomaa, A. (eds.) Membrane Computing. LNCS, vol. 2933, pp. 250–268. Springer, Heidelberg (2004)
15. Pérez-Jiménez, M.J., Romero-Campero, F.J.: Solving the Bin Packing problem by recognizer P systems with active membranes. In: Păun, G., Riscos-Núñez, A., Romero-Jiménez, A., Sancho-Caparrini, F. (eds.) Proceedings of the Second Brainstorming Week on Membrane Computing, (Report RGNC 01/04, University of Seville) pp. 414–430 (2004)
16. Pérez-Jiménez, M.J., Romero-Jiménez, A., Sancho-Caparrini, F.: A polynomial complexity class in P systems using membrane division. In: Proceedings of the 5th Workshop on Descriptional Complexity of Formal Systems, DCFS 2003, Budapest. Computer and Automation Research Institute of the Hungarian Academy of Sciences, pp. 284–294 (2003)
17. Pérez-Jiménez, M.J., Romero-Jiménez, A., Sancho-Caparrini, F.: Complexity classes in cellular computing with membranes. Natural Computing 2(3), 265–285 (2003)
18. Pérez-Jiménez, M.J., Romero–Campero, F.J.: Attacking the Common Algorithmic Problem by recognizer P systems. In: Margenstern, M. (ed.) MCU 2004. LNCS, vol. 3354, pp. 304–315. Springer, Heidelberg (2005)
19. Sosík, P.: The computational power of cell division. Natural Computing 2(3), 287–298 (2003)

Satisfiability Parsimoniously Reduces to the Tantrix™ Rotation Puzzle Problem*

Dorothea Baumeister and Jörg Rothe

Institut für Informatik, Universität Düsseldorf, 40225 Düsseldorf, Germany

Abstract. Holzer and Holzer [HH04] proved that the Tantrix™ rotation puzzle problem is NP-complete. They also showed that for infinite rotation puzzles, this problem becomes undecidable. We study the counting version and the unique version of this problem. We prove that the satisfiability problem parsimoniously reduces to the Tantrix™ rotation puzzle problem. In particular, this reduction preserves the uniqueness of the solution, which implies that the unique Tantrix™ rotation puzzle problem is as hard as the unique satisfiability problem, and so is DP-complete under polynomial-time randomized reductions, where DP is the second level of the boolean hierarchy over NP.

Keywords: computational complexity, rotation puzzle, tiling of the plane, parsimonious reduction, counting problem.

1 Introduction

Tantrix™ is a puzzle game played with hexagonal tiles firmly arranged in the plane that each can be rotated around their axes. There are four different types of tiles (called *Sint*, *Brid*, *Chin*, and *Rond*, see Figure 1) that differ by the form of the three colored lines they each have, where colors are chosen among *red*, *yellow*, *blue*, and *green*. The objective of the game is to find a rotation of the given tiles so as to create long lines and loops of the same color. Since its invention in 1991 by Mike McManaway from New Zealand and its commercial launch, the Tantrix™ rotation puzzle has become extremely popular and commercially successful.

Holzer and Holzer [HH04] considered two variants of the Tantrix™ rotation puzzle problem, one with finitely many and one with infinitely many tiles in a given problem instance. They proved that the finite variant of this problem is NP-complete by reducing the NP-complete boolean circuit satisfiability problem (restricted to circuits with AND and NOT gates only) to it. They also showed that the infinite variant of the Tantrix™ rotation puzzle problem is undecidable, again employing a circuit construction. For other results on the complexity of problems related to Domino-like strategy games, we refer to Grädel [Grä90].

We consider two variants of the finite Tantrix™ rotation puzzle problem, its counting version and its unique version. The counting problem asks for the

---

* Supported in part by DFG grant RO 1202/9-3 and the Alexander von Humboldt Foundation's TransCoop program. URL: http://ccc.cs.uni-duesseldorf.de/~rothe

J. Durand-Lose and M. Margenstern (Eds.): MCU 2007, LNCS 4664, pp. 134–145, 2007.

number of solutions of a given rotation puzzle instance. The unique problem asks whether a given rotation puzzle instance has exactly one solution. Our main result is that the satisfiability problem parsimoniously reduces to the Tantrix™ rotation puzzle problem.

The class #P was introduced by Valiant [Val79] to capture the complexity of counting the solutions of NP problems. Parsimonious reductions between NP counting problems—such as ours—preserve the precise number of solutions. This is an important property for at least two reasons. First, the structure of the solution space is preserved by a parsimonious reduction from A to B, since solutions of A are mapped bijectively to solutions of B in polynomial time. Second, parsimonious reductions can be used to prove lower bounds for the unique versions of NP problems. In particular, we apply our above-mentioned parsimonious reduction to prove that the unique Tantrix™ rotation puzzle problem is DP-complete[1] under polynomial-time randomized reductions in the sense of Valiant and Vazirani [VV86].

While many standard reductions between NP-complete problems are easily seen to be parsimonious, there are a number of exceptions. For example, Barbanchon [Bar04] showed that the (planar) satisfiability problem is parsimoniously polynomial-time reducible to the (planar) 3-colorability problem via a rather sophisticated construction. Other examples of nontrivial parsimonious reductions can be found in [Pap94]. Holzer and Holzer's reduction, however, is not parsimonious [HH04]. The main purpose of this paper is to show how to modify their reduction so as to make it parsimonious.

2 Preliminaries

2.1 Definition of Some Complexity-Theoretic Notions

Fix the alphabet $\Sigma = \{0,1\}$, and let Σ^* denote the set of strings over Σ. As is common, decision problems are suitably encoded as languages over Σ. For any language $A \subseteq \Sigma^*$, let $\|A\|$ denote the number of elements in A. For some background on computational complexity theory, we refer to any standard textbook of this field, e.g., [Pap94, Rot05]. Let NP denote the class of problems solvable in nondeterministic polynomial time. Generalizing NP, Papadimitriou and Yannakakis [PY84] introduced the class DP $= \{A - B \mid A, B \in NP\}$ to capture the complexity of NP-hard or coNP-hard problems that seemingly are neither in NP nor in coNP. In particular, they showed that DP contains a number of *uniqueness problems*, *critical graph problems*, and *exact optimization problems*, and they showed some of these problems complete for DP; see also the recent survey [RR06]. Note that DP was later generalized by Cai et al. [CGH⁺88, CGH⁺89], who introduced the boolean hierarchy over NP. Note that DP is the second level of this hierarchy.

---

[1] DP is the set of differences of any two NP sets [PY84]; so NP $\subseteq$ DP, and it is considered most unlikely that both classes are equal.

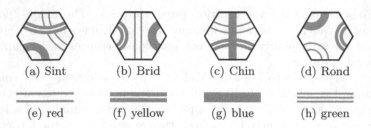

Fig. 1. Tantrix^{TM} tiles and colors

In his seminal paper, Valiant [Val79] initiated the study of counting problems and introduced the important counting class #P. Members of #P are referred to as NP *counting problems.* A well-known NP counting problem is #SAT, the counting version of the satisfiability problem: Given a boolean formula, how many satisfying assignments does it have?

Definition 1 (Valiant [Val79]). *Let NPTM be a shorthand for nondeterministic polynomial-time Turing machine. For any NPTM M and any input x, let $acc_M(x)$ denote the number of accepting computation paths of $M(x)$, i.e., acc_M is a function mapping from Σ^* to $\mathbb{N}$. Define the function class* #P = $\{acc_M \mid M$ *is an NPTM*$\}$.

We now define the notion of *(polynomial-time) parsimonious reducibility,* which will be used to compare the hardness of solving NP counting problems. Intuitively, an NP counting problem f parsimoniously reduces to an NP counting problem g if the instances of f can be transformed into instances of g such that the number of solutions of f are preserved under this transformation.

Definition 2. *Let f and g be any two given counting problems mapping from Σ^* to $\mathbb{N}$. We say f (polynomial-time) parsimoniously reduces to g (denoted by $f \leq^p_{par} g$) if there exists a polynomial-time computable function ρ such that for each $x \in \Sigma^*$, $f(x) = g(\rho(x))$. If F and G are the NP decision problems corresponding to the NP counting problems f and g with $f \leq^p_{par} g$, we will also say that F parsimoniously reduces to G.*

2.2 Variants of the Tantrix Rotation Puzzle Problem

The Tantrix^{TM} rotation puzzle has four kinds of hexagonal tiles—the *Sint,* the *Brid,* the *Chin,* and the *Rond*—each of which has three colored lines, where the colors are chosen among *red, yellow, blue,* and *green,* see Figure 1(a)–(d). This gives a total of 56 different tiles. Since we aren't using actually colored figures, we encode the colors as shown in Figure 1(e)–(h).

Holzer and Holzer [HH04] showed that the decision problem Tantrix^{TM} rotation puzzle (which we denote by TRP, for short) is NP-complete. In this paper, we introduce and study #TRP, the counting version of TRP.

We now briefly describe the formalism introduced by Holzer and Holzer [HH04] to define TRP, since the same formalism is useful for defining #TRP. In

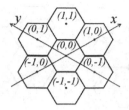

Fig. 2. A two-dimensional hexagonal coordinate system

particular, to represent the instances of both these problems, a two-dimensional hexagonal coordinate system is used, see Figure 2. In this system, two distinct pairs $a = (u, w)$ and $b = (v, x)$ from $\mathbb{Z}^2$ are adjacent if and only if one of the following four conditions is satisfied:

1. $u = v$ and $|w - x| = 1$,
2. $|u - v| = 1$ and $w = x$,
3. $u - v = 1$ and $w - x = 1$, and
4. $u - v = -1$ and $w - x = -1$.

Let T be the set of all Tantrix™ tiles. Let $\mathcal{A}$ be a (partial) function mapping the elements of $\mathbb{Z}^2$ to T, i.e., for those $v \in \mathbb{Z}^2$ on which $\mathcal{A}$ is defined, $\mathcal{A}(v)$ is the type of the tile located at v. The set $shape(\mathcal{A}) = \{v \in \mathbb{Z}^2 \mid \mathcal{A}(v) \text{ is defined}\}$ gives the positions in $\mathbb{Z}^2$ at which tiles are placed. For all $a, b \in shape(\mathcal{A})$, $\mathcal{A}(a)$ is adjacent to $\mathcal{A}(b)$ if and only if a is adjacent to b.

TRP is then defined as follows (note that the initial orientation is not specified, as it doesn't matter for the question of whether the decision problem TRP is solvable) [HH04]:[2]

Name: Tantrix™ Rotation Puzzle (TRP, for short).
Given: A finite shape function $\mathcal{A} : \mathbb{Z}^2 \to T$, appropriately encoded as a string.
Question: Is the rotation puzzle defined by $\mathcal{A}$ solvable, i.e., does there exist a rotation of the given tiles at their positions such that at each joint edge of two adjacent tiles the corresponding colors match?

For any given TRP instance $\mathcal{A}$, a *solution of $\mathcal{A}$* is a specification (in some appropriate encoding) of each tile in $shape(\mathcal{A})$ in some particular orientation such that for each joint edge of two adjacent tiles the corresponding colors match. Figure 3 gives an example of a rotation puzzle instance and its solution. Let $\text{SOL}_{\text{TRP}}(\mathcal{A})$ denote the set of solutions of a given TRP instance $\mathcal{A}$. So $\mathcal{A}$ is in TRP (viewed as a language) if and only if the set $\text{SOL}_{\text{TRP}}(\mathcal{A})$ is nonempty.

We now define the counting version and the unique version of TRP, which will be considered in Sections 3 and 4.

---

[2] As noted by Holzer and Holzer [HH04], there is a difference between their definition of TRP, which allows holes in TRP instances, and the original Tantrix™ game, which does not allow holes. The problem of whether the analog of TRP *without* holes still is NP-complete is open.

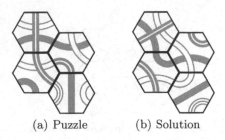

(a) Puzzle   (b) Solution

Fig. 3. An example of a TRP instance and its solution

Definition 3.   *1. The* Tantrix^{TM} *rotation puzzle counting problem is the function* $\#TRP \colon \Sigma^* \to \mathbb{N}$ *defined by*

$$\#TRP(\mathcal{A}) = \|\mathrm{Sol}_{TRP}(\mathcal{A})\|,$$

where we assume that inputs $\mathcal{A}$ are appropriately encoded as strings in Σ^* and function values are nonnegative integers (represented in binary).
   2. The unique Tantrix^{TM} *rotation puzzle problem is defined by*

$$Unique\text{-}TRP = \{\mathcal{A} \mid \#TRP(\mathcal{A}) = 1\}.$$

3   Satisfiability Parsimoniously Reduces to the Tantrix^{TM} Rotation Puzzle Problem

In this section, we prove our main result:

Theorem 4. $\#SAT \leq^p_{par} \#TRP.$

The proof of Theorem 4 will be presented in Sections 3.1, 3.2, 3.3, and 3.4.

To prove TRP NP-complete, Holzer and Holzer [HH04] gave a reduction from the NP-complete problem Circuit$_{\wedge,\neg}$-SAT (see Cook [Coo71]): Given a boolean circuit C with AND and NOT gates, does there exist a truth assignment to the input gates of C such that C under this assignment evaluates to *true*? Holzer and Holzer's construction simulates the computation of such a boolean circuit C by a Tantrix^{TM} rotation puzzle such that C evaluates to *true* for some assignment to its variables if and only if the puzzle has a solution.

Our construction will modify Holzer and Holzer's reduction [HH04] in such a way that there is a one-to-one correspondence between the solutions of the given Circuit$_{\wedge,\neg}$-SAT instance and the solutions of the resulting rotation puzzle instance; hence our reduction is parsimonious. The reduction employs planar cross-over gates (consisting of AND and NOT gates only) to avoid wire crossings of the given circuit; for technical details and examples, see [HH04].

To simulate the circuit by a rotation puzzle, a number of subpuzzles are used. The color blue in these subpuzzles will represent the truth value *true*, and the color red will represent *false*. This color encoding at the inputs and outputs of the subpuzzles thus represent the truth values of the circuit's gates and wires.

Due to space limitations, the original subpuzzles from [HH04] that are given in the full version of this paper [BR07] to allow comparison, are omitted here. Our arguments about the original subpuzzles refer to the notation used in [BR07].

3.1 Wire Subpuzzles

Wires of the circuit are simulated by the subpuzzles WIRE, MOVE, and COPY.

Figure 4 shows the modified WIRE subpuzzle, which simply represents a vertical wire. Longer wires can be built by using several WIRE subpuzzles. A single WIRE has height two, which implies that all other subpuzzles must have even height. (Otherwise it wouldn't be possible to simulate a circuit by a rotation puzzle.) It is easy to see that the original WIRE subpuzzle from [HH04] (see also [BR07, Figure 11]) has more than one valid solution with the input colors blue and red. In particular, tile a and tile b have two possible orientations for each input color, so there are four possible solutions. However, by inserting a *Rond* in the colors blue, red, and green at position x, we obtain a unique solution. If the input color is blue, there is a blue vertical line. Tiles a and b now must have red at the edge adjacent to tile x, since x doesn't have yellow. If the input color is red, tiles a and b have a choice between either blue or yellow for the edge joint with x. Again, since x doesn't have yellow, the solution is unique.

Figure 5 presents the modified MOVE subpuzzle by which a wire can be moved by two positions to the left or to the right. Consider a move to the right (a move to the left can be handled analogously). The original MOVE subpuzzle from [HH04] (see also [BR07, Figure 12]) has again more than one valid solution. To eliminate this ambiguity, we do the following. Suppose the input color is blue. Since red and yellow are symmetric in all tiles of the original MOVE subpuzzle (see [BR07, Figure 12]), there are two symmetric solutions. Also, tiles a and i have two possible orientations for each such solution. However, inserting a *Sint* in the colors red, yellow, and blue at position x enforces that the tile b has yellow at the edge adjacent to x, since e has blue at the edge adjacent to x for both possibilities. Fixing the orientation of tile b also fixes the orientation of all other tiles except a and i. Moreover, a's orientation is also uniquely determined by the tile at position x. First, for the joint edge of tiles a and x, one can choose among the colors red and yellow, but since yellow already must be the color x uses for

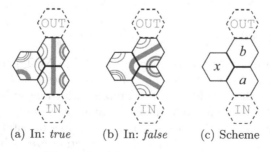

(a) In: *true*   (b) In: *false*   (c) Scheme

Fig. 4. Modified subpuzzle WIRE

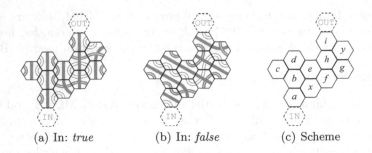

(a) In: *true*   (b) In: *false*   (c) Scheme

Fig. 5. Modified subpuzzle MOVE

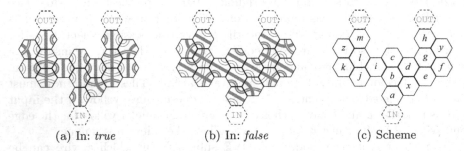

(a) In: *true*   (b) In: *false*   (c) Scheme

Fig. 6. Modified subpuzzle COPY

the edge joint with b, x must have red as the color for the edge joint with a. Second, to uniquely determine the orientation of tile i, insert another *Sint* in the colors red, yellow, and blue at position y. Since tile h has color yellow at the edge joint with y, symmetric arguments as above work for fixing the orientation of i via y. The case of red being the input color can be handled similarly.

Finally, Figure 6 presents the modified COPY subpuzzle, which can be used to "split" a wire into two copies. Its structure is akin to the MOVE subpuzzle, though it is wider and has two outputs. Due to symmetry, the original COPY subpuzzle from [HH04] (see also [BR07, Figure 13]) has again more than one valid solution. However, we can enforce a unique solution (for both input colors, blue and red) by inserting three asymmetric *Sint* tiles in the colors red, blue, and yellow at positions x, y, and z. The argument then is similar to the one for the MOVE subpuzzle.

3.2   Gate Subpuzzles

In order to simulate a boolean circuit with AND and NOT gates, we need the subpuzzles AND and NOT corresponding to these gates.

Figure 7 presents the modified NOT subpuzzle, which negates the input value by flipping the colors blue and red. In the original NOT subpuzzle from [HH04] (see also [BR07, Figure 14]), there is only one possible orientation for the tiles e, f, and g, since the tiles c, b, and f do not contain green. Thus tiles c and b must have red at the edge adjacent to tile e. It follows that for each input

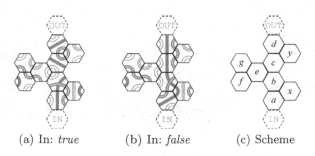

(a) In: *true*   (b) In: *false*   (c) Scheme

Fig. 7. Modified subpuzzle NOT

color only two orientations are possible for tiles a and d. Inserting a *Brid* in the colors blue, yellow, and green at position x uniquely determines the orientation of tile a. Since x does not contain red, we have that tile a is forced to choose yellow at the edge adjacent to x if the input color was blue. On the other hand, if the input color was red, a has a choice between blue and green for this color because x has blue at the edge joint with b. However, since a doesn't contain green, this uniquely determines the orientation of a. The orientation of tile d can be made unique by inserting a *Rond* in the colors yellow, red, and green at position y. For both input colors, c has yellow at the edge joint with y, so d and y can share either yellow or green. Since tile d contains no green, its orientation is uniquely determined. Thus, for both input colors, a valid solution of the NOT subpuzzle is uniquely determined.

Figure 8 presents the somewhat more complicated modified AND subpuzzles. Similarly as for the original NOT subpuzzle, in the original AND subpuzzle from [HH04] (see also [BR07, Figure 15]) the tiles o, p, and q have only one possible orientation, due to the colors at the joint edges with tiles m and n. The output of these subpuzzles is determined by the orientation of tile c. If c's color at the edge joint with j is blue, then the output color also is blue. This is the case exactly if both inputs have color blue. In all other cases, the color at the joint edge of c and j is yellow, which implies that the output color will be red. For each of these subpuzzles' upper part, the orientations are determined by the color at the joint edge of c and j. For their lower parts, however, several solutions are possible. Again, there are two possible orientations of the tiles a and d. Since the tiles h and i have only one connection to the remaining subpuzzle each, they too have two possible orientations, independent of the input color. However, since the tiles h and i do not contain blue, the input color uniquely determines the orientation of tiles b and e. The tiles c, g, and f have a different orientation for each combination of input colors, which implies that the correct output color is passed on by tile j to the upper part of the subpuzzle. However, two orientations are possible for tile g, which is a *Rond*. Due to its symmetry and since its neighbors are c and f, it cannot receive a unique orientation by the colors at the joint edges with these neighbors in the original subpuzzle (see [BR07, Figure 15]).

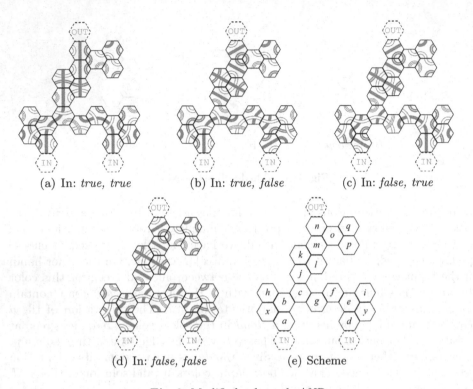

(a) In: *true, true*   (b) In: *true, false*   (c) In: *false, true*

(d) In: *false, false*   (e) Scheme

Fig. 8. Modified subpuzzle AND

The orientations of tiles a and h (respectively, of tiles d and i) can be made unique by inserting a *Sint* in the colors blue, yellow, and red at position x (respectively, at position y). The orientation of tile g cannot be made unique by inserting another tile. For these subpuzzles, there exist four possible combinations of input colors, and because of the given colors at joint edges it is not possible to insert a new tile adjacent to g. This implies that we need to replace existing tiles by different tiles. So, to obtain a unique solution, we replace the color yellow by green in the tiles j and c, and tile g is replaced by a *Sint* in the colors green, blue, and red. Replacing yellow by green in j and c is easily possible. Tile j has yellow at the edge joint with c only in some cases, and c's yellow is also replaced by green. Also, tile c has yellow at the edge adjacent to g, which now is green at this edge. By the new tile at position g, the orientation of f changes if the right input color is blue, since yellow is no longer possible as the color for the joint edge. These replacements do not alter the behavior of the AND subpuzzles, other than giving the desired effect that solutions now are unique.

The shapes of the single subpuzzles have changed by these replacements, which might imply unintended interactions between various subpuzzles. However, essentially by the argument given by Holzer and Holzer [HH04] about the minimal horizontal distance between any two wires and/or gates being at least four, such undesired interactions do not occur.

3.3   Input and Output Subpuzzles

The BOOL subpuzzle represents the input gates of the circuit. This subpuzzle has only two valid solutions, either its output is blue (if the corresponding input variable is *true*), or it is red (if the corresponding input variable is *false*). This ensures that subsequent subpuzzles can obtain only these two colors as input.

The subpuzzle TEST tests whether the function value computed by the circuit is *true* or not. This subpuzzle has only one valid solution, namely that its input is blue (which means that the circuit evaluates to *true*).

Obviously, neither of these subpuzzles, BOOL and TEST, do require any modification, and they are the only subpuzzles from [HH04] not modified. For completeness, we present them in Figures 9 and 10.

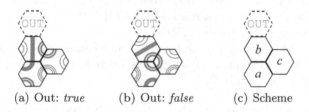

(a) Out: *true*   (b) Out: *false*   (c) Scheme

Fig. 9. Subpuzzle BOOL, see [HH04]

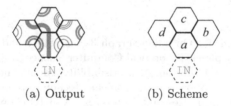

(a) Output   (b) Scheme

Fig. 10. Subpuzzle TEST, see [HH04]

3.4   Proof of Theorem 4

We are now ready to prove Theorem 4. Let SAT denote the satisfiability problem.

Lemma 5. *SAT parsimoniously reduces to Circuit$_{\wedge,\neg}$-SAT.*

Proof. Note that the problems SAT and Circuit-SAT (which is the same as Circuit$_{\wedge,\neg}$-SAT except with OR gates allowed as well) are equivalent under parsimonious reductions [Pap94]. Since OR gates can be expressed by AND and NOT gates without changing the number of solutions, this gives a parsimonious reduction from SAT to Circuit$_{\wedge,\neg}$-SAT.   ❑

Now, the parsimonious reduction from SAT to TRP immediately follows from Lemma 5 and the construction and the arguments presented in Sections 3.1, 3.2, and 3.3.

4   The Unique Tantrix™ Rotation Puzzle Problem Is DP-Complete Under Randomized Reductions

Valiant and Vazirani introduced *randomized polynomial-time reductions* in their work showing that NP is as easy as detecting unique solutions [VV86]. We will use $\leq^p_{ran}$ to denote their type of reductions. In particular, Valiant and Vazirani [VV86] proved that Unique-SAT, the unique version of SAT, is $\leq^p_{ran}$-complete in DP (see also Chang, Kadin, and Rohatgi [CKR95]).

Theorem 6.   *1. Unique-SAT parsimoniously reduces to Unique-TRP.*
2. Unique-TRP is DP-complete under $\leq^p_{ran}$-reductions.

Proof. To prove the first part, note that by Lemma 5 and Theorem 4, we obtain a parsimonious reduction from SAT to TRP. It follows that Unique-SAT parsimoniously reduces to Unique-TRP.

The second part follows from the first part and Valiant and Vazirani's above-mentioned result that Unique-SAT is $\leq^p_{ran}$-complete in DP, and from the obvious fact that Unique-TRP is in DP. $\square$

Acknowledgments. We thank the anonymous MCU 2007 referees for their helpful comments.

References

[Bar04]   Barbanchon, R.: On unique graph 3-colorability and parsimonious reductions in the plane. Theoretical Computer Science 319(1–3), 455–482 (2004)

[BR07]   Baumeister, D., Rothe, J.: Satisfiability parsimoniously reduces to the Tantrix™ rotation puzzle problem. Technical Report cs.CC/0705.0915, ACM Computing Research Repository (CoRR) (May 2007)

[CGH⁺88]   Cai, J., Gundermann, T., Hartmanis, J., Hemachandra, L., Sewelson, V., Wagner, K., Wechsung, G.: The boolean hierarchy I: Structural properties. SIAM Journal on Computing 17(6), 1232–1252 (1988)

[CGH⁺89]   Cai, J., Gundermann, T., Hartmanis, J., Hemachandra, L., Sewelson, V., Wagner, K., Wechsung, G.: The boolean hierarchy II: Applications. SIAM Journal on Computing 18(1), 95–111 (1989)

[CKR95]   Chang, R., Kadin, J., Rohatgi, P.: On unique satisfiability and the threshold behavior of randomized reductions. Journal of Computer and System Sciences 50(3), 359–373 (1995)

[Coo71]   Cook, S.: The complexity of theorem-proving procedures. In: Proceedings of the 3rd ACM Symposium on Theory of Computing, pp. 151–158. ACM Press, New York (1971)

[Grä90]   Grädel, E.: Domino games and complexity. SIAM Journal on Computing 19(5), 787–804 (1990)

[HH04]   Holzer, M., Holzer, W.: Tantrix™ rotation puzzles are intractable. Discrete Applied Mathematics 144(3), 345–358 (2004)

[Pap94]   Papadimitriou, C.: Computational Complexity. Addison-Wesley, Reading (1994)

[PY84]   Papadimitriou, C., Yannakakis, M.: The complexity of facets (and some facets of complexity). Journal of Computer and System Sciences 28(2), 244–259 (1984)

[Rot05]   Rothe, J.: Complexity Theory and Cryptology. An Introduction to Cryptocomplexity. EATCS Texts in Theoretical Computer Science. Springer, Heidelberg (2005)

[RR06]   Riege, T., Rothe, J.: Completeness in the boolean hierarchy: Exact-Four-Colorability, minimal graph uncolorability, and exact domatic number problems – a survey. Journal of Universal Computer Science 12(5), 551–578 (2006)

[Val79]   Valiant, L.: The complexity of computing the permanent. Theoretical Computer Science 8(2), 189–201 (1979)

[VV86]   Valiant, L., Vazirani, V.: NP is as easy as detecting unique solutions. Theoretical Computer Science 47, 85–93 (1986)

Planar Trivalent Network Computation

Tommaso Bolognesi

CNR-ISTI, Istituto di Scienza e Tecnologie dell'Informazione "A. Faedo", 56124,
Pisa, Italy
T.Bolognesi@isti.cnr.it

Abstract. Confluent rewrite systems for giant trivalent networks have
been investigated by S. Wolfram as possible models of space and spacetime, in the ambitious search for the most fundamental, computational
laws of physics. We restrict here to planar trivalent nets, which are shown
to support Turing-complete computations, and take an even more radi-
cal, approach: while operating on network duals, we use just *one* elementary rewrite rule and drive its application by a simple, fully deterministic
algorithm, rather than by pattern-matching. We devise effective visual
indicators for exploring the complexity of computations with elementary
initial conditions, consisting of thousands of graphs, and expose a rich
variety of behaviors, from regular to random-like. Among their features
we study, in particular, the dimensionality of the emergent space.

Keywords: Digital physics, trivalent network, complexity indicator,
cellular automata, two-dimensional Turing machine, turmite, emergent
space.

1 Introduction

The idea that physical laws and the whole evolution of our universe ultimately
reduce just to computation was first proposed by K. Zuse in 1967 [1,2], and
later investigated by scientists such as E. Friedkin, G. 't Hooft, J. Schmidhuber,
S. Lloyd. 'Digital Physics' suggests that the entire history of the universe is
precisely captured by the discrete, deterministic output of a short program, and
has been recently further developed and popularized by S. Wolfram, with his
New Kind of Science (NKS) [3].

As of today, no small program has been identified that can reproduce, say,
some fundamental physical constants. However, an intuitively convincing argument in support of the computational physics conjecture is represented by the
spectacular properties of simple programs such as elementary cellular automaton (ECA) n. 110, in which particles emerge that seem to obey the laws of some
artificial physics [3]. A remarkable property of this elementary automaton is that
it is Turing-complete [4], and this is an obvious requirement for any candidate
computational model of physics.

A weak aspect of cellular automata is that they assume the existence of an
infinite space of cells, rather than letting space and spacetime emerge from the

J. Durand-Lose and M. Margenstern (Eds.): MCU 2007, LNCS 4664, pp. 146–157, 2007.
© Springer-Verlag Berlin Heidelberg 2007

computation itself. For this reason, [3] proposes dynamic networks as a more adequate model for fundamental physics, with three dimensional space as one of the required emergent properties.

Networks for space and spacetime: the NKS approach. NKS adopts the idea that all the features of our universe emerge purely from properties of space; at the lowest level, space could be a giant, undirected, trivalent network – a graph in which all nodes have degree three. We shall use the term *trinet* for denoting this minimally structured type of object.

The *distance* between two nodes is the length of the shortest path between them, and we say that a trinet yields a space of *dimensionality* k when, given a generic node n, the number of nodes that are at distance at most d from n grows like d^k. In spite of its simplicity, a trinet can achieve any dimensionality: a ladder-shaped trinet yields a one dimensional space, the hexagonal grid yields a two dimensional space, and so on. In general, a trinet can 'implement' the structure of any graph, by replacing any node n of degree $r > 3$ by a cycle of r trivalent nodes $n_1, ..., n_r$, where each edge originally insisting on n now insists on a different n_i. (This is similar to replacing the crossing of some roads by a roundabout.)

According to Wolfram, on a small scale the net will most likely look quite random, but on a larger scale it must be arranged so as to correspond to ordinary three-dimensional space, and this feature should be preserved by the rules that make it evolve. A variety of rewrite rules can be considered, together with policies for applying them. The most elementary rule is depicted by the shaded elements of Figure 1: in this paper, we call it *node tripartition*. This rule transforms a

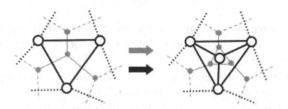

Fig. 1. Node tripartition for trinets (grey) is face tripartition for trinet duals (black)

single node into a cluster of three nodes, and, in this respect, is analogous to the rules of a *context-free* grammar. Interestingly, this transformation plays a role, with its reverse, also in the theory of Loop Quantum Gravity [1], and is one of just two fundamental transformations singled out by L. Smolin in his divulgative paper on this theory [5].

By applying the rule in parallel to each node, at each step, starting from a simple trinet such as the one formed by the edges of a tetrahedron, regular,

---

[1] Loop Quantum Gravity claims that both space and time are quantized, and uses *spin networks* (first introduced by R. Penrose in 1964) for modeling the quantum states of space. A *spin network* is a graph where every node represents an elementary "quantum of volume" and every link is a "quantum of area" delimiting it.

nested structures can be obtained. Indeed, context-free rewrite systems cannot produce, by themselves, more complexity than nesting. For this reason Wolfram investigates more elaborate trinet evolution systems, in which rewrite rules are somewhat analogous to those of *context-dependent* grammars, and transform *clusters* of nodes.

However, graph rewriting involves nondeterminism: if many rules are potentially applicable to the current trinet, which one should be applied? Using rule *priorities* does not eliminate nondeterminism completely, since even a single rule could be applicable at different locations; and insisting on applying all applicable rules simultaneously does not solve the problem, since several maximal sets of rewritings may be simultaneously enabled.

One solution explored by Wolfram consists in enriching the rewriting process by state information that records the *age* of nodes (see [3], p. 511, for details). Another approach consists in restricting to *confluent* rewrite systems, that always guarantee the same evolution in-the-large, regardless of nondeteminism in-the-small. This idea can be made precise by the notion of *causal network*, which is proposed in [3] for modeling spacetime.

A *causal network* is a directed graph in which nodes represent events (e.g. cell updating) and edges represent their causal relationship (as induced, e.g., by the cell updating process). *Causal invariance* is the property of a rewrite system to yield exactly the same causal network regardless of the rule application order. If a rewrite system is causal invariant, then its causal net retains the essential, unique partial order of events behind any contingent total ordering.

While a more detailed account of Wolfram's ideas and techniques for network rewriting is out of the scope of this paper, we wish to point out three problematic aspects of them:

- The idea to resolve nondeterminism by using time stamps appears as unnatural as, say, the requirement of a global clock for synchronizing rewritings in cellular automata.
- Causal invariance is an elegant property, that guarantees uniqueness in representing computations. However, the search for systems that guarantee this property involves a number of technical difficulties (see [3], p. 493), and the sufficient conditions "*that all the replacements that appear in the rules should be for clusters of nodes that can never overlap themselves or each other*" is perhaps too restrictive.
- While the computations of elementary cellular automata lend themselves to a very effective visualization, the direct representation of sequences of trinets of growing size is not ideal for visual inspection.

Our paper is mainly motivated by the need to overcome these limitations.

2   Planar Trinets, Duals, and Computational Universality

In this paper we shall restrict to connected, planar trinets. A graph is *planar* when it can be drawn on (or 'embedded' in) the plane so that no edges intersect;

the plane is thus partitioned into polygonal *faces*, including the external one, of infinite size. [2] In our developments we shall take advantage of the well known, *dual* representation of a planar graph, which is itself a planar graph representing the adjacency relations between faces of the original graph (Figure 1). The dual operation d is the inverse of itself: $d(d(G)) = G$. A planar trinet may in general include self-loops and/or double edges, which delimit degenerate polygonal faces. A graph without self-loops and double edges is called *simple*.

The following two facts can be easily established about planar trinets and their duals. The proofs can be found in [6].

Proposition 1. *A trinet may only have an even number of vertices.*

Proposition 2. *The dual D of a simple, planar trinet is a planar graph that satisfies the following properties: (i) D is simple; (ii) each node has degree $d \geq 3$; (iii) each face is a triangle.*

Note that the dual of a simple planar graph which is *not* a trinet, is not necessarily a simple graph. An example is provided, later, by the leftmost pair of graphs in Figure 3.

The choice of using only *planar* trinets is not excessively restrictive. First, planar trinets may well yield dimensionalities other than 2; for example, two trinets with fractal dimensionalities $\log_2 3$ and $\log_3 7$ are shown in [3] (p. 509). Second, planar trinet rewriting has maximum computing power, as established by the following proposition, whose proof is given in the Appendix.

Proposition 3. *Planar trivalent network rewriting is Turing-complete.*

3   A Fully Deterministic Planar Trinet Growth Algorithm

The system of 60 rules used in the Appendix for proving the Turing-completeness of planar trinet rewriting is fully deterministic, but the price for this is to define rules that manipulate relatively complex, ad-hoc sub-trinets. Defining a deterministic rewrite system that handles simpler sub-trinets would be much harder.

On the other hand, in line with the NKS style of investigation, we are interested in exploring the computational universe created by *very* simple rewrite systems, and in this paper, in particular, we take the extreme approach of choosing just *one* rule.

The rule we choose is node tripartition; since our algorithm is conveniently formulated in terms of trinet duals, we show in the already introduced Figure 1 how this rule operates on them, assuming *simple* trinets (in grey), thus *simple* trinet duals (in black). In terms of duals, the rule consist in placing a new node inside a face (which must be a triangle, by Proposition 2) and splitting the latter into three triangular faces. Used without further algorithmic control, the tripartition rule induces the maximum possible nondeterminism, since it can

---

[2] This external face has no real special status, as it appears by drawing the graph on a sphere.

be applied, by definition, to every node of any trinet, or, equivalently, to any face of the dual! Thus, we need a way, as simple as possible, to introduce full determinism in the rewriting process.

Informal description of the algorithm. The idea, illustrated in Figure 2, is to move across the dual graph by unit steps, from node to node, e.g. from S to T_0, without jumping, in a sort of (deterministic!) brownian motion, and to use the following simple criterion for selecting the face to split. When node T_0 is reached,

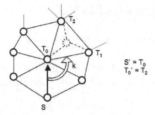

Fig. 2. Finding the triangle (T_1, T_2, T_3) for the tripartition, coming from node S

coming from node S, the cycle of radius 1 centered in T_0 is considered, and the nodes $T1$ and $T2$ at distances k and $k+1$ from S, moving counterclockwise, are selected, with T_0 itself, as the vertices of the triangle to be split. We have explored two variants, corresponding to different ways to define k. For space reasons, in this paper we discuss only the case in which k is a (small), constant nonnegative integer (see [6] for the other case). Note that k may be larger than the degree of T_0, corresponding to more than a complete cycle around that node.

The computation step assumes and returns graphs that are *simple*. Therefore, as an *initial condition* we choose the simplest trinet dual which is simple: this is the triangular graph in the lower-left corner of Figure 3. Note that the trinet corresponding to this triangle, shown above it, is not simple. Yet, any application of the node tripartition rule to this trinet yields the tetrahedron trinet, whose dual is the tetrahedron graph itself. Regardless of the different choices for k, all

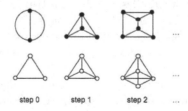

step 0   step 1   step 2   ...

Fig. 3. Trinets (black nodes) and trinet duals (white nodes) for the common prefix of the deterministic computations based on the tripartition rule

computations share the initial steps illustrated in Figure 3, and all the produced trinet duals, as well as all the corresponding trinets, are simple, except for the first trinet. Let us now analyze the computations of the algorithm, whose short *Mathematica* code can be found in [6].

4   Visual Indicators and Computations with Constant k

One of the key lessons from [3] is that important clues about the computing power of a given formal model can be obtained by inspecting the 'shape' of its computations, beyond the strategy of using it to emulate a reference model of known power. However, different models lend themselves to different visualization techniques, not all of which are as effective as the ECA diagrams thoroughly studied in [3]. Furthermore, when computations involve complex data structures, and complete visualization is unmanageable, the problem arises of which aspects to expose, as potential *indicators* of computational complexity. (A taxonomy of visual complexity indicators is proposed in [7].)

Trinet computation precisely suffers from this difficulty, since periodicity, nesting, pseudo-randomness, or other emergent properties are hardly detected by directly inspecting sequences of graphs that grow huge. But a computation of our algorithm, for a given k, is essentially a sequence of *(TND, fromNode, toNode)* triples, and this provides us with further parameters for visualizing its character, simpler than the complex adjacency-list-based graph structure *TND*. In particular, we choose two indicators:

Face size - the number of neighbors of *fromNode* in the current trinet dual
    TND, corresponding to the number of edges in the *fromFace* of the trinet.
Face id - the progressive id-number of the current face.

Both parameters offer a very localized view at the computation; the latter, in particular, is useful for revealing the extent to which the computation may go back to previously visited regions. Note that each time a polygonal face is visited, its size is increased by one.

Figure 4 shows the dynamics of our indicators for some constant values of k, and includes, for each computation, the plot of the final graph – a trinet dual.

When $k = 1$ the computation is very regular: parameter *Face size* indicates that the current *fromFace* stabilizes in three steps to an hexagon, and *Face id* indicates that the algorithm never returns to an already visited face. The graph in the right column reveals the linear overall structure of the trinet dual.

When $k = 2$ the computation is still regular, but more interesting. There is no bound to the size of the *fromFace*, and each face, except for face 1, is visited infinitely often, so that its size grows unbounded too. It turns out that face h, with $h = 2, 3, \ldots$ is the *fromFace* in steps $(2h - 3)2^n$, for $n = 1, 2, \ldots$, except that face 1, not face 2, is the *fromFace* in step 1. Face 1 is a *fromFace* only once, yet its degree is increased by 1 at each step, so that it is always the face with highest degree.

The value $k = 3$ yields a computation which stabilizes after 1229 steps to a cyclic behaviour with period 140, written, for short, 1229/140*. Similarly, case $k = 9$ yields a 7/7* computation. In case $k = 6$ the dynamics of the two indicators behaves randomly for 79 steps and then stabilizes to visiting hexagons, while never returning to already visited faces. The random-like and the regular parts are clearly visible in the final graph. The case $k = 7$ (not shown in the

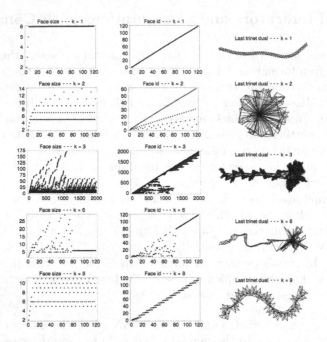

Fig. 4. 'Face size', 'Face id', and last trinet dual for computations with fixed k

picture) is quite complex, and it was necessary to look at about 30000 steps to discover a periodic, 27450/850* computation.

In conclusion, all computations illustrated for the variant of the algorithm under consideration are qualitatively similar, with the remarkable exception of the case $k = 2$, where control goes back infinitely often to infinitely many faces.

5   Emergent Dimensionality

What is the dimensionality of the spaces – the trinet dual and, more importantly, the trinet itself - created by the computations of the tripartition algorithm?

In the cases when the periodic structure of the last trinet dual graph is simple and clearly visible, it would seem natural to conclude that the graph has dimensionality one. Informally, the argument is as follows. These periodic and planar networks, whose nodes have bounded degree, appear as embedded on a cylindrical surface with uniform node density, yielding the long and thin graph structures observed in some of the plots. Then, their duals are structurally equivalent to them: periodic, with bounded-degree nodes, and embedded on the same cylindrical surface, with uniform node density. Thus, the original trinets are one-dimensional too.

Let us now present a more rigorous argument; this is useful also in light of the fact that, in some cases, we may have doubts about the precise structure of the graphs, whose appearance depends on the specific visualization method.

Plots like those for the *Face size* and *Face id* indicators, though presenting less information (and, indeed, due to that) are more effective in exposing regularity. Let us then consider a *Multiple Face id* plot that visualizes, for each step, not only the identifier of the current node T_0, but also those of the other two nodes T_1 and T_2 of the triangle being split, and the identifier X of the new node being created (an example of this type of diagram is found in [6]). Each node on the diagonal is a new node being created, while the three nodes below it, to which the new node is connected by three newly introduced edges, indentify the triangle being split. The advantage of this plot is revealed by the following proposition, which is proved in [6].

Proposition 4. *If, for a given computation c, all points of the (infinite) Multiple face id* plot fall in the region between two parallel lines, then the (infinite) trinet of c is at most one-dimensional.

It turns out that all the computations of the considered group, except for the case $k = 2$, satisfy the bounding condition of Proposition 4.

Let us finally consider the last case left (see Figure 4, $k = 2$). In the graph for the last trinet dual, a central node with high degree is clearly visible: this is node 1, whose degree is incremented at every step. We have pointed out earlier that all the other nodes have their degrees increased infinitely often, although at a rapidly decreasing rate. This circumstance is perhaps better visualized by the *radial* layout of Figure 5 (left), which hints at some nested structure. If we now

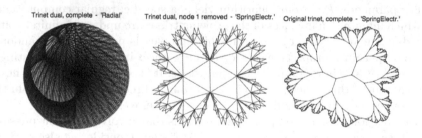

Fig. 5. 'Radial' / 'SpringElectrical' layouts for last trinet dual of a 256-step computation, with $k = 2$, and with node 1 and associated edges included / removed

remove node 1, and the edges that connect it to all the other nodes, a nested, fractal structure clearly emerges, at least when using the *SpringElectrical* layout (center). By connecting back node 1 to all the nodes in this layout, and taking the dual of the resulting graph, we readily get the original trinet, which is a double binary tree with leaves connected in circle (right).

The node count of these trinets grows exponentially with their diameter; and, given any specific (large) trinet, and a specific reference node r in it, the size of the concentric node layers around r grows exponentially too, with minor deviations as r is picked closer to the tree boundary. In this respect, the above computation is interesting because it proves that our algorithm can produce trinet-based spaces that go well beyond one dimension.

6   Conclusions

We have investigated the computing power of planar trivalent networks ('trinets'). On one hand we have proved that they are powerful in a traditional sense, since appropriate rewrite rules make them Turing-complete. On the other hand, we have explored their power by an experimental, NKS-type type of investigation and have visualized, by means of ad-hoc indicators, a variety of features. This was done by using just *one* rewrite rule – node-tripartition, a simple deterministic algorithm, and an elementary initial condition – a triangle. The contrast between this simplicity and the emergent complexity is perhaps as remarkable as that observed with cellular automata. However, the crucial advantage of the dynamic network approach over cellular automata is that space is not assumed, but *created*. We believe that, with this paper, we have proposed an original way both to create and to observe trinet-based computations, thus contributing to the study of a portion of the computational universe that, according to some researchers, might offer important insights to the ultimate law(s) of the natural universe.

Our simple indicators have been quite useful in spotting the regularity of several computations, for which plain representation of complete graphs is more costly and visually less effective. In particular, we point out two results.

1. For parameter $k = 2$ our algorithm yields a specific, regular computation in which infinitely many faces of the growing trinet are updated infinitely often: a dynamic network is obtained in which no part is permanently abandoned. This appealing property was spotted only once; it would be interesting to observe it also in random-like computations. It is remarkable that the nested structure of this trinet (Figure 5) be obtained directly by an algorithm that operates only locally, and only with unit-step moves.

2. We have found some complex computations that involve transient phases as well as periods in the order of thousands of steps (considering also a variant not covered here). Just for comparison, the computation of ECA 110 with the elementary initial state of one black cell, has a transient of about 2500 steps, and stabilizes to a shifted-period of 240 steps. In this respect we may classify some of our computations as class 4, according to Wolfram's scheme.

One desirable result that we have not yet obtained is to find class 3 trinet computations whose random-like behavior never stabilizes, similar to ECA 30.

There are similarities between our approach and two-dimensional Turing machines, sometimes called 'turmites', which move by unit steps on an infinite grid. But with turmites, again, space is given, and its regular static structure is made of stateful cells. In our approach space is created, its topology varies, and its locations are stateless.

A side result of our paper, that might possibly have some practical application, is that every periodic portion of our computations corresponds to a regular tiling of the plane; some of these involve the usage of a finite but large set of different polygons.

In [3] it is implicitly assumed that expansion rules such as node tripartition should be complemented with rewrite rules that decrease the number of nodes in the network. An obvious extension of our work would consist in considering further rules, while still driving their application by deterministic procedures.

It may be useful to study variants of our algorithm that can handle trinets with loops and double edges. By dropping the geometric, trinet-based interpretation, and by looking at the algorithm as just an abstract list manipulation procedure, one might perhaps achieve further simplifications, and make it possible to start from even simpler initial conditions.

Acknowledgment. I wish to thank Marco Tarini, at CNR-ISTI, for several lively discussions on the topics covered in this paper, and Jason Cawley for his encouraging comments on the manuscript.

References

1. Zuse, K.: Rechnender raum. Elektronische Datenverarbeitung 8, 336–344 (1967)
2. Zuse, K.: Calculating space (rechnender raum), Tech. rep., MIT, Cambridge, Mass., technical Translation AZT-70-164-GEMIT (1970)
3. Wolfram, S.: A New Kind of Science. Wolfram Media, Inc. (2002)
4. Cook, M.: Universality in elementary cellular automata. Complex Systems 15(1), 1–40 (2004)
5. Smolin, L.: Atoms of space and time. Scientific American, 56–65 (2004)
6. Bolognesi, T.: Planar trivalent network computation, Tech. rep., CNR-ISTI, Pisa, 2006-TR-41 (December 2006)
7. Bolognesi, T.: Behavioural complexity indicators for process algebra: the NKS approach, Journal of Logic and Algebraic Programming (to appear)

7   Appendix A - Proof

Proposition 3. Planar trivalent network rewriting is Turing-complete.

Proof. It is sufficient to exhibit a planar trinet rewrite system that simulates a universal Turing machine (TM). Thus we consider the smallest known universal TM, which was introduced in [3] (p. 707), and uses a tape alphabet of 5 symbols {1,2,3,4,5} and two states {s1, s2}; Table 1 provides its transitions. Figure 6 shows a coding scheme for two-state, five-symbol TMs (which can be directly extended to any other TM). The idea is to code each cell, including a tape symbol and possibly control state information, by an *elementary* sub-trinet. The trinet in (a), shown in two possible layouts, illustrates the overall structure of a coded TM configuration. The dotted edge stands for a sequence of *at least one* of the elementary sub-trinets further detailed below, which code the cells of the TM that are explicitly assigned an initial value, or are written during

Table 1. State table for smallest universal Turing machine

	1	2	3	4	5
s_1	s_1, 2, +1	s_1, 1, +1	s_1, 1, +1	s_2, 5, +1	s_2, 4, -1
s_2	s_1, 4, -1	s_1, 1, +1	s_1, 5, +1	s_2, 5, +1	s_2, 3, -1

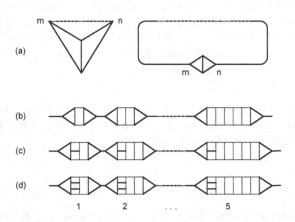

Fig. 6. Building blocks for the trinet coding a two-state, five-symbol Turing machine

the computation. The two triangles sharing one edge code the infinite portion of the tape not yet reached by the TM head, whose cells are occupied by the 'background' symbol 1. In (b) we show the coding of the pure tape symbols. In (c) (resp. (d)) we enrich this coding for representing the presence, on the tape cell, of the TM head in state s_1 (resp. s_2). Note that the elementary sub-trinets in (c) and (d) are linked only for visual clarity; such sequences may not appear in any computation, due to the presence of multiple instances of control state information!

Defining trinet rewrite rules that implement Table 1 is easy. For example, the six rewrite rules corresponding to the lower-left slot in the table, with the head in state s_2 positioned on a cell containing a '1', are depicted in Figure 7. The rewriting schema on the left, where the dots denote the coding of some of the tape symbols, accounts for five different rewrite rules; the rewriting on the right handles the case of the head moving to a portion of the tape not visited before. In conclusion, we need a total of 60 rewrite rules.

Fig. 7. Trinet rewrite rules coding the lower-left slot of Table 1

In devising the coding, one has to make sure that the rewrite rules match only the intended sub-trinets. One way to check this is to reason in terms of patterns of polygonal faces. The impossibility to apply a rewrite rule to the wrong sub-net is then guaranteed by the observation that:

- the sub-net coding a plain cell must only include polygons of arities 3 and 4;
- the sub-net coding a cell with control state $s1$ must only include polygons of arities 3, 4, 5;
- the sub-net coding a cell with control state $s2$ must only include polygons of arities 3, 4, 6;
- the net coding the whole TM configuration must always include a polygon of arity at least 8 (and the patient reader may check that the simplest initial configuration, with the tape uniformly filled by 1's, is coded by a planar trinet that already includes two octagonal faces). □

Note that the trinets used for the simulation above are simple (no loops or double edges).

On the Power of Networks
of Evolutionary Processors

Jürgen Dassow[1] and Bianca Truthe[2,*]

[1] Otto-von-Guericke-Universität Magdeburg
Fakultät für Informatik
PSF 4120, D-39016 Magdeburg, Germany
[2] Universitat Rovira i Virgili, Facultat de Lletres, GRLMC
Plaça Imperial Tàrraco 1, E-43005 Tarragona, Spain

Abstract. We discuss the power of networks of evolutionary processors where only two types of nodes are allowed. We prove that (up to an intersection with a monoid) every recursively enumerable language can be generated by a network with one deletion and two insertion nodes. Networks with an arbitrary number of deletion and substitution nodes only produce finite languages, and for each finite language one deletion node or one substitution node is sufficient. Networks with an arbitrary number of insertion and substitution nodes only generate context-sensitive languages, and (up to an intersection with a monoid) every context-sensitive language can be generated by a network with one substitution node and one insertion node.

1 Introduction

Motivated by some models of massively parallel computer architectures (see [12], [11]) networks of language processors have been introduced in [7] by E. CSUHAJ-VARJÚ and A. SALOMAA. Such a network can be considered as a graph where the nodes are sets of productions and at any moment of time a language is associated with a node. In a derivation step any node derives from its language all possible words as its new language. In a communication step any node sends those words to other nodes where the outgoing words have to satisfy an output condition given as a regular language, and any node takes words sent by the other nodes if the words satisfy an input condition also given by a regular language. The language generated by a network of language processors consists of all (terminal) words which occur in the languages associated with a given node.

Inspired by biological processes, J. CASTELLANOS, C. MARTÍN-VIDE, V. MITRANA and J. SEMPERE introduced in [4] a special type of networks of language processors which are called networks with evolutionary processors because the allowed productions model the point mutation known from biology. The sets of productions have to be substitutions of one letter by another letter or insertions of letters or deletion of letters; the nodes are then called substitution node or insertion node or deletion node,

---

* The research was supported by the Alexander von Humboldt Foundation of the Federal Republic of Germany.

J. Durand-Lose and M. Margenstern (Eds.): MCU 2007, LNCS 4664, pp. 158–169, 2007.

respectively. Results on networks of evolutionary processors can be found e. g. in [4], [5], [3], [2]. In [5] it was shown that networks of evolutionary processors are universal in that sense that they can generate any recursively enumerable language, and that networks with six nodes are sufficient to get all recursively enumerable languages. In [2] the latter result has been improved by showing that networks with three nodes are sufficient. The proof uses one node of each type (and intersection with a monoid).

Therefore it is a natural question (rised already in [2]) to study the power of networks with evolutionary processors where the nodes have only two types, i. e.,

(i) networks with deletion nodes and substitution nodes (but without insertion nodes),
(ii) networks with insertion nodes and substitution nodes (but without deletion nodes), and
(iii) networks with deletion nodes and insertion nodes (but without substitution nodes).

In this paper we investigate the power of such systems and study the number of nodes sufficient to generate all languages which can be obtained by networks of the type under consideration. We prove that networks of type (i) and (ii) produce only finite and context-sensitive languages, respectively. Every finite, context-sensitive or recursively enumerable language can be generated by a network of type (i) with one node, by a network of type (ii) with two nodes or by a network of type (iii) with three nodes, respectively.

2 Definitions

We assume that the reader is familiar with the basic concepts of formal language theory (see e. g. [14]). We here only recall some notations used in the paper.

By V^* we denote the set of all words (strings) over V (including the empty word λ). The length of a word w is denoted by $|w|$.

In the proofs we shall often add new letters of an alphabet U to a given alphabet V. In all these situations we assume that $V \cap U = \emptyset$.

A phrase structure grammar is specified as a quadruple $G = (N, T, P, S)$ where N is a set of nonterminals, T is a set of terminals, P is a finite set of productions which are written as $\alpha \to \beta$ with $\alpha \in (N \cup T)^* \setminus T^*$ and $\beta \in (N \cup T)^*$, and $S \in N$ is the axiom. The grammar G is called monotone, if $|\alpha| \leq |\beta|$ holds for every rule $\alpha \to \beta$ of P.

A phrase structure grammar is in Kuroda normal form if all its productions have one of the following forms:

$$AB \to CD,\ A \to CD,\ A \to x,\ A \to \lambda \text{ where } A, B, C, D \in N,\ x \in N \cup T.$$

We call a production $\alpha \to \beta$ a
  – substitution if $|\alpha| = |\beta| = 1$,
  – deletion if $|\alpha| = 1$ and $\beta = \lambda$.
We introduce insertions as a counterpart of a deletion. We write $\lambda \to a$, where a is a letter. The application of an insertion $\lambda \to a$ derives from a word w any word $w_1 a w_2$ with $w = w_1 w_2$ for some (possibly empty) words w_1 and w_2.

We now introduce the basic concept of this paper, the networks of evolutionary processors.

Definition 1

(i) *A network of evolutionary processors (of size n) is a tuple*

$$\mathcal{N} = (V, N_1, N_2, \ldots, N_n, E, j)$$

where
- *V is a finite alphabet,*
- *for $1 \leq i \leq n$, $N_i = (M_i, A_i, I_i, O_i)$ where*
  - *M_i is a set of evolution rules of a certain type, i. e., $M_i \subseteq \{a \to b \mid a, b \in V\}$ or $M_i \subseteq \{a \to \lambda \mid a \in V\}$ or $M_i \subseteq \{\lambda \to b \mid b \in V\}$,*
  - *A_i is a finite subset of V^*,*
  - *I_i and O_i are regular sets over V,*
- *E is a subset of $\{1, 2, \ldots, n\} \times \{1, 2, \ldots, n\}$, and*
- *j is a natural number such that $1 \leq j \leq n$.*

(ii) *A configuration C of $\mathcal{N}$ is an n-tuple $C = (C(1), C(2), \ldots, C(n))$ if $C(i)$ is a subset of V^* for $1 \leq i \leq n$.*

(iii) *Let $C = (C(1), C(2), \ldots, C(n))$ and $C' = (C'(1), C'(2), \ldots, C'(n))$ be two configurations of $\mathcal{N}$. We say that C derives C' in one*
- *evolution step (written as $C \Longrightarrow C'$) if, for $1 \leq i \leq n$, $C'(i)$ consists of all words $w \in C(i)$ to which no rule of M_i is applicable and of all words w for which there are a word $v \in C(i)$ and a rule $p \in M_i$ such that $v \Longrightarrow_p w$ holds,*
- *communication step (written as $C \vdash C'$) if, for $1 \leq i \leq n$,*

$$C'(i) = (C(i) \setminus O_i) \cup \bigcup_{(k,i) \in E} C(k) \cap O(k) \cap I(i).$$

The computation of $\mathcal{N}$ is a sequence of configurations

$$C_t = (C_t(1), C_t(2), \ldots, C_t(n)), \quad t \geq 0,$$

such that
- *$C_0 = (A_1, A_2, \ldots, A_n)$,*
- *for any $t \geq 0$, C_{2t} derives C_{2t+1} in one evolution step: $C_{2t} \Longrightarrow C_{2t+1}$,*
- *for any $t \geq 0$, C_{2t+1} derives C_{2t+2} in one communication step: $C_{2t+1} \vdash C_{2t+2}$.*

(iv) *The language $L(\mathcal{N})$ generated by $\mathcal{N}$ is defined as*

$$L(\mathcal{N}) = \bigcup_{t \geq 0} C_t(j)$$

where $C_t = (C_t(1), C_t(2), \ldots, C_t(n))$, $t \geq 0$ is the computation of $\mathcal{N}$.

Intuitively a network with evolutionary processors is a graph consisting of some, say n, nodes $N_1, N_2, \ldots, N_n$ (called processors) and the set of edges given by E such that there is a directed edge from N_k to N_i if and only if $(k, i) \in E$. Any processor N_i consists of a set of evolution rules M_i, a set of words A_i, an input filter I_i and an output filter O_i. We say that N_i is a substitution node or a deletion node or an insertion node if $M_i \subseteq \{a \to b \mid a, b \in V\}$ or $M_i \subseteq \{a \to \lambda \mid a \in V\}$ or $M_i \subseteq \{\lambda \to b \mid b \in V\}$, respectively. The input filter I_i and the output filter O_i control the words which are allowed to enter and to leave the node, respectively. With any node N_i and any time moment $t \geq 0$ we associate a set $C_t(i)$ of words (the words contained in the node at time t). Initially, N_i contains the words of A_i. In a derivation step we derive from $C_t(i)$ all words applying rules from the set M_i. In a communication step any processor N_i sends out all words $C_t(i) \cap O_i$ (which pass the output filter) to all processors to which a directed edge exists (only the words from $C_t(i) \setminus O_i$ remain in the set associated with N_i) and, moreover, it receives from any processor N_k such that there is an edge from N_k to N_i all words sent by N_k and passing the input filter I_i of N_i, i.e., the processor N_i gets in addition all words of $(C_t(k) \cap O_k) \cap I_i$. We start with a derivation step and then communication steps and derivation steps are alternately performed. The language consists of all words which are in the node N_j (j is chosen in advance) at some moment t, $t \geq 0$.

3   Networks with Only Deletion and Substitution Nodes

In this section we study the power of networks which have only deletion and substitution nodes but no insertion nodes.

Lemma 1. *For any network $\mathcal{N}$ of evolutionary processors, which has only deletion and substitution nodes, $L(\mathcal{N})$ is a finite language.*

Proof. Let $\mathcal{N} = (V, N_1, N_2, \ldots, N_n, E, j)$ be a network, which has only deletion and substitution nodes. Obviously, any evolution step and any communication step do not increase the length of a word contained in some $C_t(i)$, $1 \leq i \leq n$, $t \geq 0$. Therefore $L(\mathcal{N})$ contains only words of length at most

$$\max\{|w| \mid w \in A_i,\ 1 \leq i \leq n\}.$$

Hence $L(\mathcal{N})$ is a finite language.

On the other hand, every finite language can be generated by a network of evolutionary processors without insertion nodes.

Lemma 2
  (i) *For any finite language L, there is a network $\mathcal{N}$ of evolutionary processors which has exactly one substitution node such that $L(\mathcal{N}) = L$.*
  (ii) *For any finite language L, there is a network $\mathcal{N}$ of evolutionary processors which has exactly one deletion node such that $L(\mathcal{N}) = L$.*

Proof. Obviously, the network $\mathcal{N} = (alph(L) \cup \{a, b\}, (\{a \to b\}, L, \emptyset, \emptyset), \emptyset, 1)$ generates L and its only node is a substitution node. Therefore part (i) is shown.
In order to prove part (ii), we change the system by using $a \to \lambda$ instead of $a \to b$.

Combining the two preceding lemmas we get immediately the following statement.

Corollary 1. *The family of languages which can be generated by networks of evolutionary processors which have only deletion and substitution nodes coincides with $\mathcal{L}(FIN)$.*

4   Networks with Only Insertion and Substitution Nodes

In this section we study the power of networks which have only insertion and substitution nodes but no deletion nodes.

Lemma 3. *For any network $\mathcal{N}$ of evolutionary processors which has only insertion and substitution nodes, $L(\mathcal{N})$ is a context-sensitive language.*

Proof. The proof can be given by a simulation of the work of networks of evolutionary processors by context-sensitive contextual grammars which only generate context-sensitive languages (see [9]). For a detailed proof we refer to [10].

Lemma 4. *For any context-sensitive language L, there are a set T and a network $\mathcal{N}$ of evolutionary processors with exactly one insertion node and exactly one substitution node such that $L = L(\mathcal{N}) \cap T^*$.*

Proof. Let L be a context-sensitive language and $G = (N, T, P, S)$ be a grammar in Kuroda normal form with $L(G) = L$. Let $R_1, R_2, \ldots, R_7$ be the following sets:

$$R_1 = \{ A \to p_0, \, p_0 \to x \mid p = A \to x \in P, \, A \in N, \, x \in T \},$$
$$R_2 = \{ A \to p_1 \mid p = A \to CD \in P \text{ or } p = AB \to CD \in P, \, A, B, C, D \in N \},$$
$$R_3 = \{ B \to p_2 \mid p = AB \to CD \in P, \, A, B, C, D \in N \},$$
$$R_4 = \{ p_1 \to p_3 \mid p \in P \},$$
$$R_5 = \{ p_2 \to p_4 \mid p \in P \},$$
$$R_6 = \{ p_3 \to C \mid p = A \to CD \in P \text{ or } p = AB \to CD \in P, \, A, B, C, D \in N \},$$
$$R_7 = \{ p_4 \to D \mid p = A \to CD \in P \text{ or } p = AB \to CD \in P, \, A, B, C, D \in N \}.$$

We construct a network of evolutionary processors

$$\mathcal{N} = (V, (M_1, \{S\}, I_1, O_1), (M_2, \emptyset, I_2, V^*), \{(1, 2), (2, 1)\}, 1)$$

with

$$V = N \cup T \cup \{ p_0, p_1, p_2, p_3, p_4 \mid p \in P \},$$
$$M_1 = R_1 \cup R_2 \cup R_3 \cup R_4 \cup R_5 \cup R_6 \cup R_7,$$
$$I_1 = (N \cup T)^* \{ p_1 p_2 \mid p = A \to CD \in P \} (N \cup T)^*,$$
$$O_1 = V^* \setminus ((N \cup T)^* \bar{O} (N \cup T)^*),$$

where

$$\bar{O} = \{\lambda\} \cup \{ p_1 \mid p = AB \to CD \in P \}$$
$$\cup \{ p_1 p_2 \mid p = AB \to CD \in P \}$$
$$\cup \{ p_3 p_2 \mid p = A \to CD \in P \text{ or } p = AB \to CD \in P \}$$
$$\cup \{ p_3 p_4 \mid p = A \to CD \in P \text{ or } p = AB \to CD \in P \}$$
$$\cup \{ C p_4 \mid p = A \to CD \in P \text{ or } p = AB \to CD \in P \},$$

and

$$M_2 = \{\lambda \to p_2 \mid p = A \to CD \in P\},$$
$$I_2 = (N \cup T)^* \{p_1 \mid p = A \to CD \in P\} (N \cup T)^*.$$

First, we show that any application of a rule of the grammar G can be simulated by the network $\mathcal{N}$. In the sequel, A, B, C, D are non-terminals, x is a terminal and the word $w_1 w_2 \in (N \cup T)^*$.

Case 1. Application of the rule $p = A \to x \in P$ to a word $w_1 A w_2$.
  This is achieved by the rules $A \to p_0 \in R_1$ and then $p_0 \to x \in R_1$. After each of these two evolution steps, the word does not leave the node.

Case 2. Application of the rule $p = AB \to CD \in P$ to a word $w_1 A B w_2$.
  The word $w_1 A B w_2$ is changed to $w_1 p_1 B w_2$ (by an appropriate rule of R_2) which cannot pass the output filter, so it remains in the first node. It is then changed to $w_1 p_1 p_2 w_2$ (by R_3), and further, without leaving the first node, to $w_1 p_3 p_2 w_2$ (by R_4), to $w_1 p_3 p_4 w_2$ (by R_5), to $w_1 C p_4 w_2$ (by R_6) and finally to $w_1 C D w_2$ (by R_7). This word is not communicated in the next step, since it cannot pass the output filter. Hence the application of the rule $p = AB \to CD \in P$ to a word $w_1 A B w_2$ can be simulated in six evolution steps (the six corresponding communication steps have no effect).

Case 3. Application of the rule $p = A \to CD \in P$ to a word $w_1 A w_2$.
  The word $w_1 A w_2$ is changed to $w_1 p_1 w_2$ (by an appropriate rule of R_2). This word passes the output filter of the first node and the input filter of the second one. There, the symbol p_2 is inserted behind p_1 and the obtained word $w_1 p_1 p_2 w_2$ is communicated back to the first node. There, the word is changed to $w_1 p_3 p_2 w_2$ (by R_4) and further as in the Case 2 to the words $w_1 p_3 p_4 w_2$ (by R_5), $w_1 C p_4 w_2$ (by R_6) and $w_1 C D w_2$ (by R_7). This word is not communicated in the next step, since it cannot pass the output filter. Hence the application of the rule $p = A \to CD \in P$ to a word $w_1 A w_2$ can be simulated in six evolution steps and two effective communication steps (the other four have no effect).

Since the start symbol S also belongs to the language of the network, any derivation step in the grammar G can be simulated by evolution and communication steps in the network $\mathcal{N}$. Hence, we have the inclusion $L(G) \subseteq L(\mathcal{N}) \cap T^*$. We show now that $L(\mathcal{N}) \cap T^* \subseteq L(G)$.

Let $F(G)$ be the set of all sentential forms generated by the grammar G. We show that $L(\mathcal{N}) \cap (N \cup T)^* \subseteq F(G)$. Then $L(\mathcal{N}) \cap T^* \subseteq L(G)$ follows immediately.

The start symbol S belongs to both sets $L(\mathcal{N}) \cap (N \cup T)^*$ and $F(G)$. We now consider a word $w = w_1 A w_2$ of the set $L(\mathcal{N}) \cap (N \cup T)^*$ with $A \in N$. The word is in the first node and it is not communicated, so we start with an evolution step.

Case 1. Application of a rule $A \to p_0 \in R_1$.
  This yields the word $w_1 p_0 w_2$ in the first node. Due to the output filter, it remains there. Thereafter, the rule $p_0 \to x \in R_1$ has to be applied or we loose the word. Hence, these two evolution steps represent the derivation $w_1 A w_2 \Longrightarrow w_1 x w_2$ in G.

Case 2. Application of a rule $A \to p_2 \in R_3$.

This leads to the word $w_1 p_2 w_2$ in the first node, which is then sent out. Since the second node does not accept it, the word is lost.

Case 3. Application of a rule $A \to p_1 \in R_2$.

There are two possibilities for the rule p that belongs to p_1.

Case 3.1. $p = A \to CD$. In this case, the word $w_1 p_1 w_2$ is sent out and caught by the second node. The second node inserts a q_2. If q_2 is not p_2 or if it is p_2 but not inserted immediately behind p_1, then the obtained word is not $w_1 p_1 p_2 w_2$. It is sent back but not accepted by the first node and therefore lost. If p_2 is inserted at the correct position, then the word $w_1 p_1 p_2 w_2$ enters the first node. We set $w_2' = w_2$ and continue with the word $w_1 p_1 p_2 w_2'$ to the next evolution step.

Case 3.2. $p = AB \to CD$. In this case, the word $w_1 p_1 w_2$ remains in the first node. If the word after the next evolution step is not $w_1 p_1 p_2 w_2'$ with $w_2 = B w_2'$, then it is sent out, because applying any other rule of $R_1 \cup R_2 \cup R_3 \cup R_4$ (rules of R_5, R_6 and R_7 are not applicable) yields a word which passes the output filter. Since it cannot pass the input filter of the other node, the word gets lost. So, the word is only kept alive, if it is $w_1 p_1 p_2 w_2'$ with $w_2 = B w_2'$. This word cannot leave the first node, so we continue with $w_1 p_1 p_2 w_2'$ in the first node to the next evolution step.

In both subcases, the only word that can be obtained in the first node after two evolution steps and two communication steps starting from the word $w = w_1 A w_2$ is $w_1 p_1 p_2 w_2'$. We continue with an evolution step. Applying a rule of R_1, R_2, R_3 or R_5 leads to a word which leaves the first node and disappears. Rules of R_6 and R_7 are not applicable. By the only successful rule $p_1 \to p_3 \in R_4$, we obtain the word $w_1 p_3 p_2 w_2'$ which is kept in the first node. The next evolution step uses the rule $p_2 \to p_4 \in R_5$ because the rules of R_1, R_2, R_3 and R_6 lead to loosing the word and R_4 and R_7 are not applicable. This yields the word $w_1 p_3 p_4 w_2'$ which is also kept in the first node. In the next evolution step, the rules of R_1, R_2, R_3 and R_7 make the word disappear and R_4 and R_5 are not possible. Hence, the only next word is $w_1 C p_4 w_2'$ after applying the rule $p_3 \to C \in R_6$. It remains in the first node. Now the rules of R_4, R_5 and R_6 are not applicable; by rules of R_1, R_2 and R_3 the word will be lost. The only possible rule $p_4 \to D \in R_7$ yields the word $w_1 C D w_2'$ which is not sent out in the next communication step.

Hence, in this case, the derivation $w_1 A w_2 \Longrightarrow w_1 C D w_2'$ (which in G is obtained by the initially chosen rule p) is simulated.

Other rules are not applicable to the word w.

By the case distinction above, we have shown that every word $z \in L(\mathcal{N}) \cap (N \cup T)^*$ that is derived by the network $\mathcal{N}$ from a word $w \in L(\mathcal{N}) \cap (N \cup T)^*$ is also derived by the grammar G from the word w and, hence, belongs to the set $F(G)$.

From the inclusion $L(\mathcal{N}) \cap (N \cup T)^* \subseteq F(G)$, the required inclusion $L(\mathcal{N}) \cap T^* \subseteq L(G)$ follows. Together with the first part of the proof, we have $L(G) = L(\mathcal{N}) \cap T^* = L$.

Corollary 2. *For any context-sensitive language L, there is a network $\mathcal{N}$ of evolutionary processors with three nodes which are insertion nodes and substitution nodes such that $L = L(\mathcal{N})$.*

Proof. Let L be a context-sensitive language. Then we construct as in the proof of Lemma 4 a network $\mathcal{N} = (V, N_1, N_2, E, 1)$ with one insertion node and one substitution node such that $L = L(\mathcal{N}) \cap T^*$ and from $\mathcal{N}$ the network

$$\mathcal{N}' = (V, N_1, N_2, N_3, E \cup \{(1,3)\}, 3) \text{ with } N_3 = (\emptyset, \emptyset, T^*, \emptyset).$$

It is obvious from the proof of Lemma 4 that N_3 collects exactly the words from the set $L(\mathcal{N}) \cap T^*$. Thus $L(\mathcal{N}') = L$.

By Lemma 3 and Corollary 2 we get immediately the following statement.

Corollary 3. *The family of languages which can be generated by networks of evolutionary processors which have only insertion and substitution nodes coincides with the class $\mathcal{L}(CS)$.*

5   Networks with Only Deletion and Insertion Nodes

In this section we discuss networks which have only insertion and deletion nodes. In the paper [13], the authors have also studied systems where only insertion and deletion are allowed. However, in contrast to our definition it is possible to delete and insert words of arbitrary length (the authors show that words of length at most three are sufficient); we can delete and insert only letters. On the other hand, we can use filters which is not possible in [13]. We shall prove that networks with deletion and insertion nodes can generate any recursively enumerable language. This means that partition of the rules to nodes and the use of regular filters has the same power as deletion and insertion of words of arbitrary length.

Lemma 5. *For any recursively enumerable language L, there are a set T and a network $\mathcal{N}$ of evolutionary processors with exactly two insertion nodes and exactly one deletion node such that $L = L(\mathcal{N}) \cap T^*$.*

Proof. Let L be a recursively enumerable language and $G = (N, T, P, S)$ be a grammar in Kuroda normal form with $L(G) = L$. In the sequel, A, B, C, D, X, Y, Z designate non-terminals, x a terminal, p, r rules of P; $q \notin N \cup T$ is a new symbol, and p_1, p_2, p_3, p_4, p_5 are new symbols for every rule $p \in P$ (and only those rules). We define now sets that will be used for defining the filters (to make them more readable). Let

$$\alpha_{p_1 q} = \{ p_1 q \mid \exists A : p = A \rightarrow \lambda \},$$
$$\alpha_{p_1 x} = \{ p_1 x \mid \exists A : p = A \rightarrow x \},$$
$$\alpha_{p_1 CD} = \{ p_1 CD \mid \exists A : p = A \rightarrow CD \text{ or } \exists A, B : p = AB \rightarrow CD \},$$
$$\beta_1 = \alpha_{p_1 q} \cup \alpha_{p_1 x} \cup \alpha_{p_1 CD},$$

$$\alpha_{A p_5} = \{ A p_5 \mid p = A \rightarrow \lambda \},$$
$$\alpha_{A p_4} = \{ A p_4 \mid \exists x : p = A \rightarrow x \text{ or } \exists C, D : p = A \rightarrow CD \},$$
$$\alpha_{A B p_4} = \{ A q^n B p_4 \mid n \geq 0 \text{ and } \exists C, D : p = AB \rightarrow CD \},$$
$$\beta_2 = \alpha_{A p_5} \cup \alpha_{A p_4} \cup \alpha_{A B p_4},$$

$$\alpha_{Aqp_5} = \{\, Aqp_5 \mid p = A \to \lambda \,\},$$
$$\alpha_{Ap_2p_4} = \{\, Ap_2p_4 \mid \exists x : p = A \to x \text{ or } \exists C, D : p = A \to CD \,\},$$
$$\alpha_{ABp_2p_4} = \{\, Aq^n Bp_2p_4 \mid n \geq 0 \text{ and } \exists C, D : p = AB \to CD \,\},$$
$$\beta_3 = \alpha_{Aqp_5} \cup \alpha_{Ap_2p_4} \cup \alpha_{ABp_2p_4},$$

$$\alpha_{Aq} = \{\, Aq \mid A \to \lambda \in P \,\},$$
$$\alpha_{Ap_2} = \{\, Ap_2 \mid \exists x : p = A \to x \text{ or } \exists C, D : p = A \to CD \,\},$$
$$\alpha_{ABp_2} = \{\, Aq^n Bp_2 \mid n \geq 0 \text{ and } \exists C, D : p = AB \to CD \,\},$$
$$\alpha_{Ap_2p_3} = \{\, Ap_2p_3 \mid \exists C, D : p = A \to CD \,\},$$
$$\beta_4 = \alpha_{Aq} \cup \alpha_{Ap_2} \cup \alpha_{ABp_2},$$
$$\beta_4' = \beta_4 \cup \alpha_{Ap_2p_3}$$

$$\alpha_{p_1Aq} = \{\, p_1Aq \mid p = A \to \lambda \,\},$$
$$\alpha_{p_1Ap_2} = \{\, p_1Ap_2 \mid \exists x : p = A \to x \,\},$$
$$\alpha_{p_1ABp_2} = \{\, p_1Aq^n Bp_2 \mid n \geq 0 \text{ and } \exists C, D : p = AB \to CD \,\},$$
$$\alpha_{p_1Ap_2p_3} = \{\, p_1Ap_2p_3 \mid \exists C, D : p = A \to CD \,\},$$
$$\beta_5 = \alpha_{p_1Aq} \cup \alpha_{p_1Ap_2} \cup \alpha_{p_1ABp_2} \cup \alpha_{p_1Ap_2p_3},$$

$$\alpha_{p_1xp_2} = \{\, p_1xp_2 \mid \exists A : p = A \to x \,\},$$
$$\alpha_{p_1CBp_2} = \{\, p_1Cq^n Bp_2 \mid n \geq 0 \text{ and } \exists A, D : p = AB \to CD \,\},$$
$$\alpha_{p_1Cp_2p_3} = \{\, p_1Cp_2p_3 \mid \exists A, D : p = A \to CD \,\},$$
$$\alpha_{p_1CDp_2} = \{\, p_1CDq^n p_2 \mid n \geq 0 \text{ and } \exists A, B : p = AB \to CD$$
$$\text{or } n = 0 \text{ and } \exists A : p = A \to CD \,\},$$
$$\beta_6 = \alpha_{p_1xp_2} \cup \alpha_{p_1CBp_2} \cup \alpha_{p_1Cp_2p_3} \cup \alpha_{p_1CDp_2},$$

$$\alpha_{Ap_1qBr_4} = \{\, Aq^n p_1qq^m Br_4 \mid n, m \geq 0 \text{ and } \exists X : p = X \to \lambda$$
$$\text{and } \exists C, D : r = AB \to CD \,\},$$
$$\alpha_{p_1Cr_4D} = \{\, p_1Cr_4D \mid (\exists A : p = A \to CD \text{ or } \exists A, B : p = AB \to CD)$$
$$\text{and } (\exists x : r = C \to x \text{ or } \exists X, Y : r = C \to XY) \,\},$$
$$\alpha_{Zp_1Cr_4D} = \{\, Zq^n p_1Cr_4D \mid n \geq 0 \text{ and } (\exists A : p = A \to CD \text{ or } \exists A, B : p = AB \to CD)$$
$$\text{and } \exists X, Y : r = ZC \to XY \,\},$$
$$\alpha_{p_1CDr_4} = \{\, p_1CDr_4 \mid (\exists p = A \to CD \text{ or } \exists A, B : p = AB \to CD) \text{ and }$$
$$(\exists x : r = D \to x \text{ or } \exists X, Y : (r = D \to XY \text{ or } r = CD \to XY)) \,\},$$
$$\alpha_{p_1CDXr_4} = \{\, p_1CDq^n Xr_4 \mid n \geq 0 \text{ and } (\exists A : p = A \to CD \text{ or } \exists A, B : p = AB \to CD)$$
$$\text{and } \exists X, Y : r = DX \to YZ \,\},$$
$$\alpha_{p_1Cr_5D} = \{\, p_1Cr_5D \mid (\exists A : p = A \to CD \text{ or } \exists A, B : p = AB \to CD)$$
$$\text{and } r = C \to \lambda \,\},$$
$$\alpha_{p_1CDr_5} = \{\, p_1CDr_5 \mid (\exists A : p = A \to CD \text{ or } \exists A, B : p = AB \to CD) \text{ and } r = D \to \lambda \,\},$$
$$\beta_7 = \alpha_{Ap_1qBr_4} \cup \alpha_{p_1Cr_4D} \cup \alpha_{Zp_1Cr_4D} \cup \alpha_{p_1CDr_4} \cup \alpha_{p_1CDXr_4} \cup \alpha_{p_1Cr_5D} \cup \alpha_{p_1CDr_5},$$

$$\alpha_{p_1p_2} = \{ p_1p_2 \mid \exists A, x : p = A \to x \},$$
$$\alpha_{p_1Bp_2} = \{ p_1q^nBp_2 \mid n \geq 0 \text{ and } \exists A, C, D : p = AB \to CD \},$$
$$\alpha_{p_1Cp_2} = \{ p_1Cq^np_2 \mid n \geq 0 \text{ and } \exists A, B, D : p = AB \to CD$$
$$\text{or } n = 0 \text{ and } \exists A, D : p = A \to CD \},$$
$$\alpha_{p_1p_2p_3} = \{ p_1p_2p_3 \mid \exists A, C, D : p = A \to CD \},$$
$$\beta_8 = \alpha_{p_1p_2} \cup \alpha_{p_1Bp_2} \cup \alpha_{p_1Cp_2} \cup \alpha_{p_1p_2p_3},$$

$$T_q = (T \cup \{q\})^*,$$
$$W = (N \cup T \cup \{q\})^*.$$

Now, we construct a network of evolutionary processors

$$\mathcal{N} = (V, (M_1, \{S\}, I_1, O_1), (M_2, \emptyset, I_2, O_2), (M_3, \emptyset, I_3, O_3),$$
$$\{(1,2), (2,1), (2,3), (3,2)\}, 1)$$

with

$$V = N \cup T \cup \{q\} \cup \bigcup_{p=A\to\lambda\in P} \{p_1, p_5\} \cup \bigcup_{p=A\to x\in P} \{p_1, p_2, p_4\}$$
$$\cup \bigcup_{p=A\to CD\in P} \{p_1, p_2, p_3, p_4\} \cup \bigcup_{p=AB\to CD\in P} \{p_1, p_2, p_4\},$$
$$M_1 = \{\lambda \to q\} \cup \{\lambda \to p_i \mid 1 \leq i \leq 5 \text{ and } p_i \in V \},$$
$$M_2 = \{A \to \lambda \mid A \in N\} \cup \{p_i \to \lambda \mid 1 \leq i \leq 5 \text{ and } p_i \in V \} \cup \{q \to \lambda\},$$
$$M_3 = \{\lambda \to A \mid A \in N\} \cup \{\lambda \to x \mid x \in T\},$$

$$O_1 = V^* \setminus (W\beta_4'W),$$
$$O_2 = V^* \setminus (T_q\{p_1 \mid p \in P \text{ and } p_1 \in V\}T_q),$$
$$O_3 = V^*,$$
$$I_1 = W(\beta_1 \cup \beta_2 \cup \beta_4)W \cup T^*,$$
$$I_2 = W(\beta_3 \cup \beta_5 \cup \beta_6 \cup \beta_7)W \cup W\beta_1W\beta_2W \cup W\beta_2W\beta_1W,$$
$$I_3 = W\beta_8W.$$

By reasons of space we omit the proof that $L(\mathcal{N}) = L$ and refer to [10].

Corollary 4. *There is a network $\mathcal{N}$ of evolutionary processors with two insertion nodes and one deletion node such that $L(\mathcal{N})$ is a non-recursive language.*

Proof. Since the family of recursive languages is closed under intersection with sets T^*, where T is an alphabet, the network constructed in the proof of Lemma 5 for a non-recursive language L generates a non-recursive language.

Corollary 5. *For any recursively enumerable language L there is a network $\mathcal{N}$ of evolutionary processors with four nodes which are insertion nodes and deletion nodes such that $L = L(\mathcal{N})$.*

Proof. The proof can be given analogously to that of Corollary 2.

Obviously, any language generated by a network of evolutionary processors with only insertion and deletion nodes is recursively enumerable since arbitrary networks of evolutionary processors only generate recursively enumerable languages. Thus we get the following statement by Lemma 5.

Corollary 6. *The family of networks of evolutionary processors which have only insertion and deletion nodes coincides with the family of recursively enumerable languages.*

6   Conclusion

In the paper we have determined the power of networks of evolutionary processors if only two different types of nodes are used in the network. We have shown that

- up to an intersection with a monoid every recursively enumerable language can be generated by a network with one deletion and two insertion nodes,
- networks with an arbitrary number of deletion and substitution nodes only produce finite languages, and for each finite language one deletion node or one substitution node is sufficient, and
- networks with an arbitrary number of insertion and substitution nodes only generate context-sensitive languages, and (up to an intersection with a monoid) every context-sensitive language can be generated by a network with one substitution node and one insertion node.

The latter two results are optimal with respect to the minimal number of necessary nodes, whereas it is an open problem whether or not one deletion and one insertion node are sufficient to generate all recursively enumerable languages. In [1] it was shown that networks without substitution nodes are still powerful and can generate non-recursive languages.

   If one considers networks with all three types of nodes, it is known that it is not necessary to allow all graphs. One can obtain all recursively enumerable languages if one restricts to special graphs e. g. to those which are known as useful structures in technology as grids or rings (see [8], [6]). Obviously, the restriction to complete graphs does not restrict the power in the case of networks with nodes of two types, either, because the graph given in the proof of Lemma 4 is complete and we can extend the network of Lemma 5 to a language equivalent network with a complete underlying graph (adding the edge $(1,3)$ enforces the output filter of the first processor to be changed to $O_1 = V^* \setminus (W(\beta'_4 \cup \beta_8)W)$; for adding the edge $(3,1)$, no changes are necessary). These graphs can be extended further to complete graphs according to those given in the proofs of the Corollaries 2 and 4. Due to the input and output filters of the new nodes, the new edges have no influence to the language generated.

   Moreover, the graphs in the proofs of the Corollaries 2 and 4 are stars (if we ignore the directions) which proves that the restriction to stars does not decrease the power. The same situation holds with respect to backbones. A general investigation of special graphs remains as a task.

Analogously, one also gets all recursively enumerable languages from networks with all three types of nodes, if one restricts the form of the regular sets e. g. to random context sets, where one requires the presence and/or absence of some letters in the word (see [6]). The languages we used in our proofs are more complicated since they require absence and/or presence of some subwords. We leave as an open problem the power of networks with two types of nodes and random context regular sets.

References

1. Alhazov, A., Martín-Vide, C., Rogozhin, Y.: Networks of Evolutionary Processors with Two Nodes Are Unpredictable. In: Pre-proceedings LATA 2007, University of Tarragona, Spain. Reports of the Research Group on Math. Linguistics 35/07 (2007)
2. Alhazov, A., Martín-Vide, C., Rogozhin, Y.: On the number of nodes in universal networks of evolutionary processors. Acta Inf. 43, 331–339 (2006)
3. Castellanos, J., Leupold, P., Mitrana, V.: On the size complexity of hybrid networks of evolutionary processors. Theor. Comput. Sci. 330, 205–220 (2005)
4. Castellanos, J., Martín-Vide, C., Mitrana, V., Sempere, J.: Solving NP-complete problems with networks of evolutionary processors. In: Mira, J.M., Prieto, A.G. (eds.) IWANN 2001. LNCS, vol. 2084, pp. 621–628. Springer, Heidelberg (2001)
5. Castellanos, J., Martín-Vide, C., Mitrana, V., Sempere, J.: Networks of evolutionary processors. Acta Informatica 38, 517–529 (2003)
6. Csuhaj-Varjú, E., Martín-Vide, C., Mitrana, V.: Hybrid networks of evolutionary processors are computationally complete. Acta Informatica 41, 257–272 (2005)
7. Csuhaj-Varjú, E., Salomaa, A.: Networks of parallel language processors. In: Păun, G., Salomaa, A. (eds.) New Trends in Formal Languages. LNCS, vol. 1218, pp. 299–318. Springer, Heidelberg (1997)
8. Dassow, J.: On special networks of parallel language processors. Romanian Journal of Information Science and Technology 1, 331–341 (1998)
9. Dassow, J., Păun, G.: Regulated Rewriting in Formal Language Theory. Springer, Berlin (1989)
10. Dassow, J., Truthe, B.: On the Power of Networks of Evolutionary Processors. Otto-von-Guericke-Universität Magdeburg, Fakultät für Informatik, Technical report (2007)
11. Fahlmann, S.E., Hinton, G.E., Seijnowski, T.J.: Massively parallel architectures for AI: NETL, THISTLE and Boltzmann machines. In: Proc. AAAI National Conf. on AI, pp. 109–113. William Kaufman, Los Altos (1983)
12. Hillis, W.D.: The Connection Machine. MIT Press, Cambridge (1985)
13. Margenstern, M., Păun, G., Rogozhin, Y., Verlan, S.: Context-free insertion-deletion systems. Theor. Comput. Sci. 330, 339–348 (2005)
14. Rozenberg, G., Salomaa, A.: Handbook of Formal Languages. Springer, Berlin (1997)

Study of Limits of Solvability in Tag Systems

Liesbeth De Mol

Center for Logic and Philosophy of Science
University of Ghent, Blandijnberg 2, 9000 Gent, Belgium
elizabeth.demol@ugent.be

Abstract. In this paper we will give an outline of the proof of the solvability of the *halting* and *reachability problem* for 2-symbolic tag systems with a deletion number $v = 2$. This result will be situated in a more general context of research on limits of solvability in tag systems.

Keywords: Tag Systems, Limits of solvability, Reachability problem, Halting Problem.

1 Introduction

Tag systems were invented by Emil Post in 1921 [15],[16] and played an important role in Post's earlier work on normal systems. After 9 months of research on tag systems, he came to the conclusion that proving the Entscheidungsproblem for first-order predicate calculus solvable might be impossible. He never proved the unsolvability of this Entscheidungsproblem, but was able to show that there are certain unsolvable decision problems for normal systems [4],[5], [10], [18].

Although Post mentions some results on tag systems [15], [16] he never published any of the proofs. He considered two different decision problems for tag systems: the *halting problem* and the *reachability problem*.

Definition 1. *The halting problem for tag systems is the problem to determine for a given tag system and any initial string A_0 whether the tag system will halt.*

Definition 2. *The reachability problem for tag systems is the problem to determine for a given tag system T, a fixed initial string A_0 and any arbitrary string A over the alphabet Σ, whether T will ever produce A when started with A_0.*

Note that the halting problem for tag systems is in fact just a special case of the reachability problem. Post mentioned that he was able to prove the solvability of both decision problems for a specific class of tag systems, a result he considered as the major success of his research on tag systems. The main purpose of this paper is to give an outline of a proof of this result.

1.1 Definition of Tag Systems and Notational Conventions

A tag system T, consists of a finite alphabet $\Sigma = \{a_0, a_1, ..., a_{\mu-1}\}$ of μ symbols, a deletion number $v \in \mathbb{N}$ and a finite set of μ words, $w_0, w_1, ..., w_{\mu-1}$ defined

J. Durand-Lose and M. Margenstern (Eds.): MCU 2007, LNCS 4664, pp. 170–181, 2007.

over the alphabet, including the empty word ϵ. Each of these words corresponds with one of the letters from the alphabet as follows:

$$a_0 \quad \to a_{0,1}a_{0,2}...a_{0,n_0}$$
$$a_1 \quad \to a_{1,1}a_{1,2}...a_{1,n_1}$$
$$... \quad\quad ... \quad ...$$
$$a_{\mu-1} \to a_{\mu-1,1}a_{\mu-1,2}...a_{\mu-1,n_{\mu-1}}$$

where each $a_{i,j} \in \Sigma, 0 \leq i < \mu$. Given an initial string A_0, the tag system *first* tags the word associated with the leftmost letter of A_0 at the end of A_0, and then deletes the first v symbols of A_0.[1] This process is iterated until the tag system halts, i.e. produces the empty string ϵ. If this does not happen the tag system can become periodic or show divergent behaviour. Post mentions one example of a tag system with $v = 3$, $0 \to 00$, $1 \to 1101$ [15]. It is still not known whether this particular tag system is recursively solvable, despite its formal simplicity.

Let T be a tag system with a deletion number v with μ symbols and words $w_0, w_1, ..., w_{\mu-1}$. We shall write l_{w_i} to indicate the length of a word w_i, $l_{\mathbf{max}}$ and $l_{\mathbf{min}}$ denote the length of the lengthiest word w_i rsp. the length of the shortest word w_j of T, $0 \leq i, j < \mu$. The total sum of the number of a_i's in the words $w_0, ...w_{\mu-1}$ will be denoted as $\#a_i$. We will use $\dot{x}$ rsp. x to indicate an odd rsp. an even number. Given a string $A = a_1a_2...a_{l_A}$, we will say that A is entered with shift x, when the tag system erases its first x symbols, the first symbol scanned in A being a_{x+1}.

1.2   Results on the Limits of Solvability in Tag Systems

Post never proved that tag systems are recursively unsolvable. It was Minsky who proved the result in 1961 [8], after the problem was suggested to him by Martin Davis. He showed that any Turing machine can be reduced to a tag system with $v = 6$. The result was improved by Cocke and Minsky [2], [9]. They proved that any Turing machine can be reduced to a tag system with $v = 2$. The same result was proven by Wang [19]. Maslov generalized this result and proved that for any $v > 1$ there exists at least one tag system with an unsolvable decision problem and, independent of Wang, furthermore proved that any tag system for which $v = 1$ is solvable [7].

The result from [2], [9] can be used to determine the size of the smallest universal tag system known. If we define the size of a tag system T as the product of μ and v, it is possible to reduce any 2-symbolic Turing machine with m states to a tag system with $v = 2$, $\mu = 16m$. Using the universal Turing machine constructed by Neary in the class TM(18, 2) [14] or the machine constructed by Baiocchi which is in the class TM(19,2) [1], where TM(m, n) denotes the

---

[1] It should be noted that we follow Post's original definition of tag systems, instead of the one that is now commonly used. I.e. in the definition used here, the tagging and deletion operation are not performed in one and the same step. The proof of the main theorem only needs some minor changes in order to be applicable to a definition of tag systems where tagging and deletion operation are performed synchronously.

class of Turing machines with m states and n symbols, it is possible to construct universal tag systems in the classes TS(288, 2) rsp. TS(304,2), TS(m, v) denoting the class of tag systems with m symbols and a deletion number v.

Despite the relatively large size of the smallest universal tag systems known, there are some clear indications that proving very small classes of tag systems solvable will be very hard, if not impossible. The fact that the tag system mentioned above from the class TS(2, 3) is still not known to be solvable serves as an indication of this problem. A further indication is given by the result from [12], where it is shown that the $3n + 1$-problem can be reduced to a tag system from the class TS(3, 2), i.e., $w_0 \rightarrow w_1 w_2, w_1 \rightarrow w_0, w_2 \rightarrow w_0 w_0 w_0$. The reduction of the $3n + 1$-problem, which is known as a hard problem of number theory, to a very small tag system, illustrates how hard it might be to prove this class of tag systems solvable.

Post mentions that the halting and reachability problem for the class of tag systems for which $v = 1$ or $\mu = 1$ is trivially solvable and remarks that he completely solved the case $\mu = v = 2$ [16]. But, as was said, the proofs were never published. The case $\mu = 1$ is indeed trivially solvable. Wang [19] provided the proof for the case $v = 1$. In this paper we will outline the proof for the class $\mu = v = 2$.

Both μ and v can be regarded as *decidability criteria* [6] for tag systems, since their solvability depends on the size of these parameters. Another such criterion is the length of the words. Wang proved that any tag system for which $l_{\min} \geq v$ or $l_{\max} \leq v$ is solvable [19].

2   Solvability of the Halting and Reachability Problem of the Class TS(2,2)

In [16] Post remarks that his proof of the solvability of the halting and reachability problem of the class TS(2, 2) involved *"considerable labor"*. This is indeed true, as will become clear from the outline of the proof we will give here. The proof involves a study of a rather large number of subcases. We will merely outline the structure of the proof and restrict ourselves to detailed proofs for only some of the subcases, because of the length of the actual proof, and the fact that several subcases can be solved by using similar methods. A detailed proof is made available on-line [11].

Post differentiates between three different classes of behaviour a tag system can converge to, i.e., a tag system can halt, it can become periodic, or it can show unbounded growth. The reachability and halting problem can be proven solvable, if one can determine for any initial condition, for a given tag system, that it will lead to one of these three classes of behaviour after a finite number of steps. In case of unbounded growth, one should be able to prove that for any given number n, the tag system will always produce a string A_i of length $l_{A_i} > n$ after a finite number of iterations i, such that no string $A_j, j > i$, will ever be produced again for which $l_{A_j} \leq n$.

In our proof, we have indeed been able to show that one can determine for any tag system T from the class TS(2, 2) and any initial condition over the alphabet $\Sigma = \{0, 1\}$, that T will always become periodic, halt or show unbounded growth after a finite number of steps. We have thus been able to prove the following theorem:

Theorem 1. *For any given tag system T, if $\mu = v = 2$ then the halting problem and the reachability problem for T are solvable.*

First of all, it should be noted that we only have to consider those cases with $l_{\min} < 2, l_{\max} > 2$, given the theorem proven by Wang mentioned in Sec. 1.2. In the remainder, we assume that $l_{\max} = l_{w_1}, l_{\min} = l_{w_0}$, the symmetrical case of course being equivalent to this case.

There are three global cases to be taken into account, i.e., $w_0 = \epsilon, w_0 = 1$, $w_0 = 0$. Each of these cases is subdivided into several subcases, determined by the following parameters: l_{w_1}, the parity of l_{w_1},[2] #1, and the parity of the number of 0's separating consecutive 1's in w_1. It should be noted that, contrary to classes of Turing machines TM(m, n), the three global cases to be taken into account contain an infinite number of tag systems. In this sense it has been basic for the proof to determine certain threshold values for two of these parameters, i.e., l_{w_1} and #1. If the values of these parameters exceed a given value, the infinite class of tag systems determined by the parameters will always show unbounded growth (except for a specific class of initial strings), else they will halt or become periodic (except for a specific class of initial strings).

There is one method that has been basic to solve the majority of cases, called the *table method*. What one basically does with this method is to look at a certain number of substrings that can be produced theoretically in a given tag system, by starting from the possible productions from the respective words $w_0, ..., w_{\mu-1}$. Given a tag system T with a deletion number v, it is clear that given a word $w_i = a_{i,1} a_{i,2} ... a_{i,l_{w_i}}$, some letters in w_i will be 'scanned', others not. The sequence of letters that is scanned is determined by the number n, $0 \leq n \leq v - 1$, of leading letters of w_i that is erased but not scanned by the tag system and which leads to the concatenation or tagging of the words corresponding to the letters from the sequence at the tail of a given string. For example, if $v = 3$, there are three different sequences of letters in w_i that might be scanned by the tag system: $a_{i,1} a_{i,4} ... a_{i,t_0}$, $a_{i,2} a_{i,5} ... a_{i,t_1}$, $a_{i,3} a_{i,6} ... a_{i,t_2}$, with:

$$t_j = l_{w_i} - [(l_{w_i} - j) \bmod 3]$$

Now, given a tag system T, with deletion number v and μ letters. The table method is applied to the tag system by first looking at all the possible strings v that can be produced from each of the words w_i, $0 \leq i < \mu$, by concatenating the words corresponding to the letters of each of the different sequences in each of the w_i, determined as above. If one of these new strings is equal to one of the words w_i it is marked. If all the strings produced in this way are marked or equal to ϵ it follows that the tag system will always halt or become periodic,

---

[2] The parity of a number x is the property of it being even or odd.

since the length of the strings that can be produced from the respective words is bounded. If this is not the case, the same procedure is applied to all the strings left unmarked and not equal to ϵ,...If we e.g. apply this method to the two words 00 and 1101 of the tag system mentioned above (Sec. 1.1), only one (11011101) of the 6 possible strings produced will be left unmarked, and differs from ϵ. If we apply the method to this one string it becomes clear very soon that the method will never come to a halt, i.e., there will always remain strings left unmarked.

As will become clear in the proof, the table method is not only useful if, for a given tag system, all the strings become marked or are equal to ϵ at a given time, but can also be used to e.g. prove that a tag system will either halt or show unbounded growth. In general, it should be noted here that, although this method is very simple, it is an important instrument to study tag systems.

The method is called the table method, because the results from the method can best be represented through tables. We will explain how such a table should be read, in the first application of the method in the proof.

Note that from now on, l_{w_0} and l_{w_1} will be abbreviated as l_0 rsp. l_1.

Proof.

Case 1. $w_0 = \epsilon$

Case 1.1. #1 = 0. It is trivial to prove that tag systems from this class will always halt, since only 0's can be scanned.

Case 1.2. #1 = 1, $l_1 \equiv 0$ mod 2. Let $w_1 = 0^{x_1}10^{y_1}$. To prove this case, we need the table method mentioned above. The following table proves the case:

	w_0	w_1
S_0	ϵ	ϵ
S_1	ϵ	$w_1\checkmark$

The row headed with S_0 gives the string produced from a given string S (in this case w_0 or w_1) when the first letter of the string S is scanned by the tag system. Similarly, the row headed S_1 gives the possible productions from a given string S when its first letter is erased without being scanned. Clearly, since in this case $w_0 = \epsilon$ actually no letter in w_0 can be scanned or erased. The only possible non-empty string that can be produced for this case, is the string resulting from w_1 when entered with a shift 1, i.e., its first letter is erased but not scanned.

As is clear from the table, a tag system from this class will either halt or become periodic. It will become periodic when at least one 1 is scanned in the initial condition, such that the first letter from the word w_1 thus produced, will not be scanned. This is determined by the parity of the length of the initial condition. In all other cases, tag systems from this class halt. A similar proof can be given for the case $w_1 = 0^{x_1}10^{y_1}$.

Case 1.3. #1 = 1, $l_1 \equiv 1$ mod 2. The table that can be constructed for this class of tag systems, is identical to that of the previous case, with $w_1 = 0^{x_1}10^{y_1}$. Despite the table being identical, tag systems from this class can be proven to always halt. The reason for this is that the number of surviving 1's is at most half of what it was when the tag system has scanned (and erased) all the letters of the current word at a given stage of the computation. The reader is referred to the on-line details of the proof.

Case 1.4. #1 = 2, $l_1 \equiv 0$ mod 2. To prove the case we have to differentiate between two subcases, i.e. $w_1 = 0^{x_1}10^{y_1}10^{z_1}$ and $w_1 = 0^{x_1}10^{y_1}10^{z_1}$ (the proof for $w_1 = 0^{x_1}10^{y_1}10^{z_1}$ is similar to the first case, the proof of $w_1 = 0^{x_1}10^{y_1}10^{z_1}$ is similar to the second case).

Case 1.4.1. $w_1 = 0^{x_1}10^{y_1}10^{z_1}$. The first case is proven through the following table:

Table 2. $w_1 = 0^{x_1}10^{y_1}10^{z_1}$

	w_1
S_0	$w_1 \checkmark$
S_1	$w_1 \checkmark$

From this table it follows that any tag system from this class will always become periodic, except when no 1 is scanned in the initial condition, then it always halts.

Case 1.4.2. $w_1 = 0^{x_1}10^{y_1}10^{z_1}$. The case is proven through the following table:

Table 3. $w_1 = 0^{x_1}10^{y_1}10^{z_1}$

	w_1	w_1w_1	...	$(w_1w_1)^n$
S_0	ϵ	ϵ	...	ϵ
S_1	w_1w_1	$w_1w_1w_1w_1$	....	$(w_1w_1)^{2n}$

As is clear from the table, tag systems from this class will either halt or show unbounded growth depending on the parity of the length of the initial condition.

Case 1.5. #1 = 2, $l_1 \equiv 1$ mod 2. The proof is almost identical to that of case 1.4., except that now we have to consider the cases $w_1 = 0^{x_1}10^{y_1}10^{z_1}$ (or similarly $w_1 = 0^{x_1}10^{y_1}10^{z_1}$) and $w_1 = 0^{x_1}10^{y_1}10^{z_1}$ (or similarly $w_1 = 0^{x_1}10^{y_1}10^{z_1}$).

Case 1.6. #1 = 3, $l_1 \equiv 0$ mod 2. Again we have to consider several cases, depending on the parity of the number of 0's separating pairs of symbols 1 in w_1. The proofs of the several cases are similar to those for Case 1.4. Tag systems from this class will always show unbounded growth, halt or become periodic, depending on the parity of the initial condition and the spacings between the several 1's.

Case 1.7. #1 = 3, $l_1 \equiv 1$ mod 2. We have to differentiate between two cases: $w_1 = 0^{s_1}10^{x_1}10^{y_1}10^{t_1}$ (and all variants) or $w_1 = 0^{s_1}10^{\bar{x}_1}10^{\bar{y}_1}10^{t_1}$ (and all variants). It can be proven that tag systems from both classes will either halt (if no 1 is scanned in the string produced from the initial condition) or show unbounded growth after a finite number of steps, by applying the table method. See [11] for the detailed table.

Case 1.8. #1 > 3, $l_1 \equiv 0$ mod 2 and Case 1.9. #1 > 3, $l_1 \equiv 1$ mod 2. For any tag system from these classes and any initial condition it can be determined that it will either halt, become periodic, or show unbounded growth after a finite number of iterations. The result follows from the proofs of cases 1.4.–1.7.

Case 2. $w_0 = 1$

Case 2.1. #1 = 1 In this case the length of w_1 is a determining factor to predict the behaviour of a tag system from this class, since w_1 only consists of 0's. We have to differentiate between the following two cases: $2 < l_1 < 5$ or $5 \leq l_1$.

Case 2.1.1. $2 < l_1 < 5$ Tag systems from this class will always become periodic, except when the initial condition is equal to 0, then it will halt. The result can be proven through the table method, the details of the proof can be found on-line.

Case 2.1.2. $5 \leq l_1$ It can be easily checked that tag systems from this class will always show unbounded growth, except for a finite class of initial conditions, for which the tag systems will halt or become periodic after a finite number of steps. The proof follows from the fact that once a tag system from this class produces a string that consists of at least two times w_1 it will show unbounded growth. The proof follows from the table method (see the on-line proof).

Case 2.2. #1 = 2, $l_1 = 3$. It can be determined for any tag system from this class that it will either halt or become periodic. There are three different tag systems to be taken into account: $0 \rightarrow 1; 1 \rightarrow 100$, $0 \rightarrow 1; 1 \rightarrow 010$, and $0 \rightarrow 1; 1 \rightarrow 001$. The result can be proven for each of the cases by applying the table method. (see [11] for detailed tables.)

Case 2.3. #1 = 2, $l_1 > 3$. It can be determined for any tag system from this class that it will either halt, become periodic or show unbounded growth. To prove the result, we have to differentiate between $l_1 = 4$ and $l_1 > 4$

Case 2.3.1. $l_1 = 4$ The result of the case follows from a rather complicated application of the table method. The table is about half a page long and needs some further deductions. The details of the proof can be found on-line.

Case 2.3.2. $l_1 > 4$ For the second case it can be shown rather easily that once $w_1 w_1$ is produced as a substring, tag systems from this class will always lead to unbounded growth. For more details the reader is referred to the on-line proof.

Case 2.4. #1 > 2. Each tag system from this class will either halt, become periodic, or show unbounded growth. The proof differentiates between two sub-cases $l_1 = 3$ and $l_1 > 4$. The first case involves a more complicated application of the table method. The proof of the second case is rather straightforward and follows from case 2.3.2. See the on-line proof for more details.

Case 3. $w_0 = 0$

Case 3.1. #1 = 0, $l_1 > 2$. It is trivial to prove that any tag system from this class will halt, since any sequence of 0's always leads to ϵ.

Case 3.2. #1 = 1, $l_1 > 2$. It can be determined that any tag system from this class will either halt or become periodic by applying the table method (see the on-line proof).

Case 3.3. #1 = 2, $l_1 > 2$, $l_1 \equiv 0$ mod 2. It can be determined for any tag system from this class that it will either halt, become periodic or show unbounded growth after a finite number of iterations. From now on, we will write x instead of 0^x for the ease of notation. We have to take into account two cases. The 1's can be separated by an even or an odd number of 0's, i.e., $w_1 = t_1 1 x_1 1 s_1$ (or similarly $w_1 = t_1 1 \dot{x}_1 1 \dot{s}_1$), or $w_1 = t_1 1 \dot{x}_1 1 \dot{s}_1$ (or, similarly $w_1 = t_1 1 \dot{x}_1 1 \dot{s}_1$).

Case 3.3.1. $w_1 = t_1 1 x_1 1 s_1$ The proof of the first case results from the application of the table method. It proves that any tag system from this class will always become periodic after a finite number of steps for any initial condition except for those conditions in which no 1 is scanned by the tag system, then a halt occurs.

Case 3.3.2. $w_1 = t_1 1 \dot{x}_1 1 \dot{s}_1$ It can be shown that any tag system from this class will either halt, become periodic or show unbounded growth after a finite number of iterations. The proof of this case is more complicated, and we have to subdivide the case into two subcases: t_1, $\dot{x}_1$ or $\dot{s}_1 > 1$ and $t_1 = 0$, $\dot{x}_1 = 1$, $\dot{s}_1 = 1$.

Case 3.3.2.1. t_1, $\dot{x}_1$ *or* $\dot{s}_1 > 1$ For any tag system from this class it can be determined that it will either halt, become periodic or show unbounded growth. Set $w_1 = t_1 1 \dot{x}_1 1 \dot{s}_1$. In shift 1, the tag system will produce a sequence of 0's from w_1, ultimately leading to a halt. In shift 0, we get:

$$A_1 = t_2 w_1 \lfloor \dot{x}_1/2 \rfloor w_1 s_2 \tag{1}$$

Depending on the shift, if $\dot{s}_1 + \lfloor \dot{x}_1/2 \rfloor + t_1$ is even, we get:

$$t_3 A_1 0^{n_1} \tag{2}$$

or:

$$t_3 0^{n_1} A_1 \tag{3}$$

from (1). It thus follows that if $\dot{s}_1 + \lfloor \dot{x}_1/2 \rfloor + t_1$ is even, and at least one w_1 is produced such that its first 1 will be scanned, the tag system will ultimately become periodic, since the lengths of the possible strings produced from w_1 in this case are bounded, but never produce the empty string. If $\dot{x}_1 + \lfloor \dot{x}_1/2 \rfloor + t_1$ is odd, the tag system produces:

$$A_2 = t_4 A_1 \lfloor \dot{x}_1/4 \rfloor A_1 s_3 \tag{4}$$

from (1), or a string merely consisting of a certain number of 0's (ultimately converging to ϵ), depending on the shift. If $\dot{s}_1 + s_2 + \lfloor \dot{x}_1/4 \rfloor + t_2 + t_1$ is even, we get:

$$t_5 A_2 0^{n_2} \tag{5}$$

or:

$$t_5 0^{n_2} A_2 \tag{6}$$

from A_2, again depending on the shift. Thus if $\dot{s}_1 + s_2 + \lfloor \dot{x}_1/2 \rfloor + t_2 + t_1$ is even, the tag system will always halt or become periodic. A halt occurs, if no A_2 is produced. If $\dot{s}_1 + s_2 + (\dot{x}_1 - 1)/4$ is odd, the tag system produces:

$$A_3 = t_6 A_2 \lfloor (\dot{x}_1)/8 \rfloor A_2 s_4 \tag{7}$$

from (4), or a sequence of 0's depending on the shift.

Generally, tag systems from this class will become periodic or halt once a sequence $\dot{s}_1 + s_2 + s_3 + ... + s_n + \lfloor (\dot{x}_1)/2^n \rfloor + t_n + ... + t_2 + t_1$, separating two consecutive A_{n-1} in A_n ($n \in \mathbb{N}, A_0 = w_1$) becomes even. Indeed, given a string $A_n = t_i A_{n-1} \lfloor \dot{x}_1/2^n \rfloor A_{n-1} s_i$, with $\dot{s}_1 + s_2 + s_3 + ... + s_n + \lfloor \dot{x}_1/2^n \rfloor + t_n + ... + t_2 + t_1$ even, the tag system will produce either $t_i A_n 0^{n_j}$ or $t_i 0^{n_j} A_n$, with the number of 0's surrounding each A_n being bounded. If for a given tag system, there is no n such that the sequence $\dot{s}_1 + s_2 + s_3 + ... + s_n + \lfloor (x_1/2^n \rfloor + t_n + ... + t_2 + t_1$ between a pair of A_{n-1} in A_n is even, the tag system will either halt or show unbounded growth.

Now, it can be easily determined (in a finite number of steps) for any tag system from this class whether there exists an n such that $\dot{s}_1 + s_2 + s_3 + ... + s_n + \lfloor (x_1 - 1)/2^n \rfloor + t_n + ... + t_2 + t_1$ between a pair of A_{n-1} in A_n is even. This follows from the following lemma:[3]

Lemma 1. *For any tag system from the class 3.3.2.1. it can be proven that there is always an n, $n \in \mathbb{N}$ such that for any $i \geq n$ the sequence of 0's $\dot{s}_1 + s_2 + s_3 + ... + s_i + \lfloor (x_1 - 1)/2^i \rfloor + t_i + ... + t_2 + t_1$ between a pair of A_{i-1} in A_i is of the same length as $\dot{s}_1 + s_2 + s_3 + ... + s_n + \lfloor (x_1 - 1)/2^n \rfloor + t_n + ... + t_2 + t_1$.*

The proof of the lemma can be found in the on-line version. It follows from this lemma that one can determine for any tag system from this class whether a sequence of 0's separating two consecutive A_{i-1} in A_i will ever become even or not, since it only takes a finite number of steps before a sequence A_n is produced for which the number of 0's separating a pair of A_{n-1} becomes constant. We have

---

[3] We are indebted to an anonymous referee for pointing out a serious error in a previous proof of this case concerning the number of 0's separating a pair of A_{n-1} and having provided us with the necessary lemma and an outline of its proof to solve the case.

thus proven the case: tag systems from this class will either halt, become periodic or show unbounded growth.

Case 3.3.2.2. $t_1 = 0$, $x_1 = 1$, $s_1 = 1$ It can be proven that the only tag system in this class, with $w_1 = 1010$, will either halt or show unbounded growth. The result can easily be obtained through the table method or by pure reasoning. See the on-line proof for more details.

Case 3.4. #1 = 2, $l_1 > 2$, $l_1 \equiv 1$ mod 2. It can be determined for any tag system from this class that it will always halt or become periodic. Again we have to consider two cases, depending on the parity of the spacing between the two 1's, i.e. $w_1 = t_1' 1 x_1 1 s_1 s$ and $w_1 = t_1 1 x_1' 1 s_1$. The proof of the first case is similar to the proof of case 3.3.1. For the second case, we have to differentiate between two subcases, i.e., t_1, x_1 or $s_1 > 1$ and $t_1 = 0$, $x_1 = 1$, $s_1 = 0$. The proof of the first subcase is almost identical to that of case 3.3.2.1., the second subcase easily follows by applying the table method. See the on-line proof for more details.

Case 3.5. #1 > 2, $l_1 > 2$, $l_1 \equiv 0$ mod 2. It can be determined for each tag system from this class that it will either show unbounded growth, become periodic or halt after a finite number of iterations, depending on the initial condition. To prove this, we merely have to consider the case #1 = 3, since the generalization to #1 > 3 trivially follows from the proof of the case #1 = 3. There are two possible subcases to be proven: either all 1's are separated by an odd number of 0's, or only one pair of 1's is separated by an odd number of 0's. The proofs of both cases use methods similar to those used for Case 3.3.2. Detailed proofs are available on-line.

Case 3.6. #1 > 2, $l_1 > 2$, $l_1 \equiv 1$ mod 2. For any tag system from this class it can be determined that it will either halt, become periodic or show unbounded growth after a finite number of iterations, depending on the initial condition. The proofs for the several subcases are similar to those for case 3.5.

The proof of theorem 1 follows from the proofs of cases 1–3.   □

3   Discussion

As is clear from the outline of the main theorem of this paper, proving the solvability of the halting and reachability problem for the class TS(2, 2) indeed involves considerable labor. Most probably the proofs of some cases might be simplified. For example,the solvability of cases 1.2, 1.4, 1.6., 1.8. follows from the following theorem:

Theorem 2. *Given a tag system T with deletion number v, $\Sigma = \{a_0, a_1, ..., a_{\mu-1}\}$ and words $w_{a_0}, w_{a_1}, ..., w_{a_{\mu-1}}$. Then, if the lengths l of the words and v are not relative prime the solvability of a given decision problem for T can be reduced to the solvability of the decision problem for n different tag systems, λ being the greatest common divisor of v, $l_{w_{a_0}}, ..., l_{w_{a_{\mu-1}}}$, with deletion number $v' = v/\lambda$.*

which is proven in [13]. It follows from this theorem that the halting and reachability problem for all the tag systems with $w_0 = \epsilon, l_{w_1} \equiv 0$ mod 2 from the class TS(2, 2) can be reduced to the halting and reachability problem of tag systems with $v = 1$. Since Wang proved that these problems are solvable for any tag system with $v = 1$ (See Sec. 1.2), the result easily follows.

As was explained in Sec. 1.2, it might be very hard, if not impossible, to prove the solvability of those classes of tag systems that are closest to TS(2, 2), i.e., TS(2,3) and TS(3,2). In fact, as far as our experience goes with these classes of tag systems, they seem to be completely intractable. The methods used in the present proof do not work for these classes. The only reasonable explanation we have been capable to find for this basic difference is related to the balance between the total number $\#a_0, \#a_1, ..., \#a_{\mu-1}$ of each of the symbols $a_0, a_1, ..., a_{\mu-1}$ in the respective words for a given tag system. For each symbol a_i, we can measure the effect of scanning a_i on the length of a string produced in a tag system, i.e., it can lead to a decrease or an increase. This effect of scanning a symbol a_i on the length of a string produced, can be computed by taking the absolute value of $l_{w_{a_i}} - v$. If we then sum up the products $\#a_i \cdot (l_{w_{a_i}} - v)$ for each of the symbols, and the result is a negative rsp. a positive number, one might expect that the tag system will always halt rsp. show unbounded growth.

Although we have been able to show that this method cannot be used in general, it is clear that this method might be applied to certain infinite classes of tag systems to prove them solvable. Not taking into account the case with $w_0 = \epsilon$ it can be proven for the class TS(2, 2) that there is but a finite subclass of tag systems for which this sum is equal to 0.[4] This is in sharp contrast with the classes TS(2,3) and TS(3,2) for which it can be proven that they each contain an infinite class of such tag systems, even if no word is equal to ϵ. We consider this as a fundamental difference between the class TS(2,2) and the classes TS(3,2), TS(2,3). In fact, we suspect that further research on this method might help to considerably simplify the proof of Theorem 1. For more details on this issue the reader is referred to [13].

References

1. Baiocchi, C.: Three small universal Turing machines. In: Margenstern, M., Rogozhin, Y. (eds.) MCU 2001. LNCS, vol. 2055, pp. 1–10. Springer, Heidelberg (2001)
2. Cocke, J., Minsky, M.: Universality of tag systems with p = 2, Artificial Intelligence Project – RLE and MIT Computation Center, memo 52 (1963)
3. Davis, M.: The undecidable. Basic papers on undecidable propositions, unsolvable problems and computable functions. Raven Press, New York (1965) (Corrected republication, Dover publications, New York (2004))
4. Davis, M.: Why Gödel didn't have Church's thesis. Information and Control 54, 3–24 (1982)

---

[4] These are tag systems with $l_0 = 1, l_1 = 3, \#1 = \#0 = 2$.

5. Davis, M.: Emil L. Post. His life and work. In: [17], pp. xi–xviii (1994)
6. Margenstern, M.: Frontier between decidability and undecidability: A survey. Theoretical Computer Science 231(2), 217–251 (2000)
7. Maslov, S.J.: On E. L. Post's 'Tag' problem (russian). Trudy Matematicheskogo Instituta imeni V.A. Steklova 72, 5–56 (1964b) (English translation in: American Mathematical Society Translations Series 2, 97, 1–14 (1971))
8. Minsky, M.: Recursive unsolvability of Post's problem of tag and other topics in the theory of Turing machines. Annals of Mathematics 74, 437–455 (1961)
9. Minsky, M.: Size and structure of universal Turing machines using tag systems: a 4-symbol 7-state machine. In: Proceedings Symposia Pure Mathematics. American Mathematical Society, vol. 5, pp. 229–238 (1962)
10. De Mol, L.: Closing the circle: An analysis of Emil Post's early work. The Bulletin of Symbolic Logic 12(2), 267–289 (2006)
11. De Mol, L.: Solvability of the halting and reachability problem for tag systems with $\mu = v = 2$. Preprint 343, Center for Logic and Philosophy of Science (2007), http://logica.ugent.be/centrum/writings/pubs.php
12. De Mol, L.: Tag systems and Collatz-like functions. Theoretical Computer Science (submitted) (under revision, 2007)
13. De Mol, L.: Tracing unsolvability: A historical, mathematical and philosophical analysis with a special focus on tag systems. Ph.D. thesis, to obtain the degree of Doctor in Philosophy, University of Ghent (submitted 2007), available at: http://logica.ugent.be/liesbeth/dissertation.pdf
14. Neary, T.: Small polynomial time universal Turing machines. In: Proceedings of MFCSIT 2006, Cork, Ireland (2006)
15. Post, E.L.: Formal reductions of the general combinatorial decision problem. American Journal of Mathematics 65(2), 197–215 (1943)
16. Post, E.L.: Absolutely unsolvable problems and relatively undecidable propositions - account of an anticipation. In: [3], pp. 340–433 (1965) (also published in [17])
17. Post, E.L.: Solvability, provability, definability: The collected works of Emil L. Post, edited by Davis, M., Birkhauser, Boston (1994)
18. Stillwell, J.: Emil Post and his anticipation of Gödel and Turing. Mathematics Magazine 77(1), 3–14 (2004)
19. Wang, H.: Tag systems and lag systems. Mathematische Annalen 152, 65–74 (1963a)

Query Completeness of Skolem Machine Computations

John Fisher[1] and Marc Bezem[2]

[1] Department of Computer Science
California State Polytechnic University
Pomona, California, USA
jrfisher@csupomona.edu
[2] Department of Computer Science
University of Bergen
Bergen, Norway
bezem@ii.uib.no

Abstract. The Skolem machine is a Turing-complete machine model where the instructions are first-order formulas of a specific form. We introduce Skolem machines and prove their logical completeness. Skolem machines compute queries for the Geolog language, a rich fragment of first-order logic. The concept of complete Geolog trees is defined, and this tree concept is used to show logical completeness for Skolem machines: If the query for a Geolog theory is a logical consequence of the axioms then the corresponding Skolem machine halts succesfully in a configuration that supports the query.

1 The Geolog Language and Skolem Machines

Geolog is a language for expressing first-order geometric logic in a format suitable for computations using an *abstract machine*. *Geolog* rules are used as machine instructions for an abstract machine that computes consequences for first-order geometric logic.

A *Geolog* rule has the general form

$$A_1, A_2, \ldots, A_m \Rightarrow C_1; C_2; \ldots; C_n \qquad (1)$$

where the A_i are atomic expressions and each C_j is a conjunction of atomic expressions, $m, n \geq 1$. The left-hand side of a rule is called the *antecedent* of the rule (a conjunction) and the right- hand side is called the *consequent* (a disjunction). All atomic expressions can contain variables.

If $n = 1$ then there is a single consequent for the rule (1), and the rule is said to be *definite*. Otherwise the rule is a *splitting rule* that requires a case distinction (case of C_1 or case of C_2 or ... case of C_n).

The separate cases (disjuncts) C_j must have a conjunctive form

$$B_1, B_2, \ldots, B_h \qquad (2)$$

J. Durand-Lose and M. Margenstern (Eds.): MCU 2007, LNCS 4664, pp. 182–192, 2007.

where the B_i are atomic expressions, and $h \geq 1$ varies with j. Any free variables occurring in (2) other than those which occurred free in the antecedent of the rule are taken to be existential variables and their scope is this disjunct (2).

As an example, consider the *Geolog* rule

```
s(X,Y) => e(X,Y) ; dom(Z),r(X,Z),s(Z,Y) .
```

The variables X,Y are universally quantified and have scope covering the entire formula, whereas Z is existentially quantified and has scope covering the last disjunct in the consequent of rule. A fully quantified first-order logical formula representation of this *Geolog* rule would be

$$(\forall X)(\forall Y)[s(X,Y) \rightarrow e(X,Y) \vee (\exists Z)(dom(Z) \wedge r(X,Z) \wedge s(Z,Y))]$$

Now we come to two special cases of rule forms, the *true* antecedent and the *goal* or *false* consequents. Rules of the form

$$true \Rightarrow C_1; C_2; \ldots; C_n \tag{3}$$

are called *factuals*. Here '*true*' is a special constant term denoting the empty conjunction. Factuals are used to express initial information in *Geolog* theories. Rules of the form

$$A_1, A_2, \ldots, A_m \Rightarrow goal \tag{4}$$

are called *goal* rules. Here '*goal*' is a special constant term. A goal rule expresses that its antecedent is sufficient (and relevant) for *goal*. Similarly, rules of the form

$$A_1, A_2, \ldots, A_m \Rightarrow false \tag{5}$$

are called *false* rules. Here '*false*' is a special constant term denoting the empty disjunction. A *false* rule expresses rejection of its antecedent.

The constant terms *true*, *goal* and *false* can only appear in *Geolog* rules as just described. All other predicate names, individual constants, and variable names are the responsibility of the *Geolog* programmer.

A *Geolog theory* (or *program*) is a finite set of *Geolog* rules. A theory may have any number of factuals and any number of *goal* or *false* rules.

The logical formulas characterized by *Geolog*, and the bottom-up approach to reasoning with those logical formulas, finds its earliest precursor (1920) in a particular paper by Thoralf Skolem [5].

Geolog theories serve as the instruction set for an abstract *Skolem machine* (SM). Skolem machines resemble multitape Turing machines and the two machine models have actually the same computational power. See the discussion in the last section.

An SM starts with one tape having *true* written on it. The basic operations of an SM use the *Geolog* rules in the instruction set to

– extend a tape (write logical terms at the end)
– create new tapes (for splitting rules)

The tapes are also called *states*. An SM with more than one tape is said to be in a *disjunctive* state, comprised of multiple separate simple states or tapes.

The basic purpose of a particular SM is to compute its instruction set and to halt when all of its tapes have '*goal*' or '*false*' written on them.

In order to motivate the general definitions for the workings of SM, let us work through a small example. To this end, consider the *Geolog* rulebase (SM instructions) in Figure 1.

```
true => domain(X), p(X).                    % #1
p(X) => q(X) ; r(X) ; domain(Y), s(X,Y).    % #2
domain(X) => u(X).                          % #3
u(X), q(X) => false.                        % #4
r(X) => goal.                               % #5
s(X,Y) => goal.                             % #6
```

Fig. 1. Sample instructions

The only instruction that applies to the initial tape is instruction #1. The antecedent of the rule matches `true` on the tape, so the tape can be *extended* using the consequent of the rule. In order to extend the tape using `domain(X),p(X)` an instance for the free existential variable X is first generated and then substituted, and the resulting terms are written on the tape, as shown in Figure 2.

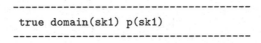

```
true domain(sk1) p(sk1)
```

Fig. 2. After applying rule

At this point in machine operation time either of the rules #2 or #3 can apply. The general definition of SM operation does not specify the order, but we will apply applicable rules in top-down order. So, applying instruction #2 we get tape *splitting*, as shown in Figure 3.

Each of the disjuncts in the consequent of rule #2 is used to extend the previous single tape. This requires that the previous tape be copied to two new tapes and then these tapes are extended.

Now, instruction #3 applies to all three tapes, even twice to the last tape, with total result shown in Figure 4.

Instruction #4 now adds `false` to the top tape, shown in Figure 5.

Now instruction #5 applies to the second tape, and then instruction #6 applies to the third tape, shown in Figure 6.

At this point the SM *halts* because each tape has either the term `goal` or the term `false` written on it.

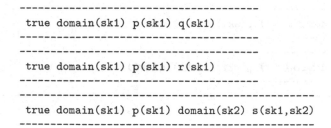

```
-------------------------------------------
true domain(sk1) p(sk1) q(sk1)
-------------------------------------------

-------------------------------------------
true domain(sk1) p(sk1) r(sk1)
-------------------------------------------

-----------------------------------------------------
true domain(sk1) p(sk1) domain(sk2) s(sk1,sk2)
-----------------------------------------------------
```

Fig. 3. After applying rule #2

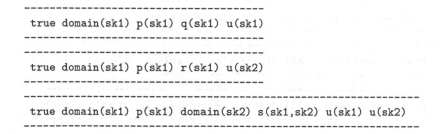

```
---------------------------------------------
true domain(sk1) p(sk1) q(sk1) u(sk1)
---------------------------------------------

---------------------------------------------
true domain(sk1) p(sk1) r(sk1) u(sk2)
---------------------------------------------

-----------------------------------------------------------------
true domain(sk1) p(sk1) domain(sk2) s(sk1,sk2) u(sk1) u(sk2)
-----------------------------------------------------------------
```

Fig. 4. After applying rule #3 four times (!)

The SM has effectively computed a proof that the *disjunction*

$$(\exists X)(u(X) \wedge q(X)) \vee (\exists X)r(X) \vee (\exists X)(\exists Y)s(X,Y)$$

is a *logical* consequence of the *Geolog* theory consisting of the first three rules in Figure 1. This is so because every tape of the halted machine either has q(sk1),u(sk1) written on it or has r(sk1) written on it or else has s(sk1,sk2) written on it. Note that the three disjuncts correspond to the *goal* and *false* rules in Figure 1. We will continue a discussion of this example (specifically, the role intended for the *false* rule) later in this section.

DEFINITION OF SKOLEM MACHINE OPERATIONS

- A *Geolog* rule $ANT \Rightarrow CONS$ is *applicable* to an SM tape T, provided that it is the case that all of the terms of ANT can be simultaneously matched against ground terms (no free variables) written on T. (It may be that ANT can be matched against T in more than one way; for example, rule #3 and the third tape of Figure 3.)
- If the rule $ANT \Rightarrow CONS$ is applicable to tape T, then for some matching substitution σ apply σ to $CONS$ and then *expand* tape T using $\sigma(CONS)$.
- In order to *expand* tape T by $\sigma(CONS) = C_1; C_2; \ldots; C_k$ copy tape T making $k-1$ new tapes $T_2, T_3, \ldots, T_k$, and then *extend* T using C_1, extend T_2 using C_2, $\ldots$, and extend T_k using C_k. (No copying if $k = 1$.)

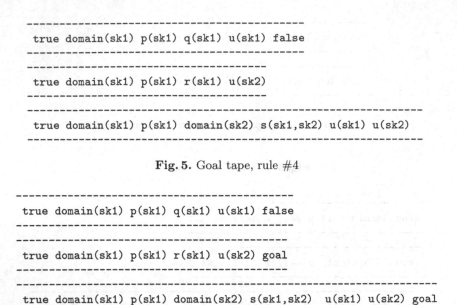

```
-----------------------------------------------------
 true domain(sk1) p(sk1) q(sk1) u(sk1) false
-----------------------------------------------
-----------------------------------------
 true domain(sk1) p(sk1) r(sk1) u(sk2)
-------------------------------------------
-----------------------------------------------------------------
 true domain(sk1) p(sk1) domain(sk2) s(sk1,sk2) u(sk1) u(sk2)
-----------------------------------------------------------------
```

Fig. 5. Goal tape, rule #4

```
------------------------------------------------
 true domain(sk1) p(sk1) q(sk1) u(sk1) false
-----------------------------------------------
-------------------------------------------
 true domain(sk1) p(sk1) r(sk1) u(sk2) goal
------------------------------------------
----------------------------------------------------------------------
 true domain(sk1) p(sk1) domain(sk2) s(sk1,sk2)  u(sk1) u(sk2) goal
----------------------------------------------------------------------
```

Fig. 6. After applying rule #5 and then #6, HALTED

- In order to *extend* a tape T using a conjunction C, suppose that $X_1,\ldots,X_p$ are all of the free existential variables in C. Create new constants c_j, $1 \le j \le p$ and substitute c_j for X_j in C, obtaining C', and then write each of the terms of C' on tape T. (It is mandatory that the constant is new with respect to the theory and the tape.)

Notice that only ground terms ever appear on any SM tape. Thus the matching algorithm does not really need the full power of general term unification. Simple left-to-right term matching suffices.

Given an SM with tapes $T_1,\ldots,T_t$, $t \ge 0$, we say a tape is *saturated* if no previously satisfied rule can be applied to it. A tape is *halted* if it is either saturated or contains *goal* or contains *false* (any of which could occur at the same time).

An SM is called *halted* if all its tapes are halted, it is *halted successfully* if it is halted with all tapes containing either *goal* or *false*.

The set of terms on any saturated tape that is not successfully halted is said to be a *counter model*.

Suppose that we write a *Geolog* theory in the form

$$T = A \cup G \cup F \tag{6}$$

where A is the *axioms*, G contains all of the affirming *goal* rules and F contains all of the rejecting *false* rules. It is intended that A contains all the rules of the theory other than the *goal* rules and the *false* rules and that A, G, and F are mutually disjoint sets.

The *Geolog query* Q for a *Geolog* theory $T = A \cup G \cup F$ is the disjunctive normal form $Q = C_1; C_2; \ldots; C_k$ consisting of all of the conjunctions C_i such that either C_i appears as antecedent of one of the *goal* rules (in G) or of one of the *false* rules (in F). As before, the free variables in Q are taken to be existential variables. The scope of a variable X appearing in a particular C_i (within Q) is restricted to C_i.

We say that a *Geolog* theory T *supports* its query Q if there is a successfully halted SM such that each tape satisfies some C_i.

Theorem 1. *If theory T supports its query Q then Q is a logical consequence of the axioms.*

2 Complete Geolog Trees

To motivate the general definitions, consider first the following simple Geolog theory, G_1.

```
true => a ; b .    % #1
true => c, d .     % #2
a => goal .        % #3
b, c => e .        % #4
e, d => false .    % #5
```

For the definition of a *Geolog trees* we consider the Geolog theory itself to be an *ordered* sequence of Geolog rules. Reference will be made to the rules of theory G_1 using their serial order (display notation: #n). The order will turn out to be irrelevant to the *branch sets* defined by the branches in these trees, and the branch sets will be the important semantic objects: They will be partial logical models (or possibly counter-models).

A complete Geolog tree of level 0, for any ordered Geolog theory, consists of just the root node *true*. The level 0 tree is, obviously, independent of the rule order. Figure 7 shows the complete Geolog tree of level 1 for the ordered theory G_1.

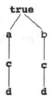

Fig. 7. Complete tree for G_1, level 1

The root of any Geolog tree is the unique atom *true*, which is the complete Geolog tree of level 0. The complete level 1 tree expands (and extends) the level 0 tree.

The first applicable rule for level 1 in our example is #1, and this constructs two branches for the growing tree. The second applicable rule (#2) adds elements to the growing tree along both branches because *true* is an ancestor for both branches. Notice that the consequents maintain a similar order of appearance (specifically, top-down) in the tree, as they appear in the consequence of rule #2 (specifically, left-to-right).

At level 2, rule #3 applies to the left branch of the complete tree for level 1, and rule #4 applies to the right branch, so a graphical depiction of the complete Geolog tree for G_1 for level 2 is given in Figure 8.

Fig. 8. Complete tree for G_1, level 2

Finally, at level 3, rule #5 applies to the right branch in Figure 8, as shown in Figure 9. At this stage, level #3, the tree is *saturated* because each branch contains either *goal* or *false*.

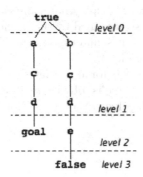

Fig. 9. Complete tree for G_1, level 3, with levels marked

Now let us suppose that the rules in the theory G_1 are reordered, for example

```
true => c, d .      % #2
true => a ; b .     % #1
b, c => e .         % #4
e, d => false .     % #5
a => goal .         % #3
```

In this case the complete Geolog trees of levels 0, 1, 2, and 3 could be depicted as shown in Figure 10.

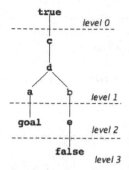

Fig. 10. Complete tree rules reordered, level 3, with levels marked

Notice that the level branch sets are the same. A *branch set* for level k consists of the set of all facts on a branch of the complete level k tree from the root of the tree down to the leaf of the branch. The branch sets for either tree, Figure 9 or 10 are

```
level 0: {true}
level 1: {a,c,d}, {b,c,d}
level 2: {a,c,d,goal}, {b,c,d,e}
level 3: {a,c,d,goal}, {b,c,d,e,false}
```

The query for theory G_1 is $Q = a; d, e$ and the level 3 branch sets also represent successfully halted tapes for a Skolem machine for G_1.

Another example is afforded by the following Geolog theory, G_2. G_2 does not support its query. Figure 11 shows some of the complete trees for G_2.

```
true => p(a) .                        % #1
p(X) => q(f(X)) ; p(f(X)) .           % #2
q(X) => goal .                        % #3
```

For G_2 the complete trees are unbounded, meaning simply that the number of nodes in the tree grows without bound as the level increases. A corresponding Skolem machine would have an unbounded number of possible tapes.

More formally, suppose that G is an arbitrary Geolog theory. We define a complete Geolog tree for G of level k by induction on k. The unique complete Geolog tree T_0 of level 0 for G is just the root tree, already describe. The single branch set for T_0 is $\{true\}$. Suppose that T_k is the complete Geolog tree for G of level k having branch sets B_i. It is assumed that any branch of T_k which contains either *goal* or *false* has that node as a leaf of the branch. Then T_{k+1} is defined as follows. The branches having leaf *goal* of *false* are not extended; they are considered to be *saturated*. For any branch B of T_k not having leaf *goal* nor

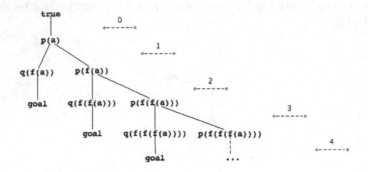

Fig. 11. The infinite tree for $G_2 \ldots$

false let us assume that r_1, r_2, $\ldots r_z$ is a complete ordered list of all possible applicable instances of *geolog* rules which are not already satisfied on B. (We assume that the specific order is determined by the order that the rules are given in G. These ground instances may have arisen from the same or from different rules.) Use r_1 to extend B in the same way as if B were a corresponding Skolem machine tape, as described in the previous section. However, if r_1 is a splitting rule, then split the branch B of T_k rather than reproduce the tape B and then extend the copies. (If r_1 is not a splitting rule then B has a unique extension.) Assume that this produces m branches $B_1, \ldots, B_m$, as shown in Figure 12.

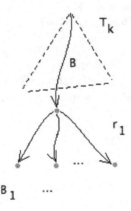

Fig. 12. Expanding branch B using first applicable rule

If any of the extended branches B_j has leaf *goal* of *false*, that branch is considered to be saturated, and it is not extended (or expanded) any further. Continuing, we now apply r_2 to each of the new branches not having leaf *goal* of *false*, then r_3 to the resulting branches, until all of the rules $\ldots r_z$ have been used to expand all of the previous branches not having leaf *goal* of *false*, using the process described for r_1, corresponding to Figure 12. The tree T_{k+1} is the result of this double induction for all branches B of T_k and all resulting applicable rules for each B (but never expand leaf *goal* of *false*).

Theorem 2. *Suppose that Q is the query for Geolog theory G and that Q is a logical consequence of G. Then G supports Q.*

Proof Sketch. The collection of all complete Geolog trees T_k for $k = 0, 1, 2, \ldots$ defines a (possibly infinite) tree T. Each node in T has finitely many children. Branch sets correspond to Herbrand models (closed term models) in the usual sense [2], but with the Herbrand basis based on the signature *plus the generated constants*. Note that, by construction, for each branch set B of T_k, any false instance of any rule is applicable and hence satisfied in all extensions of B in T_{k+1}.

If T is a finite tree and some branch set B does not satisfy any of the disjuncts of Q then B would satisfy the axioms of G but not Q. Since Q is a logical consequence of the axioms of G this case is not possible and so if T is finite then the branch sets of T correspond to a successfully halting Skolem machine and so G supports Q.

If T is infinite then, by König's lemma [3], T has an infinite branch. If none of the branch sets corresponding to this infinite branch satisfies any disjunct of Q then the set of nodes on this branch is a counter model. Since Q is a logical consequence of the axioms of G this case is not possible. Thus T is in fact a finite tree, and every disjunct of Q is satisfied on one of the branch sets of T. □

3   Discussion and Conclusion

Theorem 1 is a *logical correctness* result for Skolem machine consequences: Skolem machines compute queries for *Geolog* theories and supported queries are logical consequences of the axioms of a theory. *Theorem 2* concerns the *logical completeness* of SM computations: If the query for a Geolog theory is a logical consequence of the axioms then the corresponding Skolem machine halts succesfully in a configuration that supports the query.

It was claimed above that Skolem machines and Turing machines have the same computational power. In order to see this we remark that the following *Geolog* rules can be used to generate new constants representing natural numbers, with s the successor relation:

```
true => nat(0)
nat(X) => nat(Y),s(X,Y)
```

Given this, it is not difficult to encode one's favorite Turing-complete machine model as a Skolem machine. As shown in [1], encoding counter machines [4] (also called register machines) is particularly easy. Note that the encoding does not use function symbols.

The tree expansion definition of T_k given prior to *Theorem 2* characterizes a kind of *breadth-first* approach to proving support. The general issue of computational completeness obviously depends on ordered strategies for picking rules. It is not generally decidable whether a *Geolog* theory supports its query. Future papers will address the issue of partial completeness for ordered (*depth-first*) proof search for *Geolog* theories, as well as proof procedures that distinguish *goal* and *false* rules.

The website www.csupomona.edu/~jrfisher/www/geolog/ provides additional information about the *Geolog* language, specific interpreters for computing *Geolog*, and many mathematical examples.

References

1. Bezem, M.: On the Undecidability of Coherent Logic. In: Middeldorp, A., van Oostrom, V., van Raamsdonk, F., de Vrijer, R. (eds.) Processes, Terms and Cycles: Steps on the Road to Infinity. LNCS, vol. 3838, pp. 6–13. Springer, Heidelberg (2005)
2. Herbrand, J.: Logical Writings. Warren, D., Goldfarb, D. (eds.), Reidel Publishing Company, Springer, Heidelberg (2006)
3. König, D.: Theorie der endlichen und unendlichen Graphen, Akademische Verlagsgesellschaft. Leipzig (1936) (Translated from German by McCoart, R., Theory of finite and infinite graphs, Birkhauser (1990))
4. Minsky, M.L.: Recursive unsolvability of Post's problem of 'tag' and other topics in theory of Turing machines. Annals of Mathematics 74(3), 437–455 (1961)
5. Skolem, T.: Logisch-kombinatorische Untersuchungen über die Erfüllbarkeit und Beweisbarkeit mathematischen Sätze nebst einem Theoreme über dichte Mengen. Skrifter I, vol. 4, pp. 1–36, Det Norske Videnskaps-Akademi (1920) (also in Fenstad, J.E. (ed.), Selected Works in Logic by Th. Skolem, pp. 103–136, Universitetsforlaget, Oslo (1970))

More on the Size of Higman-Haines Sets: Effective Constructions

Hermann Gruber[1], Markus Holzer[2], and Martin Kutrib[3]

[1] Institut für Informatik, Ludwig-Maximilians-Universität München
Oettingenstraße 67, D-80538 München, Germany
gruberh@tcs.ifi.lmu.de
[2] Institut für Informatik, Technische Universität München
Boltzmannstraße 3, D-85748 Garching bei München, Germany
holzer@in.tum.de
[3] Institut für Informatik, Universität Giessen
Arndtstraße 2, D-35392 Giessen, Germany
kutrib@informatik.uni-giessen.de

Abstract. A not well-known result [9, Theorem 4.4] in formal language theory is that the Higman-Haines sets for *any* language are regular, but it is easily seen that these sets *cannot* be effectively computed in general. Here the Higman-Haines sets are the languages of all scattered subwords of a given language and the sets of all words that contain some word of a given language as a scattered subword. Recently, the exact level of unsolvability of Higman-Haines sets was studied in [10]. We focus on language families whose Higman-Haines sets are effectively constructible. In particular, we study the size of Higman-Haines sets for the lower classes of the Chomsky hierarchy, namely for the families of regular, linear context-free, and context-free languages, and prove upper and lower bounds on the size of these sets.

1 Introduction

Higman's lemma [9] and its generalization, namely Kruskal's Tree Theorem [12], can be used to show that certain rewriting systems terminate. Nevertheless, the result of Higman is not so well known and was frequently rediscovered in the literature, e.g., [8,13,14]. Although Higman's result appears to be only of theoretical interest, it has some nice applications in formal language theory. It seems that one of the first applications has been given by Haines in [8, Theorem 3], where it is shown that the set of all scattered subwords, i.e., the *Higman-Haines set* $\mathrm{DOWN}(L) = \{\, v \in A^* \mid \text{there exists } w \in L \text{ such that } v \leq w \,\}$, and the set of all words that contain some word of a given language, i.e., the *Higman-Haines set* $\mathrm{UP}(L) = \{\, v \in A^* \mid \text{there exists } w \in L \text{ such that } w \leq v \,\}$, are both regular for *any* language $L \subseteq A^*$. Here, $\leq$ refers to the scattered subword relation. As pointed out in [8], this is an exceptional property which is quite unexpected. Further applications and generalizations of Higman's result can be found, e.g., in [4,5,11,13].

J. Durand-Lose and M. Margenstern (Eds.): MCU 2007, LNCS 4664, pp. 193–204, 2007.
© Springer-Verlag Berlin Heidelberg 2007

It is worth mentioning that $\text{DOWN}(L)$ and $\text{UP}(L)$ cannot be obtained constructively in general. This is clear, because L is empty if and only if $\text{DOWN}(L)$ and $\text{UP}(L)$ are empty, but the question whether or not a language is empty is undecidable for recursively enumerable languages and decidable for regular ones. Thus, as expected, for the family of recursively enumerable languages the Higman-Haines sets are not constructible, while it is not hard to see that for regular languages the construction becomes effective. But where exactly is the borderline between language families with non-constructive and constructive Higman-Haines sets? One might expect that, e.g., the family of context-free languages has non-constructive Higman-Haines sets, but surprisingly this is not the case, as proven in [14]. On the other hand, recently it was shown in [10] that, for instance, the family of Church-Rosser languages has non-constructive Higman-Haines sets. This language family lies in between the regular languages and the growing context-sensitive languages, but is incomparable to the family of context-free languages [1]. Moreover, in [10] the exact level of unsolvability of the Higman-Haines sets for certain language families is studied. Thus, the non-constructive side of Higman-Haines sets is well studied, but is there more to be known about effective constructibility issues as presented in [14]? Moreover, are there any results about descriptional complexity issues? To our knowledge this is not the case, except for some results about regular languages accepted by nondeterministic finite automata in [10]. This is the starting point of our investigations about effective Higman-Haines set sizes. In particular we consider the problem of computing the Higman-Haines sets induced by the families of regular, context-free, and linear context-free languages. For the size of the Higman-Haines sets generated by regular languages upper and lower bounds are presented. That is, we prove that an exponential blow-up is sufficient and necessary in the worst case for a deterministic finite automaton to accept the Higman-Haines set $\text{DOWN}(L)$ or $\text{UP}(L)$ generated by some language that is represented by another deterministic finite automaton. This nicely contrasts the result about nondeterministic finite automata where a matching upper and lower bound on the size of Higman-Haines sets is shown [10]. Furthermore, we investigate the descriptional complexity of the Higman-Haines sets when the underlying device is a context-free or linear context-free grammar.

The paper is organized as follows. The next section contains preliminaries and basics about Higman-Haines sets. Then Section 3 first recalls the known upper and lower bounds for nondeterministic finite automata [10], and then studies the size of the Higman-Haines set for regular languages in terms of deterministic finite automata size. In addition, Higman-Haines sets induced by context-free and linear context-free languages are investigated.

2   Preliminaries

We denote the set of non-negative integers by $\mathbb{N}$. The powerset of a set S is denoted by 2^S. For an alphabet A, let A^+ be the set of non-empty words w over A. If the empty word λ is included, then we use the notation A^*. For the length of w we write $|w|$. For the number of occurrences of a symbol a in w we use the notation $|w|_a$. Set inclusion is denoted by $\subseteq$, and strict set inclusion by $\subset$. Let $v, w \in A^*$ be words over alphabet A. We define $v \leq w$ if and only if there are words $v_1, v_2, \ldots, v_k$ and $w_1, w_2, \ldots, w_{k+1}$, for some $k \geq 1$, $v_i \in A^*$, $w_i \in A^*$, such that $v = v_1 v_2 \ldots v_k$ and $w = w_1 v_1 w_2, v_2 \ldots w_k v_k w_{k+1}$. In case of $v \leq w$ we say that v is a scattered subword of w. Let L be a language over alphabet A. Then

$$\text{Down}(L) = \{\, v \in A^* \mid \text{there exists } w \in L \text{ such that } v \leq w \,\}$$

and

$$\text{Up}(L) = \{\, v \in A^* \mid \text{there exists } w \in L \text{ such that } w \leq v \,\}$$

are the *Higman-Haines sets* generated by L. The next theorem is the surprising result of Haines. It has been shown about half a century ago. Actually, it is a corollary of Higman's work, but let us state it as a theorem.

Theorem 1 ([8,9]). *Let L be an arbitrary language, then both* $\text{Down}(L)$ *and* $\text{Up}(L)$ *are regular.*

In order to talk about the economy of descriptions we first have to define what is meant by the *size of automata and grammars*. In general, we are interested to measure the *length of the string that defines an automaton or grammar*. In particular, we sometimes use more convenient size measures, if there is a recursive upper bound for the length of the defining string dependent on the chosen size measure. For example, for *context-sensitive and context-free grammars* M, the size $|M|$ equals the total number of occurrences of terminal and nonterminal symbols in the productions. For *deterministic and nondeterministic finite automata* M, the size $|M|$ equals the product of the number of states and the number of input symbols.

3   Effective Higman-Haines Set Sizes

Next we turn to the family of regular languages and then to the family of context-free languages, whose Higman-Haines sets can effectively be constructed [14]. We are interested in the constructions itself as well as in the sizes of the Higman-Haines sets.

3.1   Regular Languages

Let $M = (S, A, \delta, s_0, F)$ be a nondeterministic finite automaton (NFA), where S is the finite set of *internal states*, A is the finite set of *input symbols*, $s_0 \in S$ is the *initial state*, $F \subseteq S$ is the set of *accepting states*, and $\delta : S \times (A \cup \{\lambda\}) \to 2^S$ is the *partial transition function*. An NFA is deterministic (DFA) if and only if $|\delta(s, a)| \leq 1$, $|\delta(s, \lambda)| \leq 1$, and $|\delta(s, a)| = 1 \iff |\delta(s, \lambda)| = 0$, for all $s \in S$ and $a \in A$. Without loss of generality, we assume that the NFAs are always *reduced*. This means that there are no unreachable states and that from any state an accepting state can be reached.

Concerning the size of an NFA accepting $\mathrm{DOWN}(L(M))$ or $\mathrm{UP}(L(M))$ for a given NFA M, one finds the following situation, which was proven in [10].

Lemma 2. *Let M be an NFA of size n. Then size n is sufficient and necessary in the worst case for an NFA M' to accept $\mathrm{DOWN}(L(M))$ or $\mathrm{UP}(L(M))$. The NFA M' can effectively be constructed.*

In the remainder of this subsection we consider DFAs. First observe, that the results presented so far heavily rely on nondeterminism, i.e., even when starting with a DFA M, the resulting automata accepting $\mathrm{DOWN}(L(M))$ or $\mathrm{UP}(L(M))$ are nondeterministic in general. So, applying the well-known power-set construction gives an upper bound on the size of an equivalent DFA.

Corollary 3. *For any DFA M of size n, one can effectively construct a DFA accepting $\mathrm{DOWN}(L(M))$ or $\mathrm{UP}(L(M))$ whose size is at most 2^n.*   □

For the next two theorems we need some more notations. Let $L \subseteq A^*$ be an arbitrary language. Then the *Myhill-Nerode* equivalence relation $\equiv_L$ is defined as follows: For $u, v \in A^*$, let $u \equiv_L v$ if and only if $uw \in L \iff vw \in L$, for all $w \in A^*$. It is well known that the number of states of the minimal deterministic finite automaton accepting the language $L \subseteq A^*$ equals the index, i.e., the cardinality of the set of equivalence classes, of the Myhill-Nerode equivalence relation.

We continue our investigations by proving a non-trivial lower bound for DFAs accepting the language $\mathrm{DOWN}(L(M))$, for some given DFA M, that is quite close to the upper bound of the previous corollary.

Theorem 4. *For every $n \geq 1$, there exists a language L_n over an $(n+2)$-letter alphabet accepted by a DFA of size $(n+2)(n+1)^2$, such that size $2^{\Omega(n \log n)}$ is necessary for any DFA accepting $\mathrm{DOWN}(L_n)$.*

Proof. Let $A = \{a_1, a_2, \ldots, a_n\}$ and $\#, \$ \notin A$. Consider the witness language $L_n = \{\, \#^j \$ w \mid w \in A^*, j \geq 0, i = j \bmod n, |w|_{a_{i+1}} = n \,\} \subseteq (A \cup \{\#, \$\})^*$. A DFA accepting language L_3 is depicted in Figure 1. It is not hard to see that any DFA accepting L_n needs $n + 1$ states for each letter a_i to count up to n. Moreover, for the $\#$-prefix n states are used, and finally one non-accepting sink state is needed. This results in $n(n+1) + n + 1$ states, which gives size $(n+2)(n^2 + 2n + 1) = (n+2)(n+1)^2$. It is not hard to verify that the DFA is minimal. Recall the construction of an NFA for the down-set. Then one observes that $\mathrm{DOWN}(L_n) = \{\, \#^j aw \mid w \in A^*, j \geq 0, a \in \{\$, \lambda\} \text{ and } \bigvee_{i=1}^n |w|_{a_i} \leq n \,\}$.

It remains to be shown that the minimal DFA accepting $\mathrm{DOWN}(L_n)$ has at least $(n+1)^n + 2$ states. First observe that any two different words of the form $w_{i_1, i_2, \ldots, i_n} = \$ a_1^{i_1} a_2^{i_2} \ldots a_n^{i_n}$ with $0 \leq i_j \leq n$ and $1 \leq j \leq n$ are non-equivalent with respect to the Myhill-Nerode relation $\equiv_{\mathrm{DOWN}(L_n)}$. Let $w_{i_1, i_2, \ldots, i_n}$ and $w_{i'_1, i'_2, \ldots, i'_n}$ be two different words. Then $i_k \neq i'_k$, for some $1 \leq k \leq n$. Without loss of generality we assume $i_k < i'_k$. Then the word

$$w_{i_1, i_2, \ldots, i_n} \cdot a_1^{n+1} a_2^{n+1} \ldots a_{k-1}^{n+1} a_k^{(n+1)-i'_k} a_{k+1}^{n+1} \ldots a_n^{n+1}$$

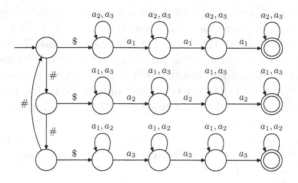

Fig. 1. A DFA of size $5 \cdot 16$ accepting $\text{DOWN}(L_3)$—the non-accepting sink state is not shown

belongs to $\text{DOWN}(L_n)$ because letter a_k appears at most n times. On the other hand, the word $w_{i'_1,i'_2,\ldots,i'_n} \cdot a_1^{n+1} a_2^{n+1} \ldots a_{k-1}^{n+1} a_k^{(n+1)-i'_k} a_{k+1}^{n+1} \ldots a_n^{n+1}$ is not member of $\text{DOWN}(L_n)$ since all letters a_i, for $1 \leq i \leq n$, appear at least $n+1$ times. Hence, there are $(n+1)^n$ different equivalence classes induced by the words $w_{i_1,i_2,\ldots,i_n}$. Moreover, none of the words λ, $w_{i_1,i_2,\ldots,i_n}$ with $0 \leq i_j \leq n$ and $1 \leq j \leq n$, and $\$a_1^{n+1} a_2^{n+1} \ldots a_n^{n+1}$ belong to the same equivalence classes. For λ and $w_{i_1,i_2,\ldots,i_n}$ this is seen by concatenating the words with $, and the remaining pairs are shown to be non-equivalent by concatenating them with the empty word λ. Therefore, we have obtained at least $(n+1)^n + 2$ equivalence classes. In fact, one can construct a DFA with exactly this number of states accepting $\text{DOWN}(L_n)$. The details are left to the reader. Therefore, $2^{\Omega(n \log n)}$ is a lower bound on the size of any DFA accepting $\text{DOWN}(L_n)$. □

The next theorem gives a lower bound for the size of any DFA accepting $\text{UP}(L(M))$, for a given DFA M. The proof is similar to the proof of the previous theorem.

Theorem 5. *For every $n \geq 1$, there exists a language L_n over an $(n+2)$-letter alphabet accepted by a DFA of size $(n+2)(n+1)^2$, such that size $2^{\Omega(n \log n)}$ is necessary for any DFA accepting $\text{UP}(L_n)$.* □

Finally, it is worth to mention that the lower bounds of the previous two theorems slightly improve when the number of states is used to measure the size of DFAs. The next theorem summarizes the lower bounds.

Theorem 6. *For every $n \geq 1$, there exists a language L_n over an $(n+2)$-letter alphabet accepted by a DFA with $(n+1)^2$ states, such that $2^{\Omega(n \log n)}$ states are necessary for any DFA accepting $\text{DOWN}(L_n)$. A similar statement is valid for $\text{UP}(L_n)$.* □

3.2   Context-Free and Linear Context-Free Languages

In this subsection we are interested in the size of NFAs accepting the Higman-Haines sets for context-free or linear context-free grammars. Recall that we use the total number of occurrences of terminal and nonterminal symbols in the productions as size measure for grammars. Let $G = (N, T, P, S)$ be a context-free grammar, where N is the finite set of *nonterminals*, T is the finite set of *terminals*, $P \subseteq N \times (N \cup T)^*$ is the finite set of productions, and $S \in N$ is the *axiom*. A context-free grammar $G = (N, T, P, S)$ is *linear context free* if $P \subseteq N \times T^*(N \cup \{\lambda\})T^*$. Without loss of generality, we assume that the context-free grammars are always *reduced*, i.e., that there are no unreachable or unproductive nonterminals. Moreover, in this section we further assume that the context-free grammars are in Chomsky normalform, i.e., the productions are of the form $P \subseteq N \times (N^2 \cup T)$. For linear context-free grammars the normalform reads as $P \subseteq N \times (NT \cup TN \cup T)$.

As in the previous subsection we first show how to construct an NFA for $\mathrm{DOWN}(L(G))$. In order to simplify the analysis we assume that the right-hand sides of the productions are described by NFAs with input alphabet $N \cup T$. We refer to such a grammar as an *extended* (linear) context-free grammar. Note, that one can assume that for each extended context-free grammar there is exactly one NFA for each nonterminal as a right-hand side. The following theorem is a detailed analysis of the inductive construction presented in [14].

Theorem 7. *Let G be a context-free grammar of size n. Then size $O(n2^{\sqrt{2^n}\log n})$ is sufficient for an NFA M' to accept $\mathrm{DOWN}(L(G))$. The NFA M' can effectively be constructed.*

Proof. First, the context-free grammar $G = (N, T, P, S)$ is transformed into an extended context-free grammar G'—the details are omitted here. Secondly, we observe that each nonterminal appears at the left-hand side of at least one production, respectively, and at least one nonterminal is rewritten by some terminal symbol. Therefore, the number of nonterminals is at most $\lfloor \frac{n}{2} \rfloor$.

Next, we inductively proceed as in [14]. For a nonterminal $A \in N$ we set the alphabet $V_A = (N \setminus \{A\}) \cup T$, and define the extended context-free grammar $G_A = (\{A\}, V_A, P_A, A)$ with $P_A = \{A \to M \mid (A \to M) \in P\}$, where M in $(A \to M) \in P$ refers to the NFA of the right-hand side of the production. Further, we set $L_A = L(G_A)$. Observe, that G_A is an extended context-free grammar with only *one* nonterminal and, thus, one can obtain an NFA M_A describing $\mathrm{DOWN}(L(G_A))$ over the alphabet V_A by a subroutine to be detailed below. Then the induction is as follows: Let $G_0 = G'$. If A is not the axiom S of G_0, we can replace each A-transition occurring in the right-hand side automata of non-A-productions of G_0 with a copy of M_A to obtain an extended grammar G_1 having one nonterminal less than G_0, and $\mathrm{DOWN}(L(G_1)) = \mathrm{DOWN}(L(G_0))$. This construction step can be iterated for at most $\lfloor \frac{n}{2} \rfloor - 1$ times, yielding extended context-free grammars $G_2, G_3, \ldots, G_{\lfloor \frac{n}{2} \rfloor - 1}$, satisfying $\mathrm{DOWN}(L(G_i)) = \mathrm{DOWN}(L(G_{i+1}))$, for $0 \le i < \lfloor \frac{n}{2} \rfloor$, where in the latter grammar $G_{\lfloor \frac{n}{2} \rfloor - 1}$ the only remaining nonterminal is the original axiom S of G. Finally, we apply the mentioned subroutine to construct the NFA M' which results in the finite automaton accepting the language $\mathrm{DOWN}(L(G))$.

It remains to describe the above mentioned subroutine and deduce an upper bound on the size of the automaton M'. The subroutine works for an extended grammar $G_A = (\{A\}, V_A, \{A \to M\}, A)$ with only *one* nonterminal. Then we distinguish two cases:

1. The production set given by $L(M)$ is linear, i.e., $L(M) \subseteq V_A^* \{A, \lambda\} V_A^*$, or
2. the production set given by $L(M)$ is nonlinear.

In the first case, we construct an NFA M_T with $L(M_T) = L(M) \cap V_A^*$, which is obtained by removing all A-transitions from M. Similarly, we build NFAs M_P and M_S for the quotients

$$L(M_P) = \{ x \in V_A^* \mid xAz \in L(M) \text{ for some } z \in (V_A \cup \{A\})^* \} \text{ and}$$
$$L(M_S) = \{ z \in V_A^* \mid xAz \in L(M) \text{ for some } x \in (V_A \cup \{A\})^* \}.$$

Then it is straightforward to construct an NFA M_A having a single start state and a single accepting state with

$$L(M_A) = \text{DOWN}(L(M_P)^* \cdot L(M_T) \cdot L(M_S)^*) = \text{DOWN}(L(G_A)).$$

The number of alphabetic transitions, i.e., non-λ-transitions, in M_A is at most three times that of M. In the second case, i.e., $L(M)$ is nonlinear, we construct automata M_P, M_T, M_S, and M_I, where the former three NFAs are as in the previous case, and M_I accepts the quotient

$$L(M_I) = \{ y \in V_A^* \mid xAyAz \in L(M) \text{ for some } x, z \in (V_A \cup \{A\})^* \}.$$

Again, it is not hard to construct an NFA M_A with a single start and a single accepting state accepting

$$L(M_A) = \text{DOWN}((L(M_T) \cup L(M_P) \cup L(M_I) \cup L(M_S))^*) = \text{DOWN}(L(G_A))$$

with no more than four times as many alphabetic transitions as M.

The upper bound on the size of an NFA accepting $\text{DOWN}(L(G))$ is deduced as follows: For an extended context-free grammar G, let $|G|_t$ denote the sum of the number of alphabet transitions in the right-hand side automata in the productions of G. We obtain the recurrence $|G_k|_t \leq 4 \cdot (|G_{k-1}|_t)^2$, for $1 \leq k < \lfloor \frac{n}{2} \rfloor$, describing the substitution step in the kth iteration to construct G_k from G_{k-1}. Taking logarithms and setting $H_k = \log |G_k|_t$, we obtain a linear recurrence $H_k \leq 2 \cdot H_{k-1} + 2$. Solving the linear recurrence, we obtain the inequality $H_k \leq 2^k \cdot H_0 + 2^{k+1} - 2$. Since $|G_0|_t \leq n$, we have

$$H_{\lfloor \frac{n}{2} \rfloor - 1} \leq 2^{\lfloor \frac{n}{2} \rfloor - 1} \cdot H_0 + 2^{\lfloor \frac{n}{2} \rfloor} - 2 \leq 2^{\lfloor \frac{n}{2} \rfloor - 1} \cdot \log n + 2^{\lfloor \frac{n}{2} \rfloor} - 2.$$

When replacing the axiom in $G_{\lfloor \frac{n}{2} \rfloor - 1}$ in the final step, the number of alphabetic transitions is increased at most by a factor of four, which results in

$$|G_{\lfloor \frac{n}{2} \rfloor}|_t \leq 2^{2^{\lfloor \frac{n}{2} \rfloor - 1} \cdot \log n + 2^{\lfloor \frac{n}{2} \rfloor}} \leq 2^{2^{\lfloor \frac{n}{2} \rfloor - 1} \cdot \log n + 2^{\lfloor \frac{n}{2} \rfloor - 1} \cdot \log n} \leq 2^{\sqrt{2^n} \log n},$$

for all $n \geq 4$. It remains to be shown that for every NFA with n alphabetical transitions, there is an equivalent NFA with at most $O(n)$ states. An easy construction can be used to remove all non-initial states having neither ingoing nor outgoing alphabetical transitions after adding some extra λ-transitions where necessary. By a simple counting argument, we find that the latter automaton has at most $2n + 1$ states. Hence, this shows that the NFA M' accepting $\text{Down}(L(G))$ has size at most $O(n \cdot 2^{\sqrt{2^n} \log n})$. $\square$

For the lower bound we obtain:

Theorem 8. *For every $n \geq 1$, there is a language L_n over a unary alphabet generated by a context-free grammar of size $3n+2$, such that size $2^{\Omega(n)}$ is necessary for any NFA accepting $\text{Down}(L(G))$ or $\text{Up}(L(G))$.*

Proof. For every $n \geq 1$, consider the finite unary languages $L_n = \{a^{2^n}\}$ generated by the context-free grammar $G = (\{A_1, A_2, \ldots, A_{n+1}\}, \{a\}, P, A_1)$ with the productions $A_i \rightarrow A_{i+1}A_{i+1}$, for $1 \leq i \leq n$, and $A_{n+1} \rightarrow a$. Obviously, grammar G has size $3n + 2$. The word a^{2^n} is the longest word in $\text{Down}(L(G))$ and the shortest word in $\text{Up}(L(G))$. In both cases, any finite automaton accepting the language takes at least as many states as the length of the word. So, it takes at least least 2^n states and, thus, has at least size 2^n. $\square$

We turn our attention to the construction of an NFA accepting $\text{Up}(L(G))$, for a context-free grammar G. To this end, we define the *basis of a language* as follows: A word $w \in L$ is called *minimal* in L if and only if there is no different $v \in L$ with $v \leq w$. The set of minimal elements in L is called a *basis* of the language $\text{Up}(L)$. Observe that any shortest word in L is minimal in L, and any such word must therefore be part of the basis. In fact, Higman's Lemma [9] says that for any arbitrary language L there exists a natural number n, which depends only on L, such that $\text{Up}(L) = \bigcup_{1 \leq i \leq n} \text{Up}(\{w_i\})$, for some words $w_i \in L$ with $1 \leq i \leq n$. Sometimes the result is called the *finite basis property*. For the construction of an NFA accepting $\text{Up}(L(G))$, where G is a context-free grammar with terminal alphabet A, we proceed as follows:

1. Determine the basis $B \subseteq A^*$ of the language $\text{Up}(L(G))$ with the algorithm presented in [14].
2. Construct an NFA M accepting language B, and apply the construction given in the previous subsection to obtain an NFA M' accepting $\text{Up}(B)$, which equals the language $\text{Up}(L(G))$ by the finite basis property.

The first step basically consists in inductively computing B starting from $B_0 = \emptyset$, and B_{i+1} is obtained by extending B_i by a shortest word w in $L(G) \setminus \text{Up}(B_i)$, i.e., setting $B_{i+1} = B_i \cup \{w\}$. This process is repeated as long as $(L(G) \setminus \text{Up}(B_i)) \neq \emptyset$. If this condition is met, the set B equals the last extended B_i. Since context-free languages are closed under set difference with regular sets, the set B can be effectively constructed.

Theorem 9. *Let G be a context-free grammar of size n. Then an NFA M' of size $O(\sqrt{n}2^{2^n \log n})$ is sufficient to accept $\text{Up}(L(G))$. The NFA M' can effectively be constructed.*

In the remainder of this section we concentrate on linear context-free languages.

Theorem 10. *Let G be a linear grammar of size n. Then an NFA M' of size $O\left(\sqrt{2^{n^2 + \frac{(3n+6)}{2}} \log n - (4 + \log e)n}\right)$ is sufficient to accept* $\text{DOWN}(L(G))$. *The NFA M' can effectively be constructed.*

Proof. Let $G = (N, T, P, A_1)$ with $N = \{A_i \mid 1 \le i \le m\}$ be a linear context-free grammar. The basic idea for the construction of M' is to inspect the derivation trees of G and to modify the underlying grammar such that any self-embedding derivation of the form $A \Rightarrow^* xAz$, for some $A \in N$ and $x, z \in T^*$, is replaced by a derivation $A \Rightarrow^* xA$ and $A \Rightarrow^* Az$, while the respective generated languages have the same DOWN-sets. In other words, the derivation that produces the "coupled" terminal words x and z is made "uncoupled" by a right-linear and a left-linear derivation. In order to make the construction work, one has to take care about these self-embedded derivation parts in an appropriate manner. For a formal treatment of the construction we need some notation.

Let $A_1 \Rightarrow^* w$ be a derivation of $w \in T^*$. Then the inner nodes of the derivation tree form a path $p = A_1 A_{i_1} A_{i_2} \cdots A_{i_k}$. We can group the inner nodes as follows: We call a subpath of p that represents a self-embedded derivation with nonterminal A, i.e., which begins and ends with the same nonterminal A, an A-block. A *splitting* of p into blocks is an ordered set $\mathcal{B}$ of blocks such that

1. any block in p is a subpath of exactly one element in $\mathcal{B}$,
2. there is at most one A-block for each nonterminal $A \in N$.

A splitting always exists, as the first condition can be ensured by adding blocks to $\mathcal{B}$ as long as necessary. Afterwards we can enforce the remaining conditions by merging blocks. The order of the set $\mathcal{B}$ is given naturally by the occurrence of blocks along the path. For such a splitting, we call a subpath connecting two consecutive blocks an (A, B)-*nonblock*, if the first is an A-block and the second one a B-block. By convention, the borders A and B are part of the nonblock. If the first or the last nonterminal of the path are not part of blocks, we agree that the paths connecting the ends to the first and last block are also nonblocks. A simple example explaining our terminology is depicted in Figure 2, where it is shown that a splitting is not necessarily unique.

Next, for each nonterminal $A \in N$ we build NFAs $M_{A,P}$ and $M_{A,S}$ for the quotients

$$L(M_{A,P}) = \{x \in T^* \mid A \Rightarrow^* xAz \text{ for some } z \in T^*\} \text{ and}$$
$$L(M_{A,S}) = \{z \in T^* \mid A \Rightarrow^* xAz \text{ for some } x \in T^*\}.$$

Then it is straightforward to construct an NFA M_A having a single start state and a single accepting state such that $L(M_A)$ is the DOWN-set of the set of all partial derivations corresponding to an A-block, i.e.,

$$L(M_A) = \text{DOWN}(L(M_{A,P})^* \cdot A \cdot L(M_{A,S})^*).$$

The number of states in M_A is at most $2|N| \leq n$, and it contains a single A-transition. Moreover, for every $A, B \in N$ we build NFAs $M_{A,I}$ and $M_{(A,B),I}$ taking care of the terminating derivation part and the nonblocks, namely

$$L(M_{A,I}) = \{y \in T^* \mid A \Rightarrow^* y \text{ is an acyclic derivation, } y \in T^*\} \text{ and}$$
$$L(M_{(A,B),I}) = \{xBz \in T^*NT^* \mid A \Rightarrow^* xBz \text{ is an acyclic derivation, } x, z \in T^*\}.$$

Here a derivation is said to be acyclic, if no nonterminal occurs more than once in the derivation. The DOWN-set of all partial derivations corresponding to some (A, B)-nonblock is given by $L(M_{(A,B)}) = \text{DOWN}(L(M_{(A,B),I}))$, the DOWN-set of the terminating derivation part by $L(M_{(A)}) = \text{DOWN}(L(M_{(A,I)}))$. We note two features of $L(M_{(A,B),I})$: First, all words in the language are at most of length $|N|$, and secondly, by [2, Lemma 4.3.2], it contains at most $2^{|P|-1}$ words. Then the construction given in [7] yields an NFA $M_{(A,B),I}$ with at most $\frac{3}{\sqrt{2}} \cdot n^{\frac{1}{4}}$ states and at most 2^{n-1} many B-transitions accepting this language, as $|\Sigma| \leq n$ and $|N|$ as well as $|P|$ cannot exceed $n/2$. The same bound on the number of states applies to $M_{A,I}$, and due to Lemma 2 and the constructions of NFAs for DOWN-sets of NFA languages, the bounds on states and transitions apply also to $M_{(A,B)}$ and $M_{(A)}$.

Finally, for every splitting $\mathcal{B} = \{A_{i_1}, A_{i_2}, \ldots, A_{i_m}\}$ containing m blocks, we obtain an NFA accepting the DOWN-set of all derivations $A_1 \Rightarrow^* w$ whose trees admit a $\mathcal{B}$-splitting by iterated substitution of transitions by NFAs. We start with the terminating derivation part, i.e, the NFA $M_{(A_{i_m})}$ with no more than $H_0 = \frac{3}{\sqrt{2}} \cdot n^{\frac{1}{4}}$ states. Next we proceed in cycles. In each cycle k, two substitution phases are performed. First, the current NFA, say with H_k states, replaces the sole (A_{i_m-k})-transition of the NFA $M_{A_{i_m-k}}$. This results in at most $H_k + n$ states. Secondly, all (A_{i_m-k})-transitions of the NFA $M_{(A_{i_m-k-1}, A_{i_m-k})}$ are replaced by the NFA constructed in the first phase. The result is an NFA with at most $2^{n-1}(H_k + n) + H_0$ states. Clearly, the construction is completed after m cycles.

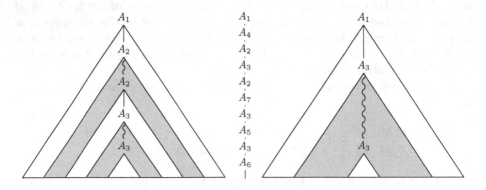

Fig. 2. Two splittings for the path $p = A_1, A_4, A_2, A_3, A_2, A_7, A_3, A_5, A_3, A_6$; blocks are gray shaded and the derivation is drawn by a curled path, while nonblocks are white and their derivation is drawn by a straight line

For the number of states, we have to solve recurrence $H_m = 2^{n-1}(H_{m-1}+n)+H_0$ with $H_0 = \frac{3}{\sqrt{2}} \cdot n^{\frac{n}{4}}$. Unrolling yields the series

$$H_m = H_0 + (H_0 + n)\sum_{i=1}^{m}(2^{n-1})^i = H_0 + (H_0 + n)\frac{2^{(n-1)(k+1)} - 1}{2^{n-1} - 1} - 1.$$

Since $m + 1 \le |N| \le n/2$, this is less than or equal to

$$H_0 + (H_0 + n)\frac{2^{\frac{(n-1)n}{2}}}{2^{n-2}} \le H_0 + (H_0 + n)4\frac{2^{\frac{n^2}{2}}}{2^{\frac{3n}{2}}} \in O\left(\frac{n^{\frac{n}{4}}2^{\frac{n^2}{2}}}{2^{\frac{3n}{2}}}\right)$$

$$= O\left(\sqrt{2^{n^2+\frac{n}{2}\log n - 3n}}\right).$$

An important observation is that this automaton also accepts the DOWN-set of all derivations whose trees admit some splitting in DOWN($\mathcal{B}$). So, it suffices to consider $|N|!$ relevant different splittings. Therefore, the number of states of the NFA M' accepting DOWN($L(G)$) is at most $O\left(\left(\frac{n}{2}\right)!\sqrt{2^{n^2+\frac{n}{2}\log n-3n}}\right)$. This implies a size of $O\left(\left(\frac{n}{2}\right)!\sqrt{2^{n^2+\frac{(n+4)}{2}\log n-3n}}\right)$. Finally, Stirling's approximation yields $O\left(\left(\frac{n}{2}\right)!\right) = O\left(\sqrt{n}\left(\frac{n}{2e}\right)^{\frac{n}{2}}\right) = O\left(\sqrt{2^{\log n}}\sqrt{2^{n\log n}}\sqrt{2^{-n(1+\log e)}}\right)$ and, thus, an upper bound of

$$O\left(\sqrt{n}\left(\frac{n}{2e}\right)^{\frac{n}{2}}\sqrt{2^{n^2+\frac{(n+4)}{2}\log n-3n}}\right) = O\left(\sqrt{2^{n^2+\frac{(3n+6)}{2}\log n-(4+\log e)n}}\right).$$

$\square$

In order to show the lower bound we use the finite witness language $L_n = \{ ww^R \mid w \in \{a,b\}^n \}$, which can be generated by a linear context-free grammar $G = (\{ A_i, A'_i, A''_i \mid 1 \le i \le n \}, \{a,b\}, P, A_1)$ with the productions $A_i \to aA'_i$, $A'_i \to A_{i+1}a$, $A_i \to bA''_i$, $A''_i \to A_{i+1}b$, for $1 \le i < n$, and $A_n \to aA'_n$, $A'_n \to a$, $A_n \to bA''_n$, $A''_n \to b$. Since any NFA accepting L_n needs at least 2^n states—see, e.g., [6]—the next theorem reads as follows. Observe, that the lower bound also holds for the up-set problem.

Theorem 11. *For every $n \ge 1$, there is a linear context-free language L_n over a binary alphabet generated by a linear context-free grammar of size $12n - 2$, such that size $2^{\Omega(n)}$ is necessary for any NFA accepting* DOWN($L(G)$) *or* UP($L(G)$).

$\square$

For the size of UP($L(G)$), for some linear context-free grammar G of size n, we argue as follows: The basis B of UP($L(G)$) contains only words whose lengths are at most n. Then by similar arguments as in the proof of Theorem 9 we obtain the following result, which is much better than that for general context-free grammars.

Theorem 12. *Let G be a linear context-free grammar of size n. Then an NFA M' of size $O(\sqrt{2^{(n+2)\log n}})$ is sufficient to accept* UP($L(G)$). *The NFA M' can effectively be constructed.*

$\square$

4   Conclusions

Several questions about the size of Higman-Haines sets remain unanswered. We mention a few of them: (1) Can one obtain better matching upper and lower bounds for context-free and linear context-free languages? Similarly, which are better bounds for *deterministic* finite automata? (2) There are some other interesting and important subfamilies of the context-free languages, e.g., unary, bounded, deterministic or turn-bounded context-free languages. The sizes of the corresponding Higman-Haines sets are worth studying. (3) Our investigations are based on the special case of the scattered subword relation. Since the result of Higman and Haines only needs a well-partially-order one may ask similar questions for other well-partially-orders as, e.g., for the Parikh subword quasi-order or for monotone well-quasi-orders—see [3,11] for further results about these well-quasi-orders.

References

1. Buntrock, G., Otto, F.: Growing context-sensitive languages and Church-Rosser languages. Inform. Comput. 141, 1–36 (1998)
2. Dassow, J., Păun, G.: Regulated Rewriting in Formal Language Theory. Springer, Berlin (1989)
3. Ehrenfeucht, A., Haussler, D., Rozenberg, G.: On regularity of context-free languages. Theoret. Comput. Sci. 27, 311–332 (1983)
4. Fernau, H., Stephan, F.: Characterizations of recursively enumerable sets by programmed grammars with unconditional transfer. J. Autom., Lang. Comb. 4, 117–152 (1999)
5. Gilman, R.H.: A shrinking lemma for indexed languages. Theoret. Comput. Sci. 163, 277–281 (1996)
6. Glaister, I., Shallit, J.: A lower bound technique for the size of nondeterministic finite automata. Inform. Process. Lett. 59, 75–77 (1996)
7. Gruber, H., Holzer, M.: Results on the average state and transition complexity of finite automata. Descriptional Complexity of Formal Systems (DCFS 2006), University of New Mexico, Technical Report NMSU-CS-2006-001, pp. 267–275 (2006)
8. Haines, L.H.: On free monoids partially ordered by embedding. J. Combinatorial Theory 6, 94–98 (1969)
9. Higman, G.: Ordering by divisibility in abstract algebras. Proc. London Math. Soc. 2, 326–336 (1952)
10. Gruber, H., Holzer, M., Kutrib, M.: The size of Higman-Haines sets. Theoret. Comput. Sci. (to appear)
11. Ilie, L.: Decision problems on orders of words. Ph.D. thesis, Department of Mathematics, University of Turku, Finland (1998)
12. Kruskal, J.B.: The theory of well-quasi-ordering: A frequently discovered concept. J. Combinatorial Theory 13, 297–305 (1972)
13. van Leeuwen, J.: A regularity condition for parallel rewriting systems. SIGACT News. 8, 24–27 (1976)
14. van Leeuwen, J.: Effective constructions in well-partially-ordered free monoids. Discrete Mathematics 21, 237–252 (1978)

Insertion-Deletion Systems with One-Sided Contexts

Artiom Matveevici[1,2], Yurii Rogozhin[2,4], and Sergey Verlan[3]

[1] Moldova State University
60, str. A.Mateevici, MD-2009, Chişinău, Moldova
`martiom@mail.md`
[2] Institute of Mathematics and Computer Science
Academy of Sciences of Moldova
5, str. Academiei, MD-2028, Chişinău, Moldova
`rogozhin@math.md`
[3] LACL, Département Informatique, Université Paris 12,
61, av. Général de Gaulle, 94010 Créteil, France
`verlan@univ-paris12.fr`
[4] Rovira i Virgili University,
Research Group on Mathematical Linguistics,
Pl. Imperial Tàrraco 1, 43005 Tarragona, Spain

Abstract. It was shown in (Verlan, 2005) that complexity measures for insertion-deletion systems need a revision and new complexity measures taking into account the sizes of both left and right context were proposed. In this article we investigate insertion-deletion systems having a context only on one side of insertion or deletion rules. We show that a minimal deletion (of one symbol) in one-symbol one-sided context is sufficient for the computational completeness if a cooperation of 4 symbols is used for insertion rules and not sufficient if an insertion of one symbol in one-symbol left and right context is used. We also prove the computational completeness for the case of the minimal context-free deletion (of two symbols) and insertion of two symbols in one-symbol one-sided context.

Keywords: insertion-deletion systems, universality, computational non-completeness.

1 Introduction

The operations of insertion and deletion are fundamental in formal language theory, and generative mechanisms based on them were considered (with linguistic motivation) since "old times", see [6] and [2]. Related formal language investigations can be found in several places; we mention only [3], [5], [8], [9]. In the last years, the study of these operations has received a new motivation, from molecular computing, see [1], [4], [10], [12].

In general form, an insertion operation means adding a substring to a given string in a specified context, while a deletion operation means removing a substring of a given string from a specified context. A finite set of insertion-deletion

J. Durand-Lose and M. Margenstern (Eds.): MCU 2007, LNCS 4664, pp. 205–217, 2007.

rules, together with a set of axioms provide a language generating device (an InsDel system): starting from the set of initial strings and iterating insertion-deletion operations as defined by the given rules we get a language. The number of axioms, the length of the inserted or deleted strings, as well as the length of the contexts where these operations take place are natural descriptional complexity measures in this framework. As expected, insertion and deletion operations with context dependence are very powerful, leading to characterizations of recursively enumerable languages. Most of the papers mentioned above contain such results, in many cases improving the complexity of insertion-deletion systems previously available in the literature. However, the power of the above operations is not necessarily related to the used context: the paper [7] contains an unexpected result: context-free insertion-deletion systems with one axiom are already universal, they can generate any recursively enumerable language. Moreover, this result can be obtained by inserting and deleting strings of a rather small length, at most three.

The further study of context-free insertion-deletion systems led in [13] to the complete description of this class. In particular, it was shown that if inserted or deleted strings are at most of length two, then a specific subclass of the family of context-free languages is obtained. This result showed that the traditional complexity measures for insertion-deletion systems, in particular the total weight based on the size of contexts, need a revision, because both systems from [12] and [13] have same total weight, but different computational power. In the same article, new complexity measures taking in account the sizes of both left and right context were proposed.

In this article we investigate insertion-deletion systems which use a context only on one side of insertion or deletion rules. Such systems are very similar to context-free insertion-deletion systems where insertions or deletions are uncontrollable and may happen an arbitrary number of times at any place. We investigate the case of a minimal deletion when the length of one context together with the length of the deleted string is at most two and we show three computational completeness results and one non-completeness result based on different combination of parameters. The article refines the borderline between universality and non-universality (and even decidability) for insertion-deletion systems and leaves a number of open problems related to other combinations of parameters.

2   Prerequisites

All formal language notions and notations we use here are elementary and standard. The reader can consult any of the many monographs in this area – for instance, [11] – for the unexplained details.

We denote by $|w|$ the length of word w and by $card(A)$ the cardinality of the set A.

An *InsDel system* is a construct $ID = (V, T, A, I, D)$, where V is an alphabet, $T \subseteq V$, A is a finite language over V, and I, D are finite sets of triples of the form

(u, α, v), $\alpha \neq \varepsilon$ of strings over V, where ε denotes the empty string. The elements of T are *terminal* symbols (in contrast, those of $V - T$ are called nonterminals), those of A are *axioms*, the triples in I are *insertion rules*, and those from D are *deletion rules*. An insertion rule $(u, \alpha, v) \in I$ indicates that the string α can be inserted in between u and v, while a deletion rule $(u, \alpha, v) \in D$ indicates that α can be removed from the context (u, v). Stated otherwise, $(u, \alpha, v) \in I$ corresponds to the rewriting rule $uv \rightarrow u\alpha v$, and $(u, \alpha, v) \in D$ corresponds to the rewriting rule $u\alpha v \rightarrow uv$. We denote by $\Longrightarrow_{ins}$ the relation defined by an insertion rule (formally, $x \Longrightarrow_{ins} y$ iff $x = x_1 uv x_2, y = x_1 u\alpha v x_2$, for some $(u, \alpha, v) \in I$ and $x_1, x_2 \in V^*$) and by $\Longrightarrow_{del}$ the relation defined by a deletion rule (formally, $x \Longrightarrow_{del} y$ iff $x = x_1 u\alpha v x_2, y = x_1 uv x_2$, for some $(u, \alpha, v) \in D$ and $x_1, x_2 \in V^*$). We refer by $\Longrightarrow$ to any of the relations $\Longrightarrow_{ins}, \Longrightarrow_{del}$, and denote by $\Longrightarrow^*$ the reflexive and transitive closure of $\Longrightarrow$ (as usual, $\Longrightarrow^+$ is its transitive closure).

The language generated by ID is defined by $L(ID) = \{w \in T^* \mid x \Longrightarrow^* w,$ for some $x \in A\}$.

The complexity of an InsDel system $ID = (V, T, A, I, D)$ is traditionally described by the vector $(n, m; p, q)$ called *weight*, where

$$n = \max\{|\alpha| \mid (u, \alpha, v) \in I\},$$
$$m = \max\{|u| \mid (u, \alpha, v) \in I \text{ or } (v, \alpha, u) \in I\},$$
$$p = \max\{|\alpha| \mid (u, \alpha, v) \in D\},$$
$$q = \max\{|u| \mid (u, \alpha, v) \in D \text{ or } (v, \alpha, u) \in D\}.$$

The *total weight* of ID is the sum $\gamma = m + n + p + q$.

However, it was shown in [13] that this complexity measure is not accurate and it cannot distinguish between universality and non-universality cases (there are families having same total weight but not the same computational power). In the same article it was proposed to use the length of each context instead of the maximum. More exactly,

$$n = \max\{|\alpha| \mid (u, \alpha, v) \in I\},$$
$$m = \max\{|u| \mid (u, \alpha, v) \in I\},$$
$$m' = \max\{|v| \mid (u, \alpha, v) \in I\},$$
$$p = \max\{|\alpha| \mid (u, \alpha, v) \in D\},$$
$$q = \max\{|u| \mid (u, \alpha, v) \in D\},$$
$$q' = \max\{|v| \mid (u, \alpha, v) \in D\}.$$

Hence the complexity of an insertion-deletion system will be described by the vector $(n, m, m'; p, q, q')$ that we call *size*. We also denote by $INS_n^{m, m'} DEL_p^{q, q'}$ corresponding families of insertion-deletion systems. Moreover, we define the total weight of the system as the sum of all numbers above: $\psi = n + m + m' + p + q + q'$. Since it is known from [13] that systems using a context-free insertion or deletion of one symbol are not powerful, we additionally require $n + m + m' \geq 2$ and $p + q + q' \geq 2$.

If some of the parameters n, m, m', p, q, q' is not specified, then we write instead the symbol $*$. In particular, $INS_*^{0,0}DEL_*^{0,0}$ denotes the family of languages generated by *context-free InsDel systems*. If some of numbers m, m', q or q' are equal to zero, then we say that corresponding families have a one-sided context.

InsDel systems of a "sufficiently large" weight can characterize RE, the family of recursively enumerable languages. A collection of these results may be found in Section 4.

3 Systems with One-Sided Context

In this section we present results about insertion-deletion systems with one-sided context, *i.e.*, of size $(n, m, m'; p, q, q')$ where either $m + m' > 0$ and $m * m' = 0$, or $q + q' > 0$ and $q * q' = 0$, *i.e.*, at least one of numbers in some couple is equal to zero.

Our proof is based on the result from [12], where it was shown that insertion-deletion systems of size $(1, 1, 1; 1, 1, 1)$ generate all recursively enumerable languages. Firstly consider following lemma which presents a kind of normal form for these systems.

Lemma 1. *For any insertion-deletion system* $ID = (V, T, A, I, D)$ *having the size* $(1, 1, 1; 1, 1, 1)$ *it is possible to construct an insertion-deletion system* $ID_2 = (V \cup \{X, Y\}, T, A_2, I_2, D_2 \cup D_2')$ *of size* $(1, 1, 1; 1, 1, 1)$ *such that* $L(ID_2) = L(ID)$. *Moreover, all rules from* I_2 *and* D_2 *have the form* (a, x, b), *where* $a, b \neq \varepsilon$ *and* $D_2' = \{(\varepsilon, X, \varepsilon), (\varepsilon, Y, \varepsilon)\}$.

Proof. Consider

$$A_2 = \{XwY \mid w \in A\},$$
$$S_2 = \{(a, x, b) \mid (a, x, b) \in S \text{ and } a, b \neq \varepsilon\} \cup$$
$$\quad \{(z, x, b) \mid (\varepsilon, x, b) \in S, z \in V \cup \{X\} \text{ and } b \neq \varepsilon\} \cup$$
$$\quad \{(a, x, z) \mid (a, x, \varepsilon) \in S, z \in V \cup \{Y\} \text{ and } a \neq \varepsilon\} \cup$$
$$\quad \{(z_1, x, z_2) \mid (\varepsilon, x, \varepsilon) \in S, z_1 \in V \cup \{X\}, z_2 \in V \cup \{Y\}\},$$
$$S \in \{I, D\}.$$

In fact, any rule having an empty left (resp. right) context is replaced by $card(V) + 1$ rules, where the left (resp. right) context is a symbol from $V \cup \{X\}$ (resp. $V \cup \{Y\}$). Any axiom $w \in A$ is surrounded by X and Y (XwY) in A_2. It is clear that if $w \in L(ID)$ then the word XwY will be obtained in ID_2 using corresponding rules and starting from the corresponding axiom. Now symbols X and Y may be erased by rules from D_2' and we obtain that $w \in L(ID_2)$. It is clear that if rules from D_2' are used before this step, then at most same w may be obtained. Hence $L(ID) = L(ID_2)$.

Moreover, following more general result holds.

Lemma 2. *For any insertion-deletion system* $ID = (V, T, A, I, D)$ *having the size* $(n, m, m'; p, q, q')$ *it is possible to construct an insertion-deletion system*

$ID_2 = (V \cup \{X, Y\}, T, A_2, I_2, D_2 \cup D_2')$ *having same size such that* $L(ID_2) = L(ID)$. *Moreover, all rules from* I_2 *have the form* (u, α, v), *where* $|u| = m$, $|v| = m'$, *all rules from* D_2 *have the form* (u', α, v'), *where* $|u'| = q$, $|v'| = q'$ *and* $D_2' = \{(\varepsilon, X, \varepsilon), (\varepsilon, Y, \varepsilon)\}$.

Proof. The proof is similar to the previous lemma. We replace each axiom $w \in A$ by the word $X^i w Y^j$, where $i = \max\{m, q\}$ and $j = \max\{m', q'\}$ and we construct rules from I_2 and D_2 similarly to the previous lemma.

Now we prove the following theorem.

Theorem 3. $INS_1^{1,2} DEL_1^{1,0} = RE$.

Proof. In order to prove the theorem it is sufficient to show that for any insertion-deletion system $ID = (V, T, A, I, D)$ of size $(1, 1, 1; 1, 1, 1)$ it is possible to construct a system $ID_2 = (V_2, T, A, I_2, D_2)$ of size $(1, 1, 2; 1, 1, 0)$ that will generate same language as ID.

From Lemma 1 it is clear that in order to show the inclusion $L(ID) \subseteq L(ID_2)$ it is sufficient to show how a deletion rule $(a, x, b) \in D$, with $a, b, x \in V$, may be simulated by using rules of system ID_2, i.e., insertion rules of type $(a', x', b'c')$ and deletion rules of type (a'', y, ε), with $a', a'', b', c' \in V_2 \cup \{\varepsilon\}$, $x', y \in V_2$.

Consider $V_2 = V \cup \{X_i, D_i^1, D_i^2, D_i^3 \mid 1 \le i \le card(D)\}$

Let us label all rules from D by integer numbers. Consider now a rule i : $(a, x, b) \in D$, where $1 \le i \le card(D)$ is the label of the rule. We introduce insertion rules (x, X_i, b), (a, D_i^1, xX_i), $(a, D_i^2, D_i^1 X_i)$, $(a, D_i^3, D_i^2 b)$ in I_2 and deletion rules (D_i^1, x, ε), $(D_i^2, D_i^1, \varepsilon)$, $(D_i^2, X_i, \varepsilon)$, $(D_i^3, D_i^2, \varepsilon)$, $(\varepsilon, D_i^3, \varepsilon)$ in D_2. We say that these rules are i-related. The rule $i : (a, x, b) \in D$ is simulated as follows. We first perform two insertions:

$$w_1 a x b w_2 \Longrightarrow_{ins} w_1 a x X_i b w_2 \Longrightarrow_{ins} w_1 a D_i^1 x X_i b w_2,$$

after that we delete x:

$$w_1 a D_i^1 x X_i b w_2 \Longrightarrow_{del} w_1 a D_i^1 X_i b w_2,$$

after that we insert D_i^2:

$$w_1 a D_i^1 X_i b w_2 \Longrightarrow_{ins} w_1 a D_i^2 D_i^1 X_i b w_2,$$

and delete D_i^1 and X_i:

$$w_1 a D_i^2 D_i^1 X_i b w_2 \Longrightarrow_{del} w_1 a D_i^2 X_i b w_2 \Longrightarrow_{del} w_1 a D_i^2 b w_2.$$

At this moment we insert D_i^3 which deletes D_i^2:

$$w_1 a D_i^2 b w_2 \Longrightarrow_{ins} w_1 a D_i^3 D_i^2 b w_2 \Longrightarrow_{del} w_1 a D_i^3 b w_2.$$

Finally symbol D_i^3 is removed:

$$w_1 a D_i^3 b w_2 \Longrightarrow_{del} w_1 a b w_2.$$

Hence, $L(ID) \subseteq L(ID_2)$. Now in order to prove the converse inclusion, we observe that the first two insertions may happen if and only if x is surrounded by a and b. Moreover, after the two insertions are performed, the only way to get rid of introduced additional symbols is to perform the sequence of insertions and deletions presented above. Indeed, the additional symbols block any insertion different from the presented above inside the site between a and b. At their turn, symbols a and b prevent the interaction of the above sequence with other possible sequences of i-related rules.

The following theorem shows the trade-off between the left context of the insertion and the size of the inserted string.

Theorem 4. $INS_2^{0,2} DEL_1^{1,0} = RE$.

Proof. We prove the theorem by simulating systems from Theorem 3. More exactly, we show that for any insertion-deletion system $ID = (V, T, A, I, D)$ of size $(1, 1, 2; 1, 1, 0)$ it is possible to construct a system $ID_2 = (V_2, T, A, I_2, D_2)$ of size $(2, 0, 2; 1, 1, 0)$ that will generate same language as ID.

From Lemma 2, but also from the proof of Theorem 3, it is clear that the inclusion $L(ID) \subseteq L(ID_2)$ will be obtained if it will be shown how an insertion rule $(a, x, bc) \in I$, with $a, b, c, x \in V$ may be simulated by using rules of system ID_2, i.e., insertion rules of type $(\varepsilon, zy, b'c')$ and deletion rules of type (a', y', ε), with $a', b', c', z \in V_2 \cup \{\varepsilon\}$, $y, y' \in V_2$.

Consider $V_2 = V \cup \{Y_i \mid 1 \leq i \leq card(I)\}$

Let us label all rules from I by integer numbers. Consider now a rule i : $(a, x, bc) \in I$, where $1 \leq i \leq card(I)$ is the label of the rule. We introduce an insertion rule $(\varepsilon, Y_i x, bc)$ in I_2 and a deletion rule (a, Y_i, ε) in D_2. We say that these rules are i-related.

We remark that since the left context is equal to zero, a rule (ε, xy, bc) may be applied any number of times, hence the language $w_1(xy)^+ bcw_2$ (we can also write it as $w_1(xy)^* xybcw_2$ or $w_1 xy(xy)^* bcw_2$) may be obtained from $w_1 bcw_2$. This behavior shall be taken into account.

The rule $i : (a, x, bc)$ is simulated as follows. We first perform an insertion:

$$w_1 abcw_2 \Longrightarrow_{ins}^+ w_1 aY_i x(Y_i x)^* bcw_2$$

after that we delete Y_i:

$$w_1 aY_i x(Y_i x)^* bcw_2 \Longrightarrow_{del} w_1 ax(Y_i x)^* bcw_2.$$

If only one insertion is performed during the insertion step, then we obtain the string $w_1 axbcw_2$. Hence, $L(ID) \subseteq L(ID_2)$.

In order to prove the converse inclusion we need to show that no other words may be obtained. Indeed, the insertion rule $(\varepsilon, Y_i x, bc)$ introduces a non-terminal symbol Y_i. This symbol may be erased if and only if its left neighbor is a. Hence, symbol x is inserted between a and bc. Let us consider a repeated application of the insertion rule. In this case symbols Y_i may be eliminated only in two cases: either $x = a$ (in this case the inserted $Y_i x$ eliminates preceding Y_i), or $x = b = c$ (in this case all Y_i are in the first position, just after a). But these cases represent an iterative application of the simulated rule (a, x, bc) (indeed, if $a = x$ or $b = c = x$, this rule may be applied any number of times). Hence, no different words may be generated and $L(ID_2) \subseteq L(ID)$.

The next result decreases the size of the insertion context at the price of increasing the deletion strings.

Theorem 5. $INS_2^{0,1} DEL_2^{0,0} = RE$.

Proof. The proof of the theorem is based on a simulation of insertion-deletion systems of size $(1, 1, 1; 2, 0, 0)$. It is known that these systems generate any recursively enumerable language [10]. Consider $ID = (V, T, A, I, D)$ to be such a system. Now we construct system $ID_2 = (V_2, T, A, I_2, D_2)$ of size $(2, 0, 1; 2, 0, 0)$ that will generate same language as ID.

Like in previous theorems we show that any rule $(a, x, b) \in I$, with $a, x, b \in V$ may be simulated by rules of system ID_2, i.e., insertion rules of type $(\varepsilon, a'b', c')$ and deletion rules of type $(\varepsilon, a'b', \varepsilon)$, with $a', b', c' \in V_2 \cup \{\varepsilon\}$, $0 < |a'b'| \leq 2$.

Consider $V_2 = V \cup \{X_i^1, X_i^2, X_i^3, Y_i^2, Y_i^3, K_i^1, K_i^2 \mid 1 \leq i \leq card(I)\}$.

Let us label all rules from I by integer numbers. Consider now a rule i : $(a, x, b) \in I$, where $1 \leq i \leq card(I)$ is the label of the rule. We introduce the following insertion rules in I_2:

$$(\varepsilon, X_i^1, b), \tag{1}$$
$$(\varepsilon, X_i^2 Y_i^2, \varepsilon), \tag{2}$$
$$(\varepsilon, X_i^3 Y_i^3, \varepsilon), \tag{3}$$
$$(\varepsilon, a K_i^1, \varepsilon), \tag{4}$$
$$(\varepsilon, x K_i^2, K_i^1), \tag{5}$$

and following deletion rules in D_2:

$$(\varepsilon, Y_i^2 a, \varepsilon), \tag{6}$$
$$(\varepsilon, X_i^2 X_i^3, \varepsilon), \tag{7}$$
$$(\varepsilon, K_i^1 Y_i^3, \varepsilon), \tag{8}$$
$$(\varepsilon, K_i^2 X_i^1, \varepsilon). \tag{9}$$

We say that these rules are i-related.

Like in previous theorem, since the left context is equal to zero, an insertion rule (ε, xy, b) may be applied any number of times, hence the language $w_1(xy)^+ bw_2$ (we can also write it as $w_1(xy)^* xybw_2$ or $w_1xy(xy)^* bw_2$) may be obtained from $w_1 bw_2$.

The rule $i : (a, x, b) \in I$ is simulated as follows. We first perform insertions of X_i^1 and $X_i^2 Y_i^2$ (in any order):

$$w_1 abw_2 \Longrightarrow_{ins}^+ w_1 a(X_i^1)^+ bw_2 \Longrightarrow_{ins}^+ w_1 (X_i^2 Y_i^2)^+ a(X_i^1)^+ bw_2.$$

After that we insert $X_i^3 Y_i^3$ and aK_i^1:

$$w_1(X_i^2 Y_i^2)^+ a(X_i^1)^+ bw_2 \Longrightarrow_{ins}^+$$
$$w_1(X_i^2 Y_i^2)^+ a((X_i^3 Y_i^3)^+ X_i^1)^+ bw_2 \Longrightarrow_{ins}^+$$
$$w_1(X_i^2 Y_i^2)^+ a((X_i^3 (aK_i^1)^+ Y_i^3)^+ X_i^1)^+ bw_2.$$

At last we insert xK_i^2:

$$w_1(X_i^2 Y_i^2)^+ a((X_i^3 (aK_i^1)^+ Y_i^3)^+ X_i^1)^+ bw_2 \Longrightarrow_{ins}^+$$
$$w_1(X_i^2 Y_i^2)^+ a((X_i^3 (a(xK_i^2)^+ K_i^1)^+ Y_i^3)^+ X_i^1)^+ bw_2.$$

We can delete $Y_i^1 a$ at this stage of computation or earlier (does not matter):

$$w_1(X_i^2 Y_i^2)^+ a((X_i^3 (a(xK_i^2)^+ K_i^1)^+ Y_i^3)^+ X_i^1)^+ bw_2 \Longrightarrow_{del}$$
$$w_1(X_i^2 Y_i^2)^* X_i^2 ((X_i^3 (a(xK_i^2)^+ K_i^1)^+ Y_i^3)^+ X_i^1)^+ bw_2.$$

After that deletion rules $(\varepsilon, X_i^2 X_i^3, \varepsilon)$, $(\varepsilon, K_i^1 Y_i^3, \varepsilon)$ and $(\varepsilon, K_i^2 X_i^1, \varepsilon)$ may be applied.

$$w_1(X_i^2 Y_i^2)^* X_i^2 ((X_i^3 (a(xK_i^2)^+ K_i^1)^+ Y_i^3)^+ X_i^1)^+ bw_2 \Longrightarrow_{del}$$
$$w_1(X_i^2 Y_i^2)^* (X_i^3 (a(xK_i^2)^+ K_i^1)^+ Y_i^3)^* (a(xK_i^2)^+ K_i^1)^* ax(X_i^1)^* bw_2.$$

If only one insertion is performed during each insertion step, then we obtain the string $w_1 axbw_2$. Hence, $L(ID) \subseteq L(ID_2)$.

Now we prove that no other words may be obtained using rules above. Indeed, by construction, any insertion rule inserts at least one symbol from $V_2 \setminus V$. So, in order to eliminate it, a corresponding deletion rule is needed. Moreover, inserted symbols may be divided in two categories that group symbols with respect to the deletion. In the first category we have X_i^2, Y_i^2, X_i^3, Y_i^3 and K_i^1. It is clear that if any of these symbols is inserted into the string, then all other symbols must be also inserted, otherwise it is not possible to eliminate them. The second group contains symbols X_i^1 and K_i^2. Now let us present some invariants which appear if we want to obtain a terminal string. Suppose that there is $(a, x, b) \in I$ and $w_1 abw_2$ is a word obtained on some step of a derivation in ID. We can deduce the following.

- One of the rules 4, 2 or 3 must be applied, otherwise nothing happens.
- In order to eliminate the introduced symbols, rules 8, 6 or 7 must be applied.
- Rule 6 may be applied if only if $X_i^2 Y_i^2$ is followed by symbol a: $(\ldots X_i^2 Y_i^2 a \ldots)$
- Rule 7 may be applied if and only if symbol X_i^3 was preceded by the string $X_i^2 Y_i^2 a$: $(\ldots X_i^2 Y_i^2 a X_i^3 \ldots Y_i^3 \ldots)$.
- Rule 8 may be applied if and only if symbol Y_i^3 is preceded by K_i^1: $(\ldots X_i^2 Y_i^2 a X_i^3 \ldots aK_i^1 Y_i^3 \ldots)$.

Hence, once one of above rules is applied, all other insertion and deletion rules above must be also applied, otherwise some non-terminal symbols are not eliminated. We also remark that if at this moment the three deletion rules 6, 7 and 8 are performed, then string w_1abw_2 is obtained, *i.e.*, no change was made with respect to the initial string (one a was deleted together with Y_i^2, but at the same time inserted together with K_i^1). To conclude, any of insertions 4, 2 or 3 introduces at least one non-terminal symbol, and in order to eliminate it a specific sequence of above rules shall be used. Moreover, this sequence does not make any changes to the string. In a more general case, it was proved in [13] that any sequence of context-free insertions and deletions of length at most 2 contributes to at most two symbols of the final terminal word. In our case, the sequence inserts only one terminal a but it also needs to delete an a in order to eliminate all non-terminals.

We are interested in the particular moment when the insertion of aK_i^1 is performed. Now, rule 5 inserts the string xK_i^2 between a and K_i^1. After that, the above sequence of insertion and deletion rules is performed and a string $w_1axK_i^2bw_2$ is obtained. At this moment, symbol x is inserted and we also know that it's left neighbor is a. Symbol K_i^2 may be eliminated if and only if it is adjacent to X_1 which is always inserted before symbol b. Hence, after eliminating all additional symbols we either obtain the same word (xK_i^2 was not inserted), or insert x between a and b which simulates corresponding rule of ID. This concludes the proof.

Remark 1. *The above proof shows how tight is the borderline between universality and decidability. In fact, using only a small number of rules with one symbol right context, it is possible to make the step that separates a decidable system (of size $(2,0,0;2,0,0)$, see [13]) and a undecidable one (of size $(2,0,1;2,0,0)$).*

Now we consider the class $INS_1^{1,1}DEL_1^{1,0}$. We show that this class is not complete. Firstly we prove the following lemma which shows that the deletion of terminal symbols may be excluded.

Lemma 6. *For any insertion-deletion system $ID = (V,T,A,I,D)$ having the size $(1,1,1;1,1,0)$ there is a system $ID' = (V \cup V',T,A \cup A',I \cup I',D')$ such that $L(ID') = L(ID)$. Moreover, for any rule $(a,b,\varepsilon) \in D'$ it holds $b \notin T$.*

Proof. Indeed, we can transform system $ID = (V,T,A,I,D)$ to an equivalent system $ID' = (V \cup V',T,A \cup A',I \cup I',D')$ as follows:

Any rule $(S,R,\varepsilon) \in D$, $S \in V$, $R \in V \setminus T$ will also be part of D'. Now consider a rule $(S,t,\varepsilon) \in D$, $S \in V$, $t \in T$. Then we add the rule (S,N_t,ε) to D', where $N_t \in V'$ is a new nonterminal. Moreover, we add also following rules to I' and strings to A':

- If $w_1tw_2 \in A$, then we add $w_1N_tw_2$ to A', where $w_1,w_2 \in V^*$,
- if $(t,S,R) \in I$, then we add (N_t,S,R) to I',
- if $(S,R,t) \in I$, then we add (S,R,N_t) to I' and
- if $(S,t,R) \in I$, then we add (S,N_t,R) to I', and analogously
- if $(t,S,\varepsilon) \in D$, then we add (N_t,S,ε) to D'.

It is clear that $L(ID') = L(ID)$ because there is no difference between erasing t or N_t.

The following result shows that the class $INS_1^{1,1}DEL_1^{1,0}$ is not computationally complete.

Theorem 7. $CF \setminus INS_1^{1,1}DEL_1^{1,0} \neq \emptyset$.

Proof. Consider the context-free language $L = \{a^i b^i \mid i > 0\}$. We claim that there is no insertion-deletion system Γ of size $(1,1,1;1,1,0)$ such that $L(\Gamma) = L$.

We shall prove the above statement by contradiction. Suppose there is such system $\Gamma = (V, \{a, b\}, A, I, D)$ and $L(\Gamma) = L$. From lemma 6 we can suppose that Γ does not delete terminal symbols.

Consider a sentential form of system Γ. It is clear that after a finite number of steps it will have the form $\alpha a w b \beta$, where $\alpha, \beta \in V^*$ and $w \in \{V \setminus \{a, b\}\}^*$, because at some moment a and b should be inserted.

Let us denote the rightmost symbol a by $\underline{a}$ and the leftmost symbol b by $\underline{b}$. Hence any word will have the form $\alpha a \underline{a} w \underline{b} b \beta$. Since there are no terminal deletion rules, this terminal symbol $\underline{a}$ cannot be deleted and it may participate in computation only in the left or right part of insertion rules: $(\underline{a}, S, R)$ or $(S, R, \underline{a})$ and in the left part of deletion rules $(\underline{a}, S, \varepsilon)$. It is clear that any insertion of a at the left of $\underline{a}$ (in α) cannot be correlated with an insertion of b at the right of $\underline{a}$ because the insertion uses one symbol context and $\underline{a}$ will be the left and correspondingly right context for both insertions. The same reasoning works for $\underline{b}$. Hence, there must be no insertions of a in α and of b in β, otherwise a word $a^i b^j$, $i \neq j$ might be obtained. This means that all insertions of symbols a and b must happen inside the word w, *i.e.*, between $\underline{a}$ and $\underline{b}$. We may also assume that $\alpha = a^{k-1}$ and $\beta = b^{m-1}$.

Consider now some terminal derivation (we suppose that there is a rule (N_s, a, M_1) in I):

$$\nu \Rightarrow^+ a^{k-1} \underline{a} N_1 \ldots N_s M_1 \ldots M_t \underline{b} b^{m-1} \tag{10}$$

$$\Rightarrow_{ins} a^k N_1 \ldots N_s \underline{a} M_1 \ldots M_t \underline{b} b^{m-1} \Rightarrow^+ a^i b^i, \tag{11}$$

where $\nu \in A$ is an axiom, and all $N_p, M_q, 1 \leq p \leq s, 1 \leq q \leq t$ are nonterminal symbols and $i > 1$. We also remark that after inserting an a between N_s and M_1 it becomes the rightmost a and it is underlined.

From the discussion above it is clear that we cannot insert symbol a in the word $N_1 \ldots N_s$ and this word must be deleted. Moreover, because we have only left-context deletion, the deletion of $N_1 \ldots N_s$ does not depend on symbol $\underline{a}$. Hence we obtain:

$$a^k N_1 \ldots N_s \Longrightarrow_{del}^+ a^k \tag{12}$$

Now consider again line (11):

$$\Rightarrow_{ins} a^k N_1 \ldots N_s \underline{a} M_1 \ldots M_t \underline{b} b^{m-1} \Rightarrow_{del}^{+} a^k \underline{a} M_1 \ldots M_t b^m$$

$$\Rightarrow^{+} a^i b^i = a a^{i-1} b^i \quad (13)$$

Thus, from (13) we conclude, that

$$a^k M_1 \ldots M_t b^m \Rightarrow^{+} a^{i-1} b^i \quad (14)$$

On the other hand from lines (10), (12) and (14) we get:

$$\nu \Rightarrow^{+} a^k N_1 \ldots N_s M_1 \ldots M_t b^m \Rightarrow_{del}^{+} a^k M_1 \ldots M_t b^m \Rightarrow^{+} a^{i-1} b^i.$$

This is a contradiction that proves the theorem.

As a corollary of the above theorems we have the symmetric variant of the results.

Corollary 8. $INS_1^{2,1} DEL_1^{0,1} = INS_2^{2,0} DEL_1^{0,1} = INS_2^{1,0} DEL_2^{0,0} = RE.$

4   Complexity Measures

We collect in table below known results on insertion-deletion systems. We indicate both traditional measures and measures proposed in [13].

Nb.	γ	$(n, m; p, q)$	family	references	ψ	$(n, m, m'; p, q, q')$
1	6	$(3, 0; 3, 0)$	RE	[7]	6	$(3, 0, 0; 3, 0, 0)$
2	5	$(1, 2; 1, 1)$	RE	[4,10]	8	$(1, 2, 2; 1, 1, 1)$
3	5	$(1, 2; 2, 0)$	RE	[4,10]	7	$(1, 2, 2; 2, 0, 0)$
4	5	$(2, 1; 2, 0)$	RE	[4,10]	6	$(2, 1, 1; 2, 0, 0)$
5	5	$(1, 1; 1, 2)$	RE	[12]	8	$(1, 1, 1; 1, 2, 2)$
6	5	$(2, 1; 1, 1)$	RE	[12]	7	$(2, 1, 1; 1, 1, 1)$
7	5	$(2, 0; 3, 0)$	RE	[7]	5	$(2, 0, 0; 3, 0, 0)$
8	5	$(3, 0; 2, 0)$	RE	[7]	5	$(3, 0, 0; 2, 0, 0)$
9	4	$(1, 1; 2, 0)$	RE	[10]	5	$(1, 1, 1; 2, 0, 0)$
10	4	$(1, 1; 1, 1)$	RE	[12]	6	$(1, 1, 1; 1, 1, 1)$
11	4	$(2, 0; 2, 0)$	$\subsetneq CF$	[13]	4	$(2, 0, 0; 2, 0, 0)$
12	$m+1$	$(m, 0; 1, 0)$	$\subsetneq CF$	[13]	$-$	$(m, 0, 0; 1, 0, 0)$
13	$p+1$	$(1, 0; p, 0)$	$\subsetneq REG$	[13]	$-$	$(1, 0, 0; p, 0, 0)$
14	5	$(1, 2; 1, 1)$	RE	Theorem 3	6	$(1, 1, 2; 1, 1, 0)$
15	6	$(2, 2; 1, 1)$	RE	Theorem 4	6	$(2, 0, 2; 1, 1, 0)$
16	5	$(2, 1; 2, 0)$	RE	Theorem 5	5	$(2, 0, 1; 2, 0, 0)$
17	4	$(1, 1; 1, 1)$	$\subsetneq RE$	Theorem 7	5	$(1, 1, 1; 1, 1, 0)$

In this table we do not present the symmetrical variants of 14, 15 and 16 which also generate all recursively enumerable languages.

We remark that the value of ψ describes in some sense the amount of cooperation between symbols in the system.

5   Conclusions

In this article we investigated insertion-deletion systems having a one-sided context, in particular, systems with minimal deletion. We showed that systems of size $(1,1,2;1,1,0)$ and $(2,0,2;1,1,0)$ generate all recursively enumerable languages, while systems of size $(1,1,1;1,1,0)$ are not computationally complete and that they cannot generate the language $\{a^i b^i \mid i \geq 0\}$. We also considered systems with a minimal context-free deletion and we showed that systems of size $(2,0,1;2,0,0)$ also generate all recursively enumerable languages.

Moreover, the proof of the above results is based on different ideas with respect to the proofs found in the literature. More precisely, previously such proofs were based on a simulation of the behavior of an arbitrary Chomsky grammar, while our proof simulates other classes of insertion-deletion systems. We think that our approach is simpler, in particular, it permits to obtain in a easy way equivalences between insertion-deletion systems from lines 1 to 10 from the table 4.

Acknowledgments

The authors would like to thank A. Alhazov for their helpful discussions. The second author acknowledge the project 06.411.03.04P from the Supreme Council for Science and Technological Development of the Academy of Sciences of Moldova and the project MolCIP, MIF1-CT-2006-021666 from the European Commission.

References

1. Daley, M., Kari, L., Gloor, G., Siromoney, R.: Circular contextual insertions/deletions with applications to biomolecular computation. In: Proc. of 6th Int. Symp. on String Processing and Information Retrieval, SPIRE'99, Cancun, Mexico, pp. 47–54 (1999)
2. Galiukschov, B.S.: Semicontextual grammars, Matematika Logica i Matematika Linguistika (in Russian), Tallin University, pp. 38–50 (1981)
3. Kari, L.: On insertion and deletion in formal languages, PhD Thesis, University of Turku (1991)
4. Kari, L., Păun, G., Thierrin, G., Yu, S.: At the crossroads of DNA computing and formal languages: characterizing RE using insertion-deletion systems. In: Proceedings of 3rd DIMACS Workshop on DNA Based Computing, Philadelphia, pp. 318–333 (1997)
5. Kari, L., Thierrin, G.: Contextual insertion/deletion and computability. Information and Computation 131(1), 47–61 (1996)
6. Marcus, S.: Contextual grammars. Rev. Roum. Math. Pures Appl. 14, 1525–1534 (1969)
7. Margenstern, M., Păun, G., Rogozhin, Y., Verlan, S.: Context-free insertion-deletion systems. Theoretical Computer Science 330, 339–348 (2005)
8. Martin-Vide, C., Păun, G., Salomaa, A.: Characterizations of recursively enumerable languages by means of insertion grammars. Theoretical Computer Science 205(1-2), 195–205 (1998)

9. Păun, G.: Marcus contextual grammars. Kluwer, Dordrecht (1997)
10. Păun, G., Rozenberg, G., Salomaa, A.: DNA Computing. New Computing Paradigms. Springer, Berlin (1998)
11. Rozenberg, G., Salomaa, A. (eds.): Handbook of Formal Languages. Springer, Berlin (1997)
12. Takahara, A., Yokomori, T.: On the computational power of insertion-deletion systems. In: Hagiya, M., Ohuchi, A. (eds.) DNA Computing. LNCS, vol. 2568, pp. 269–280. Springer, Heidelberg (2003)
13. Verlan, S.: On minimal context-free insertion-deletion systems. In: Mereghetti, C., Palano, B., Pighizzini, G., Wotschke, D. (eds.) Seventh International Workshop on Descriptional Complexity of Formal Systems, Como, Italy, June 30 - July 2, 2005, pp. 285–292 (2005) (Technical repport no. 06-05, University of Milan)

Accepting Networks of Splicing Processors with Filtered Connections

Juan Castellanos[1], Florin Manea[2], Luis Fernando de Mingo López[3], and Victor Mitrana[2,4]

[1] Department of Artificial Intelligence, Polytechnical University of Madrid
28660 Boadilla del Monte, Madrid, Spain
jcastellanos@fi.upm.es
[2] Faculty of Mathematics and Computer Science, University of Bucharest
Str. Academiei 14, 010014, Bucharest, Romania
flmanea@gmail.com
[3] Dept. Organización y Estructura de la Información
Escuela Universitaria de Informática, Universidad Politécnica de Madrid
Crta. de Valencia km. 7 - 28031 Madrid, Spain
lfmingo@eui.upm.es
[4] Research Group in Mathematical Linguistics, Rovira i Virgili University
Pça. Imperial Tarraco 1, 43005, Tarragona, Spain
mitrana@fmi.unibuc.ro

Abstract. In this paper we simplify accepting networks of splicing processors considered in [8] by moving the filters from the nodes to the edges. Each edge is viewed as a two-way channel such that input and output filters coincide. Thus, the possibility of controlling the computation in such networks seems to be diminished. In spite of this and of the fact that splicing alone is not a very powerful operation these networks are still computationally complete. As a consequence, we propose characterizations of two complexity classes, namely **NP** and **PSPACE**, in terms of accepting networks of *restricted* splicing processors with filtered connections.

1 Introduction

The origin of networks of evolutionary processors (NEP for short) is a basic architecture for parallel and distributed symbolic processing, related to the Connection Machine [6] as well as the Logic Flow paradigm [3], which consists of several processors, each of them being placed in a node of a virtual complete graph, which are able to handle data associated with the respective node. All the nodes send simultaneously their data and the receiving nodes handle also simultaneously all the arriving messages, according to some strategies, see, e.g., [4,6].

In a series of papers (see [10] for a survey) one considers that each node may be viewed as a cell having genetic information encoded in DNA sequences which may evolve by local evolutionary events, that is point mutations. Each node is specialized just for one of these evolutionary operations. Furthermore, the data in each node is organized in the form of multisets of words (each word appears

J. Durand-Lose and M. Margenstern (Eds.): MCU 2007, LNCS 4664, pp. 218–229, 2007.
© Springer-Verlag Berlin Heidelberg 2007

in an arbitrarily large number of copies), and all the copies are processed in parallel such that all the possible events that can take place do actually take place. Obviously, the computational process just described is not exactly an evolutionary process in the Darwinian sense. But the rewriting operations we have considered might be interpreted as mutations and the filtering process might be viewed as a selection process. Recombination is missing but it was asserted that evolutionary and functional relationships between genes can be captured by taking only local mutations into consideration [14].

In [8] one replaces the point mutations associated with each node by the missing operation mentioned above, that of splicing. This new processor is called splicing processor. This computing model, called accepting network of splicing processors (shortly ANSP), is similar to some extent to the test tube distributed systems based on splicing introduced in [1] and further explored in [12]. However, there are several differences: first, the model proposed in [1] is a language generating mechanism while ours is an accepting one; second, we use a single splicing step, while every splicing step in [1] is actually an infinite process consisting of iterated splicing steps; third, each splicing step in our model is reflexive; fourth, the filters of our model are based on random context conditions while those considered in [1] are based on membership conditions; fifth, at every splicing step a set of auxiliary words, always the same and proper to every node, is available for splicing. We want to stress from the very beginning that the splicing processor we discuss here is a mathematical object only and the biological hints presented above are intended to explain in an informal way how some biological phenomena are *sources of inspiration* for our mathematical computing model. Furthermore, in the case of restricted splicing processor splicing always apply to a string existing in the node and an axiom which is rather far from DNA biochemistry but mathematically attractive.

In [8] one presents a characterization of the complexity class **NP** based on accepting networks of restricted splicing processors and discusses how restricted ANSPs can be considered as problem solvers. In [9], one shows that every recursively enumerable language can be accepted by an ANSP of size 7. It has 6 fixed nodes which do not depend on the given language and one node only, the input one, which depends on the given language. In the same work one presents a method for constructing, given an **NP**-language, an ANSP of size 7 accepting that language in polynomial time. Unlike the previous case, all nodes of this ANSP depend on the given language. These results hold for both variants (restricted or not) of ANSP. A considerable improvement is reported in [7] where the size is reduced to 3.

It is clear that filters associated with each node allow a strong control of the computation. Indeed, every node has an input and output filter; two nodes can exchange data if it passes the output filter of the sender *and* the input filter of the receiver. Moreover, if some data is sent out by some node and not able to enter any node, then it is lost. In this paper we simplify the ANSP model considered in [8] by moving the filters from the nodes to the edges. Each edge is viewed as a two-way channel such that the input and output filters coincide.

Clearly, the possibility of controlling the computation in such networks seems to be diminished. For instance, there is no possibility to loose data during the communication steps. In spite of this and of the fact that splicing is not a powerful operation (remember that splicing systems generates only regular languages [2,13]) we prove here that these devices are computationally complete. As a consequence, we propose characterizations of two complexity classes, namely **NP** and **PSPACE**, in terms of accepting networks of restricted splicing processors with filtered connections.

2   Basic Definitions

We start by summarizing the notions used throughout the paper. An *alphabet* is a finite and nonempty set of symbols. The cardinality of a finite set A is written $card(A)$. Any finite sequence of symbols from an alphabet V is called *word* over V. The set of all words over V is denoted by V^* and the empty word is denoted by ε. The length of a word x is denoted by $|x|$ while $alph(x)$ denotes the minimal alphabet W such that $x \in W^*$.

A nondeterministic Turing machine is a construct $M = (Q, V, U, \delta, q_0, B, F)$, where Q is a finite set of states, V is the input alphabet, U is the tape alphabet, $V \subset U$, q_0 is the initial state, $B \in U \backslash V$ is the "blank" symbol, $F \subseteq Q$ is the set of final states, and δ is the transition mapping, $\delta : (Q \backslash F) \times U \rightarrow 2^{Q \times (U \backslash \{B\}) \times \{R,L\}}$. The variant of a Turing machine we use in this paper can be described intuitively as follows: it has a semi-infinite tape (bounded to the left) divided into cells (each cell may store exactly one symbol from U). The machine has a central unit storing a state from a finite set of states, and a reading/writing tape head which scans the tape cells; the head cannot write blank symbols. The input is a word over V stored on the tape starting with the leftmost cell while all the other tape cells initially contain the symbol B. When M starts a computation, the tape head scans the leftmost cell and the central unit is in the state q_0. The machine performs moves that depend on the content of the cell currently scanned by the tape head and the current state stored in the central unit. A move consists of: change the state, write a symbol from U on the current cell and move the tape head one cell either to the left (provided that the cell scanned was not the leftmost one) or to the right. An input word is accepted iff after a finite number of moves the Turing machine enters a final state. An instantaneous description (ID for short) of a Turing machine M as above is a word over $(U \backslash \{B\})^* Q (U \backslash \{B\})^*$. Given an ID $\alpha q \beta$, this means that the tape contents is $\alpha\beta$ followed by an infinite number of cells containing the blank symbol B, the current state is q, and the symbol currently scanned by the tape head is the first symbol of β provided that $\beta \neq \varepsilon$, or B, otherwise.

A splicing rule over the alphabet V is a quadruple written in the form $\sigma = [x, y; u, v]$, where x, y, u, v are words over V. Given a splicing rule σ over V as above and a pair of words (w, z) over the same alphabet V we define the action of σ on (w, z) by:

$$\sigma(w,z) = \begin{cases} \{t \mid w = \alpha x y \beta, z = \gamma u v \delta \text{ for some words} \\ \quad \alpha, \beta, \gamma, \delta \in V^* \text{ and } t = \alpha x v \delta \text{ or } t = \gamma u y \beta\} \\ \\ \{w\} \cup \{z\}, \text{ if the set above is empty.} \end{cases}$$

This action on pair of words can be naturally extended to a language L by $\sigma(L) = \bigcup_{w,z \in L} \sigma(w,z)$ or to a pair of languages L_1, L_2 by $\sigma(L_1, L_2) = \bigcup_{w \in L_1, z \in L_2} \sigma(w,z)$. Furthermore, if M is a finite set of splicing rules over V, then we set $M(L) = \bigcup_{\sigma \in M} \sigma(L)$ and $M(L_1, L_2) = \bigcup_{\sigma \in M} \sigma(L_1, L_2)$.

For two disjoint subsets P and F of an alphabet V and a word x over V, we define the predicates

$$\varphi^s(x; P, F) \equiv P \subseteq alph(x) \wedge F \cap alph(x) = \emptyset$$
$$\varphi^w(x; P, F) \equiv alph(x) \cap P \neq \emptyset \wedge F \cap alph(x) = \emptyset.$$

The construction of these predicates is based on *random-context conditions* defined by the two sets P (*permitting contexts/symbols*) and F (*forbidding contexts/symbols*). Informally, the former condition requires (s stands for strong) that all permitting symbols are and no forbidding symbol is present in x, while the latter (w stands for weak) is a weaker variant such that at least one permitting symbol appears in x but still no forbidding symbol is present in x.

For every language $L \subseteq V^*$ and $\beta \in \{s, w\}$, we define:

$$\varphi^\beta(L, P, F) = \{x \in L \mid \varphi^\beta(x; P, F)\}.$$

A *splicing processor* over V is a pair (S, A), where:

  – S is a finite set of splicing rules over V.

  – A is a finite set of *auxiliary words* over V. These auxiliary words are to be used by this splicing processor for splicing.

An *accepting network of splicing processors with filtered connections* (ANSPFC for short) is a 9-tuple

$$\Gamma = (V, U, <, >, G, \mathcal{N}, \alpha, x_I, x_O),$$

where:

  – V and U are the input and network alphabet, respectively, $V \subseteq U$, and, also, $<, > \in U \setminus V$ are two special symbols.
  – $G = (X_G, E_G)$ is an undirected graph without loops with the set of nodes X_G and the set of edges E_G. Each node $x \in X_G$ is seen as a splicing processor, having the set of splicing rules M_x and the set of axioms A_x. Each edge is given in the form of a binary set. G is called the *underlying graph* of the network.
  – $\mathcal{N} : E_G \longrightarrow 2^U \times 2^U$ is a mapping which associates with each edge $e \in E_G$ the disjoint sets $\mathcal{N}(e) = (P_e, F_e)$.

- $\alpha : E_G \longrightarrow \{s, w\}$ defines the *filter* type of an edge.
- $x_I, x_O \in X_G$ are the *input* and the *output* node of Γ, respectively.

We say that $card(X_G)$ is the size of Γ. As usual, we focus here on *complete* ANSPFCs, i.e., ANSPFCs having a complete underlying graph (every two nodes are connected) denoted by K_n, where n is the number of nodes. It is worth mentioning that every underlying graph of a ANSPFC can be completed without modifying the computational power; the edges that are to be added are associated with filters which make them useless. This is not possible for ANSPs.

A *configuration* of a ANSPFC Γ as above is a mapping $C : X_G \longrightarrow 2^{U^*}$ which associates a set of words with every node of the graph. A configuration may be understood as the sets of words which are present in any node at a given moment. Given a word $z \in V^*$, the initial configuration of Γ on z is defined by $C_0^{(z)}(x_I) = \{< z >\}$ and $C_0^{(z)}(x) = \emptyset$ for all $x \in X_G \setminus \{x_I\}$. Notice that the auxiliary words do not appear in any configuration.

A configuration can change either by a *splicing step* or by a *communication step*. When changing by a splicing step, each component $C(x)$ of the configuration C is changed in accordance with the set of splicing rules M_x associated with the node x and the set A_x. Formally, we say that the configuration C' is obtained in *one splicing step* from the configuration C, written as $C \Longrightarrow C'$, iff

$$C'(x) = S_x(C(x) \cup A_x) \text{ for all } x \in X_G.$$

Since each word present in a node, as well as each auxiliary word, appears in an arbitrarily large number of identical copies, all possible splicings are assumed to be done in one splicing step. If the splicing step is defined as $C \Longrightarrow C'$, iff

$$C'(x) = S_x(C(x), A_x) \text{ for all } x \in X_G,$$

then all processors of Γ are called *restricted*.

When changing by a communication step, each node processor $x \in X_G$ sends one copy of each word it has to every node processor y connected to x, provided they can pass the filter of the edge between x and y, and receives all the words sent by any node processor z connected with x providing that they can pass the filter of the edge between x and z.

Formally, we say that the configuration C' is obtained in *one communication step* from configuration C, written as $C \vdash C'$, iff

$$C'(x) = (C(x) \setminus (\bigcup_{\{x,y\} \in E_G} \varphi^{\alpha(\{x,y\})}(C(x), \mathcal{N}(\{x, y\}))))$$

$$\cup (\bigcup_{\{x,y\} \in E_G} \varphi^{\alpha(\{x,y\})}(C(y), \mathcal{N}(\{x, y\})))$$

for all $x \in X_G$.

Let Γ be an ANSPFC, the computation of Γ on the input word $z \in V^*$ is a sequence of configurations $C_0^{(z)}, C_1^{(z)}, C_2^{(z)}, \ldots$, where $C_0^{(z)}$ is the initial configuration

of Γ on z, $C_{2i}^{(z)} \Longrightarrow C_{2i+1}^{(z)}$ and $C_{2i+1}^{(z)} \vdash C_{2i+2}^{(z)}$, for all $i \geq 0$. By the previous definitions, each configuration $C_i^{(z)}$ is uniquely determined by the configuration $C_{i-1}^{(z)}$.
In other words, each computation in an ANSPFC is deterministic. A computation
halts (and it is said to be *finite*) if one of the following two conditions holds:

(i) There exists a configuration in which the set of words existing in the output
node x_O is non-empty. In this case, the computation is said to be an *accepting*
computation.

(ii) There exist two identical configurations obtained either in consecutive
evolutionary steps or in consecutive communication steps.

The *language accepted* by Γ is

$$L_a(\Gamma) = \{z \in V^* \mid \text{the computation of } \Gamma \text{ on } z$$
$$\text{is an accepting one.}\}$$

The *language accepted* by Γ with restricted processors is

$$L_a^{(r)}(\Gamma) = \{z \in V^* \mid \text{the computation of } \Gamma \text{ on } z$$
$$\text{is an accepting one.}\}$$

We say that an ANSPFC Γ (with restricted processors) decides the language
$L \subseteq V^*$, and write $L(\Gamma) = L$ iff $L_a(\Gamma) = L$ $(L_a^{(r)}(\Gamma) = L)$ and the computation
of Γ on every $z \in V^*$ halts.

In a similar way, we define two computational complexity measures using
ANSPFC with or without restricted processors as the computing model. To this
aim we consider an ANSPFC Γ with the input alphabet V that halts on every
input. The *time complexity* of the finite computation $C_0^{(x)}$, $C_1^{(x)}$, $C_2^{(x)}$, $\ldots C_m^{(x)}$
of Γ on $x \in V^*$ is denoted by $Time_\Gamma(x)$ and equals m. The time complexity of
Γ is the partial function from $\mathbf{N}$ to $\mathbf{N}$,

$$Time_\Gamma(n) = \max\{Time_\Gamma(x) \mid x \in V^*, |x| = n\}.$$

We say that Γ decides L in time $O(f(n))$ if $Time_\Gamma(n) \in O(f(n))$.

For a function $f : \mathbf{N} \longrightarrow \mathbf{N}$ we define:

$$\mathbf{Time}_{ANSPFC_p}(f(n)) = \{L \mid \text{there exists an ANSPFC } \Gamma, \text{ of size } p, \text{ deciding } L,$$
$$\text{and } n_0 \text{ such that } Time_\Gamma(n) \leq f(n) \forall n \geq n_0\}$$

Moreover, we write $\mathbf{PTime}_{ANSPFC_p} = \bigcup_{k \geq 0} \mathbf{Time}_{ANSPFC_p}(n^k)$ for all $p \geq 1$ as

well as $\mathbf{PTime}_{ANSPFC} = \bigcup_{p \geq 1} \mathbf{PTime}_{ANSPFC_p}$.

The *length complexity* of the finite computation $C_0^{(x)}$, $C_1^{(x)}$, $C_2^{(x)}$, $\ldots C_m^{(x)}$ of Γ
on $x \in L$ is denoted by $Length_\Gamma(x)$ and equals $\max_{w \in C_i^{(x)}(z), i \in \{1, \ldots, m\}, z \in X_G} |w|$.
The length complexity of Γ is the partial function from $\mathbf{N}$ to $\mathbf{N}$,

$$Length_\Gamma(n) = \max\{Length_\Gamma(x) \mid x \in V^*, |x| = n\}.$$

For a function $f : \mathbf{N} \longrightarrow \mathbf{N}$ we define

$$\mathbf{Length}_{ANSPFC_p}(f(n)) = \{L \,|\, \text{there exists an ANSPFC } \Gamma, \text{ of size } p, \text{ deciding } L,$$
$$\text{and } n_0 \text{ such that } Length_\Gamma(n) \le f(n) \forall n \ge n_0\}$$

We write $\mathbf{PLength}_{ANSPFC_p} = \displaystyle\bigcup_{k \ge 0} \mathbf{Length}_{ANSPFC_p}(n^k)$, for all $p \ge 1$, and

$$\mathbf{PLength}_{ANSPFC} = \bigcup_{p \ge 1} \mathbf{PLength}_{ANSPFC_p}.$$

The corresponding classes for ANSPFC with restricted processors are denoted by $\mathbf{PTime}_{ANSPFC_p^{(r)}}$ and $\mathbf{PLength}_{ANSPFC_p^{(r)}}$.

3   Completeness of ANSPFCs

We start this section showing that ANSPFCs with restricted processors or not are computationally complete.

Theorem 1. *For any language L, accepted (decided) by a Turing Machine M, there exists an ANSPFC Γ, of size 4, accepting (deciding) L. Moreover, Γ can be constructed such that:*
  1. if $L \in NTIME(f(m))$ then $Time_\Gamma(n) \in \mathcal{O}(f(m))$.
  2. if $L \in NSPACE(f(m))$ then $Length_\Gamma(n) \in \mathcal{O}(f(m))$.

Proof. Let $M = (Q, V, U, R, q_0, Q_f, B)$ be a Turing machine. We construct an ANSPFC that simulates, in parallel, all the computations of M on an input word. In the following we assume that $U \setminus \{B\} = \{a_1, \ldots, a_n\}$.

Let $\Gamma = (V, U', <', >', K_4, \mathcal{N}, \alpha, x_I, x_O)$, where K_4 is the complete graph with 4 nodes: $\{x_I, x_O, x_1, x_2\}$. The other parameters are defined as follows:

$$U' = V \cup U \cup Q \cup \{<', >', <, >, <^*, \#\} \cup \{<^k, >^k, <_*^k, >_*^k \,|\, 0 \le k \le 2n\}$$

and

x_I:
  • S_{x_I} is the union of the following sets:
  $\{[<', a; < q_0, \#] \,|\, a \in V \cup \{>'\}\} \cup \{[a, >'; \#, B >] \,|\, a \in V \cup \{q_0\}\}$,
  (the initialization rules)
  $\{[< q_1 a, b; < cq_2, \#] \,|\, q_1, q_2 \in Q, a, c \in U \setminus \{B\}, b \in U, (q_2, c, R) \in \delta(q_1, a)\} \cup$
  $\{[< q_1 B, b; < cq_2 B, \#] \,|\, q_1, q_2 \in Q, c \in U \setminus \{B\}, b \in U \cup \{>, >_*^0\}, (q_2, c, R) \in \delta(q_1, B)\}$,
  (rules for the simulation of a move of M to the right)
  $\{[< aq_1 b, d; < q_2 ac, \#] \,|\, q_1, q_2 \in Q, a, b, c \in U \setminus \{B\}, d \in U, (q_2, c, L) \in \delta(q_1, b)\} \cup$
  $\{[< aq_1 B, d; < q_2 acB, \#] \,|\, q_1, q_2 \in Q, a, c \in U \setminus \{B\}, d \in U \cup \{>, >_*^0\}, (q_2, c, L) \in \delta(q_1, B)\}$,
  (rules for the simulation of a move of M to the left)
  $\{[<_*^0 q_1 a, b; < cq_2, \#] \,|\, q_1, q_2 \in Q, a, c \in U \setminus \{B\}, b \in U, (q_2, c, R) \in \delta(q_1, a)\} \cup$
  $\{[<_*^0 q_1 B, b; < cq_2 B, \#] \,|\, q_1, q_2 \in Q, c \in U \setminus \{B\}, b \in U \cup \{>, >_*^0\}, (q_2, c, R) \in \delta(q_1, B)\}$,

(rules for the simulation of a move of M to the right immediately after a rotation to the right)

$\{[<^0_* aq_1b, d; < q_2ac, \#] \mid q_1, q_2 \in Q, a, b, c \in U \setminus \{B\}, d \in U, (q_2, c, L) \in \delta(q_1, b)\} \cup$
$\{[<^0_* aq_1B, d; < q_2acB, \#] \mid q_1, q_2 \in Q, a, c \in U \setminus \{B\}, d \in U \cup \{>, >^0_*\}, (q_2, c, L) \in \delta(q_1, B)\}$,

(rules for the simulation of a move of M to the left immediately after a rotation to the left)

$\{[a, >^0_*; \#, >] \mid a \in U\}$,

(rules for restoring the right marker after rotations)

$\{[< a_iq, b; <^i q, \#]\} \mid b \in U, q \in Q, 1 \leq i \leq n\} \cup$
$\{[b, >; \#, a_i >^i]\} \mid b \in U, 1 \leq i \leq n\}$,

(rules for right rotations)

$\{[< q, b; <^{i+n} a_iq, \#]\} \mid b \in U, q \in Q, 1 \leq i \leq n\} \cup$
$\{[b, a_i >; \#, >^{i+n}] \mid b \in U \cup Q, 1 \leq i \leq n\}$,

(rules for left rotations)

- $A_{x_I} = \{< q_0\#, \#B >\} \cup \{< cq\#, < cqB\# \mid c \in U \setminus \{B\}, q \in Q \setminus Q_f\} \cup$
$\{qac\#, qacB\# \mid a, c \in U \setminus \{B\}, q \in Q \setminus Q_f\} \cup \{<^i q\#, <^{i+n} a_iq\#, \#a_i >^i$
$, \# >^{i+n} \mid q \in Q \setminus Q_f, 1 \leq i \leq n\}$,

x_1:
- $S_{x_1} = \{[<^k, a; <^{k-1}_*, \#] \mid 0 < k \leq 2n, a \in U \cup Q\} \cup \{[<^0_*, a; <^*, \#] \mid a \in U \cup Q\}$,
- $A_{x_1} = \{<^k_* \# \mid 0 \leq k \leq 2n - 1\} \cup \{<^* \#\}$,

x_2:
- $S_{x_2} = \{[a, >^k; \#, >^{k-1}_*] \mid 0 < k \leq 2n, a \in U\} \cup \{[a, >^k_*; \#, >^{k-1}_*] \mid a \in U, 0 < k \leq 2n - 1\}$,
- $A_{x_2} = \{\# >^k_* \mid 0 \leq k \leq 2n - 1\}$,

x_O:
- $S_{x_O} = A_{x_O} = \emptyset$.

The filters placed on the edges of Γ are defined as follows:

- $\mathcal{N}(\{x_1, x_2\}) = (U, \{<', >', <, >, <^*, \#\})$,
  $\alpha(\{x_I, x_1\}) = (w)$
- $\mathcal{N}(\{x_1, x_2\}) = (U, \{\#, <^*, >^0_*\})$,
  $\alpha(\{x_1, x_2\}) = (w)$
- $\mathcal{N}(\{x_2, x_I\}) = (\{<^0_*, >^0_*\}, \emptyset)$,
  $\alpha(\{x_1, x_2\}) = (s)$
- $\mathcal{N}(\{x_I, x_O\}) = (Q_f, \emptyset)$,
  $\alpha(\{x_2, x_O\}) = (w)$
- For any other edge e of the underlying graph of Γ not listed above we have
  $\mathcal{N}(e) = (\emptyset, U')$ and $\alpha(e) = (s)$.

In the following we prove that Γ accepts (decides) the same language that M accepts (decides), namely L.

Assume that $<' w >'$ is the input word of Γ, for some $w \in L$. The computation of Γ on this word is divided into three major phases:

$\diamond$ *Initialization phase:* In the node x_I, the string $<' w >'$ is transformed into $< q_0 w B >$ after two splicing steps; nothing is communicated in between the two splicing steps.

$\diamond$ *Simulation phase:* At the beginning of each step of this phase the node x_I contains a string having one of the following forms:

1. $< q w_1 B w_2 >$, where $w_1, w_2 \in (U \setminus \{B\})^*$, $q \in Q$, and $w_2 q w_1$ is a configuration of M,
2. $< c q w_1 B w_2 >$, where $w_1, w_2 \in (U \setminus \{B\})^*$, $q \in Q, c \in U \setminus \{B\}$, and $w_2 c q w_1$ is a configuration of M,
3. $<_*^0 q w_1 B w_2 >_*^0$, where $w_1, w_2 \in (U \setminus \{B\})^*$, $q \in Q$, and $w_2 q w_1$ is a configuration of M, and
4. $<_*^0 c q w_1 B w_2 >_*^0$, where $w_1, w_2 \in (U \setminus \{B\})^*$, $q \in Q, c \in U \setminus \{B\}$, and $w_2 c q w_1$ is a configuration of M.

We analyze these cases:

1. x_I contains the string $< q w_1 B w_2 >$, where $w_1, w_2 \in (U \setminus \{B\})^*$, $q \in Q$, and $w_2 q w_1$ is a configuration of M (this case holds after the *Initialization phase*). If M performs a move to the right, the string is transformed, using the rules for the simulation of a move of M to the right, into $< c q' w_1' B w_2 >$, where $(q', c, R) \in \delta(q, a)$, with $a w' = w_1 B$ for some $a \in U$, $w' \in (U \setminus \{B\})^*$; further, the second case is applied.

   If the next move of M is a move to the left, a *left rotation* is applied to the string $< q w_1 B w_2 >$. In order to apply such a rotation the string w_2 must be different from λ; we assume that $w_2 = w_2' a_i$ for some $1 \le i \le n$. The string $< q w_1 B w_2 >$ is transformed into $<^{i+n} a_i q w_1 B w_2' >^{i+n}$ in two splicing steps (the intermediate string cannot be communicated), and it is communicated to the node x_1. There it becomes $<_*^{i+n-1} a_i q w_1 B w_2' >^{i+n}$ and is communicated to x_2, where it is transformed into $<_*^{i+n-1} a_i q w_1 B w_2' >_*^{i+n-1}$. The string is communicated back and forth between x_1 and x_2 until it becomes $<_*^0 a_i q w_1 B w_2' >_*^0$, and enters x_I; further, the fourth case is applied. If q is final, the string enters x_O, and the computation halts.

2. x_I contains the string $< c q w_1 B w_2 >$, where $w_1, w_2 \in (U \setminus \{B\})^*$, $q \in Q$, $c \in U \setminus \{B\}$, and $w_2 c q w_1$ is a configuration of M. If M performs a move to the left, the string is transformed, using the rules for the simulation of a move of M to the left, into $< q' c b w_1' B w_2 >$, where $(q', b, L) \in \delta(q, a)$, with $a w' = w_1 B$, $w' \in (U \setminus \{B\})^*$; further, the first case is applied.

   If the next move of M is a move to the right, a *right rotation* should be applied to the string $< c q w_1 B w_2 >$. Assume that $c = a_i$. The string $< a_i q w_1 B w_2 >$ is transformed into $<^i q w_1 B w_2 a_i >^i$, and it is communicated to the node x_1. There it becomes $<_*^{i-1} q w_1 B w e_2 a_i >^i$ and is communicated to x_2, where it is transformed into $<_*^{i-1} q w_1 B w a_i >_*^{i-1}$. The string is communicated back and forth between x_1 and x_2 until it becomes $<_*^0 q w_1 B w a_i >_*^0$, and enters x_I; further, the third case is applied. If q is final, the string enters x_O, and the computation halts.

3. x_I contains the string $<^0_* qw_1 Bw_2 >^0_*$, where $w_1, w_2 \in (U \setminus \{B\})^*$ and $w_2 q w_1$ is a configuration of M. In this case, either a right move of M is simulated, or the computation on this string is blocked. If a right move of M is simulated, we continue with the second case.

4. x_I contains the string $<^0_* cqw_1 Bw_2 >^0_*$, where $w_1, w_2 \in (U \setminus \{B\})^*$, $c \in U \setminus \{B\}$, and $w_2 cq w_1$ is a configuration of the Turing Machine M. In this case, either a left move of M is simulated, or the computation on this string is blocked. If a left move of M is simulated, we continue with the first case.

Note that after a rotation is performed, the computation blocks unless a move of M is simulated.

◇ *Acceptance phase:* Since in the simulation described above we explore all the configurations that M can reach on the input w, and $w \in L$, a string of the form $< qw_1 Bw_2 >$ or $< cqw_1 Bw_2 >$, with $q \in Q_f$, will eventually be communicated to x_O and the input word is accepted.

Therefore, we have proved that $L(M) \subseteq L(\Gamma)$. Conversely, assume that $<' w >'$ is the input word of Γ. The only strings that can be obtained from $<' w >'$, be communicated in the network, be implied in further splicing steps, and eventually reach the output node are the strings described in the three phases above. Note that during a rotation, only the strings of the form $<^i x >^i$ can be transformed and re-enter x_I or enter x_O. Indeed, if a string of the form $<^i x >^j$ leaves x_I, the superscripts will be decreased in the nodes x_1 and x_2 until one of them becomes 0; since the other is different from 0 the string is blocked, either in x_1 (when the left superscript is 0) or in x_2 (when the right superscript is 0) and it cannot influence the computation.

Thus, $L(M) = L(\Gamma)$. Moreover, M stops on a given input w if and only if Γ halts on $<' w >'$. □

The next remarks are useful:

1. Since each move of M is simulated in one splicing step, and each rotation requires at most $2n$ steps is clear that Γ makes at most $\mathcal{O}(f(|w|))$ steps (both splicing and communication), where $f(|w|)$ is the number of steps made by M on the input w.

2. The only strings that are circulated through the network and whose length grow are those encoding configurations of the Turing machine M. Therefore, if M uses $f(|w|)$ space on the input w, then $Length_\Gamma(|w|) \in \mathcal{O}(f(|w|))$.

3. The previous proof and remarks remain valid for ANSPFCs with restricted processors.

Therefore,

Corollary 1

1. $\mathbf{NP} \subseteq \mathbf{PTime}_{ANSPFC_4} \cap \mathbf{PTime}_{ANSPFC_4^{(r)}}.$

2. $\mathbf{PSPACE} \subseteq \mathbf{PLength}_{ANSPFC_4} \cap \mathbf{PTime}_{ANSPFC_4^{(r)}}.$

The reversal of Theorem 1 holds as well. The Church-Turing Thesis supports this statement; however, we do not give here a formal proof. We do not know whether the reversal of Corollary 1 holds for both variants of ANSPFCs. In the following we show that it holds for ANSPFCs with restricted processors.

Theorem 2. *For any ANSPFC Γ with restricted processors accepting (deciding) the language L, there exists a Turing machine M accepting (deciding) L. Moreover, M can be constructed such that:*

1. M works in $\mathcal{O}((Time_\Gamma(n))^2)$ computational time for an input of length n, and

2. M works in $\mathcal{O}(Length_\Gamma(n))$ space for an input of length n.

Proof. We construct a nondeterministic Turing machine M as follows:

(1) M has a finite set of states associated with each node of Γ. This set is divided into disjoint subsets such that each rule and each auxiliary word has an associated subset of states. Each edge in the underlying graph has also a finite set of states divided into two disjoint subsets each associated with the two filters on that edge.

(2) The input word of Γ is initially on the tape of M. First the Turing machine places this word between the two symbols $<, >$. Then, the Turing machine simulates nondeterministically its itinerary through the underlying network of Γ. Let us suppose that the contents of the tape of M is α; the Turing machine works according to the following strategy:

(i) When M enters a state from the subset of states associated to a rule of the node N_1: $[(x, y); (z, t)]$, it searches in α for the occurrences of the word xy. If any such occurrence is found, and there exists an auxiliary word in the node N_1 that contains an occurrence of zt as a subword (this could be checked by storing the state associated with the above splicing rule, and using the states associated with the auxiliary words of the node), the splicing rule is applied nondeterministically for any pair of such occurrences. One of the two newly obtained words, chosen nondeterministically, becomes the word whose evolution in the network is followed from now on, and M enters a state associated with a filter on an edge of Γ incident with the current node. If α does not contain any occurrence of xy, or no auxiliary word in the currently simulated node contains zt, then M blocks the computation.

(ii) When M enters a state from the subset of states associated to a filter, it checks whether α can pass that filter. If α cannot pass it, M continues its computation simulating a new splicing step in the same node. If α passes the filter, the receiving node becomes the current node.

(iii) As soon as the current node becomes the output node of Γ M halts and accepts its input word.

It is rather plain that M accepts L. Clearly, if Γ decides L, the same does M. The following complexity related observations can be made. If Γ needs at most $f(n)$ steps to accept/reject any word of length n, than the Turing machine M needs at most $\mathcal{O}(f^2(n))$ steps to accept/reject the same word. This is due to the fact that in the simulation of each of the $f(n)$ steps of the computation of Γ, M needs to perform subword matchings in the word on its tape and to replace a part of the word on its tape with another word; in both cases the number of steps needed to perform these operations is $\mathcal{O}(f(n))$. Also, if Γ produces words of length at most $f(n)$ during a computation on a word of length n, then the Turing machine M will have words of length at most $f(n)$ on its tape. $\square$

A direct consequences of the two theorems presented in this section is:

Theorem 3

1. $\mathbf{NP} = \mathbf{PTime}_{ANSPFC_4^{(r)}}$.
2. $\mathbf{PSPACE} = \mathbf{PLength}_{ANSPFC_4^{(r)}}$.

Clearly, given an ANSPFC Γ with restricted processors one can construct an ANSPFC Γ' accepting (deciding) the same language as Γ accepts (decides) and vice versa. Furthermore, if Γ works in polynomial time (space), then Γ' works in polynomial time (space). Does this remain true for the converse construction? If the answer is negative, then there are **NP**-languages that can be decided by ANSPFCs in polynomial time. In our view, this question left open here seems quite attractive.

References

1. Csuhaj-Varjú, E., Kari, L., Păun, G.: Test tube distributed systems based on splicing. Computers and AI 15, 211–232 (1996)
2. Culik, K., Harju, T.: Splicing semigroups of dominoes and DNA. Discrete Appl. Math. 31, 261–277 (1991)
3. Errico, L., Jesshope, C.: Towards a new architecture for symbolic processing. In: Artificial Intelligence and Information-Control Systems of Robots '94, pp. 31–40. World Scientific, Singapore (1994)
4. Fahlman, S., Hinton, G., Seijnowski, T.: Massively parallel architectures for AI: NETL, THISTLE and Boltzmann Machines. In: Proc. AAAI National Conf. on AI, pp. 109–113. William Kaufman, Los Altos (1983)
5. Garey, M., Johnson, D.: Computers and Intractability. A Guide to the Theory of NP-completeness. Freeman, San Francisco, CA (1979)
6. Hillis, W.: The Connection Machine. MIT Press, Cambridge (1985)
7. Loos, R.: On accepting networks of splicing processors of size 3. In: Proc. CiE 2007 (in press, 2007)
8. Manea, F., Martín-Vide, C., Mitrana, V.: Accepting networks of splicing processors: complexity results. Theoretical Computer Science 371, 72–82 (2007)
9. Manea, F., Martín-Vide, C., Mitrana, V.: All NP-problems can be solved in polynomial time by accepting networks of splicing processors of constant size. In: Mao, C., Yokomori, T. (eds.) DNA Computing. LNCS, vol. 4287, pp. 47–57. Springer, Heidelberg (2006)
10. Martín-Vide, C., Mitrana, V.: Networks of evolutionary processors: results and perspectives. In: Molecular Computational Models: Unconventional Approaches, pp. 78–114. Idea Group Publishing, Hershey (2005)
11. Păun, G., Rozenberg, G., Salomaa, A.: DNA Computing. New Computing Paradigms. Springer, Berlin (1998)
12. Păun, G.: Distributed architectures in DNA computing based on splicing: limiting the size of components. In: Unconventional Models of Computation, pp. 323–335. Springer, Heidelberg (1998)
13. Pixton, D.: Regularity of splicing languages. Discrete Appl. Math. 69, 101–124 (1996)
14. Sankoff, D., et al.: Gene order comparisons for phylogenetic inference: evolution of the mitochondrial genome. Proc. Natl. Acad. Sci. USA 89, 6575–6579 (1992)

Hierarchical Relaxations of the Correctness Preserving Property for Restarting Automata*

F. Mráz[1], F. Otto[2], and M. Plátek[1]

[1] Charles University, Faculty of Mathematics and Physics
Department of Computer Science, Malostranské nám. 25
118 00 Praha 1, Czech Republic
`mraz@ksvi.ms.mff.cuni.cz,Martin.Platek@mff.cuni.cz`
[2] Fachbereich Elektrotechnik/Informatik, Universität Kassel
34109 Kassel, Germany
`otto@theory.informatik.uni-kassel.de`

Abstract. A nondeterministic restarting automaton M is said to be *(strongly) correctness preserving*, if, for each cycle $u \vdash_M^c v$, the word v belongs to the complete language $L_C(M)$ accepted by M, if the word u does. Here, in order to differentiate between nondeterministic restarting automata that are correctness preserving and nondeterministic restarting automata in general we introduce two gradual relaxations of the correctness preserving property. These relaxations lead to an infinite two-dimensional hierarchy of classes of languages with membership problems that are decidable in polynomial time.

1 Introduction

The restarting automaton was introduced in [1] to model the so-called *analysis by reduction* of natural languages. From a theoretical point of view the restarting automaton can be seen as a tool that yields a very flexible generalization of analytical grammars. It introduces a basic syntactic system (an approximation to the formalization of the analysis by reduction), which contains the full information about the input vocabulary (set of wordforms), the categorial vocabulary, the set of reductions (rewritings), the recognized language (the input language), and the language of sentential forms (the complete language).

To each sentence of the language recognized, a restarting automaton associates all the corresponding derivations through sequences of reduction steps. These reduction steps preserve the so-called 'error preserving property' for the sentential forms derived. This is an important property that imitates a similar property of analytical grammars. It states that any cycle of any computation of a restarting automaton M that starts from a word not belonging to the complete language $L_C(M)$ accepted by M necessarily yields a word that does not belong

---

* F. Mráz and M. Plátek were partially supported by the program 'Information Society' under project 1ET100300517. F. Mráz was also partially supported by the Grant Agency of Charles University in Prague under Grant-No. 358/2006/A-INF/MFF.

J. Durand-Lose and M. Margenstern (Eds.): MCU 2007, LNCS 4664, pp. 230–241, 2007.
© Springer-Verlag Berlin Heidelberg 2007

to this language, either. On the other hand, it is only deterministic restarting automata that in general also satisfy the complementary property of being *correctness preserving*, which states that any cycle of M that starts from a word belonging to the language $L_C(M)$ will again give a word from that language. A nondeterministic restarting automaton is called *strongly correctness preserving* if it satisfies the correctness preserving property.

By extending a corresponding result for simple t-RL-automata from [3], Messerschmidt and Otto [4] have shown that for many types of restarting automata, the nondeterministic variant that is strongly correctness preserving is not more powerful than the corresponding deterministic variant. In addition, they have investigated the *error-detection distance* of nondeterministic restarting automata. If M is a nondeterministic restarting automaton that is not correctness preserving, then M will execute cycles of the form $u \vdash^c_M v$, where $u \in L_C(M)$ and $v \notin L_C(M)$, that is, M *makes a mistake*. If M detects that it has made a mistake after executing at most $i - 1$ further cycles starting from $q_0 \text{¢} v\$$, then we say that M has error-detection distance i. One might expect that based on the error-detection distance an infinite hierarchy of restarting automata and language classes is obtained. However, it is shown in [4] that nondeterministic R(W)(W)- or RL(W)(W)-automata of bounded error-detection distance are not more expressive than the corresponding deterministic types of restarting automata. Thus, it is the unbounded error-detection distance in combination with nondeterminism that makes nondeterministic restarting automata more expressive than the corresponding deterministic variants.

As the correctness preserving property, which is very desirable in linguistic applications of restarting automata, is too restrictive in practice, we introduce two gradual relaxations of this property. Based on these relaxations we will derive an infinite two-dimensional hierarchy of classes of restarting automata and of languages that are tractable. It is expected that the notions studied here will support a further development of the well-known 'Functional (Generative) Description (of Czech)' (see [2] and some previous work of P. Sgall).

The paper is structured as follows. After giving the basic definitions in Section 2 we define the notion of cyclic relaxation of degree i and the notion of error relaxation of degree j for restarting automata in Section 3. Then we prove that the membership problem for the (complete) language of an RLWW-automaton with bounded cyclic relaxation and bounded error relaxation is decidable in quadratic time. Finally we establish the announced infinite two-dimensional hierarchy of language classes based on the degree of cyclic relaxation and the degree of error relaxation.

2   Definitions and Notation

Here we describe in short the type of restarting automaton we will be dealing with. More details on restarting automata in general can be found in [6,7].

A *two-way restarting automaton*, RLWW-automaton for short, is a nondeterministic machine $M = (Q, \Sigma, \Gamma, \text{¢}, \$, q_0, k, \delta)$ with a finite-state control Q, a flexible tape, and a read/write window of a fixed size $k \geq 1$. The work space is limited by the left sentinel ¢ and the right sentinel $, which cannot be removed from the tape. In addition to the input alphabet Σ, the tape alphabet Γ of M may contain a finite number of so-called auxiliary symbols. The behaviour of M is described by the transition relation δ that associates a finite set of transition steps to each pair (q, u) consisting of a state q and a possible content u of the read/write window. There are five types of transition steps:

1. A *move-right step* (MVR) causes M to shift the read/write window one position to the right and to change the state.
2. A *move-left step* (MVL) causes M to shift the read/write window one position to the left and to change the state.
3. A *rewrite step* causes M to replace the content u of the read/write window by a shorter string v, thereby shortening the tape, and to change the state.
4. A *restart step* causes M to place its read/write window over the left end of the tape, so that the first symbol it sees is the left sentinel ¢, and to reenter the initial state q_0.
5. An *accept step* causes M to halt and accept.

If $\delta(q, u) = \emptyset$ for some pair (q, u), then M necessarily halts, and we say that M *rejects* in this situation. Further, it is required that, ignoring move operations, rewrite and restart steps alternate in each computation of M, with a rewrite step coming first. In general, the automaton M is *nondeterministic*, that is, there can be two or more instructions with the same left-hand side (q, u). If that is not the case, the automaton is *deterministic*.

A *configuration* of M is a string $\alpha q \beta$ where q is a state, and either $\alpha = \lambda$ (the empty string) and $\beta \in \{¢\} \cdot \Gamma^* \cdot \{\$\}$ or $\alpha \in \{¢\} \cdot \Gamma^*$ and $\beta \in \Gamma^* \cdot \{\$\}$; here q represents the current state, $\alpha\beta$ is the current content of the tape, and it is understood that the window contains the first k symbols of β or all of β when $|\beta| \leq k$. A *restarting configuration* is of the form $q_0 ¢ w \$$, where q_0 is the initial state and $w \in \Gamma^*$.

We observe that any finite computation of a two-way restarting automaton M consists of certain phases. A phase, called a *cycle*, starts in a restarting configuration, the window moves along the tape performing MVR and MVL operations and a single rewrite operation until a restart operation is performed and thus a new restarting configuration is reached. The part after the last restart operation is called a *tail*. By $u \vdash^c_M v$ we denote a cycle of M that transforms the restarting configuration $q_0 ¢ u \$$ into the restarting configuration $q_0 ¢ v \$$. By $\vdash^{c*}_M$ we denote the reflexive and transitive closure of $\vdash^c_M$.

A *word* $w \in \Gamma^*$ *is accepted by* M, if there is a computation which, starting with the restarting configuration $q_0 ¢ w \$$, finishes by executing an accept instruction. By $L_C(M)$ we denote the language consisting of all words accepted by M; this is the *complete language* accepted (or recognized) by M. When we restrict attention to input words only, then we obtain the language $L(M) = L_C(M) \cap \Sigma^*$, which is the *input language* recognized (accepted) by $L(M)$.

We are also interested in various restricted types of restarting automata. They are obtained by combining two types of restrictions:

(a) Restrictions on the movement of the read/write window (expressed by the first part of the class name): RL- denotes no restriction, RR- means that no MVL operations are available, R- means that no MVL operations are available and that each rewrite step is immediately followed by a restart.

(b) Restrictions on the rewrite instructions (expressed by the second part of the class name): -WW denotes no restriction, -W means that no auxiliary symbols are available (that is, $\Gamma = \Sigma$), -λ means that no auxiliary symbols are available and that each rewrite step is simply a deletion (that is, if $(q', v) \in \delta(q, u)$, then v is obtained from u by deleting some symbols).

The following properties are of central importance (see, e.g, [1]).

Definition 1. (Correctness Preserving Property)
An RLWW-*automaton* M *is* (strongly) correctness preserving *if* $u \in L_C(M)$ *and* $u \vdash_M^{c*} v$ *imply that* $v \in L_C(M)$.

Definition 2. (Error Preserving Property)
An RLWW-*automaton* M *is* error preserving *if* $u \notin L_C(M)$ *and* $u \vdash_M^{c*} v$ *imply that* $v \notin L_C(M)$.

It is rather obvious that each RLWW-automaton is error preserving, and that all deterministic RLWW-automata are correctness preserving. On the other hand, one can easily construct examples of nondeterministic RLWW-automata that are not correctness preserving.

For an RWW-automaton M, the relation $\vdash_M^c$ can be described transparently by a finite sequence of *meta-instructions* of the form $(E, u \to v)$, where E is a regular language, and $u \to v$ is a rewrite step of M (see, e.g., [7]). On trying to execute the meta-instruction $(E, u \to v)$, M will get stuck (and so reject) starting from the configuration $q_0 \text{¢} w\$$, if w does not admit a factorization of the form $w = w_1 u w_2$ such that $\text{¢} w_1 \in E$. On the other hand, if w does have factorizations of this form, then one such factorization is chosen nondeterministically, and $q_0 \text{¢} w\$$ is transformed into $q_0 \text{¢} w_1 v w_2 \$$. In order to describe the tails of accepting computations we use meta-instructions of the form $(\text{¢} \cdot E \cdot \$, \text{Accept})$, where the strings from the regular language E are accepted by M in tail computations.

Example 1. Let $L_1 := \{ a^n b^n c, a^n c b^n c \mid n \geq 0 \} \cup \{ a^n b^m d, a^n d b^m d \mid m > 2n \geq 0 \}$. Then L_1 is accepted by the RW-automaton M_1 that is given through the following sequence of meta-instructions:

    (1.) $(\text{¢} \cdot a^+, abb \to cb)$,   (4.) $(\text{¢} \cdot a^+, adbbb \to db)$,
    (2.) $(\text{¢} \cdot a^+, abbb \to db)$,   (5.) $(\text{¢} \cdot \{\lambda, ab, c, acb\} \cdot c \cdot \$, \text{Accept})$,
    (3.) $(\text{¢} \cdot a^+, acbb \to cb)$,   (6.) $(\text{¢} \cdot \{\lambda, abb, d, adbb\} \cdot b^+ \cdot d \cdot \$, \text{Accept})$.

Starting from the configuration $q_0 \text{¢} a^n b^n c \$$ for a sufficiently large value of n, M_1 can execute the cycle $a^n b^n c \vdash_{M_1}^c a^{n-1} d b^{n-2} c$. As $a^n b^n c \in L_1$, while $a^{n-1} d b^{n-2} c \notin L_1$, we see that M_1 is not correctness preserving.

Theorem 1. [4] *For any* $\mathsf{X} \in \{\mathsf{R}, \mathsf{RL}, \mathsf{RW}, \mathsf{RLW}, \mathsf{RWW}, \mathsf{RLWW}\}$, *if* M *is a correctness preserving* X-*automaton, then there exists a deterministic* X-*automaton* M' *satisfying* $L_C(M') = L_C(M)$ *and* $L(M') = L(M)$.

3   Relaxations of the Correctness Preserving Property

Here we introduce two notions that relax the strong requirements of the correctness preserving property.

Definition 3. *Let $M = (Q, \Sigma, \Gamma, \text{¢}, \$, q_0, k, \delta)$ be an* RLWW-*automaton.*

(a) *We say that M is* correctness preserving *on a word $w \in L_C(M)$, if, for all $z \in \Gamma^*$, $w \vdash_M^{c*} z$ implies that $z \in L_C(M)$, too.*

(b) *Let i be a non-negative integer. We say that M has* cyclic relaxation *of degree i, if, for all words $w \in L_C(M)$, all $m \geq i$, and all sequences of cycles of the form $w = w_0 \vdash_M^c w_1 \vdash_M^c \cdots \vdash_M^c w_m$, $w_m \in L_C(M)$ implies that M is correctness preserving on w_j for all $j \geq i$. That is, M can only make a mistake in the first $i - 1$ cycles of a (non-accepting) computation.*

Obviously, the property of being correctness preserving corresponds to cyclic relaxation of degree 0.

Definition 4. *Let $M = (Q, \Sigma, \Gamma, \text{¢}, \$, q_0, k, \delta)$ be an* RLWW-*automaton, and let j be a non-negative integer. M is said to have* error relaxation *of degree j, if $m \leq j$ holds, whenever $w \in L_C(M)$ and there are cycles (reductions) $w \vdash_M^c w_i$, $1 \leq i \leq m$, such that $w_1, \ldots, w_m \notin L_C(M)$ and $w_k \neq w_l$ for all $1 \leq k < l \leq m$. That is, for the first cycle on a word from $L_C(M)$, there are at most j different mistakes that M can possibly make.*

Obviously, the property of being correctness preserving corresponds to error relaxation of degree 0.

Notation. By c(i)-RLWW we denote the class of RLWW-automata with cyclic relaxation of degree i, by e(j)-RLWW we denote the class of RLWW-automata with error relaxation of degree j, and by ce(i, j)-RLWW we denote the class of RLWW-automata that simultaneously have cyclic relaxation of degree i and error relaxation of degree j. The corresponding classes of complete languages are denoted by $\mathcal{L}_C$(c(i)-RLWW), $\mathcal{L}_C$(e(j)-RLWW), and $\mathcal{L}_C$(ce(i, j)-RLWW), respectively. Similarly, the corresponding classes of input languages are denoted by $\mathcal{L}$(c(i)-RLWW), $\mathcal{L}$(e(j)-RLWW), and $\mathcal{L}$(ce(i, j)-RLWW), respectively.

Example 2. Let $L_{p1} := \{\, ww^R, wcw^R \mid w \in \{a, b\}^* \,\}$. This language is accepted by the RRW-automaton M_{p1} that is given through the following sequence of meta-instructions (see, e.g., [7]), where $x \in \{a, b\}$:

(1) $(\text{¢} \cdot \{a, b\}^*, xx \rightarrow c, \{a, b\}^* \cdot \$)$,   (3) $(\text{¢} \cdot \{\lambda, c\} \cdot \$, \text{Accept})$.

(2) $(\text{¢} \cdot \{a, b\}^*, xcx \rightarrow c, \{a, b\}^* \cdot \$)$,

Obviously, M_{p1} is correctness preserving on all words from the sublanguage $\{\, wcw^R \mid w \in \{a, b\}^* \,\}$. Further, for any $w \in \{a, b\}^+$, the only accepting computation of M_{p1} that begins with the restarting configuration $q_0 \text{¢} ww^R \$$ is $ww^R \vdash_{M_{p1}}^c w_1 cw_1^R \vdash_{M_{p1}}^{c*} c$, where $w = w_1 a$ or $w = w_1 b$. Thus, M_{p1} has cyclic relaxation of degree 1.

However, M_{p1} does not have error relaxation of bounded degree. Consider the word $w_m := (aabb)^m a$, where m is sufficiently large. Then

$$w_m w_m^R = (aabb)^m aa(bbaa)^m = (aabb)^{2m} aa$$

belongs to the language L_{p1}. However, starting from the restarting configuration $q_0 \text{¢} w_m w_m^R \$$, M_{p1} has $4m+1$ options to apply meta-instruction (1), that is, there are $4m+1$ possible cycles $w_m w_m^R \vdash_{M_{p1}}^c y$, but only one of them yields a word from the language $L_C(M_{p1}) = L_{p1}$.

For proving that L_{p1} is not accepted by any RRW-automaton with error relaxation of bounded degree we will use the following modification of a pumping lemma for restarting automata (see, e.g., [7]).

Proposition 1. *For any* RRWW-*automaton M there exists a constant p such that the following holds. Assume that $uvw \vdash_M^c uv'w$, where $u = u_1 u_2 \cdots u_n$ for some non-empty words $u_1, \ldots, u_n$ and a constant $n > p$. Then there exist $r, s \in \mathbb{N}$, $1 \leq r < s \leq p$, such that*

$$u_1 \cdots u_{r-1}(u_r \cdots u_{s-1})^i u_s \cdots u_n vw \vdash_M^c u_1 \cdots u_{r-1}(u_r \cdots u_{s-1})^i u_s \cdots u_n v'w$$

holds for all $i \geq 0$, that is, $u_r \cdots u_{s-1}$ is a 'pumping factor' in the above cycle. Similarly, such a pumping factor can be found in any factorization of length greater than p of w. Such a pumping factor can also be found in any factorization of length greater than p of a word accepted in a tail computation.

Lemma 1. *The language L_{p1} is not accepted by any* RRW-*automaton with error relaxation of finite degree.*

Proof. Let $\Sigma = \{a, b, c\}$, and assume that $M = (Q, \Sigma, \Sigma, \text{¢}, \$, q_0, k, \delta)$ is an RRW-automaton such that $L(M) = L_{p1}$.

Let $n_0 > 0$ be an integer. We will show that there exist a word $z \in L_{p1}$ and cycles (reductions) $z \vdash_M^c z_i$, $1 \leq i \leq n_0$, such that $z_1, \ldots, z_{n_0} \notin L_C(M)$ and $z_j \neq z_l$ for all $1 \leq j < l \leq n_0$. That is, for the first cycle on some word from $L(M)$, there are at least n_0 different mistakes that M can make.

For $m \geq 1$, let $A_m := \{ (a^{2m}b^{2m})^n a^{2m}(b^{2m}a^{2m})^n \mid n > 0 \}$. Obviously, $A_m \subset L_{p1}$. Further, the following property is easily verified:

(∗) Let uyw be a factorization of a word $x \in A_m$ such that $|y| < m$. If there exists a word y' satisfying $|y'| < |y|$ such that $uy'w \in L_{p1}$, then $|u| > |x|/2 - 2m$ and $|w| > |x|/2 - 2m$.

Let p be the constant for M from Proposition 1, and let $m > \max\{k, p\}$, $n > p$, and $v := (a^{2m}b^{2m})^n a^{2m}(b^{2m}a^{2m})^n \in L(M)$. We consider an accepting computation of M on input v. From Proposition 1 it follows easily that v cannot be accepted by a tail computation of M. Thus, the accepting computation considered begins with a cycle of the form $v \vdash_M^c \omega$ for some word $\omega \in L_{p1}$. From (∗) it follows that the corresponding rewrite operation occurs at a position in the range $[|v|/2 - 2m, |v|/2 + 2m]$, that is, a factor of the middle part $b^m a^{2m} b^m$ is being rewritten. The word v has a factorization of the form $v = \alpha_1\alpha_2 \cdots \alpha_n y \beta_1 \cdots \beta_n$ such that $\alpha_t = a^{2m}b^{2m}$ for all $t = 1, \ldots, n-1$, $\alpha_n = a^{2m}b^m$, $y = b^m a^{2m} b^m$, $\beta_1 = b^m a^{2m}$, and $\beta_t = b^{2m}a^{2m}$ for all $t = 2, \ldots, n$. Thus, according to Proposition 1 there exist indices r, s, $1 \leq r < s \leq p < n$ such that

$$\alpha_1 \cdots \alpha_{r-1}(\alpha_r \cdots \alpha_{s-1})^i \alpha_s \cdots \alpha_n y \beta_1 \cdots \beta_n \quad \vdash_M^c$$
$$\alpha_1 \cdots \alpha_{r-1}(\alpha_r \cdots \alpha_{s-1})^i \alpha_s \cdots \alpha_n y' \beta_1 \cdots \beta_n,$$

for some word y' and all exponents $i \geq 0$. Obviously, the length of the pumping factor $\alpha_r \cdots \alpha_{s-1}$ divides the number $4m \cdot p!$. Analogously a pumping factor with corresponding properties can be found in the suffix $\beta_2 \cdots \beta_n$ of v. Hence, there exist words $v_{i,j}$ and $\omega_{i,j}$ obtained by pumping the cycle $v \vdash_M^c \omega$ independently on the left and on the right of the rewritten factor y such that

$$v_{i,j} = (a^{2m}b^{2m})^{n+ip!} a^{2m} b^m y b^m a^{2m} (b^{2m}a^{2m})^{n+jp!},$$
$$\omega_{i,j} = (a^{2m}b^{2m})^{n+ip!} a^{2m} b^m y' b^m a^{2m} (b^{2m}a^{2m})^{n+jp!},$$

and $v_{i,j} \vdash_M^c \omega_{i,j}$ for all $i, j \in \mathbb{N}$. Consider the words $v_\ell := v_{\ell, n_0 - \ell}$ and $\omega_\ell := \omega_{\ell, n_0 - \ell}$ for $\ell = 0, \ldots, n_0$. Trivially,

$$v_\ell = (a^{2m}b^{2m})^{n+\ell p! + 1} a^{2m} (b^{2m}a^{2m})^{n+(n_0-\ell)p!+1} = (a^{2m}b^{2m})^{2n+n_0 p!+2} a^{2m}.$$

For any ℓ_1, ℓ_2, $0 \leq \ell_1 < \ell_2 \leq n_0$, $\omega_{\ell_1} \neq \omega_{\ell_2}$, as these words arise by shortening v_ℓ at different places. Since at most one of the words $\omega_0, \ldots, \omega_{n_0}$ is a palindrome, M can make at least n_0 mistakes in the first cycle on the word v_ℓ from $L(M)$.   □

The lemma above yields the following consequence.

Theorem 2. $L_{p1} \in \mathcal{L}(\mathsf{c}(1)\text{-RRW}) \setminus \bigcup_{j \geq 0} \mathcal{L}(\mathsf{e}(j)\text{-RRW})$.

It can be shown analogously that the language

$$L_{p2} := \{ ww^R dw_1 w_1^R, wcw^R dw_1 w_1^R, wcw^R dw_1 cw_1^R \mid w, w_1 \in \{a, b\}^* \}$$

is accepted by an RRW-automaton with cyclic relaxation of degree 2, but that it is not accepted by any RRW-automaton with cyclic relaxation of degree 1 or with bounded error relaxation. By taking more factors we obtain the corresponding result for any degree i of cyclic relaxation.

Our next results show that cyclic relaxation of bounded degree implies that the languages $L_C(M)$ and $L(M)$ are decidable in polynomial time, where the degree of the time bound depends on the degree of cyclic relaxation.

Theorem 3. *If M is a $\mathsf{ce}(i,j)$-RLWW-automaton, then the membership problems for the languages $L_C(M)$ and $L(M)$ are solvable in time $O((j+1)^i \cdot n^2)$.*

Proof. Let $i, j \geq 0$, and let $M = (Q, \Sigma, \Gamma, \mathfrak{c}, \$, q_0, k, \delta)$ be an RLWW-automaton that has cyclic relaxation of degree i and error relaxation of degree j. Given a word $w \in \Gamma^n$, we must decide whether there exists an accepting computation of M starting from the restarting configuration $q_0 \mathfrak{c} w \$$. For doing so, we construct a partial computation tree $\mathcal{G}(M, w)$. The nodes of this tree are labelled with restarting configurations of M, and there is a directed edge from a node labelled with $q_0 \mathfrak{c} x \$$ to a node labelled with $q_0 \mathfrak{c} y \$$ if and only if $x \vdash_M^c y$ holds. This tree is constructed iteratively level by level.

Level 0 consists of a single node n_w that is labelled with $q_0 \mathfrak{c} w \$$. If starting from the configuration $q_0 \mathfrak{c} w \$$, M can execute an accepting tail computation, then $w \in L_C(M)$, and we halt and accept. Otherwise, let $\nu(w)$ denote the number of words w' such that M can execute a cycle of the form $w \vdash_M^c w'$, and let $\mu(w) := \min\{\nu(w), j + 1\}$. If $\nu(w) = 0$, then starting from $q_0 \mathfrak{c} w \$$, M can only execute rejecting tail computations, implying that $w \notin L_C(M)$. Accordingly we halt and reject. Otherwise, we determine $\mu(w)$ many words w' such that M can execute a cycle $w \vdash_M^c w'$, and we add a node $n_{w'}$ labelled by $q_0 \mathfrak{c} w' \$$ and a directed edge from the node n_w to this new node for each of these words w'. These nodes form level 1 of the tree $\mathcal{G}(M, w)$.

If, for any of the words w', M can execute an accepting tail computation starting from $q_0 \mathfrak{c} w' \$$, then $w \in L_C(M)$, and we halt and accept. Otherwise, let $\nu(w')$ denote the cardinality of the number of words z such that M can execute a cycle of the form $w' \vdash_M^c z$, and let $\mu(w') := \min\{\nu(w'), j+1\}$. If $\nu(w') = 0$, then starting from $q_0 \mathfrak{c} w' \$$, M can only execute rejecting tail computations, implying that $w' \notin L_C(M)$. Otherwise, we determine $\mu(w')$ many words z such that M can execute a cycle $w' \vdash_M^c z$, and we add a node n_z labelled by $q_0 \mathfrak{c} z \$$ and a directed edge from the node $n_{w'}$ to this new node for each of these words z. Doing this for all nodes at level 1, we obtain the nodes that form level 2 of the tree $\mathcal{G}(M, w)$. If there are no nodes at level 2, then $w \notin L_C(M)$, and we halt and reject. Otherwise we continue to construct the nodes at level $3, 4, \ldots, i$.

Altogether we have constructed $O((j+1)^i)$ many nodes, which can be achieved in time $O((j + 1)^i \cdot n)$. If any of the nodes constructed is labelled by a restarting configuration such that M can execute an accepting tail computation when starting from that particular restarting configuration, then $w \in L_C(M)$, and we halt and accept. On the other hand, if for all nodes at level i, M can only execute rejecting tail computations, then $w \notin L_C(M)$, and we halt and reject. Finally, we simulate a single computation for each restarting configuration that labels a node at level i, where, at each step, we first check whether an accepting tail computation can be applied, and if that is not possible, then we execute the next cycle, provided that is possible. If one of these computations is accepting, then $w \in L_C(M)$, and we halt and accept; if all of them are rejecting, then we halt and reject. As there are at most $(j + 1)^i$ nodes at level i, this part of the computation takes time $O((j + 1)^i \cdot n^2)$.

It remains to argue that this algorithm always yields the correct answer. If it accepts, then certainly $w \in L_C(M)$, that is, this answer is correct. Conversely, assume that $w \in L_C(M)$, but that for no restarting configuration labelling a node of the tree $\mathcal{G}(M, w)$, M can execute an accepting tail computation. As M has error relaxation of degree j, we see that at least one node at level 1 is labelled by a restarting configuration $q_0 \mathfrak{c} w_1 \$$ such that $w_1 \in L_C(M)$, one successor of this node at level 2 is labelled by a restarting configuration $q_0 \mathfrak{c} w_2 \$$ such that

$w_2 \in L_C(M)$, and so forth. Thus, following the corresponding path from the root to the distinguished node at level i, we obtain a partial computation of the form $w \vdash_M^c w_1 \vdash_M^c w_2 \vdash_M^c \cdots \vdash_M^c w_i$, where $w_i \in L_C(M)$. As M has cyclic relaxation of degree i, it follows that M is correctness preserving on w_i. Thus, the computation of M that starts from the restarting configuration $q_0 \mathcal{c} w_i \$$ and that is being simulated by our algorithm will eventually accept. This implies that our algorithm will accept as well.   □

Although the proof above only mentions the complete language $L_C(M)$, it is immediate that it also works for the language $L(M)$. By abandoning the error relaxation altogether we obtain the following result.

Theorem 4. *If M is a $c(i)$-RLWW-automaton for some $i \geq 0$, then the membership problems for the languages $L_C(M)$ and $L(M)$ are solvable in time $O(n^{i+2})$.*

Proof. For a restarting configuration $q_0 \mathcal{c} x \$$, where $|x| = n$, there are at most $O(n)$ many words y such that M can execute a cycle of the form $x \vdash_M^c y$. Thus, from the proof of the previous theorem we see that we can decide membership in $L_C(M)$ and in $L(M)$ in time $O(n^{i+2})$.   □

Next we establish some hierarchy results on the degree of cyclic relaxation.

Theorem 5. *For all $i, j \geq 0$, we have the following proper inclusions:*

(a) $\mathcal{L}_C(\mathsf{c}(i)\text{-RLWW}) \subset \mathcal{L}_C(\mathsf{c}(i+1)\text{-RLWW})$,

(b) $\mathcal{L}_C(\mathsf{ce}(i,j)\text{-RLWW}) \subset \mathcal{L}_C(\mathsf{ce}(i+1,j)\text{-RLWW})$.

Proof. It remains to show that the inclusions above are proper. As we consider complete languages, it is not necessary to distinguish between input symbols and auxiliary symbols, that is, we can restrict our attention to RLW-automata. Finally, as for each RLW-automaton, an RRW-automaton can be found that has the same tape alphabet and that executes exactly the same cycles (see, e.g., [7]), we only need to consider RRW-automata. For deriving the announced separation results we consider a number of example languages.

Let $L_{1,1} := \{ a^n b^n, a^n c b^n \mid n \geq 1 \} \cup \{ a^n b^{2n}, a^n d b^{2n} \mid n \geq 1 \}$. It is easily seen that this language is accepted by the RW-automaton $M_{1,1}$ that is given through the following sequence of meta-instructions:

(1) $(\mathcal{c} \cdot a^+, abb \to cb)$,   (4) $(\mathcal{c} \cdot a^+, adbbb \to db)$,
(2) $(\mathcal{c} \cdot a^+, abbb \to db)$,   (5) $(\mathcal{c} \cdot \{ab, acb, abb, adbb\} \cdot \$, \mathsf{Accept})$.
(3) $(\mathcal{c} \cdot a^+, acbb \to cb)$,

Starting from the configuration $q_0 \mathcal{c} a^n b^n \$$ for a sufficiently large value of n, $M_{1,1}$ can execute the cycle $a^n b^n \vdash_{M_{1,1}}^c a^{n-1} d b^{n-2}$. As $a^n b^n \in L_{1,1}$, while $a^{n-1} d b^{n-2} \notin L_{1,1}$, we see that $M_{1,1}$ is not correctness preserving. On the other hand, it is easily verified that $M_{1,1}$ is a $\mathsf{ce}(1,1)$-RW-automaton.

Next consider the language $L_{2,1} := L_{1,1} \cdot L_{1,1}$. It is accepted by the RRW-automaton $M_{2,1}$ that is given through the following sequence of meta-instructions:

(1) $(\text{¢} \cdot a^+, ab \to c, b^+ \cdot a^+ \cdot \{\lambda, c, d\} \cdot b^+ \cdot \$)$,
(2) $(\text{¢} \cdot a^+, abb \to d, b^+ \cdot a^+ \cdot \{\lambda, c, d\} \cdot b^+ \cdot \$)$,
(3) $(\text{¢} \cdot (ab \cup a^+ \cdot c \cdot b^+ \cup abb \cup a^+ \cdot d \cdot b^+) \cdot a^+, ab \to c, b^+ \cdot \$)$,
(4) $(\text{¢} \cdot (ab \cup a^+ \cdot c \cdot b^+ \cup abb \cup a^+ \cdot d \cdot b^+) \cdot a^+, abb \to d, b^+ \cdot \$)$,
(5) $(\text{¢} \cdot (ab \cup a^+ \cdot c \cdot b^+ \cup abb \cup a^+ \cdot d \cdot b^+) \cdot a^+, acb \to c, b^+ \cdot \$)$,
(6) $(\text{¢} \cdot (ab \cup a^+ \cdot c \cdot b^+ \cup abb \cup a^+ \cdot d \cdot b^+) \cdot a^+, adbb \to d, b^+ \cdot \$)$,
(7) $(\text{¢} \cdot a^+, acb \to c, b^+ \cdot \{ab, acb, abb, adbb\} \cdot \$)$,
(8) $(\text{¢} \cdot a^+, adbb \to d, b^+ \cdot \{ab, acb, abb, adbb\} \cdot \$)$,
(9) $(\text{¢} \cdot \{ab, acb, abb, adbb\} \cdot \{ab, acb, abb, adbb\} \cdot \$, \text{Accept})$.

Given an input of the form $a^{2n}b^{2n}a^{2n}b^{2n}$ for a sufficiently large value of n, $M_{2,1}$ first inserts a c or a d after the prefix a^{2n-1} (by instruction (1) or (2)), and then it inserts a c or a d in the second half of the input word (by instruction (3) or (4)). Thereafter the computation proceeds deterministically. Hence, $M_{2,1}$ has cyclic relaxation of degree 2. Further, in the first step above as well as in the second step it has two choices only, which implies that it has error relaxation of degree 1. Thus, we see that $L_{2,1} \in \mathcal{L}_C(\text{ce}(2,1)\text{-RRW})$.

However, $L_{2,1}$ is not accepted by any $\text{c}(1)$-RRW-automaton. Assume that M' is an RRW-automaton such that $L_C(M') = L_{2,1}$. Consider the possible computations of M' starting from an input of the form $w := a^{2m}b^{2m}a^{2n}b^{2n}$ for some large values of m and n. As $w \in L_{2,1}$, there exists an accepting computation $w \vdash^c_{M'} w_1 \vdash^c_{M'} w_2 \vdash^c_{M'} \cdots \vdash^c_{M'} w_k$, where w_k is accepted in a tail computation. Hence, $w_1 \in L_{2,1}$, implying that in the first cycle M' has either modified the syllable $a^{2m}b^{2m}$ or the syllable $a^{2n}b^{2n}$, while the other syllable has remained unchanged. Assume that M' has rewritten the first syllable into $a^{2m-r}cb^{2m-r}$ or into $a^{2m-r}b^{2m-r}$. Using a technique similar to the proof of Lemma 1 it can be shown that M' cannot distinguish a suffix of the form $a^{2n}b^{2n}$ from a suffix of the form $a^{2n}b^{4n}$ for some values of n. Hence, M' is not correctness preserving on some words ending with the suffix $a^{2n}b^{2n}$. In particular, M' is not correctness preserving on some words of a form similar to w_1. The case that in the first cycle M' modifies the syllable $a^{2n}b^{2n}$ is dealt with analogously. Thus, M' does not have cyclic relaxation of degree 1, that is, $L_{2,1} \in \mathcal{L}_C(\text{ce}(2,1)\text{-RRW}) \smallsetminus \mathcal{L}_C(\text{c}(1)\text{-RRW})$.

For $i \geq 3$, we can show in the same way that the language $L_{i,1} := L_{1,1}^i$ belongs to $\mathcal{L}_C(\text{ce}(i,1)\text{-RRW}) \smallsetminus \mathcal{L}_C(\text{c}(i-1)\text{-RRW})$. This shows that the inclusions in (a) and (b) are indeed proper inclusions. $\qquad \square$

Corresponding hierarchy results also hold for the degree of error relaxation.

Theorem 6. *For all $i, j \geq 0$, we have the following proper inclusions:*

(a) $\mathcal{L}_C(\text{e}(j)\text{-RLWW}) \subset \mathcal{L}_C(\text{e}(j+1)\text{-RLWW})$,

(b) $\mathcal{L}_C(\text{ce}(i,j)\text{-RLWW}) \subset \mathcal{L}_C(\text{ce}(i,j+1)\text{-RLWW})$.

Proof. Again it is obvious that these inclusions hold. For proving that they are proper, we consider another family of example languages. For $m > 1$, let

$\Sigma_m := \{a, b, c_1, \ldots, c_m\}$, and $Le_{1,m} := \{a^n b^{2^i n}, a^n c_i b^{2^i n} \mid 1 \le i \le m, n \ge 1\}$. Then $Le_{1,m}$ is accepted by the RRW-automaton $M_{1,m}$ that is specified as follows, where $1 \le i \le m$:

$$(1.i)\ (\mathfrak{c} \cdot a^+, ab^{2^i} \rightarrow c_i, (b^{2^i})^+ \cdot \$),$$
$$(2.i)\ (\mathfrak{c} \cdot a^+, ac_i b^{2^i} \rightarrow c_i, (b^{2^i})^+ \cdot \$),$$
$$(3.i)\ (\mathfrak{c} \cdot a \cdot \{\lambda, c_i\} \cdot b^{2^i} \cdot \$, \mathsf{Accept}).$$

On words from $Le_{1,m}$ that contain an occurrence of a symbol c_i ($1 \le i \le m$) $M_{1,m}$ is correctness preserving. On the other hand, starting from a restarting configuration of the form $q_0 \mathfrak{c} a^n b^{2^m n}\$$, there are m possible cycles that $M_{1,m}$ can execute, but only one of them yields a word from $Le_{1,m}$. Hence, $M_{1,m}$ has cyclic relaxation of degree 1 and error relaxation of degree $m - 1$.

In fact, no RRW-automaton M for the language $Le_{1,m}$ has error relaxation of degree lower than $m - 1$. Assume that M is an RRW-automaton for $Le_{1,m}$. Given an input of the form $a^n b^{2^m r} \in Le_{1,m}$, where n is sufficiently large, M cannot accept in a tail computation. Thus, it has to execute a cycle of the form $a^n b^{2^m r} \vdash_M^c a^{n-s} c_i b^{2^m r - 2^i s}$ or $a^n b^{2^m r} \vdash_M a^{n-s} b^{2^m r - 2^i s}$ for some value of $i \in \{1, \ldots, m\}$ and a small $s \ge 1$.

By a technique similar to the one used in the proof of Lemma 1 we can show that there are m possible values for i, each of which could be the correct one, while all others are wrong. Therefore, in this situation M has at least m options, and so it has error relaxation of degree at least $m - 1$. Thus, we see that $Le_{1,m} \in \mathcal{L}(\mathsf{ce}(1, m-1)\text{-RWW}) \setminus \mathcal{L}(\mathsf{e}(m-2)\text{-RWW})$. This implies that the inclusions in (a) and in (b) are proper. $\square$

From Theorem 2 and the remark following it we also obtain the following.

Corollary 1. *For all $i \ge 1$, $\bigcup_{j \ge 0} \mathcal{L}_C(\mathsf{ce}(i, j)\text{-RLWW}) \subset \mathcal{L}_C(\mathsf{c}(i)\text{-RLWW})$.*

Also the corresponding result for the degree of error relaxation holds.

Theorem 7. *For all $j \ge 1$, $\bigcup_{i \ge 0} \mathcal{L}_C(\mathsf{ce}(i, j)\text{-RLWW}) \subset \mathcal{L}_C(\mathsf{e}(j)\text{-RLWW})$.*

Proof. Recall the language $L_{1,1}$ from the proof of Theorem 5. Here we consider the language $L_{+,1} := L_{1,1}^+$. Then an RRW-automaton can be designed that accepts this language, and that has error relaxation of degree 1. However, it can be shown that no RRW-automaton with bounded cyclic relaxation can accept the language $L_{+,1}$. Thus, $L_{+,1} \in \mathcal{L}(\mathsf{e}(1)\text{-RRW}) \setminus \bigcup_{i,j \ge 0} \mathcal{L}(\mathsf{ce}(i,j)\text{-RRW})$. $\square$

The proof above shows in fact that $L_{+,1} \notin \bigcup_{i \ge 0} \mathcal{L}_C(\mathsf{c}(i)\text{-RLWW})$. Thus, we obtain the following consequence.

Corollary 2. $\bigcup_{i \ge 0} \mathcal{L}_C(\mathsf{c}(i)\text{-RLWW}) \subset \mathcal{L}_C(\text{RLWW})$.

As the language L_{p1} is not accepted by any restarting automaton of bounded degree of error relaxation, we also have the following proper inclusion.

Corollary 3. $\bigcup_{j \ge 0} \mathcal{L}_C(\mathsf{e}(j)\text{-RLWW}) \subset \mathcal{L}_C(\text{RLWW})$.

4   Conclusion

We have seen that the two relaxations of the notion of correctness preservation yield a two-dimensional infinite hierarchy of automata and language classes. This hierarchy is depicted in the diagram below, where each arrow denotes a proper inclusion. Here $ce(i, j)$ stands for the language class $\mathcal{L}_C(ce(i, j)\text{-RLWW})$, $c(i)$ denotes the language class $\mathcal{L}_C(c(i)\text{-RLWW})$, and $e(j)$ denotes the language class $\mathcal{L}_C(e(j)\text{-RLWW})$.

$$
\begin{array}{ccccccccccc}
ce(1,1) & \to & ce(2,1) & \to & ce(3,1) & \to & \cdots \to & \bigcup_{i\geq 0} ce(i,1) & \to & e(1) \\
\downarrow & & \downarrow & & \downarrow & & & \downarrow & & \downarrow \\
ce(1,2) & \to & ce(2,2) & \to & ce(3,2) & \to & \cdots \to & \bigcup_{i\geq 0} ce(i,2) & \to & e(2) \\
\downarrow & & \downarrow & & \downarrow & & & \downarrow & & \downarrow \\
ce(1,3) & \to & ce(2,3) & \to & ce(3,3) & \to & \cdots \to & \bigcup_{i\geq 0} ce(i,3) & \to & e(3) \\
\downarrow & & \downarrow & & \downarrow & & & \downarrow & & \downarrow \\
\cdots & & \cdots & & \cdots & & \cdots & \cdots & & \cdots \\
\downarrow & & \downarrow & & \downarrow & & & \downarrow & & \downarrow \\
\bigcup_{j\geq 0} ce(1,j) & \to & \bigcup_{j\geq 0} ce(2,j) & \to & \bigcup_{j\geq 0} ce(3,j) & \to & \cdots \to & \bigcup_{i,j\geq 0} ce(i,j) & \to & \bigcup_{j\geq 0} e(j) \\
\downarrow & & \downarrow & & \downarrow & & & \downarrow & & \downarrow \\
c(1) & \to & c(2) & \to & c(3) & \to & \cdots \to & \bigcup_{i\geq 0} c(i) & \to & \mathcal{L}_C(\text{RLWW})
\end{array}
$$

It remains open whether an analogous hierarchy can be derived for the corresponding families of input languages.

References

1. Jančar, P., Mráz, F., Plátek, M., Vogel, J.: Restarting automata. In: Reichel, H. (ed.) FCT 1995. LNCS, vol. 965, pp. 283–292. Springer, Heidelberg (1995)
2. Lopatkova, M., Platek, M., Sgall, P.: Towards a formal model for functional generative description - Analysis by reduction and restarting automata. The Prague Bulletin of Mathematical Linguistics 87, 7–26 (2007)
3. Messerschmidt, H., Mráz, F., Otto, F., Plátek, M.: Correctness preservation and complexity of simple RL-automata. In: Ibarra, O.H., Yen, H.-C. (eds.) CIAA 2006. LNCS, vol. 4094, pp. 162–172. Springer, Heidelberg (2006)
4. Messerschmidt, H., Otto, F.: On determinism versus nondeterminism for restarting automata. In: Loos, R., Fazekas, S.Z., Martin-Vide, C. (eds.) LATA 2007, Preproc. Report 35/07, Research Group on Math. Linguistics, Universitat Rovira i Virgili, Tarragona, 2007, pp. 413–424 (2007)
5. Mráz, F., Plátek, M., Jurdzinski, T.: Ambiguity by restarting automata. International Journal of Foundations of Computer Science (to appear)
6. Otto, F.: Restarting automata and their relations to the Chomsky hierarchy. In: Ésik, Z., Fülöp, Z. (eds.) DLT 2003. LNCS, vol. 2710, Springer, Heidelberg (2003)
7. Otto, F.: Restarting automata. In: Ésik, Z., Martin-Vide, C., Mitrana, V. (eds.) Recent Advances in Formal Languages and Applications, Studies in Computational Intelligence, vol. 25, pp. 269–303. Springer, Heidelberg (2006)

Four Small Universal Turing Machines

Turlough Neary[1] and Damien Woods[2]

[1] TASS, Department of Computer Science,
National University of Ireland Maynooth, Ireland
tneary@cs.may.ie
[2] Department of Computer Science,
University College Cork, Ireland
d.woods@cs.ucc.ie

Abstract. We present small polynomial time universal Turing machines with state-symbol pairs of $(5, 5)$, $(6, 4)$, $(9, 3)$ and $(18, 2)$. These machines simulate our new variant of tag system, the bi-tag system and are the smallest known universal Turing machines with 5, 4, 3 and 2-symbols respectively. Our 5-symbol machine uses the same number of instructions (22) as the smallest known universal Turing machine by Rogozhin.

1 Introduction

Shannon [16] was the first to consider the problem of finding the smallest possible universal Turing machine. In 1962 Minsky [7] constructed a 7-state, 4-symbol universal Turing machine that simulates Turing machines via 2-tag systems [2]. Minsky's technique of 2-tag simulation was extended by Rogozhin [15] to construct small universal Turing machines with state-symbol pairs of $(24, 2)$, $(10, 3)$, $(7, 4)$, $(5, 5)$, $(4, 6)$, $(3, 10)$ and $(2, 18)$. Subsequently some of these machines were reduced in size to give machines with state-symbol pairs of $(3, 9)$ [5], $(19, 2)$ [1] and $(7, 4)$ [1]. Figure 1 is a state-symbol plot where the current smallest 2-tag simulators of Rogozhin et al. are plotted as circles.

Here we present universal Turing machines with state-symbol pairs of $(5, 5)$, $(6, 4)$, $(9, 3)$ and $(18, 2)$, the later two machines having previously appeared in [9]. These machines simulate Turing machines via bi-tag systems and are plotted as triangles in Figure 1. These machines improve the state of the art in small universal Turing machines and reduce the space between the universal and non-universal curves. Our 5-symbol machine uses the same number of instructions (22) as the current smallest known universal Turing machine (Rogozhin's 6-symbol machine [15]). Also, our 5-symbol machine has less instructions than Rogozhin's 5-symbol machine. Since Minsky [7] constructed his 7-states and 4-symbols machine, a number of authors [1,14,15] have decreased the number of transition rules used for 4-symbol machines. However our 4-symbol machine is the first reduction in the number of states.

Recently, the simulation overhead of Turing machines by 2-tag systems was improved from exponential [2] to polynomial [17]. More precisely, if Z is a single

J. Durand-Lose and M. Margenstern (Eds.): MCU 2007, LNCS 4664, pp. 242–254, 2007.
© Springer-Verlag Berlin Heidelberg 2007

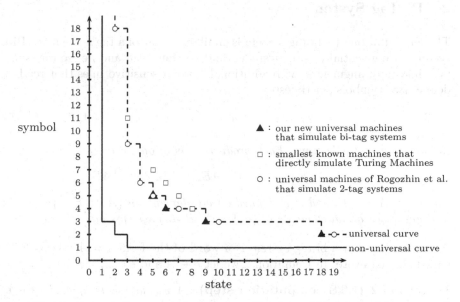

Fig. 1. Current state-symbol plot of small universal Turing machines

tape deterministic Turing machine that runs in time t, then the universal Turing machines of Minsky and Rogozhin et al. now simulate Z in $O(t^8(\log t)^4)$ time. It turns out that the time overhead can be improved to $O(t^4(\log t)^2)$ (this result is as yet unpublished). In earlier work [11] we gave the smallest known universal Turing machines that directly simulate Turing machines. These machines run in time $O(t^2)$ and are plotted as squares in Figure 1. Assuming a single instruction is reserved for halting it is known that there are no universal Turing machines for the following state-symbol pairs: $(2,2)$ [4,12], $(3,2)$ [13], $(2,3)$ (Pavlotskaya, unpublished), $(1,n)$ [3], and $(n,1)$ (trivial) for $n \geqslant 1$. These results induce the non-universal curve in Figure 1.

Our universal Turing machines simulate bi-tag systems with a quadratic polynomial increase in time. Hence from Theorem 1 our universal Turing machines simulate Turing machines efficiently in time $O(t^6(n))$. Results on alternative small universal Turing machine definitions can be found in [6,18,19].

1.1 Preliminaries

The Turing machines considered in this paper are deterministic and have one tape. Our universal Turing machine with m states and n symbols is denoted $U_{m,n}$. We write $c_1 \vdash c_2$ if a configuration c_2 is obtained from c_1 via a single computation step. We let $c_1 \vdash^t c_2$ denote a sequence of t computation steps and let $c_1 \vdash^* c_2$ denote 0 or more computation steps. Also, we let $\langle x \rangle$ denote the encoding of x and ϵ denote the empty word.

2   Bi-Tag Systems

The computation of a bi-tag system is similar to that of a tag system [8]. Bi-tag systems are essentially 1-tag systems (and so they read and delete one symbol per timestep), augmented with additional context sensitive rules that read, and delete, two symbols per timestep.

Definition 1 (Bi-tag system). *A bi-tag system is a tuple* (A, E, e_h, P)*. Here A and E are disjoint finite sets of symbols and $e_h \in E$ is the halt symbol. P is the finite set of productions. Each production is of one of the following 3 forms:*

$$P(a) = a, \quad P(e, a) \in AE, \quad P(e, a) \in AAE,$$

where $a \in A$, $e \in E$, and P is defined on all elements of $\{A \cup ((E - \{e_h\}) \times A)\}$ and undefined on all elements of $\{e_h\} \times A$. Bi-tag systems are deterministic.

A configuration of a bi-tag system is a word of the form $s = A^*(AE \cup EA)A^*$ called the dataword. In Definition 2 we let $a \in A$ and $e \in E$.

Definition 2 (BTS computation step). *A production is applied in one of two ways:*

(i) if $s = as'$ then $as' \vdash s'P(a)$,
(ii) if $s = eas'$ then $eas' \vdash s'P(e, a)$.

Theorem 1 ([10]). *Given a deterministic single tape Turing machine Z that runs in time t then there exists a bi-tag system that simulates the computation of Z using space $O(t(n))$ and time $O(t^3(n))$.*

In earlier work [10] Theorem 1 is obtained by proving bi-tag systems simulate Turing machines via clockwise Turing machines. A clockwise Turing machine is a Turing machine with a tape head that moves in one direction only, on a circular tape.

3   Universal Turing Machines

In this section we give the input encoding to our universal Turing machines. Following this we give each machine and describe its operation by explaining how it simulates bi-tag systems. Let $R = (A, E, e_h, P)$ be a bi-tag system where $A = \{a_1, \ldots, a_q\}$ and $E = \{e_1, \ldots, e_h\}$. The encoding of R as a word is denoted $\langle R \rangle$. The encodings of symbols $a \in A$ and $e \in E$ are denoted $\langle a \rangle$ and $\langle e \rangle$ respectively. The encodings of productions $P(a)$ and $P(e, a)$ are denoted as $\langle P(a) \rangle$ and $\langle P(e, a) \rangle$ respectively.

Definition 3. *The encoding of a configuration of R is of the form*

$$\ldots ccc \langle R \rangle S^* (\langle A \rangle M)^* \Big(\langle A \rangle M \langle E \rangle \cup \langle E \rangle \langle A \rangle M \Big) (\langle A \rangle M)^* Dccc \ldots \qquad (1)$$

Table 1. Encoding of P productions. Here $a_i, a_k, a_v \in A$ and $e_j, e_m \in E$. If $e_m \neq e_h$ then $L = \epsilon$. If $e_m = e_h$ then $L = g^{12q+8}$ for $U_{6,4}$ and $L = d^{10}$ for $U_{5,5}$.

	$\langle P(a_i)\rangle$	$\langle P(e_j,a_i)\rangle$ $P(e_j,a_i) = a_k e_m$	$\langle P(e_j,a_i)\rangle$ $P(e_j,a_i) = a_v a_k e_m$
$U_{5,5}$	$\delta\delta d^{16i-6}$	$\delta\delta L d^{16mq}\delta d^{16k-6}$	$\delta L d^{16mq}\delta d^{16k-2}\delta d^{16v-6}$
$U_{6,4}$	$\delta^5 g^{12i-10}\delta$	$\delta^4 L g^{12mq}\delta\delta g^{12k-10}\delta$	$\delta^2 L g^{12mq}\delta\delta g^{12hq+12k-4}\delta\delta g^{12v-10}\delta$
$U_{9,3}$	$\delta\delta cc\delta c^{8i}$	$\delta cc\delta\delta c^{8mq+2}\delta c^{8k}$	$\delta\delta c^{8mq+2}\delta c^{8k}\delta c^{8v}$
$U_{18,2}$	$cb(cc)^2 cb(cc)^{4i-2}$	$(cb)^2(cc)^{4qj+2}cb(cc)^{4k-2}$	$cb(cc)^{4qj+2}cb(cc)^{4k}cb(cc)^{4v-2}$

Table 2. Symbol values for Equations (1) and (2). The value of H for $U_{6,4}$ is given by Equation (3) in Section 3.4. There is no $\langle e_h\rangle$ for $U_{18,2}$ as this machine simulates non-halting bi-tag systems.

	$\langle a_i\rangle$	$\langle e_j\rangle$	$\langle e_h\rangle$	S	M	D	V	H
$U_{5,5}$	b^{4i-1}	b^{4jq}	$b^{4hq+2}\delta$	d^2	δ	ϵ	δ	cd
$U_{6,4}$	b^{8i-5}	b^{8jq}	$b^{8q(h+1)+5}\delta$	g^2	δ	b	δ	H
$U_{9,3}$	b^{4i-1}	b^{4jq}	b^{4hq}	c^2	δ	ϵ	δcc	$bccbc$
$U_{18,2}$	$(bc)^{4i-1}$	$(bc)^{4jq}$		$(cc)^2$	bb	$(bc)^2$	cb	cb

where $\langle R\rangle$ is given by Equation (2) and Tables 1 and 2, S is given by Table 2, and $\big(\langle A\rangle M\big)^*\big(\langle A\rangle M\langle E\rangle \cup \langle E\rangle\langle A\rangle M\big)(\langle A\rangle M)^* D$ encodes R's dataword via Table 2.

$$\langle R\rangle = H\langle P(e_{h-1},a_q)\rangle V\langle P(e_{h-1},a_{q-1})\rangle \ldots V\langle P(e_{h-1},a_1)\rangle$$

$$\vdots$$

$$V\langle P(e_1,a_q)\rangle V\langle P(e_1,a_{q-1})\rangle \ldots V\langle P(e_1,a_1)\rangle \tag{2}$$

$$V^2\langle P(a_q)\rangle V^2\langle P(a_{q-1})\rangle \ldots V^2\langle P(a_1)\rangle V^3$$

In Equation (1) the position of the tape head is over the symbol immediately to the right of $\langle R\rangle S^*$. The initial state is u_1 and the blank symbol is c.

3.1 Universal Turing Machine Algorithm Overview

Each of our universal Turing machines use the same basic algorithm. Here we give a brief description of the simulation algorithm by explaining how our machines locate and simulate a production. The encoded production to be simulated is located using a unary indexing method. The encoded production, $\langle P(a_i)\rangle$ or $\langle P(e_j,a_i)\rangle$ in Equation (2), is indexed (pointed to) by the number of symbols contained in the leftmost encoded symbol or pair of symbols in the encoded dataword (Equation (1)). For illustration purposes we assume that we are using $U_{9,3}$. If the leftmost encoded symbol is $\langle a_i\rangle = b^{4i-1}$ (Table 2) then the value $4i - 1$ is used to index $\langle P(a_i)\rangle$. If the leftmost encoded symbol is $\langle e_j\rangle = b^{4jq}$, and $\langle a_i \rangle = b^{4i-1}$ is adjacent, then the value $4jq+4i-1$ is used to index $\langle P(e_j, a_i) \rangle$. The number of b symbols in the encoded symbol, or pair of encoded symbols, is equal to the number of δc^* words between the leftmost encoded symbol and the encoded production to be simulated. To locate this production, $U_{9,3}$ simply changes each δc^* to δb^*, for each b in the leftmost encoded symbol or pair of encoded symbols. This process continues until the δ that separates two encoded symbols in the dataword is read. Note from Equation (1) that there is no δ marker between each $\langle e_j \rangle$ and the $\langle a_i \rangle$ to its right, thus allowing $\langle e_j \rangle \langle a_i \rangle$ to be read together during indexing. After indexing, our machines print the indexed production immediately to the right of the encoded dataword. After the indexed production has been printed, then $\langle R \rangle$, the encoding of R, is restored to its original value. This completes the simulation of the production.

3.2 $U_{9,3}$

Example 1 ($U_{9,3}$ simulating the execution of the production $P(a_1)$). This example is presented using three cycles. The tape head of $U_{9,3}$ is given by an underline. The current state of $U_{9,3}$ is given to the left in bold. The dataword $a_1 e_j a_i$ is encoded via Equation (1) and Table 2 as $bbb\delta b^{4jq}b^{4i-1}\delta$ and $P(a_1)$ is encoded via Table 1 as $\langle P(a_1) \rangle = \delta\delta cc\delta c^8$. From Equation (1) we get the initial configuration:

$$\boldsymbol{u_1}, \ldots \langle P(a_2) \rangle (\delta cc)^2 \delta\delta cc\delta c^8 \delta cc\delta cc\delta cc\underline{b}bb\delta b^{4jq}b^{4i-1}\delta ccc \ldots$$

Table 3. Table of behaviour for $U_{9,3}$

$U_{9,3}$	u_1	u_2	u_3	u_4	u_5	u_6	u_7	u_8	u_9
c	bRu_1	cLu_3	cLu_3	bLu_9	cRu_6	bLu_4	δLu_4	cRu_7	bLu_5
b	cLu_2	cLu_2	bLu_4	bLu_4		bRu_6	bRu_7	cRu_9	cRu_8
δ	δRu_3	δLu_2	δRu_1	δLu_4	δLu_8	δRu_6	δRu_7	δRu_8	cRu_1

Cycle 1 (Index next production). In Cycle 1 (Table 4), $U_{9,3}$ reads the leftmost encoded symbol and locates the next encoded production to execute. $U_{9,3}$ scans right until it reads b in state u_1. Then $U_{9,3}$ scans left in states u_2 and u_3 until it reads the subword δc^*. This subword is changed to δb^* as $U_{9,3}$ scans right in states u_1 and u_3. The process is repeated until $U_{9,3}$ reads b in state u_3. This indicates that we have finished reading the leftmost encoded symbol, or pair of encoded symbols, and that the encoded production to be executed has been indexed. This signals the end of Cycle 1 and the beginning of Cycle 2.

Table 4. Cycle 1 of $U_{9,3}$

$U_{9,3}$	u_1	u_2	u_3
c	bRu_1	cLu_3	cLu_3
b	cLu_2	cLu_2	bLu_4
δ	δRu_3	δLu_2	δRu_1

Table 5. Cycle 2 of $U_{9,3}$

$U_{9,3}$	u_4	u_5	u_6	u_7	u_8	u_9
c	bLu_9	cRu_6	bLu_4	δLu_4	cRu_7	bLu_5
b	bLu_4		bRu_6	bRu_7		
δ	δLu_4	δLu_8	δRu_6	δRu_7	δRu_8	

$\vdash \qquad u_2, \ldots \langle P(a_2) \rangle (\delta cc)^2 \delta \delta cc \delta c^8 \delta cc \delta cc \delta c\underline{c}cbb\delta b^{4jq}b^{4i-1}\delta ccc \ldots$

$\vdash^2 \qquad u_3, \ldots \langle P(a_2) \rangle (\delta cc)^2 \delta \delta cc \delta c^8 \delta cc \delta cc \delta \underline{c}cccbb\delta b^{4jq}b^{4i-1}\delta ccc \ldots$

$\vdash^4 \qquad u_1, \ldots \langle P(a_2) \rangle (\delta cc)^2 \delta \delta cc \delta c^8 \delta cc \delta cc \delta bbb\underline{b}b\delta b^{4jq}b^{4i-1}\delta ccc \ldots$

$\vdash^{44} \qquad u_1, \ldots \langle P(a_2) \rangle (\delta cc)^2 \delta \delta cc \delta c^8 \delta bb \delta bb \delta bb \delta bbbb \underline{b} \delta b^{4jq}b^{4i-1}\delta ccc \ldots$

$\vdash^2 \qquad u_4, \ldots \langle P(a_2) \rangle (\delta cc)^2 \delta \delta cc \delta c^8 \delta bb \delta bb \delta bb \delta bbbb \underline{b} \delta b^{4jq}b^{4i-1}\delta ccc \ldots$

In the configuration immediately above the encoded production $\langle P(a_1) \rangle$ has been indexed and we have entered Cycle 2.

Cycle 2 (Print production). Cycle 2 (Table 5) prints the encoded production, that was indexed in Cycle 1, immediately to the right of the encoded dataword. $U_{9,3}$ scans left in state u_4 and records the next symbol of the encoded production to be printed. If $U_{9,3}$ reads the subword ccc it enters state u_6, scans right, and prints b at the right end of the encoded dataword. A single b is printed for each cc pair that does not have δ immediately to its left. If $U_{9,3}$ reads the subword $c\delta cc$ it scans right in state u_7 and prints δ at the right end of the encoded dataword. This process is repeated until the end of the encoded production is detected by reading the subword $\delta \delta cc$ which causes $U_{9,3}$ to enter Cycle 3.

$\vdash^{13} \qquad u_4, \ldots \langle P(a_2) \rangle (\delta cc)^2 \delta \delta cc \delta c^6 c\underline{c}(\delta bb)^3 bbb\delta b^{4jq}b^{4i-1}\delta ccc \ldots$

$\vdash^3 \qquad u_6, \ldots \langle P(a_2) \rangle (\delta cc)^2 \delta \delta cc \delta c^6 \underline{b}b(\delta bb)^3 bbb\delta b^{4jq}b^{4i-1}\delta ccc \ldots$

$\vdash^{4(jq+i)+14} \qquad u_6, \ldots \langle P(a_2) \rangle (\delta cc)^2 \delta \delta cc \delta c^6 bb(\delta bb)^3 bbb\delta b^{4jq}b^{4i-1}\delta \underline{c}cc \ldots$

$\vdash \qquad u_4, \ldots \langle P(a_2) \rangle (\delta cc)^2 \delta \delta cc \delta c^6 bb(\delta bb)^3 bbb\delta b^{4jq}b^{4i-1}\delta \underline{b}ccc \ldots$

In the configuration immediately above the first symbol of the encoded production $\langle P(a_1) \rangle$ has been printed. Following the printing of the final symbol of the encoded production we get:

$\vdash^* \qquad u_4, \ldots \langle P(a_2) \rangle (\delta cc)^2 \delta \delta c\underline{c} \delta b^8 (\delta bb)^3 bbb\delta b^{4jq}b^{4i-1}\delta b^3 \delta ccc \ldots$

$\vdash^3 \qquad u_8, \ldots \langle P(a_2) \rangle (\delta cc)^2 \underline{\delta} \delta bb \delta b^8 (\delta bb)^3 bbb\delta b^{4jq}b^{4i-1}\delta b^3 \delta ccc \ldots$

In the configuration immediately above we have finished printing the encoded production $\langle P(a_1) \rangle$ to the right of the dataword and we have entered Cycle 3.

Cycle 3 (Restore tape). Cycle 3 (Table 6) restores $\langle R \rangle$ to its original value. The tape head of $U_{9,3}$ scans right switching between states u_8 and u_9 changing b symbols to c symbols. This continues until $U_{9,3}$ reads the δ marking the leftmost end of the dataword in u_9. Note from Table 1 and Equation (2) that there is an even number of c symbols between each pair of δ symbols in $\langle R \rangle$ hence each δ symbol in $\langle R \rangle$ will be read in state u_8. Each a_i symbol in the dataword is encoded by an odd number of b symbols ($\langle a_i \rangle = b^{4i-1}$) and hence the first δ symbol in the dataword will be read in state u_9. This δ symbol marks the left end of the new dataword and causes $U_{9,3}$ to enter state u_1 thus completing Cycle 3 and the production simulation.

Table 6. Cycle 2 of $U_{9,3}$

$U_{9,3}$	u_8	u_9
b	cRu_9	cRu_8
δ	δRu_8	cRu_1

$\vdash^{25}$ $u_9, \ldots \langle P(a_2)\rangle(\delta cc)^2\delta\delta cc\delta c^8(\delta cc)^3 ccc\underline{\delta}b^{4jq}b^{4i-1}\delta b^3\delta ccc\ldots$

$\vdash$ $u_1, \ldots \langle P(a_2)\rangle(\delta cc)^2\delta\delta cc\delta c^8(\delta cc)^3 cccc\underline{b}b^{4jq-1}b^{4i-1}\delta b^3\delta ccc\ldots$

In the configuration immediately above our example simulation of production $P(a_1)$ is complete.

Theorem 2. *Given a bi-tag system R hat runs in time t the computation of R is simulated by $U_{9,3}$ in time $O(t^2)$.*

Proof. In order to prove the correctness of $U_{9,3}$ we prove that $U_{9,3}$ simulates any possible $P(a)$ or $P(e,a)$ production of an arbitrary bi-tag system and, that $U_{9,3}$ also simulates halting when the encoded halt symbol $\langle e_h\rangle$ is encountered. In Example 1 $U_{9,3}$ simulates $P(a_1)$ for an arbitrary bi-tag system where a_1 is the leftmost symbol in a fixed dataword. This example easily generalises to any production $P(a_i)$ where a_i is the leftmost symbol in an arbitrary dataword. When some $e \in E$ is the leftmost symbol in the dataword then some production $P(e,a)$ must be executed. The simulation of $P(a_1)$ in Example 1 is also used to verify the simulation of $P(e,a)$. Note from Equation (1) that there is no δ marker between each $\langle e_j\rangle$ and the adjacent $\langle a_i\rangle$ to its right, thus $\langle e_j\rangle$ and $\langle a_i\rangle$ are read together during Cycle 1. Using the encoding in Definition 3, the number of b symbols in $\langle e_j\rangle\langle a_i\rangle$ indexes $\langle P(e,a)\rangle$. Thus, the indexing of $\langle P(e,a)\rangle$ is carried out in the same manner as the indexing of $\langle P(a)\rangle$. The printing of production $\langle P(e,a)\rangle$ during Cycle 2 and the subsequent restoring of $\langle R\rangle$ during Cycle 3 proceed in the same manner as with $P(a_1)$.

If the encoded halt symbol $\langle e_h\rangle = b^{4hq}$ is the leftmost symbol in the encoded dataword, and $\langle a_i\rangle = b^{4-i}$ is adjacent, this is encoded via Definition 3 as follows:

$$u_1, \; bccbc\langle P(e_{h-1},a_q)\rangle\delta cc\ldots\langle P(a_1)\rangle(\delta cc)^3(cc)^*\underline{b}b^{4hq-1}b^{4i-1}\delta(\langle A\rangle\delta)^*ccc\ldots$$

During Cycle 1, immediately after reading the $(4hq+3)^{\text{th}}$ b symbol in the dataword, $U_{9,3}$ scans left in u_2 and we get the following:

$\vdash^* \; u_2, \; bccb\underline{c}\langle P(e_{h-1},a_q)\rangle\delta cc\ldots\langle P(a_1)\rangle(\delta cc)^3(cc)^*c^{4hq+3}b^{4i-4}\delta(\langle A\rangle\delta)^*ccc\ldots$

$\vdash^4 \; u_5, \; \underline{b}bbbc\langle P(e_{h-1},a_q)\rangle\delta cc\ldots\langle P(a_1)\rangle(\delta cc)^3(cc)^*c^{4hq+3}b^{4i-4}\delta(\langle A\rangle\delta)^*ccc\ldots$

There is no transition rule in Table 3 for the case 'when in u_5 read b', hence the computation halts. □

The proof of correctness given for $U_{9,3}$ can be applied to the remaining machines in a straightforward way, so we do not restate it.

3.3 $U_{5,5}$

The dataword $a_1 e_j a_i$ is encoded via Equation (1) and Table 2 as $bbb\delta b^{4jq}b^{4i-1}\delta$, and $P(a_1)$ is encoded via Table 1 as $\langle P(a_1)\rangle = \delta\delta d^{10}$. From Equation (1) we get the initial configuration:

$$\boldsymbol{u_1}, \dots \delta^2\langle P(a_2)\rangle \delta^2 \delta\delta d^{10}\delta\delta\delta\underline{b}bbb\delta b^{4jq}b^{4i-1}\delta ccc\dots$$

Table 7. Table of behaviour for $U_{5,5}$

$U_{5,5}$	u_1	u_2	u_3	u_4	u_5
g	bLu_1	gRu_1	bLu_3		
b	gLu_1	gRu_2	dRu_5	gRu_4	dRu_3
δ	cRu_2	cRu_2	δRu_3	cRu_4	dRu_1
c	δLu_1	bLu_3	δLu_3	δLu_3	
d	bLu_1	gRu_2	bLu_5	bLu_2	bLu_4

Cycle 1 (Index next production). In Cycle 1 (Table 8) when $U_{5,5}$ reads b in state u_1, it changes it to g and scans left until it reads δ. This δ is changed to c and $U_{5,5}$ then enters state u_2 and scans right until it reads g which causes it to re-enter state u_1. This process is repeated until $U_{5,5}$ reads the δ that separates a pair of encoded symbols in the encoded dataword. This signals the end of Cycle 1 and the beginning of Cycle 2.

Table 8. Cycle 1 of $U_{5,5}$

$U_{5,5}$	u_1	u_2
g	bLu_1	gRu_1
b	gLu_1	gRu_2
δ	cRu_2	cRu_2
c	δLu_1	
d	bLu_1	

Table 9. Cycle 2 of $U_{5,5}$

$U_{5,5}$	u_2	u_3	u_4	u_5
g		bLu_3		
b	gRu_2		gRu_4	
δ	cRu_2	δRu_3	cRu_4	
c	bLu_3	δLu_3	δLu_3	
d	gRu_2	bLu_5	bLu_2	bLu_4

Table 10. Cycle 3 of $U_{5,5}$

$U_{5,5}$	u_3	u_5
b	dRu_5	dRu_3
δ	δRu_3	dRu_1

$$\vdash^3 \qquad \boldsymbol{u_1}, \dots \delta^2\langle P(a_2)\rangle \delta^2 \delta\delta d^{10}\delta\delta cg\underline{b}b\delta b^{4jq}b^{4i-1}\delta ccc\dots$$

$$\vdash^{18} \qquad \boldsymbol{u_1}, \dots \delta^2\langle P(a_2)\rangle \delta^2 \delta\delta d^{10}ccggg\underline{\delta}b^{4jq}b^{4i-1}\delta ccc\dots$$

$$\vdash \qquad \boldsymbol{u_2}, \dots \delta^2\langle P(a_2)\rangle \delta^2 \delta\delta d^{10}cccgggc\underline{b}b^{4jq-1}b^{4i-1}\delta ccc\dots$$

Cycle 2 (Print production). Cycle 2 (Table 9) begins with $U_{5,5}$ scanning right and printing b to the right of the encoded dataword. Following this $U_{5,5}$ scans left in state u_3 and records the next symbol of the encoded production to be printed. If $U_{5,5}$ reads the subword $dddd$ it enters state u_2, scans right, and prints b at the right end of the encoded dataword. If $U_{5,5}$ reads the subword δdd it scans right in state u_4 and prints δ at the right end of the encoded dataword. This process is repeated until the end of the encoded production is detected by reading δ in state u_3, which causes $U_{5,5}$ to enter Cycle 3.

$$\vdash^* \qquad u_3, \ldots \delta^2 \langle P(a_2)\rangle \delta^2 \delta\delta d^6 dddd\underline{d}\delta\delta\delta bbbb\delta b^{4jq}b^{4i-1}\delta bccc\ldots$$

$$\vdash^3 \qquad u_2, \ldots \delta^2 \langle P(a_2)\rangle \delta^2 \delta\delta d^6 \underline{d}bbbb\delta\delta\delta bbbb\delta b^{4jq}b^{4i-1}\delta bccc\ldots$$

$$\vdash^* \qquad u_3, \ldots \delta^2 \langle P(a_2)\rangle \delta^2 \delta\delta dd\underline{b}^8 \delta\delta\delta bbbb\delta b^{4jq}b^{4i-1}\delta bbbbccc\ldots$$

$$\vdash^2 \qquad u_4, \ldots \delta^2 \langle P(a_2)\rangle \delta^2 \delta\underline{\delta}bbb^8 \delta\delta\delta bbbb\delta b^{4jq}b^{4i-1}\delta bbbbccc\ldots$$

$$\vdash^* \qquad u_3, \ldots \delta^2 \langle P(a_2)\rangle \delta^2 \underline{\delta}\delta bbb^8 \delta\delta\delta bbbb\delta b^{4jq}b^{4i-1}\delta bbbb\delta ccc\ldots$$

Cycle 3 (Restore tape). In Cycle 3 (Table 10) the tape head of $U_{5,5}$ scans right switching between states u_3 and u_5 changing b symbols to d symbols. This continues until $U_{5,5}$ reads the δ marking the leftmost end of the encoded dataword in u_5. Note from Table 1 and Equation (2) that there is an even number of d symbols between each pair of δ symbols in $\langle R\rangle$ hence each δ symbol in $\langle R\rangle$ will be read in state u_3. Each a_i symbol in the dataword is encoded by an odd number of symbols ($\langle a_i\rangle = b^{4i-1}$) and hence the first δ symbol in the dataword will be read in in state u_5. This causes $U_{5,5}$ to enter state u_1 thus completing Cycle 3 and the production simulation.

$$\vdash^{19} \qquad u_1, \ldots \delta^2 \langle P(a_2)\rangle \delta^2 \delta\delta d^{10} \delta\delta\delta dddd\underline{d}bb^{4jq-1}b^{4i-1}\delta bbb\delta ccc\ldots$$

Halting for $U_{5,5}$. If the encoded halt symbol $\langle e_h\rangle = b^{4hq+2}\delta$ is the leftmost symbol in the encoded dataword then this is encoded via Definition 3 as follows:

$$u_1, cd\langle P(e_{h-1}, a_q)\rangle \delta \ldots \delta^2 \langle P(a_1)\rangle \delta^3 (dd)^* \underline{b}b^{4hq+1}\delta(\langle A\rangle\delta)^* ccc\ldots$$

The computation continues as before until $U_{5,5}$ enters Cycle 2 and scans left in u_3. Immediately after $U_{5,5}$ reads the leftmost d during this leftward scan we get:

$$\vdash \qquad u_5, \underline{c}b\langle P(e_{h-1}, a_q)\rangle'\delta \ldots \delta^2 \langle P(a_1)\rangle'\delta^3 (dd)^* b^{4hq+2}\delta(\langle A\rangle\delta)^* bccc\ldots$$

In the configuration above, $\langle P\rangle'$ denotes the word in which all the d symbols in $\langle P\rangle$ are changed to b symbols. There is no transition rule in Table 7 for the case 'when in u_5 read c' hence the computation halts.

3.4 $U_{6,4}$

The dataword $a_1 e_j a_i$ is encoded via Equation (1) and Table (2) as $bbb\delta b^{8jq}b^{8i-5}\delta b$. From Equation (1) we get the initial configuration:

$$u_1, \ldots \delta^2 \langle P(a_2)\rangle \delta^2 \langle P(a_1)\rangle \delta\delta\delta\underline{b}bb\delta b^{8jq}b^{8i-5}\delta bccc\ldots$$

Table 11. Table of behaviour for $U_{6,4}$

$U_{6,4}$	u_1	u_2	u_3	u_4	u_5	u_6
g	bLu_1	gRu_1	bLu_3	bRu_2	bLu_6	bLu_4
b	gLu_1	gRu_2	bLu_5	gRu_4	gRu_6	gRu_5
δ	cRu_2	cRu_2	δLu_5	cRu_4	δRu_5	gRu_1
c	δLu_1	gRu_5	δLu_3	cRu_5	bLu_3	

Cycle 1 (Index next production). In Cycle 1 (Table 12) when $U_{6,4}$ reads b in state u_1 it scans left until it reads δ. This δ is changed to c and $U_{6,4}$ then enters state u_2 and scans right until it reads g which causes it to re-enter state u_1. This process is repeated until $U_{6,4}$ reads the δ that separates a pair of encoded symbols in the encoded dataword. This signals the end of Cycle 1 and the beginning of Cycle 2.

Table 12. Cycle 1 of $U_{6,4}$

$U_{6,4}$	u_1	u_2
g	bLu_1	gRu_1
b	gLu_1	gRu_2
δ	cRu_2	cRu_2
c	δLu_1	

Table 13. Cycle 2 of $U_{6,4}$

$U_{6,4}$	u_2	u_3	u_4	u_5	u_6
g		bLu_3	bRu_2	bLu_6	bLu_4
b	gRu_2	bLu_5	gRu_4		
δ	cRu_2	δLu_5	cRu_4	δRu_5	
c	gRu_5	δLu_3	cRu_5	bLu_3	

Table 14. Cycle 3 of $U_{6,4}$

$U_{6,4}$	u_5	u_6
b	gRu_6	gRu_5
δ	δRu_5	gRu_1

Cycle 2 (Print production). Cycle 2 (Table 13) begins with $U_{6,4}$ scanning right and printing bb to the right of the encoded dataword. Following this, $U_{6,4}$ scans left in state u_3 and records the next symbol of the encoded production to be printed. If $U_{6,4}$ reads the subword $ggg\delta$ or $gggb$ it enters state u_2, scans right, and prints bb at the right end of the encoded dataword. If $U_{6,4}$ reads the subword δggb or $\delta gg\delta$ it scans right in state u_4 and prints δb at the right end of the encoded dataword. This process is repeated until the end of the encoded production is detected by reading δ in state u_5, which causes $U_{6,4}$ to enter Cycle 3.

Cycle 3 (Restore tape). In Cycle 3 (Table 14) the tape head of $U_{6,4}$ scans right switching between states u_5 and u_6, changing b symbols to g symbols. This continues until $U_{6,4}$ reads the δ marking the leftmost end of the encoded dataword in u_6. Note from Table 1 and Equation (2) that there is an even number of g symbols between each pair of δ symbols in $\langle R \rangle$, hence each δ symbol in $\langle R \rangle$ is read in state u_5. Each a_i symbol in the dataword is encoded by an odd number of symbols ($\langle a_i \rangle = b^{8i-5}$) and hence the first δ symbol in the dataword is read in state u_6. This causes $U_{6,4}$ to enter state u_1, thus completing Cycle 3 and the production simulation.

Special case for $U_{6,4}$. If we are simulating a production of the form $P(e, a) = a_v a_k e_m$ we have a special case. Note from Table 2 and Cycle 2 that the simulation of $P(e, a) = a_v a_k e_m$ for $U_{6,4}$ results in the word $b^{8v-5}\delta b^{8hq+8k-3}\delta b^{8mq}b$ being printed to the right of the dataword. From Table 2 note that a_k is not encoded in this word in its usual from. However when $U_{6,4}$ reads the subword $b^{8hq+8k-3}\delta$ it indexes $\langle P(a_k) \rangle$ in H which results in $\langle a_k \rangle$ being printed to the dataword. To see this, note that the value of H from Equation (2) for $U_{6,4}$ is as follows:

$$H = cgbV^2\langle P(a_q)\rangle V^2\langle P(a_{q-1})\rangle \ldots V^2\langle P(a_1)\rangle V^3 \tag{3}$$

The halting condition for $U_{6,4}$ occurs in a similar manner to that of $U_{5,5}$. Halting occurs during the first scan left in Cycle 2 when $U_{6,4}$ reads c in state u_6 at the left end of $\langle R \rangle$.

3.5 $U_{18,2}$

The example dataword $a_1 e_j a_i$ is encoded via Equation (1) and Table (2) as $bcbcbcbb(bc)^{4jq}(bc)^{4i-1}bb(bc)^2$. From Equation (1) we get the initial configuration:

$$\boldsymbol{u_1}, \ldots \langle P(a_2)\rangle (cb)^2 \langle P(a_1)\rangle cbcbcb\underline{b}cbcbcbb(bc)^{4jq}(bc)^{4i-1}bb(bc)^2 ccc\ldots$$

Table 15. Table of behaviour for $U_{18,2}$

$U_{18,2}$	u_1	u_2	u_3	u_4	u_5	u_6	u_7	u_8	u_9
c	bRu_2	cRu_1	cLu_5	cLu_5	cLu_4	bRu_2	cLu_8	bRu_{12}	bLu_{10}
b	bRu_3	bRu_1	bLu_9	bLu_6	cLu_4	cLu_4	bLu_9	bLu_7	bLu_7

$U_{18,2}$	u_{10}	u_{11}	u_{12}	u_{13}	u_{14}	u_{15}	u_{16}	u_{17}	u_{18}
c	cRu_{13}	bLu_7	cRu_{11}	cLu_{15}	cRu_{13}	bLu_9	cRu_{17}		cRu_{15}
b	bRu_{15}	bRu_{12}	bRu_{11}	bRu_{14}	bRu_{13}	cRu_{16}	bRu_{15}	cRu_{18}	cRu_1

Cycle 1 (Index next production). In Cycle 1 (Table 16) $U_{18,2}$ scans right in states u_1, u_2 and u_3 until it reads the subword bc. Following this, it scans left in states u_4, u_5 and u_6 until it reads the subword cb. This cb is changed to bb and $U_{18,2}$ re-enters state u_1 and scans right. This process is repeated until $U_{18,2}$ reads the bb that separates a pair of encoded symbols in the encoded dataword during a scan right. This signals the end of Cycle 1 and the beginning of Cycle 2.

Table 16. Cycle 1 of $U_{18,2}$

$U_{18,2}$	u_1	u_2	u_3	u_4	u_5	u_6
c	bRu_2	cRu_1	cLu_5	cLu_5	cLu_4	bRu_2
b	bRu_3	bRu_1	bLu_9	bLu_6	cLu_4	cLu_4

Cycle 2 (Print production). In Cycle 2 (Table 17) $U_{18,2}$ scans left in states u_7, u_8 and u_9 and records the next symbol of the encoded production to be printed. If $U_{18,2}$ reads the subword cc then it scans right in states u_{11} and u_{12} and changes the cc immediately to the right of the encoded dataword to bc. If $U_{18,2}$ reads the subword ccb it scans right in states u_{13} and u_{14} and changes the rightmost bc in the encoded dataword to bb. This process is repeated until the end of the encoded production is detected by reading the subword bcb during the scan left. This causes $U_{18,2}$ to enter Cycle 3.

Cycle 3 (Restore tape). In Cycle 3 (Table 18) the tape head of $U_{18,2}$ scans right in states u_{15}, u_{16}, u_{17} and u_{18} changing each bc to cc and each bb to cb. This continues until $U_{18,2}$ reads the bb marking the leftmost end of the dataword in u_{17} and u_{18}. Note from Table 1 and Equation (2) that the number of cc subwords between each pair of δ symbols in $\langle R\rangle$ is even, hence each bb pair is read in states u_{15} and u_{16} and restored to cb. Each a_i symbol in the dataword is encoded by an odd number of bc subwords ($\langle a_i\rangle = (bc)^{4i-1}$) and hence the first bb pair in

Table 17. Cycle 2 of $U_{18,2}$

$U_{18,2}$	u_7	u_8	u_9	u_{10}	u_{11}	u_{12}	u_{13}	u_{14}	u_{15}
c	cLu_8	bRu_{12}	bLu_{10}	cRu_{13}	bLu_7	cRu_{11}	cLu_{15}	cRu_{13}	bLu_9
b	bLu_9	bLu_7	bLu_7	bRu_{15}	bRu_{12}	bRu_{11}	bRu_{14}	bRu_{13}	

Table 18. Cycle 3 of $U_{18,2}$

$U_{18,2}$	u_{15}	u_{16}	u_{17}	u_{18}
c			cRu_{17}	cRu_{15}
b	cRu_{16}	bRu_{15}	cRu_{18}	cRu_1

the dataword is read in states u_{17} and u_{18}, which causes $U_{18,2}$ to enter state u_1 thus completing Cycle 3 and the production simulation.

There is no halting condition for $U_{18,2}$ and as such $U_{18,2}$ simulates bi-tag systems that have no halting symbol e_h. Such bi-tag systems complete their computation by entering a simple repeating sequence of configurations.

Acknowledgements. Turlough Neary is supported by the Irish Research Council for Science, Engineering and Technology and Damien Woods is supported by Science foundation Ireland grant number 04/IN3/1524.

References

1. Baiocchi, C.: Three small universal Turing machines. In: Margenstern, M., Rogozhin, Y. (eds.) MCU 2001. LNCS, vol. 2055, pp. 1–10. Springer, Heidelberg (2001)
2. Cocke, J., Minsky, M.: Universality of tag systems with $P = 2$. Journal of the ACM 11(1), 15–20 (1964)
3. Hermann, G.: The uniform halting problem for generalized one state Turing machines. In: Proceedings, Ninth Annual Symposium on Switching and Automata Theory, New York, October 1968, pp. 368–372. IEEE, Los Alamitos (1968)
4. Kudlek, M.: Small deterministic Turing machines. Theoretical Computer Science 168(2), 241–255 (1996)
5. Kudlek, M., Rogozhin, Y.: A universal Turing machine with 3 states and 9 symbols. In: Kuich, W., Rozenberg, G., Salomaa, A. (eds.) DLT 2001. LNCS, vol. 2295, pp. 311–318. Springer, Heidelberg (2002)
6. Margenstern, M., Pavlotskaya, L.: On the optimal number of instructions for universality of Turing machines connected with a finite automaton. International Journal of Algebra and Computation 13(2), 133–202 (2003)
7. Minsky, M.: Size and structure of universal Turing machines using tag systems. In: Recursive Function Theory, Symposium in Pure Mathematics, Provelence, vol. 5, pp. 229–238. AMS (1962)
8. Minsky, M.: Computation, finite and infinite machines. Prentice-Hall, Englewood Cliffs (1967)

9. Neary, T.: Small polynomial time universal Turing machines. In: Hurley, T., Seda, A., et al. (eds.) 4th Irish Conference on the Mathematical Foundations of Computer Science and Information Technology(MFCSIT), Cork, Ireland, August 2006, pp. 325–329 (2006)
10. Neary, T., Woods, D.: A small fast universal Turing machine. Technical Report NUIM-CS-TR-2005-12, National university of Ireland, Maynooth (2005)
11. Neary, T., Woods, D.: Small fast universal Turing machines. Theoretical Computer Science 362(1–3), 171–195 (2006)
12. Pavlotskaya, L.: Solvability of the halting problem for certain classes of Turing machines. Mathematical Notes (Springer) 13(6), 537–541 (1973)
13. Pavlotskaya, L.: Dostatochnye uslovija razreshimosti problemy ostanovki dlja mashin T'juring. Problemi kibernetiki, 91–118 (1978) (Sufficient conditions for the halting problem decidability of Turing machines) (in Russian))
14. Robinson, R.: Minsky's small universal Turing machine. International Journal of Mathematics 2(5), 551–562 (1991)
15. Rogozhin, Y.: Small universal Turing machines. Theoretical Computer Science 168(2), 215–240 (1996)
16. Shannon, C.E.: A universal Turing machine with two internal states. Automata Studies, Annals of Mathematics Studies 34, 157–165 (1956)
17. Woods, D., Neary, T.: On the time complexity of 2-tag systems and small universal Turing machines. In: FOCS. 47th Annual IEEE Symposium on Foundations of Computer Science, Berkeley, California, October 2006, pp. 132–143. IEEE, Los Alamitos (2006)
18. Woods, D., Neary, T.: The complexity of small universal Turing machines. In: Cooper, S.B., Lowe, B., Sorbi, A. (eds.) Computability in Europe 2007. CIE, Sienna, Italy, June 2007. LNCS, vol. 4497, pp. 791–798. Springer, Heidelberg (2007)
19. Woods, D., Neary, T.: Small semi-weakly universal Turing machines. In: Durand-Lose, J., Margenstern, M. (eds.) Machines, Computations, and Universality (MCU), Orélans, France, September 2007. LNCS, vol. 4664, pp. 306–323. Springer, Heidelberg (2007)

Changing the Neighborhood of Cellular Automata

Hidenosuke Nishio

ex. Kyoto University
Iwakura Miyake-cho 204-1, Sakyo-ku, 606-0022 Kyoto
yra05762@nifty.com

Abstract. In place of the traditional definition of a cellular automaton $CA = (S, Q, N, f)$, a new definition (S, Q, f_n, ν) is given by introducing an injection called *the neighborhood function* $\nu : \{0, 1, ..., n-1\} \rightarrow S$, which provides a connection between the variables of local function f_n of arity n and neighbors of CA: image(ν) is a neighborhood of size n. The new definition allows new analysis of cellular automata. We first show that from a single local function countably many CA are induced by changing ν and then prove that equivalence problem of such CA is decidable. Then we observe what happens if we change the neighborhood. As a typical research topics, we show that reversibility of 2 states 3 neighbors CA is preserved from changing the neighborhood, but that of 3 states CA is not.

Keywords: cellular automaton, neighborhood, decision problem, reversibility, simulator.

1 Introduction

The cellular automaton (CA for short) is a uniformly structured information processing system, which is traditionally defined by a 4-tuple (S, Q, N, f), where S is a discrete space consisting of (infinitely) many cells, Q is a finite set of states of each cell, N is a finite subset of S called *the neighborhood* of CA and f is a function $Q^N \rightarrow Q$ called *the local function*. Among others, the neighborhood is most important constituent of CA.

Most studies on CA first assume some standard neighborhood (von Neumann, Moore) and then investigate the global behaviors (properties) or look for a local function that would meet a given problem, say, the self-reproduction [1], the Game of Life [2] and so on. In 2003, however, H.Nishio and M.Margenstern began a general study of the neighborhood in its own right, where the neighborhood N can be an arbitrary finite subset of S and particularly the problem if N generates (*fills*) S has been discussed [3]. Following such a framework, we asked the question: How does the Neighborhood Affect the Global Behavior of Cellular Automata? It has been shown that there are some properties which depend on the choice of the neighborhood, while there are some neighborhood-independent properties [4]. Following such research works, the notion of *the neighborhood*

J. Durand-Lose and M. Margenstern (Eds.): MCU 2007, LNCS 4664, pp. 255–266, 2007.

function, though not named so, was first introduced by T. Worsch and H. Nishio (2007) for achieving universality of CA by changing neighborhoods [5].

CA is now defined by a 4-tuple (S, Q, f_n, ν), where f_n is an n-ary local function and ν is an injection $\{0, 1, ..., n-1\} \rightarrow S$ called *the neighborhood function* which provides a connection between n variables of f_n and n neighbors for each cell. range(ν) is considered to be a usual neighborhood N. For instance, the von Neumann neighborhood in $\mathbb{Z}^2$ is redefined by a neighborhood function ν such that $\nu(0) = (0,0), \nu(1) = (0,1), \nu(2) = (0,-1), \nu(3) = (1,0)$ and $\nu(4) = (-1,0)$.

This paper first gives the new definition of CA, then Section 3 shows that infinitely many CA are induced from a single local function by changing the neighborhoods and in Section 4 the equivalence problem of CA is proved decidable. In later sections, we observe what happens if we change the neighborhood (function). In particular we show that reversibility of CA is preserved by changing the neighborhood, if CA has 2 states but not if it has 3 states. Appendix gives some illustrative simulations of Rule 110 by a newly made Java Applet simulator which affords to change the neighborhood.

2   Definitions

Though the theory applies to higher dimensional CA, we describe definitions only for 1-dimensional CA. 1-dimensional CA is defined by a 4-tuple $(\mathbb{Z}, Q, f_n, \nu)$, where

1. $\mathbb{Z}$ is the set of integers, each cell being identified by an integer,
2. Q is the set of states of a cell and assumed to be a finite field $GF(q)$ where $q = p^k$ with a prime p and a positive integer k,
3. $f_n : Q^n \rightarrow Q$ is the local function of arity $n \geq 1$: $f_n(x_0, x_1, ..., x_{n-1})$ and
4. ν is an injection from $\{0, 1, ..., n-1\}$ to $\mathbb{Z}$ which we call *the neighborhood function*. The neighborhood function defines connection between variables of f_n and neighbors for CA: x_i is connected to $\nu(i)$ for $0 \leq i \leq n-1$. In this way, range(ν) $= (\nu(0), \nu(1), ..., \nu(n-1))$ defines *the neighborhood* of CA in the ordinary sense. Note that range(ν) or the neighborhood is not simply a subset of $\mathbb{Z}$, but an *ordered list* of integers (neighbors). That is $(-1, 0, 1) \neq (-1, 1, 0)$. The *degenerate neighborhood* where ν is not injective (many to one mapping) also will do, but we will not discuss such a case in this paper.

$f_n(x_0, x_1, x_2, ..., x_{n-1})$ is expressed by a polynomial over Q in n variables, see [6]. In case of ternary function, it reads

$$f_3(x, y, z) = u_0 + u_1 x + u_2 y + \cdots + u_i x^h y^j z^k + \cdots$$
$$+ u_{q^3-2} x^{q-1} y^{q-1} z^{q-2} + u_{q^3-1} x^{q-1} y^{q-1} z^{q-1},$$
$$where \; u_i \in Q, \; 0 \leq i \leq q^3 - 1. \quad (1)$$

Furthermore, if $Q = GF(2) = \{0, 1\}$, we have

$$f_3(x, y, z) = u_0 + u_1 x + u_2 y + u_3 z + u_4 xy + u_5 xz + u_6 yz + u_7 xyz,$$
$$\text{where } u_i \in \{0, 1\}, \ 0 \le i \le 7. \quad (2)$$

A local function f_3 expressed by Equation (2) is called Elementary Local Function (ELF for short). From Equation (2) there are $2^8 = 256$ ELF. The neighborhood function ν_E such that $\text{range}(\nu_E) = (-1, 0, 1)$ is called Elementary Neighborhood function (ENB for short). $(\mathbb{Z}, GF(2), f_3, \nu_E)$ or $(\mathbb{Z}, GF(2), f_3, (-1, 0, 1))$ is an Elementary Cellular Automaton (ECA for short) as usually called. ECA have been extensively investigated by many authors like S.Wolfram [8], where every ECA(ELF) is identified by a Wolfram number. There is a clear one-to-one correspondence between the polynomial expression and the Wolfram number; for example $f = x + z$ over $GF(2)$ is rule 90. In this paper both expressions are exploited wherever neccessary.

Finally, the global map $F_\nu : Q^{\mathbb{Z}} \to Q^{\mathbb{Z}}$ is defined. For any global configuration $c \in Q^{\mathbb{Z}}$ and $j \in \mathbb{Z}$, $c(j)$ means the state of cell j in c. Then we have

$$F_\nu(c)(j) = f(c(j + \nu(0)), c(j + \nu(1)), ..., c(j + \nu(n - 1))). \quad (3)$$

Illustrations

Traditional CA. $(\mathbb{Z}, Q, N, f)$, with space $\mathbb{Z}$, cell states Q, neighborhood $N = (-1, 0, 1)$ and local function $f : Q^N \to Q$ is illustrated by Fig.1.

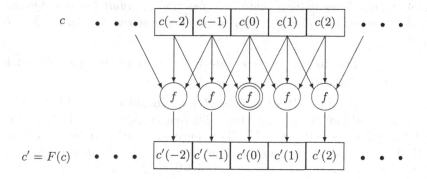

Fig. 1. Traditional definition of CA

New CA. $(\mathbb{Z}, Q, f_3, \nu)$, where ternary function $f_3(x_0, x_1, x_2)$ and neighborhood function $\nu : \{0, 1, 2\} \to \mathbb{Z}$ together define a CA, which has the local state transition rule $f : Q^{(\nu(0), \nu(1), \nu(2))} \to Q$. Fig. 2 illustrates the case $\text{range}(\nu) = (-2, 0, 1)$.

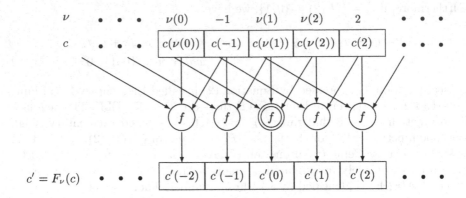

Fig. 2. New definition of CA

3   Infinitely Many CA Induced by Changing the Neighborhood

In this section, we show a basic theorem which formally proves that changing the neighborhood induces infinitely many CA from a single local function. The theorem is given for the case of 1-dimensional CA with local functions in 3 variables, but it will be enough for showing the power of changing the neighborhood. In the next section, an equivalence problem of CA by new definition is proven to be decidable.

Theorem 1. *By changing the neighborhood function ν, infinitely many different global CA functions are induced by any single local function $f_3(x, y, z)$ which is not constant.*

Proof. It is clear that to each non-constant function f_3 at least one of the following three cases applies.

1) If $f_3(a, b, c) \neq f_3(a, b, c')$ for $a, b, c \neq c' \in Q$, consider CA and CA' which have the same local function $f_3(x, y, z)$ and different neighborhoods $(-1, 0, 1+k)$ and $(-1, 0, 1+k')$ where $0 \leq k < k'$. Then, for configuration $W = vab\delta c\delta' c'w$, where $W(0) = b$, δ and δ' are words of lengths $k - 1$ and $k' - k - 1$ and v, w are semi-infinite words over Q, we have $F(W)(0) = f_3(a, b, c) \neq f_3(a, b, c') = F'(W)(0)$. That is $F(W) \neq F'(W)$.

$$
\begin{array}{ccccccccc}
 & & -1 & 0 & & k & & k' & \\
W & \cdots\ v & \boxed{a} & \boxed{b} & \boxed{\delta} & \boxed{c} & \boxed{\delta'} & \boxed{c'} & w \cdots \\[4pt]
F(W) & \cdots\ v' & \boxed{} & \boxed{f_3} & \zeta & \boxed{} & \zeta' & \boxed{} & w' \cdots
\end{array}
$$

In this way, countably many different CA $\{(\mathbb{Z}, Q, f_3, (-1, 0, 1 + k)),\ k \geq 1\}$ are induced from a single local function f_3.

2) If $f_3(a, b, c) \neq f_3(a, b', c)$ for $a, b \neq b', c \in Q$, consider CA and CA' which have the same local function $f_3(x, y, z)$ and different neighborhoods $(-1, 2+k, 1)$ and $(-1, 2+k', 1)$, where $0 \leq k < k'$. Then, for configuration $W = vadc\delta b\delta' b' w$, where $W(0) = d$, δ and δ' are words of lengths $k - 1$ and $k' - k - 1$ and v, w are semi-infinite words over Q, we have $F(W)(0) = f_3(a, b, c) \neq f_3(a, b', c) = F'(W)(0)$. That is $F(W) \neq F'(W)$.

$$
\begin{array}{ccccccccc}
 & & -1 & 0 & 1 & & k & & k' \\
W & \cdots \ v & \boxed{a} & \boxed{d} & \boxed{c} & \delta & \boxed{b} & \delta' & \boxed{b'} & w \cdots \\
\\
F(W) & \cdots \ v' & \boxed{} & \boxed{f_3} & \boxed{} & \zeta & \boxed{} & \zeta' & \boxed{} & w' \cdots
\end{array}
$$

In this way, countably many different CA $\{\{(\mathbb{Z}, Q, f_3, (-1, 2+k, 1)), \ k \geq 1\}$ are induced from a single local function f_3.

3) If $f_3(a, b, c) \neq f_3(a', b, c)$ for $a \neq a', b, c \in Q$, consider CA and CA' which have the same local function $f_3(x, y, z)$ and different neighborhoods $(-k-1, 0, 1)$ and $(-k' - 1, 0, 1)$ where $0 \leq k < k'$. Then, for configuration $W = va'\delta'a\delta bcw$, where $W(0) = b$, δ and δ' are words of lengths $k - 1$ and $k' - k - 1$ and v, w are semi-infinite words over Q, we have $F(W)(0) = f_3(a, b, c) \neq f_3(a', b, c) = F'(W)(0)$. That is $F(W) \neq F'(W)$.

$$
\begin{array}{ccccccccc}
 & & k' & & k & & 0 & 1 & \\
W & \cdots \ v & \boxed{a'} & \delta' & \boxed{a} & \delta & \boxed{b} & \boxed{c} & w \cdots \\
\\
F(W) & \cdots \ v' & \boxed{} & \zeta' & \boxed{} & \zeta & \boxed{f_3} & \boxed{} & w' \cdots
\end{array}
$$

In this way, countably many different CA $\{(\mathbb{Z}, Q, f_3, (-1 - k, 0, 1)), \ k \geq 1)$ are induced from a single local function f_3. ∎

Corollary 1. *There are infinitely many 2 states 3 neighbors CA different from any ECA.*

4   Equivalence Problem of CA

When $\mathbb{Z}$ and Q are understood, we denote $(\mathbb{Z}, Q, f_n, \nu)$ simply by (f_n, ν).

Definition 1. *Two CA (f_n, ν) and $(f'_{n'}, \nu')$ are called equivalent, denoted by $(f_n, \nu) \cong (f'_{n'}, \nu')$, if and only if their global maps are equal.*

Note that there is a local function which induces an equivalent CA for different neighborhood functions, while different local functions may induce an equivalent CA by changing the neighborhood function. For example, $(R85, (-1, 0, 1)) \cong (R51, (-1, 1, 0))$, where R85 and R51 are ELF in Wolfram number which give reversible ECA on ENB, see proof of Theorem 7.

We have here a decidability theorem whose proof is independent of dimensionality.

Theorem 2. *The equivalence problem of CA is decidable.*

Proof: Consider two CA (f_n, ν) and $(f'_{n'}, \nu')$ for the same set Q of states. Let $N = \text{range}(\nu) \cup \text{range}(\nu')$. We will consider finite "subconfigurations" $\ell : N \to Q$.

Changing in c the states of cells outside the finite part N has no influence in the computation of $F(c)(0)$ or $F'(c)(0)$. Thus any subconfiguration ℓ determines states $F(c)(0)$ or $F'(c)(0)$ which we denote $G(\ell)$ and $G'(\ell)$.

- Now assume, that the two CA are not equivalent: $(f_n, \nu) \not\equiv (f'_{n'}, \nu')$, i.e. the corresponding global maps F and F' are not the same. Then there is a configuration c such that $F(c) \neq F'(c)$. Since global maps commute with the shift, it is without loss of generality to assume that $F(c)(0) \neq F'(c)(0)$. Hence in this case there is an $\ell = c|_N$ such that $G(\ell) \neq G'(\ell)$.
- On the other hand, when there exists an ℓ such that $G(\ell) \neq G'(\ell)$, then obviously F and F' will be different for any configuration c satisfying $c|_N = \ell$ and hence the CA are not equivalent.

For deciding the equivalence it is therefore sufficient to check whether for all $\ell : N \to Q$ holds: $G(\ell) = G'(\ell)$. If this is the case, the two CA are equivalent, if not they are not. ∎

In the following, we generally discuss the case $n = n'$ (local functions are of the same arity). For an example of the case $n \neq n'$, see Proposition 1 below.

The following easily proved proposition shows that for CA defined by the neighborhood function ν, there is an equivalent CA having the ordinary neighborhood of scope $2r + 1$.

Proposition 1. *For (f_n, ν), let $r = \max\{|\nu(i)| \mid 0 \leq i \leq n - 1\}$. Then there is an equivalent (f'_{2r+1}, ν') such that $\text{range}(\nu') = (-r, -r+1, ..., 0, ..., r-1, r)$ and f'_{2r+1} takes the same value as f_n on $\text{range}(\nu)$, while variables x_i are don't care for i such that $\nu'(i) \notin \text{range}(\nu)$.*

5   Neighborhood Family and Permutation Family

We define two families of CA which are obtained by changing or permuting the neighborhood being the local function fixed and investigate what properties are preserved from changing or permuting the neighborhood.

Definition 2. *The neighborhood family $\mathcal{F}(f_n)$ of f_n is an infinite set of global functions defined by*

$$\mathcal{F}(f_n) = \bigcup_{\nu \in N_n} \{(f_n, \nu)\}, \tag{4}$$

where N_n is the set of all injections $\nu : \{0, \ldots, n-1\} \to \mathbb{Z}$.

Definition 3. *A permutation π of* range(ν) *is denoted by $\pi(\nu)$ or simply π when ν is known. The permutation family $\mathcal{P}(f_n, \nu)$ of (f_n, ν) is a finite set of global functions defined by*

$$\mathcal{P}(f_n, \nu) = \bigcup_{i=0}^{n!-1} \{(f_n, \pi_i(\nu))\}. \tag{5}$$

Example: In case of n=3 there are 6 permutations of ENB.

$$\pi_0 = (-1, 0, 1), \pi_1 = (-1, 1, 0), \pi_2 = (0, -1, 1),$$
$$\pi_3 = (0, 1, -1), \pi_4 = (1, -1, 0), \pi_5 = (1, 0, -1).$$

Proposition 2. *The set of CA $\{(f_n, \nu) \mid f_n : n\text{-ary function}\}$ is closed under permutation of the neighborhood. That is*

$$\bigcup_{f_n} \mathcal{P}(f_n, \nu) = \bigcup_{i=0}^{n!-1} \{(f_n, \pi_i(\nu))\} = \bigcup_{f_n} \{(f_n, \nu)\}. \tag{6}$$

Proof. Since a permutation of the neighborhood amounts to a permutation of the variables of the local function with the neighborhood being fixed to ν, for any f_n there is a function g_n and permutation π_i such that $(f_n, \nu) \cong (g_n, \pi_i(\nu))$ for some $1 \le i \le n! - 1$. ∎

Here are three properties of CA which are preserved from changing the neighborhood. See also [4].

Proposition 3. *$f_n(x_1, ..., x_n)$ is called totalistic if it is a function of $\sum_{i=1}^{n} x_i$. If f_n is totalistic, then any $(f_n, \nu) \in \mathcal{F}(f_n)$ is totalistic.*

Proposition 4. *An affine CA is defined by a local function*

$$f_n(x_1, x_2, ..., x_n) = u_0 + u_1 x_1 + \cdots + u_n x_n, \text{ where } u_i \in Q, \ 0 \le i \le n.$$

If f_n is affine, then any $(f_n, \nu) \in \mathcal{F}(f_n)$ is affine.

Proposition 5. *A local function $f : Q^n \to Q$ is called balanced if $|f^{-1}(a)| = |Q|^{n-1}, \ \forall a \in Q$. A finite CA is called balanced if any global configuration has the same number of preimages. In case of finite CA, if (f_n, ν) is balanced then $(f_n, \pi(\nu))$ is balanced for any π.*

In contract, here is a property which is sensitive to permutation of the neighborhood.

Proposition 6. *The number-conserving ECA is sensitive to permutation.*

Proof. The only number-conserving ECA are $(R184, \pi_0)$ and its conjugate $(R226, \pi_0)$ [7]. It is seen that $(R184, \pi_2) \cong (R172, \pi_0)$ which is not number-conserving. A similar relation holds for $R226$. ∎

6   Reversibility of CA

This section addresses the problem how the reversibility of 2 and 3 states 3 neighbors CA is affected by changing the neighborhood.

Proposition 7. *The set of 6 reversible ECA is closed under permutation.*

Proof. There are 6 reversible ECA; R15, R51, R85, R170, R204, R240 expressed by Wolfram numbers, see page 436 of [8]. Their local functions are listed in Table 1. In the sequel such 6 functions are called *elementary reversible functions*(ERF for short). Note that R204 is the conjugate of R51, R240 is the conjugate of R15 and R170 is the conjugate of R85.

Table 1. Reversible CA with 2 states 3 neighbors

local configuration	000	001	010	011	100	101	110	111
R15	1	1	1	1	0	0	0	0
R51	1	1	0	0	1	1	0	0
R85	1	0	1	0	1	0	1	0
R170	0	1	0	1	0	1	0	1
R204	0	0	1	1	0	0	1	1
R240	0	0	0	0	1	1	1	1

For instance, from R51, by permuting ENB, we obtain R15 and R85. Summing up, we see that

$$(R51, \pi_1) \cong (R85, \pi_0), \quad (R51, \pi_2) \cong (R15, \pi_0), \quad (R51, \pi_3) \cong (R15, \pi_0)$$
$$(R51, \pi_4) \cong (R15, \pi_0), \quad (R51, \pi_5) \cong (R51, \pi_0) \quad x \leftrightarrow z \text{ symmetry.}$$

Similarly from R204 we obtain R170 and R240 by permutation. Note, however, that R170 can not be obtained by permutation of R51 but by taking conjugate. In other word, $\mathcal{P}(R51, \nu_E) \cap \mathcal{P}(R170, \nu_E) = \emptyset$. ∎

Proposition 8. *Any 2 states 3 neighbors local function f_{ERF} from Table 1 induces a reversible CA (f_{ERF}, ν) for any ν, particularly for $\nu \neq ENB$.*

Proof. $R15 = x + 1$, where variables y and z are don't care, and CA $(R15, ENB)$ is essentially *a right shift by 1 cell*. Now, it is seen that $(R15, (-k, l, m))$ is a right shift by k cells for any integers k, l, m, which is a reversible CA. Since $R51 = y + 1$ and $R85 = z + 1$, we have the same conclusion that they define reversible CAs for any neighborhood functions. As for $R170 = z, R204 = y$ and $R240 = x$, we have the same conclusion. ∎

Since in $\mathbb{Z}^n$, too, a reversible local function f_{ERF} from Table 1 is a shift by one cell, summing up the above propositions we have

Theorem 3. *n-dimensional CA* $(\mathbb{Z}^n, GF(2), f_{ERF}, \nu)$ *is reversible for any* ν : $\{0, 1, 2\} \to \mathbb{Z}^n$.

Problem 1. Are there irreversible ECA which become reversible by permuting or changing the neighborhood?

Problem 2. Investigate the same problem for CA having local functions of arity larger than 3 and corresponding neighborhoods of size larger than 3: $(\mathbb{Z}, GF(2), f_n, \nu), n \geq 4$.

In contrast to the binary state case, we see that a reversible 3 states CA on ENB becomes irreversible on neighborhoods different from ENB.

Proposition 9. *Reversible 3 states CA* $(\mathbb{Z}, GF(3), f_3, ENB)$ *is not always reversible, when the neighborhood is different from ENB.*

Proof. We give a counter example for 3 stats 3 neighbors CA; Among 3^{3^3} 3 states CA on ENB, 1800 are reversible. A reversible CA R270361043509 appearing in p.436 of [8] is proved not reversible when the neighborhood is changed to $(-1, 0, 2)$ as is shown below;

Injectivity: R270361043509 on neighborhood $(-1, 0, 2)$ maps both global configurations $\bar{0}1\bar{0}$ and $\bar{0}11\bar{0}$ to $\bar{1}0\bar{1}$. So, it is not injective.

Surjectivity: David Sehnal [9], student of the University of Bruno (CZ), showed by Mathematica computation that R270361043509 is not surjective on $(-1, 0, 2)$. Naonori Tanimoto [10], graduate student of the Hiroshima University (JP), also confirmed Sehnal's conclusion by his C-code computation.

Recently Clemens Lode [11], student of the University of Karlsruhe (DE), wrote a Java program called *catest105* which checks injectivity and surjectivity of CA for arbitrary neighborhoods. The program classifies R270361043509 as not injective and not surjective on $(-1, 0, 2)$. Moreover, catest105 can test injectivity and surjectivity of arbitrary local functions on all (6) permutations of ENB. Owing to the program, we see that R270361043509 is reversible on ENB $= (-1, 0, 1)$ and $(1, 0, -1)$ but not on the other neighborhoods. ∎

Conjecture 1. By use of the above mentioned program by C. Lode we see that another 3 states reversible CA R277206003607 in [8] is reversible on *all permutations* of ENB and on permutations of many other neighborhoods such as $(-1, 0, 2), (-1, 0, 3)$ and $(-2, 0, 1)$. From this, we conjecture that R277206003607 is reversible for *arbitrary* neighborhoods of size 3 in $\mathbb{Z}$.

7 Concluding Remarks and Acknowledgements

In the paper, a new definition of CA with the neighborhood function was given , which triggered new research of CA. The results established here are limited to basic ones and many interesting problems are being left to be solved. Apart from those already mentioned, the computer simulation given in Appendix suggests for example the following problems: Is Rule 110 universal for a neighborhood different from ENB? Is there any other ELF which gives a universal CA for a cleverly chosen neighborhood?

The author expresses his thanks to Thomas Worsch for his cooperation throughout the research work at the University of Karlsruhe, October-December 2006 as well as the preparation of this paper later on.

References

1. von Neumann, J., Burks(ed.), A.W.: Theory of Self-reproducing Automata. Univ. of Illinois Press (1966)
2. Gardner, M.: The fantastic combinations of John Conway's new game of 'life'. Scientific American **223** (1970) 120–123
3. Nishio, H., Margenstern, M., von Haeseler, F.: On algebraic structure of neighborhoods of cellular automata –Horse Power Problem– to appear in Fundamenta Informaticae, 2006.
4. Nishio, H.: How does the neighborhood affect the global behavior of cellular automata? In: Proceedings of ACRI2006, eds. El Yacouybi, B. Chopard and S. Bandini. Volume LNCS 4173. (2006) 122–130
5. Worsch, T., Nishio, H.: Variations on neighborhoods in CA—How to simulate different CA using only one local rule. Eurocast2007, Workshop on CA, February 2007.
6. Nishio, H., Saito, T.: Information dynamics of cellular automata I: An algebraic study. Fundamenta Informaticae **58** (2003) 399–420
7. Boccara, N.: Randomized cellular automata. arXiv:nlin/0702046v1 (2007)
8. Wolfram, S.: A New Kind of Science. Wolfram Media, Inc. (2002)
9. Sehnal, D.: private communication, June 2006.
10. Tanimoto, N.: private communication, November 2006.
11. Lode, C.: private communication, February 2007.
12. Scheben, C.: http://www.stud.uni-karlsruhe.de/ uoz3/cgi/main.cgi/ menu=submenuPrograms&view=view/ca.html.

Appendix: Java Applet Simulator for 1-Dimensional CA

We are using a Java Applet simulator of 1-dimensional CA coded by Christoph Scheben for the Institute of Informatics, University of Karlsruhe [12]. It works for arbitrary local function, number of states, neighborhood and initial configuration (including random configurations) up to 1,000 cells with cyclic boundary and 1,000 time steps. The simulator is the first of this kind —arbitrary neighborhoods. It has been well finished and proved very useful for our research work.

The following three figures are outputs of the simulator, where the local function Rule 110 is fixed while the neighborhood is changed. Number of cells × time is 100 × 100 with cyclic boundary. The initial configuration is random $(p(0) = p(1) = 0.5)$ and the same for three cases.

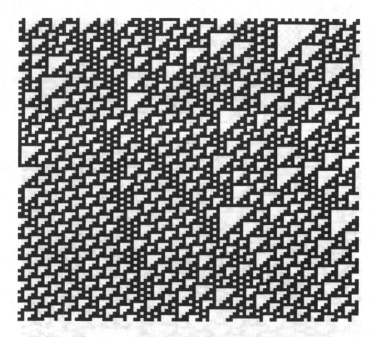

Fig. 3. Rule 110 with neighborhood $(-1, 0, 1)$=ENB

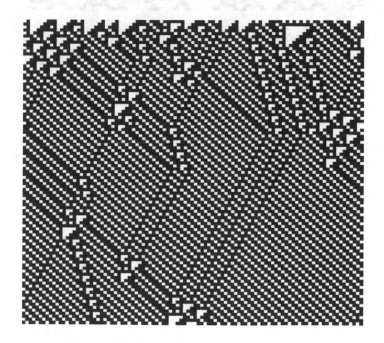

Fig. 4. Rule 110 with neighborhood $(-2, 0, 1)$

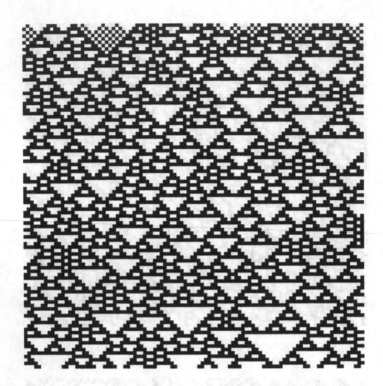

Fig. 5. Rule 110 with neighborhood $(0, -1, 1)$

A Simple P-Complete Problem and Its Representations by Language Equations*

Alexander Okhotin

Academy of Finland *and*
Department of Mathematics, University of Turku, FIN-20014 Turku, Finland
alexander.okhotin@utu.fi

Abstract. A variant of Circuit Value Problem over the basis of Peirce's arrow (NOR) is introduced, in which one of the inputs of every k-th gate must be the $(k-1)$-th gate. The problem, which remains P-complete, is encoded as a simple formal language over a two-letter alphabet. It is shown that this language can be naturally and succinctly represented by language equations from several classes. Using this representation, a small conjunctive grammar and an even smaller LL(1) Boolean grammar for this language are constructed.

1 Introduction

The notion of a language complete for a family of languages with respect to one of the standard types of reductions is one of the main concepts in computation theory. For every noteworthy class of automata or grammars, such that the language family they generate contains a complete set, it is interesting to find a succinct specification of such a set. For instance, for the class of recursively enumerable (r.e.) sets, the standard specification of a complete set is a *universal Turing machine*, and finding the smallest such machine has been a subject for research, see Rogozhin [19]. Recently there have been numerous papers on small descriptions of r.e.-complete sets using non-standard formal systems.

Similar research is occasionally done for automata and grammars of a restricted computational power, which can sometimes solve complete problems for the complexity class that bounds their expressive power. Let us note a paper by Sudborough [20], who constructed a linear context-free grammar for an NL-complete language, at the same time proving that all linear context-free languages to lie in NL. Similarly, Galil [3] found a P-complete language accepted by a two-way deterministic pushdown automaton; his construction was improved by Ladner [9]. The existence of a trellis automaton accepting a P-complete language was demonstrated by Ibarra and Kim [7]. A linear conjunctive grammar for a P-complete problem was constructed by the author [13]. An amazing example of P-completeness in elementary cellular automata was recently found by Neary and Woods [10].

---

* Supported by the Academy of Finland under grants 118540 and 206039.

J. Durand-Lose and M. Margenstern (Eds.): MCU 2007, LNCS 4664, pp. 267–278, 2007.

This paper considers a class of *language equations* [14,15,17], whose solutions are known to lie in P, and which are already known to specify some P-complete sets. The goal is to construct very succinct specifications of such sets. For this purpose, a new variant of the *Circuit Value Problem* [9,5,6] is proposed in Section 2 and proved to be P-complete. The set of yes-instances of this problem is encoded as a formal language in Section 3, and four different representations of this language using language equations with different sets of operations are constructed in Section 4.

These representations are next used to construct formal grammars for this problem. The classes of grammars considered are closely related to language equations: these are *conjunctive grammars* [11], which generalize context-free grammars with an explicit conjunction operation, and *Boolean grammars* [15], which further add negation to the formalism. An up-to-date survey of these grammars has recently appeared [18].

Conjunctive grammars for P-complete problems have been constructed before, using a mechanical simulation of a 45-state trellis automaton over a 9-letter alphabet [13]. The resulting linear conjunctive grammar contains $45^2 \cdot 9^2 + 1 = 164026$ rules. Using a conjunctive grammar with unrestricted concatenation, it is sufficient to have around $45^2 + 9 + 1 = 2035$ rules. Though the majority of these rules are not actually needed, reducing their number would require a tedious proof.

The proposed variant of the circuit value problem results in a significant reduction in size. The conjunctive grammar given in Section 5 uses only 8 rules, while the Boolean grammar constructed in Section 6 contains as few as 5 rules. In addition, one can obtain an equivalent LL(1) Boolean grammar [16] with 8 rules; this is a subclass of Boolean grammars that can be parsed using generalized recursive descent. The latter result implies P-completeness of some variants of the recursive descent parsing used in software engineering [2].

2   A Variant of the Circuit Value Problem

A circuit is an acyclic directed graph, in which the incoming arcs in every vertex are considered ordered, every source vertex is labelled with a variable from a certain set $\{x_1, \ldots, x_m\}$ $(m \geqslant 1)$, each of the rest of the vertices is labelled with a Boolean function of k variables (where k is its in-degree), and there is a unique sink vertex. For every Boolean vector of input values $(\sigma_1, \ldots, \sigma_m)$ assigned to the variables, the value computed at each gate is defined as the value of the function assigned to this gate on the values computed in the predecessor gates. The value computed at the sink vertex is the output value of the circuit on the given input.

The *Circuit Value Problem* (CVP) is stated as follows: given a circuit with gates of two types, $f_1(x) = \neg x$ and $f_2(x, y) = x \wedge y$, and given a vector $(\sigma_1, \ldots, \sigma_m)$ of input values assigned to the variables $(\sigma_i \in \{0, 1\})$, determine whether the circuit evaluates to 1 on this vector. The pair *(circuit, vector of input values)* is called an instance of CVP. This is the fundamental problem complete for P, which was proved by Ladner [9]. A variant of this problem is the *Monotone Circuit Value Problem* (MCVP), in which only conjunction and disjunction gates are allowed. As shown by Goldschlager [5], MCVP remains P-complete.

A multitude of other particular cases of CVP are known to be P-complete [6]. Let us define one more version of this standard computational problem:

- The notion of an input variable is eliminated, and the circuit is deemed to have a single source vertex, which, by definition, assumes value 1.
- A single type of gate is used. This gate implements *Peirce's arrow* $x \downarrow y = \neg(x \vee y)$, also known as the NOR function. It is well-known that every Boolean function can be expressed as a formula over this function only.
- The first argument of every k-th NOR gate has to be the previous $(k-1)$-th gate, while the second argument can be any preceding gate. Because of that, these gates will be called *restricted NOR gates*.

Let us call this kind of circuit a *sequential NOR circuit*, and let the problem of testing whether such a circuit evaluates to 1 be called *sequential NOR circuit value problem*. We shall now see that instances of the ordinary CVP can be mechanically translated to this restricted form.

Let any circuit with conjunction and negation gates be given. The first two gates of the output sequential NOR circuit have to be $C_0 = 1$ and $C_1 = C_0 \downarrow C_0 = 0$. Every time the input circuit refers to a variable, the output circuit refers to C_0 or C_1. Each negation gate $\neg C_j$ in the input circuit can be expressed via two restricted NOR gates as follows:

$$C_i = C_{i-1} \downarrow C_0 \qquad\qquad (= \neg(C_{i-1} \vee 1) = \neg 1 = 0)$$
$$C_{i+1} = C_i \downarrow C_j \qquad\qquad (= \neg(C_i \vee C_j) = \neg(0 \vee C_j) = \neg C_j)$$

Note that the first gate C_i resets the computation to 0 regardless of the value computed in C_{i-1}, while the second gate C_{i+1} substitutes this constant 0 into Peirce's arrow to obtain negation.

Similarly, a conjunction of two gates, C_j and C_k, can be implemented using the following five restricted NOR gates[1]:

$$C_i = C_{i-1} \downarrow C_0 \qquad\qquad\qquad (= 0)$$
$$C_{i+1} = C_i \downarrow C_j \qquad\qquad\qquad (= \neg C_j)$$
$$C_{i+2} = C_{i+1} \downarrow C_0 \qquad\qquad\qquad (= 0)$$
$$C_{i+3} = C_{i+2} \downarrow C_k \qquad\qquad\qquad (= \neg C_k)$$
$$C_{i+4} = C_{i+3} \downarrow C_{i+1} \qquad (= \neg(\neg C_j \vee \neg C_k) = C_j \wedge C_k)$$

The gates C_i and C_{i+1} compute $\neg C_j$ as above, the gates C_{i+2} and C_{i+3} similarly compute $\neg C_k$, and the last gate C_{i+4} computes Peirce's arrow of C_{i+1} and C_{i+3}, which is exactly the conjunction of C_j and C_k.

---

[1] Actually, there exist several shorter four-gate implementations (e.g., $C_i = C_{i-1} \downarrow C_0$, $C_{i+1} = C_i \downarrow C_j$, $C_{i+2} = C_{i+1} \downarrow C_k$, $C_{i+3} = C_{i+2} \downarrow C_{i+1}$), but they are not as easy to understand as the slightly larger circuit given in the text.

The resulting sequential NOR circuit evalutes to 1 if and only if the original circuit evaluates to 1. In addition, this transformation can be carried out by a logarithmic-space transducer. This proves that the sequential NOR circuit value problem is P-complete.

3 Encoding of Circuits

Let us now give a simple encoding of sequential NOR circuits as strings over the alphabet $\{a, b\}^*$. Consider any such circuit

$$C_0 = 1$$
$$C_1 = C_0 \downarrow C_0$$
$$C_2 = C_1 \downarrow C_{j_2}$$
$$\vdots$$
$$C_{n-1} = C_{n-2} \downarrow C_{j_{n-1}}$$
$$C_n = C_{n-1} \downarrow C_{j_n}$$

where $n \geqslant 0$ and $0 \leqslant j_i < i$ for all i. The gate C_0 is represented by the empty string. Every restricted NOR gate $C_i = f(C_{i-1}, C_{j_i})$ is represented as a string $a^{i-j_i-1}b$. The whole circuit is encoded as a concatenation of these representations in the reverse order, starting from the circuit C_n and ending with $\dots C_1 C_0$:

$$a^{n-j_n-1}b\, a^{(n-1)-j_{n-1}-1}b \,\dots\, a^{2-j_2-1}b\, a^{1-j_1-1}b$$

The set of syntactically correct circuits can be formally defined as follows:

$$\{a^{n-j_n-1}ba^{(n-1)-j_{n-1}-1}b\dots a^{2-j_2-1}ba^{1-j_1-1}b \mid n \geqslant 0 \text{ and, for each } i, 0 \leqslant j_i < i\}$$

This language is already non-context-free, but it is computationally easy: one can straightforwardly construct a logspace Turing machine to test a string for being a description of a circuit.

The language of correct circuits that have value 1 has the following fairly succinct definition:

$$\{a^{n-j_n-1}ba^{(n-1)-j_{n-1}-1}b\dots a^{2-j_2-1}ba^{1-j_1-1}b \mid n \geqslant 0 \text{ and } \exists y_0, y_1, \dots, y_n, \text{ s.t.}$$
$$y_0 = y_n = 1 \text{ and } \forall i\ (1 \leqslant i \leqslant n),\ 0 \leqslant j_i < i \text{ and } y_i = \neg(y_{i-1} \vee y_{j_i})\}$$

This is a P-complete language, and it has a simple structure that reminds of the examples common in formal language theory. As it will now be demonstrated, this set can indeed be very succinctly defined by language-theoretic methods.

4 Representation by Language Equations

Language equations with Boolean operations and concatenation will now be used to replicate the above definition of the problem. In general, such equations are known to have computationally universal expressive power, and most of their properties are undecidable [14]. However, all constructed equations will belong to a special class of *strict systems* [1,12], which are known to have unique solutions. The membership of strings in these solutions can be tested in cubic time [15].

Let us start with an equivalent inductive definition of the set of syntactically correct circuits.

- ε is a well-formed circuit.
- A string $a^m bw$ is a well-formed circuit if and only if w is a well-formed circuit, and the latter circuit contains at least m gates besides C_0, that is, $w = (a^*b)^m x$ for some $x \in \{a, b\}^*$.
- Nothing else is a well-formed circuit.

The set of well-formed circuits that have value 1 (that is, the yes-instances of the CVP) can be defined inductively as follows:

- The circuit ε has value 1.
- Let $a^m bw$ be a syntactically correct circuit. Then $a^m bw$ has value 1 if and only if both of the following statements hold:
    1. w is *not* a circuit that has value 1 (in other words, w is a circuit that has value 0);
    2. w is in $(a^*b)^m u$, where $m \geqslant 0$ and u is *not* a circuit that has value 1 (that is, u is a circuit that has value 0).

Checking the representation $a^m b(a^*b)^m u$ requires matching the number of as in the beginning of the string to the number of subsequent blocks (a^*b), as shown in Figure 1. This can naturally be specified by a context-free grammar for the following language:

$$L_0 = \bigcup_{m \geqslant 0} a^m b(a^*b)^m \tag{1}$$

To be precise, the language L_0 is linear context-free and deterministic context-free; furthermore, there exists an LL(1) context-free grammar for this language.

Using L_0 as a constant, one can construct the following language equations, which are the exact formal representation of the above definitions:

$$X = \overline{a^*bX} \cap \overline{L_0 X} \tag{2a}$$

$$Y = \varepsilon \cup (a^*bY \cap L_0\{a, b\}^*) \tag{2b}$$

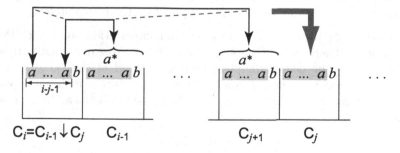

Fig. 1. Looking up a gate

The equation for Y defines well-formed descriptions of circuits: its unique solution is the language of all such descriptions. The equation for X similarly transcribes the definition of the set of circuits that have value 1. According to the definition, a string is a well-formed circuit that has value 1 if and only if it is syntactically correct and it satisfies (2a). Thus the final result is obtained by intersecting X and Y using an additional equation:

$$Z = X \cap Y \tag{3}$$

Now the system of equations (2a, 2b, 3) has a unique solution $X = L$, $Y = L'$, $Z = L''$, in which L' is the set of syntactically correct circuits, while L'' is the requested set of yes-instances of the given encoding of CVP.

Furthermore, since $L \cap L' = L''$, the language L contains a valid description of a circuit if and only if this circuit has value 1, so L, in spite of containing garbage that does not describe any circuits, still correctly represents the yes-instances of the circuit value problem. Therefore, the unique solution of the individual equation (2a) is P-complete.

This is worth being stated as the main result of this paper:

Theorem 1. *There exists an LL(1) context-free language $L_0 \subseteq \{a, b\}^+$, which is at the same time linear context-free, such that the unique solution of the language equation $X = \overline{a^* b X} \cap \overline{L_0 X}$ is a P-complete language. The language L_0 is given by the grammar $\{S \to aSAb,\ S \to b,\ A \to aA,\ A \to \varepsilon\}$.*

Two constants in this equation can be combined into one, resulting in the following variant of this equation:

Corollary 1. *Consider the linear context-free language $L_1 = L_0 \cup a^* b \subseteq \{a, b\}^+$. Then the language equation $X = \overline{L_1 X}$ has a P-complete unique solution.*

Yet another variant of this equation is obtained by substituting it in itself: the equation $X = \overline{L_1 \overline{L_1 X}}$ has the same unique solution. Here nested concatenation and complementations form a monotone operation on languages known as *the dual of concatenation* [17]:

$$K \odot L = \overline{\overline{K} \cdot \overline{L}} = \{w \mid \forall u, v : w = uv \Rightarrow u \in K \text{ or } v \in L\}$$

In terms of this operation the above equation is reformulated as follows:

Corollary 2. *Let $L_2 = \overline{L_1}$, which is also a linear context-free language. Then the unique solution of the equation $X = L_2 \odot (L_1 \cdot X)$ is P-complete.*

The equation (2a) uses complementation and intersection to specify Peirce's arrow as it is. There is another way of specifying the same condition, which does not require the use of complementation. Instead of the variable X from (2a), consider two variables, T and F (*true* and *false*), which correspond to circuits evaluating to 1 and 0, respectively. Now the problem can be represented as follows:

$$T = (a^* b F \cap L_0 F) \cup \varepsilon \tag{4a}$$
$$F = a^* b T \cup L_0 T \tag{4b}$$

This is also a strict system, which has a unique solution (L_T, L_F). Intersected with the set of syntactically correct circuits, as in (2b, 3), L_T and L_F yield exactly the sets of circuits that have value 1 and 0, respectively.

Hence the following variation of Theorem 1:

Theorem 2. *There exists an LL(1) context-free language $L_0 \subseteq \{a, b\}^+$ (see Theorem 1), such that both components of the unique solution of the system of language equations (4) are P-complete languages.*

Four completely formal representations of the circuit value problem have been given. Let us use these representations to obtain succinct formal grammars for the set of yes-instances of this problem. The first task is to specify the system (4) as a conjunctive grammar.

5   Representation by a Conjunctive Grammar

Conjunctive grammars [11] were introduced by the author in 2000 and studied in a series of papers [11,12,13]. These grammars are generalize the context-free grammars by adding an explicit intersection operation, and despite a substantial increase in the generative power, they inherit a number of their attractive properties, most notably, some of the parsing algorithms.

A *conjunctive grammar* is a quadruple $G = (\Sigma, N, P, S)$, where

- Σ and N are disjoint finite nonempty sets of *terminal* and *nonterminal* symbols;
- P is a finite set of *rules*, each of the form

$$A \to \alpha_1 \& \ldots \& \alpha_n,$$

  where $A \in N$, $n \geqslant 1$ and $\alpha_i \in (\Sigma \cup N)^*$;
- $S \in N$ is a nonterminal designated as the *start symbol*.

For every rule $A \to \alpha_1 \& \ldots \& \alpha_n \in P$ and for every i $(1 \leqslant i \leqslant n)$, an object $A \to \alpha_i$ is called a *conjunct*.

The semantics of conjunctive grammars is defined using term rewriting, which generalizes the context-free derivation. The difference is in that the context-free derivation operates with strings over $\Sigma \cup N$ (that is, terms over a single associative operation, the concatenation), while the derivation in conjunctive grammars uses terms over two operations, concatenation and conjunction.

These terms can be formally specified as strings over the alphabet $\Sigma \cup N \cup \{$ "(", ")", "&"$\}$ as follows:

1. ε is a term;
2. Every symbol from $\Sigma \cup N$ is a term;
3. If $\mathcal{A}$ and $\mathcal{B}$ are terms, then $\mathcal{A}\mathcal{B}$ is a term;
4. If $\mathcal{A}_1, \ldots, \mathcal{A}_n$ $(n \geqslant 1)$ are terms, then $(\mathcal{A}_1 \& \ldots \& \mathcal{A}_n)$ is a term.

Define the following term rewriting:

1. A subterm A can be replaced by the body of any rule for A. Using the string representation of terms,

$$s_1 A s_2 \Longrightarrow s_1(\alpha_1 \& \ldots \& \alpha_n) s_2 \tag{5}$$

for all $s_1, s_2 \in (\Sigma \cup N \cup \{\text{``(''}, \text{``)''}, \text{``\&''}\})^*$ and for every rule $A \to \alpha_1 \& \ldots \& \alpha_n \in P$. For the clarity of notation, let us assume that the parentheses are omitted in case $n = 1$:

$$s_1 A s_2 \Longrightarrow s_1 \alpha_1 s_2 \tag{5'}$$

2. Conjunction of several identical terminal strings can be replaced by one such string:

$$s_1 \underbrace{(w \& \ldots \& w)}_{n} s_2 \Longrightarrow s_1 w s_2 \tag{6}$$

for all $s_1, s_2 \in (\Sigma \cup N \cup \{\text{``(''}, \text{``)''}, \text{``\&''}\})^*$, for all $w \in \Sigma^*$ and for all $n \geqslant 1$.

Let $\Longrightarrow^*$ be the reflexive and transitive closure of $\Longrightarrow$.

The language generated by a term $\mathcal{A}$ with respect to a grammar G can now be defined as the set of all strings over Σ derivable from $\mathcal{A}$ in zero or more steps:

$$L_G(\mathcal{A}) = \{w \mid w \in \Sigma^*, \mathcal{A} \Longrightarrow^* w\} \tag{7}$$

The language generated by a grammar is the set of all strings over its terminal alphabet derivable from its start symbol: $L(G) = L_G(S)$.

The most important basic property of conjunctive grammars is their representation by language equations, which is a direct generalization of a similar property of context-free grammars established by Ginsburg and Rice [4]. The system of language equations associated with a conjunctive grammar $G = (\Sigma, N, P, S)$ uses the set N as the set of variables and, for each variable $A \in N$, there is the following equation:

$$A = \bigcup_{A \to \alpha_1 \& \ldots \& \alpha_m \in P} \bigcap_{i=1}^{m} \alpha_i$$

A solution of such a system is a vector of languages $(\ldots, C, \ldots)_{C \in N}$, such that the substitution of L_C for C, for all $C \in N$, turns each equation into an equality. Like in the context-free case, it is known that this system always has solutions, and that among them there is a least one with respect to componentwise inclusion. This least solution is exactly the vector $(\ldots, L_G(A), \ldots)_{A \in N}$ [12]. This, in particular, shows that the conjunction operation in the rules of conjunctive grammars indeed has the assumed semantics of intersection of languages.

Having recalled the definition of conjuctive grammars and their relationship with language equations, we can now proceed to expressing the system (4) constructed Section 4. It is represented by the following small conjunctive grammar,

$$T \to AbF \& CF \mid \varepsilon$$
$$F \to AbT \mid CT$$
$$A \to aA \mid \varepsilon$$
$$C \to aCAb \mid b$$

in which the nonterminal C generates exactly the language (1) used in the equations (4). This establishes the following result:

Theorem 3. *There exists an 8-rule conjunctive grammar that generates a P-complete language.*

A certain drawback of this grammar is that it is not LL(k) for any k, that is, it cannot be used with the recursive descent parsing method for conjunctive grammars [16]. The same applies to the previously known very large conjunctive grammar for another P-complete language [13]: though it is linear, it is still not LL(k). The question of whether there exists an LL(k) conjunctive grammar for any P-complete language thus remains open.

In the following section it will be demonstrated that if a somewhat more expressive family of grammars is used, then the accordingly generalized LL condition can be met.

6 Representation by an LL(1) Boolean Grammar

Boolean grammars, introduced by the author in 2003 [15], are a generalization of the context-free grammars that allows the use of all Boolean connectives in the rules. In other words, Boolean grammars are a further extension of conjunctive grammars that supports negation.

A Boolean grammar is a quadruple $G = (\Sigma, N, P, S)$, where

- Σ and N are disjoint finite nonempty sets of terminal and nonterminal symbols, respectively;
- P is a finite set of rules of the form

$$A \to \alpha_1 \& \ldots \& \alpha_m \& \neg\beta_1 \& \ldots \& \neg\beta_n, \tag{8}$$

  where $m + n \geqslant 1$, $\alpha_i, \beta_i \in (\Sigma \cup N)^*$; similarly to the case of conjunctive grammars, $A \to \alpha_i$ is called a *positive conjunct*, while $A \to \neg\beta_j$ is a *negative conjunct*;
- $S \in N$ is the start symbol of the grammar.

The intuitive semantics of a Boolean grammar is clear: a rule (8) means that every string w over Σ that satisfies each of the syntactical conditions represented by $\alpha_1, \ldots, \alpha_m$ and none of the syntactical conditions represented by $\beta_1, \ldots, \beta_m$ therefore satisfies the condition defined by A.

The formal semantics of Boolean grammars is defined using language equations similar to those used to characterize context-free and conjunctive grammars [4,12]. The system of language equations associated with G uses N as its set of variables, and the equation for each variable $A \in N$ is

$$A = \bigcup_{A \to \alpha_1 \& \ldots \& \alpha_m \& \neg\beta_1 \& \ldots \& \neg\beta_n \in P} \left[\bigcap_{i=1}^{m} \alpha_i \cap \bigcap_{j=1}^{n} \overline{\beta_j} \right] \tag{9}$$

Assume that this system has a unique solution $(\ldots, L_C, \ldots)_{C \in N}$, and further assume that for every finite language $M \subset \Sigma^*$ (such that for every $w \in M$ all substrings of w are also in M) there exists a unique vector of languages $(\ldots, L_C^{(M)}, \ldots)_{C \in N}$ $(L_C^{(M)} \subseteq M)$, such that a substitution of $L_C^{(M)}$ for C, for each $C \in N$, turns every equation (9) into an equality modulo intersection with M. Then, for every $A \in N$, the language $L_G(A)$ is defined as L_A, while the language generated by the grammar is $L(G) = L_G(S)$. An alternative definition of the semantics of Boolean grammars has been given by Kountouriotis et al. [8], but it is known to be equivalent to this in power.

Let us now rewrite the language equation (2a) as a Boolean grammar:

$$S \to \neg AbS \& \neg CS$$
$$A \to aA \mid \varepsilon$$
$$C \to aCAb \mid b$$

This grammar uses negation to specify Peirce's arrow exactly as it is defined. It also has another advantage over the conjunctive grammar for a similar language given in the previous section: it can be used with the recursive descent parsing [16]. The main condition is that whenever $w \in L(X)$ for $X \in \{S, A, C\}$, the rule for X which produces w is completely determined by the first symbol of w. One small change has to be made to the above grammar in order to meet the formal definition of an LL(1) Boolean grammar [16]: namely, the rule for S should contain a positive conjunct. Then the grammar takes the following form:

$$S \to E \& \neg AbS \& \neg CS$$
$$A \to aA \mid \varepsilon$$
$$C \to aCAb \mid b$$
$$E \to aE \mid bE \mid \varepsilon$$

The following result can be stated:

Theorem 4. *There exists a 5-rule Boolean grammar that generates a P-complete language. The same language is generated by a 8-rule LL(1) Boolean grammar.*

Taking a closer look at the recursive descent parser for this grammar (see the corresponding paper [16] for details), it is worth note that all branches of computation of the procedure $S()$ in the parser corresponding to this grammar terminate at the end of the input, and hence all comparisons between pointers in the parser's code always hold true. Therefore, these checks become redundant and can be removed from the generated program.

In this simplified form, the parser becomes similar to *ad hoc* extensions of recursive descent parsing, such as the one recently proposed by Ford [2]. Viewing specifications of those parsers as formalisms for language definition, we now see that those formalisms are capable of expressing the same P-complete set in exactly the same way as shown in this section.

7 Conclusion

The new variant of the circuit value problem allows representing P-complete sets using language equations and formal grammars of a fairly small size. It is very likely that their size can be further reduced (for instance, from 5 to 4 rules in a Boolean grammar), or it can be reduced with respect to a different descriptional complexity measure (e.g., by constructing a 5-rule 2-nonterminal Boolean grammar); constructing such grammars could be a challenging exercise.

Let us mention two research problems left open in this paper. First, it remains unknown whether there exists an $LL(k)$ conjunctive grammar for any P-complete problem. Another task is to construct a reasonably small and understandable linear conjunctive grammar for any P-complete problem, as well as a trellis automaton satisfying these criteria.

References

1. Autebert, J., Berstel, J., Boasson, L.: Context-free languages and pushdown automata. In: Rozenberg, G., Salomaa, A. (eds.) Handbook of Formal Languages, vol. I, pp. 111–174. Springer, Heidelberg (1997)
2. Ford, B.: Parsing expression grammars: a recognition-based syntactic foundation. In: Proceedings of POPL 2004, Venice, Italy, January 14–16, 2004, pp. 111–122 (2004)
3. Galil, Z.: Some open problems in the theory of computation as questions about two-way deterministic pushdown automaton languages. Mathematical Systems Theory 10(3), 211–228 (1977) (Earlier version In: 15th Annual Symposium on Automata and Switching Theory (1974))
4. Ginsburg, S., Rice, H.G.: Two families of languages related to ALGOL. Journal of the ACM 9, 350–371 (1962)
5. Goldschlager, L.M.: The monotone and planar circuit value problems are log space complete for P. SIGACT News 9(2), 25–29 (1977)
6. Greenlaw, R., Hoover, H.J., Ruzzo, W.L.: Limits to Parallel Computation: P-Completeness Theory. Oxford University Press, Oxford (1995)
7. Ibarra, O.H., Kim, S.M.: Characterizations and computational complexity of systolic trellis automata. Theoretical Computer Science 29, 123–153 (1984)
8. Kountouriotis, V., Nomikos, C., Rondogiannis, P.: Well-founded semantics for Boolean grammars. In: Ibarra, O.H., Dang, Z. (eds.) DLT 2006. LNCS, vol. 4036, pp. 203–214. Springer, Heidelberg (2006)
9. Ladner, R.E.: The circuit value problem is log space complete for P. SIGACT News 7(1), 18–20 (1975)
10. Neary, T., Woods, D.: P-completeness of cellular automaton rule 110. In: Bugliesi, M., Preneel, B., Sassone, V., Wegener, I. (eds.) ICALP 2006. LNCS, vol. 4051, pp. 132–143. Springer, Heidelberg (2006)
11. Okhotin, A.: Conjunctive grammars. Journal of Automata, Languages and Combinatorics 6(4), 519–535 (2001)
12. Okhotin, A.: Conjunctive grammars and systems of language equations. Programming and Computer Software 28, 243–249 (2002)
13. Okhotin, A.: The hardest linear conjunctive language. Information Processing Letters 86(5), 247–253 (2003)

14. Okhotin, A.: Decision problems for language equations with Boolean operations. In: Baeten, J.C.M., Lenstra, J.K., Parrow, J., Woeginger, G.J. (eds.) ICALP 2003. LNCS, vol. 2719, pp. 239–251. Springer, Heidelberg (2003)
15. Okhotin, A.: Boolean grammars. Information and Computation 194(1), 19–48 (2004)
16. Okhotin, A.: Recursive descent parsing for Boolean grammars. Acta Informatica (to appear)
17. Okhotin, A.: The dual of concatenation. Theoretical Computer Science 345(2-3), 425–447 (2005)
18. Okhotin, A.: Nine open problems for conjunctive and Boolean grammars. Bulletin of the EATCS 91, 96–119 (2007)
19. Rogozhin, Y.: Small universal Turing machines. Theoretical Computer Science 168(2), 215–240 (1996)
20. Sudborough, I.H.: A note on tape-bounded complexity classes and linear context-free languages. Journal of the ACM 22(4), 499–500 (1975)

Slightly Beyond Turing's Computability for Studying Genetic Programming

Olivier Teytaud

TAO, INRIA Futurs, LRI, UMR 8623 (CNRS - Univ. Paris-Sud),
olivier.teytaud@inria.fr

Abstract. Inspired by genetic programming (GP), we study iterative algorithms for non-computable tasks and compare them to naive models. This framework justifies many practical standard tricks from GP and also provides complexity lower-bounds which justify the computational cost of GP thanks to the use of Kolmogorov's complexity in bounded time.

1 Introduction

Limits of Turing-computability are well-known [28,20]; many things of interest are not computable. However, in practice, many people work on designing programs for solving non-computable tasks, such as finding the shortest program performing a given task, or the fastest program performing a given task: this is the area of genetic programming (GP) [9,13,15]. GP in particular provides many human-competitive results
(http://www.genetic-programming.com/humancompetitive.html), and contains 5440 articles by more than 880 authors according to the GP-bibliography [5]. GP is the research of a program realizing a given target-task roughly as follows:

1. generate (at random) an initial population of algorithms ;
2. select the ones that, after simulation, are "empirically" (details in the sequel) the most relevant for the target-task (this is dependent of a distance between the results of the simulation and the expected results, which is called the *fitness*) ;
3. create new programs by randomly combining and randomly mutating the ones that remain in the population ;
4. go back to step 2.

Theoretically, the infinite-computation models [6] are a possible model for studying programs beyond the framework of Turing Machines (TM). However, these models are far from being natural: they are intuitively justified by e.g. time steps with duration divided by 2 at each tick of the clock. We here work on another model, close to real-world practice like GP: iterative programs. These programs iteratively propose solutions, and what is studied is the convergence of the iterates to a solution in $\equiv_f$ with good properties (speed, space-consumption, size), and not the fact that after a finite time the algorithm stops and proposes a solution. The model, termed iterative model, is presented in algorithm 1. We point out that we can't directly compare the expressive power of our model and

J. Durand-Lose and M. Margenstern (Eds.): MCU 2007, LNCS 4664, pp. 279–290, 2007.
© Springer-Verlag Berlin Heidelberg 2007

the expressive power of usual models of computation; we here work in the framework of symbolic regression. Classically, programs work with a program as input, and output something (possibly a program). Here, the input can be a program, but it can also be made of black-box examples provided by an oracle. Therefore, we study algorithms with: (i) inputs, provided by an oracle (precisely, the oracle provides examples $(x_i, f(x_i))$); (ii) possibly, an auxiliary input, which is a program computing f; (iii) outputs, which are programs supposed to converge to the function f underlying the oracle *and* satisfying some constraints (e.g. asymptotically optimal size or asymptotically optimal speed). This is symbolic regression. We can encode decision problems in this framework (e.g., deciding if $\forall n, f(n) = 1$ by using x_i independent and $\forall n \in \mathbb{N}, P(x_i = n) > 0$); but we can not encode the problems as above as decision problems or other classical families of complexity classes. However, the links with various Turing degrees might be studied more extensively than in this paper.

Algorithm 1. GP - Iterative-algorithms

Set $p = 1$.
while true **do**
    Read an input $I_p = (x_p, y_p)$ with $y_p = f(x_p)$ on an oracle-tape.
    Perform standard computations of a TM (allowing reading and writing on an internal tape).
    Output some O_p.
    $p \leftarrow p + 1$
end while

This model is the direct translation of genetic programming in a Turing-like framework. A different approach consists in using also f as input. Of course, in that case, the important point is that O_p is "better" than f (faster, more frugal in terms of space-consumption, or smaller). We will see that at least in the general framework of f Turing-computable, the use of f as an input (as in algo. 2), and not only as a black-box (as in 1), is not so useful (theorem 3).

We will in particular consider the most standard case, namely symbolic regression, i.e. inputs $I_1, \ldots, I_p, \ldots$ that are independently identically distributed on $\mathbb{N} \times \mathbb{N}$ according to some distribution. We assume that there exists some f such that with probability 1, $\forall i, f(x_i) = y_i$. Inputs are examples of the relation f (see e.g. [29,10] for this model). The goal is that O_p converges, in some sense (see theorem 2 for details), to f. We will in particular study cases in which such a convergence can occur whereas without iterations f can not be built even with a black-box computing f as oracle; we will therefore compare the framework above (alg. 1) and the framework below (alg. 3). We point out that in algo. 3 we allow the program to both (i) read f on the input tape (ii) read examples (x_i, y_i) with $y_i = f(x_i)$. (i) allows automatic optimization of code and (ii) allows the use of randomized x. In cases in which (i) is allowed, what is interesting is the convergence to some $g \equiv f$ such that g is in some sense "good" (frugal in terms of space or time). In contrast, algorithm 1 only uses examples. We will see that in the general case of Turing-computable functions f, this is not a big weakness (th. 3).

Algorithm 2. Iterative-algorithms using more than a black-box.

Set $p = 1$.
Read an input f (this is not black-box!).
while true **do**
    Read an input $I_p = (x_p, y_p)$ with $y_p = f(x_p)$ on an oracle-tape[1].
    Perform standard computations of a TM (allowing reading and writing on an internal tape).
    Output some O_p (there are therefore infinitely many outputs, but each of them after a finite time).
    $p \leftarrow p + 1$
end while

Algorithm 3. Finite-time framework.

Possibly read f on the input tape (if yes, this is not black-box).
Set $p = 1$.
while Some computable criterion **do**
    Possibly read an input $I_p = (x_p, y_p)$ on the input tape.
    Perform standard computations of a TM (allowing reading and writing on an internal tape).
    $p \leftarrow p + 1$
end while
Output some O.

In this spirit, we compare baseline standard (already known) results derived from recursion theory applied to finite-time computations (algo. 3), and results on iterative algorithms derived from statistics and optimization in a spirit close to GP (algo. 1). Interestingly, we will have theoretically-required assumptions close to the practice of GP, in particular (i) penalization and parsimony [26,30,16,17], related to the bloat phenomenon which is the unexpected increase of the size of automatically generated programs ([11,1,14,22,19,27,2,12]), and (ii) necessity of simulations (or at least of computations as expensive as simulations, see th. 3 for precise formalization of this conclusion). We refer to standard programs as "finite-time algorithms" (alg. 3), in order to emphasize the difference with iterative algorithms. Finite-time algorithms take something as input (possibly with infinite length), and after a finite-time (depending upon the entry), give an output. They are possibly allowed to use an oracle which provide 2-uples (x_i, y_i) with the x_i's i.i.d and $y_i = f(x_i)$. This is usually what we call an "algorithm". The opposite concept is iterative algorithms, which take something as input, and during an infinite time provide outputs, that are e.g. converging to the solution of an equation. Of course, the set of functions that are computable in finite time is included in (and different from) the set of functions that are the limit of iterative algorithms (see also [21]). The (time or space) complexity of iterative algorithms is the (time or space) complexity of *one computation* of the infinite loop with one entry and one output. Therefore, there are two questions quantifying the overall complexity: the convergence rate of the outputs to a nice solution, and the computation time for each run through the loop. We study the following questions about GP:

- What is the natural formalism for studying GP ? We propose the algorithm 1 as a Turing-adapted-framework for GP-analysis.
- Can GP paradigms (algo. 1) outperform baseline frameworks (algo. 3) ? We show in theorem 2, contrasted with standard non-computability results summarized in section 3, that essentially the answer is positive.
- Can we remove the very expensive simulations from GP ? Theorem 3 essentially shows that simulation-times can not be removed.

2   Framework and Notations

We consider TM [28,20] with:

- one (read-only) binary input tape, where the head moves right if and only if the bit under the reading head has been read;
- one internal binary tape (read and write, without any restriction on the allowed moves);
- one (write-only) output binary tape, which moves of one and only one step to the right at each written bit.

The restrictions on the moves of the heads on the input and on the output tapes do not modify the expressive power of the TMs as they can simply copy the input tape on the internal tape, work on the internal tape and copy the result on the output tape. TM are also termed programs. If x is a program and e an entry on the input tape, then $x(e)$ is the output of the application of x to the entry e. $x(e) = \perp$ is the notation for the fact that x does not halt on entry e. We also let $\perp$ be a program such that $\forall e; \perp (e) = \perp$. A program p is a total computable function if $\forall e \in \mathbb{N}; p(e) \neq \perp$ (p halts on any input). We say that two programs x and y are equivalent if and only if $\forall e \in \mathbb{N}; x(e) = y(e)$. We denote this by $x \equiv y$. We let $\equiv_y = \{x; x \equiv y\}$.

All tapes' alphabets are binary. These TM can work on rational numbers, encoded as 2-uples of integers. Thanks to the existence of Universal TM, we identify TM and natural numbers in a computable way (one can simulate the behavior of the TM of a given number on a given entry in a computable manner). We let $< x_1, \ldots, x_n >$ be a n-uple of integers encoded as a unique number thanks to a given recursive encoding.

We use capital letters for programming-programs, i.e. programs that are aimed at outputting programs. There is no formal definition of a programming-program; the output can be considered as an integer; we only use this difference for clarity. A decider is a total computable function with values in $\{0, 1\}$. We denote by D the set of all deciders. We say that a function f recognizes a set F among deciders if and only if $\forall e; (e \in F \cap D \rightarrow f(e) = 1$ and $e \in D \setminus F \rightarrow f(e) = 0)$ (whatever may be the behavior, possibly f does not halt on e i.e. $f(e) = \perp$, for $e \notin D$). We let $\mathbf{1} = \{p; \forall e, p(e) = 1\}$, the set of programs always returning 1. The definition of the size $|x|$ of a program x is any usual definition such that there are at most 2^l programs of size $\leq l$. The space complexity is with respect to the internal tape (number of visited elements of the tape) *plus* the size of the program. We let (with a small abuse of notation as it depends on f and x and not only on $f(x)$) $time(f(x))$ (resp. $space(f(x))$) be the computation time (resp. the space complexity) of program f on entry x. $\mathbb{E}$ is the expectation operator. $Proba(.)$ is the probability operator ; by abuse, depending on the context, it is sometimes with respect to (x, y) and sometimes with respect to a sample $(x_1, x_2, \ldots, x_m, y_1, y_2, \ldots, y_m)$. Iid is a short notation for "independent identically distributed".

Section 3 presents non-computability results for finite-time algorithms. Section 4 which shows positive results for GP-like iterative algorithms. Section 5 studies the complexity of iterative algorithms. Section 6 concludes.

3   Standard Case: Finite Time Algorithms

We consider the existence of programs $P(.)$ such that when the user provides x, which is a Turing-computable function, the program computes $P(x) = y$, where $y \equiv x$ and y is not too far from being optimal (for size, space or time). It is known that for reasonable formalizations of this problem, such programs do not exist. This result is a straightforward extension of classical non-computability examples (the classical case is $C(a) = a$, we slightly extend this case for the sake of comparison with usual terminology in learning or genetic programming and in order to make the paper self-contained).

Theorem 1 (Undecidability). *Whatever may be the function $C(.)$ in $\mathbb{N}^{\mathbb{N}}$, there does not exist P such that for any total function x, $P(x)$ is equivalent to x and $P(x)$ has size $|P(x)| \leq C(\inf_{y \equiv x} |y|)$.*

Moreover, for any $C(.)$, for any such non-computable $P(.)$, there exists a TM using $P(.)$ as oracle, that solves a problem in $0'$, the jump of the set of computable functions.

Due to length constraints, we do not provide the proof of this standard result; but the proof is sketched in remark 1. We also point out without proof that using a random generator does not change the result:

Corollary 1 (No size optimization). *Whatever may be the function $C(.)$, there does not exist any program P, even possibly using a random oracle providing independent random values uniformly distributed in $\{0, 1\}$ such that for any total function x, with probability at least $2/3$, $P(x)$ is equivalent to x and $P(x)$ has size $|P(x)| \leq C(\inf_{y \equiv x} |y|)$.*

The extension from size of programs to time complexity of programs requires a more tricky formulation than a simple total order relation "is faster than" ; a program can be faster than another for some entries and slower for some others. A natural requirement is that a program that suitably works provides a (at least nearly) Pareto-optimal program [18], i.e. a program f such that there's no program that is as fast as f for all entries, and better than f for some specific entry, at least within a tolerance function $C(.)$. The precise formulation that we propose is somewhat tricky but indeed very general; once again, we do not include the proof of this result (the proof is straightforward from standard non-computability result):

Corollary 2 (Time complexity). *Whatever may be the function $C(.)$, there does not exist any program P, even possibly using a random oracle providing independent random values uniformly distributed in $\{0,1\}$, such that for any total function x, with probability at least $2/3$,*

$P(x) \equiv x$ and there's no $y \equiv x$ such that y Pareto-dominates $P(x)$ (in time complexity) within $C(.)$, i.e. $\nexists y \in \equiv_x$ such that

$$\forall z; time(P(x)(z)) \geq C(time(y(z)))$$
$$and \; \exists z; time(P(x)(z)) > C(time(y(z)))$$

The result is also true when restricted to x such that a Pareto-optimal function exist.

After size (corollary 1) and time (corollary 2), we now consider space complexity (corollary 3). The proof in the case of space complexity relies on the fact that we include the length of programs in the space complexity.

Corollary 3 (Space complexity). *Whatever may be the function $C(.)$, there does not exist any program P, even possibly using a random oracle providing independent random values uniformly distributed in $\{0,1\}$, such that for any total function x, with probability at least $2/3$,*

$P(x) \equiv x$ and there's no $y \equiv x$ such that y dominates $P(x)$ (in space complexity) within $C(.)$, i.e., $\nexists y, y \equiv x$ and

$$\forall z; space(P(x)(z)) \geq C(space(y(z)))$$

$$and \; \exists z; space(P(x)(z)) > C(space(y(z)))$$

Remark 1 (Other fitnesses and sketch of the proofs). We have stated the non-computability result for speed, size and space. Other fitnesses (in particular, mixing these three fitnesses) lead to the same result. The key of the proofs above (th. 1, corollaries 1, 2, 3) is the recursive nature of sets of functions optimal for the given fitness, for at least the **1**-class of programs, which is a very stable feature. In results above, the existence of P, associated to this recursiveness in the case of **1**, shows the recursive nature of **1**, what is a contradiction.

4   Iterative Algorithms

We recalled in section 3 that finite-time algorithms have deep limits. We now show that to some extent, such limitations can be overcome by iterative algorithms. The following theorem deals with learning deterministic computable relations from examples.

Theorem 2. *Assume that $y = f(x)$ where f is computable and $Proba(f(x) = \perp)$ $= 0$ (with probability 1, f halts on x) and $\mathbb{E}time(f(x)) < \infty$. Assume that $(x_1, y_1), \ldots, (x_m, y_m)$ is an iid (independently identically distributed) sample with the same law as (x, y). We denote $ACT_m(g) = \frac{1}{m}\sum_{i=1}^{m} Time(g(x_i))$ and $c(a, b)$ any computable function, increasing as a function of $a \in \mathbb{Q}$ and increasing as a function of $b \in \mathbb{N}$, such that $\lim_{a\to\infty} c(a, 0) = \lim_{b\to\infty} c(0, b) = \infty$. We let*

$$f_m = P(< x_1, \ldots, x_m, y_1, \ldots, y_m >) \tag{1}$$

and suppose that almost surely in the x_i's, $\forall i; f_m(x_i) = y_i$ (2)

and suppose that f_m is minimal among functions satisfying eq. 2 for criterion

$$c(ACT_m(f_m), |f_m|). \tag{3}$$

Then, almost surely in the x_i's, for m sufficiently large

$$Proba(P(< x_1, \ldots, x_m, y_1, \ldots, y_m >)(x) \neq y) = 0. \tag{4}$$

Moreover, $c(\mathbb{E}time(f_m(x)), |f_m|)$ converges to the optimal limit:

$$c(\mathbb{E}time(f_m(x)), |f_m|) \to \inf_{f; Proba(f(x)\neq y)=0} c(\mathbb{E}time(f_m(x)), |f|) \tag{5}$$

and there exists a computable P computing f_m optimal for criterion 3 and satisfying eq. 2.

Proof:
The computability of f_m is established by the following algorithm:

1. Build a naive function h such that h terminates on all entries and $\forall i \in [[1, m]], h(x_i) = y_i$ (simply the function h that on entry x checks $x = x_i$ and replies y_i if such an x is found).

2. Consider a such that $c(a/m, 0) \geq c(ACT_m(h), |h|)$ and b such that $c(0, b) \geq c(ACT_m(h), |h|)$.

3. Define G as the set of all functions g with size $\leq b$.

4. Set $G' = G \setminus G''$, where G'' contains all functions in G such that $g(x_i)$ is not computed in time a or $g(x_i) \neq y_i$.

5. Select the best function in G' for criterion $c(ACT_m(g), |g|)$.

Any satisfactory f_m is in G and not in G'' and therefore is in G'; therefore this algorithms finds g in step 5.

We now show the convergence in eq. 5 and equation 4:

1. Let f^* be an unknown computable function such that $Proba(f^*(x) \neq y) = 0$, with $\mathbb{E}time f^*(x)$ minimal.

2. The average computation time of f^* on the x_i converges almost surely (by the strong law of large numbers). Its limit is dependent of the problem ; it is the expected computation time $\mathbb{E}f^*(x)$ of f^* on x.

3. By definition of f_m and by step 2, $f_m = P(< x_1, \ldots, x_m, y_1, \ldots, y_m >)$ is such that $c(ACT_m(f_m), |f_m|)$ is upper bounded by $c(ACT_m(f^*), |f^*|)$, which is

itself almost surely bounded above as it converges almost surely (Kolmogorov's strong law of large numbers [7]).

4. Therefore, f_m, for m sufficiently large, lives in a finite space of computable functions $\{f; c(0, |f|) \leq c(\sup_i ACT_i(f^*), |f^*|)\}$.

5. Consider $g_1, \ldots, g_k$ this finite family of computable functions.

6. Almost surely, for any $i \in [[1, k]]$ such that $Proba(g_i(x) \neq y) > 0$, there exists m_i such that $g_i(x_{m_i}) \neq y_{m_i}$. These events occur simultaneously as a finite intersection of almost sure events is almost sure ; so, almost surely, these m_i all exist.

7. Thanks to step 6, almost surely, for $m > \sup_i m_i$, $Proba(f_m(x) \neq y) = 0$.

8. Combining 5 and 7, we see that $f_m \in \arg\min_G c(ACT_m(g), |g|)$ where $G = \{g_i; i \in [[1, k]]$ and $Proba(g_i(x) \neq y) = 0\}$.

9. $c(ACT_m(g_i), |g_i|) \to c(\mathbb{E}time(g_i(x)), |g_i|)$ almost surely for any $i \in [[1, k]] \cap \{i; \mathbb{E}time(g_i(x)) < \infty\}$ as $c(.,.)$ is continuous with respect to the first variable (Kolmogorov's strong law of large numbers). As this set of indexes i is finite, this convergence is uniform in i.

10. $c(ACT_m(g_i), |g_i|) \to \infty$ uniformly in i such that $\mathbb{E}time(g_i(x)) = \infty$ as this set is finite.

11. Thanks to steps 9 and 10, $c(\mathbb{E}time(f_m(x)), |f_m|) \to \inf_{g; Proba(g(x) \neq y) = 0} c$ $(\mathbb{E}time(g(x)), |g|)$.   □

5   Complexity

We recalled above that finite time algorithms could not perform some given tasks (theorem 1, corollaries 1,2,3, remark 1). We have also shown that iterative methods combining size and speed are Turing-computable (theorem 2) and converge to optimal solutions. The complexity of Turing-computable programs defined therein (in theorem 2) is mainly the cost of simulation. We now show that it is not possible to avoid the complexity of simulation. This emphasizes the necessity of simulation (or at least, of computations with the same time-cost as simulation) for automatic programming in Turing spaces. Kolmogorov's complexity was introduced by Solomonov ([24]) in the field of artificial intelligence. Some versions include bounds on resource's ([24,25,8]), in particular on the computation-time ([3,4,23]):

Definition 1 (Kolmogorov's complexity in bounded time). *An integer x is T,S-complex if there is no TM M such that $M(0) = x \wedge |M| \leq S \wedge time(M(0)) \leq T$.*

Consider an algorithm A deciding whether an integer x is T, S-complex or not. Define $C(T, S)$ the worst-case complexity of this algorithm $(C(T, S) = \sup_x time(A(< x, T, S >)))$. $C(T, S)$ implicitly depends on A, but we drop the dependency as we consider a fixed "good" A. Let's see "good" in which sense; there is some A which is "good" in the sense that with this A, $\forall T, S$, $C(T, S) < \infty$. This is possible as for x sufficiently large, x is T,S-complex, whatever may be its value; A does not have to read x entirely.

These notions are computable, but we will see that their complexity is large, at least larger than the simulation-parts. The complexity of the optimization of the fitness in theorem 4 is larger than the complexity $C(.,.)$ of deciding if x is T,S-complex ; therefore, we will lower bound $C(.,.)$.

Lemma 1 (The complexity of complexness). *Consider now T_n and $S_n = O(\log(n))$, computable increasing sequences of integers computable in time $Q(n)$ where Q is polynomial. Then there exists a polynomial $G(.)$ such that*

$$C(T_n, S_n) > (T_n - Q(n))/G(n),$$

and in particular if T_n is $\Omega(2^n)$, $C(T_n, S_n) > \dfrac{T_n}{P(n)}$ where $P(.)$ is a polynomial.

Essentially, this lemma shows that, within polynomial factors, we can not get rid of the computation time T_n when computing T_n, S_n-complexity. The proof follows the lines of the proof of the non-computability of Kolmogorov's complexity by the so-called "Berry's paradox", but with complexity arguments instead of computability arguments. In short, we will use y_n, the smallest number that is "hard to compute".

Proof: Let y_n be the smallest integer that is T_n, S_n-complex.

Step 1: y_n is T_n, S_n-complex, by definition.

Step 2: But it is not $Q(n) + y_n \times C(T_n, S_n), C + D \log_2(n)$-complex, where C and D are constants, as it can be computed by (i) computing T_n and S_n (in time $Q(n)$) (ii) iteratively testing if k is T_n, S_n-complex, where $k = 1, 2, 3, \ldots, y_n$ (in time $y_n \times C(T_n, S_n)$).

Step 3: $y_n \leq 2^{S_n}$, as: (i) there are at most 2^{S_n} programs of size $\leq S_n$, (ii) therefore there are at most 2^{S_n} numbers that are not T_n, S_n-complex. (iii) therefore, at least one number in $[[0, 2^{S_n}]]$ is T_n, S_n-complex.

Step 4: if $S_n = C + D \log_2(n)$, then y_n is upper bounded by a polynomial $G(n)$ (thanks to step 3).

Step 5: combining steps 1 and 2, $y_n C(T_n, S_n) > T_n - Q(n)$.

Step 6: using step 4 and 5, $C(T_n, S_n) > (T_n - Q(n))/G(n)$, hence the expected result. $\qquad\square$

Consider now the problem $\mathcal{P}_{n,x}$ of solving in f the following inequalities:

$$Time(f(0)) \leq T_n, \ |t| \leq S_n, \ f(0) = x$$

Theorem 3 below shows that we can not get rid of the computation-time T_n, within a polynomial. This shows that using f in e.g. algo. 2 does not save up the simulation time that is requested in algorithm 4.

Theorem 3. *If $T_n = \Omega(2^n)$ and $S_n = O(\log(n))$ are computable in polynomial time from n, then there exists polynomials $P(.)$ and $F(.)$ such that*

- *for any n and x, algorithm 4 solves problem $\mathcal{P}_{n,x}$ with computation-time at most $T_n F(n)$;*

- *there's no algorithm solving $\mathcal{P}_{n,x}$ for any n and x with computation-time at most $T_n/P(n)$.*

Proof: The computation time of algorithm 4 is straightforward. If an algorithm solves $\mathcal{P}_{n,x}$ for any x with computation-time at most $T_n/P(n)$, then this algorithm decides if x is T_n,S_n-complex in time at most $T_n/P(n)$, which contradicts lemma 1 if $P(n)$ is bigger than the polynomial of lemma 3.   □

Algorithm 4. Algorithm for finding a program of size $\leq S$ and computation time $\leq T$ generating x.

---

   for f of size $\leq S$ **do**
      Simulate T steps of f on entry 0.
      if output $= x$ **then**
         Return f
         Break
      end if
   end for
   Return "no solution".

---

6   Conclusion

The iterative-model (algo. 1) is relevant for modeling GP in the sense that (i) it is very natural, as genetic programming tools work iteratively (ii) it reflects parsimony pressure (iii) by the use of Kolomogorov's complexity with bounded time, one can show that simulation as in genetic programming is necessary (at least the computation-time of simulation is necessary). (ii) and (iii) are typically formal elements in favor of genetic programming. Let's now sum up and compare our results, to see the relevance with the state of the art in genetic programming:

- In corollaries 1, 2, 3 we have shown that finite-time programming-programs can not perform the required task, i.e. finding the most efficient function in a space of Turing-equivalent functions. This, contrasted with th. 2, shows that algorithms as algo. 1 definitely can compute things that can not be computed by algorithms as algo 3.
- In theorem 2, we have shown that an iterative programming-program could asymptotically perform the required target-tasks, namely satisfying simultaneously (i) consistency, i.e. $f_m(x) = y$ with probability 1 on x and y as shown in eq. 4; (ii) good compromise between size and speed, as shown in eq. 5. Interestingly, we need parsimony pressure in theorem 2 (short programs are preferred); parsimony pressure is usual in GP. This is a bridge between mathematics and practice. This leads to the conclusion that algo. 1 has definitely a larger computational power than algo. 3.
- The main drawback of GP is that GP is slow, due to huge computational costs, as a consequence of intensive simulations during GP-runs; but anyway one can not get rid of the computation time. In theorem 3, using a modified form of Kolmogorov's complexity, we have shown that getting rid of the

simulation time is anyway not possible. This shows that the fact that f is not directly used, but only black-box-calls to f, in algo. 1, is not a strong weakness (at least within some polynomial on the computation time).

This gives a twofold theoretical foundation to GP, showing that (i) simulation + selection as in th. 2 outperforms any algorithm of the form of algo. 3 (ii) getting rid of the simulation time is not possible, and therefore using algo. 2 instead of 1 will not "very strongly" (more than polynomially) reduce the computational cost. Of course, this in the case of mining spaces of Turing-computable functions; in more restricted cases, with more decidability properties, the picture is very different. Refining comparisons between algorithms 1, 2, 3, is for the moment essentially an empirical research in the case of Turing-computable functions, termed genetic programming. The rare mathematical papers about genetic programming focus on restricted non-Turing-computable cases, whereas the most impressive results concern Turing-computable functions (also in the quantum case). This study is a step in the direction of iterative-Turing-computable models as a model of GP.

References

1. Banzhaf, W., Langdon, W.B.: Some considerations on the reason for bloat. Genetic Programming and Evolvable Machines 3(1), 81–91 (2002)
2. Blickle, T., Thiele, L.: Genetic programming and redundancy. In: Hopf, J. (ed.) Genetic Algorithms Workshop at KI-94. Max-Planck-Institut für Informatik, pp. 33–38 (1994)
3. Buhrman, H., Fortnow, L., Laplante, S.: Resource-bounded kolmogorov complexity revisited. SIAM Journal on Computing (2001)
4. Fortnow, L., Kummer, M.: Resource-bounded instance complexity. Theoretical Computer Science A 161, 123–140 (1996)
5. Gustafson, S.M., Langdon, W., Koza, J.: Bibliography on genetic programming. In: The Collection of Computer Science Bibliographies (2007)
6. Hamkins, J.D.: Infinite time turing machines. Minds Mach. 12(4), 521–539 (2002)
7. Khintchine, A.Y.: Sur la loi forte des grands nombres. Comptes Rendus de l'Academie des Sciences, 186 (1928)
8. Kolmogorov, A.N.: Logical basis for information theory and probability theory. IEEE trans. Inform. Theory IT-14, 662–664 (1968)
9. Koza, J.R.: Genetic Programming: On the Programming of Computers by Means of Natural Selection. MIT Press, Cambridge, MA, USA (1992)
10. Lugosi, G., Devroye, L., Györfi, L.: A probabilistic theory of pattern recognition. Springer, Heidelberg (1997)
11. Langdon, W.B.: The evolution of size in variable length representations. In: ICEC'98, pp. 633–638. IEEE Computer Society Press, Los Alamitos (1998)
12. Langdon, W.B., Poli, R.: Fitness causes bloat: Mutation. In: Koza, J. (ed.) Late Breaking Papers at GP'97, Stanford Bookstore, pp. 132–140 (1997)
13. Langdon, W.B., Poli, R.: Foundations of Genetic Programming. Springer, Heidelberg (2002)
14. Langdon, W.B., Soule, T., Poli, R., Foster, J.A.: The evolution of size and shape. In: Spector, L., Langdon, W.B., O'Reilly, U.-M., Angeline, P. (eds.) Advances in Genetic Programming III, pp. 163–190. MIT Press, Cambridge (1999)

15. Langdon, W.B.: Genetic Programming and Data Structures: Genetic Programming + Data Structures = Automatic Programming! April 24, 1998. Genetic Programming, vol. 1. Kluwer, Boston (1998)
16. Luke, S., Panait, L.: Lexicographic parsimony pressure. In: Langdon, W.B., et al. (eds.) GECCO 2002: Proceedings of the Genetic and Evolutionary Computation Conference, pp. 829–836. Morgan Kaufmann Publishers, San Francisco (2002)
17. Nordin, P., Banzhaf, W.: Complexity compression and evolution. In: Eshelman, L. (ed.) Genetic Algorithms: Proceedings of the Sixth International Conference (ICGA95), Pittsburgh, PA, USA, July 15-19, 1995, pp. 310–317. Morgan Kaufmann, San Francisco (1995)
18. Pareto, V.: Manuale d'Economia Politica. Società Editrice, Libraria, Milano (1906)
19. Ratle, A., Sebag, M.: Avoiding the bloat with probabilistic grammar-guided genetic programming. In: Collet, P., Fonlupt, C., Hao, J.-K., Lutton, E., Schoenauer, M. (eds.) EA 2001. LNCS, vol. 2310, Springer, Heidelberg (2002)
20. Rogers, H.: Theory of recursive functions and effective computability. McGraw-Hill, New York (1967)
21. Schmidthuber, J.: Hierarchies of generalized kolmogorov complexities and nonenumerable universal measures computable in the limit. International Journal of Foundations of Computer Science 13(4), 587–612 (2002)
22. Silva, S., Almeida, J.: Dynamic maximum tree depth: A simple technique for avoiding bloat in tree-based gp. In: Cantú-Paz, E., Foster, J.A., Deb, K., Davis, L., Roy, R., O'Reilly, U.-M., Beyer, H.-G., Kendall, G., Wilson, S.W., Harman, M., Wegener, J., Dasgupta, D., Potter, M.A., Schultz, A., Dowsland, K.A., Jonoska, N., Miller, J., Standish, R.K. (eds.) GECCO 2003. LNCS, vol. 2724, pp. 1776–1787. Springer, Heidelberg (2003)
23. Sipser, M.: A complexity theoretic approach to randomness. In: Proceedings of the 15th ACM Symposium on the Theory of Computing, pp. 330–335. ACM Press, New York (1983)
24. Solomonoff, R.: A formal theory of inductive inference, part 1. Inform. and Control 7(1), 1–22 (1964)
25. Solomonoff, R.: A formal theory of inductive inference, part 2. Inform. and Control 7(2), 222–254 (1964)
26. Soule, T., Foster, J.A.: Effects of code growth and parsimony pressure on populations in genetic programming. Evolutionary Computation 6(4), 293–309 (1998)
27. Soule, T.: Exons and code growth in genetic programming. In: Foster, J.A., Lutton, E., Miller, J., Ryan, C., Tettamanzi, A.G.B. (eds.) EuroGP 2002. LNCS, vol. 2278, pp. 142–151. Springer, Heidelberg (2002)
28. Turing, A.: On computable numbers, with an application to the entscheidungsproblem. In: Proceedings of the London Mathematical Society, vol. 2, 45, pp. 161–228 (reprinted in Davis, M.: The Undecidable, pp. 155-222, Raven Press, Ewlett, NY (1965)) (1936-1937)
29. Vapnik, V.: The nature of statistical learning. Springer, Heidelberg (1995)
30. Zhang, B.-T., Muhlenbein, H.: Balancing accuracy and parsimony in genetic programming. Evolutionary Computation 3(1), 17–38 (1995)

A Smallest Five-State Solution to the Firing Squad Synchronization Problem

Hiroshi Umeo and Takashi Yanagihara

Univ. of Osaka Electro-Communication,
Neyagawa-shi, Hastu-cho, 18-8, Osaka, 572-8530, Japan
{umeo,yanagihara}@cyt.osakac.ac.jp

Abstract. An existence or non-existence of five-state firing squad synchronization protocol has been a long-standing, famous open problem for a long time. In this paper, we answer partially to this problem by proposing a smallest five-state firing squad synchronization algorithm that can synchronize any one-dimensional cellular array of length $n = 2^k$ in $3n - 3$ steps for any positive integer k. The number *five* is the smallest one known at present in the class of synchronization protocols proposed so far.

1   Introduction

We study a synchronization problem that gives a finite-state protocol for synchronizing a large scale of cellular automata. The synchronization in cellular automata has been known as a firing squad synchronization problem since its development, in which it was originally proposed by J. Myhill in Moore [1964] to synchronize all parts of self-reproducing cellular automata. The firing squad synchronization problem has been studied extensively for more than 40 years [1-15]. The optimum-time (i.e., $(2n - 2)$-step) synchronization algorithm was devised first by Goto [1962] for one-dimensional array of length n. The algorithm needed many thousands of internal states for its realization. Afterwards, Waksman [1966], Balzer [1967], Gerken [1987] and Mazoyer [1987] developed an optimum-time algorithm and reduced the number of states realizing the algorithm, each with 16, 8, 7 and 6 states. On the other hand, Balzer [1967], Sanders [1994] and Berthiaume et al. [2004] have shown that there exists no four-state synchronization algorithm. Thus, an existence or non-existence of five-state firing squad synchronization protocol has been a long-standing, famous open problem for a long time.

In this paper, we answer partially to this problem by proposing a smallest five-state firing squad synchronization algorithm that can synchronize any one-dimensional cellular array of length $n = 2^k$ in $3n - 3$ steps for any positive integer k. The number *five* is the smallest one known at present in the class of synchronization protocols proposed so far. Due to the space availability we only give informal descriptions of the five-state solution.

J. Durand-Lose and M. Margenstern (Eds.): MCU 2007, LNCS 4664, pp. 291–302, 2007.
© Springer-Verlag Berlin Heidelberg 2007

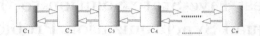

Fig. 1. A one-dimensional cellular automaton

2   Firing Squad Synchronization Problem

2.1   Firing Squad Synchronization Problem

Figure 1 shows a finite one-dimensional cellular array consisting of n cells. Each cell is an identical (except the border cells) finite-state automaton. The array operates in lock-step mode in such a way that the next state of each cell (except border cells) is determined by both its own present state and the present states of its left and right neighbors. All cells (*soldiers*), except the left end cell (*general*), are initially in the quiescent state at time $t = 0$ with the property that the next state of a quiescent cell with quiescent neighbors is the quiescent state again. At time $t = 0$, the left end cell C_1 is in the *fire-when-ready* state, which is the initiation signal for the array. The firing squad synchronization problem is to determine a description (state set and next-state function) for cells that ensures all cells enter the *fire* state at exactly the same time and for the first time. The set of states and the next-state function must be independent of n.

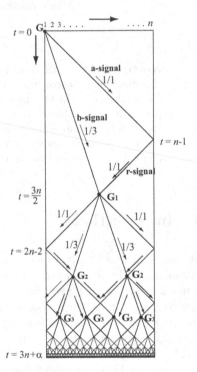

Fig. 2. A time-space diagram for $3n$-step firing squad synchronization algorithms

2.2   A Class of $3n$-Step Synchronization Algorithms

The $3n$-step algorithm that synchronizes n cells in $3n$ steps is an interesting class of synchronization algorithms due to its simplicity and straightforwardness and it is important in its own right in the design of cellular algorithms. Minsky and MacCarthy [1967] gave an idea for designing the $3n$-step synchronization algorithm and Fischer [1965] implemented the $3n$-step algorithm, yielding a 15-state implementation. Afterwards, Yunès [1994] proposed a seven-state $3n$-step firing squad synchronization algorithm. Umeo et al. [2006] also proposed a six-state $3n$-step symmetrical synchronization algorithm.

Figure 2 shows a time-space diagram for the well-known $3n$-step firing squad synchronization algorithm. The synchronization process can be viewed as a typical divide-and-conquer strategy that operates in parallel in the cellular space. An initial "*General*" G, located at left end of the array of size n, generates two special signals, referred to as *a-signal* and *b-signal*, which propagate in the right direction at a speed of $1/1$ (i.e., 1 cell per unit step) and $1/3$ (1 cell per three steps), respectively. The a-signal arrives at the right end at time $t = n - 1$, reflects there immediately, then continues to move at the same speed in the left direction. The reflected signal is referred to as *r-signal*. The b- and r-signals meet at a center cell(s), depending on the parity of n. In the case that n is odd, the cell $C_{\lceil n/2 \rceil}$ becomes a *General* at time $t = 3\lceil n/2 \rceil - 2$. The new *General* works for synchronizing both its left and right halves of the cellular space. Note that the *General* is shared by the two halves. In the case that n is even, two cells $C_{\lceil n/2 \rceil}$ and $C_{\lceil n/2 \rceil + 1}$ become the next *General* at time $t = 3\lceil n/2 \rceil$. Each *General* works for synchronizing its left and right halves of the cellular space, respectively.

Thus at time

$$t = \begin{cases} 3\lceil n/2 \rceil - 2 & n\text{: odd} \\ 3\lceil n/2 \rceil & n\text{: even,} \end{cases} \tag{1}$$

the array knows its center point(s) and generates one or two new *General(s)* G_1. The new *General(s)* G_1 generates the same $1/1$- and $1/3$-speed signals in both left and right directions and repeat the same procedures as above. Thus, the original synchronization problem of size n is divided into two sub-problems of size $\lceil n/2 \rceil$. In this way, the original array is split into equal two, four, eight, ..., subspaces synchronously. In the last, the original problem of size n can be split into small sub-problems of size 2. Most of the $3n$-step synchronization algorithms developed so far [3, 7, 12, 15] are based on similar schemes.

3 Five-State Synchronization Algorithm

In this section we present a five-state synchronization algorithm $\mathcal{A}$ for synchronizing any cellular array of length $n = 2^k$, where k is any positive integer. In the design of the $3n$-step synchronization algorithms, what is important is to find a center cell(s) of the cellular space to be synchronized. It is noted that two center cells can be always found at each iteration of centering processes in the case where $n = 2^k$. How can we implement those a-, b- and r-signals shown in Fig. 2 as a four-state transition table? Note that the fifth firing state cannot be used during the computation. First, we consider a special four-state cellular automaton M_0 with internal state set {Q, R, L, S} that can find center cells of a given array, initially staring from a configuration such that: all of the cells, excluding a left end cell, are in quiescent state Q and the left end cell is in a special *General* state R. By constructing the transition rule sets step-by-step, we show how to develop the final five-state synchronization protocol. The state "*" that will appear in the state transition rules below is a border state for the

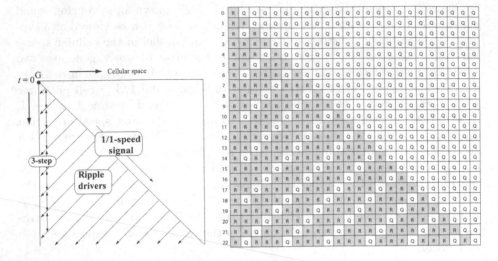

Fig. 3. Time-space diagram for generating ripple drivers propagating in the left direction (left) and its two-state implementation (right)

left and right end cells. According to conventions, the border state "*" is not counted in the number of states.

3.1   Two-State Implementation for Ripple Drivers

In this subsection first we give a two-state implementation of *ripple drivers* that enable the propagation of the b-signal at 1/3 speed. The a-signal is also realized within the two-state implementation. See Fig. 3. The *General* at the left end is in state R and all other cells $C_i, 2 \leq i \leq n$, are in state Q at time $t = 0$. Those quiescent cells keep the quiescent state with the rules: Q Q Q $\to$ Q; Q Q * $\to$ Q. At time $t = 0$ the *General* in state R generates an a-signal represented in state R. The a-signal propagates in the right direction. A rule: R Q Q $\to$ R is used for the generation of the a-signal and its propagation. At every two steps the a-signal generates a 1/1 speed signal in state Q. The 1/1 speed signal is transmitted in the reverse direction. Any cell in state R with a left neighbor in state R and a right neighbor in Q takes a state Q with a rule: R R Q $\to$ Q. The state Q is propagated in the left direction at 1/1 speed with the next two rules: R R Q $\to$ Q; R Q R $\to$ R. This yields many ripple drivers (described later) propagating toward its left end. Any cell that has received the a-signal keeps the R state as long as no Q state in its right neighbor. The following four rules: Q R R $\to$ R; Q R Q $\to$ R; * R Q $\to$ R; * R R $\to$ R are used for this purpose. The next rule set r_1 consisting of ten local rules given above is used for the generation and propagation of the a-signal and generating ripple drivers. Figure 3 shows the time-space diagram and its two-state implementation. Note that we need no counter for the generation of ripple drivers that arrives at C_1 at every three steps.

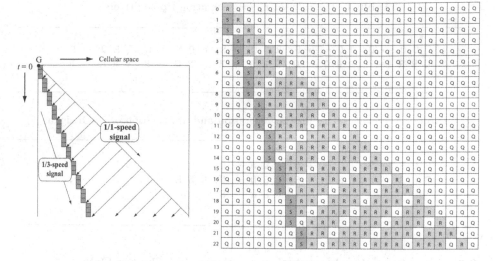

Fig. 4. Time-space diagram for generating the 1/3 speed b-signal and its three-state implementation

3.2 Three-State Implementation for a- and b-Signals

In this subsection, we show that three states suffice for the implementation of the b-signal with 1/3 speed. The time separation of each consecutive ripple driver is three-step. The b-signal is represented as a state S staying at a cell for three steps. The b-signal on the leftmost cell C_1 takes a state R, S, S in order for the first three steps, i.e. at time $t = 0, 1$ and 2. Each ripple driver can be used to drive the propagation of the b-signal to its right neighbor. The three-step separation of two consecutive ripples enables the b-signal to propagate at 1/3 speed.

To implement the b-signal we first delete the next two rules from r_1:

$$* \ R \ Q \ \rightarrow \ R; \quad * \ R \ R \ \rightarrow \ R;$$

which involve the state transition on C_1, yielding the rule set $r_{1'}$. Then we add the following rule set r_2 to the rule set $r_{1'}$. A cell in state S keeps the state for three steps and a ripple driver described above arrives at its right neighbour at every three steps. Then at the next step the state S disappears from the cell and its right neighbor cell takes the state S. In this way, the b-signal in state S can be propagated at 1/3 speed in the right direction. Figure 4 (left) shows the time-space diagram for the propagation of the b-signal and its three-state implementation based on $r_{1'} \cup r_2$ is given in Fig. 4 (right). We omit the details of each rule in r_2, since it is easily seen with the help of those snapshots in Fig. 4 (right) that which rule in r_2 is used for the propagation of the b-signal. Thus we can show that three states suffice for the generation and propagation of the a- and b-signals. It is noted that any cell where the b-signal passes by keeps the quiescent state again.

Table 1. The rule set r_1 for generating ripple drivers

Q Q Q → Q; Q Q * → Q; R Q Q → R; R Q R → R; Q R Q → R;
Q R R → R; R R Q → Q; R R R → R; * R Q → R; * R R → R.

Table 2. The rule set r_2 for the generation and propagation of the b-signal

S Q R → S; * Q Q → Q; * Q S → Q; Q Q S → Q; S R Q → Q;
S R R → R; * R Q → S; Q S Q → Q; Q S R → S; * S Q → Q;
* S R → S.

3.3 Four-State Implementation for Searching Center Cells

The fourth state L is used for the reflected r-signal. The following rule set r_3 includes rules for generation and propagation of the reflected signal. At time $t = n-1$, the a-signal arrives at C_n and the reflected signal in state L is generated at time $t = n$ on C_n. The return signal propagates in the left direction at 1/1 speed. Any cell where the return signal passes by keeps a quiescent state. At time $t = 3n/2$, the b-signal and the return signal meet on $C_{n/2}$ and $C_{n/2+1}$. At the next step, the cells $C_{n/2}$ and $C_{n/2+1}$ take a state L and R with rules: S L Q → R; Q S L → L. The state L and R act as a *General* for the left and right half of the array, respectively. For these purposes we add the following rule set r_3 to the original rule set $r_{1'} \cup r_2$, thus yielding the rule set $\mathcal{R}_0 = r_{1'} \cup r_2 \cup r_3$.

Table 3. The rule set r_3 for the return signal

R Q * → R; R R * → L; L Q Q → Q; L Q * → Q; R R L → L;
S R L → L; R L Q → Q; R L * → Q; S L Q → R; Q S L → L;
L R Q → S; S S R → S; S S Q → Q.

Let S_i^t denote the state of C_i at time t. The next state transition function $\mathcal{R}_0$ of M_0, shown in Fig. 5, consists of four sub-tables for each state in $\{Q, R, L, S\}$. Each state on the first row (column) indicates a state of right (left) neighbor cell, respectively. Each entry of the sub-tables shows a state at the next step. In general the border state "*" is not counted as a number of states. We have the following [Lemma 1] on finding a center of the given array.

State Q

Left\Right	Q	R	L	S	*
Q	Q			Q	Q
R	R	R			R
L	Q				Q
S		S			
*	Q				Q

State R

Left\Right	Q	R	L	S	*
Q	R	R			
R	Q	R	L		L
L	S				
S	Q	R	L		
*	S				

State L

Left\Right	Q	R	L	S	*
Q					
R	Q				Q
L					
S	R				
*					

State S

Left\Right	Q	R	L	S	*
Q	Q	S	L		
R					
L					
S	Q	S			
*	Q	S			

Fig. 5. A four-state transition table $\mathcal{R}_0$ for finding center cells of cellular arrays.

```
    1 2 3 4 5 6 7 8
 0  R Q Q Q Q Q Q Q
 1  S R Q Q Q Q Q Q
 2  S Q R Q Q Q Q Q
 3  Q S R R Q Q Q Q
 4  Q S R Q R Q Q Q
 5  Q S Q R R R Q Q
 6  Q Q S R R Q R Q
 7  Q Q S R Q R R R
 8  Q Q Q S R R R L
 9  Q Q Q S R R L Q
10  Q Q Q S R L Q Q
11  Q Q Q S L Q Q Q
12  Q Q Q L R Q Q Q
```

```
    1 2 3 4 5 6 7 8 9 10 11 12 13 14 15 16
 0  R Q Q Q Q Q Q Q Q Q  Q  Q  Q  Q  Q  Q
 1  S R Q Q Q Q Q Q Q Q  Q  Q  Q  Q  Q  Q
 2  S Q R Q Q Q Q Q Q Q  Q  Q  Q  Q  Q  Q
 3  Q S R R Q Q Q Q Q Q  Q  Q  Q  Q  Q  Q
 4  Q S R Q R Q Q Q Q Q  Q  Q  Q  Q  Q  Q
 5  Q S Q R R R Q Q Q Q  Q  Q  Q  Q  Q  Q
 6  Q Q S R R Q R Q Q Q  Q  Q  Q  Q  Q  Q
 7  Q Q S R Q R R R Q Q  Q  Q  Q  Q  Q  Q
 8  Q Q S Q R R R Q R Q  Q  Q  Q  Q  Q  Q
 9  Q Q Q S R R R R Q R  Q  Q  Q  Q  Q  Q
10  Q Q Q S R Q R R R Q  R  Q  Q  Q  Q  Q
11  Q Q Q S Q R R R Q R  R  R  Q  Q  Q  Q
12  Q Q Q Q S R R Q R R  Q  R  Q  Q  Q  Q
13  Q Q Q Q S R Q R R Q  R  R  R  Q  Q  Q
14  Q Q Q Q S Q R R R Q  R  R  R  Q  R  Q
15  Q Q Q Q Q S R R Q R  R  R  Q  R  R  R
16  Q Q Q Q Q S R Q R R  R  Q  R  R  R  L
17  Q Q Q Q Q S Q R R R  Q  R  R  R  L  Q
18  Q Q Q Q Q Q S R R Q  R  R  R  L  Q  Q
19  Q Q Q Q Q Q S R Q R  R  R  L  Q  Q  Q
20  Q Q Q Q Q Q S Q R R  R  L  Q  Q  Q  Q
21  Q Q Q Q Q Q Q S R R  L  Q  Q  Q  Q  Q
22  Q Q Q Q Q Q Q S R L  Q  Q  Q  Q  Q  Q
23  Q Q Q Q Q Q Q S L Q  Q  Q  Q  Q  Q  Q
24  Q Q Q Q Q Q Q L R Q  Q  Q  Q  Q  Q  Q
```

Fig. 6. Snapshots for searching for center cells

[**Lemma 1**]. Let k be any positive integer such that $k \geq 2$ and M_0 be a four-state cellular automaton of length $n = 2^k$ with the transition table $\mathcal{R}_0$. We assume that M_0 has an initial configuration such that:

1. $S_1^0 = L$, $S_i^0 = Q, 2 \leq i \leq n$,

Then, M_0 takes the following configuration at time $t = 3n/2$:

2. At time $t = 3n/2$,
$S_{n/2}^t = L$, $S_{n/2+1}^t = R$, $S_i^t = Q$, for any i such that $1 \leq i \leq n, i \neq n/2, i \neq n/2 + 1$.

Figure 6 shows how the cellular automaton M_0 can find the center cells of the cellular space using only four states. Thus the rules in $\mathcal{R}_0$ are used for searching center cells of arrays in which a *General* R is stationed at its left end. To look for center cells of arrays in which a *General* L is posted at its right end, we develop the following rule set $\mathbf{r}_4$ based on the previous way. The a- and r-signals are

Table 4. The rule set r_4 for finding center cells

$$
\begin{array}{l}
\text{Q Q L} \rightarrow \text{L}; \ \text{Q L R} \rightarrow \text{S}; \ \text{L S S} \rightarrow \text{S}; \ \text{Q L S} \rightarrow \text{Q}; \ \text{Q L Q} \rightarrow \text{L}; \\
\text{L Q S} \rightarrow \text{S}; \ \text{Q S S} \rightarrow \text{Q}; \ \text{L S Q} \rightarrow \text{S}; \ \text{S Q Q} \rightarrow \text{Q}; \ \text{L L S} \rightarrow \text{L}; \\
\text{Q L L} \rightarrow \text{Q}; \ \text{L Q L} \rightarrow \text{L}; \ \text{L L Q} \rightarrow \text{L}; \ \text{L L L} \rightarrow \text{L}; \ * \ \text{Q L} \rightarrow \text{L}; \\
* \ \text{L L} \rightarrow \text{R}; \ * \ \text{R L} \rightarrow \text{Q}; \ \text{R L L} \rightarrow \text{R}; \ * \ \text{Q R} \rightarrow \text{Q}; \ \text{Q R L} \rightarrow \text{Q}; \\
\text{Q Q R} \rightarrow \text{Q}; \ \text{R L S} \rightarrow \text{R}; \ \text{Q R S} \rightarrow \text{L}; \ \text{R S Q} \rightarrow \text{R}. \ \text{R L R} \rightarrow \text{Q}; \\
\quad\quad \text{L R L} \rightarrow \text{Q}; \ * \ \text{L S} \rightarrow \text{R}; \ \text{S R} * \rightarrow \text{L}.
\end{array}
$$

---

represented by the state L and R, respectively. By letting $\mathcal{R}_1 = \mathcal{R}_0 \cup r_4$, we get the next [Lemma 2].

[Lemma 2]. Let k be any positive integer such that $k \geq 2$ and M_1 be the four-state cellular automaton of length $n = 2^k$ with the transition table $\mathcal{R}_1$. We assume that M_1 has an initial configuration such that:

1. $S^0_{n/2} = L$, $S^0_{n/2+1} = R$, $S^0_i = Q$, for any i such that $1 \leq i \leq n, i \neq n/2, i \neq n/2 + 1$.

   Then, M_1 takes the following configuration at time $t = 3n/4$.

2. At time $t = 3n/4$, $S^t_{n/4} = L$, $S^t_{n/4+1} = R$, $S^t_{3n/4} = L$, $S^t_{3n/4+1} = R$, $S^0_i = Q$, for any i such that $1 \leq i \leq n, i \neq n/4, i \neq n/4 + 1, i \neq 3n/4, i \neq 3n/4 + 1$.

3.4 Transition Rules for Synchronizing Small Subarrays of Length $n = 2$

By using the halving [Lemma 1, 2] recursively, the original problem is reduced to many small synchronization problems of size 2. In Fig. 8, we illustrate snapshots for synchronizing an array of size 2. Each *General* in state L and R works for synchronizing each left and right sub-arrays independently. Both of them can be synchronized at exactly three steps. To synchronize them at exactly three steps, we add the following seven rules:

3.5 Five-State Synchronization Protocol

A five-state cellular automaton M is defined as follows: The set of internal states of M is $\{Q, L, R, S, F\}$, where Q is the *quiescent* state, R is the initial *General* state and F is the *firing* state, respectively. In Fig. 9 we give our final transition rule set $\mathcal{R} = \mathcal{R}_1 \cup r_f$. Let $T(n)$ be time complexity for synchronizing any array of length $n = 2^k$, for any integer $k \geq 1$. Then we have:

$$
T(n) = \begin{cases} T(n/2) + 3n/2 & n = 2^k, k \geq 2, \\ 3 & n = 2. \end{cases} \tag{2}
$$

	1	2	3	4	5	6	7	8	9	10	11	12	13	14	15	16
0	O	O	O	O	O	O	O	O	L	R	O	O	O	O	O	O
1	O	O	O	O	O	O	L	S	S	R	O	O	O	O	O	O
2	O	O	O	O	O	L	O	S	S	O	R	O	O	O	O	O
3	O	O	O	O	L	L	S	O	O	S	R	R	O	O	O	O
4	O	O	O	L	O	L	S	O	O	S	R	O	R	O	O	O
5	O	O	L	L	L	O	S	O	O	S	R	R	R	O	O	O
6	O	L	O	L	L	S	O	O	O	O	S	R	R	R	O	R
7	L	L	L	O	L	S	O	O	O	O	S	R	O	R	R	R
8	R	L	L	L	O	S	O	O	O	O	S	O	R	R	R	L
9	O	R	L	L	S	O	O	O	O	O	O	S	R	R	L	O
10	O	O	R	L	S	O	O	O	O	O	O	S	R	L	O	O
11	O	O	O	R	S	O	O	O	O	O	O	S	L	O	O	O
12	Q	Q	Q	L	R	Q	Q	Q	Q	Q	Q	L	R	Q	Q	Q

Fig. 7. Snapshots for searching for center cells

	size 2		size 2	
$t = 0$	Q	L	R	Q
1	L	L	R	R
2	R	S	S	L
3	F	F	F	F

Fig. 8. Snapshots for synchronizing an array of size 2

State Q

Left\Right	Q	R	L	S	*
Q	Q	Q	L	Q	Q
R	R	R			R
L	Q		L	S	Q
S	Q	S			
*	Q	Q	L	Q	

State R

Left\Right	Q	R	L	S	*
Q	R	R	Q	L	
R	Q	R	L		L
L	S		Q	F	
S	Q	R	L		L
*	S		Q	F	

State L

Left\Right	Q	R	L	S	*
Q	L	S	Q	Q	
R	Q	Q	R	R	Q
L	L		L	L	
S	R	F			F
*			R	R	

State S

Left\Right	Q	R	L	S	*
Q	Q	S	L	Q	
R	R			F	
L	S			S	
S	Q	S	F		
*	Q	S	F		

Fig. 9. A state transition table $\mathcal{R}$ for the five-state $3n$-step firing squad synchronization algorithm $\mathcal{A}$

Table 5. The rule set $\mathbf{r}_f$ for synchronizing an array of lengh $n = 2$

$$* \text{ R S} \rightarrow \text{F}; \ \text{R S S} \rightarrow \text{F}; \ \text{S S L} \rightarrow \text{F}; \ \text{S L R} \rightarrow \text{F}; \ \text{L R S} \rightarrow \text{F};$$
$$\text{S L} * \rightarrow \text{F}; \ * \text{ S L} \rightarrow \text{F}.$$

The recurrence equation can be expressed as $T(n) = 3n - 3$. Thus we have:

[Theorem 3]. There exists a 5-state cellular automaton that can synchronize any array of length $n = 2^k$ in $3n - 3$ steps, where k is any positive integer.

Figure 10 shows snapshots for the 5-state firing squad synchronization algorithm on 8 and 16 cells.

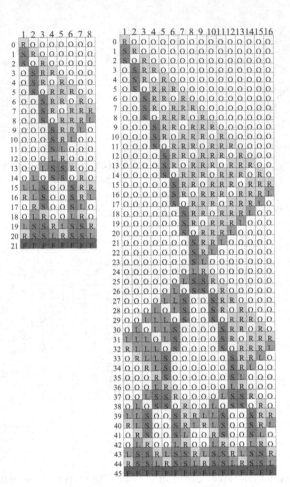

Fig. 10. Snapshots for the 5-state firing squad synchronization algorithm on 8 and 16 cells

4   State-Change Complexity

Vollmar [1981] introduced a state-change complexity in order to measure the efficiency of cellular algorithms and showed that $\Omega(n \log n)$ state changes are required for the synchronization of n cells in $(2n - 2)$ steps.

[Theorem 4].[13] $\Omega(n \log n)$ state-change is necessary for synchronizing n cells. Let $S(n)$ be total number of state changes for the five-state synchronization algorithm $\mathcal{A}$ on n cells. We have $S(n) = \alpha n^2 + 2S(n/2) = O(n^2)$ for some constant α. Thus we have:

[Theorem 5]. The five-state synchronization algorithm $\mathcal{A}$ has $O(n^2)$ state-change complexity.

Table 6. A comparison of $3n$-step firing squad synchronization algorithms

Algorithm	# States	# Rules	Time complexity	State-change complexity	Generals's position	Type	Notes	Ref.
Minsky and MaCcarthy [1967]	13	–	$3n + \theta_n \log n + c$	$O(n \log n)$	left	thread	$0 \leq \theta_n < 1$	[7]
Fischer [1965]	15	–	$3n - 4$	$O(n \log n)$	left	thread	–	[3]
Yunès [1994]	7	105	$3n \pm 2\theta_n \log n + c$	$O(n \log n)$	left	thread	$0 \leq \theta_n < 1$	[15]
Yunès [1994]	7	107	$3n \pm 2\theta_n \log n + c$	$O(n \log n)$	left	thread	$0 \leq \theta_n < 1$	[15]
Settle and Simon [2002]	6	134	$3n + 1$	$O(n^2)$	right	plane	–	[10]
Settle and Simon [2002]	7	127	$2n - 2 + k$	$O(n^2)$	arbitrary	plane	–	[10]
Umeo et al. [2006]	6	78	$3n + O(\log n)$	$O(n^2)$	left	plane	–	[12]
Umeo et al. [2006]	6	115	$\max(k, n - k + 1)$ $+ 2n + O(\log n)$	$O(n^2)$	arbitrary	plane	–	[12]
this paper	5	67	$3n - 3$	$O(n^2)$	left	plane	$n = 2^k$	–

5 Conclusions

An existence or non-existence of five-state firing squad synchronization protocol has been a long-standing, famous open problem for a long time. In this paper, we have answered partially to this problem by proposing a smallest five-state firing squad synchronization protocol that can synchronize any one-dimensional cellular array of length $n = 2^k$ in $3n - 3$ steps for any positive integer k. The number *five* is the smallest one known at present in the class of synchronization protocols proposed so far. Here, in the last, we present Table 6 that shows a quantitative comparison of $3n$-step synchronization protocols proposed so far with respect to the number of internal states of each finite state automaton, the number of transition rules realizing the synchronization and state-change complexity.

References

1. Balzer, R.: An 8-state minimal time solution to the firing squad synchronization problem. Information and Control 10, 22–42 (1967)
2. Berthiaume, A., Bittner, T., Perkovic, L., Settle, A., Simin, J.: Bounding the firing squad synchronization problem on a ring. Theoretical Computer Science 320, 213–228 (2004)
3. Fischer, P.C.: Generation of primes by a one-dimensional real-time iterative array. J. of ACM 12(3), 388–394 (1965)
4. Gerken, H.-D.: Über Synchronisations - Probleme bei Zellularautomaten. Diplomarbeit, Institut für Theoretische Informatik, Technische Universität Braunschweig, p. 50 (1987)
5. Goto, E.: A minimal time solution of the firing squad problem. Dittoed course notes for Applied Mathematics, vol. 298, pp. 52–59. Harvard University, Cambridge (1962)

6. Mazoyer, J.: A six-state minimal time solution to the firing squad synchronization problem. Theoretical Computer Science 50, 183–238 (1987)
7. Minsky, M.L.: Computation: Finite and infinite machines, pp. 28–29. Prentice-Hall, Englewood Cliffs (1967)
8. Moore, E.F.: The firing squad synchronization problem. In: Moore, E.F. (ed.) Sequential Machines, Selected Papers, pp. 213–214. Addison-Wesley, Reading MA (1964)
9. Sanders, P.: Massively parallel search for transition-tables of polyautomata. In: Jesshope, C., Jossifov, V., Wilhelmi, W. (eds.) Proc. of the VI International Workshop on Parallel Processing by Cellular Automata and Arrays, pp. 99–108. Akademie (1994)
10. Settle, A., Simon, J.: Smaller solutions for the firing squad. Theoretical Computer Science 276, 83–109 (2002)
11. Umeo, H., Hisaoka, M., Sogabe, T.: A Survey on Firing Squad Synchronization Algorithms for One-Dimensional Cellular Automata. International Journal of Unconventional Computing 1, 403–426 (2005)
12. Umeo, H., Maeda, M., Hongyo, K.: A design of symmetrical six-state $3n$-step firing squad synchronization algorithms and their implementations. In: El Yacoubi, S., Chopard, B., Bandini, S. (eds.) ACRI 2006. LNCS, vol. 4173, pp. 157–168. Springer, Heidelberg (2006)
13. Vollmar, R.: On cellular automata with a finite number of state changes. Computing, Supplementum 3, 181–191 (1981)
14. Waksman, A.: An optimum solution to the firing squad synchronization problem. Information and Control 9, 66–78 (1966)
15. Yunès, J.B.: Seven-state solution to the firing squad synchronization problem. Theoretical Computer Science 127, 313–332 (1994)

Small Semi-weakly Universal Turing Machines

Damien Woods[1] and Turlough Neary[2]

[1] Department of Computer Science,
University College Cork, Ireland
d.woods@cs.ucc.ie
[2] TASS, Department of Computer Science,
National University of Ireland Maynooth, Ireland
tneary@cs.may.ie

Abstract. We present two small universal Turing machines that have 3 states and 7 symbols, and 4 states and 5 symbols respectively. These machines are semi-weak which means that on one side of the input they have an infinitely repeated word and on the other side there is the usual infinitely repeated blank symbol. This work can be regarded as a continuation of early work by Watanabe on semi-weak machines. One of our machines has only 17 transition rules making it the smallest known semi-weakly universal Turing machine. Interestingly, our two machines are symmetric with Watanabe's 7-state and 3-symbol, and 5-state and 4-symbol machines, even though we use a different simulation technique.

1 Introduction

Shannon [22] was the first to consider the question of finding the smallest possible universal Turing machine, where size is the number of states and symbols. From the early sixties, Minsky and Watanabe had a running competition to see who could come up with the smallest machines [10,11,23,24,25]. In 1962, Minsky [11] found a small 7-state, 4-symbol universal Turing machine. Minsky's machine worked by simulating 2-tag systems, which where shown to be universal by Cocke and Minsky [2]. Rogozhin [20] extended Minsky's technique of 2-tag simulation and found small machines with a number of state-symbol pairs. Subsequently, some of Rogozhin's machines were reduced in size or improved by Robinson [19], Rogozhin [21], Kudlek and Rogozhin [6], Baiocchi [1]. Neary and Woods [12,15] have recently found small machines that simulate another variant of tag systems called bi-tag systems. All of the smallest known Turing machines, that obey the standard definition (deterministic, one tape, one head), simulate either 2-tag or bi-tag systems. They are plotted as circles and triangles in Figure 1.

Interestingly, Watanabe [23,24,25] managed to find small machines (some were smaller than Minsky's) by generalising the standard Turing machine definition. Instead of having an infinitely repeated blank symbol to the left and right of the input, Watanabe's machines have an infinitely repeated word to one side of the input and an infinitely repeated blank symbol to the other side. We call such machines semi-weak. Watanabe found 7-state, 3-symbol, and 5-state, 4-symbol semi-weakly universal machines that are plotted as hollow diamonds in Figure 1.

J. Durand-Lose and M. Margenstern (Eds.): MCU 2007, LNCS 4664, pp. 303–315, 2007.

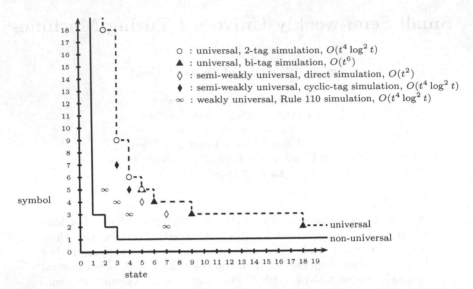

symbol

state

Fig. 1. State-symbol plot of the smallest universal Turing machines to date. Our semi-weak machines are shown as solid diamonds and Watanabe's as hollow diamonds. The standard and semi-weak machines are symmetric about the line where state = symbol.

A further generalisation are weak machines where we allow an infinitely repeated word to the left of the input and another to the right. Cook [3] and Wolfram [26] have found very small weakly universal machines which are illustrated as ∞ symbols in Figure 1. These weak machines simulate the cellular automaton Rule 110. Cook [3] proved (the proof is also sketched in Wolfram [26]) that Rule 110 is universal by showing that it simulates cyclic tag systems, which in turn simulate 2-tag systems.

The non-universal curve in Figure 1 is shown for the standard Turing machine definition. The 1-symbol case is trivial, and the 1-state case was shown by Shannon [22] and, via another method, Hermann [4]. Pavlotskaya [16] and, via another method, Kudlek [5], proved that the halting problem is decidable for 2-state, 2-symbol machines, where one transition rule is reserved for halting. Pavlotskaya [17] proved that the halting problem is decidable for 3-state, 2-symbol machines, and also claimed [16], without proof, that the halting problem is decidable for 2-state, 3-symbol machines. Both cases assume that one transition rule is reserved for halting. It is not difficult to generalise these results to (semi-)weak machines with 1 state or 1 symbol. It is currently unknown if all lower bounds in Figure 1 generalise to (semi-)weak machines.

It is also known from the work of Margenstern [7] and Michel [9] that the region between the non-universal curve and the smallest standard universal machines contains (standard) machines that simulate the $3x + 1$ problem and other related problems. These results, along with the weakly and semi-weakly universal machines, lend weight to the idea that finding non-universal lowerbounds in this region is difficult. For results on other generalisations of the Turing machine model see [8,18], for example.

Figure 1 shows our two new semi-weak machines as solid diamonds. These machines simulate cyclic tag systems, which were used [3] to show that Rule 110 is universal. It is interesting to note that our machines are symmetric with those of Watanabe, despite the fact that we use a different simulation technique. Our 4-state, 5-symbol machine has only 17 transition rules, making it the smallest known semi-weakly universal machine (Watanabe's 5-state, 4-symbol machine has 18 transition rules). The time overhead for our machines is polynomial. More precisely, if M is a single tape deterministic Turing machine that runs in time t, then M is simulated by each of our semi-weak machines in time $O(t^4 \log^2 t)$. See [13,14,27,28] for further results and discussion related to the time complexity of small universal Turing machines.

1.1 Preliminaries

All of the Turing machines considered in this paper are deterministic and have one tape. Our 3-state, 7-symbol universal Turing machine is denoted $U_{3,7}$ and our 4-state, 5-symbol machine is denoted $U_{4,5}$. We let $\langle x \rangle$ denote the encoding of x. We write $c_1 \vdash c_2$ when configuration c_2 follows from c_1 in 1 computation step, and $c_1 \vdash^t c_2$ when c_2 follows from c_1 in t steps.

2   Cyclic Tag Systems

We begin by defining cyclic tag systems [3].

Definition 1 (cyclic tag system). *A cyclic tag system* $C = \alpha_0, \alpha_1, \ldots, \alpha_{p-1}$ *is a list of binary words* $\alpha_m \in \{0,1\}^*$ *called appendants.*

A *configuration* of a cyclic tag system consists of (i) a *marker* $m \in \{0, 1, \ldots, p-1\}$ that points to a single appendant α_m in C, and (ii) a *dataword* $w = x_0 x_1 \ldots x_{l-1} \in \{0,1\}^*$. Intuitively the list C is a program with the marker pointing at instruction α_m. At the initial configuration the marker points at appendant α_0 and w is the binary input word.

Definition 2 (computation step of a cyclic tag system). *A computation step is deterministic and acts on a configuration in one of two ways:*

- *If* $x_0 = 0$ *then* x_0 *is deleted and the marker moves to appendant* $\alpha_{(m+1) \mod p}$.
- *If* $x_0 = 1$ *then* x_0 *is deleted, the word* α_m *is appended onto the right end of* w, *and the marker moves to appendant* $\alpha_{(m+1) \mod p}$.

A cyclic tag system completes its computation if (i) the dataword is the empty word, or (ii) it enters a repeating sequence of configurations. The complexity measures of time and space are defined in the obvious way.

Example 1. (cyclic tag system computation) Let $C = 00, 1010, 10$ be a cyclic tag system with input word 0010010. Below we give the first four steps of the computation. In each configuration C is given on the left with the marked appendant highlighted in bold font.

$$\textbf{00}, 1010, 10 \quad 0010010 \qquad \vdash \qquad 00, \textbf{1010}, 10 \quad 010010$$
$$\vdash \qquad 00, 1010, \textbf{10} \quad 10010 \qquad \vdash \qquad \textbf{00}, 1010, 10 \quad 001010$$
$$\vdash \qquad 00, \textbf{1010}, 10 \quad 01010 \qquad \vdash \qquad \dots$$

Cyclic tag systems were proved universal by their ability to simulate 2-tag systems [3]. Recently we have shown that cyclic tag systems simulate Turing machines in polynomial time:

Theorem 1 ([13]). *Let M be a single-tape deterministic Turing machine that computes in time t. There is a cyclic tag system C_M that simulates the computation of M in time $O(t^3 \log t)$.*

Note that in order to calculate this upper bound we substitute space bounds for time bounds whenever possible in the analysis.

3   3-State, 7-Symbol Universal Turing Machine

$U_{3,7}$ simulates cyclic tag systems. The cyclic tag system binary input dataword is written directly to the tape, no special encoding is required. The cyclic tag system's list of appendants is reversed and encoded to the left of the input. This encoded list is repeated infinitely often to the left. $U_{3,7}$ computes by erasing one encoded appendant for each 0 on the dataword. If the symbol 1 is read then the next available (encoded) appendant to the left is appended to the dataword, and the appendant is erased. Since the appendants are repeated to the left, this process increments (mod p) through the list of appendants.

3.1 $U_{3,7}$

	u_1	u_2	u_3
0	$\lambda L u_1$	$\cancel{1} R u_2$	$\cancel{1} R u_3$
1	$\lambda L u_2$	$z R u_2$	$z R u_3$
λ	$b R u_1$	$b R u_2$	$b R u_3$
$\emptyset$	$\lambda L u_1$	$\lambda L u_3$	$b R u_2$
$\cancel{1}$		$0 L u_2$	$1 L u_2$
z	$b R u_1$	$1 L u_2$	$b R u_1$
b	$\lambda L u_1$	$\lambda L u_2$	$b R u_3$

Table of behaviour for $U_{3,7}$. The start state is u_1 and the blank symbol is $\cancel{1}$.

3.2   Encoding

For our 3-state, 7-symbol machine an appendant $\alpha \in \{0, 1\}^*$ is encoded in the following manner. Firstly, the order of the symbols in α is reversed to give α_R. Then the symbol 0 is encoded as $\emptyset\emptyset$, and 1 is encoded as $b\emptyset$. The encoded α_R is then prepended with the two symbols $z\emptyset$. For example, if $\alpha = 100$ then this appendant is encoded as $\langle \alpha \rangle = z\emptyset\emptyset\emptyset\emptyset\emptyset b\emptyset$. Finally the order of appendants are also reversed so that the list of appendants $\alpha_0, \alpha_1, \ldots, \alpha_{p-1}$ are encoded as $\langle \alpha_{p-1} \rangle \langle \alpha_{p-2} \rangle \ldots \langle \alpha_0 \rangle$. This encoded list is repeated infinitely often, to the left, on the tape of $U_{3,7}$. The blank symbol for $U_{3,7}$ is $\bar{1}$ and the cyclic tag system input is written directly on the tape of $U_{3,7}$. Thus the initial configuration of the cyclic tag system given in Example 1 is encoded as

$$u_1, \ldots z\emptyset\emptyset\emptyset b\emptyset \; z\emptyset\emptyset\emptyset b\emptyset\emptyset\emptyset b\emptyset \; z\emptyset\emptyset\emptyset\emptyset\emptyset \; \underline{0}010010 \; \bar{1}\bar{1}\bar{1} \ldots \tag{1}$$

where the underline denotes the tape head position, the three encoded appendants are repeated infinitely to the left, and the extra whitespace is for human readability purposes only.

3.3 Simulation

To show how $U_{3,7}$ computes we simulate the first 3 steps of the cyclic tag computation from Example 1.

Example 2. Beginning with the configuration given in Equation (1), $U_{3,7}$ reads the leftmost 0 in the input, in state u_1, and then indexes the second encoded appendant to the left, changing each symbol to λ until it reaches z, to give the configuration

$$u_1, \ldots z\emptyset\emptyset\emptyset b\emptyset \; z\emptyset\emptyset\emptyset b\emptyset\emptyset\emptyset b\emptyset \; \underline{z}\lambda\lambda\lambda\lambda\lambda \; \lambda 010010 \; \bar{1}\bar{1}\bar{1} \ldots$$

These steps have the effect of reading and erasing the first 0 in the dataword (input), and simulating the incrementing of the marker to the next (second) appendant. The head then scans right, to read the second dataword symbol.

$$u_1, \ldots z\emptyset\emptyset\emptyset b\emptyset \; z\emptyset\emptyset\emptyset b\emptyset\emptyset\emptyset b\emptyset \; bbbbbb \; b\underline{0}10010 \; \bar{1}\bar{1}\bar{1} \ldots$$

Again we read 0 in the dataword which causes us to index the third appendant

$$u_1, \ldots z\emptyset\emptyset\emptyset b\emptyset \; \underline{z}\lambda\lambda\lambda\lambda\lambda\lambda\lambda\lambda \; \lambda\lambda\lambda\lambda\lambda\lambda \; \lambda\lambda10010 \; \bar{1}\bar{1}\bar{1} \ldots$$

and then return to the third input symbol.

$$u_1, \ldots z\emptyset\emptyset\emptyset b\emptyset \; bbbbbbbb \; bbbbbb \; bb\underline{1}0010 \; \bar{1}\bar{1}\bar{1} \ldots$$

The input symbol 1 causes $U_{3,7}$ to enter a 'print cycle' which iterates the following: we scan left in state u_2, if we read $\emptyset\emptyset$ then we scan right in state u_2 and print 0, if we read $b\emptyset$ then we scan right in state u_3 and print 1. We exit the cycle if we read $z\emptyset$. We now contine our simulation to the point where we are about to read an encoded 1 in the third appendant

$$u_3, \ldots z\emptyset\emptyset\emptyset \underline{b}\lambda \; \lambda\lambda\lambda\lambda\lambda\lambda\lambda\lambda \; \lambda\lambda\lambda\lambda\lambda\lambda \; \lambda\lambda\lambda0010 \; \bar{1}\bar{1}\bar{1} \ldots$$

This causes $U_{3,7}$ to scan right, append a 1 to the dataword, and return left to read the next encoded symbol in the third appendant

$$u_3, \ldots z\emptyset\emptyset\underline{\lambda}\lambda\lambda \; \lambda\lambda\lambda\lambda\lambda\lambda\lambda\lambda \; \lambda\lambda\lambda\lambda\lambda\lambda \; \lambda\lambda\lambda0010 \; 1\bar{1}\bar{1}\bar{1} \ldots$$

which causes a 0 to be printed, and we return left

$$u_3, \quad \ldots \underline{z} \lambda\lambda\lambda\lambda\lambda \ \lambda\lambda\lambda\lambda\lambda\lambda\lambda\lambda \ \lambda\lambda\lambda\lambda\lambda\lambda \ \lambda\lambda\lambda 0010 \ 10\cancel{1}\cancel{1}\cancel{1} \ldots$$

where the string $z\emptyset$ marks the end of the encoded appendant and causes $U_{3,7}$ to exit the print cycle and return to state u_1; the index cycle.

$$u_1, \quad \ldots z\cancel{\emptyset}\cancel{\emptyset}\cancel{\emptyset}b\cancel{\emptyset} \ z\cancel{\emptyset}\cancel{\emptyset}\cancel{\emptyset}b\cancel{\emptyset}\cancel{\emptyset}\cancel{\emptyset}b\cancel{\emptyset} \ z\cancel{\emptyset}\cancel{\emptyset}\cancel{\emptyset}\cancel{\emptyset}\cancel{\emptyset} \ bbbbb \ bbbbbbbb \ bbbbb \ bbb\underline{0}010 \ 10\cancel{1}\cancel{1}\cancel{1} \ldots$$

The latter configuration shows the next set of encoded appendants to the left. At this point we have simulated the third computation step in Example 1.   □

As can be seen in the preceding example, the computation of $U_{3,7}$ is relatively straightforward, so we refrain from giving a full proof of correctness.

Section 2 gives two conditions for a cyclic tag system completing its computation (halting). The first condition (empty dataword) is simulated by $U_{3,7}$ in a very straightforward way: if the dataword is empty then $U_{3,7}$ reads a blank symbol $\cancel{1}$ in state u_1, and immediately halts. The second condition (repeating sequence of cyclic tag configurations) causes $U_{3,7}$ to simulate this loop in an easily detectable way, where some fixed sequence of appendants are repeatedly appended to the dataword.

4   4 State, 5 Symbol Machine

$U_{4,5}$ bears some similarities to the previous machine in that it simulates cyclic tag systems which are encoded to the left. However its computation is somewhat more complicated. $U_{4,5}$ simulates a restricted cyclic tag system where the dataword does not contain consecutive 1 symbols. In particular, we say that the dataword and all appendants are words from $\{0, 10\}^*$. Such a cyclic tag system simulates an arbitrary cyclic tag system with only a small constant factor slowdown (using the simulation from [13]). Furthermore, in two different cycles, $U_{4,5}$ makes special use of whether specific substrings on the tape are of odd or even length. Intuitively this kind of encoding helps to keep the program small.

4.1 $U_{4,5}$

	u_1	u_2	u_3	u_4
0	$\lambda L u_1$	$\lambda L u_2$	$\emptyset R u_3$	$\emptyset R u_4$
1	$\emptyset R u_2$	$1 L u_2$	$1 R u_3$	$1 R u_4$
λ	$0 R u_2$	$0 R u_1$	$0 R u_4$	$0 R u_3$
$\emptyset$		$0 L u_2$	$0 L u_2$	$1 L u_2$
$\cancel{1}$	$0 L u_2$	$\lambda L u_3$		

Table of behaviour for $U_{4,5}$. The start state is u_1 and the blank symbol is $\emptyset$.

4.2 Encoding

An appendant $\alpha \in \{0, 10\}^*$ is encoded in the following manner. Firstly, the order of the symbols in α is reversed to give α_R. Then the symbol 0 is encoded as $0\lambda\bar{1}0$, and 1 is encoded as $00\lambda\bar{1}$. The encoded α_R is then prepended with the symbol λ. For example, if $\alpha = 100$ then this appendant is encoded as $\langle\alpha\rangle = \lambda0\lambda\bar{1}00\lambda\bar{1}000\lambda\bar{1}$. Finally the order of appendants are also reversed so that the list of appendants $\alpha_0, \alpha_1, \ldots, \alpha_{p-1}$ are encoded as $\langle\alpha_{p-1}\rangle\langle\alpha_{p-2}\rangle\ldots\langle\alpha_0\rangle$. This encoded list is repeated infinitely often, to the left, on the tape of $U_{4,5}$. The blank symbol for $U_{4,5}$ is $\emptyset$ and the cyclic tag system input, an element of $\{0, 10\}^*$, is written directly on the tape of $U_{4,5}$. Thus the initial configuration of the cyclic tag system given in Example 1 is encoded as

$$\boldsymbol{u_1}, \quad \ldots\lambda0\lambda\bar{1}000\lambda\bar{1}\ \lambda0\lambda\bar{1}000\lambda\bar{1}0\lambda\bar{1}000\lambda\bar{1}\ \lambda0\lambda\bar{1}00\lambda\bar{1}0\ \underline{0}010010\ \emptyset\emptyset\emptyset\ldots \qquad (2)$$

where the underline denotes the tape head position, the three encoded appendants are repeated infinitely to the left, and the extra whitespace is for human readability purposes only.

4.3 Simulation

In order to show how $U_{4,5}$ computes, we simulate the first 4 steps of the cyclic tag computation from Example 1. Example 3 shows $U_{4,5}$ reading two 0 symbols in the dataword and indexing appendants. Example 4 shows $U_{4,5}$ reading a 10 in the dataword, printing one appendant and indexing the next. Lemmata 1 and 2 build on these examples to give a proof of correctness.

Example 3 ($U_{4,5}$; reading 0). Beginning with the configuration given in Equation (2), $U_{4,5}$ reads the leftmost 0 in the input, in state u_1, and begins the process of indexing the second appendant to the left, using states u_1 and u_2.

$\vdash^3 \quad \boldsymbol{u_2}, \quad \ldots\lambda0\lambda\bar{1}000\lambda\bar{1}\ \lambda0\lambda\bar{1}000\lambda\bar{1}0\lambda\bar{1}000\lambda\bar{1}\ \lambda0\lambda\bar{1}00\underline{\lambda}0\lambda\ \lambda010010\ \emptyset\emptyset\emptyset\ldots$

$\vdash \quad \boldsymbol{u_1}, \quad \ldots\lambda0\lambda\bar{1}000\lambda\bar{1}\ \lambda0\lambda\bar{1}000\lambda\bar{1}0\lambda\bar{1}000\lambda\bar{1}\ \lambda0\lambda\bar{1}000\underline{0}\lambda\ \lambda010010\ \emptyset\emptyset\emptyset\ldots$

$\vdash^4 \quad \boldsymbol{u_1}, \quad \ldots\lambda0\lambda\bar{1}000\lambda\bar{1}\ \lambda0\lambda\bar{1}000\lambda\bar{1}0\lambda\bar{1}000\lambda\bar{1}\ \lambda0\lambda\underline{\bar{1}}\lambda\lambda\lambda\lambda\ \lambda010010\ \emptyset\emptyset\emptyset\ldots$

until we read $\lambda0$, to give the configuration

$\vdash^5 \quad \boldsymbol{u_1}, \quad \ldots\lambda0\lambda\bar{1}000\lambda\bar{1}\ \lambda0\lambda\bar{1}000\lambda\bar{1}0\lambda\bar{1}000\lambda\bar{1}\ \underline{\lambda}\lambda\lambda\lambda\lambda\lambda\lambda\lambda\ \lambda010010\ \emptyset\emptyset\emptyset\ldots \qquad (3)$

Upon reading λ in state u_1, $U_{4,5}$ scans right, switching between states u_1 and u_2. There are an even number of consecutive λ symbols, thus we exit the string of λ symbols in state u_1, ready to read the next input symbol.

$\vdash^{10} \quad \boldsymbol{u_1}, \quad \ldots\lambda0\lambda\bar{1}000\lambda\bar{1}\ \lambda0\lambda\bar{1}000\lambda\bar{1}0\lambda\bar{1}000\lambda\bar{1}\ 000000000\ 0\underline{0}10010\ \emptyset\emptyset\emptyset\ldots$

It can be seen from the proceeding configurations, that whenever $U_{4,5}$ enters an encoded appendant from the right and in state u_1, then the encoded appendant is erased. Assume, for the moment, that every symbol in the dataword is 0. Then

for each erased appendant it is the case that exactly one dataword symbol has
also been erased. Encoded appendants are of odd length. Therefore the string
of consecutive λ symbols is always of even length immediately after erasing an
appendant, e.g. in configurations of the form given in Equation (3). Thus it can
be seen that even though $U_{4,5}$ switches between two states, u_1 and u_2, while
scanning right through the string of λ symbols, it always exits this string on the
right to read the next binary dataword symbol in state u_1.

We continue our simulation: the next dataword symbol (again 0) is erased and
the next appendant is erased to give:

$$\vdash^{35} \quad u_1, \quad \ldots \lambda 0\lambda 1̸000\lambda 1̸ \ \underline{\lambda}\lambda\lambda\lambda\lambda\lambda\lambda\lambda\lambda\lambda\lambda\lambda\lambda\lambda\lambda\lambda \ \lambda\lambda\lambda\lambda\lambda\lambda\lambda\lambda \ \lambda\lambda 10010 \ \emptyset\emptyset\emptyset\ldots$$

We then scan right through the (even length) string of λ symbols, switching
between states u_1 and u_2, to read the next dataword symbol in state u_1:

$$\vdash^{28} \quad u_1, \quad \ldots \lambda 0\lambda 1̸000\lambda 1̸ \ 00000000000000000 \ 000000000 \ 00\underline{1}0010 \ \emptyset\emptyset\emptyset\ldots \quad (4)$$

The example is complete.   □

The following example illustrates how $U_{4,5}$ simulates the reading of 10 in the
dataword. Specifically, the 10 is erased from the dataword, we append and erase
the indexed appendant, and finally we erase the following appendant.

Example 4 ($U_{4,5}$; reading 10). Recall that, for $U_{4,5}$, any 1 in the dataword is
immediately followed by a 0. When $U_{4,5}$ reads a 1 in the dataword it then
(i) erases the 10 pair, (ii) enters a print cycle (to simulate appending the indexed
appendant) and then enters (iii) an index cycle (to simulate the reading of the
0 and indexing the next appendant).

We continue from configuration (4) above.

$$\vdash \quad u_2, \quad \ldots \lambda 0\lambda 1̸000\lambda 1̸ \ 00000000000000000 \ 000000000 \ 00\emptyset\underline{0}010 \ \emptyset\emptyset\emptyset\ldots$$

$$\vdash \quad u_2, \quad \ldots \lambda 0\lambda 1̸000\lambda 1̸ \ 00000000000000000 \ 000000000 \ 00\emptyset\lambda 010 \ \emptyset\emptyset\emptyset\ldots$$

$$\vdash \quad u_2, \quad \ldots \lambda 0\lambda 1̸000\lambda 1̸ \ 00000000000000000 \ 000000000 \ 0\underline{0}0\lambda 010 \ \emptyset\emptyset\emptyset\ldots$$

$$\vdash^{27} \quad u_2, \quad \ldots \lambda 0\lambda 1̸000\lambda 1̸ \ \underline{0}\lambda\lambda\lambda\lambda\lambda\lambda\lambda\lambda\lambda\lambda\lambda\lambda\lambda\lambda\lambda \ \lambda\lambda\lambda\lambda\lambda\lambda\lambda\lambda \ \lambda\lambda 0\lambda 010 \ \emptyset\emptyset\emptyset\ldots$$

We now begin reading the encoded appendant, which encodes 10.

$$\vdash \quad u_2, \quad \ldots \lambda 0\lambda 1̸000\lambda \underline{1̸} \ \lambda\lambda\lambda\lambda\lambda\lambda\lambda\lambda\lambda\lambda\lambda\lambda\lambda\lambda\lambda\lambda \ \lambda\lambda\lambda\lambda\lambda\lambda\lambda\lambda \ \lambda\lambda 0\lambda 010 \ \emptyset\emptyset\emptyset\ldots$$

This encoded appendant tells us that the symbol 1 (encoded as $00\lambda 1̸$), and then
the symbol 0 (encoded as $0\lambda 1̸0$), should be appended to the dataword.

$$\vdash \quad u_3, \quad \ldots \lambda 0\lambda 1̸000\underline{\lambda}\lambda \ \lambda\lambda\lambda\lambda\lambda\lambda\lambda\lambda\lambda\lambda\lambda\lambda\lambda\lambda\lambda\lambda \ \lambda\lambda\lambda\lambda\lambda\lambda\lambda\lambda \ \lambda\lambda 0\lambda 010 \ \emptyset\emptyset\emptyset\ldots$$

$U_{4,5}$ now scans right, switching between state u_3 and u_4, eventually appending
either 0 or 1 to the dataword. If there are an odd number of λ symbols on, and
to the right of, the tape head then 1 is appended, if there is an even number

then 0 is appended. Such a printing mechanism uses a relatively small number of transition rules.

$\vdash$ u_4, ... $\lambda0\lambda\not10000\underline{\lambda}$ $\lambda\lambda\lambda\lambda\lambda\lambda\lambda\lambda\lambda\lambda\lambda\lambda\lambda\lambda\lambda\lambda$ $\lambda\lambda\lambda\lambda\lambda\lambda\lambda\lambda$ $\lambda\lambda0\lambda010$ $\emptyset\emptyset\emptyset$ ...

$\vdash$ u_3, ... $\lambda0\lambda\not100000$ $\underline{\lambda}\lambda\lambda\lambda\lambda\lambda\lambda\lambda\lambda\lambda\lambda\lambda\lambda\lambda\lambda\lambda$ $\lambda\lambda\lambda\lambda\lambda\lambda\lambda\lambda$ $\lambda\lambda0\lambda010$ $\emptyset\emptyset\emptyset$ ...

$\vdash^{30}$ u_4, ... $\lambda0\lambda\not100000$ 00000000000000000 000000000 $00\emptyset0\underline{0}10$ $\emptyset\emptyset\emptyset$ ...

We now pass over the dataword and append a 1.

$\vdash^3$ u_4, ... $\lambda0\lambda\not100000$ 00000000000000000 000000000 $00\emptyset0\emptyset1\emptyset$ $\emptyset\emptyset\emptyset\emptyset$ ...

$\vdash$ u_2, ... $\lambda0\lambda\not100000$ 00000000000000000 000000000 $00\emptyset0\emptyset1\underline{\emptyset}$ $1\emptyset\emptyset\emptyset$ ...

We now scan left to find the next symbol to be appended

$\vdash^{37}$ u_2, ... $\lambda0\lambda\not1\underline{0}\lambda\lambda\lambda$ $\lambda\lambda\lambda\lambda\lambda\lambda\lambda\lambda\lambda\lambda\lambda\lambda\lambda\lambda\lambda$ $\lambda\lambda\lambda\lambda\lambda\lambda\lambda\lambda$ $\lambda\lambda0\lambda010$ $1\emptyset\emptyset\emptyset$ ...

which is an encoded 0. We erase this encoded 0:

$\vdash^2$ u_3, ... $\lambda0\underline{\lambda}\lambda\lambda\lambda\lambda\lambda\lambda$ $\lambda\lambda\lambda\lambda\lambda\lambda\lambda\lambda\lambda\lambda\lambda\lambda\lambda\lambda\lambda$ $\lambda\lambda\lambda\lambda\lambda\lambda\lambda\lambda$ $\lambda\lambda0\lambda010$ $1\emptyset\emptyset\emptyset$ ...

Now we are ready to scan right, switching between states u_3 and u_4. There are an even number of λ symbols on, and to the right of, the tape head. This will result in a 0 being appended to the dataword.

$\vdash^{41}$ u_3, ... $\lambda00000000$ 00000000000000000 000000000 $00\emptyset0\emptyset1\emptyset$ $1\underline{\emptyset}\emptyset\emptyset$ ...

$\vdash$ u_2, ... $\lambda00000000$ 00000000000000000 000000000 $00\emptyset0\emptyset1\emptyset$ $\underline{1}\emptyset\emptyset\emptyset$ ...

$U_{4,5}$ now scans left, in state u_2, and since there are no more encoded 0 or 1 symbols, it eventually reads the 'end of appendant' marker λ.

$\vdash^{42}$ u_2, ... $\underline{\lambda}\lambda\lambda\lambda\lambda\lambda\lambda\lambda\lambda$ $\lambda\lambda\lambda\lambda\lambda\lambda\lambda\lambda\lambda\lambda\lambda\lambda\lambda\lambda\lambda\lambda$ $\lambda\lambda\lambda\lambda\lambda\lambda\lambda\lambda$ $\lambda\lambda0\lambda010$ $10\emptyset\emptyset\emptyset$ ...

Reading this λ in state u_2 sends us to the right in the index cycle (switching between states u_2 and u_1); however we enter the cycle in the 'incorrect' state u_2 (we usually enter this cycle in state u_1), but when we read the leftmost 0 in the dataword

$\vdash^{37}$ u_1, ... 000000000 00000000000000000 000000000 $00\underline{0}\lambda010$ $10\emptyset\emptyset\emptyset$ ...

this forces us to index another appendant (after which we will enter the next index cycle in state u_1; the 'correct' state). This is the main reason why we insist that each 1 in the dataword is immediately followed by a 0.

We duplicate the configuration immediately above (while introducing some shorthand notation for erased appendants and showing the next two encoded appendants to the left).

u_1, ... $\lambda0\lambda\not1000\lambda\not10\lambda\not1000\lambda\not1$ $\lambda0\lambda\not100\lambda\not10$ 0^9 0^{17} 0^9 $00\underline{0}\lambda010$ $10\emptyset\emptyset\emptyset$ ...

As already noted, we are forced to index the next appendant:

$$\vdash^{50} \quad \boldsymbol{u_1}, \quad \ldots \lambda 0 \lambda \cancel{1} 000 \lambda \cancel{1} 0 \lambda \cancel{1} 000 \lambda \cancel{1} \ \underline{\lambda \lambda \lambda \lambda \lambda \lambda \lambda \lambda} \ \lambda^9 \ \lambda^{17} \ \lambda^9 \ \lambda \lambda \lambda \lambda 010 \ 10 \cancel{\emptyset} \cancel{\emptyset} \ldots$$

We then scan right through the (even length) string of λ symbols, switching between states u_1 and u_2 to read the next dataword read symbol in state u_1:

$$\vdash^{48} \quad \boldsymbol{u_1}, \quad \ldots \lambda 0 \lambda \cancel{1} 000 \lambda \cancel{1} 0 \lambda \cancel{1} 000 \lambda \cancel{1} \ 000000000 \ 0^9 \ 0^{17} \ 0^9 \ 0000\underline{0}10 \ 10 \cancel{\emptyset} \cancel{\emptyset} \ldots$$

The example is complete. □

The halting conditions for $U_{4,5}$ are the same as those for $U_{3,7}$; if the cyclic tag systems halts then $U_{4,5}$ reads a $\emptyset$ in state u_1 and halts, if the cyclic tag systems enters a repeating sequence of configurations then $U_{4,5}$ simulates this loop in an easily detectable way.

The previous two examples provide the main mechanics for the workings of $U_{4,5}$. The two lemmata below generalise these examples, and cover the cases of read symbols 0 and 1 respectively. We assume that the cyclic tag dataword and appendants are from $\{0, 10\}^*$, as described at the beginning of Section 4.

Lemma 1. *Let c_1 be a configuration of cyclic tag system C with read symbol 0, and let c_2 be the unique configuration that follows c_1 using C (i.e. $c_1 \vdash_C c_2$). Given an encoding of C and c_1, then $U_{4,5}$ computes the encoding of c_2.*

Proof. In the encoding of c_1, $U_{4,5}$ is reading 0 in state u_1. This causes the head to move left leaving a string of λ symbols. An encoded appendant is a word over $\lambda\{\langle 0 \rangle, \langle 1 \rangle \langle 0 \rangle\}^*$. Notice if we enter either $\langle 0 \rangle = 0\lambda\cancel{1}0$ or $\langle 1 \rangle = 00\lambda\cancel{1}$ from the right, in state u_1, then we exit to the left, in the same state, leaving $\lambda\lambda\lambda\lambda$ on the tape. Eventually the entire appendant is erased (converted into a string of λ symbols), and $U_{4,5}$ is reading the leftmost λ in the encoded appendant, in state u_1.

From the encoding, the length of each encoded appendant is odd. Furthermore, the number of erased appendants is equal to number of erased dataword symbols. Thus, the sum of the number of erased dataword symbols plus the number of symbols in the erased appendants is even. We begin reading this even length string of λ symbols from the left in state u_1, alternating between states u_1 and u_2 as we scan right. We exit the string of λ symbols in state u_1. We have completed the index cycle and are reading the the leftmost (next read) symbol from the dataword in state u_1. From above, the next appendant is indexed. Thus the tape encodes configuration c_2. □

Lemma 2. *Let c_1 be a configuration of cyclic tag system C with read symbol 1, and let c_2 be the unique configuration that follows c_1 using C (i.e. $c_1 \vdash_C c_2$). Given an encoding of C and c_1, then $U_{4,5}$ computes the encoding of c_2.*

Proof. Recall that any 1 in the dataword is immediately followed by a 0. Thus our proof has two parts, a print cycle followed by an index cycle.

In the encoding of c_1, $U_{4,5}$ is reading 1 in state u_1. This 1 is changed to $\emptyset$, and the head moves to the right and erases an extra 0 symbol. The $\emptyset$ is changed to 0 (which is used to trigger an extra index cycle below). The head then scans left in state u_2 leaving a string of λ symbols until we read the first (rightmost) non-erased encoded appendant. An encoded appendant is a word over $\lambda\{\langle 0\rangle, \langle 1\rangle\langle 0\rangle\}^*$.

Notice that if we enter $\langle 0\rangle = 0\lambda\cancel{1}0$ from the right in state u_2, we then (i) exit to the right in state u_4. However if we enter $\langle 1\rangle = 00\lambda\cancel{1}$ from the right in state u_2 we then (ii) exit to the right in state u_3. In both cases we then scan to the right, reading an *odd* number of λ symbols (a string of the form $\lambda^{2i}0\lambda$, $i \in \mathbb{N}$), while switching between states u_3 and u_4. We pass to the right over the dataword, which does not cause us to change state. Then in case (i) we append 0 to the dataword and in case (ii) we append a 1 to the dataword.

We continue appending 0 or 1 symbols until we reach the leftmost end of the (currently indexed) appendant by reading the symbol λ in state u_2. We then scan right, through a string of the form $\lambda^{2j+1}0\lambda$, $j \in \mathbb{N}$, switching between states u_2 and u_1. After $2j + 1$ steps we read 0 in state u_1, which triggers an index cycle (Lemma 1). After the index cycle we pass over the rightmost λ (which occupies the location of the extra erased 0 mentioned above) and we are reading the next encoded dataword symbol in state u_1. Thus the tape encodes configuration c_2.

$\square$

Let C be a cyclic tag system that runs in time t. After simulating t steps of C, machines $U_{3,7}$ and $U_{4,5}$ have used $O(t)$ workspace. Therefore both machines simulate the computation of C in time $O(t^2)$. By applying Theorem 1 directly we find that given a single-tape deterministic Turing machine M that computes in time t, then machines $U_{3,7}$ and $U_{4,5}$ both simulate M in time $O(t^6 \log^2 t)$. We observe that in the simulation from [13] the space used by C is only a constant times that used by M. This observation, along with an (as yet unpublished) improvement to [13], improve the time bound to $O(t^4 \log^2 t)$ for $U_{3,7}$ and $U_{4,5}$ simulating Turing machines M.

Acknowledgements

DW is supported by Science Foundation Ireland grant number 04/IN3/1524. TN is supported by the Irish Research Council for Science, Engineering and Technology.

References

1. Baiocchi, C.: Three small universal Turing machines. In: Margenstern, M., Rogozhin, Y. (eds.) MCU 2001. LNCS, vol. 2055, pp. 1–10. Springer, Heidelberg (2001)
2. Cocke, J., Minsky, M.: Universality of tag systems with $P = 2$. Journal of the Association for Computing Machinery 11(1), 15–20 (1964)
3. Cook, M.: Universality in elementary cellular automata. Complex Systems 15(1), 1–40 (2004)

4. Hermann, G.T.: The uniform halting problem for generalized one state Turing machines. In: FOCS. Proceedings of the ninth annual Symposium on Switching and Automata Theory, Schenectady, New York, October 1968, pp. 368–372. IEEE Computer Society Press, Los Alamitos (1968)
5. Kudlek, M.: Small deterministic Turing machines. Theoretical Computer Science 168(2), 241–255 (1996)
6. Kudlek, M., Rogozhin, Y.: A universal Turing machine with 3 states and 9 symbols. In: Kuich, W., Rozenberg, G., Salomaa, A. (eds.) DLT 2001. LNCS, vol. 2295, pp. 311–318. Springer, Heidelberg (2002)
7. Margenstern, M.: Frontier between decidability and undecidability: a survey. Theoretical Computer Science 231(2), 217–251 (2000)
8. Margenstern, M., Pavlotskaya, L.: On the optimal number of instructions for universality of Turing machines connected with a finite automaton. International Journal of Algebra and Computation 13(2), 133–202 (2003)
9. Michel, P.: Small Turing machines and generalized busy beaver competition. Theoretical Computer Science 326, 45–56 (2004)
10. Minsky, M.: A 6-symbol 7-state universal Turing machines. Technical Report 54-G-027, MIT (August 1960)
11. Minsky, M.: Size and structure of universal Turing machines using tag systems. In: Recursive Function Theory: Proceedings, Symposium in Pure Mathematics, Provelence, vol. 5, pp. 229–238. AMS (1962)
12. Neary, T.: Small polynomial time universal Turing machines. In: MFCSIT'06. Fourth Irish Conference on the Mathematical Foundations of Computer Science and Information Technology, Ireland, pp. 325–329. University College Cork (2006)
13. Neary, T., Woods, D.: P-completeness of cellular automaton Rule 110. In: Bugliesi, M., Preneel, B., Sassone, V., Wegener, I. (eds.) ICALP 2006. LNCS, vol. 4051, pp. 132–143. Springer, Heidelberg (2006)
14. Neary, T., Woods, D.: Small fast universal Turing machines. Theoretical Computer Science 362(1–3), 171–195 (2006)
15. Neary, T., Woods, D.: Four small universal Turing machines. In: Margenstern, M., Rogozhin, Y. (eds.) MCU 2007. LNCS, vol. 4664, pp. 242–254. Springer, Heidelberg (2007)
16. Pavlotskaya, L.: Solvability of the halting problem for certain classes of Turing machines. Mathematical Notes (Springer) 13(6), 537–541 (June 1973) (Translated from Matematicheskie Zametki 13(6), 899–909 (June 1973))
17. Pavlotskaya, L.: Dostatochnye uslovija razreshimosti problemy ostanovki dlja mashin T'juring. Avtomaty i Mashiny (Sufficient conditions for the halting problem decidability of Turing machines) (in Russian), 91–118 (1978)
18. Priese, L.: Towards a precise characterization of the complexity of universal and nonuniversal Turing machines. SIAM J. Comput. 8(4), 508–523 (1979)
19. Robinson, R.M.: Minsky's small universal Turing machine. International Journal of Mathematics 2(5), 551–562 (1991)
20. Rogozhin, Y.: Sem' universal'nykh mashin T'juringa. Systems and theoretical programming, Mat. Issled. 69, 76–90 (1982) (Seven universal Turing machines, in Russian)
21. Rogozhin, Y.: Small universal Turing machines. Theoretical Computer Science 168(2), 215–240 (1996)
22. Shannon, C.E.: A universal Turing machine with two internal states. Automata Studies, Annals of Mathematics Studies 34, 157–165 (1956)
23. Watanabe, S.: On a minimal universal Turing machines. Technical report, MCB Report, Tokyo (August 1960)

24. Watanabe, S.: 5-symbol 8-state and 5-symbol 6-state universal Turing machines. Journal of the ACM 8(4), 476–483 (1961)
25. Watanabe, S.: 4-symbol 5-state universal Turing machines. Information Processing Society of Japan Magazine 13(9), 588–592 (1972)
26. Wolfram, S.: A new kind of science. Wolfram Media, Inc. (2002)
27. Woods, D., Neary, T.: On the time complexity of 2-tag systems and small universal Turing machines. In: FOCS. 47th Annual IEEE Symposium on Foundations of Computer Science, Berkeley, California, October 2006, pp. 439–446. IEEE, Los Alamitos (2006)
28. Woods, D., Neary, T.: The complexity of small universal Turing machines. In: CiE 2007. Computation and Logic in the Real World: Third Conference of Computability in Europe, Siena, Italy, June 2007. LNCS, vol. 4497, Springer, Heidelberg (2007)

Simple New Algorithms Which Solve the Firing Squad Synchronization Problem: A 7-States $4n$-Steps Solution

Jean-Baptiste Yunès

LIAFA - Université Paris 7 Denis Diderot
175, rue du chevaleret
75013 Paris - France
Jean-Baptiste.Yunes@liafa.jussieu.fr

Abstract. We present a new family of solutions to the firing squad synchronization problem. All these solutions are built with a few finite number of signals, which lead to simple implementations with 7 or 8 internal states. Using one of these schemes we are able to built a 7-states $4n + \mathcal{O}(\log n)$-steps solution to the firing squad synchronization problem. These solutions not only solves the unrestricted problem (initiator at one of the two ends), but also the problem with initiators at both ends and the problem on a ring.

1 Introduction

The Firing Squad Synchronization Problem (FSSP) is one of the oldest problem in Cellular Automata. It has also been studied all over the years from the beginning of the field up to these days. There exists a lot of solutions, for many different variants of the problem but the subject is far from exhausted. Recent progress in the quest for minimal states or minimal time solution to the problem reveals that some intrinsic properties of that computation model are not so well known.

1.1 The Problem

A linear cellular automata, simply CA, is a finite array of identical finite automata, each one having two direct neighbors. The whole machine operates at discrete time-steps; every automaton reads its inputs (states of its neighbor cells and its own state) and changes its state according to a transition function. Its new state is then made available to its neighbors at the next time-step. As usual, we define the quiescent state such as any quiescent cell remains quiescent when its neighborhood is quiescent.

Then, we can define the Firing Squad Synchronization Problem, in short FSSP, as follows. Consider arrays of identical automata which are initially all in the quiescent state except the first one called the initiator. The FSSP is to design a transition function such that after some steps all cells are in the same

J. Durand-Lose and M. Margenstern (Eds.): MCU 2007, LNCS 4664, pp. 316–324, 2007.

firing state which never occurred before. What is really challenging is that such a transition function mustn't depend on the length of the line: the same function must be used for every possible finite line.

That problem has been long studied. First stated by J. Myhill in 1957, reported by E. Moore in 1964 (see [5]), and since then, a very rich set of solutions has grown up. The very first published solution is due to J. McCarthy & M. Minsky in 1967 (see [4]). E. Goto (in 1962, see [2]) has built a so-called minimal-time solution: one which takes only $2n - 2$ steps to synchronize a line of n automata. After that and independently, A. Waksman and R. Balzer in 1966 and 1967, see [10,1]) have got minimal-time solutions with very few states (resp. 16 and 8 states). R. Balzer also proved that no 4-state minimal-time solution exists. A famous record is held by J. Mazoyer who exhibited a 6-states minimal-time solution in 1987 (see [3]). Since then the design of a 5-states solution remains an open problem and actually nobody knows how to solve that question.

During late years, surprising 6-states non minimal time solutions emerged. A. Settle & J. Simon in 2002 (see [6]) built a tricky $3n$-steps solution based on Mazoyer's solution, H. Umeo in 2006 (see [9]) exhibited a $3n$ Minsky's solution, and J.-B. Yunès in 2007 (see [12]) showed another $3n$ but thread-like Minsky's solution. Let's also mention recent H. Umeo's works (see [7,8]) on 6-states solutions to the problem in two dimensions. These solutions contradict Mazoyer's claim that to minimize the number of states it is necessary to synchronize in minimal-time and to break the symmetry of the solution. Settle and Simon's solution violates the first assertion: they synchronize a line of length n in $3n$-steps. Umeo's and Yunes's solutions violate both assertions as they are intrinsically non minimal-time (in about $3n$) and symmetric.

Much remains to be done to investigate non-minimal time solutions which can be obtained with few states.

1.2 Our Contribution

In this paper, we focus our attention on the following features of solutions to the FSSP:

- the number of states used by the transition function,
- the synchronization time,
- the number of different signals (and their slopes),
- the density of the solution (total amount of work),
- the flexibility of the ignition (location of initiator(s)).

We present different schemes which can be used to synchronize a line of n cellular automata in time $\mathcal{T}(n) = 4\sigma n$ or $\mathcal{T}(n) = (3 + \sigma)n$ (for any $\sigma \geq 1$). We will also show that such schemes are so simple that they lead, for $\sigma = 1$, to two 7-states $4n$-steps solutions to the problem and some other 8-states interesting solution. As the described processes are, by nature, symmetric, their implementation also is, leading to symmetric solutions which solve the unrestricted problem (with an initiator on the left or on the right end), the problem with initiators at both ends and the problem on a ring. Two of these solutions are thread-like and use, for a line of length n, an amount of work (*i.e.* the number of executed transitions different from $\bullet\bullet\bullet\rightarrow\bullet$, $\bullet$ being the convenient representation of the quiescent state) in the order of $n\log n$ and one work in the order of n^2.

2   A Solution in 8-States 4n-Steps

As figure 1(a) shows, the guideline to synchronize a line of n automata in time $4n$ is very simple, and only use two different slopes for signals: a signal of slope 1 and another one of slope 2. As one can see, the lightspeed signal (slope 1) and a $\frac{1}{2}$-lightspeed (slope 2) signal are launched from the initiator located at one end. The first signal reaches the other border and then bounces back. Then one can easily note that the two signals respectively reach the two borders at the same time $2n$. Then the process is launched again from the two borders and in a symmetric way: each new run synchronizes two sub-lines of length $\frac{n}{2}$.

Theorem 1. *With two signals of slope 1 and 2, it is possible to synchronize a line of n automata in time $4n$.*

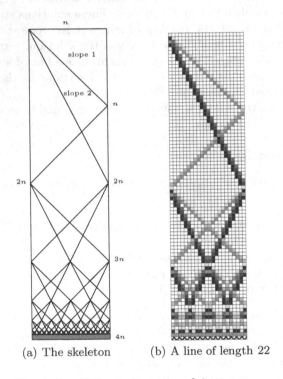

(a) The skeleton   (b) A line of length 22

Fig. 1. A solution in 8-states and $4n$-steps

Proof. The total time is the limit

$$\lim_{p\to\infty}\sum_{i=0}^{i=p}\frac{2n}{2^i} = 2n\lim_{p\to\infty}\sum_{i=0}^{i=p}\frac{1}{2^i} = 4n$$

□

2.1   An Implementation

Figure 1(b) shows a run on a line of length 22 (we used different greytones to represent the states), and figure 2 gives the used transition rules. This solution uses only 8 states, the initiator is 'A' and the firing state 'G'. For convenience we used '$' to symbolize the border and '•' for the quiescent state.

That transition function use 195 rules, and one can easily verify that the function is symmetric, *i.e.* that if xyz→v is defined then so is zyx→v. The *virtual border* property, *i.e.* that if xy$→v is defined then so are xyx→v and xyy→v, is also verified (see [12] for details).

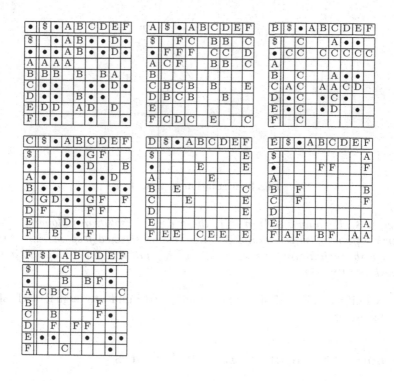

Fig. 2. The transition rules of our 8-states 4*n*-steps solution

Theorem 2. *There exists a 8-states cellular automata synchronizing any line of length n in time* $4n + \mathcal{O}(\log n)$ *and work in* $\mathcal{O}(n\log n)$. *That cellular automata also solves the unrestricted problem, the problem with initiators at both ends and the problem on a ring.*

3   Solutions in $4\sigma n$, $\sigma \in \mathbb{Q}$

The preceding scheme can easily be generalized to produce a synchronization of a line of length n in time $4\sigma n$ (if $\sigma \geq 1$) and still work in $\mathcal{O}(n \log n)$. The trick is to obtain two initiators, one on each border at the same time. Figure 3 illustrates the construction. At the limit the line is synchronized at time

$$\lim_{p \to \infty} \sum_{i=0}^{i=p} \frac{2\sigma n}{2^i} = 4\sigma n$$

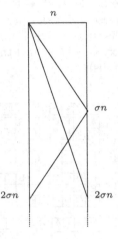

Fig. 3. A solution in time $4\sigma n$

Theorem 3. *For any $\sigma \in \mathbb{Q}$, $\sigma \geq 1$, there exists a solution following a scheme with two signals of slopes σ and 2σ, to the unrestricted fssp in time $4\sigma n$, the problem with an initiator at each end, and the problem on a ring in time $2\sigma n$, and work in $\mathcal{O}(n \log n)$.*

Proof. A finite number of states is sufficient to build any signal with slope a rational number.   □

4   Another Solution in 4n But 7-States

We can also use Minsky's strategy to construct a $4n$-steps solution. This is illustrated in figure 4(a). Minsky looks for the middle to launch, from the middle, the two half sub-lines. In our solution, we look for the middle to mark the two half sub-lines, but ignition takes place on the opposite ends of the sub-lines.

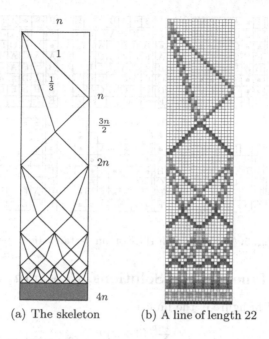

(a) The skeleton   (b) A line of length 22

Fig. 4. A solution in 7-states and 4n-steps

Theorem 4. *With two signals of slope 1 and 3, it is possible to synchronize a line of n automata in $4n + \mathcal{O}(\log n)$ steps with $\mathcal{O}(n \log n)$ work.*

Proof. The total time is the limit

$$\lim_{p \to \infty} \sum_{i=0}^{i=p} (\frac{3n}{2} + \frac{n}{2})/2^i = 2n \lim_{p \to \infty} \sum_{i=0}^{i=p} \frac{1}{2^i} = 4n \qquad \square$$

4.1   An Implementation

Figure 5 gives the transition function of the 7-states solution to the problem.

It is based on our 6-states 3n-steps (see [12]) and it consists of 162 rules (the initiator is 'A' and the firing state 'F'). It is easy to verify that the function is symmetric, *i.e.* that if xyz→v is defined then is zyx→v. The *virtual border* property, *i.e.* that if xy\$→v is defined then are xyx→v and xyy→v, is also verified (see [12] for details).

Theorem 5. *There exists a 7-states cellular automata synchronizing any line of length n in time $4n + \mathcal{O}(\log n)$ and work in $\mathcal{O}(n \log n)$. That cellular automata also solves the unrestricted problem, the problem with an initiator at both ends and the problem on a ring.*

•	$	•	A	B	C	D	E
$		•	C	B	•	•	E
•	•	•	C	B	•	•	E
A	C	C	C	B		C	
B	B	B	B	B	B	A	
C	•	•		A	•	•	
D	•	•	C		•	•	
E	E	E				E	

A	$	•	A	B	C	D	E
$	F	B	F	A	C	C	
•	B	B	B		A		
A	F	B	F	A	C	C	
B	A		A	A		E	
C	C	A	C		C	C	
D	C		C	E	C	C	
E							

B	$	•	A	B	C	D	E
$		D	A		A	B	
•	D	D	C	D	D	D	
A	A	C	A	A		E	
B		D	A		A	B	
C	A	D		A	A		
D	B	D	E	B		B	
E							

C	$	•	A	B	C	D	E
$		D	B		C	D	
•		D	B		C	•	
A	D	D	D	D	D	D	
B	B	B	D	B	B		
C		D	B		C	D	
D	C	C			C	C	
E	D	•		D		D	

D	$	•	A	B	C	D	E
$			•	•		•	
•			•	•	A	•	
A	•	•	•		E	•	
B	•	•		•		•	
C	A	E			A		
D		•	•	A		•	
E	•	•			•	•	

E	$	•	A	B	C	D	E
$					A		
•		D			D	D	
A							
B							
C				E			
D	A	D			A	A	
E		D			A		

Fig. 5. The transition rules of our 7-states $4n$-steps solution

5   Other Linear-Time Solutions, $(3 + \sigma)n$, $\sigma \in \mathbb{Q}$

As illustrated in figure 6, the limit is

$$\lim_{p \to \infty} \sum_{i=1}^{i=p} \frac{(3 + \sigma)n}{2^i} = (3 + \sigma)n$$

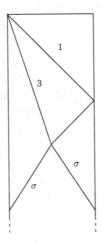

Fig. 6. A solution in time $(3 + \sigma)n$

Theorem 6. *For any $\sigma \in \mathbb{Q}$, $\sigma \geq 1$, there exists a solution in time $(3+\sigma)n$ and work $\ell(n \log n)$, following a scheme with 3 signals of slopes 1, 3 and σ, for the unrestricted FSSP, the problem with an initiator at each end, and the problem on a ring in time $\frac{3+\sigma}{2}n$.*

6   An Alternate Solution in 7-States 4n-Steps

Here, we used the same scheme as in section 4 but based our implementation on Umeo's 6-states solution (see [9]) on which some slight modifications have been made. Those modifications lead to a solution which verify the *virtual border* property (see [12]) and then solves not only the unrestricted problem but also the problem with initiators at both ends and the problem on a ring. But doing so, we lost the *generalization* property (ability to synchronize whatever is the position of the initiator). That solution is not thread-like but plain (work in $\mathcal{O}(n^2)$).

The figure 7(a) shows a run on a line of length 20.

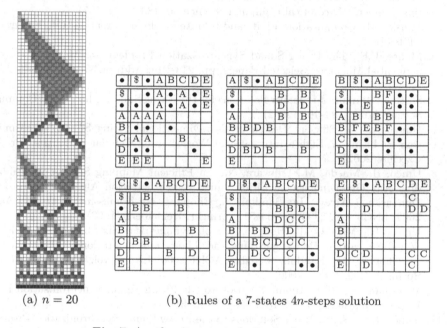

(a) $n = 20$ (b) Rules of a 7-states 4n-steps solution

Fig. 7. Another 7-states solution in 4n-steps

The transition function is made of 108 rules and is shown in figure 7(b). As all the preceding constructions, this one also solves the unrestricted problem, the problem with an initiator at both ends and the problem on a ring.

7   Conclusion

In this paper, we present two new simple schemes to build new non minimal time solutions to the problem and some extensions (both ends, ring). The intrinsic simplicity of these schemes is illustrated by our construction of three simple implementations which synchronizes in about 4n: two with 7-states and one with 8-states. These schemes naturally leads to thread-like solutions which total amount of work in the order of $n \log n$, but also work if we use plain solutions which work in the order of n^2.

We don't know if it is possible to build a 6-states solution with such constructions.

References

1. Balzer, R.: An 8-State Minimal Time Solution to the Firing Squad Synchronization Problem. Information and Control 10, 22–42 (1967)
2. Goto, E.: A Minimum Time Solution of the Firing Squad Problem. Course Notes for Applied Mathematics, vol. 298. Harvard University, Cambridge (1962)
3. Mazoyer, J.: A Six-State Minimal Time Solution to the Fring Squad Synchronization Problem. Theoretical Computer Science 50, 183–238 (1987)
4. Minsky, M.: Computation: Finite and Infinite Machines. Prentice-Hall, Englewood Cliffs (1967)
5. Moore, E.F.: The Firing Squad Synchronization Problem. In: Moore, E.F. (ed.) Sequential Machines. Selected Papers, pp. 213–214. Addison-Wesley, Reading MA (1964)
6. Settle, A., Simon, J.: Smaller Solutions for the Firing Squad. Theoretical Computer Science 276(1), 83–109 (2002)
7. Umeo, H.: An Efficient Design of Two-Dimensional Firing Squad Synchronization Problem. In: Eighth International Workshop on Cellular Automata, Prague, Czechia (2002)
8. Umeo, H., Maeda, M., Fujiwara, N.: An Efficient Mapping Scheme for Embedding Any One-Dimensional Firing Squad Synchronization Algorithm onto Two-Dimensional Arrays. In: Bandini, S., Chopard, B., Tomassini, M. (eds.) ACRI 2002. LNCS, vol. 2493, pp. 69–81. Springer, Heidelberg (2002)
9. Umeo, H., Maeda, M., Hongyo, K.: of Symmetrical Six-State 3n-Step Firing Squad Synchronization Algorithms and Their Implementations. In: El Yacoubi, S., Chopard, B., Bandini, S. (eds.) ACRI 2006. LNCS, vol. 4173, pp. 157–168. Springer, Heidelberg (2006)
10. Waksman, A.: An Optimum Solution to the Firing Squad Synchronization Problem. Information and Control 9, 66–78 (1966)
11. Yunès, J.-B.: Seven States Solutions to the Firing Squad Synchronization Problem. Theoretical Computer Science 127(2), 313–332 (1994)
12. Yunès, J.-B.: An Intrinsically Non Minimal-Time Minsky-like 6-States Solution to the Firing Squad Synchronization Problem. In: RAIRO (submitted, 2007)

Author Index

Lecture Notes in Computer Science

For information about Vols. 1–4409

please contact your bookseller or Springer

Vol. 4546: J. Kleijn, A. Yakovlev (Eds.), Petri Nets and Other Models of Concurrency – ICATPN 2007. XI, 515 pages. 2007.

Vol. 4545: H. Anai, K. Horimoto, T. Kutsia (Eds.), Algebraic Biology. XIII, 379 pages. 2007.

Vol. 4533: F. Baader (Ed.), Term Rewriting and Applications. XII, 419 pages. 2007.

Vol. 4528: J. Mira, J.R. Álvarez (Eds.), Nature Inspired Problem-Solving Methods in Knowledge Engineering, Part II. XXII, 650 pages. 2007.

Vol. 4527: J. Mira, J.R. Álvarez (Eds.), Bio-inspired Modeling of Cognitive Tasks, Part I. XXII, 630 pages. 2007.

Vol. 4525: C. Demetrescu (Ed.), Experimental Algorithms. XIII, 448 pages. 2007.

Vol. 4514: S.N. Artemov, A. Nerode (Eds.), Logical Foundations of Computer Science. XI, 513 pages. 2007.

Vol. 4513: M. Fischetti, D.P. Williamson (Eds.), Integer Programming and Combinatorial Optimization. IX, 500 pages. 2007.

Vol. 4510: P. Van Hentenryck, L.A. Wolsey (Eds.), Integration of AI and OR Techniques in Constraint Programming for Combinatorial Optimization Problems. X, 391 pages. 2007.

Vol. 4507: F. Sandoval, A. Prieto, J. Cabestany, M. Graña (Eds.), Computational and Ambient Intelligence. XXVI, 1167 pages. 2007.

Vol. 4501: J. Marques-Silva, K.A. Sakallah (Eds.), Theory and Applications of Satisfiability Testing – SAT 2007. XI, 384 pages. 2007.

Vol. 4497: S.B. Cooper, B. Löwe, A. Sorbi (Eds.), Computation and Logic in the Real World. XVIII, 826 pages. 2007.

Vol. 4494: H. Jin, O.F. Rana, Y. Pan, V.K. Prasanna (Eds.), Algorithms and Architectures for Parallel Processing. XIV, 508 pages. 2007.

Vol. 4493: D. Liu, S. Fei, Z. Hou, H. Zhang, C. Sun (Eds.), Advances in Neural Networks – ISNN 2007, Part III. XXVI, 1215 pages. 2007.

Vol. 4492: D. Liu, S. Fei, Z. Hou, H. Zhang, C. Sun (Eds.), Advances in Neural Networks – ISNN 2007, Part II. XXVII, 1321 pages. 2007.

Vol. 4491: D. Liu, S. Fei, Z.-G. Hou, H. Zhang, C. Sun (Eds.), Advances in Neural Networks – ISNN 2007, Part I. LIV, 1365 pages. 2007.

Vol. 4490: Y. Shi, G.D. van Albada, J. Dongarra, P.M.A. Sloot (Eds.), Computational Science – ICCS 2007, Part IV. XXXVII, 1211 pages. 2007.

Vol. 4489: Y. Shi, G.D. van Albada, J. Dongarra, P.M.A. Sloot (Eds.), Computational Science – ICCS 2007, Part III. XXXVII, 1257 pages. 2007.

Vol. 4488: Y. Shi, G.D. van Albada, J. Dongarra, P.M.A. Sloot (Eds.), Computational Science – ICCS 2007, Part II. XXXV, 1251 pages. 2007.

Vol. 4487: Y. Shi, G.D. van Albada, J. Dongarra, P.M.A. Sloot (Eds.), Computational Science – ICCS 2007, Part I. LXXXI, 1275 pages. 2007.

Vol. 4484: J.-Y. Cai, S.B. Cooper, H. Zhu (Eds.), Theory and Applications of Models of Computation. XIII, 772 pages. 2007.

Vol. 4475: P. Crescenzi, G. Prencipe, G. Pucci (Eds.), Fun with Algorithms. X, 273 pages. 2007.

Vol. 4474: G. Prencipe, S. Zaks (Eds.), Structural Information and Communication Complexity. XI, 342 pages. 2007.

Vol. 4459: C. Cérin, K.-C. Li (Eds.), Advances in Grid and Pervasive Computing. XVI, 759 pages. 2007.

Vol. 4449: Z. Horváth, V. Zsók, A. Butterfield (Eds.), Implementation and Application of Functional Languages. X, 271 pages. 2007.

Vol. 4448: M. Giacobini (Ed.), Applications of Evolutionary Computing. XXIII, 755 pages. 2007.

Vol. 4447: E. Marchiori, J.H. Moore, J.C. Rajapakse (Eds.), Evolutionary Computation, Machine Learning and Data Mining in Bioinformatics. XI, 302 pages. 2007.

Vol. 4446: C. Cotta, J. van Hemert (Eds.), Evolutionary Computation in Combinatorial Optimization. XII, 241 pages. 2007.

Vol. 4445: M. Ebner, M. O'Neill, A. Ekárt, L. Vanneschi, A.I. Esparcia-Alcázar (Eds.), Genetic Programming. XI, 382 pages. 2007.

Vol. 4436: C.R. Stephens, M. Toussaint, D. Whitley, P.F. Stadler (Eds.), Foundations of Genetic Algorithms. IX, 213 pages. 2007.

Vol. 4433: E. Şahin, W.M. Spears, A.F.T. Winfield (Eds.), Swarm Robotics. XII, 221 pages. 2007.

Vol. 4432: B. Beliczynski, A. Dzielinski, M. Iwanowski, B. Ribeiro (Eds.), Adaptive and Natural Computing Algorithms, Part II. XXVI, 761 pages. 2007.

Vol. 4431: B. Beliczynski, A. Dzielinski, M. Iwanowski, B. Ribeiro (Eds.), Adaptive and Natural Computing Algorithms, Part I. XXV, 851 pages. 2007.

Vol. 4424: O. Grumberg, M. Huth (Eds.), Tools and Algorithms for the Construction and Analysis of Systems. XX, 738 pages. 2007.

Vol. 4423: H. Seidl (Ed.), Foundations of Software Science and Computational Structures. XVI, 379 pages. 2007.

Vol. 4422: M.B. Dwyer, A. Lopes (Eds.), Fundamental Approaches to Software Engineering. XV, 440 pages. 2007.

Vol. 4421: R. De Nicola (Ed.), Programming Languages and Systems. XVII, 538 pages. 2007.

Vol. 4420: S. Krishnamurthi, M. Odersky (Eds.), Compiler Construction. XIV, 233 pages. 2007.

Vol. 4419: P.C. Diniz, E. Marques, K. Bertels, M.M. Fernandes, J.M.P. Cardoso (Eds.), Reconfigurable Computing: Architectures, Tools and Applications. XIV, 391 pages. 2007.

Vol. 4416: A. Bemporad, A. Bicchi, G. Buttazzo (Eds.), Hybrid Systems: Computation and Control. XVII, 797 pages. 2007.

Vol. 4415: P. Lukowicz, L. Thiele, G. Tröster (Eds.), Architecture of Computing Systems - ARCS 2007. X, 297 pages. 2007.